Art and its Worlds
Exhibitions, Institutions and Art Becoming Public

Exhibition Histories

First published 2021 by Afterall in association with Asia Art Archive, the Center for Curatorial Studies, Bard College and the Faculty of Fine, Applied and Performing Arts, University of Gothenburg

Edited by Bo Choy, Charles Esche, David Morris and Lucy Steeds

Afterall
Central Saint Martins
Granary Building
1 Granary Square
London N1C 4AA
www.afterall.org

Afterall is a Research Centre of University of the Arts London, located at Central Saint Martins

Project Coordinators
Camille Crichlow and Beth Bramich

Project Managers
Chloe Ting and Lauren Houlton

Editorial Director
Mark Lewis

Associate Director
Charles Esche

Distribution
Verlag der Buchhandlung Walther und Franz König (Europe: verlag@buchhand-lung-walther-koenig.de); Cornerhouse Publications Ltd. - HOME (UK & Ireland: publications@cornerhouse.org); and D.A.P. / Distributed Art Publishers, Inc. (outside Europe: orders@ dapinc.com)

Exhibition Histories **Series Editors**
Lauren Cornell, Tom Eccles, Charles Esche, Sanne Kofod Olsen, Pablo Lafuente, Lucy Steeds, John Tain and Mick Wilson

Research Fellow and Managing Editor
David Morris

Assistant Editor
Bo Choy

Copy Editor
Deirdre O'Dwyer

Design
Andrew Brash

Print
die Keure

British Library Cataloguing-in-Publication Data
A catalogue record for this book is available from the British Library
ISBN 978-3-96098-917-2 (Koenig Books, London)
ISBN 978-1-84638-256-7 (Afterall Books, London)
© 2021 Afterall, Central Saint Martins, University of the Arts London, the artists and the authors

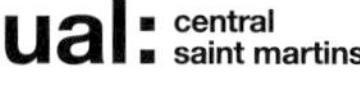

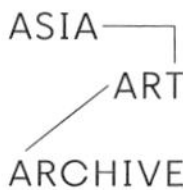
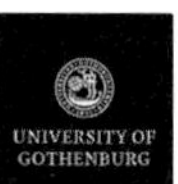
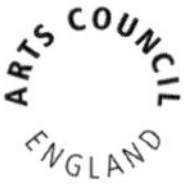

Contents

Art and its Worlds

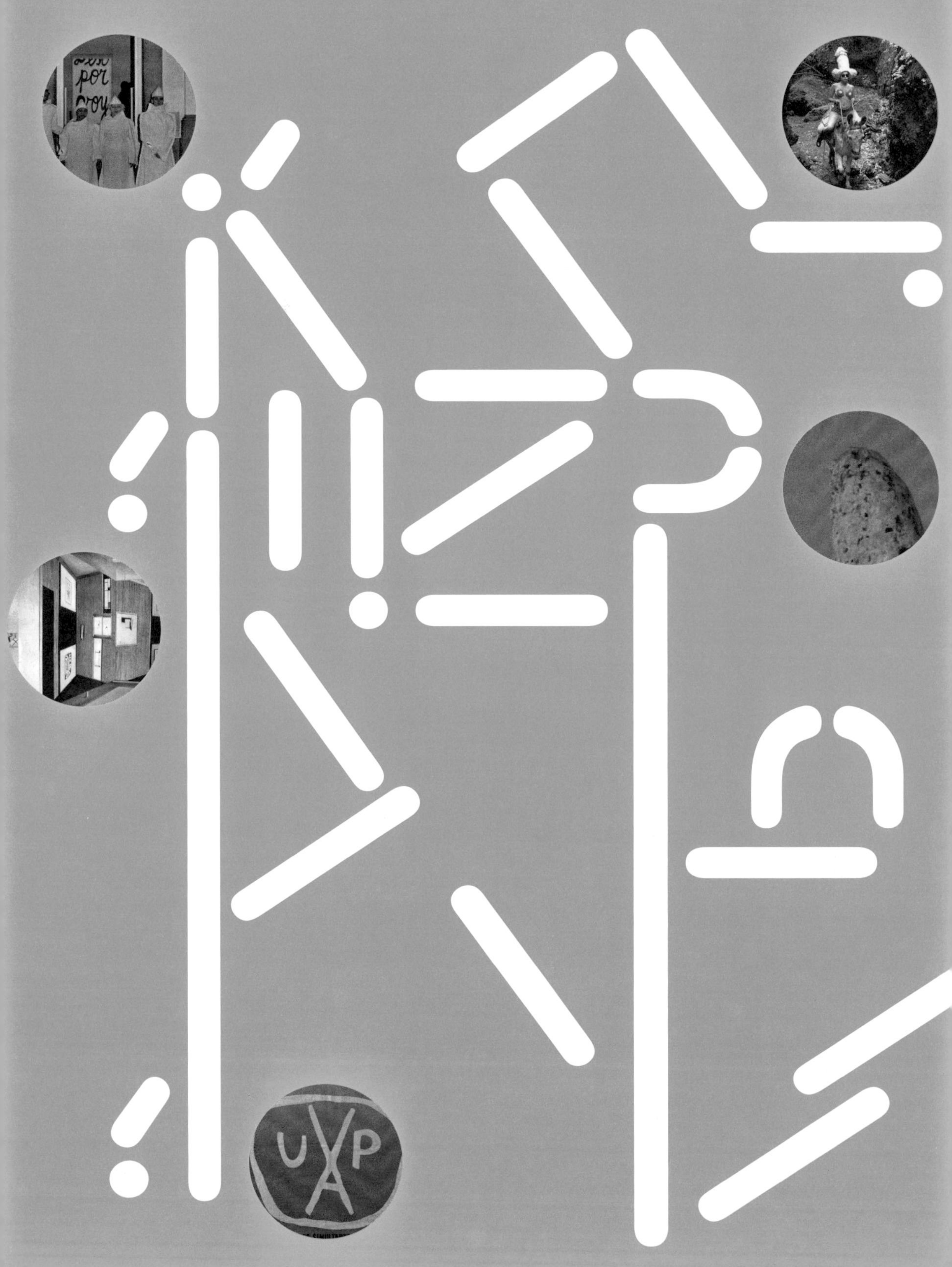

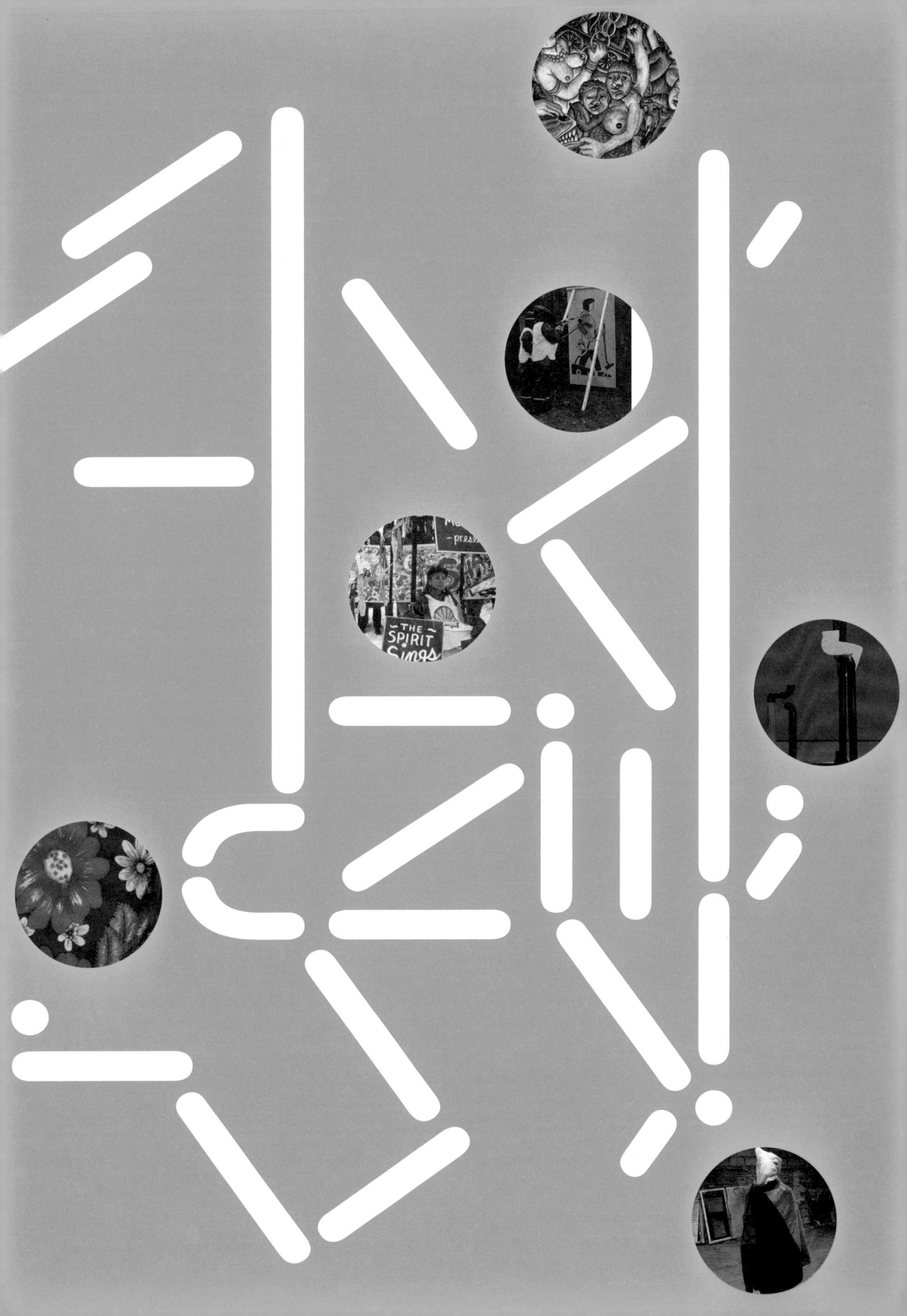

Exhibition Histories Through the Shared Art of Memory

Lucy Steeds, David Morris, Charles Esche and Bo Choy

The title of this text draws on a mantra we have learnt from Chimurenga: 'History is the science of the state, while memory is the art of the stateless.'[1] In what ensues here, we reflect on our work in the name of exhibition histories for contemporary art, while acknowledging that what we have always named with these words and what we now mean, different from before, are not universal. This acknowledgement is performed, perhaps, by the work of many that is anthologised in *Art and its Worlds: Exhibitions, Institutions and Art Becoming Public*. Given that we care for art beyond ownership – for art as belonging to whatever and whomever it convenes in any particular place, for any particular duration – then our commitment in this book is to sharing art, on that basis, further and wider.

The bulk of *Art and its Worlds* is constituted by essays published in *Afterall* journal between 2007 (issue 15) and 2019 (issue 44), precisely coinciding with the first ten books in the publication series *Exhibition Histories*, to which the present book forms the twelfth volume. Indeed, there is more than coincidence: the eighteen such essays republished here, on the one hand, and the ten books produced alongside, on the other, arise from research concerns nurtured by overlapping teams throughout that period. We here also revisit online articles and public discussions we previously initiated, while presenting newly commissioned contributions from long-standing and more recent interlocutors, each with a distinct approach.

In assembling the selection here, we decided to focus on contemporary art and its worlds since the late 1980s or early 1990s. Processes of social and political upheaval at this moment within Europe have lent the year 1989 a particular symbolism – although this is certainly not the only story to be told and no such precise date can be given to the Cold War ending, the internet emerging or capitalism spreading and mutating.[2] It is true that the artistic responses to this period of change around the world were not immediately abundant, notably in modern art's Western heartlands, although we stand by the significance, in terms of sampling the complexity of the changes, of certain exhibitions that took place in 1989.[3] Certainly, we hope that more of the diversity or pluriversality of exhibition practices in the past three decades or so is reflected in the multifarious work with text and image that follows.

The selection seeks to interconnect disparate moments of making art public while being attuned to potential reverberations; it tries to indicate the field's manifold variety, to jointly articulate what might be at stake in art's becoming public before now, *for now*. If an exhibition is an enfolding of collective experience and discursive activity enabled by artworks, which operates most powerfully through pooling a sense of authorship, then we see our task as stepping in to extend something of its earlier significance to other places and times. If art relies on a show, or showing, to come to life, then the exhibition similarly refuses self-sufficiency, relying on its social, political and economic context and contingencies (the land and the weather) to determine its vitality and sustainability (onwards germination). In this way, art is subject to a world that surrounds it and, if it moves around, the worlds proliferate. These are only tangentially connected to an apocryphal 'art world', a phenomenon that is itself increasingly shifting and multiplying, according to the criteria of hard commercial value and contested cultural value. The title 'art and its worlds' is an attempt to recognise a wider and more permissive field of activity, in which the makers and users of art have a certain agency but are always also subject to the where, when, how and why of their positions.

In this introduction we offer a short retrospective description of our practices to date. We then go into how our books have both shaped and been shaped by these practices. Third and finally, we speculate on what this might mean now, if not exactly where we might head together next. As our study of exhibition histories and art becoming public has matured, we have become less interested in marking boundaries around art, exhibitions, institutions, publics and worlds. Encouraged by each other's curiosity – and hopefully by yours – we would like to open up overlapping possibilities and permeable positions.

1. Exhibition Histories: An Evolving Research Concern

Under the banner of *Exhibition Histories* for contemporary art we have sought, with colleagues for the last fifteen years, to sustain a growing field of research and enquiry. The book series of this name is probably the most tangible outcome of these endeavours, which more broadly strive to counter the neoliberal imperatives that marketise the art, research and education in our lives, insisting on the commodified production of objects, outputs and qualifications, which we resist. To this end, it seems important to clarify that the books emerge – are trialled and developed – in the context of teaching situations and symposia.[4] Art historians and curators – alongside artists, theorists, designers and those merging or refusing these and other categories – have all contributed powerfully to our classes, public discussions and publications. We hope this field-in-becoming of exhibition histories can be multidisciplinary, interdisciplinary and transdisciplinary all at the same time, and it feels precious for that reason.[5] Certainly, we seek to inhabit the field with increasing plurality and fluidity. We value that at its core is an activity of publicness that involves a holding in common, where different interpretations build the discourse and inform the practice for everyone who is interested to be involved. This is also why we have adjusted the banner for our studying to *Art Becoming Public*, while retaining *Exhibition Histories* for the series of publications.[6]

The research questions that we currently start out with might be phrased in various ways. How is the becoming public of art – which is of its time, but in the past – relevant for a distributed 'here', in the present 'now'? How can we engage cultural entanglements today through the study and exploration of the public life of art – for instance, its affective, discursive, social and political agency – in previous conjunctures? How can the conjuring, mobilising and questioning of worlds that were once achieved when art resonated within a historical situation address a wider context now? How may we extend, revisit or open back up a former durational field for works of contemporary art, in order to invite in people from new places and times to reshape meanings in the present? We feel passionately about the possibility for exhibition histories to be geo-politically open and anti-imperialist. This is a fragile possibility, of course, and one that requires sensitive nurturing through anti-hegemonic acts in re-lation to what has come before: challenging dominant art historical narratives by shifting *what* is paid attention to and rethinking *how*; destabilising familiar triumphalism through amplifying alternative resonances.

In the absence of a preferred, disciplinary regime, the methods and indeed methodologies of exhibition histories are to be inspired by the perceived needs of whatever is selected for study. In other words, the theories and practices used within the field work best, we believe, when responding to what they are particularly focussed on. To elaborate this, albeit somewhat simplistically, the modes of approach suited to a relatively recent edition of a long-standing and ongoing biennial in a wealthy nation, for instance, will ill serve the un-subsidised initiatives of a disbanded collective who have worked aside from the markets for art and are no longer *in situ*. This highlights, perhaps, that the definition of 'exhibition' is as productively uncircumscribed as the mean-ing of 'art' and 'publics'.[7] Nevertheless, we are committed to publics (viewers, visitors, users, audiences, receivers, participants, etc.) as being both plural and temporally united – and, on this basis, exhibitions are neither one thing nor preservable: their life is defined by the durational field instigated by art in a given context. As such, exhibition histories should always reflect on a missing physical experience and be aware of the paradoxes of revisiting its legacy in terms of discursivity, transience and pastness, *regardless of the chosen locus of study*. At the same time, the relevance of that focus, and its choice before oth-ers, should be articulated and/or activated, *in particular*.

The 'histories', plural, of 'exhibition histories' marks the multiple intersecting realities prompted by any single show. Of course, history is always embodied when lived and then disputed when written, but there is something about exhibitions – their public eventhood, we might say – that demands a polyvocal account. As already indicated, we oppose History's imperial claims upon The Future, and the associated modern and modernist logic of innovation through creative destruction. The plurality of 'histories' further indicates mediation via varying conditions *now*: from contingent standpoints, looking back. On both counts, uncertainty will be to the fore in what is produced; the aim being to achieve an enabling complexity without a disabling confusion, inviting engagement and effective repositioning in response. Perhaps 'histories', in the plural, also suggests the *doing of* history. This means referring to historical – or merely 'past' – events for the purposes of reanimation, for a marshalling now to distinct ends. While refusing the master discipline of History, however, exhibition histories is not without discipline, if only in the sense that declared facts can be adjusted in light of more convincing 'evidence', nor is it lacking in disciplines, in that values may be disputed and ranked among different constituencies against differing criteria. Perhaps this is just us upholding the involvement of scholarly labour: studious care, with an attendant role for playfulness and a collegiality that rejects elitism. Accordingly, thinking is to be demonstrated; learning, insights and imagination to be shared. Whatever traditions are passed on generationally, there is at best an aliveness – intellectually and creatively – to matters in a situated present. There is an engagement with the 'real world' while exercising 'academic freedom' in relation to it.

However, we are perhaps now at risk of saying rather than showing. To make these proclaimed ideals concrete, we will turn to how we have striven for all this in the *Exhibition Histories* book series. In some ways, we seek to rethink what exhibition histories might be every time we make a book. Since we have deliberately found our way forwards through practice, rather than working fixedly from an initial plan, this current text, written together, amounts to a taking stock.

2. Exhibition Histories: Books

When we say 'our' with regards to the *Exhibition Histories* books, there are various communities invoked: those involved in instigating the research and publishing project, back in 2007; those who work, or have worked, on this project in the London production office;[8] specific collaborative partners at institutions on three continents;[9] and our many contributors, some of whom have transformed our thinking and remained part of us even after the book they have shaped is finalised. We cannot reliably speak for everyone who has played a role in the books, of course, but our point is to emphasise that this is fundamentally a communal project with evolving mutual responsibility for and use of what has been produced.

There have been eleven books in the *Exhibition Histories* series prior to this one, published annually since 2010. Each of these books takes an issue in art becoming public that seems engaging to us. It examines this issue through study of a past exhibition, or a pair or cluster of shows, involving art that is contemporary to that given moment in time. To date, we have looked back as far as 1957 (which stretched our interest in living memory) and as recently as 2000. The books have zoomed in on art events in: Amsterdam/Bern, Chiang Mai, Chicago, Havana, Lagos, Moscow, Newcastle/London, Paris, São

Paulo and Shanghai – and an evolving US project that took in Vancouver and Buenos Aires. We have an ongoing concern to decentralise situations for art in the West, First World or Global North, beginning to address the necessity and explore the potential to denaturalise our research from the English language and open it up beyond Anglo-American and associated readerships.

The books do not imagine eternal or universal relevance for the case studies they foreground. Each book is crafted and received in its own moment, addressing particular constituencies and seeking its own durational field, perhaps. We do not propose a map of 'landmark' shows around the globe, to be preserved and defended, and we rarely know which project will be the subject of the next study until it is already begun. If asked about a 'global canon' of exhibitions, we would venture that this exists only on the understanding that everyone constantly fashions (or ignores) their own. The politics of nationhood and associated exclusionary operations have taught us to be wary of presuming we can ever get close to sampling or representing. So, how do we pick the exhibitions we choose to study? Only on the basis of ongoing discussions with an unconstituted group of interlocutors, often through public seminars and always with the anguish of knowing we are condemned to negligence, but in tandem with the hope of learning something useful for the next book. Moreover, the factual multiplicity of shows can always be emphasised, with cross-referencing used to insist that no one project is unimpeachable or worth considering in isolation.

All the books up until now have included two key elements – revisitation and polyvocality. Revisitation requires us to have access to images, texts, witnesses, accounts or memories that will enable collective study. Each book is then plurally authored, bringing together archival and reminiscent material with newly commissioned essays, interviews and design. Space is given to curatorial and organisational intention or recollection, but equally to artistic positioning and to appraisal from independent perspectives. The polyvocality of each book insists on the many who experienced an exhibition, or might engage with it now, and on the plurality of those producing it. A dispersed agency is assumed in production and reception and through their chiasmus.

The ambition to revisit the exhibitionary events we publish books about, and to do this on the pages of these books, is a more mercurial proposition, which we have come to realise needs to take different form each time and will always, in some senses, fail. A map, documentary images, a verbalised tour or photographic 'walk-through', may be possible and useful in some instances, but not all.[10] The broader insufficiency – or inevitable failure to offer actual access to the past – is a challenge we have come to embrace. The desire to do justice to the complex phenomena of a former encounter between artworks and publics is indeed a desire, not compelled by law, and so to be explored playfully as well as seriously. Perhaps we mean 'be faithful' rather than 'do justice'? We usually have photographic and other extant material to work with and many people to consult. Through careful study, critical proximity, time spent seeking testimony and time spent *with* this testimony, we seek to clarify where there are indications that complicate received opinions.[11] Like the translator of a novel, poem or playscript who is working between languages with the dual imperatives of fidelity and felicity, we develop an intense relationship to a remote original and simultaneously to imagine new audiences. When the sincerity of adequate representation weighs heavily, reviewing the significances in the present offers refreshed direction, reminding us what spirits of the past might need in order to feel invited to animate matters again today. Ways of using images and words – and working with them on the printed page – have to be found in order to conjure up events from traces, making them available for discussion now.[12] This latter in particular is why we moved away from the initial, formulaic design of the books to embrace eclecticism led by appropriateness.

We want to flick through particular books with you now, drawing out some other features of our approach to exhibition histories.

First, when studying art shows that are well celebrated – canonised, for instance, within long-established curatorial courses – we have sought to complicate the achievements hailed and to foreground other exhibitions that have been occluded by that canon. On this basis, when we tackled 'When Attitudes Become Form', we did so in tandem with 'Op Losse Schroeven': if the former notoriously opened up, in 1969, the traditional exhibition space at the Kunsthalle Bern to improvisation in situ by West European and US artists (and, on this basis, is often assigned a nascent role in relation to the lauded curatorial personage of Harald Szeemann), then the latter, overlappingly initiated by Wim Beeren at the Stedelijk Museum, Amsterdam has been marginalised by comparison.[13] We followed that European, masculine pairing with a book dedicated to the related conceptual art exhibitions organised by Lucy Lippard, specifically elaborating a political trajectory marked by her move into feminism.[14] Differently seeking to destabilise a solidifying canon or curriculum of 'landmark shows', we published paired books that jointly reflected on a topic – the 'global' or 'worldwide' curation of contemporary art – from distinct geo-political perspectives but at the same moment in time, 1989.[15] One exhibition, 'Magiciens de la Terre' in Paris, was arguably overexposed when our book came out, with homage and vilification deeply entrenched in opposing camps (hence begging re-examination from new positions); while the other initiative, the third Bienal de la Habana, was then rarely discussed in the same circles, yet brought new light to bear. Publishing on the 'other' exhibition initiative, the Cuban biennial, *first* – before 'Part 2' on 'Magiciens' – was important to us.

A second strand of the book series has involved challenging our understandings of what an exhibition might be. For instance, for one book we focussed on a gallery installation that is usually discussed as a unified artwork, not as an inhabited show.[16] Several books reconsidered projects that did not rely on gallery space in order to engage publics with art, with the scattered-site and dispersed temporalities of 'Culture in Action' in Chicago in 1993,[17] comparable in that regard with the otherwise distinct initiatives of Chiang Mai Social Installation (CMSI) in northern Thailand from 1992–98.[18] A book on the APTART 'anti-shows' in a Moscow flat late in the Soviet era allowed us to question the very status of 'publics' in relation to art, when those gathered come together in defiance of state sanction – a situation that resonates more and more with the politics of the current time.[19] Our subsequent publication – marking the first decade of the series – put in question the very status of 'art' and 'exhibition' in relation to publics via FESTAC in Lagos in 1977, a self-proclaimed 'festival of arts and culture';[20] in this context, gallery-style visual arts exhibitions were only a small component, in amongst formal and informal music, theatre and literature gatherings and much else. Yet we understood the month-long mega event to be suggestive of a whole panoply of artistic practice, exemplary precisely because of its capacity to convene multitudinous publics.

Implicit in this second strand of our *Exhibition Histories* publishing is a concern to credit the work not only of professional exhibition-makers or curators – with Mary Jane Jacob or Gerardo Mosquera as worthy of celebration as Lippard or Szeemann, for instance – but also to acknowledge the equal achievements of those who operated primarily as artists, for instance in Chiang Mai, or who were mobilised (often outside of defined roles) by state-led initiatives such as FESTAC. The collective agency, or dispersal of responsibility, that characterises these less curatorially authored endeavours is of active interest to us.

Thirdly, we have learnt to work more openly and collaboratively in producing books in the *Exhibition Histories* series. Our first step was to invite those expert in the case studies at issue not just to make a discrete contribution but to inform the overall editorial process – co-determining the content and texture – for that particular book. In this way, Lisette Lagnado guided our response to the 'anthropophagy biennial' in São Paulo in 1998 and David Teh shaped the book on the Chiang Mai festivals of the mid 1990s. More recently we have collaborated with partner outfits that bring many years of concerted work to bear. We celebrated our tenth volume in the series by joining forces with Chimurenga to produce the bespoke publication in which they advance their ongoing exploration of FESTAC's imaginaries. Learning from this, we freed the next books from elements of conformity that we had (sometimes inadvertently) developed for ourselves and happily now allow ourselves to trial new models. Increasingly, each book is written and illustrated, assembled and designed, in a way that responds to the exhibitionary events at issue. Last year's book was the first entirely born of our institutional partnership with Asia Art Archive, drawing on their specific resources – materials, expertise and relationships – to jointly consider contemporary art shows staged in Shanghai in 2000.[21]

The two most recent publications – centred respectively on Lagos in 1977 and Shanghai in 2000 – might be said to revisit the 'global' or 'worldwide' curation of contemporary art as we previously addressed it through the lens of Paris and Havana in 1989, and indeed also via São Paulo in 1998. This may be identified as a fourth strand of our ongoing work in the field of exhibition histories,[22] and it recognises the fundamentally localised claims to globalism or worldliness.[23] At the same time, we concern ourselves with more avowedly local initiatives, while selecting these for their potential translocal, transnational and transcontinental resonances.

Increasingly, through our partners and interlocuters, we have come to acknowledge the problem of our anchorage in London, with its dominant narrative of British exceptionalism. The focus and commissioning of future books, we realise, must be an even more determinedly collective task. Certainly, we feel strongly that, even within our ongoing book series, exhibition histories may take myriad forms – or rather, exhibition histories *must* in the effort to respond appropriately to the particularity and complexity of art's exposure. Yet, we are also adamant that no one publisher can own or control the field on this basis, for it is the pluralised and distributed nature of field formation – involving independent activity, like that of Chimurenga in Cape Town or *Huakan* in Beijing,[24] with which we may cross pollinate – that ensures the vitality.

3. From Exhibition Histories to Art Becoming Public and Back Again

We have discussed moving out from the under the umbrella of 'exhibition histories' many times in recent years. To summarise rather coarsely what we have heard, prompting our debates, there are two camps. From one side we hear those not keen to loosen their grasp on what an exhibition might be and how it might operate. Their insistence on tying 'exhibition' to display in the museum, gallery, biennial or art fair seems a way to orientate themselves – which might be justified, though we sometimes find it too demanding of curatorial privilege, or of leaning hubristically on 'the curatorial'. Many in this camp seem to be similarly fixed in their grip of what history – also an artist, or a curator – is or does. Yet the relative valency of these terms, for different proponents, is interestingly contrasting: compare an artistic conservative who may be powerfully *pro* the exhibition and history as narrowly understood through traditions rooted in Europe, with someone committed to the rhetorics of 'the curatorial' who may be powerfully *contra* the same. Simultaneously, there is another camp, distinct from the positions just outlined, which has very little intellectual, creative or emotional investment in any of this language – although their particular concerns and practices are just as pertinent to the field for us as exhibitions understood by those in the first camp. So, in sum, it is not only mindful of the inadequacies of terminology that we persist with exhibition histories, but in the hope of steering a course that brings more people together – from all camps and, for instance, across generations, geopolitics, class or caste – on the basis of curiosity about art and its sociocultural potential.

For us, there are as many overlaps as discrepancies, with work that is pursued under terms such as 'art history' and 'cultural history'; 'curatorial studies', 'museum studies' and 'cultural studies'; 'anthropology' and 'area studies'; 'artistic', 'curatorial' and 'cultural practice'.[25] We celebrate the dialogue and ricochets between these approaches, finding brilliant inspiration as well as interesting problems. We most often sense problems if art production and curating – and discussion of these practices – risk overshadowing the work of exhibition.

As may be obvious just from this text, we have consistently referenced this 'work' of art's exhibition as that of becoming public. As we contemplate the possibility of another decade of research and publishing in the name of exhibition histories, we wish to foreground the becoming public of art still more. So, how to move that centre stage, to dilate or amplify it? To attempt an answer, we will draw on Fred Moten's writing from 2016, about an exhibition curated by Charles Gaines in Los Angeles in 1993, 'The Theater of Refusal: Black Art and Mainstream Criticism'.[26] Moten first notes that 'the blur of spirit admits of no personhood', before drawing an analogy to art and its 'constant violation of the artist, the viewer and the work that is the mobile location of their entangled differentiation'.[27] We suggest taking this up and seeing art as a constant violation of the artist, the curator, the viewer and all other agents open to its – and their own – exposure. On this basis, we see the exhibition as the 'mobile location of the entangled differentiation' of art's producers and its publics. The task of exhibition histories, for us, is then the material, embodied and political practice that, through the 'blur of spirit', invites a new location for past art, bringing it into the present for what is to come.

Notes

1 Wendell Marsh, 'Re-Membering the Name of God', *Chimurenga Chronic*, 19 March 2015. Quoted in, for instance, Ntone Edjabe, 'How to Eat a Forest', in this volume. See also 'Performing Pan-Africanism: Ntone Edjabe in Conversation with David Morris', in Paul O'Neill, Simon Sheikh, Lucy Steeds and Mick Wilson (ed.), *Curating after the Global, Roadmaps for the Present*, London and Cambridge, MA: MIT Press, 2019, pp.273–91.

2 On the significance of 1989, see Charles Esche and Maria Hlavajova, 'FORMER WEST: Introductory Notes', 5 November 2009, available at https://formerwest.org/ResearchCongresses/1st FormerWestCongress/Text/IntroductoryNotes. Events beyond the North Atlantic, including the fall of military governments in various parts of Latin America, or the struggle against apartheid in South Africa, suggest a wider transitional time frame; moreover, an acknowledgement of multiple temporalities recommends against any such reading of events according to any teleology.

3 See 'Exhibitions and the World at Large', hosted by Afterall and TrAIN (both of University of the Arts London) at Tate Britain, 3 April 2009, https://www.afterall.org/events/exhibitions.and.the. world.at.large. See also the ensuing books 2 and 4 in the *Exhibition Histories* series (see n.15) and 'The "Other Story", 1989', available at https://www.afterall.org/exhibition/the-other-story/.

4 The *Exhibition Histories* books complement and are complemented by a research-based masters course in Art: Exhibition Studies and by disparate doctoral projects each defined by the students leading them, all based at Central Saint Martins, a college of University of the Arts London (UAL). The external partners on the books (see n.9) all have their own, also complementary, educational remits. Many books have further been shaped through public symposia and open editorial meetings, hosted by disparate generous collaborators.

5 On the 'indiscipline' of exhibition histories, see L. Steeds, 'What is the Future of Exhibition Histories? Or, Toward Art in Terms of Its Becoming-Public', in P. O'Neill, L. Steeds and M. Wilson (ed.), *The Curatorial Conundrum: What to Study? What to Research? What to Practice?*, London and Cambridge, MA: MIT Press, 2016, p.17. If the hope in that essay was to repurpose the curatorial rhetoric of 'indiscipline' and the 'undisciplined' after Okwui Enwezor and Irit Rogoff (see, for instance, O. Enwezor, 'Documentary/Vérité: Bio-Politics, Human Rights and the Figure of "Truth" in Contemporary Art', *Australian and New Zealand Journal of Art*, vol.5, no.1, 2004, pp.11–42), then we are now more indebted to the thinking of Yaiza Hernández Velázquez, who has flagged the danger – by 'positioning ourselves *a priori* in this "undisciplined" terrain' – of 'remaining obdurately blind to our own academicism.' See Y. Hernández Velázquez, introduction to her edited volume *Inter/multi/cross/trans: The Uncertain Territory of Art Theory in the Age of Academic Capitalism*, Vitoria: Montehermoso, 2011, p.188.

6 See https://www.afterall.org/research/art-becoming-public/.

7 A philosophical discourse on the exhibition as such – a bid to grasp all public occasions for art within a unified ontology – does not interest us, as this would deny the lived and shifting, historical (and geo-political) nature of exhibitions as we see them. For eloquence on this and many issues relevant to the present essay, from someone more than capable when it comes to philosophy, see Y. Hernández Velázquez, 'Who Needs "Exhibition Studies"?', in this volume.

8 Afterall is based at Central Saint Martins, a college of UAL, and core funded by Arts Council England as a National Portfolio Organisation.

9 The collaborative partners on 'Exhibition Histories' are currently: Central Saint Martins, UAL; Asia Art Archive, Hong Kong; the Center for Curatorial Studies at Bard College, Annandale-On-Hudson, New York; and the Faculty of Fine, Applied and Performing Arts, University of Gothenburg.

10 Maps and an illustrated 'walk-through' make most sense where there is a *parcours* or 'red thread' through an exhibition (while presupposing obedience to a dogmatic display mode). On one adjusted 'revisitation' mode that we have used in the *Exhibition Histories* series, see Lucy Steeds's contribution 'Return and/as Response: Minding the Memory of "an Exhibit"' to a book on the methodologies of exhibition histories edited by Rike Frank and Beatrice von Bismarck: *O(f)f Our Times: Curatorial Anachronics*, Berlin: Sternberg Press, 2019. As live events contribute to art's engagement with a public, such modes become more evidently wanting.

11 On testimony, forensics and yet a lack of neutrality – the rejection of empirical objectivity as an ambition – in our book series, see 'Things After the Event: Publishing Exhibition Histories – Lucy Steeds in conversation with Beatrice von Bismarck and Benjamin Meyer-Krahmer' in B. von Bismarck and Benjamin Meyer-Krahmer (ed.), *Curatorial Things*, Berlin: Sternberg Press, 2019, pp.325–333. The insights articulated there lean on those of Geeta Kapur as conveyed in panel 7 of 'Showing, Telling, Seeing: Exhibiting South Asia in Britain 1900–Now', 30 June and 1 July 2016, organised by the Paul Mellon Centre for Studies in British Art and Asia Art Archive in collaboration with Tate Modern. Audio recording available at http://www.paul-mellon-centre.ac.uk/whats-on/past/showing-telling-seeing-conference.

12 The opportunities and challenges of producing exhibition histories online offer exciting alternatives, of course. We have only started to explore the possibilities ourselves, with this initial foray awaiting development: https://www.afterall.org/exhibition/the-other-story/

13 Christian Rattemeyer et al., *Exhibiting the New Art: 'Op Losse Schroeven' and 'When Attitudes Become Form' 1969*, London: Afterall Books, 2010. The idiomatic Dutch phrase 'op losse schroeven' literally means 'on weak screws', implying weak foundations or loose connections; it was not widely translated into English as an exhibition title at the time, although 'Square Pegs in Round Holes' was sometimes proffered.

14 Cornelia Butler et al., *From Conceptualism to Feminism: Lucy Lippard's Number's Shows 1969–74*, London: Afterall Books, 2012. Related New York initiatives that we neglected in this book include the exhibitionary activities of the collective 'Where We At' Black Women Artists, featured in the FESTAC book (see n.20), and Ana Mendieta, Kazuko Miyamoto and Zarina in 'Dialectics of Isolation: An Exhibition of Third World Women Artists of the United States' at the A.I.R. Gallery, New York in 1980.

15 Rachel Weiss et al., *Making Art Global (Part 1): The Third Havana Biennial 1989*, London: Afterall Books, 2011. Lucy Steeds et al., *Making Art Global (Part 2): 'Magiciens de la Terre' 1989*, London: Afterall Books, 2013. On flagging some neglected context for the exhibitions covered in these paired volumes, see Anthony Gardner and Charles Green, 'Biennials of the South on the Edges of the Global', *Third Text*, vol.27, no.4, 2013, pp.442–55.

16 Elena Crippa and L. Steeds (ed.), *Exhibition, Design, Participation: 'an Exhibit' 1957 and Related Projects*, London: Afterall Books, 2016. For critical reflection on this book, see L. Steeds 'Return and/as Response', *op. cit.*

17 Joshua Decter and Helmut Draxler et al., *Exhibition as Social Intervention: 'Culture in Action' 1993*, London: Afterall Books, 2014.

18 David Teh and David Morris (ed.), *Artist-to-Artist: Independent Art Festivals in Chiang Mai 1992–98*, London: Afterall Books, 2018.

19 Margarita Tupitsyn, Victor Tupitsyn and D. Morris (ed.), *Anti-Shows: APTART 1982–84*, London: Afterall Books, 2017. For analysis of the expanded context in play here, see D. Morris, 'Underground Museology: A Research Report', in *Centre for Experimental Museology, Almanac, No.1*, Moscow: V–A–C Foundation, 2020 (in Russian) and forthcoming 2021 (in English).

20 *FESTAC '77: The 2nd World Black and African Festival of Arts and Culture – Decomposed, an-arranged and reproduced by Chimurenga*, Cape Town and London: Chimurenga and Afterall, 2019.

21 *Uncooperative Contemporaries: Art Exhibitions in Shanghai in 2000*, London: Afterall Books, 2020.

22 These four strands offer a somewhat alternative categorisation to the three sections of this book. The point here is that there are many ways of dividing up the same field, with no one way abiding. Likewise, the book sections that follow are not hard and fast, with a contribution positioned within one likely to sit as comfortably in another.

23 For reflection on this strand of our work, see Lucy's introduction to 'Section 2: Exhibition Histories', in P. O'Neill, S. Sheikh, L. Steeds and M. Wilson (ed.), *Curating after the Global, op. cit.*, pp.221–27.

24 See Mia Yu's recent project on exhibition histories for *Huakan* (画刊, *Art Monthly*), 2021, and Panafest '66'69'74'77 as hosted by Chimurenga online at https://www.panafest.org.za.

25 For various stances on the relationship to art history as recently discussed online, see 'Why Exhibition Histories?', available at http://britishartstudies.ac.uk/issues/issue-index/issue-13/why-exhibition-histories; and 'A história das exposições é a nova história da arte?' ('Is the history of the exhibitions the new history of art?'), https://www.select.art.br/a-historia-das-exposicoes-e-a-nova-historia-da-arte/.

26 Fred Moten was invited to frame thoughts in response to 'The Theater of Refusal' for a public event at LAXART, Los Angeles in 2016. His paper was then published in the first volume of his trilogy *consent not to be a single being* (see n.27). Charles Gaines discussed 'The Theater of Refusal' in a 2019 talk for our *Exhibition Histories* series at Whitechapel Gallery, London with the support of the International Curator's Forum. Recording available online at https://www.afterall.org/article/exhibition-histories-talks-charles-gaines-video-online.

27 Fred Moten, *Black and Blur*, Durham, NC and London: Duke University Press, 2017, p.259.

I.
Making
Art
Global?

Charles Esche, David Morris and Lucy Steeds

We have looped the loops of art's 'global contemporary', while also getting lost down its cul-de-sacs. This book covers the period from the late 1980s onwards, without trying to present a coherent teleology of progress or a timeline that leads towards a satisfying set of closures. Instead, much of the past thirty years for art would be better characterised in terms of intermittent pulses from different locations that become stronger and weaker over time, while yet to fade out entirely. Our task in this first section of the book has been to study these pulses through the lenses of exhibitions. Methodologically, the approaches here depart from our initial understanding of exhibition histories, which looked for shows that shaped the way art is experienced, made and discussed, often centring on the substantial reassessment of famous or infamous examples within the history of contemporary art.[1] Such 'materialist' studies of public moments for art – invested in the materiality of works and bodies in space, as well as the material conditions of their socio-political realities – here intersect with a number of more reflexive and speculative interventions that interrogate the ways in which such exhibition histories are formed. Moving with care through certain categories and moments, we trace the shifting fortunes of the 'global contemporary' and what it has to tell us about the present.

Perhaps the dominant category of the past three decades for 'making art global', or the presiding form of recent times, has been the biennial. Let us widen this to consider all exhibitions that seek to carry certain ideas from one place to another. In their search for continuities between the contexts they serve, such projects often have an awkward, implicated relationship with the needs of global capital for market access and the instrumentalisation of desire. Of course, this is unlikely to be the explicit agenda of anyone involved – the commitments of artists, curators, commissioners, institutions, patrons and audiences are more often directed towards the potentialities of art, including the capacity to radically reimagine world(s). Such tensions, elsewhere described as the art world's ability to operate simultaneously as a dream of liberation and a structure of exclusion,[2] lie at the heart of this section. This recognises that exhibitions can hold out the promise of exceeding the institutional frame while only being made available to us – and to some of us more than others – by the funding and infrastructure of those same institutions. Providing the basis for an analysis of the difference between intention and experience, these tensions allow space for criticality that can also be propositional – we hope. This also introduces the quality of location and circumstance, in which exhibitions happen in a place and context that determine much of their possibility and consequence. This being so, a linear, progressive unfolding of exhibition experience historically over time cannot offer much guidance. It is by jumping between contexts while studying them closely that something of a sense of art's changing prospects might be gleaned.

With this in mind, then, we will start this introduction in the middle: in Central Asia, in between the late 1980s and the time of writing this introduction. Francesca Recchia characterises the mood of the art community in Kabul in the early 2010s, amid a surge of cultural activities initiated from 'elsewhere':

Foreigners come and go, and with them various initiatives and endless streams of good intentions. … [T]he small art community in Kabul has kept struggling to survive, just as it did before the event. Artists constantly try to negotiate new spaces and possibilities; they have become cynically aware of the transience of international initiatives, but they smile at the succession of newcomers who arrive promising bright opportunities and lasting change.[3]

The presence of dOCUMENTA (13) in Kabul and Bamiyan in Afghanistan in 2012 marks the height of a certain kind of 'global' exhibition-making. Recchia's argument goes wider than the specifics of the Kassel-based mega-exhibition, to consider the ambitions of many similar projects in the art worlds of the late 2000s: 'they all want(ed) to be *the first* – to open new borders, to include new territories, to explore new routes. This quest for novelty, this myth of primacy, is engrained in the mentality of the frontier and has grown to become an inevitable part of the contemporary cultural gold rush.' The legacy of coloniality – a meme of modern European power – is key to understanding exhibition histories of the recent past, particularly with reference to the 'global'. Centring this reflection of our post-1989 period in Afghanistan takes on an added significance given that country's role in the political and military history of the world at that moment. What Recchia reveals in her understated way about the misfortune of dOCUMENTA (13) in Kabul then serves as a location to look back to the dawn of the 1990s, as well as forward to today.

Exhibition Histories has revisited 1989 through a number of our projects. From the vantage point of the early 2010s, the third Bienal de la Habana still held out some prospects of a global contemporary that might shape itself into a meaningful civic cultural form of resistance to capital.

As we wrote:

The idea of a global poetics draws us into one of the most intractable yet central tensions of the growth of global art production in the past twenty years. Who is this global art for? What kind of public can imaginatively transform, for itself, the references and internal logics of international contemporary art into meaningful life experiences? These questions still lie unanswered as the second decade of the 2000s [opens]. *If there is such a thing as an emerging global public for this global art and if it is to be sustainable in any sense, then it must be accompanied by a still mysterious notion of a global politics, one that has yet to develop. In the absence of such a notion, the answer to the question of what global art may and can be will be reduced to affirmation for a nomadic international elite.*[4]

The text goes on to cite the 2011 Arab Spring as arguably a moment when a form of global resistance led by artists and intellectuals might take real political shape. Sadly, that hope proved forlorn; but it could easily be said that the curators of dOCUMENTA (13) were equally invested not only in the hopes of the Arab Spring but that their idea to engage with Afghanistan was a route towards an emancipatory global politics. The latter has so far proved elusive, meaning that the category of global contemporary art has become, against all its intentions, a decorative alibi for those mired in global capital that is in turn largely grounded in earth-shattering extractivism and its financial benefits. Nevertheless, the tension between complicity and reform remains, and art's trump card is still its possibility to imagine the world otherwise and, by doing so, to help in eventually turning capital against itself.

The 'global' visions of this era resonated with a rejection of the nation-state as a framework for understanding artistic and exhibition-making practice. Around the time that *Exhibition Histories* published paired books on the Bienal de la Habana and 'Magiciens de la Terre' (initiatives both staged in 1989), the ambitions of these projects to *transcend* national boundaries seemed to reflect the direction of travel of the 'global contemporary'.[5] Yet this assumption would also be overtaken by historical events. As we wrote more recently:

> [I]*t is now painfully clear – as xenophobia and the borders between countries are re-entrenched – that national anchorage is not as easily discounted as it felt possible to celebrate* [circa 2010]. *Moreover, the cultural ills (to say nothing of the humanitarian and ecological perils) of the neoliberal take on globalism are also now clearer – resounding with (and financialising) the imperial advances of modernist universalism. Both resurgent nationalism and pernicious globalisation demand a rethinking of 'the global' in more ethical and responsible terms. Prioritising a popular critical openness to ideas and practice from around the world, solidarities that exceed market imperatives are now crucial.*[6]

These considerations bring attention to the shifting circumstances in which local understandings of 'global contemporaneity' may take form. Our publication on exhibition-making in Shanghai in 2000 considered state-led and artist-led initiatives in the city as part of a wider shift in this 'global' trajectory, 'perhaps indicating an understanding of globalisation as a process no longer grounded in the West', as John Tain writes in the introduction to that book. An exhibition project such as 'Cities on the Move', which may be understood in the context of this moment, was formative of the idea of an Asian modernity that would, in both economic and cultural terms, inherit the universal rationalist model from the West; whereas it was perhaps only in Bangkok, the project's only iteration in Asia, in which the hype heralding the Asian century confronted itself.[7] What (dis)continuities may be found between the modernities articulated here and the 'inverted modernity' proposed by another multisite exhibition project that travelled between locations in Europe and Latin America some years later?[8] The artist-led initiatives and networks established in Southeast Asia from the late 1980s offer another story still, of a contemporaneity that is regionally and temporally specific, and produced through the complex configurations of a modernity that remains 'unfinished'.[9]

These stories include any number of critical tensions and contradictions – not least between the dual totalising ambit of 'global' and 'contemporary', and the particularity and locality of each articulation. Contemporaneity as a historical-temporal form is an articulation of the temporal logic of global capitalist modernity, yet it is not reducible to it. Consider Geeta Kapur, invited from Delhi to address art communities gathered in Havana for the 1989 biennial, and presenting her shared task, shouldered together with artists and other intellectuals, as being 'to bring existential urgency to questions of contemporaneity', specifically from a Third World perspective.[10] Compare Gayatri Spivak, invited that same year from Pittsburgh into the Parisian art scene convened by 'Magiciens de la Terre'. Addressing the show's title as well as its billing as 'the first worldwide exhibition of contemporary art', she highlighted significances anchored in French-language particularities and emphasised deep cultural associations in connection; noting that it was a 'worldwide' (as opposed to 'global') claim that was made by the show's strapline, she offered a feminist critique of the notion, via Martin Heidegger, that a world (*monde*, masculine) is inscribed on virgin land or earth (*terre*, feminine).[11]

The last three decades have also seen the emergence of a 'global' art history, or worldwide histories, aiming to intervene retroactively on the discipline's traditional geographical allegiances. As Reiko Tomii describes:

> *Hitherto unrecognised or overlooked movements, individual artists and groups from non-Western backgrounds of the postwar decades are now more frequently and routinely incorporated into canonical narratives of twentieth-century art history and introduced into museum collections and exhibitions. That is to say, multiple practices that did exist but were omitted from history have been reclaimed to complete what may be called the world atlas of contemporary art – an atlas that had been originally delineated within the perimeters of the West, with sporadic notations of activity in terrae incognitae beyond. In some sense, a perception of contemporaneity is thus reconstituted retroactively to construct a whole and all-inclusive view of the immediate past.[12]*

An exemplary case of this retroactive reconstitution of the Western contemporary's 'world atlas' is 'Global Conceptualism: Points of Origin, 1950s–1980s', an exhibition that presented itself as 'challeng[ing] the canonical perception that conceptual art was simply one movement which spread internationally and acknowledg[ing] the important local circumstances which gave birth to conceptualist art in regions around the world'. Yet as Miguel López, writing for *Afterall* in 2010, asked: 'How do we know what Latin American conceptualism looks like?' For López, to answer this question is 'no longer a matter of tirelessly continuing to accommodate events in the endless container we believe history to be, but of questioning the ways in which they reappear and the roles they play within it.'[13] His suggestion is that we look not only at the artistic representations themselves, but at specific variations and displacements within a Western category such as conceptualism, understanding them as 'machines of political transformation'.

Rather than continuing to fill the 'endless container' of art history, then, it is through challenging the dominant categories and cartographies of art, representation and exhibition that a new sort of planetary exchange of experiences could be forthcoming.[14] The contributions in the current section are typical of the present publication as a whole in that they reflect a plurality of approaches, moving from close readings of particular case studies; to critical, theoretical and historiographic considerations on the terms and concepts upon which such studies are grounded; into more speculative or collaborative modes of thinking. These latter include a number of speculative cartographies that move towards a comprehensive undoing of the global contemporary's rigid spatio-temporal teleology:

> *The task is to develop maps that are based on a multiplicity of scales and projections, and a multiplicity of symbolisation – a river can be a body of water and can be a sacred being. Scales, set squares and compasses alone will not work; we also require hands, feet and hearts. And memory.*[15]

As we move into the third decade of the twenty-first century, the idea of a global contemporary art no longer seems an adequate vessel through which to establish alternatives to the dominant mode of planetary relationships established through modernity-coloniality.[16] The ecosystems that Silvia Rivera Cusicanqui describes in this section, for instance, are simply beyond the epistemology of the global contemporary to understand – however much it may, out of ignorance, attempt to tame and control them. The apparent endlessness and divided realities of digital space, another development from the early 1990s, is similarly contingent on these forces.[17] Perhaps here we finally reach the ultimate cul-de-sac of global contemporary art: we refuse its bid to contain and control every culturally significant object on earth, turning our backs on its claim to global universalism once and for all. This feels like a more optimistic position from which to listen to other knowledges and coexist with different traditions of 'art', understood as a pluriversal, non-linear experience with 'the Energy of the cosmos … the dialectic without synthesis in which the *kupi* half, state and masculine, encounters/collides with the *chiqa* half, earthly and feminine'.[18] Brook Andrew offers another answer to what the decolonial might mean in exhibition-making practice, to its participants:

> *They felt represented and in a community. Many artists said to me that often they were in exhibitions and they were the only black, trans, PoC, queer whatever from that group in their country – they were artists ticked off in boxes. This horrified me. But I understand and have experienced it. Swing around to yindyamarra and how this philosophy isn't about comparing or fixing the western dilemma of the decolonial. It's about being present.*[19]

Perhaps rather than the 'contemporary' as a framework for thinking about art, publics and exhibition-making today, we may remain with the condition of being 'present' and sharing presence.

Notes

1 This paraphrases the frontispiece description offered in the first nine volumes of our *Exhibition Histories* books, 2010–18.

2 See Nika Dubrovsky and David Graeber, 'Another Art World', parts 1 and 2, *e-flux*, no.102 and 104, September 2019–November 2020, https://www.e-flux.com/journal/102/284624/another-art-world-part-1-art-communism-and-artificial-scarcity/ and https://www.e-flux.com/journal/104/298663/another-art-world-part-2-utopia-of-freedom-as-a-market-value/.

3 Francesca Recchia, 'Aftermaths? dOCUMENTA (13) in Kabul', in this volume. For a perspective on the wider context of internationally funded cultural initiatives in Afghanistan in this period, see F. Recchia, 'Kabul Good: Cultural Politics of an Endless War', available at http://www.tanqeed.org/2015/08/kabul-good-cultural-politics-of-an-endless-war/.

4 Charles Esche, 'Introduction: Making Art Global: A Good Place or a No Place?', in Rachel Weiss et al., *Making Art Global (Part 1): The Third Havana Biennial 1989*, London: Afterall Books, 2011, p.12.

5 The fortunes of the nation also depend on where one is looking. Ntone Edjabe here describes the African nation state 'under extreme duress. In the context of the colonial instrument of the land survey and its counterpart, the land legislation regime, our continent seems to be reverting to its earlier knowledges of territory against the more recent colonial and postcolonial instrument of cartography – against "survey" – while also exerting newly emerging knowledges and ways of thinking against the same instrument.' See N. Edjabe, 'How to Eat a Forest', in this volume.

6 L. Steeds, 'Introduction: Activating What Might Have Happened to Shape What Could Be', in Paul O'Neill, Simon Sheikh, Lucy Steeds and Mick Wilson (ed.), *Curating After the Global: Roadmaps for the Present*, Cambridge, MA: MIT Press, 2019, p.224.

7 See '"Cities on the Move" in Public Space: A Journey Through the Archive', in this volume.

8 See Luiza Proença, 'Potosí Principle: Following the Devil's Tail', in this volume.

9 This notion of 'incomplete modernity' is employed by David Teh in 'Who Cares a Lot? ruangrupa as Curatorship', in this volume. Questions of contemporaneity in this context were the subject of the 2016 symposium 'Regions of the Contemporary: Transnational Art Festivals and Exhibitions in Southeast Asia', co-organised by Afterall and the School of Culture and Communication, University of Melbourne. See also D. Teh and David Morris (ed.), *Artist-to-Artist: Independent Art Festivals in Chiang Mai 1992–98*, London: Afterall Books, 2018; and Bo Choy, 'On Womanifesto' and Võ Hồng Chương-Đài, 'Viva ExCon: Itinerant Indeterminacy', both in this volume.

10 See Geeta Kapur, 'Contemporary Cultural Practice: Some Polemical Categories', in R. Weiss et al., *Making Art Global (Part 1)*, *op. cit.*, p.203. Kapur reflects on the subsequent developments of this position in her conversation with Natasha Ginwala 'On the Curatorial in India', in this volume.

11 See Gayatri Chakravorty Spivak, 'Looking at Others', in L. Steeds et al., *Making Art Global (Part 2): 'Magiciens de la Terre' 1989*, London: Afterall Books, pp.260–66.

12 Reiko Tomii, 'Historicizing "Contemporary Art": Some Discursive Practices in Gendai Bijutsu in Japan', *positions*, vol.12, no.3, 2004, pp.612–13.

13 Miguel A. López, 'How do we know what Latin American conceptualism looks like?', in this volume.

14 For instance, Pablo Lafuente explores how the early 2000s exhibition project 'Contemporary Arab Representations' employed the notion of 'representations' in favour of 'art'. See P. Lafuente, 'Art and the Foreigner's Gaze: A Report on Contemporary Arab Representations', in this volume. Miguel A. López, *op. cit.*, also addresses how Tucumán Arde exceeded the attempts to represent it via its archive in subsequent exhibition representations in European institutions.

15 N. Edjabe, 'How to Eat a Forest', in this volume. Adjoa Armah extends and expands on these cartographic imaginaries via a consideration of the 'Black ungeographic' for 'In our language the word for the sea means "the spirit that returns"', in this volume.

16 Coloniality is how Walter Mignolo defines the continuing force of the colonial matrix of power that remains the dominant frame through which planetary relations are managed today. He argues it is through decolonising minds and knowledge that societies can develop other options to the Western universal. See, for instance, W. Mignolo and Catherine E. Walsh, *On Decoloniality: Concepts, Analytics, Praxis*, Durham, NC: Duke University Press, 2014.

17 See Adeena Mey and D. Morris, 'In Real Life – A Reflection on the Online Exhibition', in this volume.

18 Silvia Rivera Cusicanqui, 'Amo la montaña / I Love the Mountain', in this volume.

19 See Brook Andrew and Anthony Gardner, 'NIRIN WURRUNMARRA', in this volume.

How to Eat a Forest

Ntone Edjabe

Over the past two centuries the visible, material and symbolic boundaries of Africa have constantly expanded and contracted. … New forms of territoriality and unexpected forms of locality have appeared. Their limits do not necessarily intersect with the official limits, norms or language of states.
– Achille Mbembe[1]

History is the science of the state, while memory is the art of the stateless.
– Wendell Hassan Marsh[2]

It has often been said that cartography is the tool of the colonial project. But it is rarely acknowledged that mapping has remained a major instrument of political and economic interests beyond the colonial project. A few years ago writer Billy Kahora travelled to a region on the southern edge of the Great Rift Valley in Kenya that forms part of the Mau Forest Complex, the largest forest area in East Africa.[3] The complex is a water catchment of more than ten rivers and numerous lakes in both East and Central Africa. It was once said to occupy 273,300 hectares, three times the size of Nairobi's administrative district. Kahora was there to write about the eviction of what were being described as 'encroachers', or landless peasants from neighbouring tribes; he noted the buzzword, which proved as unyielding as the claims of the people being described thus. 'Squatter' had always been the term of choice in such circumstances, and Kahora became curious about this relatively new term, encroacher, and its connotations. The difference, in the context of the Mau, is simply that an encroacher is seen to be a 'foreign invader', and a squatter is a propertyless individual from within. The squatter is considered to be relatively harmless, while the encroacher seizes and intrudes on property that has been clearly mapped and is already owned. There is a primordial hatred towards encroachers by locals, while some impatient tolerance seems to exist for the squatter. At the heart of all this was an attempt by the encroachers to change the map. Encroachers seize territory, change maps to their advantages. Squatters do not threaten the cartographical status quo.

This seemingly harmless distinction completely changed things in the Mau scenario. These so-called encroachers were the tip of an attempt at one of the largest land grabs in Kenya's history: they were the most visible manifestation of the attempted abuse of one of two instruments that govern the process of land ownership, cartography, which in this context can be described using the less grand term 'survey'.

Survey, like encroachment, was a ubiquitous term in the Mau saga, used invariably by both the communal owners of the land and the encroachers. This modern word had entered the lingo to justify illegal actions – 'survey this' and 'survey that' – and had also been appropriated by the victims into something that was itself illegal, hostile to the old ways. So, as Kahora discovered in the depths of the Mau, one of the biggest untold stories about our continent is the abuse of the technical aspects of the land survey. What is measured point by point on the ground, and the representation that tallies this exact measurement, can be changed arbitrarily if no one is fighting for a neutral and epic-sized territory such as the natural space of a forest. A land surveyor might be instructed by powerful political and economic interests to redraw a map of the original piece of land, to eat up a forest. This disregard of natural boundaries in favour of new and recreated boundaries is at the heart of the problems of our knowledge of self, of our spaces and of our territories. But a contestation of who the land belongs to and who is new, who is local and who is an encroacher, is at the heart of the struggles against our official atlas.

More than the abuse of law, especially as regards land, it is this disregard for pre-existing boundaries and organically emerging ones that has given lie to what our territories really are and what they mean. And so, lately, the primary entity of how we understand our spaces, the nation-state – the result of the colonial survey, accepted by the independent African nation – is for this exact reason coming under extreme duress. In the context of the colonial instrument of the land survey and its counterpart, the land legislation regime, our continent seems to be reverting to its earlier knowledges of territory against the more recent colonial and postcolonial instrument of cartography – against 'survey' – while also exerting newly emerging knowledges and ways of thinking against the same instrument.

Our atlas is therefore now being reshaped into territories of new religious ecumenisms that are related to Christianity, Islam and African religions; sexual and pleasure territories; contemporary migratory phenomena manifested in refugee camps that produce armies without a state, making war a phenomenon that is disconnected from the state; and resource-based territorialities where water is especially key (issues around the Nile indicate this phenomenon).

So, we ask: What were the precolonial visible, material and symbolic boundaries and what is their relationship with official state boundaries today? What are the new forms of territoriality and unexpected forms of locality? How does one now represent Greater Somalia? What of the Swahili Coast that extends from Kenya through Tanzania and Northern Mozambique, of its reluctance to be integrated into any national project other than its own, which goes back to the fourteenth century? What of the transnational identity of the Tuareg across the Sahel belt, who are at the core of several conflicts in that region, from Libya to Mali and Chad? What are the African names of the Indian Ocean? And as a site of world-making, what role did this ocean-territory play in the emergence of Third World politics? What are the new divisions of the world and how do they affect our continent – from the war on terror to the Sahara-Mediterranean as boundary? Who are the neo-pats and re-pats (new and returning migrants), and where do they come from? What are the new capitals – for the church-industrial complex of Anglophone West Africa, for example? Or for the drug trade in East Africa?

So, we ask: What if maps were made by Africans for their own use, to understand and make visible their own realities or imaginaries? How do we, on the continent, create a cartography that is so exactingly representative of our fluidities, complexities and material realities?

Jorge Luis Borges's fable 'Del rigor en la ciencia' ('On Exactitude in Science', 1946) might be a good start for such work. An exacting representation, cartography or series of maps can only start with an attempt to understand every inch, foot, unit of measurement of the thing we claim to stand on as our own, our continent. The territory we claim as collectively ours. The reality we all take on. The knowledge we herald as our own. This approach suggests that the optimal way to real ownership is to map one's reality; to make an exacting representation, point for point, centimetre for centimetre, whether it is land, water, dreams. Then, after possibly understanding one's reality in its minutiae, to earn the right to work on a replication, to create real understanding and knowledge. If this is done right, the representation should be directly proportional to the confidence of one's knowledge.

This work requires that we reaffirm lived experience, improvisation and imagination as forms of knowledge. It calls for a knowing-through-seeking and a constant transforming and renewing of our image of the world.

This is important because over time the few and powerful on our continent have excelled, to their advantage, in creating an atlas without exactitude. Therefore, our knowledge of the territory is never ours. At the same time, a too exacting knowledge would be useless; a too representative approach would distance us from the real. We also need our own modes of representation on our own terms, our own materialities and needs.

The task is to develop maps that are based on a multiplicity of scales and projections, and a multiplicity of symbolisation – a river can be a body of water and can be a sacred being. Scales, set squares and compasses alone will not work; we also require hands, feet and hearts. And memory.

The following maps are part of an atlas of our discontent at misrepresentations, an ongoing attempt to represent our knowledge of our spaces with some exactitude. It is also an attempt to balance exactitude and representation.

Notes

[1] Achille Mbembe, 'At the Edge of the World: Boundaries, Territoriality, and Sovereignty in Africa' (trans. Steven Rendall), *Public Culture*, vol.12, no.1, 2000, p.261.
[2] Wendell Hassan Marsh, 'Re-Membering the Name of God', *Chronic*, March 2015, p.19, available at http://chimurengachronic.co.za/re-membering-the-name-of-god/.
[3] See Billy Kahora, 'How to Eat a Forest', *Chronic*, March 2015, pp.28–31 and 34–35, available at http://chimurengachronic.co.za/how-to-eat-a-forest/.

SOFT POWER DESIRE MACHINES AND

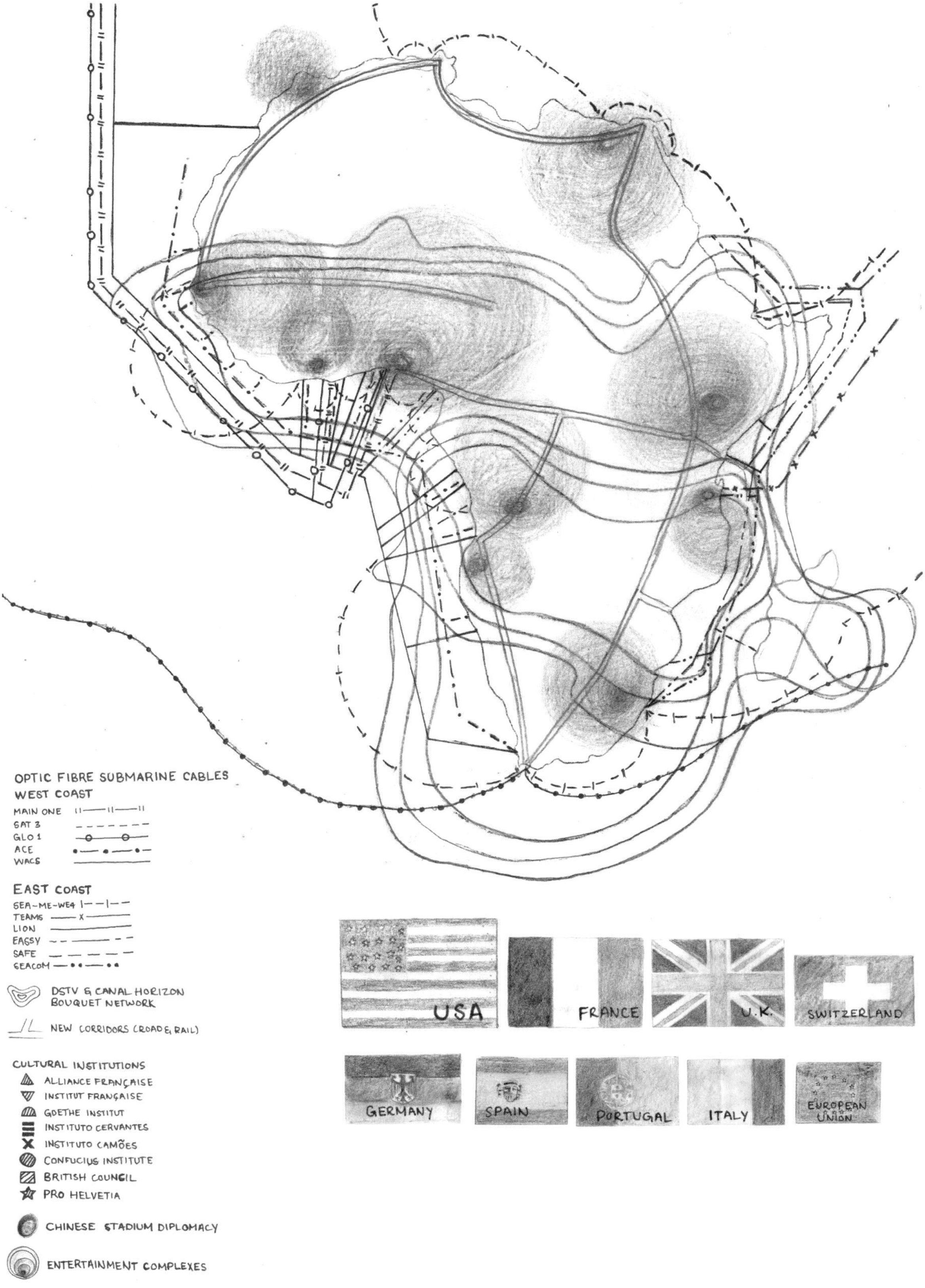

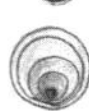

THE PRODUCTION OF AFRICA RISING

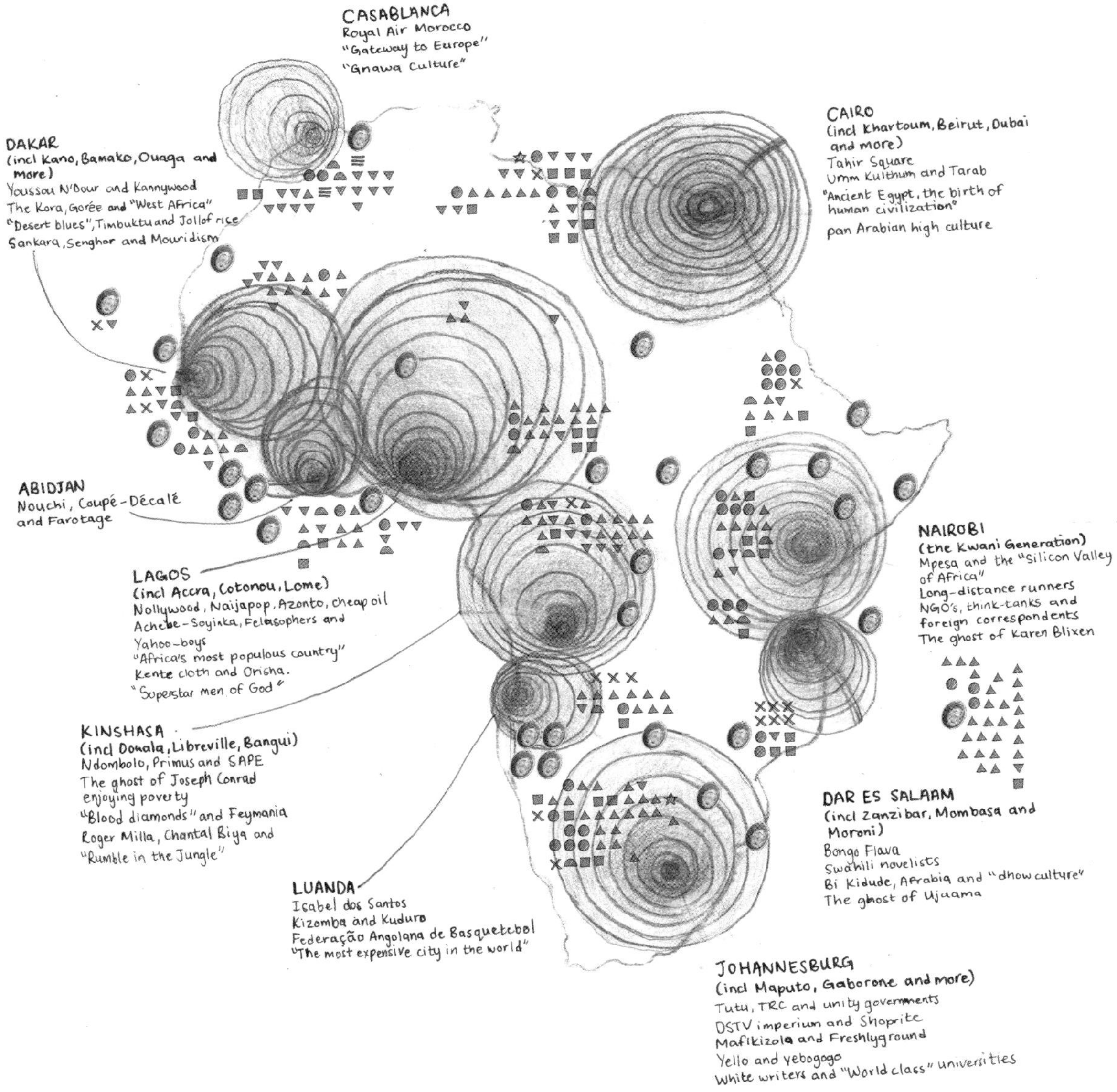

CASABLANCA
Royal Air Morocco
"Gateway to Europe"
"Gnawa Culture"

CAIRO
(incl Khartoum, Beirut, Dubai and more)
Tahir Square
Umm Kulthum and Tarab
"Ancient Egypt, the birth of human civilization"
pan Arabian high culture

DAKAR
(incl Kano, Bamako, Ouaga and more)
Youssou N'Dour and Kannywood
The Kora, Gorée and "West Africa"
"Desert blues", Timbuktu and Jollof rice
Sankara, Senghor and Mouridism

ABIDJAN
Nouchi, Coupé-Décalé and Farotage

NAIROBI
(the Kwani Generation)
Mpesa and the "Silicon Valley of Africa"
Long-distance runners
NGO's, think-tanks and foreign correspondents
The ghost of Karen Blixen

LAGOS
(incl Accra, Cotonou, Lome)
Nollywood, Naijapop, Azonto, cheap oil
Achebe-Soyinka, Felasophers and Yahoo-boys
"Africa's most populous country"
Kente cloth and Orisha.
"Superstar men of God"

KINSHASA
(incl Douala, Libreville, Bangui)
Ndombolo, Primus and SAPE
The ghost of Joseph Conrad enjoying poverty
"Blood diamonds" and Feymania
Roger Milla, Chantal Biya and "Rumble in the Jungle"

DAR ES SALAAM
(incl Zanzibar, Mombasa and Moroni)
Bongo Flava
Swahili novelists
Bi Kidude, Afrabia and "dhow culture"
The ghost of Ujaama

LUANDA
Isabel dos Santos
Kizomba and Kuduro
Federação Angolana de Basquetebol
"The most expensive city in the world"

JOHANNESBURG
(incl Maputo, Gaborone and more)
Tutu, TRC and unity governments
DSTV imperium and Shoprite
Mafikizola and Freshlyground
Yello and yebogogo
White writers and "World class" universities

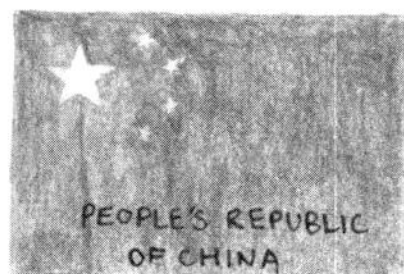

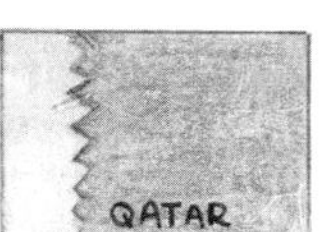

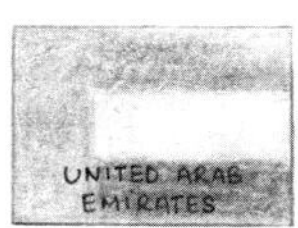

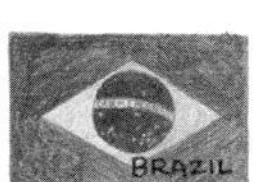

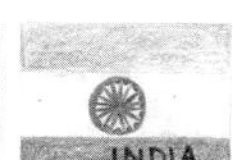

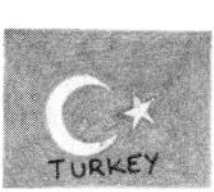

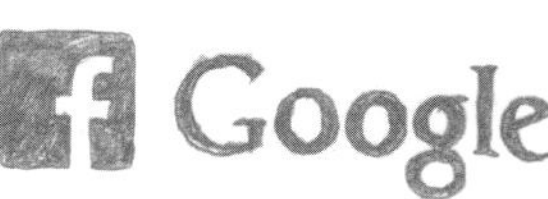

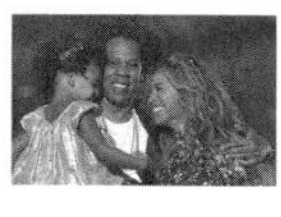

Sources:
TeleGeography submarine cable map http://www.submarinecablemap.com/
Culture Means Business British Council Report
Gregory Paschalidis, 'Exporting National Culture: History of Cultural Institutes Abroad', International Journal of Cultural Policy
Rui Yang, 'Soft Power and Education: an examination of China's Confucius Institutes', Globalication, Societies and Education
Jesse Weaver Shipley, 'Living the Hiplife: Celebrity and Entrepreneurship in Ghanaian Popular Music

British Council www.britishcouncil.org
Alliance Francaise – www.alliancefr.org
Institut Francais – www.institutfrancais.com
Goethe Institut – www.goethe.de
Confucius Institute – www.chinesecio.com
Instituto Camões – www.Instituto-Camões.pt
Instituto Cervantes – www.londres.cervantes.es

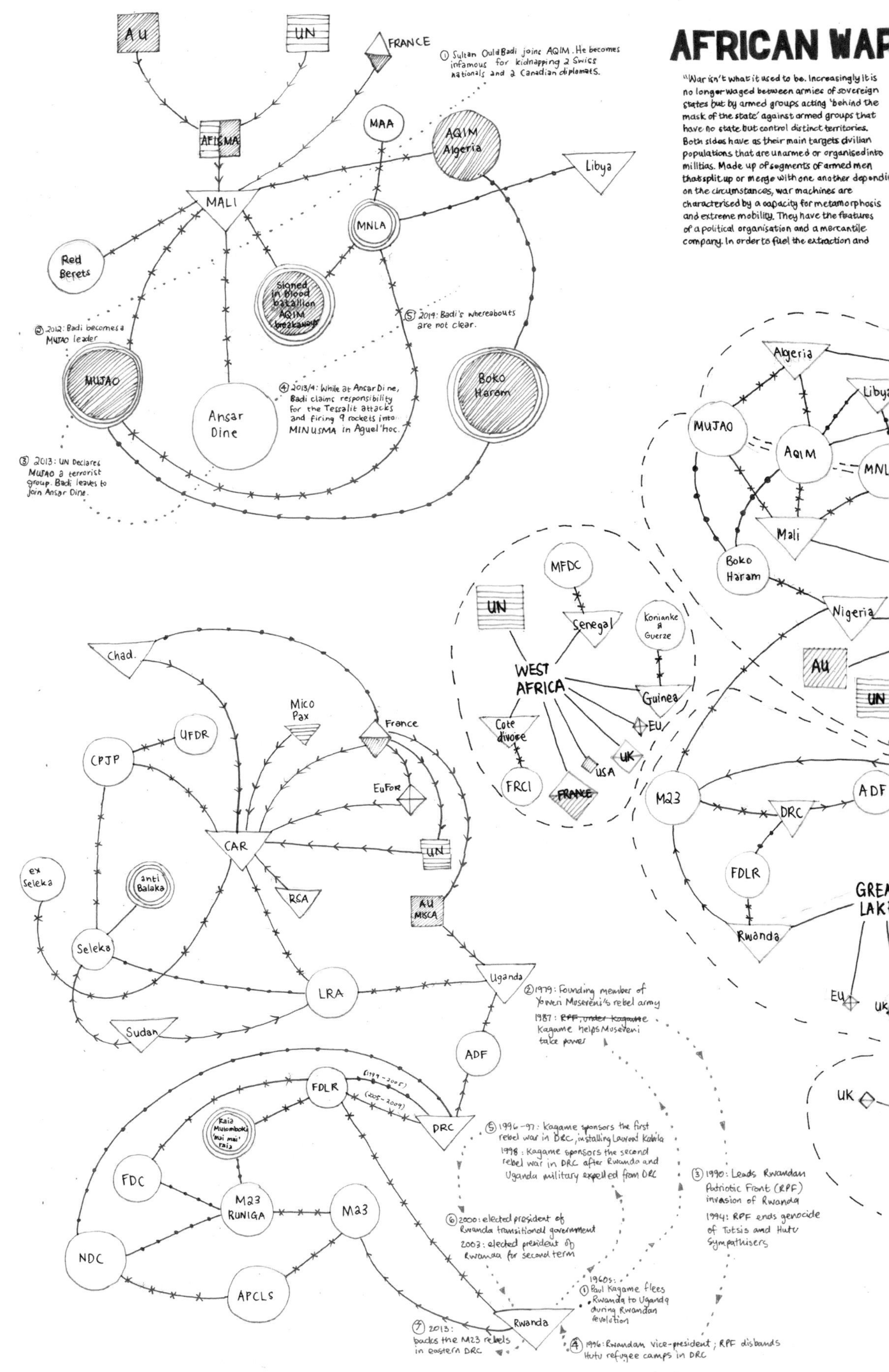

AFRICAN WAR

"War isn't what it used to be. Increasingly it is no longer waged between armies of sovereign states but by armed groups acting 'behind the mask of the state' against armed groups that have no state but control distinct territories. Both sides have as their main targets civilian populations that are unarmed or organised into militias. Made up of segments of armed men that split up or merge with one another depending on the circumstances, war machines are characterised by a capacity for metamorphosis and extreme mobility. They have the features of a political organisation and a mercantile company. In order to fuel the extraction and

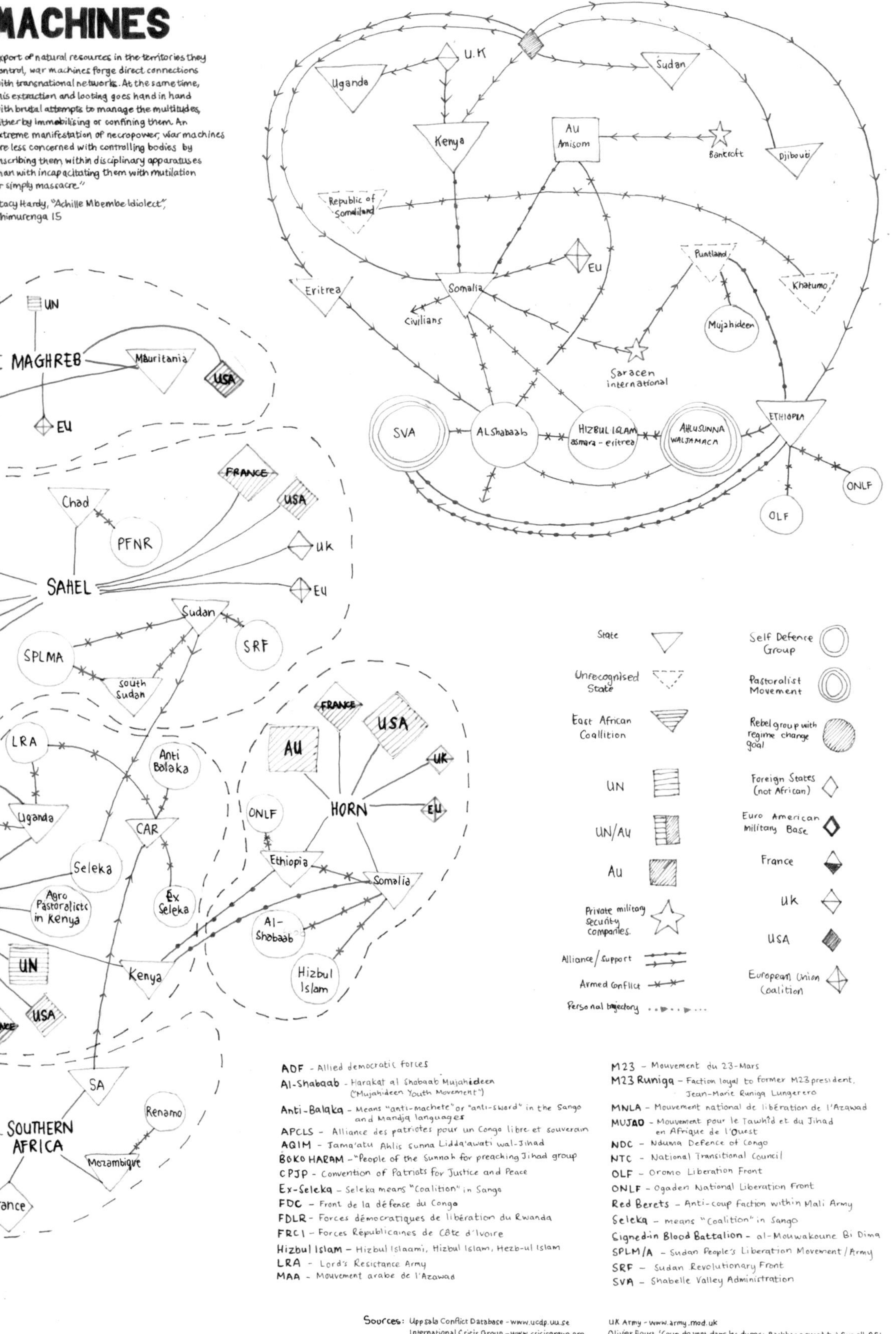
MACHINES
xport of natural resources in the territories they
ontrol, war machines forge direct connections
with transnational networks. At the same time,
his extraction and looting goes hand in hand
with brutal attempts to manage the multitudes,
ither by immobilising or confining them. An
xtreme manifestation of necropower, war machines
re less concerned with controlling bodies by
nscribing them within disciplinary apparatuses
han with incapacitating them with mutilation
r simply massacre."
Lacy Hardy, "Achille Mbembe Idiolect",
Chimurenga 15

UN
MAGHREB
Mauritania
USA
EU

FRANCE
Chad
USA
PFNR
uk
SAHEL
EU
Sudan
SRF
SPLMA
South
Sudan

LRA
FRANCE
USA
Anti
Balaka
AU
UK
Uganda
ONLF
EU
CAR
HORN
Seleka
Ethiopia
Agro
Pastoralists
in Kenya
Ex
Seleka
Somalia
Al-
Shabaab
UN
Kenya
Hizbul
Islam
USA
NCE
SA
SOUTHERN
AFRICA
Renamo
Mozambique
ance

U.K
Uganda
Sudan
Kenya
Au
Amisom
Bancroft
Djibouti
Republic of
Somaliland
EU
Puntland
Khatumo
Eritrea
Somalia
Mujahideen
Civilians
Saracen
international
SVA
AL Shabaab
HIZBUL ISLAM
asmara - eritrea
AHLUSUNNA
WALJAMACA
ETHIOPIA
ONLF
OLF

State
Self Defence
Group
Unrecognised
State
Pastoralist
Movement
East African
Coalition
Rebel group with
regime change
goal
UN
Foreign States
(not African)
UN/AU
Euro American
Military Base
Au
France
Private military
security
companies.
uk
USA
Alliance / support
European Union
Coalition
Armed conflict
Personal trajectory
ADF - Allied democratic forces
Al-Shabaab - Harakat al Shabaab Mujahideen
("Mujahideen Youth Movement")
Anti-Balaka - Means "anti-machete" or "anti-sword" in the Sango
and Mandja languages
APCLS - Alliance des patriotes pour un Congo libre et souverain
AQIM - Jama'atu Ahlis sunna Lidda'awati wal-Jihad
BOKO HARAM - "People of the Sunnah for preaching Jihad group"
CPJP - Convention of Patriots for Justice and Peace
Ex-Seleka - Seleka means "Coalition" in Sango
FDC - Front de la défense du Congo
FDLR - Forces démocratiques de libération du Rwanda
FRCI - Forces Républicaines de Côte d'Ivoire
Hizbul Islam - Hizbul Islaami, Hizbul Islam, Hezb-ul Islam
LRA - Lord's Resistance Army
MAA - Mouvement arabe de l'Azawad

M23 - Mouvement du 23-Mars
M23 Runiga - Faction loyal to former M23 president,
Jean-Marie Runiga Lungerero
MNLA - Mouvement national de libération de l'Azawad
MUJAO - Mouvement pour le Tawhid et du Jihad
en Afrique de l'Ouest
NDC - Nduma Defence of Congo
NTC - National Transitional Council
OLF - Oromo Liberation Front
ONLF - Ogaden National Liberation Front
Red Berets - Anti-coup faction within Mali Army
Seleka - means "Coalition" in Sango
Signed-in Blood Battalion - al-Mouwakoune Bi Dima
SPLM/A - Sudan People's Liberation Movement / Army
SRF - Sudan Revolutionary Front
SVA - Shabelle Valley Administration

Sources: Uppsala Conflict Database - www.ucdp.uu.se
International Crisis Group - www.crisisgroup.org
United Nations Peacekeeping - www.un.org
AU Peacekeeping - www.peaceau.org

UK Army - www.army.mod.uk
Olivier Fourt, 'Coup de vent dans les dunes: Barkhane succède à Serval', RFI
Nick Turse, 'America's Proxy Wars in Africa', The Nation

In our language the word for the sea means the 'spirit that returns'

Adjoa Armah

The tendency of disciplinary conventions (e.g. cartography) to stand as statements of fact cannot survive an ongoing confrontation with their own virtuality – that part of their diagrammatic function which stands as a structure of possibility, in plural, not universal. While any diagram propagates through actual power, its virtuality simultaneously reveals the limits of that power. Ironically a diagram's power is bounded (limited) by its inherent unboundedness. Which is to say, a diagram is always only an option.
– Nolan Oswald Dennis[1]

As much as the map re-presents a geographical territory, landscape or space, it is infused with time and temporality, usually at the intersection of the distance between two points on it. The map is also infused with several intersecting and conflicting temporal domains. There are the past(s) – of the mapmaker, of the mapped territory that lies inert on the map – the present(s) – of the map user, of the mapped terrain's changes in reality – and the future(s) of all of those events. These interactive temporal domains fuse together as a 3-D invisible hologram layered over the body of the map.
– Rasheedah Phillips[2]

Starting from near nowhere

I found my way to the land closest to nowhere after Google Maps said there was no road to follow. My eyes told me different and I kept going. To get there that first night, especially alone after dark, I was far more reliant on strangers' knowledges of well-travelled roads than any formal map or its timings. Nowhere is an invention. Real or not, it enables navigation, not on land but at sea:

Latitude 0°
Longitude 0°
Altitude 0°

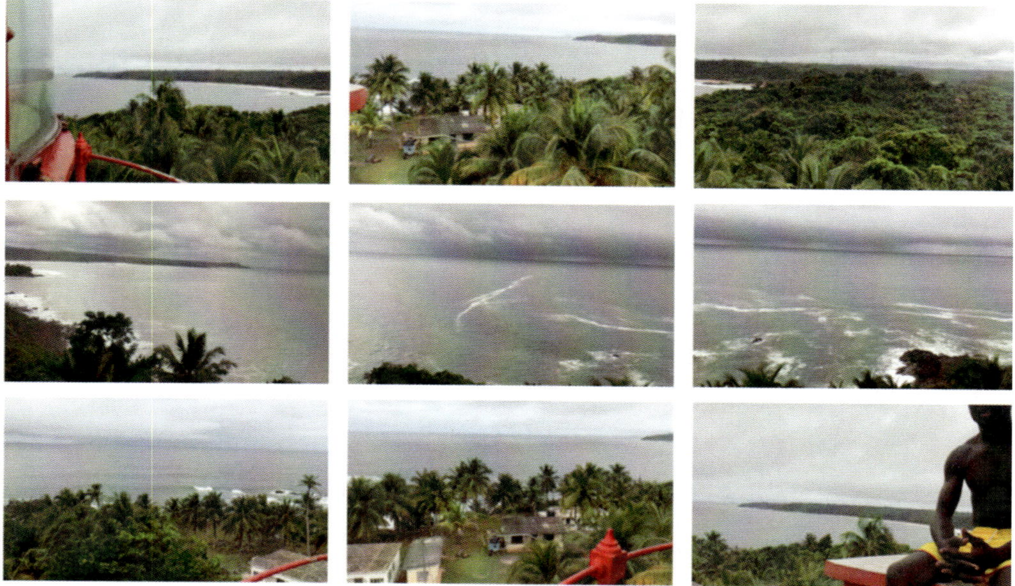

Nowhere is the centre of the surface of the world. It is on the longitude line that links Britain and Ghana. Nowhere sets its clocks to Greenwich Mean Time. This nowhere is *the* nowhere because the British were best at sea. The land closest to nowhere is a cape jutting out into the Atlantic, not to one point, but three: nowhere is never somewhere you get to one way.

From near nowhere I found my way to, and now attempt to map, Princes Town, Akwidaa, Dixcove and Butre. Tracing the routes to, from, between and within Fort Fredericksburg, Fort Dorothea, Fort Metal Cross and Fort Batenstein. From the land closest to nowhere my work is to know where Brandenburg territory became Dutch or British, and when, and what that meant. The work is also to listen for why what had long been Pokesu became Princes Town, and who decided the land under control of Chief Dekyi should be known as Dixcove.

When people of the African Diaspora come to Ghana searching, relatively few end up this far west. At least not specifically for the forts – the beaches are a bigger draw and there are more significant forts elsewhere. More often, Cape Coast and Elmina are both the primary destinations and points of departure. From there, routes are followed inland, towards particular markets or water bodies, or out to the sea from Cape Coast and Elmina castles. It's far less common for forts to initiate the type of journey I'm on, border to border along the Trans-West African Coastal Highway, searching. And why would they?

> These sites were never for Africans on the continent.
> Black people of the New World have different routes.
> Europeans seldom come looking.

Views from Cape Three Points Lighthouse, Ghana, 2019. Courtesy of the author

Of intervals to be traversed[3]
Several years ago in *Afterall* Ntone Edjabe of Chimurenga asked:

> *What if maps were made by Africans for their own use, to understand and make visible their own realities and imaginaries? How do we, on the continent, create a cartography that is so exactingly representative of our fluidities, complexities and material realities?*[4]

Before that nowhere was understood as such, and a near nowhere could be positioned relative to it, there were long histories here. Nowhere's legibility was ordered by the destructions, displacements, disappearances and desecrations of these histories. Yet, life never stopped. Not enough would be made visible without attending to these histories. Before, during and after this nowhere making its mind up about itself, there were innumerable lives taken, as in ended and transported. Those lives kept much from here and made much elsewhere. Not enough would be made visible without attending to these.

What would it take to map these sites? Really map for time and movement? Map for sets of relationships? Map for hopes, dreams, and possibility? Map for different registers of knowledge and modes of knowing? Ntone ended his call for an Africa-centred cartography thus:

> *The task is to develop maps that are based on a multiplicity of scales and projections, and a multiplicity of symbolisation – a river can be a body of water and can be a sacred being. Scales, set squares and compasses alone will not work; we also require hands, feet and hearts. And memory.*[5]

In addressing these questions and needs, allow me to attend to a constellation of moments, thinking and a set of practices that might support one in adequately orienting themselves in a cartographic endeavour of this sort.

A brief consideration of the Black (un)geographic

Black geographies, and the Black *ungeographic*,[6] are action, not discipline. Instead they are the work of un-disciplining, bringing disparate worlds into correspondence, negating dominant protocols, casting place-making as a set of ideas and not strictly a knowable geography.[7] Black geographies do not fix knowledge or affirm knowability. They are open, infinite possibility. They are not, and should not only be, the rejection of cartography as a colonial tool, a rejection of the abuses of power, and a move towards the possibility of claims of ownership. Black geographies help us question the desire to own. They enable us to perhaps approach the coast of Western Africa as part of the shoals of normative theorising of the spatio-temporalities of New World conquest,[8] constituting moments 'of convergence, gathering, reassembling and coming together (or apart)'.[9]

I begin a consideration of African cartography with an insistence, also, on Black geographies because the project that is being embarked on is not only in knowing our land, and ourselves, in relation to the erasures of the colonial project, and abuses that followed it *here* on the continent, but in relay with,

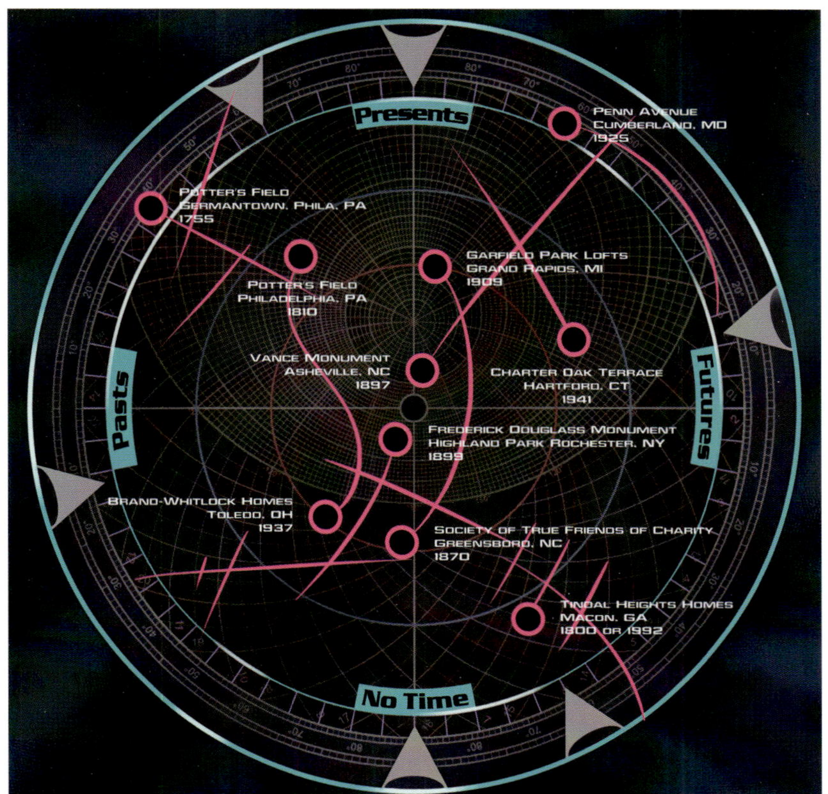

Black Quantum Futurism, *Time Capsule Map*, 2021. Courtesy Black Quantum Futurism

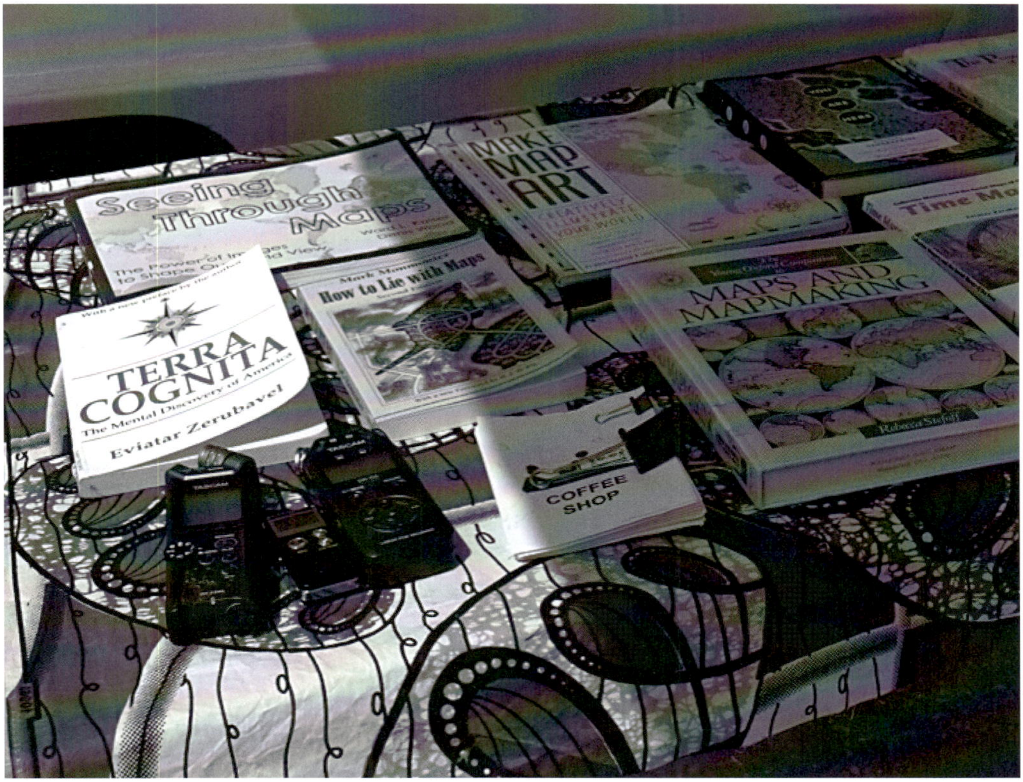

Below: 'You are now here', workshop, 2017. Courtesy Black Quantum Futurism

and relation to, ourselves as Black people, *anywhere*. Black geographies ensure we can stand at numerous doors of no return[10] and allow them to be animated both by those who went through and those who didn't. They account for befores, durings and afters, asking:

What else happened?[11]

What is happening?
What could happen?
What should happen?

What are the relationships between these what's? In the questioning, too, is a drawing forth.

'I want to find a way to draw a map home when I am already at home'[12]

I am interested in Nolan Oswald Dennis's and Black Quantum Futurisms' (BQF)[13] cartographic practices and the guidance and strategies they provide. From Johannesburg-based Dennis is a systems- rather than site-specific approach towards topology and a diagrammatics of Black spatial consciousness. In his practice, various differences are made concurrently traversable as multiple social fictions are stitched together. From Philadelphia-based BQF, initiated by Rasheedah Phillips and Camae Ayewa (stage name Moor Mother), is a community-embedded spatio-temporal practice: ranging from housing journey maps, sonic mappings, communal memory mapping and a digital temporal portal.[14] In each of these cartographies is the offering of a strategy for being (in)/(with) time otherwise than with Western space-time constructions. Both practices grapple with the ontological and existential impacts of colonialism, a project that Phillips acknowledges did 'different versions of the same thing to all Black people everywhere'.[15]

By attuning their assumptions about reality to the laws of quantum physics, BQF open up not only simultaneous *elsewheres,* but also *elsewhens.* Their alignment with a scientific episteme, so valued by the Western imagination, confirms at the quantum scale realities as Africans have always understood them, opening radical possibilities for imagination and relation. In this gesture, BQF establish a particular deconstructive relationship with the Western project. Considering their work with the master's clock and map,[16] the physical assumptions of their practice are an extension of concerns with what might constitute and how one may use a tool. Additionally, Phillips's work as a housing lawyer extends the possibilities offered by the tools not calibrated towards the dignity of Black life. As she explains: 'When I approach my work as a community lawyer I also become a specific kind of instrument or tool. This tool has to work with facticity in different ways to my artistic practice but there are ways it can allow people to access spaces that are privileged.'[17]

Dennis also considers this terrain, asking when certain tools stop being a master's and can become yours: 'What do I need to do for it to do something else?'[18] And arriving at the import of using 'small gestures for holding secrets:

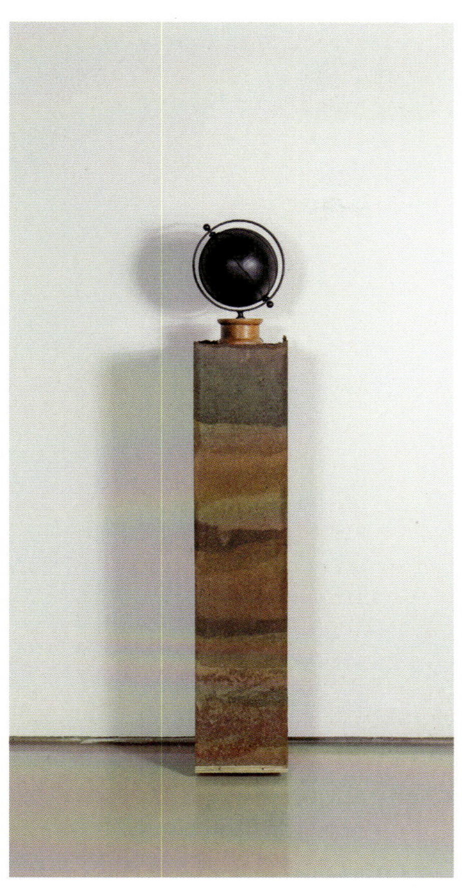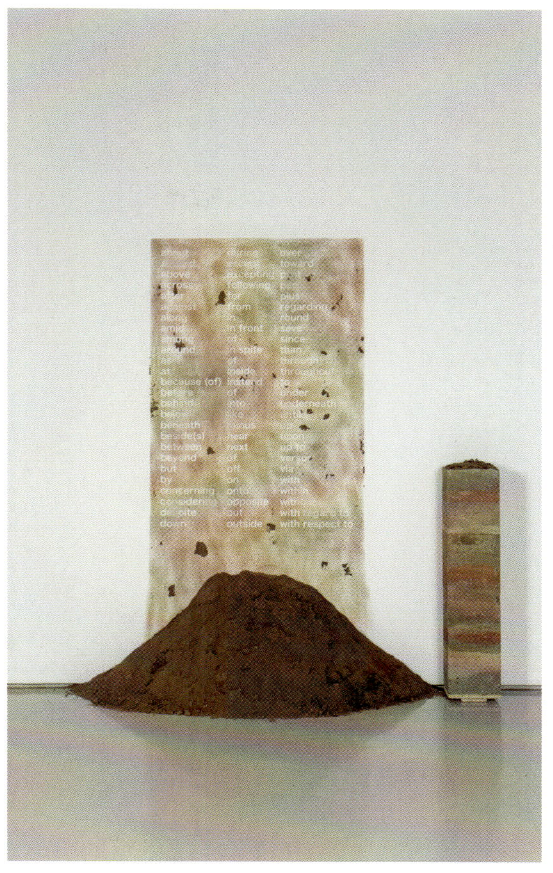

marks, notations, clues'.[19] Whether in cartography itself, writing, or drawing, 'the task is not to be so familiar with something that I now know its inner secrets and can perform some kind of transmutation … the task is to be with the tool in ways that can be delinked from the antagonistic or general project'.[20]

In Dennis's being with differently, is a drawing forth. Particularly through his relationship with drawing, his draughtsmanship developed through an architectural training that makes assumptions about space at odds with Black spatial consciousness. His is a being with a technology of spatial representation in ways that recognise that, 'African people have learnt how to move through this world while knowing that this world is not real'.[21] They are not drawings of, but drawings as, space. They get at the things underneath: the blood vessels, the guts, the underground tunnels. Their systems approach allows one to meet as many of the interactions that make space possible as possible. They are projections in systems in need of projections. In this practice of being, and drawing forth, with graphite and paper, to draw is also 'simply, to equalise. As in 1–1, a draw. To draw is to equivocate, in the abstract, such that what is drawn can stand for what is not.'[22]

Left:
Nolan Oswald Dennis, *xenolith IV*, 2018

Right:
Nolan Oswald Dennis, *xenolith V: prepositions*, 2018. Courtesy the artist and Goodman Gallery

Next spread:
Nolan Oswald Dennis, *No Conciliation is possible (compensation set)*, 2019, installation. Courtesy the artist and Goodman Gallery

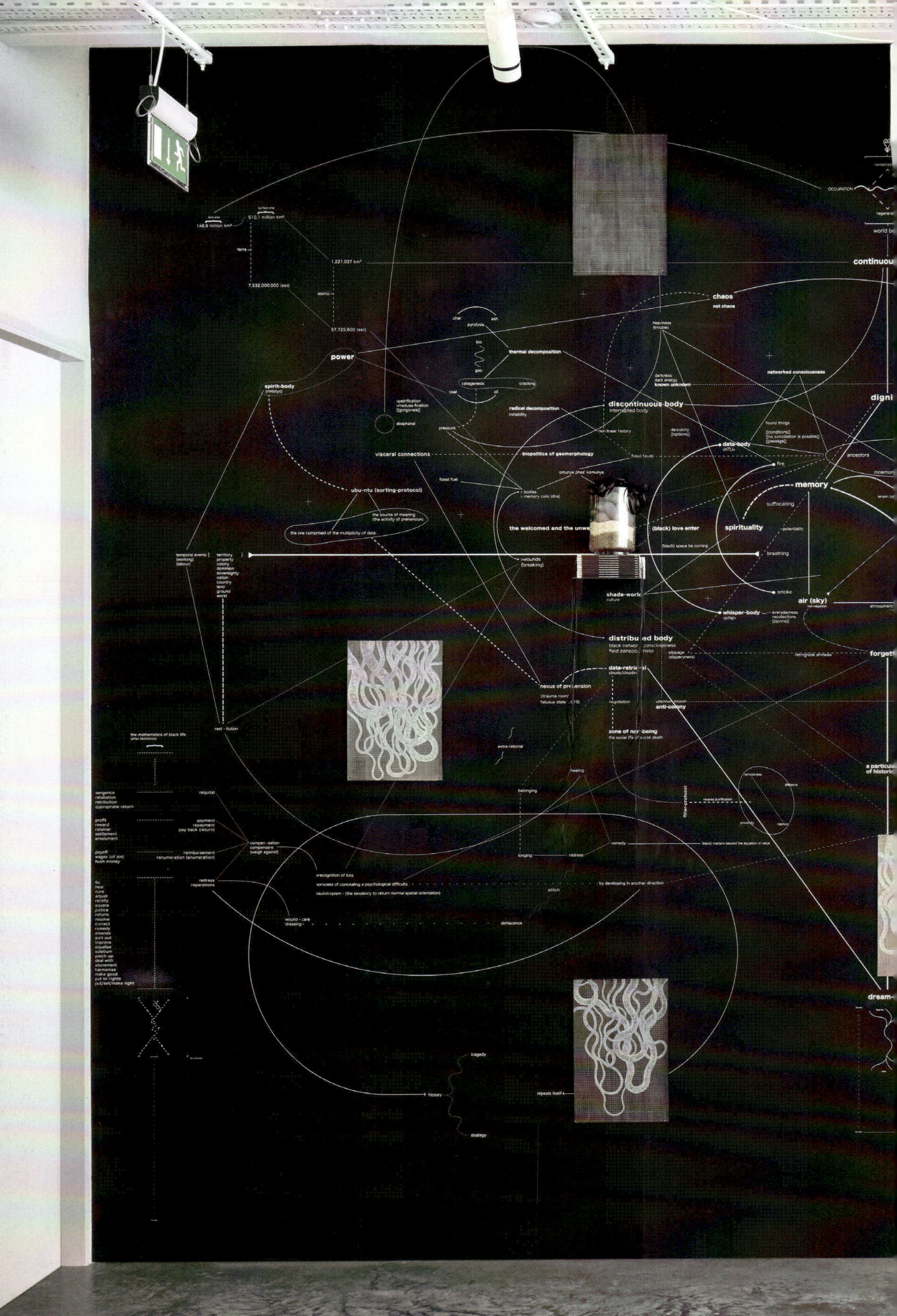
land area
148,9 million km²
surface area
510,1 million km²
terra
1.221.037 km²
7.532.000.000 (est)
aqua
57.725.500 (est)
power
spirit-body
[inkinyo]
char pyrolysis ash
bio
thermal decomposition
geo
catagenesis cracking
coal oil
abaphansi
pressure
radical decomposition
instability
chaos
not chaos
heaviness
[trouble]
darkness
dark energy
known unknown
networked consciousness
discontinuous body
interrupted body
continuous
digni
visceral connections
biopolitics of geomorphology
non linear history
de-colony
[optional]
found things
[conditions]
[no conciliation is possible]
[passage]
data-body
<NTU>
ancestors
fossil feuds
fire
memory
ubu-ntu (sorting-protocol)
fossil fuel
omunye phezi komunye
> bodies
> memory coils (dna)
suffocating
the source of meaning
(the activity of prehension)
the one comprised of the multiplicity of data
the welcomed and the unwe
(black) love enter
spirituality
potentiality
(black) space be coming
breathing
temporal events {   territory
[working]   property
[labour]   colony
dominion
sovereignty
nation
country
land
ground
world
>wounds
[breaking]
shade-world
culture
smoke
air (sky)
whisper-body
<ofaji>
everydayness
recollections
[ipona]
atmospheric
distributed body
black network consciousness
field consciousness
slippage
[slipperyness]
rethignics ahhelia
forget
the mathematics of black life
after McKittrick
nexus of prehension
[trauma room]
fabulous state - .118)
data-retrieval
clouds/clouding
negotiation
unknown known
anti-colony
rest - itution
zone of non-being
the social life of social death
a particula
of historica
extra-rational
healing
vengence
retaliation
retribution
appropriate return
requital
belonging
remoteness
transcendent
reverse purification
remedy
(black) matters beyond the equation of value
profit
reward
retainer
settlement
emolument
payment
repayment
pay back (return)
compen-sation
compensare
[weigh against]
payoff
wages (of sin)
hush money
reimbursement
renumeration (enumeration)
longing
redress
fix
heal
cure
adjust
rectify
square
justice
reform
resolve
correct
remedy
amends
sort out
improve
equalize
solatium
patch up
deal with
atonement
harmonize
make good
put to rights
put/set/make right
redress
reparations
recognition of loss
process of concealing a psychological difficulty
autotropism - (the tendency to return normal spatial orientation)
by developing in another direction
stitch
wound - care
dressing -
dehiscence
tragedy
history
repeats itself
strategy
dream-
OCCUPATION
regenera
world be
dream-

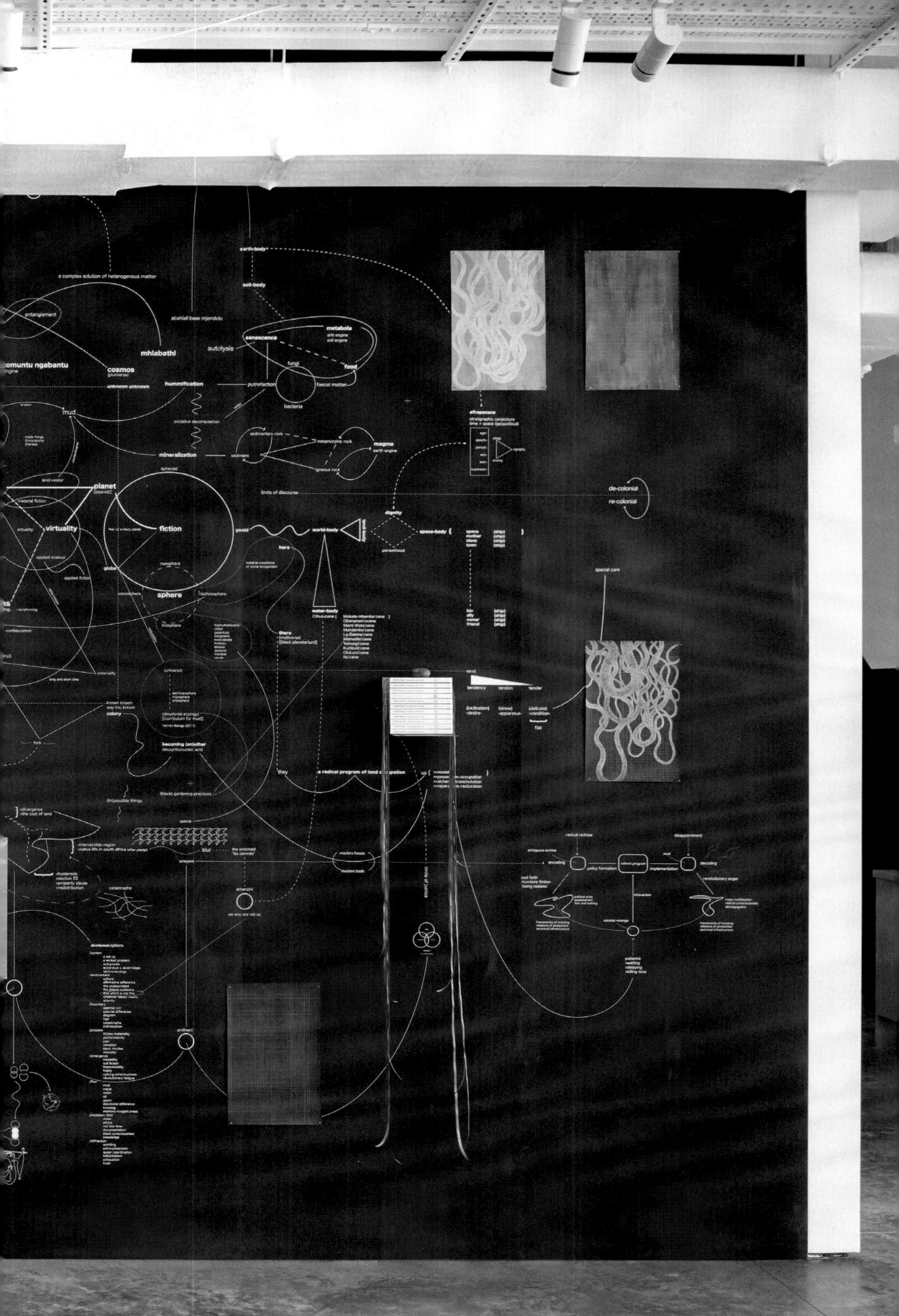
earth-body
soil-body
a complex solution of heterogenous matter
entanglement
abahlali base mjondolo
mhlabathi
senescence
autolysis
metabola
shit engine
soil engine
omuntu ngabantu
engine
cosmos
(pluriverse)
food
fungi
hummification
putrefaction
faecal matter
unknown unknown
bacteria
mud
oxidative decomposition
mineralization
sediment
sedimentary rock
metamorphic rock
magma
earth engine
igneous rock
afropocene
stratigraphic conjecture
time + space (geopolitical)
planet
(bizarre)
limits of discourse
de-colonial
re-colonial
dignity
virtuality
fiction
geoid
world-body
land-body
space-body
space
mother
sister
here
personhood
globe
noosphere
sphere
sociosphere
technosphere
special care
biosphere
water-body
Cthulucene
Mokele-mbembe'cene
Otoananem'ocene
Mami Wata'cene
Mamjambo'cene
La Baleine'cene
Mamarbo'cene
Yemanja'cene
Kunbukuti'cene
Olokuru'cene
Nu'cene
there
(multiverse)
(black planetarium)
tend
tendency
tendon
tender
(universe)
(inclination)
(sinew)
(delicate)
desire
apparatus
condition
known known
way too known
colony
(decolonial ecology)
(curriculum for mud)
Vermin Beings (2011)
becoming (an)other
deoxyribonucleic acid
fork
they
a radical program of land occupation
us
remodel
re-occupation
(black) gardening practices
(impossible) things
(divergence
the cost of land
radical redress
disappointment
astrica
encoding
policy formation
implementation
decoding
the wretched
blur
masters house
masters tools
revolutionary anger
hysteresis
section 25
property clause
redistribution
catastrophe
emihleri
colonial revenge
patience
waiting
delaying
killing time

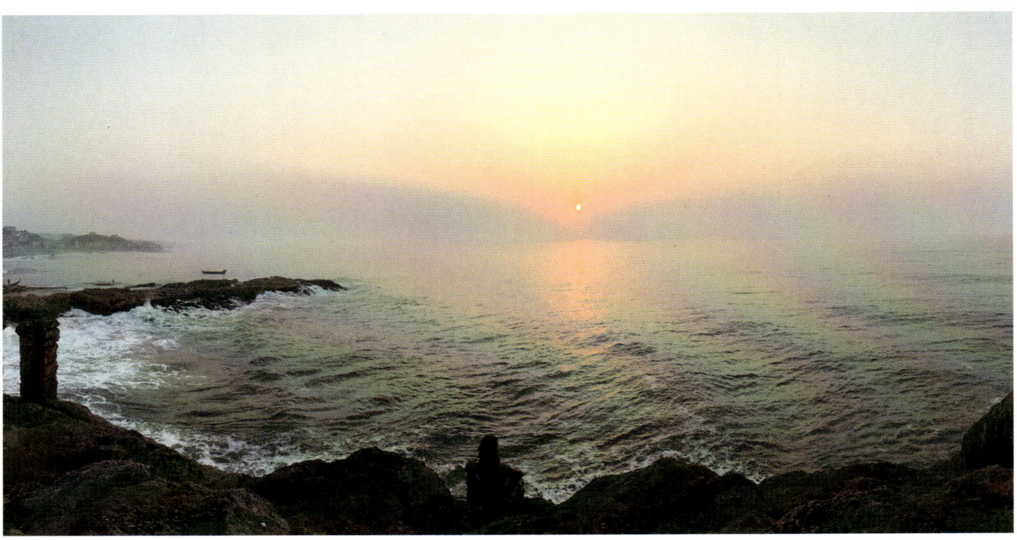

'Mereko Oguaa aba'

I'd wake up with the fishermen's songs and go watch the sunrise on those rocks behind the fort. From that spot, if the sky was clear enough, when the rising sun reflected on the surface of the sea, it looked as though the heavens were opening up. I'd sit and think, and sometimes the fishermen would end up on the rocks too. Pulling their rope, singing their songs. Balanced far too close to the edge.

I was always trying to find a good time to go into the fort. I'd been before. Twice. And I'd done the tour. Twice. But it felt like too much now. So I'd sit at that spot where heaven opened up, avoiding history. It would be Ekow and I every morning. On the first morning I met him there, a man walked past and asked me to talk to him. I seemed decent and maybe I'd have some sense for the boy. I asked why he wasn't going to school and he said his mother couldn't pay. So I asked if he'd go if I paid, and he said no.

I didn't push. We'd just talk about the odd jobs he was picking up in town. He is the one that told me about the part of the beach, just left of the fort, that was still called the white men's beach because that's where the ships came. One morning, we got stuck, and I couldn't find a word, and he couldn't meet me halfway. I asked him if he liked talking to me, and he said yes. And I told him, we wouldn't ever need to get stuck like this if he went to school. And he told me, it wasn't his problem if I didn't speak my own language well enough. That he spoke as much English as he needed to, and Fante was good enough for him.

In the evenings, I would sit with Ras Kwame and his friend Poppee. Poppee would talk about George Best, the premier league and those boys he would avoid at the betting shop if he had DStv at home. We'd talk about land, too:

46

You know, this place was important before. Cape Coast isn't a Fante name. This is Oguaa *(Cape Coast). You still hear people say,* Mɛrekɔ Oguaa aba. *It was important long before that castle that has never had any king living there. There are 77 deities here. One of their shrines is next to the room you sleep in. Don't you see people pour libations in the water sometimes? You know, in our language the real word for the sea means 'the spirit that returns'.*[23] *We believe whatever you give it comes back to you. Sometimes it's the pure water sachets and plastic bottles that washed out to sea from the gutters when it rained. Sometimes it's bits of bodies. On good days it's people from Kingston Town and New York City, searching.*

Key to the Map

◊ Black Quantum Futurism, *blackwomxntemporal*, https://www.blackwomxntemporal.net

◊ Dionne Brand, *A Map to the Door of No Return: Notes to Belonging*, Toronto: Vintage Canada, 2003

◊ Nolan Oswald Dennis, 'A fragment on diagrams and dreams' (2020), available at: https://www.nolanoswalddennis.com/studio_theory/a%20fragment%20on%20diagrams%20and%20dreams%20.pdf

◊ Nolan Oswald Dennis, 'drawn out: notes for a (k)new world' (2001), available at https://www.nolanoswalddennis.com/studio_theory/drawn%20out-notes%20for%20a%20(k)new%20world.pdf

◊ Ntone Edjabe, 'How to Eat a Forest', *Afterall*, issue 43, Spring/Summer 2017, pp.70–73, and in this volume

◊ Rubén Gaztambide-Fernández, 'Decolonial options and artistic/aestheSic entanglements: An interview with Walter Mignolo', *Decolonization: Indigeneity, Education & Society*, vol.3, no.1, 2014, pp.196–212

◊ Tiffany Lethabo King, *The Black Shoals: Offshore Formations of Black and Native Studies*, Durham, NC: Duke University Press, 2019

◊ Katherine McKittrick, *Demonic Grounds: Black Women and the Cartographies of Struggle*, Minneapolis: University of Minnesota Press, 2006

◊ Katherine McKittrick, 'Mathematics Black Life', *The Black Scholar*, vol.44, no.2, 2014, pp.16–28

◊ Katherine McKittrick (@demonicground), 'this puts the black "ungeographic" (and a black sense of place) to work in productive ways because it casts place-making as a set of ideas and rebellions rather than a knowable geography. to be ungeographic is heretical', Twitter, 5 August 2019, 4.49 p.m., https://twitter.com/demonicground/status/1158404706135433216

◊ Nkgopoleng Moloi, 'Nolan Oswald Dennis embraces misreading and misinterpretation, *Artskop*, 15 March 2019, https://www.artskop.com/artmedia/en/nolan-oswald-dennis-embraces-misreading-and-misinterpretation

◊ Fred Moten, 'Blackness and Nothingness (Mysticism in the Flesh)', *South Atlantic Quarterly*, vol.11, no.4, 2013, pp.737–80

◊ Rasheedah Phillips, 'Placing Time, Timing Space: Dismantling the Master's Map and Clock', *The Funambulist* [online magazine], 5 July 2018, https://thefunambulist.net/magazine/cartography-power/placing-time-timing-space-dismantling-masters-map-clock-rasheedah-phillips

◊ Koen Vermeir and Jonathan Regier (ed.), *Boundaries, Extents and Circulations: Space and Spatiality in Early Modern Natural Philosophy*, New York: Springer, 2016

Notes

1 Nolan Oswald Dennis, 'A fragment on diagrams and dreams' (2020), available at https://www.nolan oswalddennis.com/studio_theory/a%20fragment%20on%20diagrams%20and%20dreams%20.pdf, p.1. For more information on Dennis's articulation of the 'option', see Rubén Gaztambide-Fernández, 'Decolonial options and artistic/aestheSic entanglements: An interview with Walter Mignolo', *Decolonization: Indigeneity, Education & Society*, vol.3, no.1, 2014, pp.196–212.

2 Rasheedah Phillips, 'Placing Time, Timing Space: Dismantling the Master's Map and Clock', *The Funambulist* [online magazine], 5 July 2018, https://thefunambulist.net/magazine/cartography-power/placing-time-timing-space-dismantling-masters-map-clock-rasheedah-phillips.

3 'In early Western maps, gaps and the spaces between locations pointed to the fact of intervals to be traversed. A reflection of the itinerary, or intention, of traveller.' Koen Vermeir and Jonathan Regier (ed.), *Boundaries, Extents and Circulations: Space and Spatiality in Early Modern Natural Philosophy*, New York: Springer, 2016, p.2.

4 Ntone Edjabe, 'How to Eat a Forest', *Afterall*, issue 43, Spring/Summer 2017, p.73, and in this volume.

5 *Ibid.*

6 I draw here particularly on Katherine McKittrick's analysis of black women's geographies in the black diaspora and her engagement with the possibilities that arise at the encounter between black studies and human geography: 'The relationship between black populations and geography – and here I am referring to geography as space, place and location in their physical materiality and imaginative configurations – allows us to engage with a narrative that locates and draws on black histories and black subjects in order to make visible social lives which are often displaced, rendered ungeographic'. K. McKittrick, *Demonic Grounds: Black Women and the Cartographies of Struggle*, Minneapolis: University of Minnesota Press, 2006, p.x. To be rendered ungeographic is to be denied the capacity to produce space: 'the ungeographic is a colonial fiction, sometimes cast in real life, thus functioning to determine how we only seem to see black geographies in hierarchical, stereotypical, human/inhuman terms, and therefore as ostensible impossibilities'. *Ibid.*, p.5.

7 '[T]his puts the black "ungeographic" (and a black sense of place) to work in productive ways because it casts place-making as a set of ideas and rebellions rather than a knowable geography. to be ungeographic is heretical.' Katherine McKittrick (@demonicground), Twitter, 5 August 2019, 4.49 p.m., available at https://twitter.com/demonicground/status/1158404706135433216.

8 *Shoal, n.* a place where the water is of little depth; a shallow, a sand-bank or bar. *adj.* of water, etc.; not deep; shallow. 'Because the shoal's shape, expanse and density change over time, the shoal is as much a dynamic and moving set of processes and ecological relations as it is a longitudinal and latitudinal coordinate that cartographers attempt to fix in time and space. It is a mobile, always changing and shifting state of flux. As an ecological space, it represents an errant and ecotonal location made of both water and not water. Ecotones are classified within environmental science as a combination or meeting of at least two distinct ecological zones. The shoal is liminal, indeterminate and hard to map.' Tiffany Lethabo King, *The Black Shoals: Offshore Formations of Black and Native Studies*, Durham, NC: Duke University Press, 2019, p.3.

9 *Ibid.*, p.4.

10 For figuring of the Door of No Return, see Dionne Brand, *A Map to the Door of No Return: Notes to Belonging* (Toronto: Vintage Canada, 2003, p.49): 'to live at the Door of No Return is to live self-consciously. To be always aware of your presence as a presence outside yourself.'

11 This orientation towards 'what else happened' refers to strategies for reading the archive that rest on 'encountering, thinking about and articulating black absented presences: the unspeakable, the unwritten, the unbearable and unutterable, the unseeable and invisible, the uncountable and un-indexed, outside the scourge, that which cannot be seen or heard or read but is always there'. K. McKittrick, 'Mathematics Black Life', *The Black Scholar*, vol.44, no.2, 2014, p.22.

12 Nolan Oswald Dennis, interviewed by the author, July 2020.

13 See www.blackwomxntemporal.net.

14 See Camae Ayewa, 'Sights and Sounds of the Passage', in Rasheedah Phillips and Dominique Matti (ed.), *Black Quantum Futurism – Space-time Collapse I: From the Congo to the Carolinas*, Philadelphia: AfroFuturist Affair, 2016, pp.9–13.

15 Rasheedah Phillips, interviewed by the author, July 2020.

16 R. Phillips, 'Placing Time, Timing Space', *op. cit.*

17 R. Phillips, interviewed by the author, July 2020.

18 Nkgopoleng Moloi, 'Nolan Oswald Dennis embraces misreading and misinterpretation', *Artskop*, 15 March 2019, https://www.artskop.com/artmedia/en/nolan-oswald-dennis-embraces-misreading-and-misinterpretation.

19 *Ibid.*

20 N.O. Dennis, interviewed by the author, July 2020.

21 *Ibid.*

22 Dennis elaborates this point: 'The drawing body is an extension of the human body under these inertial conditions. More precisely, it is a prosthetic transformation of that body in conditions where acting becomes a type of inaction: a game played against time, or put simply: planning. The drawing body is called into being wherever an apparatus is put to work to draw out, as a matter of practice, a (k)new body in violation of colonial assumptions of linear time and normative value. Some kind of mark-making instrument that shivers and trembles, and moves forward only in indeterminate scribbles. This drawing body is the inverted agency of a planning exercise performed in a situation where consequences must precede their causes.' N.O. Dennis, 'drawn out: notes for a (k)new world' (2001), https://www.nolanoswalddennis.com/studio_theory/drawn%20out-notes%20for%20a%20(k)new%20world.pdf.

23 To enliven this conversation, please consider the thinking on seaborne sociality in North American scholarship, of which Fred Moten wrote that it is 'terrible to have come from nothing but the sea, which is nowhere, navigable only in its constant auto dislocation.' F. Moten, 'Blackness and Nothingness (Mysticism in the Flesh)', *South Atlantic Quarterly*, vol.11, no.4, 2013, p.744. This articulation of nothing, and nowhere, draws on an 'affirmative negation', particularly the Afro Pessimist thought of Jared Sexton and Frank B. Wilderson, wherein: 'We study our seaborne variance, sent by its prehistory into arrivance without arrival, as a poetics of lore, of abnormal articulation. … Having defied degradation, the moment becomes a theory of a moment, of the feeling of a presence that is ungraspable in the way that it touches.' *Ibid.*, pp.743–44.

How Do We Know What Latin American Conceptualism Looks Like?

Miguel A. López

A piece that is essentially the same as a piece made by any of the first Conceptual artists, dated two years earlier than the original and signed by somebody else.
– Eduardo Costa[1]

I

On 28 April 1999 the exhibition 'Global Conceptualism: Points of Origin, 1950s–1980s' opened at New York's Queens Museum of Art. Organised by Luis Camnitzer, Jane Farver and Rachel Weiss, consisting of eleven geographically defined sections and curated by a large, international group of art historians and researchers, the exhibition formulated one of the riskiest and most controversial interpretations of so-called Conceptual art at an international level. The show was ambitious. Its structure created a geographical spill-over that called into question the lesser or secondary place to which certain critical productions had been consigned. The framework of analysis was the global set of social and political transformations that have taken place since 1950, and the emergence of new forms of political action that formed the backdrop to a renewed repertoire of visual language. Such a scope allowed the curators to gather aesthetic proposals not defined in the exhibition by a Conceptualist 'aesthetics of immateriality', but instead by their capacity for intervention.[2] This approach, without doubt, shifted the very rules according to which the history of Conceptual art had been written. Those radical changes of the *modes of producing* and *giving value* to art exposed by 'Global Conceptualism' reveal complex processes in which political subjectivities oppose the consensual organisation of power and its distribution of places and roles, mobilising singular and collective resistances and dissenting energies.

Ten years on, the shock waves can still be felt, perhaps even more intensely than at the time. In different ways, 'Global Conceptualism' updated some of the debates that had been attempting to raise the issue of subjectivity in social practices from a postcolonial perspective, disputing the geographical and temporal orders of a modern or colonial Occidentalism.[3] Hence, it was no surprise that the show became one of the most quoted (and most questioned)

50

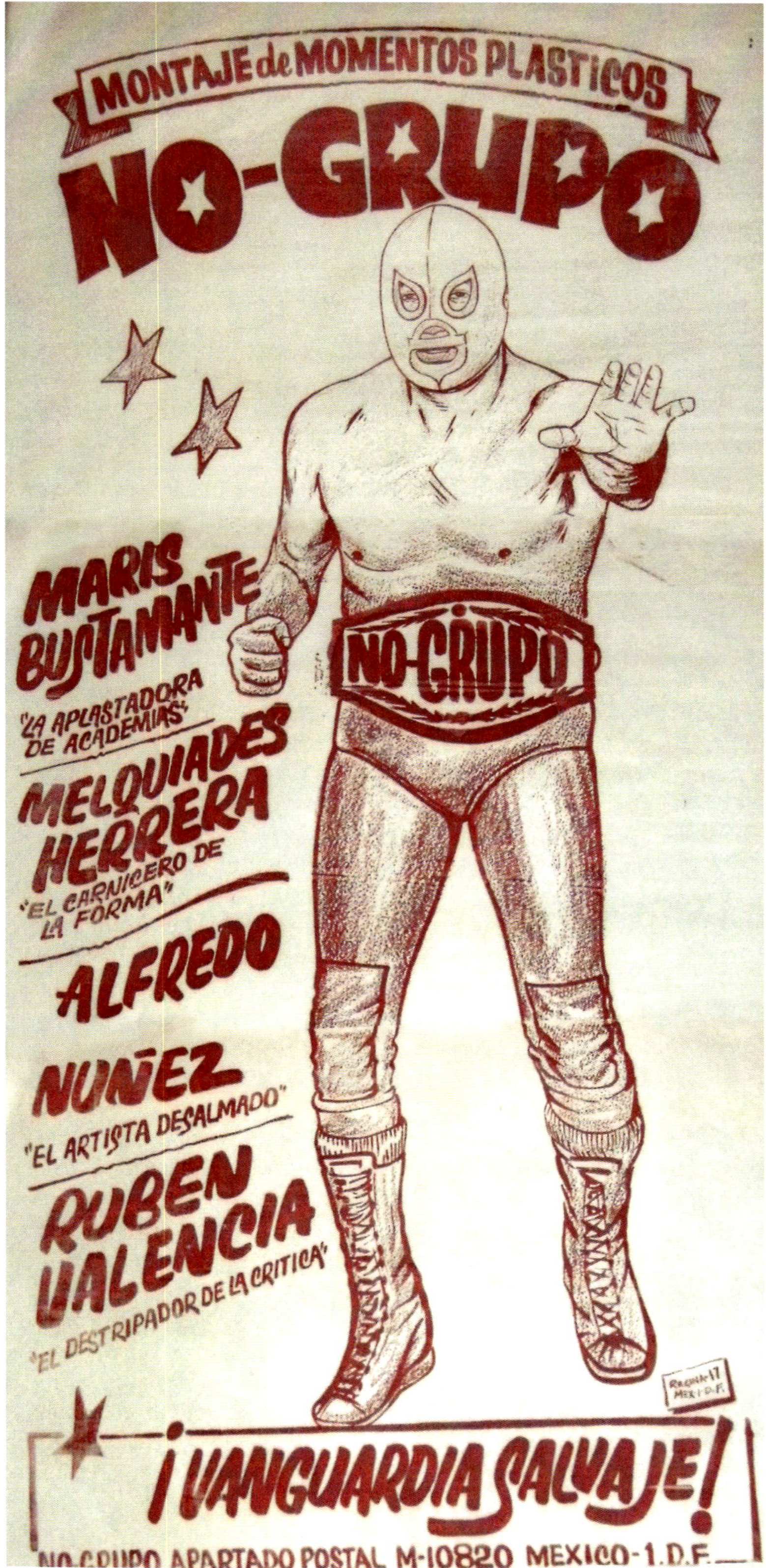

No-Grupo (Maris Bustamante, Melquíades Herrera, Alfredo Núñez and Rubén Valencia), poster of the action *Montaje de Momentos Plásticos* (*Assemblage of Fine Art Moments*), presented at the Primer Coloquio de Arte No-Objetual y Arte Urbano (First Congress on Non-Object and Urban Art), Medellín, Colombia, 1981, offset print in three parts, 57 × 87cm each

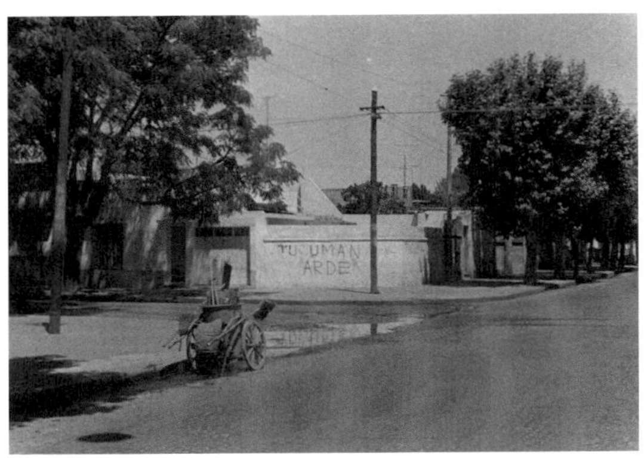

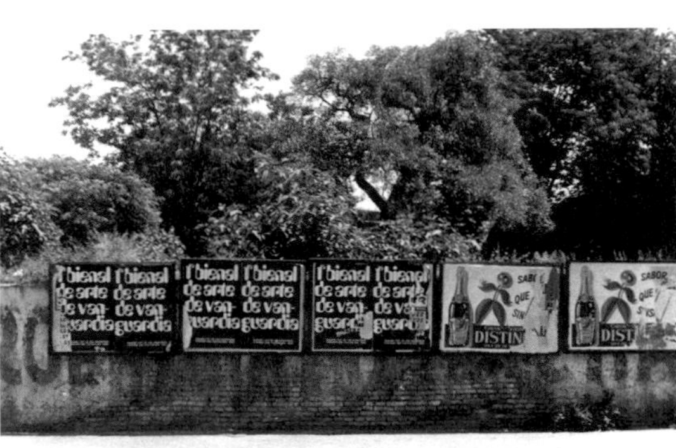

'Tucumán Arde', 1968. Above: Graffiti in the streets of Rosario for second phase of the campaign. Below: Posters calling for the 1st Bienal de Arte de Vanguardia during third phase

referents of the revival of 1960s and 70s critical production that has taken place over the past decade in exhibitions, seminars and publications around the world.

While much has been said about the decentralising virtues of 'Global Conceptualism', in retrospect its most significant legacy appears not only to be the broadening of the Conceptual art map (a move that had a bearing on several subsequent curatorial projects), but the way in which the exhibition questioned the identity of a Conceptual art with universal aspirations. The curatorial operation of 'Global Conceptualism' started from a categorical distinction between 'Conceptual art' – understood as a North American and Western European aesthetic development associated with a formalist reduction inherited from abstraction and Minimalism – and 'Conceptualism', a term denoting a critical return to an 'ordering of priorities' that made visible certain aesthetic processes on a transnational level, allowing for diverse historical, cultural and political narratives to be set in place.[4] Conceptualism was presented as a phenomenon that took place in a 'federation of provinces', with the 'traditional hegemonic centre [being] one among many', drawing a multiplicity of points of origin and questioning the privileged position claimed by Western modernity and its politics of representation.[5] The exhibition seemed to work as a performative apparatus determined to re-politicise, reconfigure and rewrite the memory of

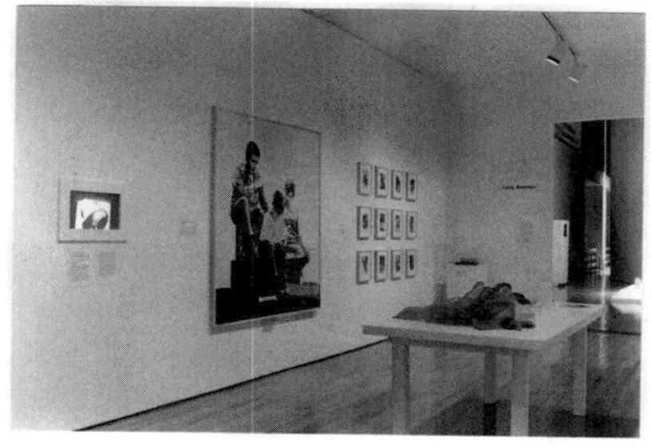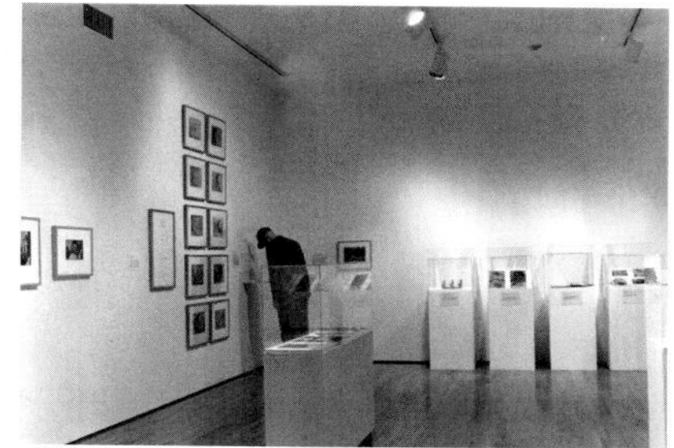

those decades. As a result, Conceptual art, which from the perspective of the United States and Western Europe had until then been an unavoidable prism for reading other critical productions, appeared fractured.

The shrewdness of the 'Global Conceptualism' gesture no doubt managed to effectively dominate the critical framework from which one would contemplate and validate those antagonistic practices. But more importantly, and perhaps without intending to, it allowed for the reconsideration of Conceptualism as the effect of a discourse (or multiplicity of discourses) that had itself caused breaks and a major questioning of the fabric of certain local memories – albeit in some cases at the expense of reinforcing lineages and typologies. These are complex manoeuvres, and their political implications must be addressed. What do we achieve today by reflecting on Conceptual art's radical dimension from the perspective of the ways in which it has been historicised? How should we assess the political impact of such histories, and their effect on possible forms of recognition? Furthermore, how might we assess this effect on the production of certain forms of subjectivisation and sociability?[7]

II

The struggle of Latin American historiography to place local episodes within global narratives, in an attempt to counter the dominant geographies of art, has been successful. For some time now, artists such as Hélio Oiticica, León Ferrari, Lygia Clark, Alberto Greco, Luis Camnitzer, Cildo Meireles, Oscar Bony and Artur Barrio, or collective experiences such as 'Tucumán Arde' ('Tucumán Burns', 1968) and 'Arte de los medios' ('Art of Media', 1966), have become unavoidable references in virtually all recent accounts that trace the so-called inaugural landmarks of Conceptualism on a transcontinental scale. Today, however, this apparent expansion of discourse seems to demand renewed reflection, as it is no longer a matter of tirelessly continuing to accommodate events in the endless container we believe history to be, but of questioning the ways in which they reappear and the roles they play within it. Such reflection will enable us to examine the anachronisms and discontinuities of historical discourse – its fragments, snippets, shreds – and activate their ability to disrupt once again the logic of the 'verified facts'.

In the recent essay 'Cartografías Queer' (2008),[7] the theorist Paul B. Preciado discusses the formation of historiographic models of the so-called sexual difference from the perspective of a queer epistemological critique that

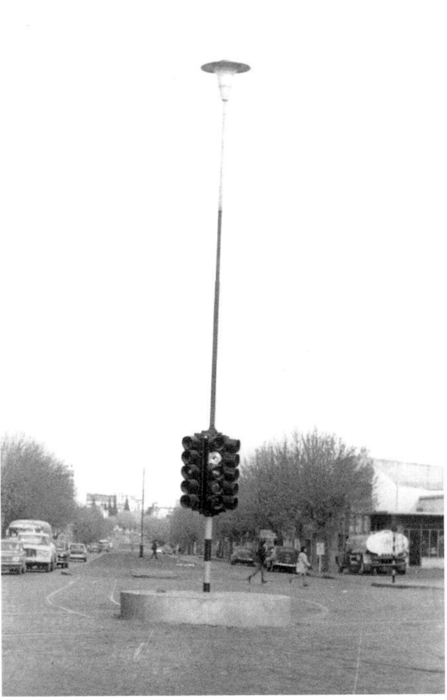

Edgardo Antonio Vigo, *Señalamiento 1: Manojo de Semáforos* (*Appointment 1: Handful of Traffic Lights*), 25 October 1968. Courtesy Centro de Arte Experimental Vigo, La Plata

could be very useful for us in this task. Considering the political scope of the historical exercise, Preciado avoids the taxonomy of places, situations or individuals and instead proposes, in direct dialogue with Félix Guattari's 'schizoanalytic cartographies', a map that gives an account of the *technologies of representation* and *modes of production* of subjectivities.[8] This map makes explicit how certain dominant diagrams of representation of sexual minorities come dangerously close to becoming mechanisms of social control and discipline. Can we envision a way of reading and representing that does not result in an illustrative exercise of description, but that instead allows for the perception of variations and displacements that appear as forms of subjectivisation, or even as *machines of political transformation* that disrupt previously established arrangements?

Preciado brings into play two antagonistic historiographic figures: the conventional model of 'identity cartography' (or 'cartography of the lion', as he terms it), concerned with seeking, defining and classifying the identities of bodies; and a 'critical cartography' ('queer cartography' or 'cartography of the bitch'), which sidesteps writing as a topography of established representations in order to instead 'sketch out a map of the modes of production of subjectivity', observing the 'technologies of representation, information and communication' as *genuine performative machines*.[9] These two models are divergent not only in their modes of producing visibility, but also in their ways of battling the technologies that mediate the political construction of knowledge. These issues are pervaded by the relationship between power and knowledge, and to an even greater extent by biopolitical modes of production linked to the codes of representation and the allocation of places in social space.[10] Such crucial issues must be considered at a time when 'dematerialised' logic has begun to strike up an effective dialogue with the dynamics of global capitalism on immaterial goods.[11]

Following (or perhaps perverting) Preciado's reflections, it may not be difficult to acknowledge that until recently most historiographies of modern and contemporary art have been 'cartographies of identities'. Among these, 'Conceptual art' surfaced as a sanctionable identity, and the historiographic task resembled that of a detective tracking down the still unfound remains of Conceptualism in order to introduce them into the topography of the visible. It strives to offer a genealogy and geography of that which is totally representable – bringing those experiences into historical account, dispelling the mists that surrounded them and clarifying a place apparently recovered.[12]

But let's try the opposite exercise too. Let's imagine a cartography not interested in seeking out the fragments of Conceptual art, one that even doubts the existence of such pieces. Let's imagine a map that instead aims to explore the label itself, observing its uses and noting how it produces identities in different contexts – a map that, before attempting to function as a technique of representation, tries to expose power relations, 'the architecture, displacement and spatialisation of power as a technology for the production of subjectivity'.[13] Here it would no longer be a question of establishing formal resemblances between works, or of dating those that can effectively guide us in recognising the 'Conceptual' or 'Conceptualist' category (and its regional derivatives such as 'Argentinean', 'Brazilian' or 'Latin American'), but, rather, of finding out how those narratives *have determined the materiality and forms of visibility* of what they hoped to describe, how they have negotiated their place within and without the institution and distributed it after having transformed these critical art forms into received knowledge.

Taking that tension between the cartographic models in their identitarian and queer versions as a starting point, I would like to pose a series of questions concerning some of the recent cartographical representations of Conceptual art: first, by revisiting one of the most influential accounts of so-called Latin American Conceptualism and the re-inscription of the 'ideological' as a category from which to consider aesthetic trends in the region; and second, by analysing a recent, almost unnoticed Argentinean exhibition that proposed a strategy for reflecting politically on how it is possible to reassess the ruptures triggered by 1960s avant-garde movements and the 'Tucumán Arde' episode. The show, notably, put forward an approach to the archive that refuses to treat this event as a chapter in the history of art and instead reactivates the anachronistic heterogeneity of meanings borne by the documentary remnants.

III

It was not until the early 1990s that one of the first programmatic essays of Latin American Conceptualism was published, and its ideological reverberations have accompanied many of the considerations on the subject since. Art historian Mari Carmen Ramírez wrote the essay 'Blueprint Circuits:

Conceptual Art and Politics in Latin America' (1993) for the catalogue of the exhibition 'Latin American Artists of the Twentieth Century', curated by Waldo Rasmussen and organised by the Museum of Modern Art in New York in 1992.[14] The exhibition, which was first opened to the public in Seville and produced in the context of the celebrations commemorating the fifth centenary of the 'discovery of America' – a controversial exhibition on account of its perceived condescending and stereotyping discourse – was one of the culminating stages of the boom of Latin American art that began in the mid-1980s and fostered a depoliticised representation of Latin American culture and history,[15] which was strongly associated with private promotional and funding interests in both the US and Latin America. The political landscape at that time included the reestablishment of democratic governments throughout the subcontinent, the internal crisis of the Left and the introduction of neoliberal policies following the Washington Consensus.[16] For several of the intellectuals who were symbolically mediating the cultural production between North and South America at the time, such as the Cuban art historian and curator Gerardo Mosquera, the Chilean feminist cultural critic Nelly Richard or Ramírez herself, it was clear that what was at stake were the mechanisms of representation of the American continent at the end of the Cold War, and therefore a totally renewed political economy of signs catalysed by a sequence of exhibitions of Latin American art outside of Latin America – exhibitions that effectively were beginning to draw a new exotic, formalist and neocolonial framework of interpretation.[17]

The very title of the text, 'Conceptual Art and Politics in Latin America', announces Ramírez's focus on disruptive aesthetic forms and their sociocultural conditions, something that was not in Rasmussen's exhibition. The essay attempts to provide a unitary legibility to radical experiences that had until then been in large part unrelated (some of which not only had remained indifferent to the nomenclature but even rejected it),[18] and by doing so gives the label 'Latin American Conceptualism' one of its first major concrete manifestations. Ramírez's intention was to challenge the then common assumption that Latin American Conceptual art was a poor, late imitation of Conceptual art 'from the centre', and hoped to politicise its readings by means of an argument that assigned positive value to an apparent Latin American difference. In opposition to the limited North American and British 'analytical' or 'tautological' model, the Latin American model was presented as 'ideological Conceptualism'. Ramírez traced this binary distinction back to 1974, when it was discussed by the Spanish critic Simón Marchán Fiz, but did not go as far as to question it.[19]

Ramírez believed the dichotomy revealed the prominence of the ideas of a sadly self-referential Joseph Kosuth, heir apparent to the positivist legacy of modernism. 'In Kosuth's model the artwork as conceptual proposition is reduced to a tautological or self-reflexive statement. He insisted that art consists of nothing other than the artist's idea of it, and that art can claim no meaning outside itself',[20] Ramírez says, echoing – voluntarily or not – some of the criticism that art historian Benjamin H.D. Buchloh had put forward fiercely just four years before,[21] and indirectly playing down the political dimension implicit in the linguistic turn and its break with late-modern formalism. She thereby created an interpretative formula repeated almost to the letter in several of her subsequent essays, opposing, in general terms, a 'depoliticised' North American canon with a 'political' Latin American Conceptualism that subverts the structure of the former and actively intervenes in social space. The assertion, though somewhat provocative, traces a particularly narrow and dichotomous path of analysis, indebted to essentialist nuances that fail to establish a genuine antagonism.[22]

However, our intention here is not to denounce an 'incorrect' reading of Conceptualism, to dispute labels or to reduce Ramírez's discourse to the use of such categories (conversely, her work puts forward noteworthy observations on the political use of communication and the 'recovery' of the mass-produced object in these processes). Rather, it instead is to note how that 'difference' shaped a specific visibility and morphology, making the distinction part of many of the debates surrounding the interpretations of the situation and, surprisingly or not, part of the 'central', dominant narratives, where it functions as a mystifying cliché in a process of categorisation and normalisation. Returning to some of Ramírez's ideas, the philosopher and art theorist Peter Osborne observes:

> *'Ideological content' is the key term of Latin American Conceptual art. In distinction from the more formal ideational concerns of most US and European Conceptual art (the act/event, mathematical series, linguistic propositions or the structures of cultural forms), this was an art for which 'ideology itself became the fundamental "material identity" of the conceptual proposition'.*[23]

Along similar lines, though without circumscribing the 'analytical-linguistic' to North American Conceptualism, Alexander Alberro repeats the argument:

> [T]*he most extreme alternatives to models of analytic Conceptualism in the late 1960s and early 70s are those that developed in the deteriorating political and economic climate of a number of Latin American countries including Argentina, Brazil, Uruguay and Chile.*[24]

And in a more recent book, formulated as a Conceptualist 'census' of Spain with categories such as 'poetic', 'political' and 'peripheral', the historian Pilar Parcerisas revisits Ramírez's thesis,[25] scorning 'the premises of the analytical orthodoxy of Conceptual art in English-speaking countries' by attempting to elaborate on the political character of the 'periphery'. From a range of perspectives in Latin America, that difference has been repeatedly recovered, with variations, in several recent accounts of the 1960s and 70s.[26]

Rather than objecting to the use of the term or any of its related epithets, what I am attempting to do is underline the need to deploy it as a diagram of power, to assess which meanings and distinctions, and which processes of normalisation and resistance, are concealed in such consensual representations. This reconsideration demands a different articulation to the other concepts used by critics and artists when considering their own positions:

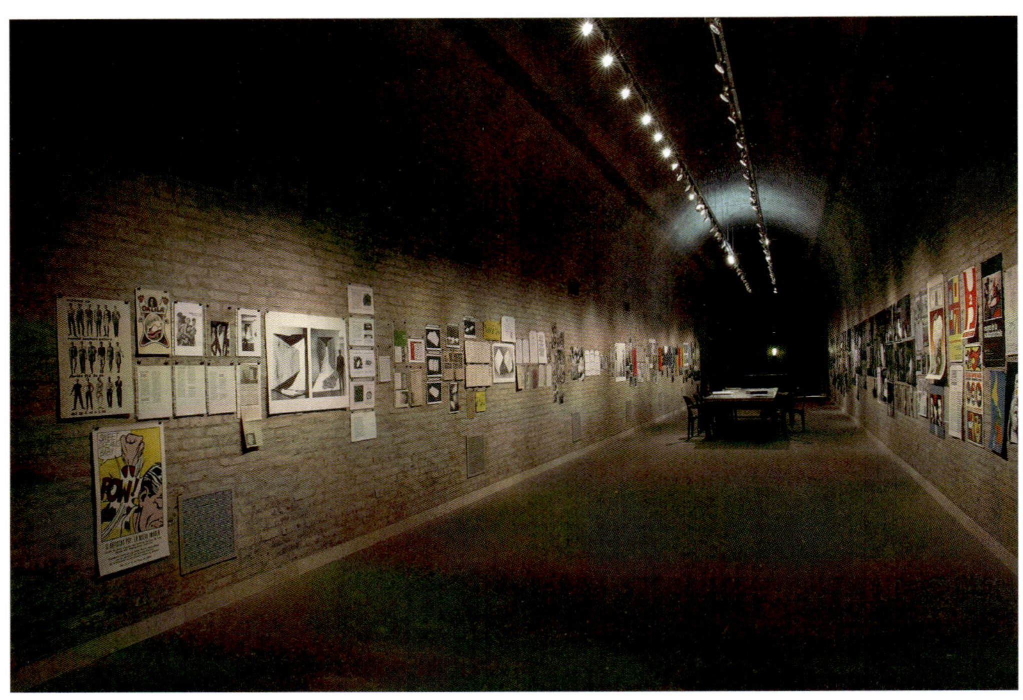

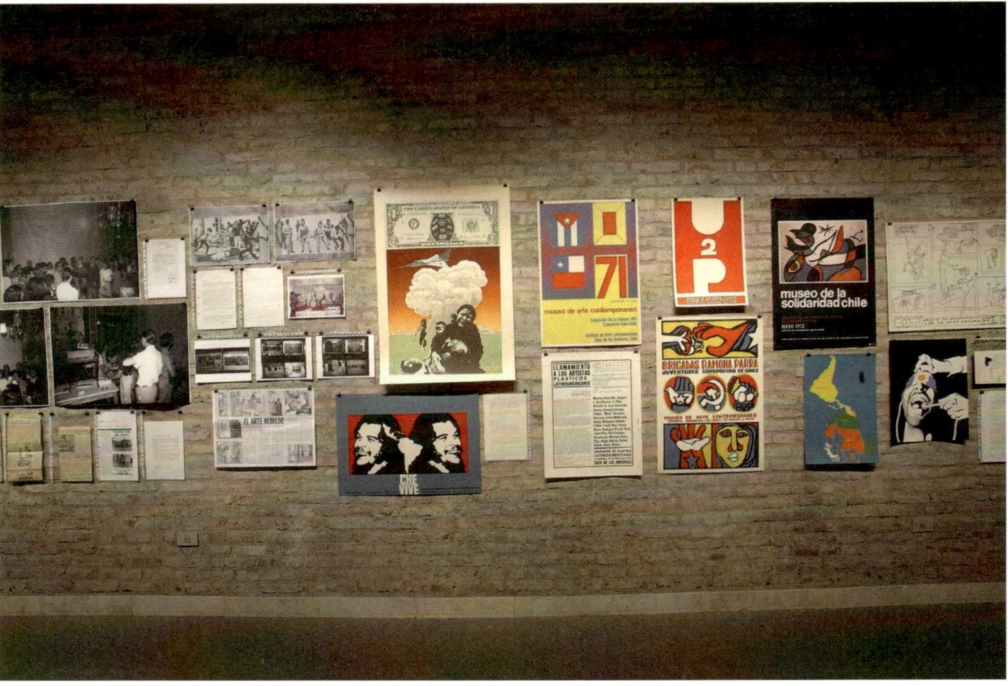

minor expressions (to paraphrase Gilles Deleuze and Félix Guattari),[27] the gradual erosion of which has contributed to the standardisation of radical experiences in order that they may establish an 'appropriate' exchange with centralist discourses.[28]

For example, it would be provocative to consider the term 'dematerialisation' in the context of Argentina's experimental art scene in the 1960s – as the Argentinean theoretician Oscar Masotta proposed in 1967, independently from Lucy R. Lippard – as deriving from El Lissitsky and his plan to integrate artists into the publishing industry of revolutionary Russia in the 1920s.[29] It also would be challenging to rethink a term such as 'no-objetualismo' (non-object-based art), coined in Mexico by Peruvian critic Juan Acha around 1973, as part of a Marxist approach to countercultural protest and collective artistic experiences of the Mexican 'grupos' (Proceso Pentagono, Grupo Suma and No-Grupo among others), but most significantly to indigenous aesthetic processes, such as popular art and design, that question Western art history.[30] Or to re-examine concepts that artists employ to reflect on their own practice: Argentinean Ricardo Carreira uses the term 'deshabituación' (dishabituation) to refer to an aesthetic theory based on the political transformation of the environment through estrangement.[31] In the early 1960s Alejandro Jodorowsky spoke of 'efímeros' (ephemerals) in reference to his series of improvised and provocative actions confronting conventional theatre, halfway between psychotropic mysticism and fantastic esotericism,[32] while Edgardo Antonio Vigo's 'revulsive' aesthetic agenda pledged to destabilise the roles of the artist – on other occasions Vigo defined himself as an 'unmaker of objects'.[33] These are but a few of the entries in the critical repertoire still in the shadow of the hegemonic rhetoric. Such subterranean theoretical constructs pose a latent conflict, a *multitude* of not-yet-articulated and potential genealogies. Beyond mere naming, these words appear as proof of the fact that there is something irreducible – a discordant crossing of stories pointing to divergent ways of living and constructing the contemporary – its capacity to unfold other times.

IV

Forty years after 'Tucumán Arde', the exhibition 'Inventario 1965–1975. Archivo Graciela Carnevale', organised in 2008 in the Argentinean city of Rosario, offered one of the sharpest readings among the host of curatorial approaches that have explored episodes of radicalism and rupture in Argentina in 1968.[34] That year, several groups of artists, film-makers, journalists and intellectuals organised a series of experiences that connected cultural and artistic production with dissenting forms of political intervention – often with revolutionary claims – in collaboration with militant sectors of the workers' movement. These collaborations dramatically modified artistic and cultural practices, resulting in progressively radicalised experiences in several contexts. In this context, a group of artists – invited to the exhibition 'Experiencias 68' that was organised by the pre-eminent Instituto Di Tella – broke with the institution, exhibiting, in 'Experiencias,' politically critical artworks. When the police banned one of these – an installation of a public toilet, in which the public wrote slogans critical of the military dictatorship

– the artists protested, destroying their works in the streets and distributing a text denouncing the increasing repression in the country. This incident became the trigger for a major rethinking of their commitment to the artistic avant-garde, formulating the new programme of action that comprised the 'Tucumán Arde' episode. Once outside of the institution, the artists began a process of documentation and social intervention aimed at generating counter-information about the causes and consequences of the crisis that was affecting the Tucumán province after the closure of several sugar mills, and then mounting two public displays in the labour unions in Rosario and Buenos Aires, which were closed by the police. The project connected artists with sociologists, journalists, theorists, unions, the workers' movement and others in a process of dispute and intervention in which aesthetic and political strategies were interchanged.[35]

The 'Inventario' exhibition tried to reassess the celebrated entry of 'Tucumán Arde' into the canonical historiography of international art,[36] as well as its recognition as a foundational episode of Latin American, even global, 'ideological Conceptualism' (or 'the mother of all political works', as artist and sociologist Roberto Jacoby has ironically called it).[37] The project introduced itself as a questioning of the process of legitimisation and institutionalisation of 'political art' that in recent years had focussed on the 1968 events, in particular on 'Tucumán Arde', and resulted in a global tour that took it, among other places, to documenta 12 in Kassel in 2007.[38] What is won and what is lost in the process of 'Tucumán Arde' becoming a legend? How should we approach the complex and heterogeneous weft of political subjectivities inscribed in the rupture of the Argentinean avant-garde of the 1960s? Is 'Tucumán Arde', as a landmark, a watershed moment, capable of giving an account of the most intense and radical moments of that process?

The exhibition took the transformation of 'Tucumán Arde' into an artwork as its starting point, approached through a selection of photographs and documents from the Carnevale archive in an attempt to visually compose a chronological micro-narrative that would describe the events of 1968. The adoption of this origin not only implied returning to the several narratives in which the Argentinean event had been inscribed over the past decade, but also exploring the documentary framework, the material background from which those reconstructions seemed to appear and disappear. The archive was put forward as capable of disrupting all narrative certainty. The exhibition had four sections, and its focus was on the display of the Carnevale archive, the most comprehensive archive of Argentinean art in the 1960s. The installation made the archive freely available (providing desks and the possibility of consulting and copying documents), enabling the circulation of conflicting accounts coming from other people involved at the time. If the fetishising logic had managed to fix the image of 'Tucumán Arde', reducing its complexities to mere forms with seemingly immediate meaning, this exhibition attempted to suggest a totally different cartography based on the analysis of the processes of institutional legibility, their discursive production, exhibition formats, economic transformations and publishing products, uncovering their interrelations and tensions.

'Inventario' opened with a long, empty corridor in which beams of light were aimed at the walls and floor. At the end of the tunnel a large number of archival images (many of them photographs taken by the group of artists from Buenos Aires and Rosario in 1968) were projected, accompanied by audio fragments of interviews held in the 1990s with trade unionists, artists and student leaders, protagonists and witnesses of several of the actions.[39] The entrance thereby presented an empty architecture that both revealed its own modes of display and suggested the impossibility of establishing a single story, disrupting, implicitly, the idea of the singular official version.

A second corridor presented a substantial part of Carnevale's archive on walls and tables: photographs, posters, catalogues, writings and manifestos of the various Argentinean avant-garde events, alongside graphic work, pictures and other documents of experiences that connected art and politics in other contexts (from silkscreen prints by Taller 4 Rojo in Colombia to posters of the Brigadas Ramona Parra, made before or during Salvador Allende's socialist government in Chile, and others of the Encuentros de Plástica Latinoamericana in Havana). A panel in a third corridor traced the numerous events and exhibitions in which 'Tucumán Arde' had been recovered, quoted, exhibited or referenced, including information about the political and economic protocols in place in each institution, and photographs of how it was installed on each occasion. Materials related to the exhibition venue of 'Inventario' and the catalogue of the project (a detailed inventory of all the material in Carnevale's archive) were displayed on several of the tables, where each publication, catalogue and edition referenced in the gallery was made available. Finally, a space presented the contributions of two recent archives generated by Argentinean activist-artists more recently involved in local experiences, posing questions about the different ways of granting visibility to those practices in an exhibition space.

The show was constructed as a series of interludes that paradoxically reformulated the collisions that had initially configured the history of the archive. The passage between one space and another acted as a distancing effect that rejected any possible teleology of facts. While the first gallery had seemed to point out the impossibility of a narrative through the random polyphony of voices and images, the third gave an account of an 'excess of narratives' on 'Tucumán Arde' and on its own construction (historiographic, curatorial, institutional, economic and social) through its recognisable trajectories and the multiple ways in which it was activated.[40] Conversely, in the second gallery, the archive appeared as a potential story, an exhibited archive in use that offered its own migratory movements, its excesses and absences, its revolutions to come.

Put to use, the archive not only attempted to misplace 'Tucumán Arde', but to question its simple narration, re-enacting its original misidentification (its initial refusal to describe its practice as art, but also its dissolution as an event driven by urgency), opening and exposing the layers of sedimentation it had accumulated. Unlike some recent interpretations that have tried to make it legible as a work of art either by taking a small number of documents and images accompanied by comments, a system of marks and footnotes for illustration purposes, or else by a total lack of comments or stories (dangerously verging on aestheticisation, as in documenta 12), this *mise en scène* brought fragments together according to their differences, including everything that was usually excluded from the consensual art historical configurations that repeated its name. The installation of this exhibition rejected from the start all 'reasonable' understanding, showing, as Georges Didi-Huberman would say, not only the direction of its movement but the locus of its agitations.[41]

By presenting the actual archive, 'Inventario' also fell into contradictions: in spite of an attempt to present a multiplicity of times and events, as reflected by the heterogeneous archival material presented in the second tunnel, the inclusion of images of some of the most recognisable actions within 'Tucumán Arde' contributed to a repetition of the excessive prominence that 'Tucumán Arde' had already been given in written accounts of the late 1960s experiences. The photographs displayed throughout the gallery space, which had been enlarged for previous exhibitions in which they had been shown, provided an imposing presence themselves, at times even offering an unwitting chronology, especially if compared to the assemblage of documents that pointed to the complexity and impossibility of offering full descriptions. And yet, is it possible to escape from this already constructed significance?

V

In his most recent book, Luis Camnitzer establishes two key events for the reading of Latin American Conceptualism: the Tupamaro guerrilla group of the late 1960s in Uruguay, and the experience of rupture that led to 'Tucumán Arde' in 1968.[42] What is important for me here is the invocation of the Argentinean experience in relation to politics from the point of view of militants, or even armed conflict. Despite the possible good intentions behind its attempt to politicise historiographic accounts, we should ask ourselves whether the twosome Tupamaros/'Tucumán Arde' and the idealised image of 'resistance' in which it places Latin American Conceptual art history implies a pre-established consensus that reaffirms a certain stereotype of subversive art. If that is the case, does this point to a dead end for the politicisation of Conceptualism, and for its criticism? To what extent has an experience such as 'Inventario' managed to suggest an alternative representation of the usual story, to fracture narrative certainties or to dispute its stereotyped places? Is it possible to establish a topography of that which cannot yet be named, an index that refuses nomenclatures and stands alone, only to become disorder and pure unpredictability?

I have followed two clues in what I consider the cartographic or diagrammatic forms of critical reading that operate in tension with recent processes of historicisation of 'Latin American Conceptualism'. The first is an open question that speculates on the interpretative categories stabilised and legitimised in a specific order of discourse, and other secondary notions subsumed in that particular configuration of the 'Latin American', which presents itself as a uniform fabric – decentred concepts that would otherwise distort the usual flows of meaning and expose us to dissenting testimonies. The second is the gap between the conventional exhibition formats of 'Tucumán Arde', between the individuation of a set of documents that present the chronology of what is considered the artistic 'episode', and the presentation of the archive that disrupts and dismantles the order of this appearance. Besides its obvious limitations, the return to the archive is also a misidentification of an event countless times named – classified, arranged, defined – and whose name and materiality are repeatedly questioned in an attempt to bring difference to the surface. On display are merely temporary installations that enable us to return to those operations as a potential space from which to redefine relations between spaces, words and bodies.[43]

Over fifty years ago the Argentinean artist Eduardo Costa made a piece in which he proposed a counter-history of Latin American Conceptualism, one based on mixing up the dates: *A piece that is essentially the same as a piece made by any of the first conceptual artists, dated two years earlier than the original and signed by somebody else.* In this short text, written for the exhibition 'Art in the Mind', Costa suggested stealing history as a political activation of Conceptual practice, challenging 'reasonable' consolidations by historical narrative – a historiographic practice deliberately formulated around error.[44] His work seemed to insist on the possibility of thinking that rationalist history has been permanently mistaken – that there is no possible story, but merely a circumstantial sum of paradoxes, trades and sleights of hand, and that an erratic alteration in its diagram of successions simply adds to its most joyous (in)coherence, celebrating its impossibility.

Costa's work reminds us that history is never neutral, and if there should be any pending task it is precisely to be unfaithful to it, to betray it. This does not mean giving up on historical reflection, but rather corrupting whatever degree of Christian fidelity and Calvinist obedience history still inspires, unravelling its destiny and ultimate causes. Looking back at those events consigned to oblivion should allow us to recover their salutary force, their emancipatory thrill, and at the same time to activate a nostalgia for the future. We do not recover the past in order to make it exist as a bundle of skeletons, but to disturb the orders and assurances of the present. The task of reintegrating the subversive component of whatever we happen to be historicising can't be resolved by communicating as truth what we apparently know. It is neither a question of producing exhibitions or books on a certain theme, nor of drawing up lists, directories or summaries. It is a question of making the event spill over and break down established modes of thinking about the past and the future, and generating ways of allowing for whatever is excluded to eventually challenge the consensus and bring back the parts of an unresolved conflict.

Translated from Spanish by Josephine Watson.

Notes

[1] Eduardo Costa, quoted in Athena T. Spear (ed.), *Art in the Mind* (exh. cat.), Oberlin, OH: Allen Memorial Art Museum, 1970, n.p.

[2] The term 'dematerialisation', introduced by Lucy R. Lippard and John Chandler in 1968, for a long time was used as the key term to identify Conceptual art in North America and Western Europe. See L.R. Lippard and J. Chandler, 'The Dematerialization of Art', *Art International*, vol.12, no.2, February 1968, pp.31–36, and L.R. Lippard (ed.), *Six Years: The Dematerialization of the Art Object from 1966 to 1972*, New York: Praeger, 1973.

[3] In Latin America those discussions happened around the Bienal de La Habana, which, since its creation in 1984, has become an important forum of discussion disengaged from the international art market. Another significant moment at an international scale is the coinciding in 1997 of documenta X, curated by Catherine David, and the second Johannesburg Biennial, curated by Okwui Enwezor.

[4] Luis Camnitzer points out that 'while "conceptual art" is an anecdotal little label in the history of universal art, "conceptualism" as a strategy created a rupture in the appreciation of all art and in the behaviour of artists, regardless of their location'. Fernando Davis, 'Entrevista a Luis Camnitzer: "Global Conceptualism fue algo intestinal e incontrolable, al mismo tiempo que presuntuoso y utópico"', *Ramona*, no.86, November 2008, p.29. See also Rachel Weiss, 'Re-writing Conceptual Art', *Papers d'Art*, no.93, 2007, pp.198–202. Translation the author's.

[5] F. Davis, 'Entrevista a Luis Camnitzer', *op. cit.*, p.26.

[6] This last question was put forward by theoretician José Luis Brea in his considerations of the political effects of visuality. See J.L. Brea, 'Los estudios visuales: por una epistemología política de la visualidad', in J.L. Brea (ed.), *Los estudios visuales: La epistemología de la visualidad en la era de la globalización*, Madrid: Akal, 2005, pp.5–14.

[7] [Paul] B. Preciado, 'Cartografías *Queer*. El *flâneur* perverso, la lesbiana topofóbica y la puta multicartográfica, o cómo hacer una cartografía "zorra" con Annie Sprinkle', in José Miguel Cortés (ed.), *Cartografías disidentes*, Madrid: SEACEX, 2008, n.p.

[8] See Félix Guattari, *Cartographies schizoanalytiques*, Paris: Éditions Galilée, 1989.

[9] [P.]B. Preciado, 'Cartografías *Queer*', *op. cit.*

[10] As Antonio Negri and Michael Hardt remind us, these biopolitical modes of production do not only involve the production of tangible goods in a purely economic sense, but 'affect all spheres of social, economic, cultural and political life, at the same time as they produce them'. A. Negri and M. Hardt, 'Preface', *Multitude: War and Democracy in the Age of Empire*, Cambridge, MA and London: Harvard University Press, 2001, p.xi.

[11] Boris Groys has clearly expressed some of the effects of this paradox in art: 'If life is no longer understood as a natural event, as fate, as Fortuna, but rather as time artificially produced and fashioned, then life is automatically politicised, since the technical and artistic decisions with respect to the shaping of the lifespan are always political decisions as well. The art that is made under these new conditions of biopolitics – under the conditions of an artificially fashioned lifespan – cannot help but take this artificiality as its explicit theme. Now, however, time, duration and thus life too cannot be shown directly but only documented. The dominant medium of modern biopolitics is thus bureaucratic and technological documentation, which includes planning, decrees, fact-finding reports, statistical inquiries and project plans. It is no coincidence that art also uses the same medium of documentation when it wants to refer to itself as life.' B. Groys, 'Art in the Age of Biopolitics: From Artwork to Art Documentation', *Documenta 11_Platform 5: Exhibition* (exh. cat.), Ostfildern: Hatje Cantz, 2002, p.109.

[12] The issue also involves the critical modes of working around the concepts that sustain these historiographic exercises. It is possible to say, for instance, that to a certain extent 'Global Conceptualism' adopted the task of the ethnologist, raking up experiences in different geographies and marking its affinities and Conceptualist identities, and yet, paradoxically, its strategy facilitated the *mise-en-critique* of identity itself. An acritical example of the identity discourse is provided by Álvaro Barrios's book *Orígenes del arte conceptual en Colombia* (1999), which offers a narrative made up of interviews in which several leading figures of the 1960s and 70s guide the story's main character (Barrios himself), who appears increasingly convinced of his ability to truly recover the unrecognised Conceptualist element. Á. Barrios, *Orígenes del arte conceptual en Colombia (1968–1978)*, Bogotá: Alcaldía Mayor de Bogotá, 1999.

[13] [P.]B. Preciado, 'Cartografías *Queer*', *op. cit.*

[14] Mari Carmen Ramírez, 'Blueprint Circuits: Conceptual Art and Politics in Latin America', in Waldo Rasmussen, Fatima Bercht and Elizabeth Ferrer (ed.), *Latin American Artists of the Twentieth Century* (exh. cat.), New York: Museum of Modern Art, 1993, pp.156–67.

[15] The exhibition presented Latin American art production as a tame continuation of modern Western aesthetic movements, avoiding any type of political reflection on the colonial history of the subcontinent. Most critics agreed in characterising it as a blatant attempt to 'maintain a total

control of the ideological and aesthetic premises [...] and of their interpretation' from categories projected from the outside. Shifra M. Goldman, 'Artistas latinoamericanos del siglo XX, MoMA' (trans. Magdalena Holguín), *ArtNexus*, no.10, September–December 1993, pp.84–89.

[16] Drawn up in 1989 and promoted by the International Monetary Fund, the World Bank and the US Treasury Department, the Washington Consensus is a list of measures for economic reform that presented itself as the 'best' programme to face the crisis and 'underdevelopment' of Latin America, among which were liberalisation of trade and investment, deregulation and a general withdrawal of the state from economic matters.

[17] Some of these debates, from a Latin American cultural perspective opposed to European and North American dominance, can be found in Gerardo Mosquera (ed.), *Beyond the Fantastic: Contemporary Art Criticism from Latin America*, London: Institute of International Visual Arts, 1995.

[18] Juan Pablo Renzi, a driving force in 'Tucumán Arde', was emphatic about this. In a work titled *Panfleto no.3. La nueva moda* (*Pamphlet no.3. The New Fashion*, 1971), which he contributed to the 'Arte de Sistemas' exhibition organised by the Museo de Arte Moderno/Centro de Arte y Comunicación in Buenos Aires in 1971, he stated: 'What is in fashion now is Conceptual art [...] and it turns out that (at least for some critics like Lucy Lippard and Jorge Glusberg) I am one of those responsible for the onset of this phenomenon (together with my colleagues from the ex-groups of revolutionary artists in Rosario and Buenos Aires from 67 to 68). This assertion is mistaken. Just as any intention of linking us to that aesthetic speculation is mistaken.' And he concluded: 'REGARDING OUR MESSAGES: 1. We are not interested in them being considered aesthetic. 2. We structure them according to their contents. 3. They are always political and are not always transmitted by official channels like this one. 4. We are not interested in them as works but as a means of denouncing exploitation.'

[19] The same reference to Marchán Fiz's 'ideological Conceptualism' had already been made one year earlier by the North American critic Jacqueline Barnitz in the catalogue of the exhibition 'Encounters/ Displacements. Luis Camnitzer, Alfredo Jaar, Cildo Meireles', curated by Ramírez and Beverly Adams. However, Ramírez's voice was the one that consolidated and furthered the argument most effectively, making it an indispensable reference for many subsequent interpretations. A decisive factor in this consolidation was the repetition of the line of argument in the catalogue of 'Global Conceptualism' and later on in two large-scale international surveys of Latin American art she was also in charge of: 'Heterotopías. Medio siglo sin lugar 1918–1968', at the Museo Nacional Centro de Arte Reina Sofía, Madrid, 2000; and 'Inverted Utopias: Avant-Garde Art in Latin America', at Museum of Fine Arts, Houston, 2004. Marchán Fiz doesn't quite completely confine the 'ideologisation' to Conceptual art from Latin American nor self-referentiality to European/North American work. See J. Barnitz, 'Conceptual Art in Latin America: A Natural Alliance', in M.C. Ramírez and B. Adams (ed.), *Encounters/Displacements: Luis Camnitzer, Alfredo Jaar, Cildo Meireles* (exh. cat.), Austin: Archer M. Huntington Art Gallery, University of Texas, 1992, pp.35–47; M.C. Ramírez, 'Tactics for Thriving on Adversity: Conceptualism in Latin America, 1960–1980', in L. Camnitzer, J. Farver and R. Weiss (ed.), *Global Conceptualism: Points of Origin, 1950s–1980s* (exh. cat.), New York: Queens Museum of Art, 1999, pp.53–71; and S. Marchán Fiz, *Del arte objetual al arte de concepto*, Madrid: Alberto Corazón Editor, 1974 (1972).

[20] M.C. Ramírez, 'Blueprint Circuits', *op. cit.*, p.156.

[21] Benjamin H.D. Buchloh, 'From the Aesthetic of Administration to Institutional Critique (Some Aspects of Conceptual Art, 1962–1969)', in *l'art conceptuel, une perspective* (exh. cat.), Paris: Musée d'Art Moderne de la Ville de Paris, 1989, pp.41–53.

[22] Historian Jaime Vindel has also noted the contradictions in responding to the centre/periphery relationship through an equally binary opposition: 'By basing their position on an antagonist with no real voice, these discourses run the risk of making their publicity dependent on the centre/periphery logic against which they declare they stand and to which they are still yielding.' J. Vindel, 'A propósito [de la memoria] del arte político: Consideraciones en torno a "Tucumán Arde" como emblema del conceptualismo latinoamericano', lecture at the Fifth International Conference of Theory and History of the Arts – Thirteenth CAIA Symposium, Buenos Aires, October 2009.

[23] Peter Osborne, *Conceptual Art*, London and New York: Phaidon Press, 2002, p.37.

[24] Alexander Alberro, 'Reconsidering Conceptual Art, 1966–1977', in A. Alberro and Blake Stimson (ed.), *Conceptual Art: A Critical Anthology*, Cambridge, MA and London: MIT Press, 1999, pp.xxv–xxvi.

[25] Pilar Parcerisas, *Conceptualismo(s) Poéticos, Políticos, Periféricos: En torno al arte conceptual en España. 1964–1980*, Madrid: Akal, 2007, p.27.

[26] In a 1997 text, Camnitzer celebrated Ramírez's argument, which he found enlightening for its understanding of the regional differences of Conceptualism, which emphasised the relationship between Marcel Duchamp and the modern tradition of Mexican muralism, starting from its foray into the social sphere with communicative goals. Broadly speaking, however, Camnitzer

shares Ramírez's view of North American Conceptual art, which Caminitzer brands 'a quasi-mystical search for the imponderable'. L. Camnitzer, 'Una genealogía del arte conceptual latino-americano', *Continente Sul Sur*, no.6, November 1997, p.187. Other historians who have used the expression 'ideological Conceptualism' more or less critically over the past few years include Andrea Giunta, Ana Longoni, María José Herrera, Ivonne Pini, Miguel González, Cristina Freire and Alberto Giudici. Due to problems of space, this text will not compare the conflicting meanings and the implications inscribed in their uses.

[27] 'A minor literature doesn't come from a minor language; it is rather that which a minority constructs within a major language. [...] The second characteristic of minor literatures is that everything in them is political. Minor literature is completely different; its cramped space forces each individual intrigue to connect immediately to politics. [...] We might as well say that minor no longer designates specific literatures but the revolutionary conditions for every literature within the heart of what is called great (or established) literature.' Gilles Deleuze and Félix Guattari, *Kafka: Toward a Minor Literature* (trans. Dana B. Polan), Minneapolis: University of Minnesota Press, 1986, pp.16–18.

[28] See Ana Longoni, 'Other Beginnings of Conceptualism (Argentinean and Latin-American)', *Papers d'Art*, no.93, 2007, pp.155–58.

[29] See Oscar Masotta, 'Después del pop, nosotros desmaterializamos' (1967), in O. Masotta, *Revolución en el arte: Pop-art, happenings y arte de los medios en la década del sesenta*, Buenos Aires: Edhasa, 2004, pp.335–76. For Lucy Lippard's use of the term, see L.R. Lippard, *Six Years, op. cit.*

[30] As yet, there is no study dealing with Juan Acha's critical thinking of the 1960s and 70s, and the political process that led to the emergence of 'no-objetualismo'. For a first, partial attempt, see Miguel A. López and Emilio Tarazona, 'Juan Acha y la Revolución Cultural. La transformación de la vanguardia artística en el Perú a fines de los Sesenta', in J. Acha, *Nuevas referencias sociológicas de las artes visuales: Mass-media, lenguajes, represiones y grupos* (1969), Lima: IIMA – Universidad Ricardo Palma, 2008, pp.1–17.

[31] A. Longoni, 'El Deshabituador: Ricardo Carreira in the Beginnings of Conceptualism', in Viviana Usubiaga and A. Longoni, *Arte y literatura en la Argentina del siglo XX*, Buenos Aires: Fundación Telefónica, Fundación Espigas and FIAAR, 2006, pp.159–203.

[32] See Cuauhtémoc Medina, 'Recovering Panic', in Olivier Debroise (ed.), *The Age of Discrepancies: Art and Visual Culture in Mexico, 1968–1997*, Mexico City: UNAM, 2007, pp.97–103.

[33] In October 1968, in a newspaper and on local radio, Vigo made the surprising call for his first 'señalamiento' (appointment), titled *Manojo de Semáforos* (*A Handful of Traffic Lights*). The proposal called for people to look at an ordinary object for its aesthetic potential to cause 'revulsion'. See F. Davis, 'Prácticas "revulsivas": Edgardo Antonio Vigo en los márgenes del conceptualismo', in C. Freire and A. Longoni (ed.), *Conceitualismos do Sul/Sur*, São Paulo: Annablume, USP-MAC and AECID, 2009, pp.283–98.

[34] 'Inventario 1965–1975. Archivo Graciela Carnevale', Centro Cultural Parque de España, Rosario (3 October–9 November 2008). The team working on the show was made up of the artist Graciela Carnevale; historians Ana Longoni and Fernando Davis; and Ana Wandzik, an artist from Rosario. This project constituted the first curatorial experiment in political activation by the Red Conceptualismos del Sur group.

[35] For further discussion of the experiences of 1968 in Argentina, see G. Carnevale et al. (ed.), *Tucumán Arde. Eine Erfahrung: Aus dem Archiv von Graciela Carnevale*, Berlin: b_books, 2004.

[36] While its earliest mentions date back to the late 1960s, its incorporation within the canon since the late 1990s, through a series of essays, exhibitions and publications, quickly multiplied its visibility. International exhibitions include: I Bienal de Artes Visuais do Mercosul, Porto Alegre, Brazil, 1997; 'Global Conceptualism', 1999, and 'Heterotopías', 2000; 'Ambulantes. Cultura Portátil', curated by Rosa Pera, Centro Andaluz de Arte Contemporáneo, Seville; 'Inverted Utopias', Museum of Fine Arts, Houston, 2004; and 'Be what you want but stay where you are', curated by Ruth Noack and Roger M. Buergel, Witte de With, Rotterdam, 2005.

[37] Roberto Jacoby, 'Tucucu mama nana arara dede dada', *Ramona*, no.55, October 2005, pp.86–91.

[38] Even though the most prevalent reading of 'Tucumán Arde' places it within the 'Conceptual' genealogy, others have tried to relate it to a history of political intervention, collective production or militant research. Examples of this are the dossier 'Les fils de Marx et Mondrian: Dossier argentine', *Robho*, no.5–6, 1971, pp.16–22; or anthropologist Néstor García Canclini's discussion of 'Tucumán Arde' in the context of the process of integration of artistic avant-gardes with popular organisations. See N. García Canclini, 'Vanguardias artísticas y cultura popular', *Transformaciones*, no.90, 1973, pp.273–75. More recently, Brian Holmes has noted the impact this experience had on several activist groups operating in Europe in the late 1990s. See A. Longoni, Daniela Lucena et al., '"Un sentido como el de Tucumán Arde lo encontramos hoy en el zapatismo": Entrevista colectiva a Brian Holmes', *Ramona*, no.55, October 2005, pp.7–22. Similar readings are proposed

by exhibitions such as: 'Antagonismes. Casos d'estudi', curated by Manuel Borja-Villel and José Lebrero, Museu d'Art Contemporani de Barcelona, 2001; 'Collective Creativity: Common Ideas for Life and Politics', curated by What, How and for Whom, Kunsthalle Fridericianum, Kassel, 2005; and the project *ExArgentina*, organised by Alice Creischer and Andreas Siekmann.

[39] The interviews were conducted by Mariano Mestman and A. Longoni; some were eventually published in their book *Del Di Tella a 'Tucumán Arde'. Vanguardia artística y política en el '68 argentino*, Buenos Aires: El cielo por asalto, 2000.

[40] See F. Davis and A. Longoni, 'Apuntes para un balance difícil: Historia mínima de "Inventario 1965–1975. Archivo Graciela Carnevale"', unpublished text presented at the Second Red Conceptualismos del Sur Reunion, Rosario, October 2008.

[41] 'Politics are only displayed by exposing the conflicts, the paradoxes, the reciprocal clashes that weave history', says Didi-Huberman in his considerations of the Brechtian notion of montage. '[M]ontage appears as the procedure *par excellence* in this exposition: its objects are not revealed when taking position but once they have been taken apart, as is said in French to describe the violence of a "unbridled" storm, wave against wave, or as is said of a watch "dismantled", i.e., analysed, explored and therefore spread by the passion of knowing applied by a philosopher or a Baudelairian child.' G. Didi-Huberman, *Cuando las imágenes toman posición*, Madrid: A. Machado Libros, 2008, p.153. Translation the editors'.

[42] See L. Camnitzer, *Conceptualism in Latin American Art: Didactics of Liberation*, Austin: University of Texas Press, 2007, pp.44–72. Camnitzer, however, points at alternative coordinates, such as the writings of nineteenth-century Venezuelan writer and educator Simón Rodríguez, who taught Simón Bolívar. For Camnitzer, the Tupamaros's use of 'aestheticised military operations' and Rodríguez's 'ideological aphorisms' contribute to what he calls a 'didactics of liberation': communication process aimed at generating actual changes in society.

[43] 'Politics is a specific rupture in the logic of *arche*. It does not simply presuppose the rupture of the "normal" distribution of positions between the one who exercises power and the one subject to it. It also requires a rupture in the idea that there are dispositions "proper" to such classifications.' Jacques Rancière, 'Dix thèses sur la politique', *Aux Bords du Politique*, Paris: Gallimard, p.229.

[44] A.T. Spear, *Art in the Mind, op. cit.*

NIRIN WURRUNMARRA

Brook Andrew

Anthony Gardner

LET'S PLAY ▶ NIRIN WURRUNMARRA

So what have we got? 8 pages? **whatever they give us**

- Do we have 4 double spreads? **Whatever they will give ngajuu**

- An individual page, followed by 3 double spreads and another individual page? **Call and response and some dual/duel**

- Those individual pages could be for brief amounts of text (1 or 2 separate texts) **is anything individual? When we are alone are we ever really alone?**

MAKING ~~METHODS~~ PRESENT

Thinking through NIRIN's methods rather than specific works per se? **action**

Jota Mombaça, THE DAUGHTERS OF THE DRIEST RAIN, 2020. 22nd Biennale of Sydney (2020). Photograph: Zan Wimberley

Key ideas: nothing is fixed — key ideas are always in flux and sometimes don't exist. People change their minds and protocols are always shifting even when they seem solid and still.

- Opacity **some things are not clear and will never be**

- Retraining the perspective of the book **look to the side**

- Layerings rather than juxtapositions? **Conciliation was always in the complex forms of colonisation**

- Display and resisting display **they have always been there**

- How other narratives of past/present can emerge and entwine **they have always been there**

Handwritten annotations:

DON'T KNOW THE WORDS?

LET'S PLAY

NGAJUU NGAY NGINDUWURR

TURN YOURSELF OVER INSIDE-OUT

TURN THE WRITING / THE BOOK UPSIDE DOWN!

IS LAYERING A CONCILIATION? A MONTAGE? A (SUPER-) ~~IMPOSITION~~? TO SEE

YES, BUT WHAT IS THE HISTORY OF RESISTING DISPLAY? HOW CAN WE PRESENT THIS? ARE WE STILL NEGOTIATING?

Indigenisation of curation, not just decolonisation of curation? Parallel universes

- Practice-led reimagining of how knowledge is articulated, developed and shared **no comment**

- Powerful objects and how they release their stories and/or resist need for "didactic" history-telling **some objects were not made to be preserved**

- How the experience of an exhibition can be articulated, rather than an exhibition be archived - first person narrative? Dialogue? To up-root they very understanding of exhibition making requires one to at times, to forget.

- The non-archivability of experiencing an exhibition, yet still somehow trying to activate that exhibition, those experiences, after deinstallation? **Continual cultural practices**

NIRIN provoked questions and doubt, possibilities and frustrations that exhibitions so often shy away from — so how to think through doubt and with responses that are unusual given how safe (and sometimes overdetermined) exhibitions have become.

What was an aspect of this doubt? Trying to find some of the works on Cockatoo Island that weren't present yet in that first few days, that were still finding their form or that were hiding away from becoming public yet. **This isn't a terrible thing, because sometimes works need to resist their publicness.** They spark curiosity instead, a curiosity to develop a conversation with a work that's in hiding, a conversation based on shyness and modesty (in a biennale!) and getting to know each other slowly.

I'm thinking about those curatorial passages or episodes that initially seemed surprising, not baffling but very affective, very unsettling. Like in the MCA and the passage of relationships between Pedro's work with the ceremonial poles, shifting into Aziz's installation and the Giordano painting of the rape of the Sabine women, into the Aboriginal land rights posters and then back out again, through the painting and the video and the poles. The relationships between the works — especially the sound bleed, the song and lament in Pedro's work and its re-presencing of log memorials on the beach, that first site of encounter and farewell, the wails and sound of screaming wind above Kabul in Aziz's work, the silent stilled violence against the Sabine Women and the way the lighting was so delicate, so gentle that the painting only emerged very slowly from the darkness of the gallery walls. This multiple sense of bleeding given the violence in all of the works, of sound and substance, blood and song come together in a curatorial space. How to make that sense of passage, of bleed, apparent now that the exhibition has come down? Splicing the images together like a montage won't work. Do the images need to be all overlapped in one image, bleeding into each other? What happens to sound, to movement, to doubt when we remember an exhibition?

CURATORIA[L] METHODS OF SOUNDBLEED, DELIBERATE A[N] POLYVOCAL, RELEASING TH[E] CHARGE OF VIOLENCE, O[F] BLOOD AND SCREA[M] IN COLONIAL (NEO-) TIMES

I'M ALSO THINKING ABOUT HOW AN EXHIBITION THINKS THROUGH, AND WITH, THE HISTORIES/STORIES OF OTHER EXHIBITIONS — EXHIBITIONS THAT HAVE BEEN REALLY CRUCIAL TO THE DEVELOPMENT OF LATER ONES, EXHIBITIONS THAT HAVE BEEN PROBLEMATIC & NEED TO BE RESPONDED TO. BROOK, YOU SHOWED BERNHARD LÜTHI'S ARCHIVES FROM MAGICIENS DE LA TERRE AND ARATJARA AT THE ART GALLERY OF NEW SOUTH WALES. WHY THESE EXHIBITIONS? DO THEY RESONATE IN THE SAME WAY? AND WHY WERE SOME OF THE ARCHIVAL MATERIALS VISIBLE IN THEIR VITRINES AND OTHERS WERE STILL HIDDEN AWAY, UNDERNEATH OTHER DOCUMENTS AND OBSCURED FROM VIEW?

THERE'S TOO MUCH OF A MESS — WILL IT EVER BE RESOLVED? THIS IS THE PROBLEM. HUMANS DON'T REALLY WANT TO NEGOTIATE OR SEE SOMETHING DIFFERENT — IT'S LIKE PUSHIN[G] SHIT UP HILL. STINKY

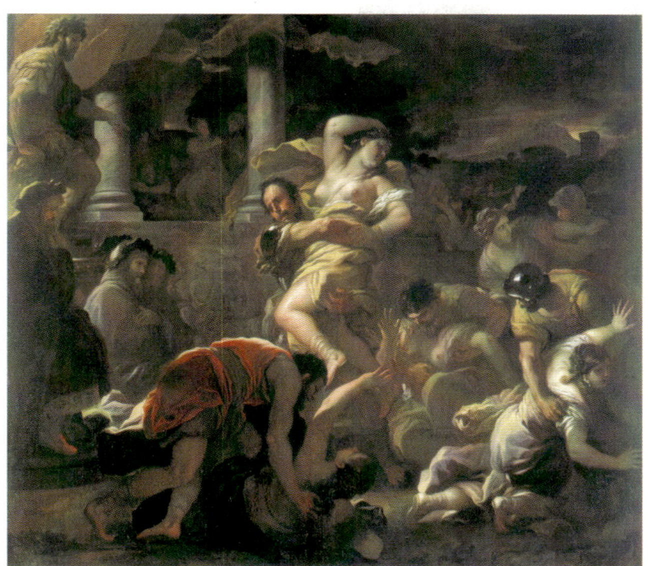

Luca Giordano.
Il ratto delle Sabine [The rape of the Sabine women] c.1672-74
Collection of National Gallery of Victoria.

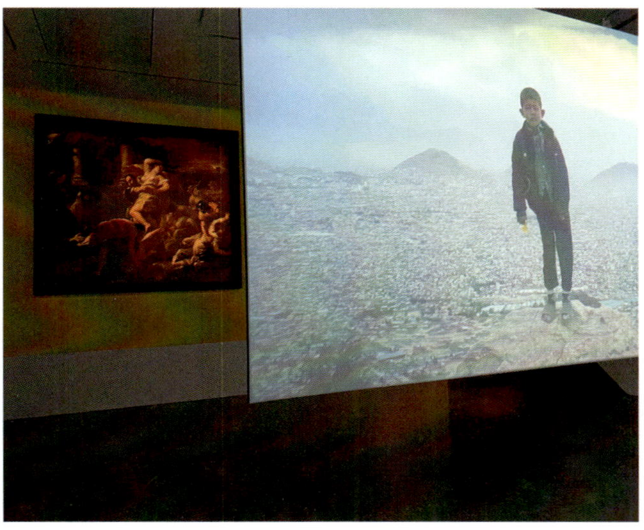

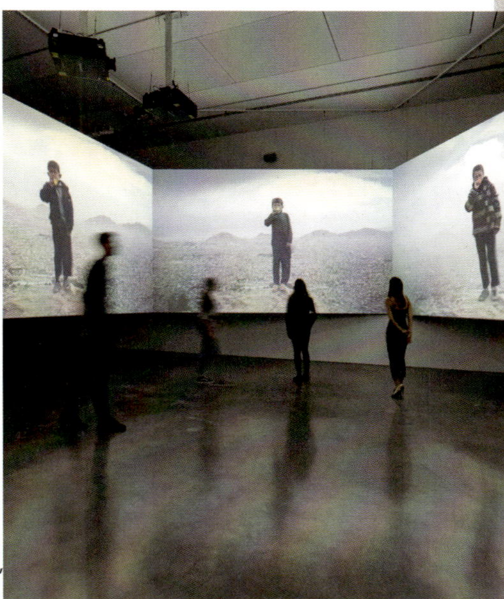

z Hazara, *Bow Echo*, 2019. Installation view for the 22nd Biennale of Sydney (2020),
seum of Contemporary Art Australia. Presented at the 22nd Biennale of Sydney
duced by Han Nefkens Foundation. Courtesy the artist. Photograph: (L) Brook Andrew, (R) Ken Leanfore, Museum of Contemporary Art Austral

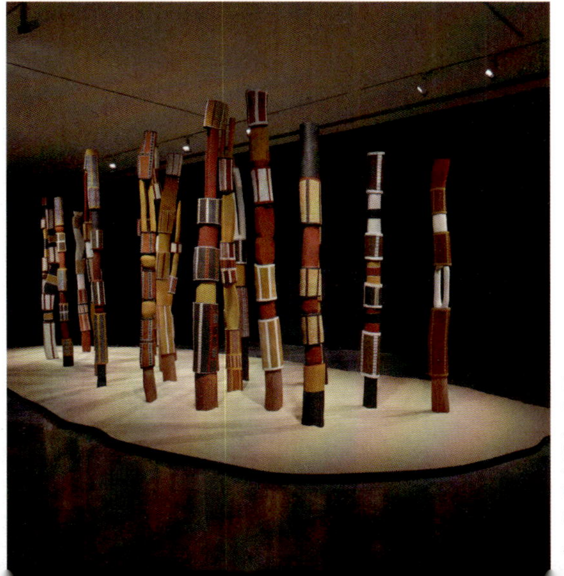

Pedro Wonaeamirri (with Patrick Freddy Puruntatameri),
'kurrujupuni, arrikininga, yarringa, tunuwuni kapi katukuni (white,
yellow, red, black on ironwood)', 2020. Installation view for the
22nd Biennale of Sydney (2020), Museum of Contemporary Art Australia
Courtesy the artist; Jilamara Arts and Craft, Milikapiti; and Alcaston
Gallery, Melbourne. Additional carving by Gerry Mungatopi,
Jason Palipuaminni and Pius Tipungwuti. Photograph: Zan Wimberley.

NIRIN is expressing a ceremony, an emotionality between space, movement and sound, it's not just visual and conceptual – it's through a whole host of other experiences and sensations that bring histories and the way we experience and reflect on histories into different dialogues and clashes.

Yindyamarra Winhanganha
The wisdom of respectfully knowing how to live well in a world worth living in.
Yindyamarra: to be gentle and care, which expands to respect, give honour, go slow, and take responsibility; Winhanganha: to know, remember and think.

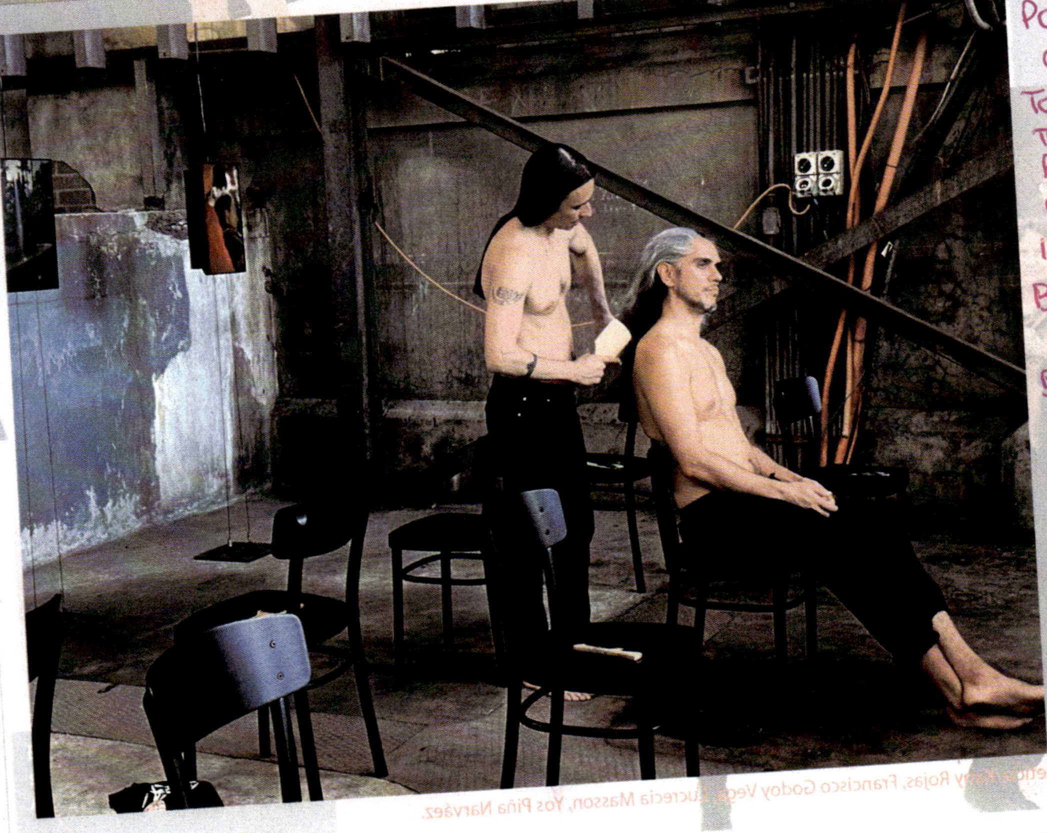

Hair is a sacred substance. It is cared for in Indigenous cultures, and is not a simple gesture, many often do not understand the power of hair.

S.J.Norman. Magna Mater. 2020. Performance view at Cockatoo Island with video installation. 12 channel video. Biennale of Sydney. Photograph: Brook Andrew.

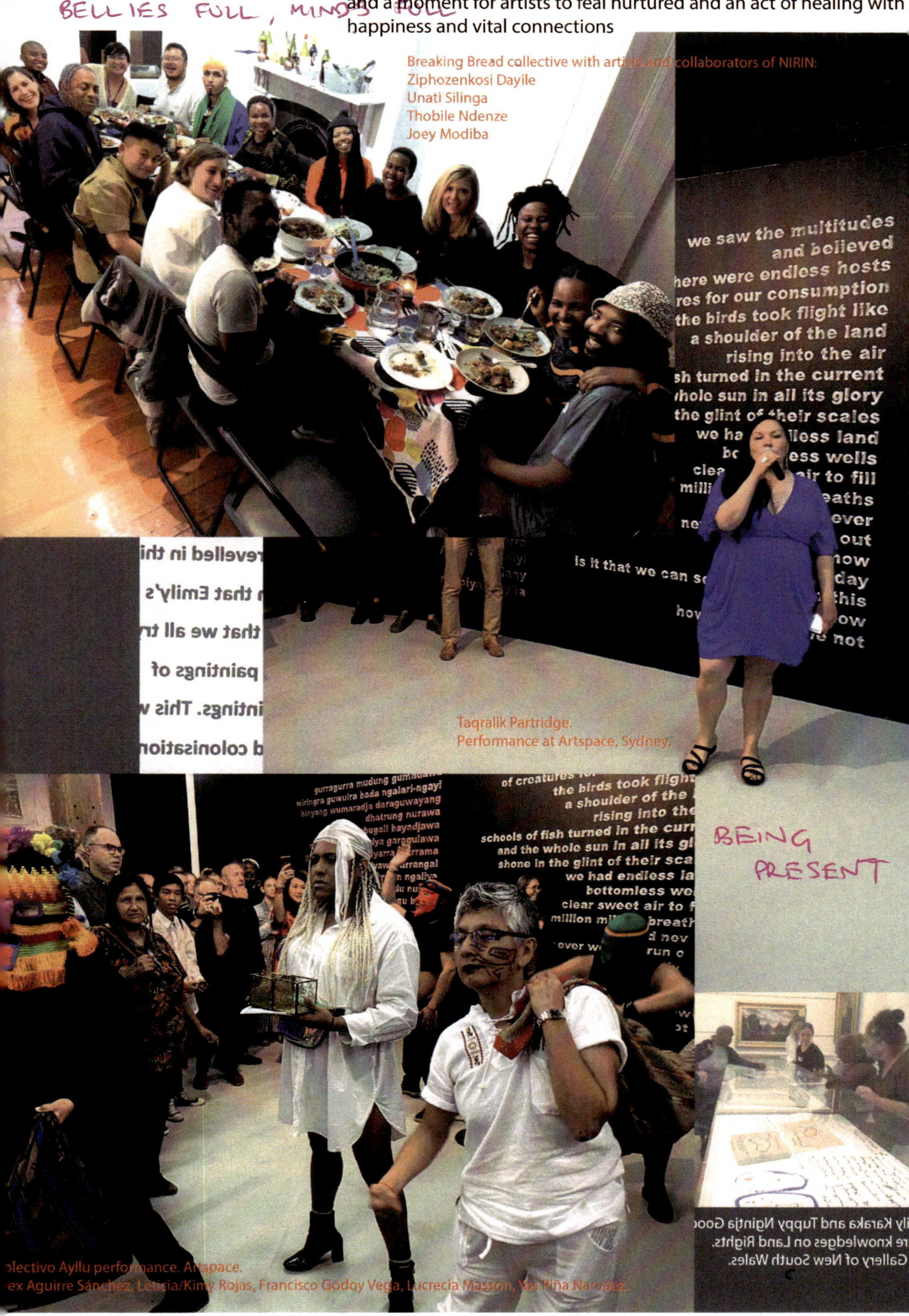

Taqralik Partridge.
Performance at Artspace, Sydney.

olectivo Ayllu performance. Artspace.
ex Aguirre Sánchez, Leticia/Kimy Rojas, Francisco Godoy Vega, Lucrecia Masson, Yos Piña Narváez.

ily Karaka and Tuppy Ngintja Goo
re knowledges on Land Rights.
Gallery of New South Wales.

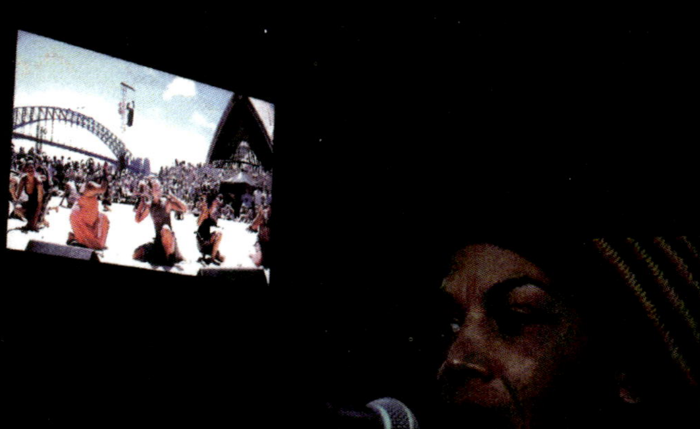

Barbara McGrady (with John Janson-Moore), Ngiyaningy Maran Yaliwaunga Ngaara-li (Our Ancestors Are Always Watching), 2020. Installation view for the 22nd Biennale of Sydney (2020), Campbelltown Arts Centre. Photograph: Anthony Gardner.

Juxtapositions, interventions – so often when an object is made to juxtapose with another, or with a gallery (think a Wiradjuri entity made to "intervene" in a colonial display), the objects are made didactic, they can't speak for themselves, there is no agency, they simply respond to the ongoing power and focus on the master narrative of a colonial display, determined by a master curator. What happens when all that curatorial apparatus – the livery, the accoutrements, the straitjacket – is stripped away, and the object finally speaks for itself and not for others – is that the power of the powerful objects? Does that power happen when the objects draw themselves open and are present without the need for curatorial ventriloquism – like the shackles that had enslaved people that were presented in the Campbelltown Arts Centre – and the people that have been touched and hurt by these objects and how these presentations connect to other presentations of slavery and shackles regardless of where they are? These shackles connect with the lives of those enslaved as the foundation of settler Australia, they connect with our lives as viewers in settler Australia today, they connect with the lives of other enslaved peoples whose enslavement founded other settler colonies, and they connect with other displays (in anthropological museums, in smart exhibitions like Fred Wilson's in the early 1990s) in which shackles are silent, present reminders of

I'M THINKING ABOUT, BUT N ONLY, MININ THE MUSEUM

OR VIEWING THE INVISIBLE AT THE POTTER MUSEUM OF ART IN NARRM/MELBOURNE IN 1998!

how knowledge, nation, histories and remembering are made and
denied.

And so each object is polyvocal, it has so many stories that can come
out if we want to feel them and listen to them and sense them – by
taking away the confinement of the curatorial discourse and
translations. The object can open up in any way it wants to – it could
touch on many histories, on protracted forms of physical and cultural
and interpersonal violence, and can be all these things together. It's
confronting for some and everyday for others, often those of us
silenced. Or not heard above the dominant racket of muselogical
circus games.

People just want to fix everything – and you can't. So, what do you
do about it. And this is not a question. Most of the time it's because
people don't want to give up their jobs.

CAN YOU SAY MORE ABOUT THIS?

Transition

WHAT KIND OF TRANSITION?
DOES IT MATTER?!

What does the decolonial mean in theory and in practice – what does
it do? Especially in curating, which is so often still fixated on the
heroic authorial voice, excluding all the collaborations and
negotiations that are central to curatorial work.

DOES A "DISPERSED" CURATING – SUCH AS ENWEZOR'S OR CHRISTOV-BAKARGIEV'S – REALLY "DE-COLONISE" CURATORIAL AUTHORSHIP? OR IS THAT NOT THE POINT?

WHO IS NIRIN FOR?
CHANGE. A PROPOSITION. A VISIBILITY. A POWER.

They felt represented and in a community. Many artists said to me
that often they were in exhibitions and were the only black, trans,
POC, queer whatever person or from that group in their country –
they were artists ticked off in boxes. This horrified me. But I
understand and have experienced it. Swing around to yindyamrra
and how this philosophy isn't about comparing or fixing the
western dilemma of the decolonial. It's about being present.

I'D LIKE TO KNOW MORE ABOUT THIS!

How has this denial of presence informed exhibition histories? If
artists who identify as non-heteronormative western have been
excluded from being present or prescribed in a certain role or
visibility, then how can we understand the exclusions and analyse

Not every path finds a place that is out of the mess that colonialism or other bad decisions made through creating a level playing field. This kind of control or optimism is sometimes a reflection of privilege or someone being out of touch with another culture or people. It is ok to be out of touch, just don't try to always fix it - allow others to take control and be well with this.

real falsity to try to magic histories of exhibitions that are inclusive or thinking differently in terms of community or not box ticking. Do we rectify those histories? Tell them again, but with commentary? Deny them or leave them as they are? Struggling through this is good.

Some people are blinded by their own Eurocentricity its confounding. But I understand because they are surrounded by the cultural objects of people outside of their own language and geographical positioning broadly collected through the colonial hole.

The word struggle can be a buzz word for those who do not struggle. To struggle is like being in poverty or being bashed or raped or experiencing racism or prejudice. People get angry about this...being in this space sitting in this space is essential in order to understand that being out of the struggle doesn't mean that one is complacent, it is after all allowing for space.

In Europe, someone said to me that a person who screams to the forest ... the voice that comes back is your own voice – but in my culture, when you scream to the forest or call to the forest it is not you who calls back it is the trees, water, rocks and animals and the

I wouldn't think it's poetic - it is for me another form to express culture through an Indigenous way, and in many ways the translation of the word poetry does not stand up to the immensity of an Indigenous methodology - but it does help out of touch people some kind of hook to enter. Elicura was a powerful presentation regarding this:

Handwritten marginalia:

FINDING PATHS OUT OF STRUGGLE. CAN AN EXHIBITON, A BIENNALE, PROVIDE ANY ANSWERS TO THIS STRUGGLE?

DOUBT IS SO IMPORTANT. IT'S A SPACE, A VULNERABILITY, AN OPENNESS, THAT MANY OF US DENY BUT WHICH NIRIN COULD OPEN UP

LET'S UNSETTLE THIS TERM!

AND IMPORTANT TO THINK ABOUT POETIC WAYS, OTHER WAYS, TO SCREAM

Elicura Chihuailaf Nahuelpán, *Machiluwvn / Iniciación / Initiation*, 2020.
Installation view for the 22nd Biennale of Sydney (2020), Art Gallery of New South Wales.
Commissioned by the Biennale of Sydney with assistance from NIRIN 500 patrons.
Courtesy the artist. Photograph: Zan Wimberley.

...ortunately there are not enough curatorial strategies that can dismantle the view of specific cultural trajectories - the people in power are charged with museums that evoke and stabilise dominant views of history that are not only outdated but need to be disappeared and replaced with new visions that are inclusive of indigenous and other methadologies which reflect the balanced view of humanity, spirituality and the animal world.

Can we think about Emily Karaka's paintings here, too, in the Art Gallery of New South Wales? Set amongst the colonial paintings of the land that the settlers were stealing, these paintings that are the pride of the Sydney gallery, Karaka's work shows the land and its custodians from a very different aesthetic and cultural and political sensibility. Did the colonial paintings go into storage, hidden away, or maybe hiding away, embarrassed by how they've been hung and instrumentalised by the Gallery's settler directors and curators for so long?

Emily Karaka is a land rights activist and long dedicated respected senior elder in Aotearoa. When I first spoke with Emily about the old court galleries of the Art Gallery of NSW, she like other artists were both perplexed and surprised by the context. Emily's works are bright and bold and have figurative animals like octopus as well as landscapes and text which is from the court cases of the land claims. Like Arthur Jafa's video work *The White Album* blasting out to historical paintings, Emily revelled in this contrast whereas some Europeans who visited the gallery space though that Emily's work didn't 'match' – interesting this aspect, it's like the market cringe that we all try to avoid but is absolutely embedded in the art market – this is that the paintings of Emily didn't fit well aesthetically with the calm landscape European paintings. This was the point of difference and of the serious nature of contrast to land and colonisation. After all, to turn the system on its head is to accept that there are other pathways.

too difficult to reproduce here seeing in person is the aim to then see the real power of an intervention that disrupts the regular Western display of often out of touch art that does not assist in dealing with the hugs issues of power and control in this century

[handwritten annotations: THE ARTIST STRATEGIES; SUSTAIN LOOKING TWICE; THE WAYS COLOUR AND SOUND BLAST OUT BUT HOW THA...; THE SHOCK WITH BLASTING THE HISTORICAL?; CAN (SHOULD) THAT DISTURBING AND NECESSARY VIOLENCE BE CAPTURED?]

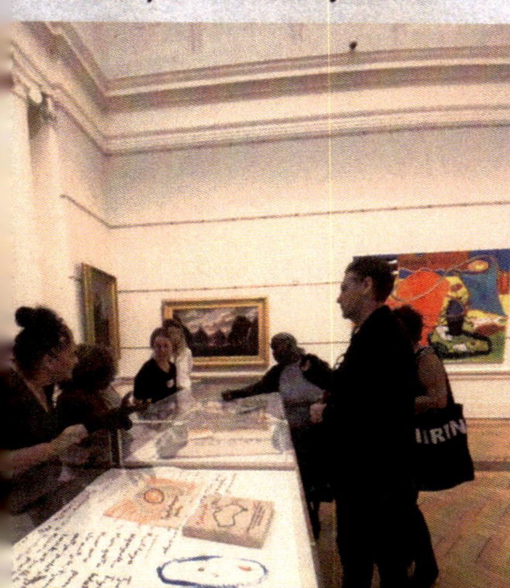

...y Karaka and Tuppy Ngintja Goodwin and family ...e knowledges on Land Rights. ...Gallery of New South Wales. ...tograph: Jessyca Hutchens

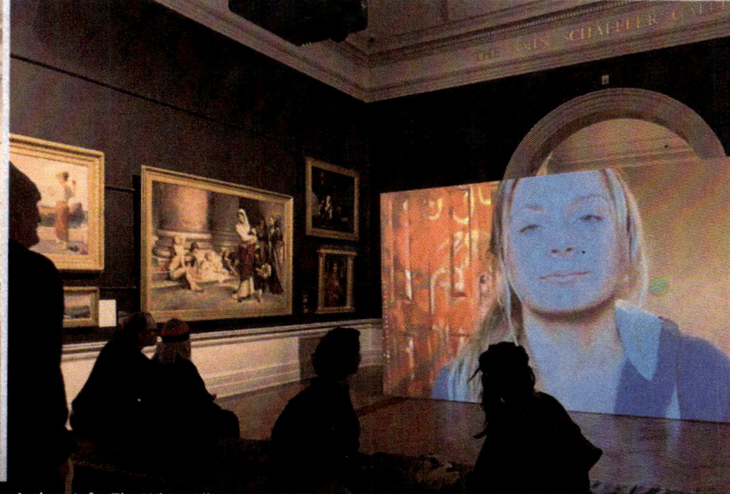

Arthur Jafa, *The White Album*, 2018-19. Installation view for the 22nd Biennale of Sydney (2020), Art Gallery of New South Wales. Originally commissioned by the UC Berkeley Art Museum and Pacific Film Archive (BAMPFA). Presented at the 22nd Biennale of Sydney with assistance from the United States Government. Courtesy the artist and Gavin Brown's enterprise, New York / Rome. Photograph: Brook Andrew.

People in power are terrified of letting it go - this is what that often scary word 'privilege' is all about...and within museums and cultural structures where this hits the most. After all, what would a museum or galle look like if the decision making was made by the living ancestors of the cultural objects in collections? Ar what does this say about a juxtaposition or a new layering or return of these objects? What then would b in the museums and hence what then would the museum's usefulness be? This is a terrifying thought for

Anger and Reconciliation: A Very Brief History of Exhibiting Contemporary Indigenous Art in Canada

Lee-Ann Martin

In 1986, while working in a university museum in the US state of Maine, I began to hear media reports regarding the planning of an exhibition titled 'The Spirit Sings: Artistic Traditions of Canada's First Peoples'.[1] Organised by the Glenbow Museum in Calgary, Alberta to coincide with the 1988 Olympics held in that location, 'The Spirit Sings' was to include over 650 historical objects borrowed from national and international ethnographic collections.[2] I was angry and frustrated to learn that the curatorial committee included no Indigenous curators. My anger was exacerbated by the fact that the exhibition would include only historical objects, without regard to contemporary realities – typical of the exclusionary practices of museums that had amassed significant collections of Indigenous historical objects while denying intellectual and physical access to the objects by the very communities from which they were taken.

I was not alone in my anger. 'The Spirit Sings' was part of a sequence of exhibitions and events during the late 1980s and early 90s that profoundly impacted the content of, and contexts for, exhibitions of Indigenous art. Artistic and community activism, exhibitions, conferences and a task force forever transformed relationships between museums and Indigenous peoples in Canada; this essay is an attempt to weave together a history of the turbulent dynamic of this time.

The fact that 'The Spirit Springs' came to my attention as early as 1986 can be attributed to a widely publicised campaign by the Lubicon Cree Nation – a small Aboriginal community living sovereignly in northern Alberta – to boycott the exhibition, which brought issues of museum representation and First Nations cultural heritage to the forefront of the national debate. From the perspective of the Lubicon Cree, the exhibition glorified numerous romantic stereotypes associated with historical Aboriginal cultural objects while denying complex contemporary realities. In their case, that reality was the destruction wrought on their culture and livelihood by Shell Canada, the corporate sponsor of the exhibition, as well as the complicity of major cultural institutions in Shell's corporate agenda, through organising or lending works to the show. Indigenous artists, communities and political organisations across the nation strongly supported Lubicon's perspective and boycott.

On 12 January 1988, three days before 'The Spirit Sings' opened to the public, Rebecca Belmore burst into the national arts consciousness with her performance piece *Artifact #671B*. In minus 18 degrees Celsius weather, she sat immobile on the frozen ground in a museum case outside the Thunder Bay Art Gallery in Ontario. Her performance expressed the collective anger of the many Indigenous people throughout Canada who condemned the organisers and sponsor of 'The Spirit Sings'. Four days earlier, the exhibition 'Revisions' had opened at the Walter Phillips Gallery in Banff, Alberta (about an hour from Calgary). Strategically timed to coincide with 'The Spirit Sings', 'Revisions' included eight Indigenous artists from both Canada and the US.[3] Conceived to counter the historic and ethnographic focus of 'The Spirit Sings', 'Revisions' asserted the significance of contemporary Indigenous culture and arts practices. The artists sabotaged ethnographic stereotypes in order to redress their present and future cultural identities. They were concerned with 'deconstructing Eurocentric versions of native history and proposing their own counternarratives';[4] for example, Jimmie Durham and Joane Cardinal-Schubert both angrily parodied the devices of museum display as they created their own contemporary artefacts as history lesson and ethnographic critique. These interventions responded to the housing of Indigenous artefacts in Caucasian museums in North America and in Europe and the categorisation of Indigenous art practices in ethnographic terms. (These conditions are largely still the case.) Even with the growing public awareness of Indigenous sovereignty in the late 1980s, sympathy for Indigenous peoples was usually based on paternalistic notions of cultures forever locked in history. While 'Revisions' was important as one of the first exhibitions to focus on the disruption of institutional practices through an Indigenous lens, its impact was limited until the accompanying catalogue was published in 1992.

In conjunction with the last days of the second presentation of 'The Spirit Sings', from 1 July–6 November 1988 at the Canadian Museum of Civilization[5] in Gatineau, Quebec (across the river from Ottawa), the Assembly of First Nations and the Canadian Museums Association jointly organised a conference to debate the full range of concerns voiced by the Lubicon Cree. 'Preserving Our Heritage: A Working Conference Between Museums and First Peoples' brought together over 150 academics, artists, curators, museum professionals, politicians and Indigenous knowledge keepers. Sponsorship, representation, access to collections and training were some aspects of the vital and multifaceted discussions at this conference. Following the recommendations of conference participants, and officially initiated by the Assembly of First Nations and the Canadian Museums Association in 1990,

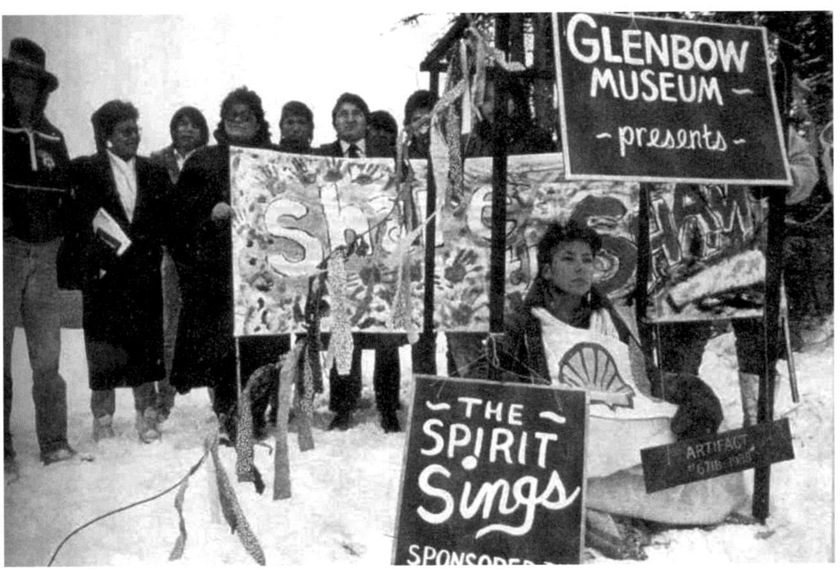

Rebecca Belmore, *Artifact #671B*, performance, Thunder Bay, Ontario, 1988. Courtesy the artist

the Task Force on Museums and First Peoples – for which I was coordinator – convened consultations and meetings and conducted research over a two-year period. The final report, *Turning the Page: Forging New Partnerships Between Museums and First Peoples* (1992), contains guidelines and recommendations 'to develop an ethical framework and strategies for Aboriginal Nations to represent their history and culture in concert with cultural institutions'.[6]

At this time I also conducted an independent survey on the status of contemporary Native art within 29 contemporary Canadian art institutions; this involved studying a number of museum functions: acquisitions, exhibitions, publications, programming, staffing and relationships to Aboriginal (arts) communities.[7] Written acquisition policies of the period contained subtle exclusionary phrases such as 'highest quality collections', 'finest visual art available' and 'important artists'; such language was used to denote a single acceptable standard, to perpetuate the myth of the Western European model of race hierarchy and to deny the complex issues of diverse art discourses and practices. The study concluded by detailing the systemic exclusion of contemporary Indigenous art from Canada's foremost art museums.

With few exceptions, curators and directors rationalised this exclusion with statements that they didn't want to 'segregate' or 'reduce to a ghetto status' these works. Although many stated that they were fearful of 'different' treatment for these artists, they overlooked the fact that contemporary Aboriginal artists had been treated differently and negatively for far too long. The majority of the museums displayed an aversion to thematic exhibitions based 'solely on cultural origins' of artists; the integration of contemporary Indigenous art with contemporary Canadian art seems to have been beyond their scope at that time.

The mobilisation around 'The Spirit Sings' built upon years and decades of Indigenous activism, organisation and resistance. I became increasingly aware of this as of 1987, when I began graduate work in museum studies at the University of Toronto, to research, critique and enter into a field less travelled by Indigenous peoples at that time. I soon learned about the third National Native Indian Artists Symposium that was organised at K'san, British Columbia in 1983, where Kwakwaka'wakw and Haida artists who had worked on museum projects in Victoria and Vancouver during the previous two decades shared their skills with over a hundred artists and students.[8] (The symposium itself was held on the site of the Kitanmax School of Northwest Coast Indian Art, which in 1967 had initiated an artist training programme to revitalise Nisga'a art and cultural traditions.) Immediately following the symposium, a working group was organised to address the ongoing exclusion of Indian art by mainstream art institutions; the group incorporated as the Society of Canadian Artists of Native Ancestry (SCANA) in January 1985. Two artists highly respected as innovators within their respective traditions of Iroquoian sculpture and Northwest Coast sculpture, David General and Doreen Jensen, were the first co-chairs of SCANA. Throughout the 1980s and the early 90s, the group worked tirelessly to increase the recognition of contemporary First Nations artists. The mandate of SCANA, as an informally organised national group, was to act as liaison amongst the growing number of Native artists, the provincial and federal funding agencies, and art museums. It was a strong advocate in the many debates around museum representation in this period; amongst its accomplishments was the organisation in 1987 of 'Networking', the fourth National Native Indian Arts Symposium, at the University of Lethbridge, Alberta.[9]

Importantly, SCANA also collaborated with several cultural institutions to develop exhibition projects, including the pioneering 'Beyond History', presented at the Vancouver Art Gallery in 1989.[10] A partnership involving SCANA, the Woodland Cultural Centre and the Vancouver Art Gallery, this exhibition signalled 'the creation of a new ideology which is highly personal and political, unlike the collective tribal response proclaimed during the sixties'.[11] 'Beyond History' included mixed media works by artists who came to prominence in the 1980s, and who shared a critique of popular ethnographic stereotypes and a focus on the impact of colonisation in Canada on Indigenous peoples. However, these artists were by no means a homogeneous group: they came from different cultural heritages, art traditions, political persuasions and personal experiences.

Parallel to the activist history of Aboriginal artists, First Nations artist-run centres also emerged throughout Canada beginning in the 1980s. This movement exemplified the ways in which artists seized control of how their art was presented, providing alternative spaces free from the limitations of public institutions. The Native Indian/Inuit Photographers' Association in Hamilton, Ontario was the first such collective, created in 1985; by the mid-90s other centres were operating with broad, multidisciplinary mandates, amongst

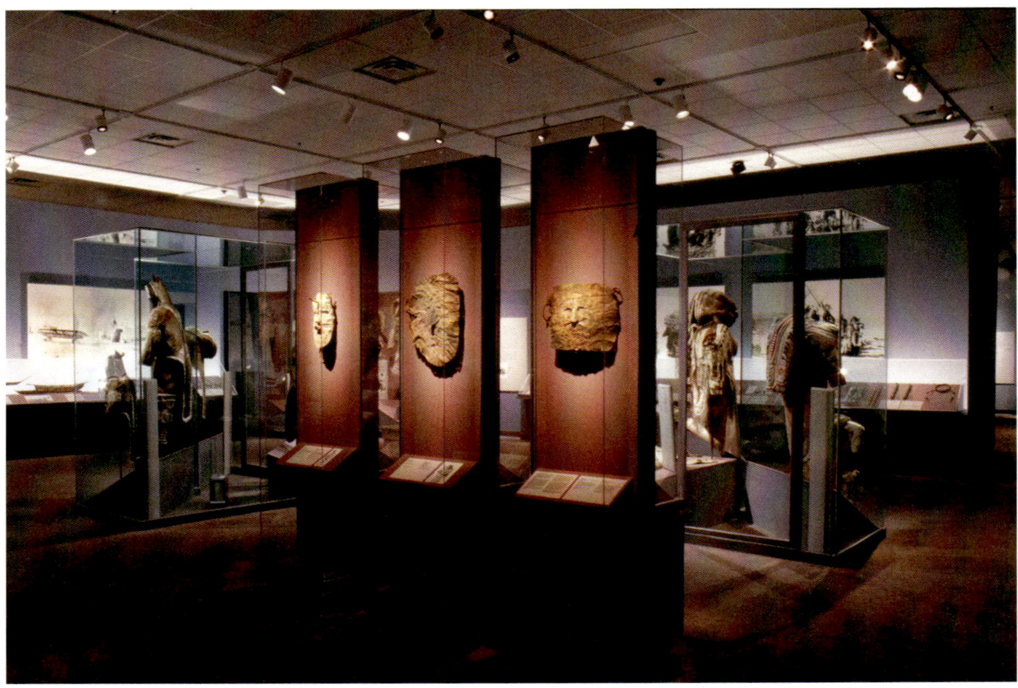

them Sâkêwêwak Artists' Collective in Regina, Saskatchewan (1993); Tribe Inc. in Saskatoon, Saskatchewan (1995); and Urban Shaman Contemporary Gallery in Winnipeg, Manitoba (1996). Additionally, the Aboriginal Film and Video Art Alliance (formed in 1991) was instrumental in developing the framework for the multidisciplinary Aboriginal Arts Program at the Banff Centre in 1995.

During the late 1980s, the mounting debates surrounding the inclusion of contemporary Indigenous art and access to historical collections were compounded by a turbulent sociopolitical landscape in Canada. Land claims and struggles against corporate development resulted in direct action by First Nations communities throughout the country. By 1990, political events galvanised Indigenous solidarity and provided the impetus for heightened activities that would resonate throughout the next decade. Massive land claims were slowly proceeding in British Columbia, Ontario and the Yukon; the Quebec government announced plans to begin the second phase of the James Bay hydroelectric project; and the late Elijah Harper, a Cree member of the Manitoba Legislative Assembly, said 'No' to the Meech Lake Accord, the proposed constitutional legislation that would have denied recognition of Aboriginal peoples while affirming the province of Quebec as a distinct society with special status.

And then there was Oka. For 78 days in the summer of 1990, the Mohawk people of Kanehsatake defended their land against the impending encroachment of a golf course in the neighbouring town of Oka, in Quebec. The Canadian Armed

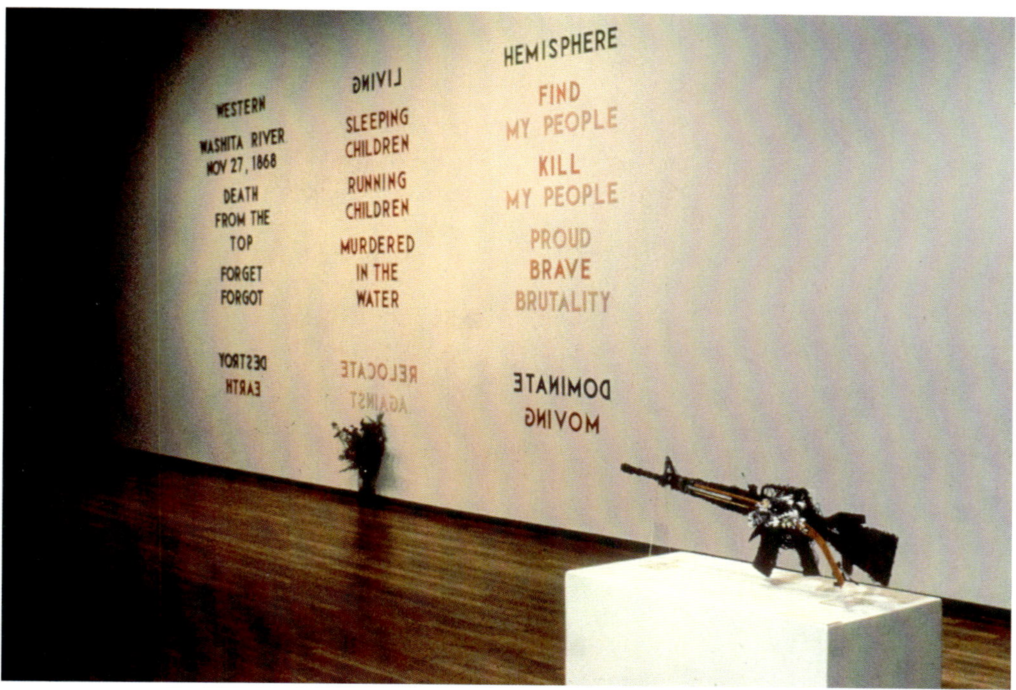

Forces and the Quebec Provincial Police used physical force against the many people who struggled to defend their land. Once again, artist Rebecca Belmore produced a powerful artwork. For her community-based performance and sound installation *Ayum-ee-aawach Oomama-mowan: Speaking to their Mother* (1991–96), Belmore travelled to First Nation communities and urban areas throughout Canada and the US, inviting people to address the land directly in response to the Oka standoff. Hundreds of Indigenous and non-Indigenous people joined in addressing Mother Earth through a megaphone encased in a massive wooden amplifier bound together with leather and animal hides.

***

In 1992, official events marked the 500th anniversary of the arrival of Christopher Columbus in the Americas, a largely Italian-American celebration of 'discovery' that was receiving considerable funding and media attention on both sides of the Atlantic. Indigenous peoples did not share this celebratory spirit, as the legacy of European colonisation has largely rendered Indigenous peoples invisible in their own territories. But 1992 was also the culmination of a decade-long escalation of Indigenous frustration in Canada, with a colonial state that steadfastly refused to uphold the rights that had been recognised and affirmed in the Constitution Act of 1982. Once again, artists raised their voices in anger, reflection, conciliation and affirmation of cultural identity. Following 500 years of oppression and exclusion, Indigenous peoples tenaciously affirmed their own histories, experiences and identities within a thoroughly contemporary context.

Edward Poitras, *Lost for Words (M-16)*, 1987. Installation view, 'Revisions', Walter Phillips Gallery, Banff Centre for Arts and Creativity, Alberta, 1988. Courtesy the Walter Phillips Gallery, Banff Centre for Arts and Creativity

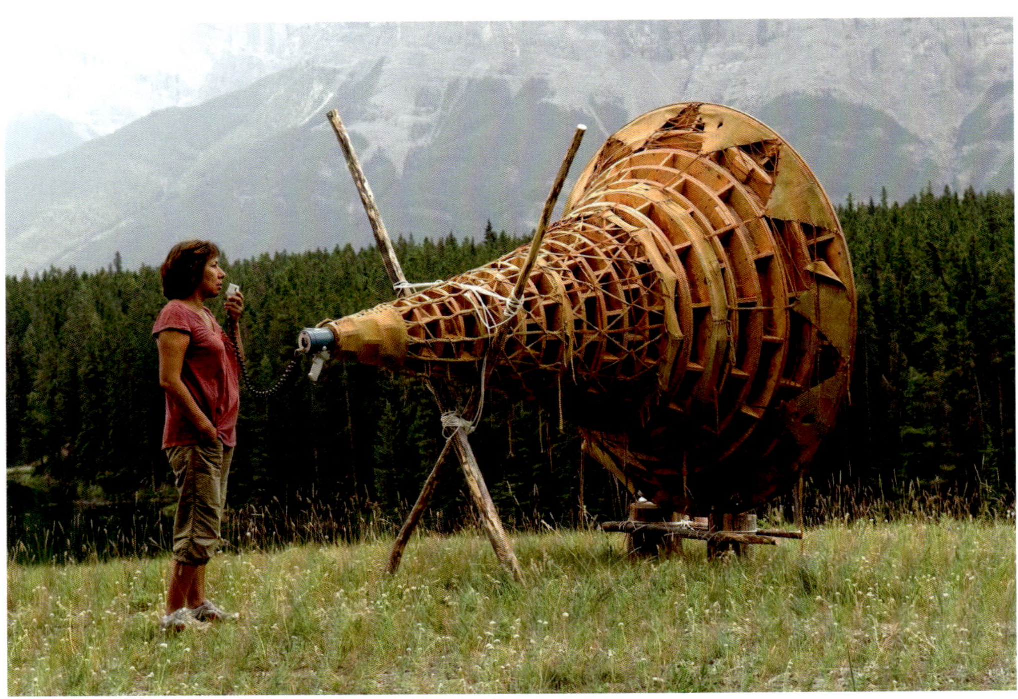

That year, two international touring exhibitions heralded a significant new direction for the production and presentation of contemporary Aboriginal art in Canada. 'INDIGENA: Perspectives of Indigenous Peoples on Five Hundred Years', curated by myself and Gerald McMaster, opened at the Canadian Museum of Civilization; across the Ottawa River, 'Land Spirit Power: First Nations at the National Gallery of Canada' was the result of the curatorial collaboration of that institution's Diana Nemiroff, independent curator and Saulteaux artist Robert Houle and anthropologist Charlotte Townsend-Gault. 'INDIGENA' was the first Indigenous-curated internationally touring exhibition organised by a high-profile national institution. Its organisation began in the mid-1980s, while I was living in the US, where I worked with colleagues – Tewa curator Margaret Archuleta and Tlingit artist Jim Schoppert – to develop a national project to de-celebrate the impending quincentennial of Columbus's arrival; I continued the project in Canada in collaboration with McMaster. (SCANA also supported the exhibition project by providing a grant for my curatorial fee.) Our primary audiences were the Euro-Canadian and US occupiers of the Americas. We hoped to shock non-Indigenous viewers out of their complacency and ignorance of Indigenous history and contemporary realities. But we also hoped to connect with Indigenous audiences throughout North America who knew about and lived this painful history.

The government of Canada chose not to recognise the quincentennial of the United States. But they did plan to celebrate the 125th anniversary of Canada. As Indigenous curators, we could not acknowledge any such celebrations of

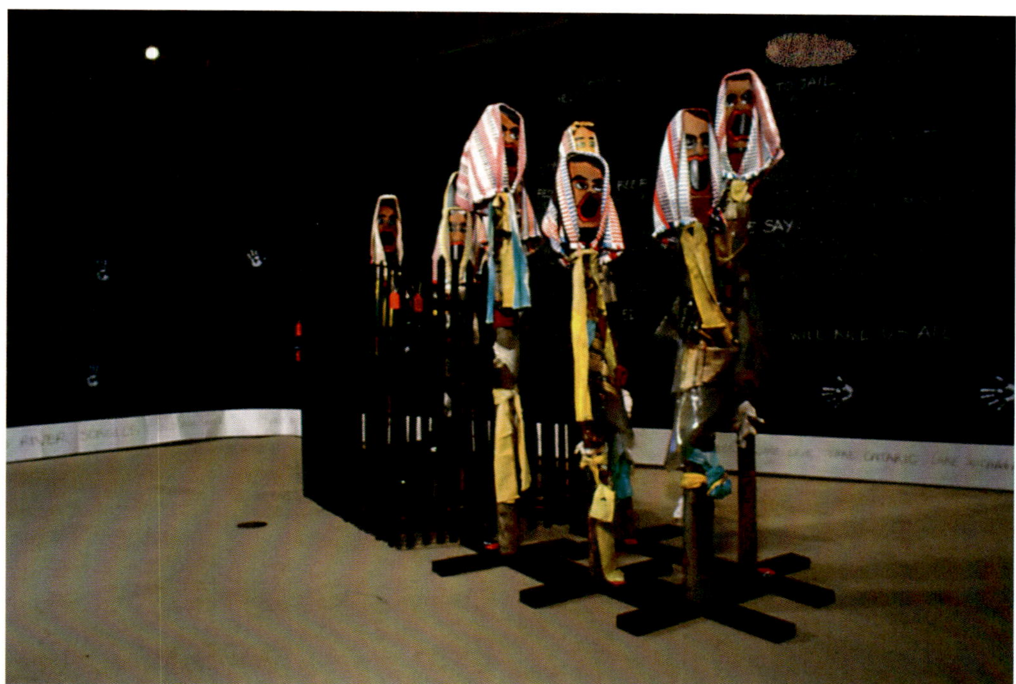

Western dominance and oppression, so we seized that moment to present, on our own terms, issues of importance to our communities. 'INDIGENA' was a logical extension of the Canadian Museum of Civilization's commitment to contemporary Indigenous art; the museum had opened three years earlier, and many of its staff members were participants on the Task Force on Museums and First Peoples. The exhibition brought together works by visual, literary and performing artists from across the country that engaged in an Indigenous critique of 500 years of colonial history. Essays, performances, paintings, installations, videos and photographs examined the tangled complex of history, language, identity, stereotypes and contemporary realities that defined Indigenous cultures at the time. The primacy of Indigenous voices, representation and community support were central tenets of the project; hosting venues in both Canada and the US were selected based upon the involvement of local Indigenous communities.

Opening in September 1992, and overlapping with 'INDIGENA' for one month, 'Land Spirit Power' was the first major international exhibition of contemporary First Nations art from Canada and Native American artists from the US to be held at the National Gallery of Canada. The curatorial premise sought to 'recognise a new generation of First Nations artists whose work was individual and personal, yet reflected a distinct cultural experience within mainstream North American art'.[12] Most of the artists, including three who were also exhibiting in 'INDIGENA' (Carl Beam, Domingo Cisneros and Lawrence Paul Yuxweluptun), worked within contemporary mainstream idioms. 'Land Spirit Power' also presented the work of artists who contemporised their culture-specific and customary practices (Dempsey Bob, Robert Davidson and Dorothy Grant were noteworthy in this respect). This exhibition was significant in including diverse artists who expressed their 'distinct cultural experiences' through individual notions of the land as a spiritual and political legacy.

As two of the first major exhibitions of art and contemporary issues as seen through Indigenous lenses, 'INDIGENA' and 'Land Spirit Power' disrupted long-held institutional discourses and practices. They mark an important turning point, and the point at which I will end this brief history. Writing today, 25 years later, I remain angry and frustrated. Indigenous arts professionals throughout Canada and the world have developed a formidable intellectual force that challenges the basic premise of Western mandates and practices. But drastic conditions still exist throughout Canada – evidence of the persistence of the country's colonial history and its lingering effects today. Thousands of missing and murdered women, high rates of suicide amongst our youth, the incarceration of Indigenous men, poverty, lack of drinking water and educational needs plague our communities – not to mention the constant struggle for sovereignty over traditional lands. Much work remains to be done.

Notes

[1] Note on terminology: 'Indigenous' is the preferred terminology used today with specific reference to the arts in the Canadian context and internationally. However, throughout this text, I use the terms 'Native', 'Indian' and 'First Nations' to respect their historic context and usage in Canada.

[2] The exhibition ran from 15 January–1 May 1988 at the Glenbow Museum, before travelling to the Canadian Museum of Civilization in Ottawa, 1 July–6 November 1988.

[3] 'Revisions' took place 8–28 January 1988. The participating artists were Joane Cardinal-Schubert, Jimmie Durham, Hachivi Edgar Heap of Birds, Zacharias Kunuk, Mike MacDonald, Alan Michelson, Edward Poitras and Pierre Sioui.

[4] Helga Pakasaar, in *Revisions* (exh. cat.), Banff, Alberta: Walter Phillips Gallery, 1992, p.3.

[5] Now the Canadian Museum of History.

[6] *Turning the Page: Forging New Partnerships Between Museums and First Peoples*, a report jointly sponsored by the Assembly of First Nations and the Canadian Museums Association, Ottawa, Ontario, 1992.

[7] The study was supported by the Canada Council as part of a residency I was then undertaking at the Canadian Museum of Civilization, Gatineau, Quebec.

[8] Funded in part by the federal Department of Indian Affairs and Northern Development (now Indigenous and Northern Affairs Canada), previous symposia included: Symposium I, Manitoulin Island, Ontario, October 1978; and Symposium II, Saskatchewan Indian Federated College, Regina, Saskatchewan, September 1979.

[9] At this event, artists and representatives of Canadian arts and funding institutions debated issues surrounding the definitions of and contexts for contemporary Indigenous art. See Alfred Young Man (ed.), *Networking: Proceedings of the Fourth National Native Indian Arts Symposium*, Lethbridge, Alberta: University of Lethbridge, 1987.

[10] Karen Duffek and Tom Hill, *Beyond History* (exh. cat.), Vancouver: Vancouver Art Gallery, 1989.

[11] *Ibid.*, p.5.

[12] Diana Nemiroff, Robert Houle and Charlotte Townsend-Gault, 'Land, Spirit, Power', in *Land Spirit Power: First Nations at the National Gallery of Canada* (exh. cat.), Ottawa: National Gallery of Canada, 1992, p.11.

Art and the Foreigner's Gaze: A Report on Contemporary Arab Representations

Pablo Lafuente

*Who hijacked my religion? No, seriously! Who hijacked my religion? I turn
on the TV and see this guy explaining Islam. But he's talking nonsense. What
religion is this guy talking about?*
– Baba Ali[1]

*Does a land that has great poets have the right to control a land that has no
poets?*
And is the lack of poetry amongst a people enough reason to justify its defeat?
Is poetry a sign or is it an instrument of power?
Can't a people be strong without having its own poetry?
[…]
A people with no poetry is a defeated people.
– Mahmoud Darwish[2]

While, according to a poll [conducted in 2006, around the time of writing],
80 per cent of the British believe that 'political correctness' inhibits them from
discussing Islam,[3] news programmes in the UK (like the rest of the European
media and, perhaps to a lesser extent, that of the US) are pregnant with 'Muslim
issues', from reports on the war in Iraq or the Israel-Palestine conflict to polemics around the wearing of the veil by students or staff in comprehensive
schools. Behind the reports and the discussions stands one common assumption: there are a certain set of values and practices, characteristically Muslim,
which are incompatible with the typically Western, progressive mode of social organisation. The discussion that followed the publication of cartoons of
Prophet Mohammed in the Danish newspaper *Jyllands-Posten* in September
2005 perfectly laid down the arguments at play. Flemming Rose, its culture
editor, defended the commission and publication of the cartoons as simple
freedom of expression, 'in response to several incidents of self-censorship in
Europe caused by widening fears and feelings of intimidation in dealing with
issues related to Islam'.[4] This he claims he did not as a 'fundamentalist' – as
he would not publish dead bodies or pornographic images – but as someone

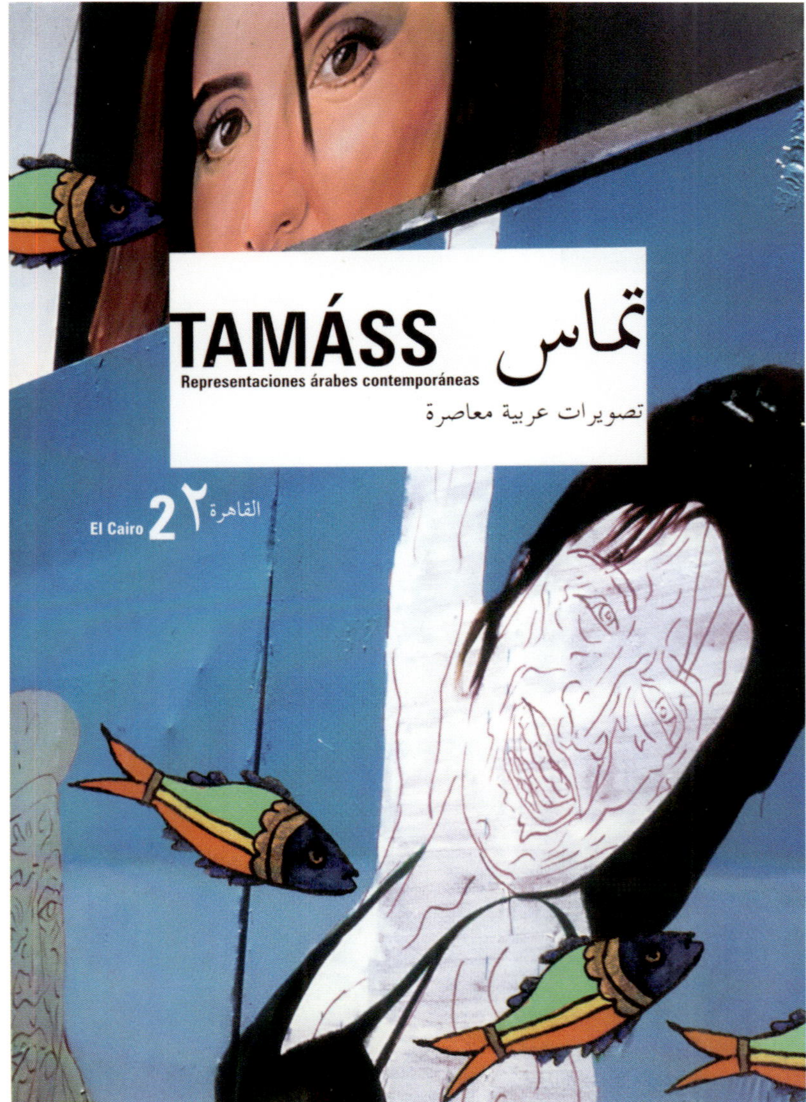

Cover of *Tamáss 2. Contemporary Arab Representations, Cairo*, Barcelona: Fundació Antoni Tàpies, 2004

determined to act against a force challenging liberal democracy. Thanks to the publication, he concluded, 'perhaps we do not need to fight the battle for the Enlightenment all over again in Europe'.

Like liberal democracy, contemporary art is a typically Western product.[5] Both emerged at the turn of the eighteenth century, when a new model of political organisation – as imagined by the French Revolution – and a new notion of aesthetic experience – as initiated by Kant – offered the possibility of a new world. But while some sectors within liberal democracy have identified Islam – or, indifferently, the Muslims and/or the Arab world – as a threat, the contemporary art context hasn't paid too much attention to it and, until

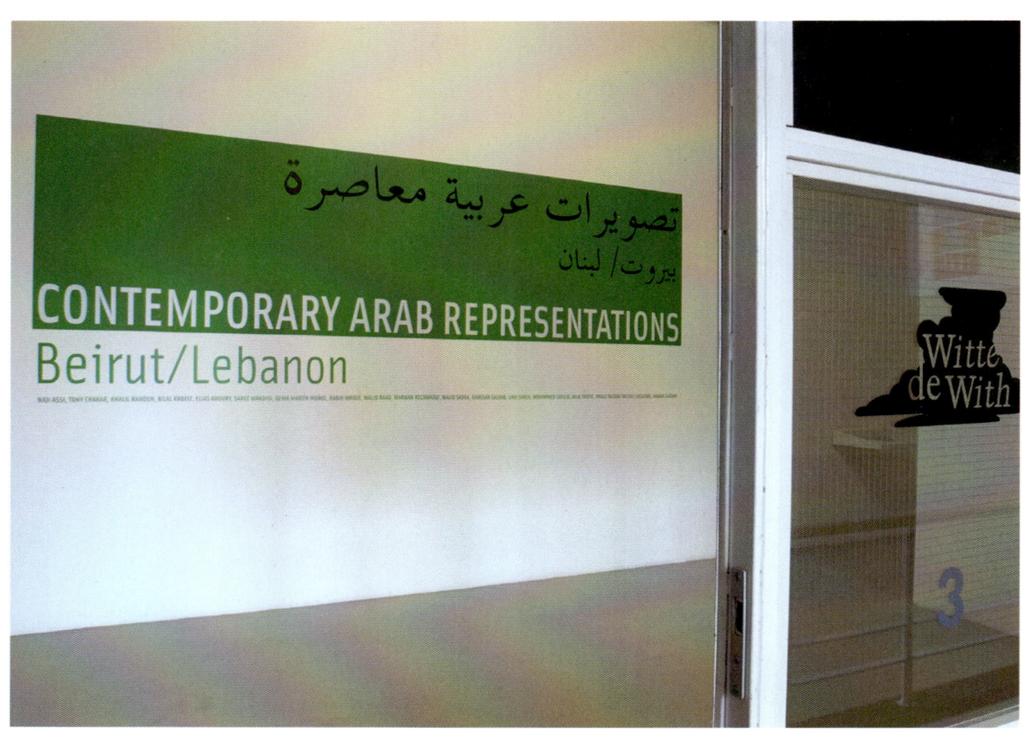

تصويرات عربية معاصرة
بيروت / لبنان
CONTEMPORARY ARAB REPRESENTATIONS
Beirut/Lebanon
Witte de With
3

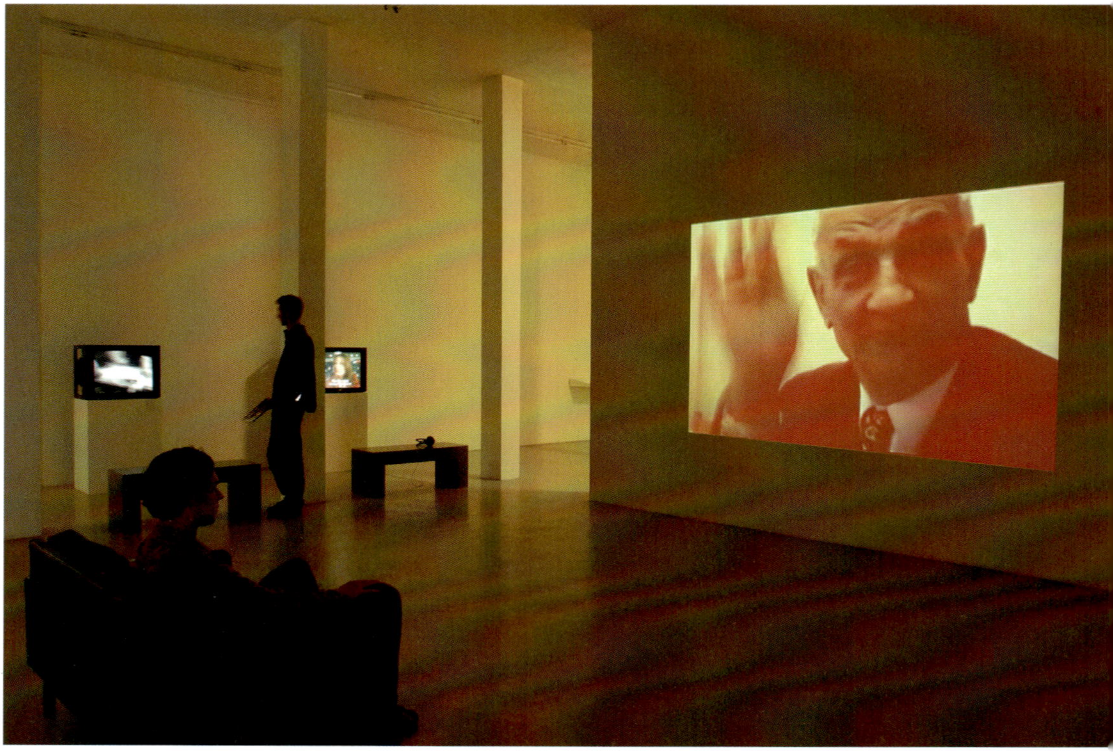

now, hasn't been able to incorporate much of its production, with the exception, perhaps, of work made by a few Lebanese artists, as well as others like Shirin Neshat or Ghada Amer whose language and ideas seem tailored for a Western viewer.

Contemporary Arab Representations, a project directed by Catherine David, is one of the first major attempts at presenting contemporary art and other types of cultural production from Arab countries within both a Western and Arab context. The project started as an exhibition, two publications and a series of seminars and conferences that, under the general name of 'Contemporary Arab Representations. Beirut/Lebanon', focussed on contemporary art and cultural production from Lebanon, specifically, the city of Beirut.[6] The exhibition opened in 2002 at Fundació Antoni Tàpies in Barcelona and later travelled to Witte de With in Rotterdam and the BildMuseet in Umeå. It featured photography, film and research-based work by, amongst others, Tony Chakar, Walid Raad, Walid Sadek, Jalal Toufic and Paola Yacoub and Michel Lasserre, offering a set of critical and experimental approaches to cultural production from the city of Beirut and, by extension, Lebanon, twelve years after the official end of the civil war and two years after the Israeli withdrawal in 2000. The exhibition was preceded by a seminar held at Universidad Internacional de Andalucía (UNIA) in Seville in October 2001, gathering some of the participants in the show to discuss cohabitation, representation and the relationship between disaster and tradition.[7] The publication *Tamáss 1. Contemporary Arab Representations. Beirut/Lebanon* (2002) later included contributions by some of those authors as well as others, in the form of texts and artists' projects, with a focus on urbanism, reconstruction and urban renewal. *Beirut is a Magnificent City: Synoptic Pictures*, a book by Paola Yacoub and Michel Lasserre, followed shortly after.[8]

The seminars, publications and exhibition reflected a country that if in the past had been seen as a bridge between the East and the West – or, as Maxime Rodinson puts it, a shop window[9] – it had considerably changed after fifteen years of civil war and the lengthy Israeli and Syrian occupations. However, Lebanon's Western heritage, its complex national identity and its active cultural scene after the war made it the perfect choice for a project dealing with contemporary artistic and cultural production. Several of the works included in the exhibition and publications dealt with urban regeneration in Beirut, addressing the confluence of private interests in the urban renewal process undertaken in the city centre. There also was an overriding interest in truth and fabrication, from Elias Khoury and Rabih Mroué's study of the rehearsal of martyrdom manifestos (*Three Posters*, 2000) to Walid Raad's investigation of recent political history through his fictional Atlas Group archive. At Witte de With, a green mural displaying the title in English and Arabic (not Dutch) welcomed the visitors, with the names of artists and other authors underneath it. Inside the galleries, there was little object-based work; a profusion of benches, screens and headphones dominated the space. The installation was clearly designed to look functional and accessible – something stressed by the visual documentation of the exhibition, as almost all of the photographs show people looking at works, reading texts, watching films or browsing through documentation.

The exhibition format was decidedly discursive. Writing was present not only on the walls or screens, but also as soundtracks to the many films and videos included. Reading sections and computer screens shared the space with video projections in a situation of equality. Contemporary Arab Representation's presence in Francesco Bonami's 'Dreams and Conflicts: The Dictatorship of the Viewer' at the 2003 Venice Biennale replicated this format. In two consecutive rooms within the Arsenale, David set up a reading space, followed by a series of large-scale projection screens – installed in two rows facing the viewer – showing film and video work from 'CAR. Beirut/Lebanon'. The installation not only communicated to the viewer an imperative to research (read, listen, talk) in order to be able to access what was to come; it also suggested that, even with the help of printed matter, the works might still remain inaccessible, leaving the viewer no choice other than circumventing them. This laying bare of the viewing conditions of the Arsenale and the culture of spectatorship characteristic of such an environment may have been a self-defeating exercise (it is hard to imagine anyone actually looking at the work in full in that context), but its stubbornness felt refreshing within the general lack of engagement that characterised the curatorial premise of 'Dreams and Conflicts'.

The Biennale show underlined the relative importance of the exhibition form in the framework of Contemporary Arab Representations. Within it, the exhibition is used as an instance of the project's crystallisation, but just one, and probably not more important than the others. It is necessary to the extent that several of the institutions involved need it to complete a programme, and it serves as a way to create a nodal point which is the occasion for other elements to happen – the production of works for it, the organisation of seminars around it, the publication of books or articles after it, the publicising of the project through it or the establishing of collaborative relations for, during and after it. As a consequence, the project offers a new 'exhibition' model that is relatively independent from the institutions involved, and whose audience is no longer composed mainly of people who visit contemporary art institutions, but a series of more-or-less-involved participants in seminars, spectators of performances, and viewers and readers of first- or second-hand material. *Tamáss*, which is published in English, Spanish and Arabic, is key in this respect. Despite being 'attached' to the exhibition project, its independent vocation makes it a platform on its own, one that can reach audiences the average art institutions can only imagine.

The emphasis on discourse doesn't imply a functional inclusion of artworks or other visual or cultural manifestations. Paintings, poems, films and photographs, whether in the publications or the exhibition, were allowed their own space, equal in value to the one given to textual practice. The discursive element was a direct consequence of the objectives David set for the overall project. In the opening text of *Tamáss 1*, she described it as

> *a long-term project which includes seminars, presentations of works by different authors – visual artists, architects, writers and poets – performances and publications, with the aim of encouraging production, circulation and exchange between the different cultural centres of the Arab world and the*

rest of the world. The project thus aims to tackle heterogeneous situations and contexts which may sometimes be antagonistic or conflictive, to acquire more specific knowledge of what is going on in certain parts of the Arab world at present, to look at the complex dimensions of aesthetics in relation to social and political situations, and to help to think more deeply about the role played today by cultural practices in our own countries.[10]

The remit was, then, double: the production and presentation of art and cultural production of Arab origin within an Arab context as well as outside of it, and an exercise in self-reflection on the wider role of cultural practices. This was to be done through a diversity of means, paying attention to detail, recognising the existence of 'conflict', and with the objective of producing a 'knowledge' of the context. The unusual frankness of this programmatic statement is echoed by the descriptive title: no 'Africa Remix' or 'Uncertain States of America' – to name a few recent high-profile international shows with a geographical remit – but 'Contemporary Arab Representations'.

Art vs. Representation

The apparent simplicity of the title is, however, just that: apparent. The fact that the word 'art' appears nowhere in the title or the subtitles, even though a majority of the participating institutions and authors specialise in contemporary art practice, is a strategic choice. It is a way of avoiding the semantic network the term 'art' implies, including notions such as avant-garde, modern, market, museum and, ultimately, progress conceived within a linear historicity and the consequent hierarchy between different cultural contexts. In a word, the avoidance of the term 'art' is an attempt to escape the particularities of a Western perspective, a shot at discussing contemporary (artistic) production within a different set of discursive tropes. Interestingly, David's strategy here formally echoes the claim by certain Islamic movements to an alternative universality in the face of the European or dominant Western figure, which is, necessarily, exclusive. Denouncing the particularity of Western universalism does not imply that there is no universality – as a comment of the type 'Human Rights are a Western invention' would seem to imply. It suggests that the way the West addresses Islam often involves, as Étienne Balibar says, 'an appropriation of the universal, a monopoly of the interpretation that western powers assume for themselves'.[11] If that is the case, ideological conflict within a world context does not adopt the form of a conflict between one universalism and several particularisms, but 'the scene of conflicts between fictitious universalities, antagonistic claims to universality and conflicts within universality itself'. When 'art' is substituted by 'representation', this dynamics of universality doesn't imply that the 'representations' expose 'art' as a mere product of a class and context (as a sociological analysis like Pierre Bourdieu's points out); on the contrary, instead of reducing different modes of artistic production to their conditions of emergence, it opens up the door for them to stake their claims in their own, different ways.

However, if the elimination of the word 'art' clears the field of a set of problems, the word that David chose instead – 'representations' – as well the one that accompanies it – 'Arab' – introduces new ones.

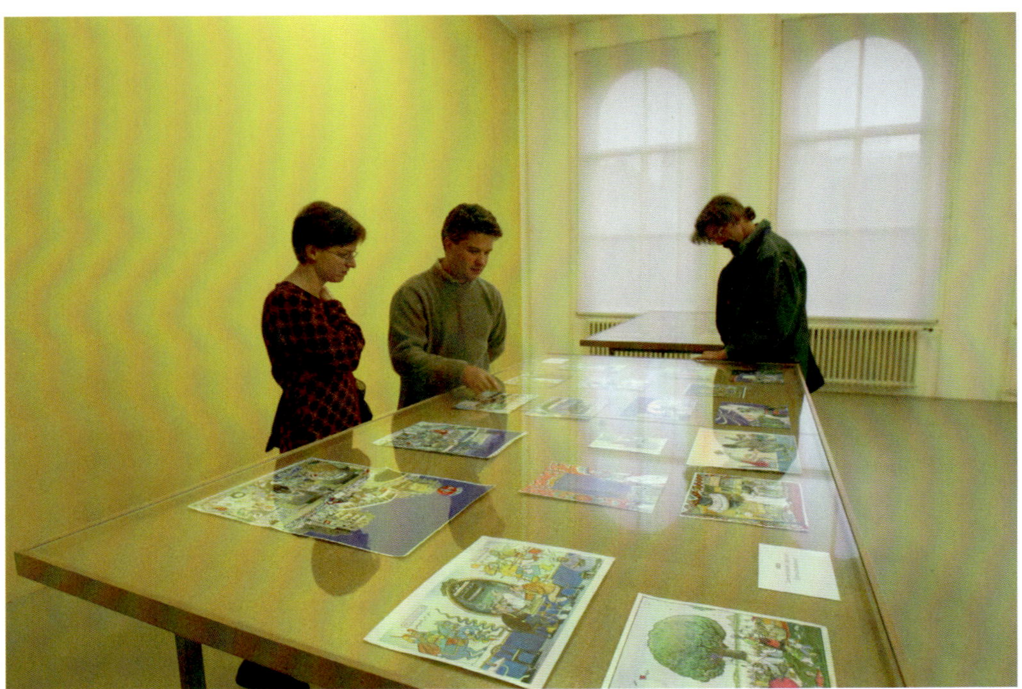

The term 'representation' is obviously not circumscribed to a cultural realm. It traditionally relates to epistemological considerations of truth as adequation – or, at least, it implies questions about the fairness of the representation. Furthermore, when the objects of that representation are human beings, a political dimension comes into play. When 'representation' appears together with 'Arab', misrepresentation is an inevitable consideration. The West's relation to the Arab world, currently and historically, combines ignorance with a 'will to knowledge' (in a Foucauldian sense, as a desire to acquire an immediate knowledge of social relations with a regulatory goal). This, according to Balibar, are the two main mechanisms of racism.[12] Following the lines of Samuel P. Huntington's 'clash of civilisations', this is not a racism based on biological factors but a 'differential racism', one grounded on the irreducibility of cultural differences; it is 'a racism that, at first sight, doesn't postulate the superiority of certain groups or people in relation to others, but "just" the harmful consequences of erasing borders, the incompatibility of types of life and traditions'.[13] While anti-Semitism is the classic example of differential racism, the notion can be applied to the current view of Islam as a religion and culture incompatible with European and Western values.

Contemporary Arab Representations, as David's reference to 'knowledge' reveals, intends to act upon this context by addressing that ignorance and contributing to the production of something closer to a fair representation. But in a political context that representation cannot be done from the outside: the local cultural agents are to be responsible for their own image. The stress on self-representation is an essential part of May '68, from Jean-Paul

96

Sartre ('We want the *actors* of an event to be those whom we consult, we want them to be the ones to speak') to Michel Foucault (with his 'chronicle of workers' memory' or the 'life of infamous men') and *Libération* ('Information comes from the people and returns to the people').[14] It is also the impulse around which, more than a century earlier, workers' movements originated, as Jacques Rancière argues in *La Nuit des prolétaires* (*The Nights of Labour*, 1981). The representation imposed by the dominant gaze, coming from the outside, 'doesn't only justify the power of the dominant class, it constitutes the dominated class as such'.[15] The working class is produced by a decision of the masters, and kept in its place by a perspective that, 'in the materiality of its work, the vulgarity of its pleasures, the emptiness of its thought and its condemned flesh, sees the marks of its belonging to an inferior race'. In order to change their situation, a modification of the material conditions is not enough; it is also necessary to create conflicting representations. To some extent, the latter comes first.

The articulation of self-expression, within Contemporary Arab Representations, is done in three levels: individual (the invited authors), regional/ national (through the focus on a geographical area) and cultural (through the generic title 'Arab'). In an Arab context, the relationship between the last two presents specific problems. The essence of a nation, as Ernest Renan said, 'is that all the individuals have lots of things in common, and also that all of them have forgotten many things'.[16] But, more deeply, the Arab Awakening, the term used by Arab intellectuals to describe the process of 'modernisation'[17] at the end of the nineteenth century, was not the result of a spontaneous awareness, but of the challenge that the West represented in social, political, economic and psychological terms.[18] This implies that nations are, as reads the title of Benedict Anderson's 1983 book, 'imagined communities', in which individual existence is ingrained in a collective narrative, under a common name and with the background of traditions lived as the trace of an immemorial past. In the case of the Arab countries, the history of these narratives, as well as the institutions that effect them and the physical territories where they are established, has too often been conditioned by the West. To begin with, 'every political boundary in the Arab world has been directly or indirectly drawn by western interests'.

Arab nationalism owes its inception not to the revivalism that Islamic reformist movements proposed in the late-nineteenth century, but to the Christian, non-religious definition of Arab society and its cultural traditions.[19] The secularisation effort of Christian intellectuals, in its attempt to rationalise Islamic history and define Christian Arabs' relation to it, resulted in the earliest concrete distinction between Arab and Muslim. As a consequence, a notion of love of the fatherland appeared beside the religious bond. Arab nationalism's rationalising effort wasn't anti-Muslim or pro-European: it was born as a response to the domination of both the Ottoman Empire and the European powers, while the principal contradiction for most Arab nationalists was with Europe.[20] From then on, Arabism became the common name under which an imaginary community was created in the region. As Frantz Fanon pointed out, cultural experience is from then on not circumscribed to a country, but becomes Arab. The perceived problem is not how to build a national culture or take control over the destiny of the nation, but how 'to assume an Arab or African culture in the face of the global condemnation effected by the dominant power'.[21]

Secularisation was only partial, however, and Islam remains a strong factor of social cohesion. To some extent, this is an effect of Arabism's 'diffuse ethnic consciousness' and the consideration of Islam as a value of national or cultural identification – something not dissimilar from the recent attempts to introduce a mention of the shared Christian heritage in the European Constitution.[22] The idea of Islamism implied a 'step backward', but as a nostalgia for an ideal that could be established in Muslim terms, a political appeal, a positive call for action against the external – Western – aggressive forces.

The choice of 'Arab' as a generic title for a project of cultural representations is, therefore, obliged to deal with this history, the term's ethnic acception (though a diffuse one), its status as a form of political and ideological resistance, its Christian origins, its intimate connection to Islam and its complex relation to nationalism (considerably affected by the Arab-Israeli war of 1967). Despite this, it seems a better choice than 'Islamism', a term that Susan Buck-Morss proposes in her recent book *Thinking Past Terror: Islamism and Critical Theory on the Left* (2006) as a discursive position from which to enact a critique of (Western) modernity. Because of its religious genealogy, 'Islamism' conditions the types of phenomena that can originate within it, while the generic 'Arab' provides a loose framework from which to construct individual or collective positions (be they ethnic, geographical, cultural or political). While the first ultimately defines what is possible within it, the second refuses to decide beforehand.

✱✱✱

The second chapter of Contemporary Arab Representations, 'CAR. Cairo', took place in 2003 with another exhibition,[23] two more publications – *Tamáss 2. Contemporary Arab Representations. Cairo* and Randa Shaath's *Under the Same Sky: Cairo*[24] – and a seminar.[25] In contrast to 'CAR. Beirut/Lebanon', 'CAR. Cairo' had a much more orthodox exhibition format: photographs and drawings were lined up on the gallery walls; more drawings were displayed on table/vitrines; and several short films were shown on a (considerably smaller) number of monitors. This was determined by the more conventional form of the works themselves, possibly a consequence of what David identified in the accompanying literature as a lack of structures within the country's artistic scene (of training, information, distribution and debate). As artists based in Egypt hadn't been exposed to international contemporary art production to the same extent as Lebanese artists, the techniques they used were mostly 'traditional' (i.e. photography, painting and drawing). However, this characterisation doesn't involve a value judgement or a hierarchy – what matters is not the contemporaneity of the work in relation to an international or technical standard, but the relation between a language, a content and a context. As in the Lebanese exhibition, discussions of urban structures and their effect on populations featured prominently, but this time, instead of issues of truth and fabrication, representation came to the fore – perhaps because, in contrast to Lebanon, political and geographical identity is not an issue in contemporary Egypt. The focus of the work was on the depiction of Egyptian realities, as in Golo's graphic stories, Anna Boghiguian's drawings of populated urban scenes and Randa Shaath's black-and-white photographs of urban landscapes, cultural figures or life on the banks of the Nile.

The important role of photography as a cultural form within Arab countries was also punctuated by the inclusion of a large number of pictures from the Arab Image Foundation within the third and, for the moment, last chapter of Contemporary Arab Representations, 'CAR. The Iraqi Equation' – which opened as an exhibition in 2006,[26] preceded by two seminars in Seville,[27] and to be followed by a third issue of *Tamáss* in 2007. A non-profit organisation set up in Lebanon in 1996, the foundation's role is to promote photography within the Middle East and North Africa by locating, collecting and preserving photographs made in the region or taken by local amateur or professional photographers. Here again, the selection is not based on artistic criteria, but on a mixture of aesthetic, historical and cultural considerations. In 'The Iraqi Equation' images of Iraq from the 1930s to the 1970s were projected onto several suspended screens, showing portraits, images of leisure scenes and archaeological and urban landscapes.

However, that was the only apparent continuity between both exhibitions, because with 'The Iraqi Equation' both the focus of the show and the type of work exhibited changed dramatically. David's inability to undertake actual research in a war zone resulted in an exhibition with barely any art (only four artists: Samir, Nedim Kufi, Faisel Laibi and Talal Refit) and a large number of television monitors and projections, books and computer screens. At Fundació Tàpies, a number of small rooms were built within the exhibition space to show films such as *The Baghdad Blogger* (2004), *Voting Amidst Violence* (2005) and *Three Years On* (2006) by blogger Salam Pax; *16 Hours in Baghdad* (2004) by Tariq Hashim; and *On Democracy in Iraq* (2003) by Hana al-Bayaty. More monitors scattered around the exhibition space showed films on Iraqi cultural figures, and several computers granted access to a selection of websites and blogs, as well as recordings of discussions on Iraqi literature and culture.[28] The amount of information available was enough to take up days, but, somehow, the impression was never one of overload – just of lack of time.

Art, Intervention and Knowledge Production

'CAR. The Iraqi Equation' was the exhibition that perhaps best reflected David's aim to produce and disseminate knowledge of a concrete cultural and political situation: most of the material collected in the show offered direct representations of historical or present-day Iraq that were in conflict with dominant views. With its focus on knowledge production it followed the lines of the seminar 'CAR. Critical Discourses and Political Thinking' at Arteleku, San Sebastián in June 2004, which, under the direction of Gema Martín Muñoz, discussed the political history of the Arab region and the role of Islam within it, as well as its relation to the West after September 11. This impulse must

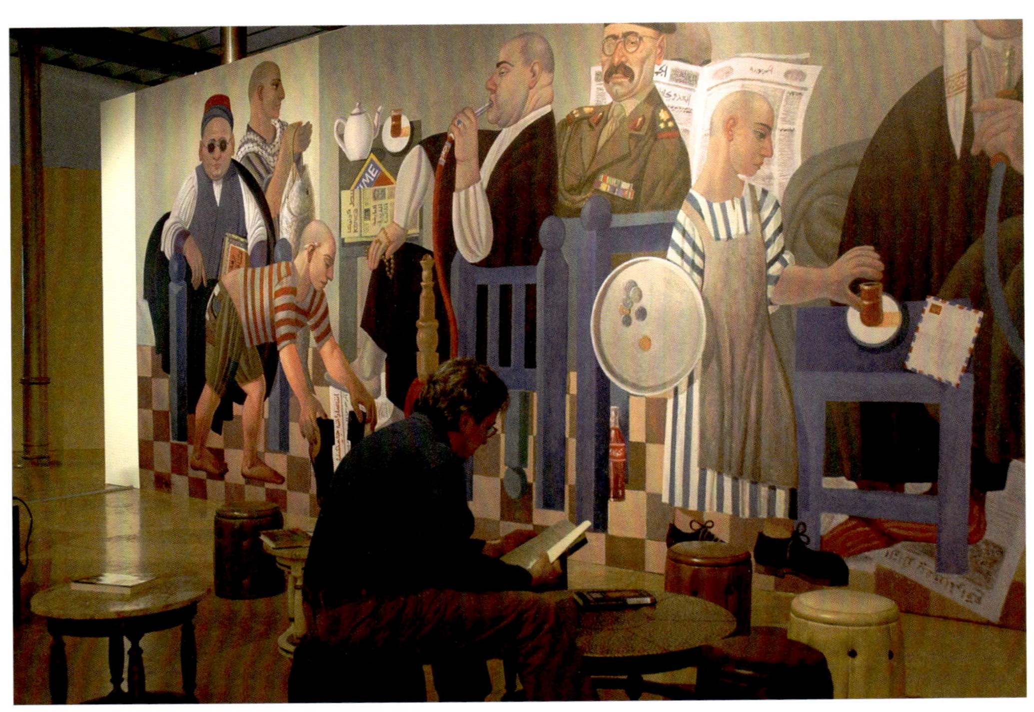

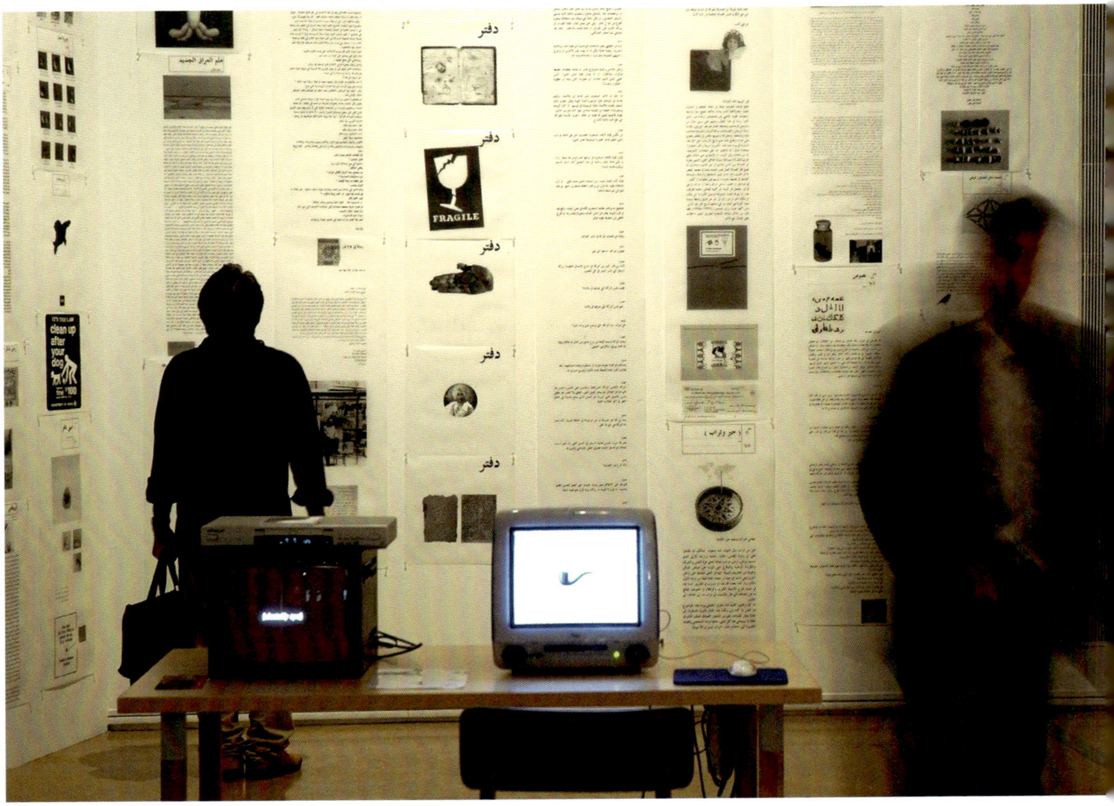

be understood within the interventionist character of the project as a whole: rather than offering a general overview of the cultural scene from the featured regions, or an opportunity for local artists to present their work elsewhere, Contemporary Arab Representations aims to assist in the consolidation of a cultural situation by addressing misrepresentations, establishing collaborations and setting up new contexts. This goal is directly opposed to the presentation of an artistic or cultural reality through discreet examples – as exhibitions such as 'Africa Remix', 'Uncertain States of America' and many of their kind do, practising a sort of hijacking of the cultural scene on which they focus. Consequently, measuring the success of the project can only be done in the medium or long term. But here is also where the other goal of Contemporary Arab Representations – the reflection on the role of cultural or aesthetic production within a political context – comes to the fore. As Mahmoud Darwish says, 'a people with no poetry is a defeated people'. The development of artistic, cultural forms in a concrete situation is essential to the articulation of how people (the artist, the viewer) relate to that situation, and can perhaps create the conditions for a possibility of change. It is not that the role of those cultural forms is to effect the change, but that their ability to imagine is intimately connected to the possibility of change itself. In the case of Iraq, however, the situation was perhaps too extreme to allow for much more than sociopolitical analysis and a reflection on how different things were in the past.

Some aspects of 'CAR. The Iraqi Equation' resemble Chris Gilbert's 'Now-Time Venezuela', a recent series of exhibitions expressing solidarity with Hugo Chávez's Bolivarian revolution.[29] Gilbert intended to express support for a political process through the direct display of some of its mechanisms and effects at the Berkeley Art Museum at the University of California – a cultural institution in a faraway land. But by opting for a direct representation of a political process, he failed to take advantage of the conditions that the institution and the more-general discourses of art and culture provide. David's Contemporary Arab Representations differs not only in her reluctance to establish alliances with singular political positions, but also in her focus: when the situation allowed it, she didn't explore the mechanisms of a political process or how change is enacted by cultural forms, but how art can propose a reorganisation of the way we look at the world. What art, when freed from a narrative of progress, can do is open the doors to situations that reveal a different system of organisation, a different way of dealing with things. This doesn't need to be abstract, as is shown by works as diverse as the ones included in the project, or others from a similar context – such as Michel Khleifi and Eyal Sivan's *Route 181: Fragments of a Journey in Palestine-Israel* (2004) – or a completely different one – such as Pedro Costa's *Vanda's Room* (2000). A project like Contemporary Arab Representations offers a platform in which this can happen, by proposing a set of images that take their viewer (Arab or not) to places where he/she no longer knows where he/ she is. But if that is the case, what self-representation means in this context must be readdressed. There is a gap between what an artist from Cairo is expected to produce and what an artist from Cairo actually produces. This doesn't suggest that art production is completely independent from its context (such defence of absolute artistic autonomy would be a curious conclusion for a text that dedicates

Installation views, 'Contemporary Arab Representations. The Iraqi Equation', Fundació Antoni Tàpies, Barcelona, 2002. Photography: Lluís Bover © Fundació Antoni Tàpies, Barcelona a large section to an exposition of context); it proposes that art is not a direct expression of a place and moment or a culture – as Vico thought of Homer in relation to Ancient Greece – or a direct consequence of a social (i.e. class) structure. No sociological, political, biographical, historical or even cultural account is able to exhaust a work of art, as, if what is possible is already decided from the beginning, little could things change. In that sense, the self-representation that the artist offers is similar to that of a foreigner: not really a knowledge, in the strong sense of the word, but something closer to a fiction that is in conflict with the dominant representation. This reveals a tension between the goals that David set for her project and her insistence on the production of knowledge. Presenting the work of an artist or author as knowledge strips it from its ability to effect the displacement that is typical of the art form. With 'The Iraqi Equation', the necessary focus on knowledge resulted in a more coherent presentation than the previous chapters, but at the same time, by muting part of the work's strangeness with a large amount of information, it did away with the precarious (and productive) articulation of culture and sociopolitical reality that could be found in 'Beirut/Lebanon' and 'Cairo'. It offered a remarkable amount of knowledge about Iraq, and, perhaps, a parallel reflection on how artistic and cultural production actually relates to it – but there wasn't much art to be seen attempting to do so. Somehow, in the urgency of the situation, it forgot that 'it is the foreigner's gaze that puts us in touch with the truth of a world' – not a tourist's gaze, but a gaze that is able to imagine what is, and also what is not.[30]

Notes

[1] Baba Ali in his *Who Hijacked Islam??!* (2006), available at http://www.youtube.com/watch?v=VqmMdPKw378.

[2] Mahmoud Darwish in Jean-Luc Godard's *Notre musique* (*Our Music*, 2004).

[3] See Mukul Devichand, 'Telling Muslim Tales', openDemocracy.org, http://www.opendemocracy.net/conflict-terrorism/muslim_tales_4219.jsp.

[4] See http://www.jp.dk/udland/artikel:aid=3566642:fid=11328.

[5] This statement and the elaboration that follows echo the historical genealogy that Jacques Rancière has presented in several of his books, including *Le Partage du sensible* (Paris: La Fabrique, 2000).

[6] Organised by Fundació Antoni Tàpies, Barcelona, in association with Witte de With, Rotterdam (where David was director at the time), the Universidad Internacional de Andalucía (UNIA), Seville, Arteleku, San Sebastián and Akademie Schloss Solitude, Stuttgart.

[7] See http://www.unia.es/arteypensamiento02/world/proy_1.htm.

[8] Paola Yacoub and Michel Lasserre, *Beirut is a Magnificent City: Synoptic Pictures*, Barcelona: Fundació Antoni Tàpies, 2003.

[9] '… a double shop window. The Arabs who cannot go further come to admire in Beirut the marvels of capitalist economy. The westerners discover with rapture a special, seducing, reassuring, quiet Arabism.' Maxime Rodinson, 'Le Liban et l'arabisme', in *Marxisme et monde musulman*, Paris: Seuil, 1972, p.666.

[10] Catherine David, 'Presentation', in *Tamáss 1. Contemporary Arab Representations. Beirut/Lebanon*, Barcelona: Fundació Antoni Tàpies, 2002, p.10. 'Our own countries' was substituted by 'in our own locations, under our own circumstances' for 'CAR. Cairo'. The change addresses the apparent initial suggestion that CAR is to be considered from an exclusively nationalistic and, perhaps, Western perspective.

[11] Étienne Balibar, 'Algérie, France: une ou deux nations?' (1995), in *Droit de cité*, Paris: Quadrige/PUF, 2002, p.85. All French references in this text are translated by the author.

[12] See É. Balibar, 'Y a-t-il un "néo-racisme"?' (1988), in É. Balibar and Immanuel Wallerstein, *Race, nation, classe. Les identities ambiguës*, Paris: La Découverte, 1997, p.30.

[13] *Ibid.*, p.33. Balibar borrows this term from Pierre-André Taguieff.

[14] All quoted in Kristin Ross, *May '68 and Its Afterlives*, Chicago: Chicago University Press, 2002, p.115.

[15] Jacques Rancière, *La Nuit des prolétaires. Archives du rêve ouvrier*, Paris: Librairie Anthème Fayard/Hachette Littératures, 1981, p.270.

[16] Ernest Renan, 'Qu'est-ce qu'une nation?', quoted in Benedict Anderson, *Imagined Communities: Reflections on the Origin and Spread of Nationalism*, London and New York: Verso, 2006, p.6.

[17] Hisham Sharabi, *Arab Intellectuals and the West: The Formative Years, 1875–1914*, Baltimore: Johns Hopkins Press, 1970, p.134.

[18] See *ibid.*, p.ix.

[19] See *ibid.*, pp.63–64.

[20] See M. Rodinson, 'Nature et fonction des mythes dans les mouvements socio-politiques d'après deux exemples comparés: communisme marxiste et nationalisme arabe', in *Marxisme et monde musulman, op. cit.*, p.257.

[21] Frantz Fanon, *Les Damnés de la terre*, Paris: La Découverte, 2002, p.204.

[22] M. Rodinson, 'Développement et structure de l'arabisme', in *Marxisme et monde musulman, op. cit.*, p.587.

[23] This time without Akademie Schloss Solitude as partner and with Centro José Guerrero in Granada as an additional venue.

[24] *Tamáss 2. Contemporary Arab Representations. Cairo*, Barcelona: Fundació Antoni Tàpies, 2004; and Randa Shaath, *Under the Same Sky: Cairo*, Barcelona: Fundació Antoni Tàpies, 2003.

[25] 'CAR. Cairo', UNIA, April 2004.

[26] Witte de With, of which David is no longer director, wasn't a partner this time. Kunst-Werke, Berlin, occupied its place.

[27] 'Contemporary Arab Representations. The Iraqi Equation', UNIA, November 2005 and June 2006.

[28] A list of links is available at http://www.fundaciotapies.org/site/article.php3?id_article=4811.

[29] See Chris Gilbert, 'Statement on Resigning, 21 May 2006', http://www.stretcher.org/archives/rl_a/2006_05_23_rl_archive.php.

[30] J. Rancière, *Short Voyages to the Land of the People* (trans. James B. Swenson), Stanford, CA: Stanford University Press, p.125.

On the Curatorial in India

Geeta Kapur

Natasha Ginwala

(2011)

Natasha Ginwala: What are the possible reasons for a lack of institutional as well as extra-institutional discourse on curatorial practice in India thus far?

Geeta Kapur: Since our institutional infrastructure is entirely undeveloped – our museum structures are weak and our art history departments likewise impoverished – where could curatorial studies or curatorial experiments have been nurtured? But, elaborating on our institutional scene in a more particularised way, there *is* some preparatory discourse which can be tapped for future curatorial projects. Since the 1960s there has been a sustained pedagogic understanding of modern and contemporary art at the Fine Arts Faculty in Maharaja Sayajirao University (MSU) in Baroda (/Vadodara); and, later, a pedagogical renewal at Kala Bhavana, Visva-Bharati University at Santiniketan, Bengal. The former began to alter the course of conventional art history by developing the field of visual culture, wherein potentially the question of publics would have to be raised and, thereby, the question of curating – as an expositional activity in the public domain. This agenda, in a more complex configuration of disciplines and curricula, is now being fulfilled by the School of Art and Aesthetics at Jawaharlal Nehru University (JNU), Delhi.

Simultaneous to the opening up of contemporary art to the broader discursive frame of visual studies, artists began to travel extensively. Art historians and critics participated in international conferences where questions of critical curating were gaining prominence. Opportunities emerged in the 1990s for Indian critic-curators to show Indian art internationally. Non-Indian curators, exhibiting contemporary Indian art in their own contexts, brought in transcultural criteria. Private galleries in India entered the international circuit through auctions, art fairs and, later, exhibitory collaborations.

India has a conspicuously backward infrastructure for almost all museums. The state museums are run in the manner of government departments with little scope for even public programming. However, there are now experimental platforms like Khoj International Artists' Association developing workshop formats and radical curation. Private collections are opening up: the Jehangir Nicholson

Collection in Mumbai is now housed in Chhatrapati Shivaji Maharaj Vastu Sangrahalaya (formerly Prince of Wales Museum), and in Delhi, the Devi Art Foundation has taken a lead in innovative curation. The inauguration of the Kiran Nadar Museum of Art in 2010 holds out great promise.

NG: How do you view the use of the lens of popular culture in exhibition-making and the study of contemporary creative processes?

GK: Many of my academic colleagues whom I greatly respect have chosen to reframe the field of art history through the lens of visual culture. This was an intentional pedagogic turn chosen by scholars at the M.S. University, Baroda and Jawaharlal Nehru University, Delhi. I work within the frame of what used to be called high (modernist) art in conjunction with avant-garde art, also referred to as 'critical' or cutting-edge art. Rather than expanding the art historical frame to include all sign systems that constitute visual culture, I want to engage with the semiotics of art such that its criticality is foregrounded and thus its contingent, consequent politics.

NG: I would like to understand your distinctive usage of the term 'avant-garde' and what it has meant to speak from the 'Third World' position.

GK: In India I am almost alone in my use of the term 'avant-garde' and I always have to explain! I use the term because I wish to distinguish it from modernist art; and because I want to both historicise the original movement in early twentieth-century art history and track how it splits and diversifies in the 1960s–70s. And then to transform its usage on fresh ground in the way that's been done in Central and South America, and now Asia. I believe the concept of the avant-garde places a wedge in the morphological/formalist readings of art language, allows an alteration of prevalent equations, promotes alterity in actual practice.

I was more pugnacious when the category of the 'Third World' was still operative. I am speaking about the 1950s–70s, when liberation and decolonisation movements were sweeping across many parts of the world and artists were proclaiming this third formation as the one that would dialectically mediate and transcend the impasse of the 'First' and 'Second' World (broadly the capitalist West and the socialist bloc). With the twentieth century now periodised – politically and discursively – the term in use since the 1980s is 'postcolonial'. This very quickly developed an academic status that came in time to be (almost excessively) theorised. Just as postcolonial discourse overtook the 'Third World' rhetoric, globalism has overtaken the postcolonial prerogative. In a globalised world, terms such as 'transnational' and 'transcultural' have greater purchase, but there is little that is contestatory about 'trans' – it covers gaps and differences, thereby creating an illusion of a continuity-in-difference. The point to reiterate is that discourse is now so mobile as to be slippery and one must learn to enunciate both firmly and flexibly in order to be heard.

NG: While performing the role of critic-curator, you seem to create an epistemological bridge, with your writing often feeding your curatorial practice.

GK: Many art professionals prefer to name themselves as curators first, since they undertake criticism as part of their curatorial studies, and sometimes because it is simply more practical. Exhibition-making, the actual display, the phenomenology of the exhibition space, the dialogue between objects, the unexpectedness of the encounter and the meanings that surface in the setting up of an itinerary thrill me quite separately from the conceptual paradigm. Yet, concept and criticality form the foundation of my curation, so I conscientiously maintain the difference: it is my discursive and critical formation that is primary, therefore I am critic first, then curator.

NG: Could you provide instances of your curatorial practice – how in the last decade you have negotiated the poly-vocality of Indian modern and contemporary art in both national and transnational terrain.

GK: Let me begin with 'Place for People' (1981).[1] This was a self-generated project of six artists and a critic. We did not anyway use the term 'curator' at the time and I functioned as a member of the group or collective. This was therefore *not my* exhibition – which stands in contrast with later battles where I, among others, would claim the nomenclature and rights of a curator.

'Place for People' began with the theorising of narrativity. The works developed simultaneously and even as a consequence of the discourse on contemporary narration as a still-valid mode within an inclusive art historical frame. The first round of discussions took place among Bombay and Baroda artists, followed up by the vociferous English artist and critic Timothy Hyman. We were all inspired by Bhupen Khakhar; he had set the agenda to think audaciously about what it meant to belong to a place, to respond to vernacular cultures and narrativise the self within the everyday. Jogen Chowdhary belonged within this genre. Artist-pedagogue Gulam Sheikh provided the art historical dimension to pictorial narratives, ranging from Siennese paintings to Persian miniatures. During the artist workshop at Kasauli Art Centre, the issues became contentious with Vivan Sundaram, Nalini Malani, Sudhir Patwardhan and I exploring the more ideological dimensions of historical narrativisation. What emerged was an engagement with history and subjectivity, and the politics of *place,* whether the nation or city or an imagined and contested site. 'Place for People' artists, committed to a *dialogic* basis for their evolving practice, believed a critic was a necessary colleague.

To go on with the story: I was co-curator of a very large two-part exhibition, 'Contemporary Indian Art', mounted in the upper galleries of Royal Academy of Arts, London, during the state-sponsored Festival of India in Britain (1982).[2] In 1994 I was invited to work with the collection of the National Gallery of Modern Art (NGMA) in Delhi. I rehung a selection of Indian art from across a hundred years with a 'deviant' itinerary. It raised the ire of some senior artists and culture bureaucrats and the exhibition received a melodramatic press coverage![3]

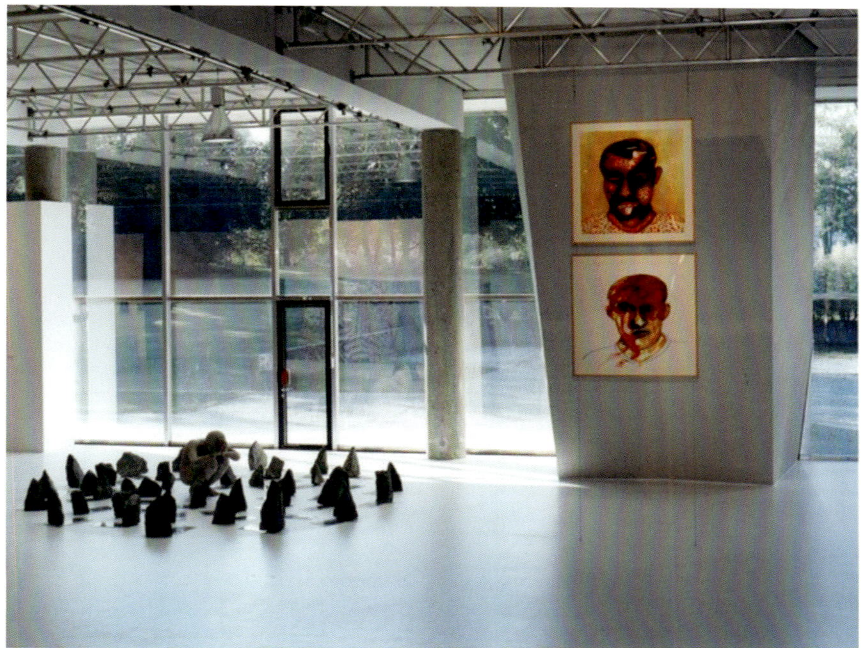

At the turn of the twenty-first century, Tate Modern developed its inaugural exhibition with a consortium of curators, to which I was invited. The project sought to mark certain historical conjunctures in the twentieth century and relate these to the dynamic of art and visual culture igniting a particular *city*: thus the title, 'Century City: Art and Culture in the Modern Metropolis'. The exhibition evolved into nine 'chapters': Paris, Vienna, Moscow, Rio de Janeiro, Lagos, Tokyo, New York, London – and Bombay. Co-curating with the film theorist Ashish Rajadhyaksha, we beheld Bombay as a significant twentieth-century metropolis framed by its historic cosmopolitanism and multi-religious citizenry; the vicissitudes of its economy – a national (capitalist) bourgeoisie and major working class movements; its archipelago-like space; and a public sphere that includes an alluring film industry. (Bombay was renamed Mumbai in 1995, so this section of Century City was titled: 'Bombay/Mumbai 1992–2001'.) The curation of artworks aimed at spectatorial extrapolation, enhanced by Bombay's 'location' in the great Turbine Hall of the Tate Modern. Here, London and Bombay, both referencing the 1990s, became precipitate claimants to the status of Century City![4]

In between these large exhibitions, I curated 'Dispossession', a small, focussed show of four women artists at the First Johannesburg Biennale in 1995.[5] And in continued investigation of contemporary art in urban India, I curated 'subTerrain: artworks in the cityfold', as part of a multi-arts project 'body.city', at Haus der Kulturen der Welt (HKW), Berlin in 2003.[6]

NG: There has been an increasing tendency to draw parallels between the contemporary art scene in China and India by art experts from the West, but also

N.N. Rimzon, *Speaking Stones*, 1998; Bhupen Khakhar, *Blind Babubhai and Injured Head of Raju*, 2001. Installation view from 'subTerrain: artworks in the cityfold', Haus der Kulturen der Welt (HKW), Berlin, 2003, curated by Geeta Kapur

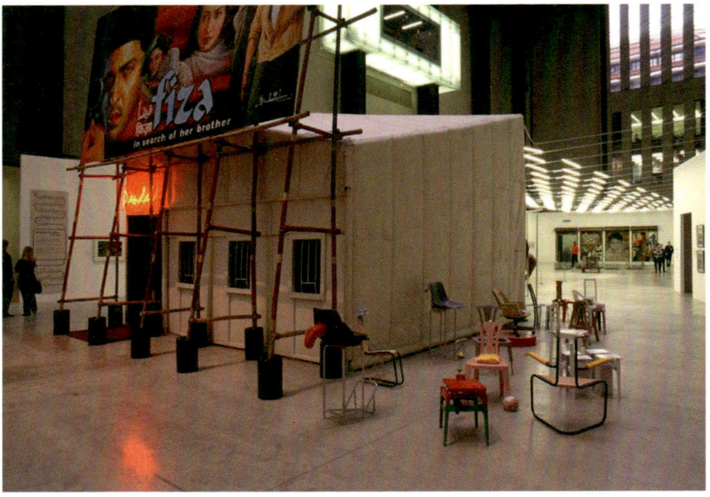

Installation view, 'Bombay/Mumbai: 1992–2001', curated by Geeta Kapur and Ashish Rajadhyaksha, as part of the multi-part exhibition 'Century City: Art and Culture in the Modern Metropolis', Tate Modern, London, 2001. Photography: © Tate

some closer to home. Could you put the matter in perspective – are there any genuine shared concerns, and how do the two nations compare in relation to creative infrastructure?

GK: The Chinese are pushing their infrastructural development with breath-taking ambition. The state is determined to promote Chinese art so that it becomes a front runner in the international arena; they are building academies with technologically equipped studios, museum and exhibition venues. They invite experts from all over the world, offering bold creative assignments. On the one hand, state control, including censorship in the cultural domain; on the other, state capitalism that easily rides globalism. This is a strategy and a lure, and the more powerful for that. And while there may be dissent and censorship at the ground level, Chinese artists know how to fly high and make pragmatic adjustments within the system – so long as it serves their artistic fabulations. Even, maybe, so long as they can contribute, with a degree of cynical patriotism, to China's gaining distinction as a global player in all things, including contemporary art.

Does that sound like the Indian scenario? Economy and politics, democracy and citizen's rights, cultural policy, pedagogy and futuristic visions – the two countries are on altogether different planes. All equations ring false, including comparisons based on artists' stardom, art markets and international exposure that competitive globalisation promotes.

That said, I would like to mention a project linking China and India. Partially coinciding with the Eighth Shanghai Biennale, an exhibition featuring Indian and Chinese artists was realised in 2010. With Johnson Chang as project commissioner, Chaitanya Sambrani as curator, the exhibition was titled 'Place.Time.Play: Contemporary Art from the West Heavens to the Middle Kingdom'. This exhibition, part of a larger project initiated by Chang (with the cooperation of Gao Shiming) was preceded by a dialogue between contemporary philosophers, historians and artists from India and China. This sought to invoke a civilisational poetics of traversed geographies and conjured temporalities, which might then frame actual traversal by participating artists from both countries. Mapping situational concerns, time loops, cultural imaginings and reciprocal aesthetics – this experiment sought to break open such glibly conflated futures that global rhetoric encourages.[7]

NG: Are there any other countries you would suggest we could look at in order to develop a clearer understanding of contemporary art cultures from a non-Western perspective?

GK: It would be more interesting to shift our gaze towards countries like Mexico, Cuba, Brazil. They 'belonged' within the 'Third World', developed a cultural ethos on that basis, and (given the tortuous history of encounter between European and indigenous cultures) nurtured a highly complex discourse on modernity – by developing distinct allegories, metaphors and models of the subject-in-history. Though our history is very different, our debates on identity, ethnicity and modernism produce an equally complex historical discourse; and the narratives coincide over conditions of dire poverty, liberation struggles, social heterogeneity.

I also find this to be the right time to look towards contemporary art and culture in West Asia since these societies are defining their own contemporaneity under civilisational, religious and often authoritarian pressures, while their struggle for democracy is hijacked by operations of capital and militaristic strategies. To me it seems more pertinent to engage with art and politics in, say, Iran, Lebanon, Egypt – and Palestine, the wounded country – rather than looking towards Beijing and Seoul.

NG: Could you share your thoughts on the curatorial frameworks employed when 'Indian' contemporary art is exhibited abroad?

GK: The national format has produced so many permutation-combinations of exhibition-making that it has now become difficult to produce something different in the name of India. Even as diasporic dilemmas widen the political base of global issues tackled by art, they tend to produce, within the transnational space, a straitened convergence. If the form of address of an artwork is coextensive with the site of production, even confrontational work addressed to the 'First World' or, to the centripetal heart of capitalism, marginalises region and nation, societies and living communities, into the category of *geo-political context*. These imponderables of identity and address require the interlocutors to assume a multiplicity of agential roles, so as to move back and forth between a speculative transculturalism and a declared partisanship. It is still necessary to ask how art situates itself in the highly differentiated national economies/political societies that bear the name of countries; and how, from those sites, it reckons with divergent forces at work within globalisation. More pointedly, what are the countercultural tendencies generated in the contested sites of the nation-state itself? With what strategies is a neoliberal, anti-poor developmental agenda and/or a (covertly) authoritarian state opposed? What

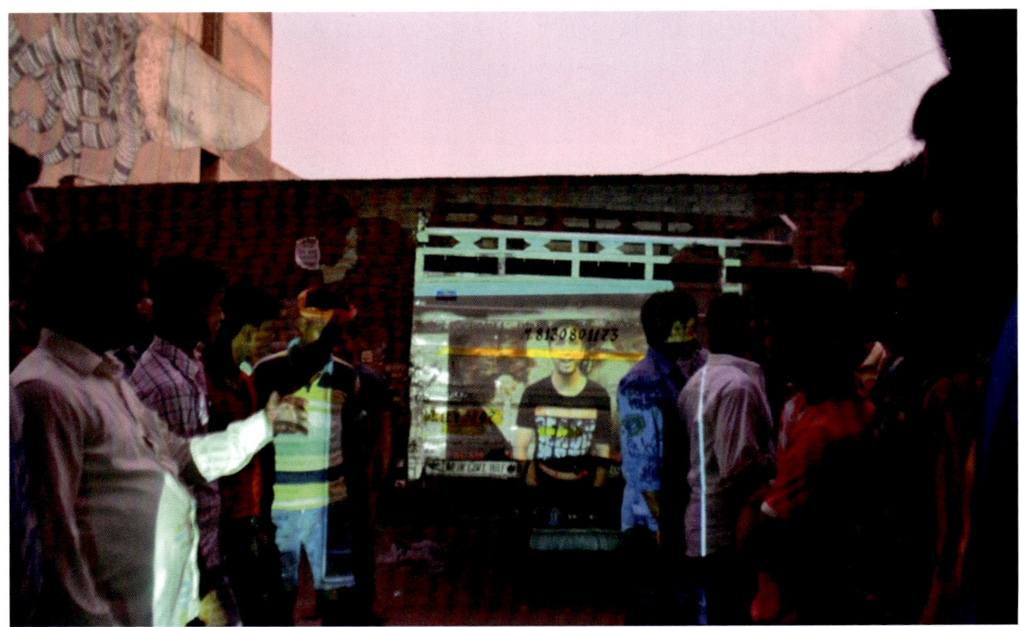

Public screening
as part of
the Khirkee
Storytelling
Project organised
by Swati Janu
during their
Coriolis residency
at Khoj, Delhi.
Photography:
Suresh Pandey.
Courtesy Khoj

political positions are upheld by the recognisable protagonists of radical change? Further, how, in the broad attempt to build and sustain democratic structures of governance, institutions for a functioning civil society and a public sphere, does the cultural vanguard in its anarchist gestures come to be positioned?

Billed under a country banner, the aura of national affiliation still survives. A critic-curator from India will have to go beyond sentiment to claim that artists from a particular country, properly conceptualised under a theme and a problematic, can, in the consequent exposition, address 'universal' issues of global contemporaneity. This, incidentally, is assumed to have been the case with selections of European or American artists throughout the twentieth century. A substantial partisanship from the southern end should add both to art historical knowledge and to political agendas that go beyond a mere counterbalancing polemic against the global.

Postscript by Geeta Kapur, 2021

Almost as if on cue, everything relating to curatorial opportunities changed in India around 2011, the year that *Afterall* published my interview with Natasha Ginwala. While there was already by then vigorous production, distribution and critical evaluation of artworks, what came about was a curatorial upsurge backed at last by institutional infrastructures within India. These allowed potential curators to develop their contextual positioning, their aesthetic priorities, their spatial and choreographic imagination. With these opportunities came pedagogical backing through the introduction of curating courses as part of visual culture curricula, notably at the School of Arts and Aesthetics at Jawaharlal Nehru University and at the School of Culture and Creative Expressions at Ambedkar University, in Delhi.

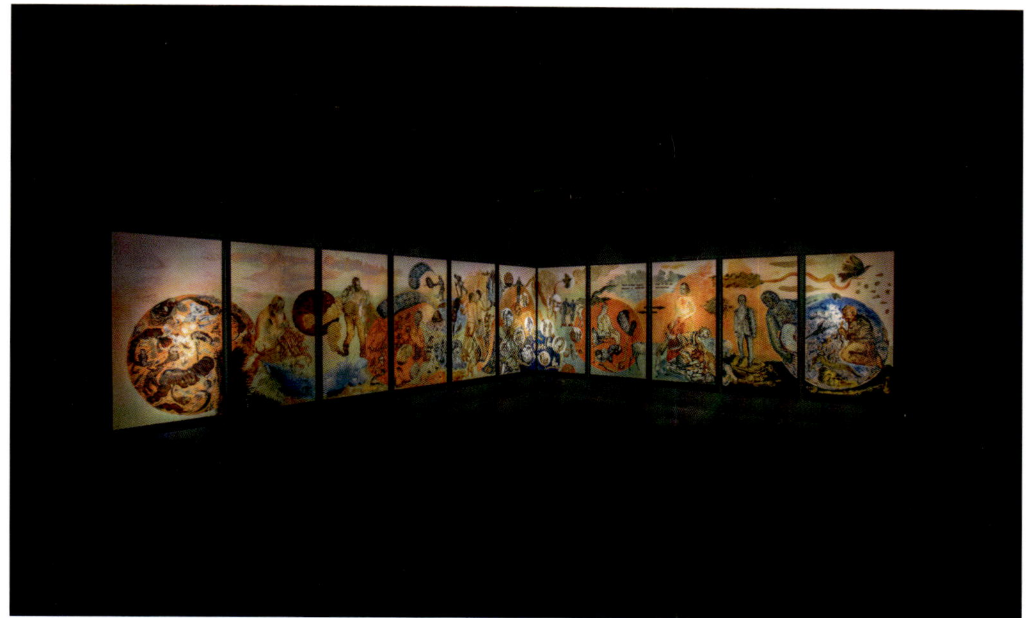

Khoj, the artist-initiated platform led by its dynamic director, Pooja Sood, is where curation has made uncharted forays. Prompting artist collectives in India and South Asia; testing materials and technologies; staging artists' performances, installations and dialogic platforms conducive to locational priorities and avant-garde initiatives, Khoj offers definitional alternatives within an international setting.[8] Pooja Sood, in her independent capacity, was Artistic Director of '48ºC. Public Art.Ecology' (sponsored by German institutions and the Delhi Government in 2008), which commissioned Indian and international artists to install 25 public installations relating to Delhi's urban urgencies.

Differently positioned, Delhi-based FICA, led by Vidya Shivadas, seeks artists' long-term solidarity at communitarian levels. Addressing India's grossly inequitable society in pedagogical frameworks, FICA turns curation into social praxis.

What was awaited now in India was a formal institution, a museum space (other than the National Gallery of Modern Art in Delhi – more on that later) that could unfold India's mid-century modernism into the contemporary. Since its establishment in 2010, the Kiran Nadar Museum of Art in Delhi has developed an outstanding and exponentially growing collection supported by Kiran Nadar, as chairperson, and programmed by Roobina Karode, the institution's director and chief curator, whose distinct aesthetic prioritises women artists and abstraction.[9] Karode has curated major retrospectives as well as thematic and intersectional exhibitions featuring multimedia presentations and architectural, socially engaged and documentary material.[10] Already KNMA has collaborated with international museums; in the coming years a major museum complex will house the collection and expand its interactive activities on the global stage.

Nalini Malani, *Twice Upon a Time*, 2014, acrylic, ink and enamel reverse painting on acrylic sheet. Installation view, 'Narrating from the Museum Archives and Collection: 10 Years of KNMA', Kiran Nadar Museum of Art, Noida, 2020, curated by Roobina Karode. Courtesy KNMA

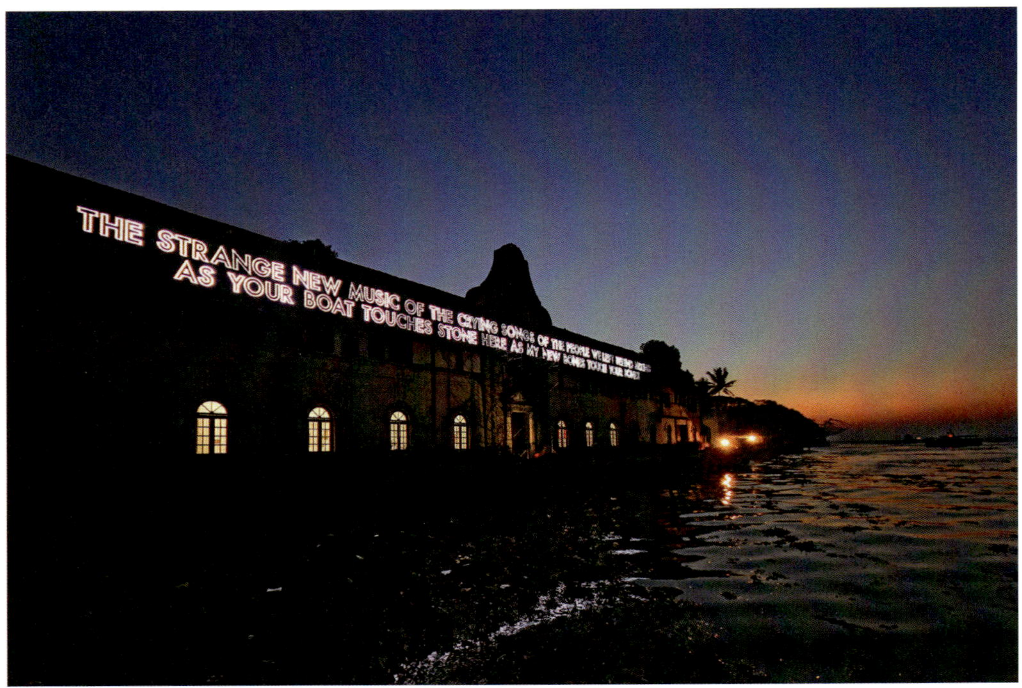

And as if to complement and in certain ways counterbalance the private museum aesthetic, the marvellously conceived Kochi-Muziris Biennale appeared on the Indian scene in 2012 in the southern state of Kerala. As co-founders, artists-turned-curators Riyas Komu and Bose Krishnamachari inspired the enlightened bureaucrats of this left-oriented state along with its fully literate population, the private sector and a generous community of artists from India and abroad to help create – with little money or infrastructure – this near-miracle of a biennale. As a site, Kerala is cosmopolitan, multi-ethnic, multi-religious, progressive and, with its ancient trade port at Kochi, fortuitously enchanting! As conceptualised by the artist-curators, Kochi-Muziris Biennale has marked a difference: its vision statement emerges from artists' creative obsessions, and there is perhaps a more elliptical form that surfaces in the curatorial display across Kochi – elegant spaces and, just as often, roughly converted former warehouses.[11]

The programming teams of KMB have emphasised discursive and pedagogical aspects. These include dialogues meant equally for international arts-related visitors and for Keralites across all classes and professions – so that the slogan launched by Riyas Komu, 'A Peoples' Biennale', comes true. In continuation with this ideological orientation, there is now a Students' Biennale involving very young curators and art school students. This has a separate yet interstitial life in the many *godams* of this port town. You can see here how the art scene in India has diversified: the museum exhibitions at KNMA and the rhizomatic expositions at KMB span the full range of aesthetic and interventionist strategies.

These two utterly disparate institutions of substantial scale then bring into question the National Gallery of Modern Art in Delhi, an institution inaugurated in 1954 in post-independence India. In its very conception, the NGMA recognised modernity and the modern movements of Indian art as integral to a modernising ethos – as in many new-born nations. While the institution remains a good repository of artworks from the first eight decades of the twentieth century (in some cases, artists' entire oeuvres), the NGMA, facing vicissitudes of definition, priorities, budget and ideology, has failed to become properly contemporary in terms of its collection and curation. Its years of earned merit should be mentioned – in the 1970s, under the directorship of art historian Laxmi P. Sihare; in the 1990s, with some thematic exhibitions, including my own unconventional rehang (discussed in the 2011 interview); and between 2001–16, under the directorship of Rajeev Lochan, when a series of important exhibitions were facilitated. Starting with Anish Kapoor and leading on to India-based mid-career artists, the series underscored the nature of these artists' express contemporaneity.[12] Today, NGMA's destiny, handled by a culturally retrogressive and politically bigoted regime, depends on (dire) state command rather than vision.

Meanwhile, there have been institutional breakthroughs providing curatorial opportunities, for instance at the Dr. Bhau Daji Lad Museum in Mumbai, a magnificently renovated museum from the nineteenth century, where Tasneem Zakaria Mehta, as honorary director, invites contemporary artists to stage their installations in the *mise-en-scène* of colonial artefacts.[13]

And there has been the honing of curatorial intelligence by gallerists in Mumbai, Delhi, Kolkata and Bengaluru.[14] Here, I would like to introduce 'Aesthetic Bind' (2013–14), my curatorial project with one of Mumbai's earliest galleries, Kekoo and Khorshed Gandhy's Chemould Gallery (which in 2007 relocated to become Chemould Prescott Road, led by Shireen Gandhy). To mark the gallery's fiftieth anniversary, I conceptualised five exhibitions with shifting curatorial themes: 'Subject of Death', 'Citizen Artist', 'Phantomata', 'Cabinet Closet Wunderkammer' and 'Floating World'. My curatorial premise was driven by the need for a renewed form of subjective *knowing* that has come to be centrally placed in contemporary discourse, including that of the political.[15] Here, as Giorgio Agamben says, *poiesis* becomes the minimum condition for unveiling, experiencing and knowing, to be paired and contrasted with *praxis*, 'to do', to gain freedom through action.[16]

I see this in conjunction with Jacques Rancière's theoretical proposition for the 'distribution of the sensible', wherein special importance is given to the aesthetic regime – triangulated with, yet distinct from, the ethical and representative regimes. A glossed interpretation in Rancière's book *The Politics of Aesthetics* (2004) instructs that meaning is inscribed like hieroglyphs on the body of things, waiting to be deciphered, while at the same time an unfathomable silence functions as an insurmountable obstacle to signification and meaning.[17] With Rancière, these competing conceptions of the unconscious, this paradoxical unity of *logos* and *pathos*, emerges always on *historical terrain* and is thus seen to have political consequence. Using the concept of 'distribution' to account for inclusion as basic democratic criteria, we see aesthetics and politics as coeval, reciprocal and the more dynamic.

My focus as a critic is on developing a grammar and vocabulary in tune with the immanent meaning of a given work; on translating a phenomenological encounter into an interpretative mode and inscribing this into a critical paradigm. Thence a *mise-en-scène* is set up and within it a curatorial itinerary, turning artworks into myriad signs. Yet, the active presence of the art-object in an exhibition is capable of, even perhaps intent on, deconstructing the very conditions of context and contingency that overdetermine curatorial meaning. For these reasons, an exhibition tests our disposition to confront or surrender, to activate our cognitive functions or celebrate states of immersion.

As the very title 'Aesthetic Bind' suggests, my own proclivities – an existential tilt counterposed with a political tilt – require a precariously maintained balance. This is not necessarily successful, but always usefully tendentious.

***

I return now to a wide-angle view of the curatorial field in India today. From the 1990s, art from here was spiritedly introduced into the international arena by curators at home and abroad. But it was in the second decade of the twenty-first century that Indian curators began to curate across transnational sites, entering what is called, in shorthand, 'the global contemporary'.

Foremost here are Raqs Media Collective (Jeebesh Bagchi, Monica Narula and Shuddhabrata Sengupta), who work with art and discourse and a remarkable curatorial imagination, introducing eliding themes, wayward itineraries and a phenomenology conducive to time-navigation. Their major exhibitions are curated like riddles accompanied by distributive strategies to figure a poetic-philosophic locus – pointedly different from any assignable social *context*. I refer to their curation of Manifesta 7, Bolzano ('The Rest of Now', 2008); Shanghai Biennale ('Why Not Ask Again', 2016–17) and Yokohama Triennale ('Afterglow', 2020). As curators in India they introduce an anarchy of choices to democratise the field into a kind of 'commons' – rendering it audaciously accessible! I refer to their Sarai Media Lab projects: 'City as Studio' (2010–13) and 'Sarai 09: The Exhibition' (Devi Art Foundation, 2012–13). And to the magical 'Five Million Incidents' (Goethe-Institute – Max Mueller Bhavan, Delhi and Kolkata, 2019–20).

Mumbai-based CAMP (film-maker Shaina Anand, architect Ashok Sukumaran and their collective) has developed research-based engagement with urban economy; with conditions of labour and terms of exchange. For example, *As If,* a series of five exhibitions in the cities of Kolkata, Delhi and Mumbai (2014–15), is a project denoting a full inhabitation of alternate realities. *As If,* part III, 'Country of the Sea', brought together a six-year project on the Western Indian Ocean that began in Sharjah, including the *boat-modes* project from dOCUMENTA (13) and *The Annotated Gujarat and the Sea Exhibition.* In 2019, they premiered *Housing Histories in a Cultural Matrix,* a six-hour video assemblage project at the Chicago Architecture Biennial. For a decade, they have used their rooftop studio as a venue for programmed gatherings, film screenings and dialogue around explorative technologies.

Continuing with Indian critics and curators, Deepak Ananth, Chaitanya Sambrani and Gayatri Sinha have curated extensively. Concisely for now: Ranjit Hoskote was invited by Okwui Enwezor to be one of the co-curators of the 7th Gwangju Biennale (2008); Nancy Adajania was co-artistic director on an all-woman curatorial team for the 9th Gwangju Biennale (2012). Hoskote curated the Indian Pavilion, 'Everyone Agrees: It's About to Explode', at the 54th Venice Biennale (2011).

Among those working primarily with international institutions, Nida Ghouse, also from Mumbai, traverses intriguing curatorial routes at once topical and esoteric. She co-curated the punctually positioned exhibition 'Parapolitics: Cultural Freedom and the Cold War' (2017–18), at the Haus der Kulturen der Welt (HKW), Berlin. She also curated, again at HKW, the marvellously resonant exhibition 'A Slightly Curving Place' (2020), where she collaborated with Umashankar Manthravadi, an acoustic archaeologist engaged in the measurement of sound in ancient performative and architectural spaces in India. She has frequently worked in West Asia, including projects with the Bombay collective, CAMP.

And I end this curatorial mapping with none other than Natasha Ginwala. In the decade after our 2011 exchange for *Afterall*, her curatorial practice has vastly amplified. Presently an associate curator at Gropius Bau, Berlin and the artistic director of Colomboscope arts festival in Sri Lanka, she was a member of the artistic team for the 8th Berlin Biennale for Contemporary Art (2014) and Adam Szymczyk's curatorial team for Documenta 14 (2017). She curated the Contour Biennale 8 in Mechelen, Belgium, titled 'Polyphonic Worlds: Justice as Medium' (2017) and 'Corruption: Everybody Knows'(2015) with e-flux, New York. As artistic director with Defne Ayas, 'Minds Rising, Spirits Tuning', 13th Gwangju Biennale (2021), their curation researches indigenous art worlds, unfolding a dream of coded objects that can be seen to merge use- and fetish-value – and to thus gain what is arguably, in our time, an 'aura' that inversely serves to de-commoditise the aesthetic.

***

This postscript is an account of the past decade's exuberant turns and twists, of peer camaraderie and necessary agonisms where curatorial imaginaries intersect and delineate the contemporary – aesthetically, culturally, politically. In exhibition-making we contemplate the material, the phenomenological *presencing*, of art. We also understand the conjunction of criticality and the curatorial, and the paradigm that Okwui Enwezor – the curator of our time – called 'thinking historically in the present'.[18]

Notes

Editors' note: The original conversation between Geeta Kapur and Natasha Ginwala was published by *Afterall* in 2011 and is available online; see text credits page in this publication for details. The interview has been edited for length and revised for this publication.

[1] Geeta Kapur, co-curator, 'Place for People', Lalit Kala Akademi, New Delhi and Jehangir Art Gallery, Bombay, 1981. See Geeta Kapur, 'Partisan Views about the Human Figure', in *Place for People* (exh. cat.), Bombay, Delhi, 1981.

[2] 'Contemporary Indian Art', co-curated by Richard Bartholomew, G. Kapur and Akbar Padamsee at the Festival of India in Britain, Royal Academy of Arts, London, 1982. See G. Kapur 'Contemporary Indian Art', in *Contemporary Indian Art* (exh. cat.), New Delhi: Festival of India in Britain, 1982.

[3] 'Hundred Years: From the NGMA Collection', curated by G. Kapur, National Gallery of Modern Art, New Delhi, 1994.

[4] See G. Kapur and Ashish Rajadhyaksha,'Bombay/ Mumbai: 1992–2001', in Iwona Blazwick (ed.), *Century City: Art and Culture in the Modern Metropolis* (exh. cat.), London: Tate Publishing, 2001.

[5] 'Dispossession: four women artists from India', curated by G. Kapur as part of 'Africus: Johannesburg Biennale', Johannesburg, South Africa, 1995.

[6] *Body.City: Siting Contemporary Culture in India*, Berlin: Haus der Kulturen der Welt; Delhi: Tulika Books, 2003.

[7] Tsongzung Johnson Chang, Yun Chen and Chaitanya Sambrani (ed.), *Place.Time.Play: Contemporary Art from the West Heavens to the Middle Kingdom* (exh. cat.), Hong Kong: Hanart TZ Gallery, 2012.

[8] Among Khoj's powerful initiatives: performance art residencies, including Khoj Live (2008) with Hassan Khan, Boris Nieslony, DA MOTUS, Steven Cohen, Ray Langenbach, Nikhil Chopra and Neha Choksi; from 2010 onward, artist projects involving rural ecology and urban neighborhoods; on a dialogic plane, 'KHOJ Marathon' (2011) with Hans Ulrich Obrist; and the conference 'Asia Assemble' (2017) with seminal speakers from India and across Asia, including Patrick Flores and Ashish Rajadhyaksha (keynotes), Ho Tzu Nyen, Zoe Butt, Gridthiya Gaweewong, Iftikhar Dadi, CAMP, Shilpa Gupta and Amar Kanwar.

Two retrospective views are required here. Artists' collectives in India (and South Asia) emerged from 2000 onwards. In Mumbai guerilla-like interventions were made by the 'Open Circle' collective (led by artist-activists Tushar Joag and Sharmila Samant, the collective was disbanded in 2008). Others, starting in the first decade (from 2004–10), took flight as curation hubs in the second decade of this century: in Guwahati, 'Desire Machine Collective' (led by Sonal Jain and Mriganka Madhukaillya); in Bengaluru, 'I Shanti Road'(led by Suresh Jayaram); in Mumbai, CAMP (led by Shaina Anand and Ashok Sukumaran) and Clark House Collective (started by Sumesh Sharma and Zasha Colah).

The second retrospect compresses the trajectory of the activist platform Sahmat (1989 to date) with a left-wing core group building solidarity against the state's curtailment of democratic rights, of artists and academics, of Indian citizens. Sahmat's numerous programmes include exhibitions like the declarative 'Ways of Resisting' (2002–03), curated by artist Vivan Sundaram following the massacre of Muslims in Gujarat; and several exhibitions marking historical junctures have been curated by photographer Ram Rahman. Here, I also mention Majlis in Mumbai, its arts component galvanized by film-maker Madhushree Dutta. Mumbai artists, often led by Tushar Joag, enacted protest politics with carnivalesque energy as at World Social Forums in Mumbai (2004), Porto Allegre, Brazil (2005) and Nairobi (2007). Majlis's cross-over expositions on art and visual culture continued until 2016.

[9] At KNMA, Roobina Karode has curated magnificent exhibitions of women artists. Her priorities were set in 2013 with Nasreen Mohamedi ('A view to infinity: A retrospective (1937–1990)'; this was accompanied with the exhibition 'Seven Contemporaries' of mid-career women artists including Sheela Gowda and Sheba Chhachhi. The exhibition 'Is It What You Think?' (2014) was a complex interrogation of India's social and ethical crises, relating especially to religious and gender violence. It included major works by both male and female artists; the title was borrowed from the late Rummana Hussain's extraordinary 1998 performance rendering the dilemmas of a Muslim woman. A three-part retrospective of Nalini Malani ('You Can't Keep Acid in a Paper Bag, 1969–2014') was held in 2014; Sonia Khurana's labyrinthine install ('Oneiric House / round about midnight') was staged offsite in 2014; Dayanita Singh's 'Conversation Chambers: Museum Bhavan' was held in 2016. Nasreen re-emerged as an iconic figure with Karode's exhibition 'Waiting is a Part of Intense Living' (2015). Beautifully displayed at the Museo Nacional Centro de Arte Reina Sofia in Madrid, it was then co-curated with Sheena Wagstaff and shown at the Metropolitan Museum of Art, New York (2016). Then Arpita Singh's retrospective ('Submergence: Six decades of Painting') was held in 2019; and a retrospective of Zarina ('A Life in Nine Lines') was mounted in 2020, with a complementary exhibition of younger women abstractionists from South Asia.

[10] A parallel list of KNMA exhibitions includes retrospectives of senior artists (the late Jeram Patel in 2016, Himmat Shah in 2017, and Vivan Sundaram in 2018). Exhibitions related to architecture and photography; ambitiously scaled shows of video installations such as 'Enactments and Each Passing Day' (2016–17) and, more recently, 'Delirium // Equilibrium' (2018), featuring major works by, for example, Amar Kanwar and Shahzia Sikander. KNMA has shown group exhibitions based on region (Bengal, Kerala); genre (political satire); and 'indigenous' contemporaneity (a retrospective of the late Jangarh Singh Shyam). Younger curators have interrogated the politics of the marginalised and peripheral aspects of Indian art and pedagogy in 'Zones of Contact' (2013) and 'Hangar for the Passerby' (2017–18). The KNMA team led by Roobina Karode curated the Indian Pavilion at the 58th Venice Biennale, 'Our time for a future caring', in 2019.

[11] Subsequent editions of the Kochi-Muziris Biennale have been curated by artists: Jitish Kallat, 'Whorled Explorations' (2014); Sudarshan Shetty, 'forming in the pupil of an eye' (2016); Anita Dube, 'Possibilities for a Non-Alienated Life' (2018); and Shubigi Rao, 'In our veins flow ink and fire' (postponed to 2021).

A brief retrospect here: a state-sponsored Triennale-India was inaugurated in 1968 by the progressive writer, Mulk Raj Anand, inheritor of Bandung and Third World politics. Despite major conflicts, it had a good ten-year run, then declined due to bureaucratic apathy. In 2005, artist Vivan Sundaram brought together a consortium of artists and critics to form the Delhi Biennale Society. This generated two international conferences (in 2005 and 2007) where major international curators were invited to conduct an intensive dialogue on the biennale phenomenon. While this initiative did not produce an actual biennale, the discourse generated a vision conducive to the artist-led Kochi-Muziris Biennale.

[12] Amongst the exhibitions of contemporary art held at the NGMA during and immediately following the directorship or Rajeev Lochan: a retrospective of Anish Kapoor (2010); 'Sooni Taraporevala: Through a Lens, By a Mirror, the Parsis 1977–2013'; a retrospective of Homai Vyarawalla (curated by Sabeena Gadihoke, 2010); Ketaki Sheth, 'A Certain Grace, the Sidi: Indians of African Descent' (2013); 'Experiments With Truth: Atul Dodiya Works: 1981–2013' (curator Ranjit Hoskote, 2013); 'Subodh Gupta: Everything is Inside' (curated by Germano Celant, 2014); and exhibitions of senior architects Raj Rewal and Balkrishna Doshi (2014). These were followed by another set of important solos: 'Transfigurations: The Sculpture of Mrinalini Mukherjee' (curated by Peter Nagy, 2015); Sudarshan Shetty, 'Shoonya Ghar' (2016); Jitish Kallat, 'Here after Here' (curated by Catherine David, 2017).

[13] Dr. Bhau Daji Lad Museum has held exhibitions of contemporary artists, such as: Sudarshan Shetty ('this too shall pass', 2010); L.N. Tallur ('Quintessential', 2011); Jitish Kallat ('Fieldnotes: Tomorrow Was Here Yesterday', 2011); Atul Dodiya ('7000 Museums: A Project for the Republic of India', 2015).

[14] Experimenter, a private gallery in Kolkata, holds an annual 'Curators' Hub', inviting major curators such as Adam Szymczyk, Hoor-Al-Qasimi, Hans Ulrich Obrist and Reem Fadda to share their exhibitions and develop curatorial discourse. Natasha Ginwala has participated in and moderated the 'Hub' over several years.

[15] See my curatorial essay in *Aesthetic Bind: 50 Years of Chemould* (exh. cat.), Mumbai: Chemould Prescott Road, 2018.

[16] Giorgio Agamben, 'Poiesis and Praxis', in *The Man Without Content* (trans. Georgia Albert), Stanford, CA: Stanford University Press, 1999.

[17] Jacques Rancière, 'The Distribution of the Sensible: Politics and Aesthetics', in *The Politics of Aesthetics* (trans. Gabriel Rockhill), London: Continuum, 2004.

[18] The Sharjah Biennial 15, postponed to 2022, is titled, as Okwui had it, 'Thinking Historically in the Present'.

Aftermaths?: dOCUMENTA (13) in Kabul

Francesca Recchia

A Road Map

In a world that fantasises about its global interconnectedness, questions of origin, location, proximity and distance are central to debates on contemporary art and curatorial practice.

This article, written in 2015, looks back at the decision to have dOCUMENTA (13) 'travel' in 2012 to Kabul on the grounds that the Afghan capital and the city of Kassel – where the exhibition is traditionally hosted – share a common (generic?) post-conflict heritage. Taking issue with the widespread commodification of 'elsewhere' in contemporary art, it interrogates the exhibition's choice of language and its conceptual framework, examining the repercussions of spoken and unspoken expectations towards the symbolic significance of Afghanistan. It also addresses the risks of the Western developmental approach that often seep through contemporary art's interactions with localities 'beyond the frontier' to ask if this is not a sort of *excusatio non petita, accusatio manifesta* – the unrequested reassurance of abiding by the rules of good intentions and political correctness thus betraying a need to excuse the colonial underpinnings of Western institutions' incursions into the Global South. Finally, the article ends with a note from Afghanistan, a reflection on the challenges of establishing equal grounds for the dialogue with the elsewhere.

Commodification of Provenance

Questions of origins, identity and locality are central both to the production of contemporary art and its imagination, while the discovery and conquest of new frontiers play a particularly important role in current curatorial practice. Over the last decade, national pavilions at the Venice Biennale have multiplied in an incremental rush to represent more diverse geographies, at the same time as the main exhibition's geo-political horizon has substantially broadened. dOCUMENTA (13) travelled all the way to Afghanistan on the basis of a parallel post-conflict geography, and Documenta 14 (held in 2017) also partially displaced itself from its own roots – this time, Kassel went to

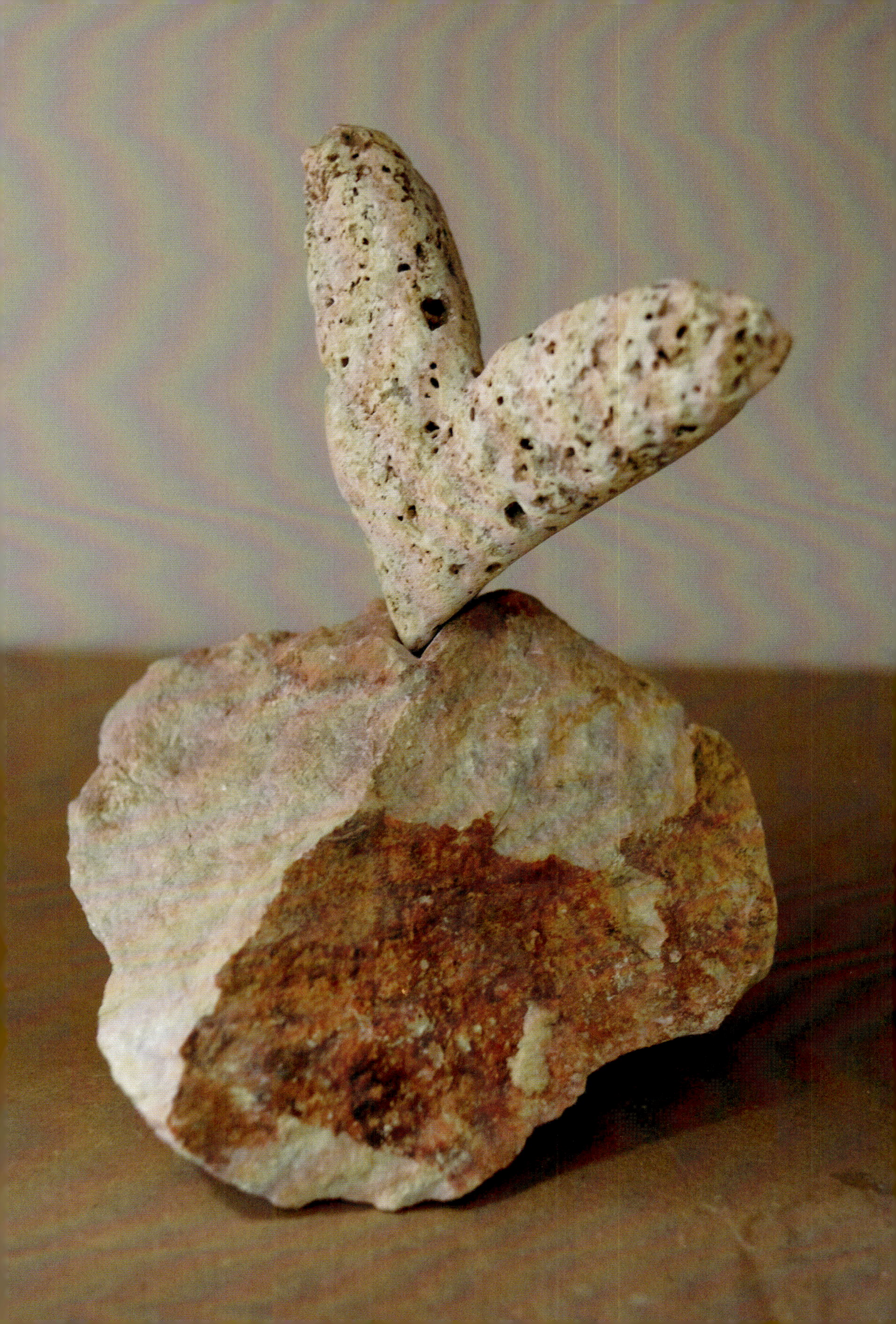

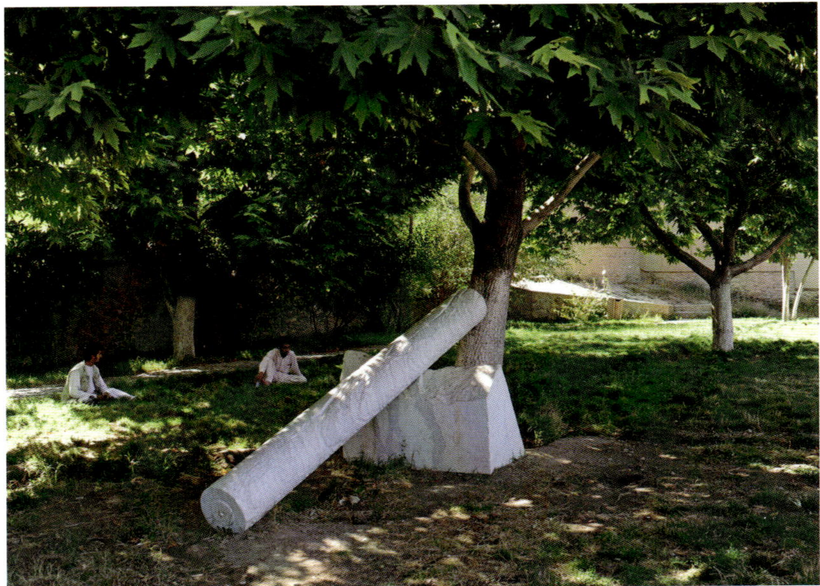

learn from Athens.[1] The terms are different, but the claims seem not to be: they all want to be *the first* – to open new borders, to include new territories, to explore new routes. This quest for novelty, this myth of primacy, is engrained in the mentality of the frontier and has grown to become an inevitable part of the contemporary cultural gold rush.

Writer, curator and urban designer Brendan Cormier has coined the term 'the commodification of provenance' to characterise this widespread phenomenon.[2] In the context of Milan Design Week 2015, he commented that the so-called 'exotic' origin of an object adds surplus value to it as a collected artefact because it enhances the uniqueness that buyers and collectors pursue; in other words, it enlarges its aura, and inflates its price. With its purchase, therefore, collectors gain a story to tell: a story about faraway makers, about reviving remote artisanal traditions, about their own moral profile as supporters of a humanitarian cause, be it impoverished ceramicists in Africa, Afghan women carpet weavers, Rajasthani dyers or the like. This sort of self-referential narrative says more about the owner than the craftspeople themselves: hardly any of this reverberates to the very source of the narrative, and if it does, it has scarcely any relevance to the actual lives of the makers.

Similar issues around the commodification of place can be considered in connection to the journeying of a curatorial project to a place that may qualify as elsewhere. When commissioned to write this article, I was specifically asked to look at the aftermaths of Documenta in Afghanistan from the viewpoint of someone who lives and works in Kabul. I was not part of the organisation, but I have been deeply involved in the Kabul arts community in different capacities since I moved here in 2012. The editors wanted me to look, as a direct observer on the ground, at what was left after the events of dOCUMENTA (13) had passed. As I started working on this essay, I found myself problematising the very terms of the commission. Why do we look in terms of impact when we relate to contexts like Afghanistan? Why do we expect that our cultural actions as intellectual outsiders may reverberate in these frontier lands? How is it that concepts such as 'aftermaths' are applied to places like Kabul, but not, for example, to Venice, Paris or New York?

dOCUMENTA (13) from Kassel to Kabul

Carolyn Christov-Bakargiev, the artistic director of dOCUMENTA (13), acted to push the exhibition beyond the scope of its original venue in Kassel by taking it on a journey to Banff, Canada; Alexandria, Egypt; and Kabul and Bamiyan, Afghanistan. Each of the venues – included on the horizon of Documenta because of their 'phenomenal spatialities' – would embody a fluid combination of the four 'conditions' around which Christov-Bakargiev articulated the project: being under siege; being in a state of hope; being on retreat, or in a state of withdrawal; and being on stage. These conditions were to interpellate both a collective dimension of mutual interrelations and a disposition towards the world at an individual level.

> *Each position is a state of mind, and relates to time in a specific way: while the retreat suspends time, being on stage produces a vivid and lively time of the here and now, the continuous present; while hope releases time through the sense of a promise, of time opening up and being unending, the sense of being under siege compresses time, to the degree that there is no space beyond the elements of life that are tightly bound around us.*[3]

In what Christov-Bakargiev defines as the '"locational" turn' of the exhibition, Kabul and Bamiyan were deemed to present a convergence of these conditions, making them the perfect setting for 'highlighting the significance of a physical place, but at the same time aiming for dislocation and for the creation of different and partial perspectives'.[4] Conceived as an educational programme including artists, writers and thinkers, the 'Kabul – Bamiyan: Seminars and Lectures' consisted of three two-week workshops held in February, April and May 2012, which aimed to foster dialogue and prepare the ground for a local exhibition to be held in Kabul that summer, just days after the grand inauguration in Kassel.

> *Stemming from these seminars, the exhibition comprised works mainly produced in Afghanistan that engaged the audience in a dialogue full of correspondences between siege and diaspora, collapse and recovery, memory and fantasy, past and future. They also proposed mutual evocations of the history of two cities, Kabul and Kassel, both of which have witnessed destruction through war and the need for physical reconstruction and mental retrieval, becoming stages where our present is represented or transcended.*[5]

The exhibition in Kabul took place in the National Gallery and in the beautiful Qasr-e-Malika, or Queen's Palace, scenically located at the top of Bagh-e Babur, the most visited public park in Kabul. As the contemporary art scene in the city has only started consolidating in the last ten years, there is not

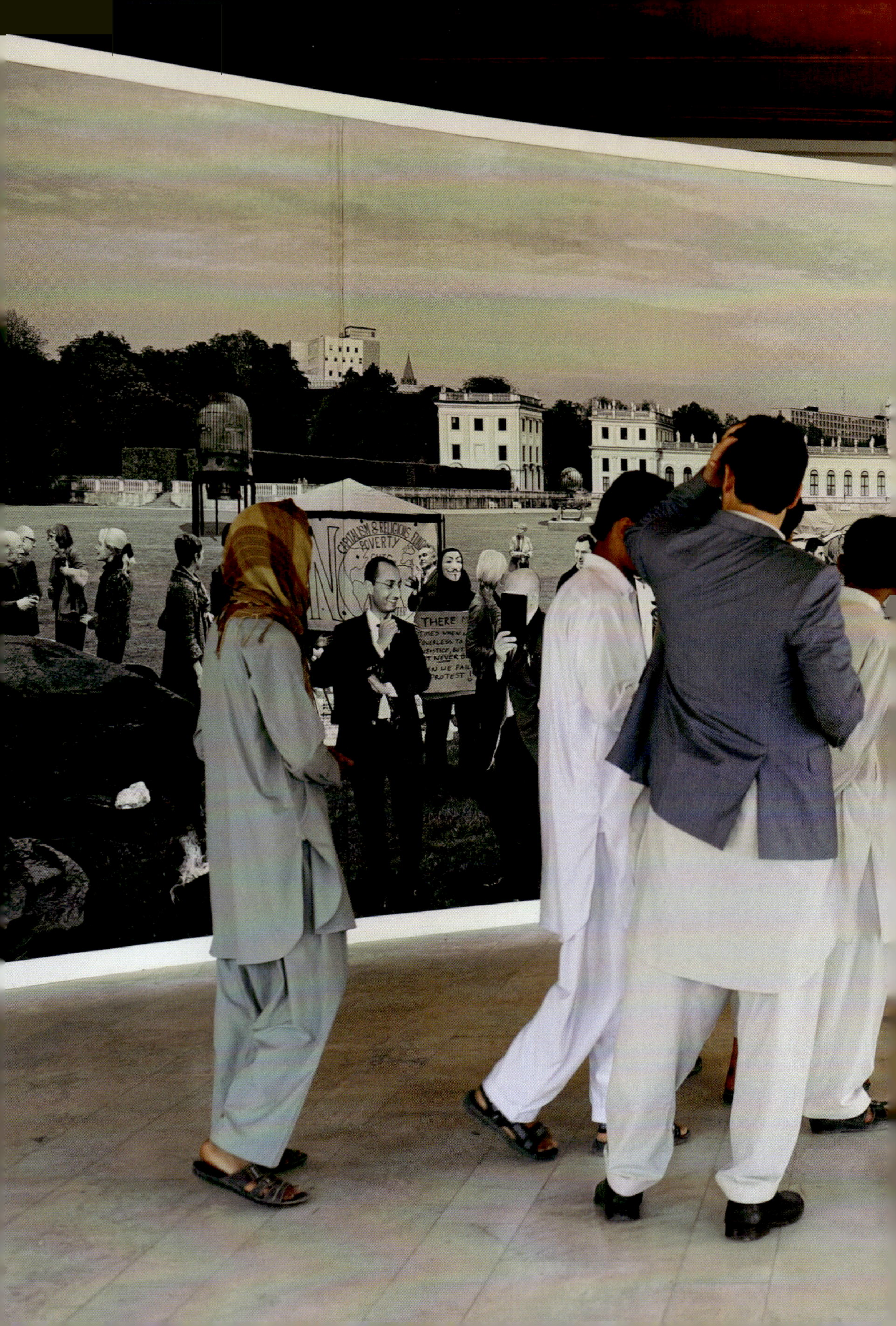

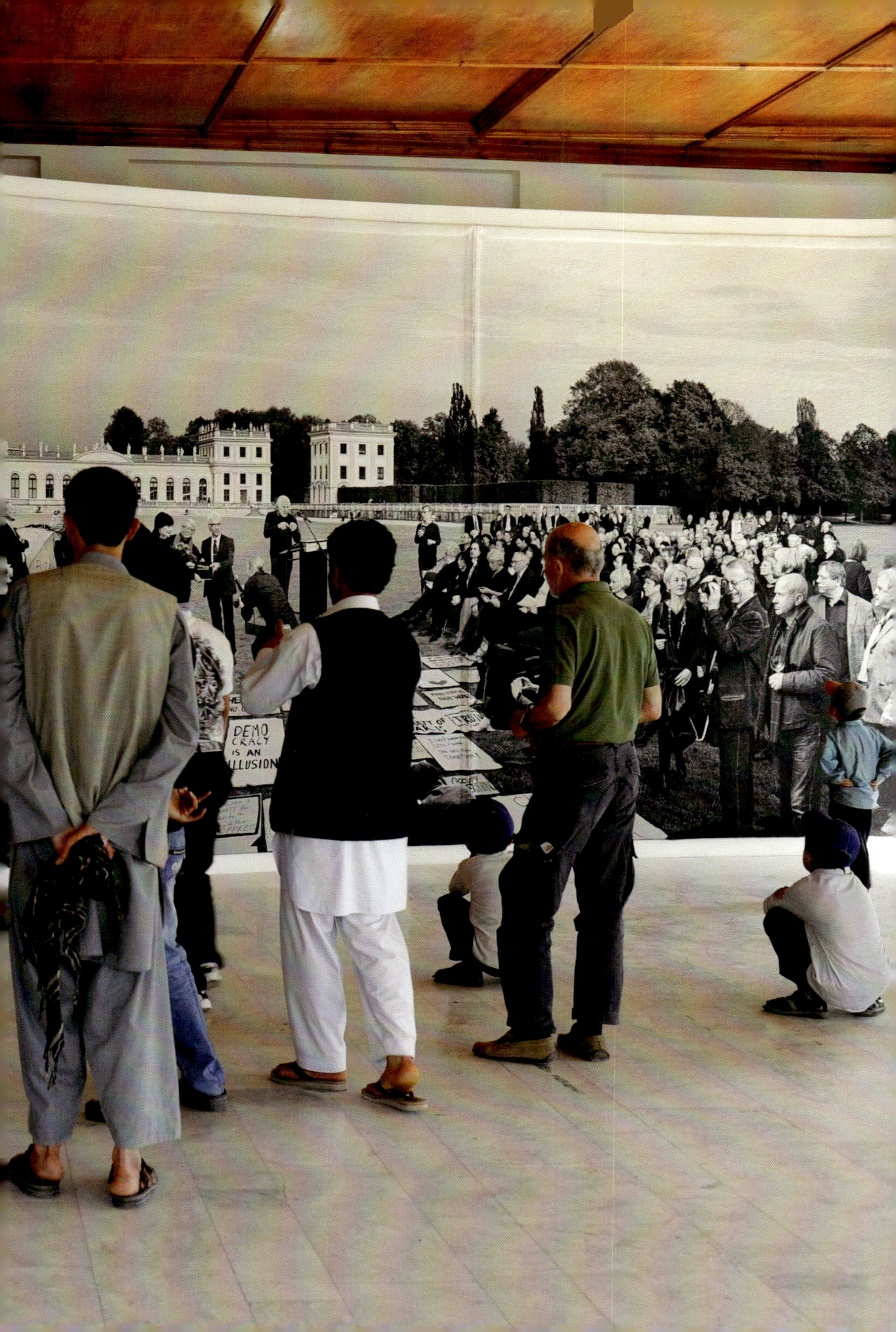
DEMO
CRACY
IS AN
ILLUSION

yet a wide, fully articulated audience with firm critical approaches and attitudes. Because of these multiple factors, the 'dialogue' may not have been as full of 'correspondences', nor the 'evocations' as mutual as might have been hoped. Most of the exhibition's visitors were in fact non-art specialists and passers-by who found themselves in the park for other reasons. According to Nabila Horakhsh, an artist who assisted curators Andrea Viliani and Aman Mojadidi during the project, both the participating Afghan artists and the visitors reported a deep sense of disconnect with the exhibition's content, claiming that, despite the attempts at mediation, the general public found the works alien and obscure.

Words Shape Worlds?

Aman Mojadidi is an Afghan-American artist who was involved since the beginning in the organisation of the satellite project of dOCUMENTA (13) in Afghanistan. His work was included in both the Kassel and Kabul exhibitions, and he was also recruited one-and-a-half years before the opening as one of the experts – dubbed 'curatorial agents' – advising on the exhibition's development. These agents were to be the project's international eyes and sensors, who, besides looking after the logistics of the travelling components in their own territories, helped the artistic director in identifying the artists to be invited to the exhibition from various elsewheres. Placed in a perspective of frontier exploration, and if we believe at all that words shape worlds, their definition as agents in places like Alexandria or Kabul carries the disquieting echo of that old anthropological specimen, the native informant. It also brings to mind the role attributed to these 'informants' as translators of cultural meaning, building bridges that could facilitate the colonial endeavour and ensure intelligibility. As the project unfolded in Kabul, and despite the organisers' claims of forfeiting a set agenda, the Afghan participants saw in dOCUMENTA (13) the reiteration of these flawed cultural hierarchies.

Mojadidi, whose work sarcastically questions the processes of othering inherent in the encounter with those who come from elsewhere, has often been vocally critical of the developmental mentality that informs many cultural interventions in Afghanistan. When asked to comment on the very Western expectation that a foreign institution parachuted into Afghanistan could generate visible aftermaths, he argued that the initial discussions of dOCUMENTA (13) were intent on avoiding its transformation into a colonial project, but something, somehow got lost in the process. 'The project started very well,' he conceded. 'Unlike many other foreign projects, it started without an agenda. However, the content of the seminars came for the most part from the outside, from what those who led the workshops envisioned as a good intervention rather than from what Afghan artists may have wanted or needed.'[6] Combining theory and practice, the seminars – which for security reasons were strictly by invitation only – addressed questions of translation, inclusion and exclusion within the contemporary art system, as well as ideas around the archive or the relation between the personal and the political. Mojadidi critiqued the project at large in a text for the exhibition catalogue of Francis Alÿs's 'REEL-UNREEL (Afghan Projects, 2010–2014)', on view at the Museo Madre in Naples in 2014.[7] (REEL-UNREEL (2011) was a video commissioned and produced by dOCUMENTA (13) that Alÿs realised during a trip to Afghanistan.) Mojadidi wrote that initially dOCUMENTA (13) presented itself as a 'refreshing change from the formulaic art projects often simply transplanted to new development soil, or the arrogant hierarchy of Western knowledge understood as a gift bestowed upon the noble savages'. As things went on, though, the project morphed

> *to take the form of whatever shape is already serving as the dominant blob within which so much happens. And in Afghanistan today that blob, that form, is the largely Western-led, White Man's Burden of International Aid & Development. [...] So the approach still became problematic, and to some extent only furthered the West's romanticised, exaggerated glamourisation of contemporary culture in the country in a way that ultimately creates, like cultural carnival mirrors, a distorted reflection of reality.*[8]

A similar narrative of disconnection emerged in my interview with Qasem Foushanji, another participating artist in both Kassel and Kabul. Foushanji lamented having been included in the exhibition because of the curators' interest in drawing geographical and historical parallels between Kabul and Kassel. He spoke about his personal struggle to be recognised internationally for his artistic merits: 'Being in Documenta in itself does not make me an artist equal to others: it is the fact that I was born in Afghanistan that brought me there. How do I feel about it? Not very good, to be honest.'[9] Most Afghan artists' work was exhibited in a separate venue in Kassel, the former Elisabeth Hospital, which was founded in 1297 and used as a leprosarium and a home for the elderly before being destroyed in World War II and later renovated as private housing.[10] As Documenta has never traditionally featured geographically specific pavilions or thematic exhibitions, the decision took many by surprise. There was in fact no official explanation but an informal rumour that justified it as a display of the results of the 'Kabul – Bamiyan: Seminars and Lectures'.[11] The place, to the great displeasure of the artistic director, was dubbed 'the Afghan ghetto'. Foushanji stopped short of using such language, but he did not find the choice 'very respectful' either. He added: 'I just did not expect Documenta to do something like that. I thought it was about "here is what the latest art is" and then again you find yourself immersed in this whole cliché, this political, passport-related thing.'[12]

The choice of segregating Afghan artists in Kassel was of great concern to Leeza Ahmady, a curator born and raised in Afghanistan and based in New York, who was one of the core agents engaged in the organisation of the events in Kabul.[13] In our conversation, she recalled her disappointment at not being consulted about the decision to show the artists from Afghanistan in a separate venue, and the simmering unease on the part of the artists themselves. This issue then unexpectedly exploded at the opening press conference; Ahmady remembered being saddened to see that rather than considering what could have been the reasons for the artists' discomfort, Christov-Bakargiev took offence at the bad taste of calling it a ghetto, since they were in Germany and words have meanings: 'This word was being thrown around by the artists, jokingly expressing the uncertainty of their representation in Kassel. On the

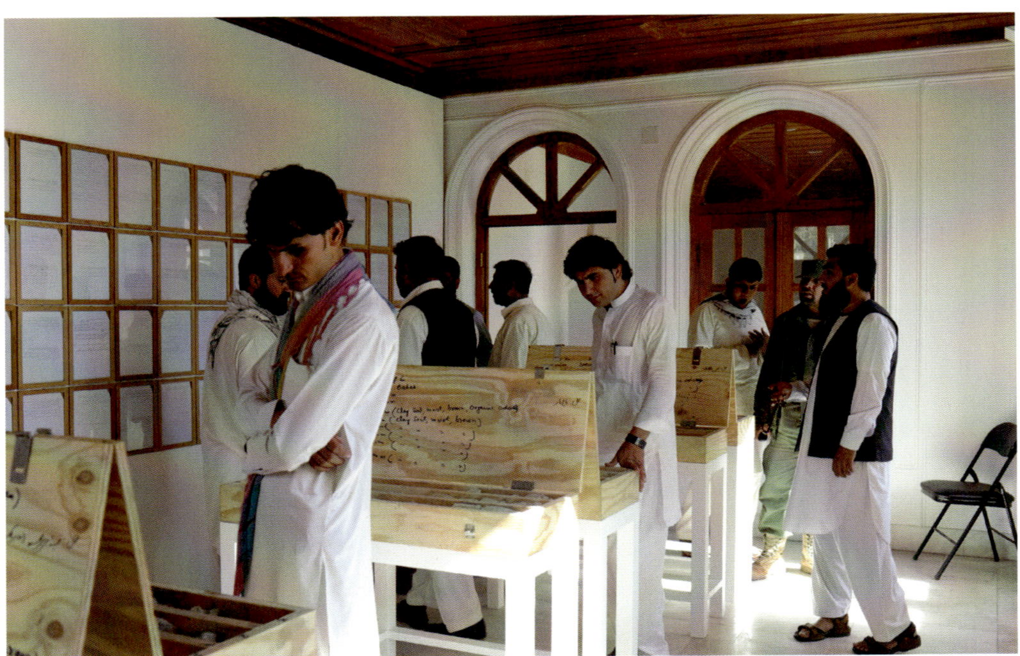

part of the curators, there was a great fear of judgement from the art world, so the defence mechanisms were so high that even a brilliant person like Carolyn had no space for reflection.'[14]

Global art showbiz is endemically permeated by a frontier mentality that leads to a frantic drive towards the accumulation of exotica and elsewheres. The margins of reflexivity and mutuality are squeezed by the event-driven nature of international collaborations and the muddled relationships between artistic and geo-political representations. We are thus left to wonder whether 'Documenta needed Afghanistan more than Afghanistan needed Documenta', as Ahmady put it.

A Note from Afghanistan

Assessing the dynamics triggered by dOCUMENTA (13) opens broader questions on relations with the elsewheres. Considering the globalised landscape within which cultural practitioners navigate, is there any way to move beyond what may be seen as a colonial impasse? Is there any chance of a dialogue on equal grounds that could challenge hierarchical power structures and exotic expectations? And more importantly, how do we build the basis for a common language and awareness from which to address these questions? Reflecting on the factors that influence today's global circulation of cultural objects, Arjun Appadurai has argued:

We need to understand more about the ways in which the forms of circulation and the circulation of forms create the conditions for the production of locality. I stress locality because, in the end, this is where our vitally important archives

As I write from Kabul – and as I write also because of my locality – I put
myself in the equation and interpellate my own position.

Three years have passed since dOCUMENTA (13) ended. Much in the city
has changed and the country is undergoing a phase of political redefinition
that is profoundly impactful on social relations and cultural production.
Artists are struggling to find spaces of expression and to give financial sustainability to their practices. The international presence is renegotiating its
engagement with the country. Foreigners come and go, and with them various initiatives and endless streams of good intentions.[16] dOCUMENTA (13)
was one of them: it happened and passed; it gave some artists the chance
to meet, some ideas the chance to be exchanged, some critics the chance to
write, some adventurers the chance to travel.

Since dOCUMENTA (13) left, the small art community in Kabul has kept
struggling to survive, just as it did before the event. Artists constantly try to
negotiate new spaces and possibilities; they have become cynically aware of
the transience of international initiatives, but they smile at the succession of
newcomers who arrive promising bright opportunities and lasting change.
To nurture the possibility of establishing a relation and a common production
of meaning that can last – in Kabul or any other elsewhere – it is necessary to
accept a different temporality and to address a different geography.

A temporal dedication that goes beyond the transient scope of event-based engagements may allow all those who take part in the conversation to question
the scope of utilitarian self-interest. This relational approach is premised upon
a political and personal commitment to a game that changes you as much as
it may affect your interlocutor and surroundings. This certainly does not happen overnight or with prefabricated answers that can fit questions grounded
on politically correct or generic commonalities. We may end up interrogating
the very notion of expertise and the sustainability of building this kind of
authority through parachuted trips and sanitised encounters that are pleasing
to the eye, ready to showcase and intellectually acceptable.

Rethinking geography may also help us to challenge the removed authority
of external, think-tank-like experts. As an alternative, fostering regional dialogues could open critical spaces of knowledge production beyond the global
display systems where provenance ticks an often-exoticising box. Investing in
the regional dimension may be an appropriate cultural strategy to overcoming
the tokenism of what Foushanji called the 'passport-related thing'. It could
also be a way to throw into question narrow and conservative expressions of
localism while dismantling the assumption that there is no 'internationalism'
unless the West is involved.

Notes

1 This dislocation is still built around the argument of the social and economic divide between North and South – even with the necessary, almost customary caveats aimed at rejecting all binary logics. See http://http://www.documenta14.de.

2 Conversation with the author, 17 April 2015.

3 Carolyn Christov-Bakargiev, 'Introduction to dOCUMENTA (13): Artistic Director's Statement' (press release), dOCUMENTA (13), available at http://d13.documenta.de/uploads/tx_presssection/3_Introduction.pdf. dOCUMENTA (13) was held in Kassel from 9 June to 16 September 2012. Satellite events included: 'The Cairo Seminar', Alexandria, 1–8 July 2012; 'The Retreat', The Banff Centre, 2–15 August 2012; and 'Kabul – Bamiyan: Seminars and Lectures', with seminars held in February, April and May 2012, and exhibitions held at the National Gallery, the Queen's Palace and Bagh-e Babur, Kabul, 20 June–19 July 2012.

4 *Ibid.*

5 'Other Positions' (press release), dOCUMENTA (13), available at http://www3.documenta.de/fileadmin/press/for_the_press/press_kit/en/7_Other_Positions.pdf.

6 Conversation with the author, 27 February 2015.

7 '*REEL-UNREEL* (Afghan Projects, 2010–2014)', Madre – Museo d'arte contemporanea Donnaregina, Naples, 14 June–22 September 2014, and Centre for Contemporary Art Ujazdowski Castle, Warsaw, 10 October–11 January 2015, curated by Andrea Viliani and Eugenio Viola.

8 Aman Mojadidi, 'The Sand Mandala', in *Francis Alÿs: REEL-UNREEL* (exh. cat.), Milan, Naples and Warsaw: Electa, Madre – Museo d'arte contemporanea Donnaregina and Centre for Contemporary Art Ujazdowski Castle, 2014, pp.181–82.

9 Conversation with the author, 6 April 2015.

10 Qasem Foushanji, Lida Abdul, Barmak Akram, Khadim Ali, Jeanno Gaussi, Mariam Ghani, Masood Kamandy, Aman Mojadidi, Rahraw Omarzad, Zalmaï, Mohsen Taasha and Zainab Haidary had their work exhibited both in Kabul and Kassel. Zolaykha Sherzad/Zarif Design only participated in the Kabul iteration. Mohammad Yusuf Asefi had a work in the 'brain', a central space in the Fridericianum in Kassel conceived as a curatorial mind map of sorts.

11 In Kassel there was no separate venue showcasing the activities organised in Banff or Alexandria.

12 Conversation with the author, 6 April 2015.

13 As Leeza Ahmady's disagreement with the artistic director grew, her role became increasingly marginal and she had little say in the curatorial decisions around the presence of Afghan artists in Kassel. Conversation with the author, 30 March 2015.

14 Ahmady had not made this public prior to our interview in Kabul on 30 March 2015 because of 'time and respect'. During our conversation, she explained that she had decided to share it because she felt the need to openly question certain attitudes in order to be able to learn from them and find healthier forms of interaction.

15 Arjun Appadurai, 'How Histories Make Geographies: Circulation and Context in a Global Perspective', *TransCultural Studies*, no.1, 2010, available at http://journals.ub.uni-heidelberg.de/index.php/transcultural/article/view/6129/1760.

16 I have discussed this in depth in my article 'Kabul Good: Cultural Politics Of An Endless War', *Tanqeed: A Magazine of Politics and Culture*, issue 9 ('Enduring Imperialisms'), 2015, available at http://www.tanqeed.org/2015/08/kabul-good-cultural-politics-of-an-endless-war/.

In Real Life – A Reflection on the 'Online Exhibition'

Adeena Mey

David Morris

Is the move to exhibit online really defined by a distinction of space – 'IRL' physical space versus the internet?[1] At the time of writing, almost a year into the Covid-19 pandemic, the way we access museums and galleries begs questions of this supposed divide between digital and physical worlds. What is more, what has become, at an impressive speed, an almost compulsory generalised drive to deliver online projects has resulted in a variable explosion of 'content' – virtual renderings of actual shows, curated web-specific initiatives, digital viewing booths, video festivals, discursive programmes and so on – a situation that also, at its core, calls into question the nature and definition of exhibition.

Let us start with the 'online exhibition'. To try and gain some perspective, it might be helpful to flash back to some of its prehistories. Art as a form of telematics has long been articulated in various ways: in the late 1960s, curator Gerry Schum founded Television Gallery, using TV broadcasting for artists' film and video to question the relationship between the work of art and the artistic process; and in 1984, with *Good Morning Mr. Orwell*, Nam June Paik made what is considered the first international 'satellite installation', aired live via the Bright Star Satellite.[2] Similarly internationalist are the early experiments in exhibition cybernetics and computer art emerging in the 1960s, including 'Cybernetic Serendipity' in London, Centro de Arte y Comunicación (CAyC) in Buenos Aires, and Nova tendencija (New Tendencies) in Zagreb – to name just three nodes in an expansive transnational network. In a more recent phase, Rhizome's valuable 'Net Art Anthology' (https://anthology.rhizome.org/) offers historical perspective on the emergence of 'net art', tracing a timeline between 1984 and 2016, which also serves as a reminder that internet art is one specific tendency from a much wider shift in cultural life; or to put it another way, *all* art produced since the mid-80s is post-internet art.

An alternative approach to understand the notion of 'online exhibition' may be to zoom out to some more general considerations: What do exhibitions do? What are they for? Who are they for? The approach of many practitioners in the field of exhibition studies is to approach exhibitions in terms of audiences encountering artworks, through publics that gather in and through them: rather than an individuated, object-based encounter, an exhibition is understood primarily as a collective experience. The most fundamental operation of the exhibition is perhaps one of modulation. It modulates the multiple mediations between objects, viewers, institutions and the sensibility of the visitor. Understood in such terms, it is clear that an 'online exhibition' could be many things and take diverse forms not indexed on the model of the white cube. It is clear that there is no reason that online exhibitions should follow the parameters of their 'offline' counterparts; and furthermore, that this binary between 'on-' and 'offline' is neither descriptive nor particularly useful for thinking through these questions.

At the suggestion of the editors of *Critique d'art*, we look up an example of the kind of '360 degree online exhibition' offered by many large-scale cultural institutions. Via the Google Arts & Culture platform, we click into an image of the lobby of the MAXXI National Museum of XXI Century Arts in Rome. In the top left corner, an overlaid text tells us where we are. In the bottom right, there is a compass and other navigation symbols. More symbols appear at the tip of the cursor as it is moved across the image; when an arrow appears, we click and fade into a new image, giving the impression of movement across the lobby. The text on the wall for a temporary exhibition reveals that we are navigating the museum as it was in mid-2013. The interface is that of Google Street View; using it we are able to navigate around three large-scale sculptures from the collection (Giuseppe Penone, Maurizio Mochetti, Anish Kapoor) as well as the extent of the lobby area, including a wall work by Sol LeWitt, the ticket desk and café – an encounter bounded by the kind of 'invisible wall' familiar from three-dimensional video game environments.[3]

Is this experience emblematic of a particular dominant approach to the 'online exhibition'? It is tempting to dismiss it in simple terms, as a crude digital rendering of the experience of visiting a museum or exhibition 'in real life' – its crudeness only amplified by its rigid fixity in space and time (we are stuck in an experiential space of the museum lobby and three works as they were nearly a decade ago). But it is worth paying more careful attention to how such an encounter is historically constructed, and how it functions. What, for example, are we to make of its deployment of Google Street View as a technology of exhibition? Street View produces interactive panoramas from stitched images as an augmentation of GPS and mapping technologies, and forms one small part of a multinational data-capital empire with a corporate mission 'to organise the world's information and make it universally accessible and useful'.[4] This particular conception of the online exhibition can thus be read as the expression of a universalist desire to collect and render the world as information.

As such, rather than being a crude distortion of 'in real life' exhibitions, the exhibition as rendered by the Google Street View museum might be seen as a logical end point of one dominant lineage of modern exhibition practice. It echoes the much older universalisms to be found in the history of exhibition-making (from nineteenth-century World Fairs to the colonial formation of the modern museum). It is unsurprising that visuality and spatiality are the key exhibition characteristics produced by such technologies – and that these are the primary sources of information to be collected – given the prioritisation of visual and object-based practice (painting and sculpture) within this same tradition. It is unsurprising too that the original research project that became Street View positions itself in the tradition of linear perspective visualisations in Western art, upgrading the floating-eye vision of modern subjectivity to a car-mount webcam.[5] And it is worth noting the insatiable expansion and accumulation embedded in these logics: the technologies and renderings will improve, no doubt, and with them new forms of capture and extraction.

But if this is one dominant mode of 'online exhibition', there are many alternative variations. Among the first exhibitions to be launched online in the wake of the pandemic was 'Art Is Still Here: A Hypothetical Show for a Closed Museum', curated by Victor Wang and hosted by Beijing institution M WOODS. We visited this exhibition as part of a group Zoom session with students from the MRes Art: Exhibition Studies programme at Central Saint Martins, University of the Arts London. The idea of gathering a group together online to visit some shows emerged from an observation that such experiences tend more often to happen in solitary, atomised, asynchronous ways – each visitor alone with their browser, attention spread across windows and tabs. It is more rare, perhaps anachronistic, to come together as a group to experience an online show in shared time. We entered the M WOODS show from different locations and time zones (London, Beijing, and several points in between) via the institution's main website; the show, listed as 'ongoing', at the time of writing consists of nine weekly 'rooms', each of which contains a 30–60 minute showreel of moving-image works. Each showreel begins with a minute or so of intense advertising – video games, apps, films and TV shows – before a short sequence panning through a three-dimensional rendering of the museum, leading us to the virtual location of the screenings we are about to see. Elsewhere on the page are other works and contributions as well as artist biographies and work synopses, overlapping with decontextualised images, gifs, three-dimensional site maps and other elements.

The experience is disorientating and overwhelming. As a group we quickly realised that a main point of mediation was the museum's social media – Weibo, WeChat, Instagram and Facebook – and that these weekly updates, if we had been following, could offer more thematic flow and rhythm as well embedding the exhibition's presentations of works with already existing social spaces online (however good or bad or non-existent the critical art discourse on such platforms may be). Some works resonate with these surroundings: in 'room 4', video game ads segue into Lawrence Lek's *'Unreal Estate' (The Royal Academy)* (2015), a digital 3D tour of the Royal Academy of Arts in London,

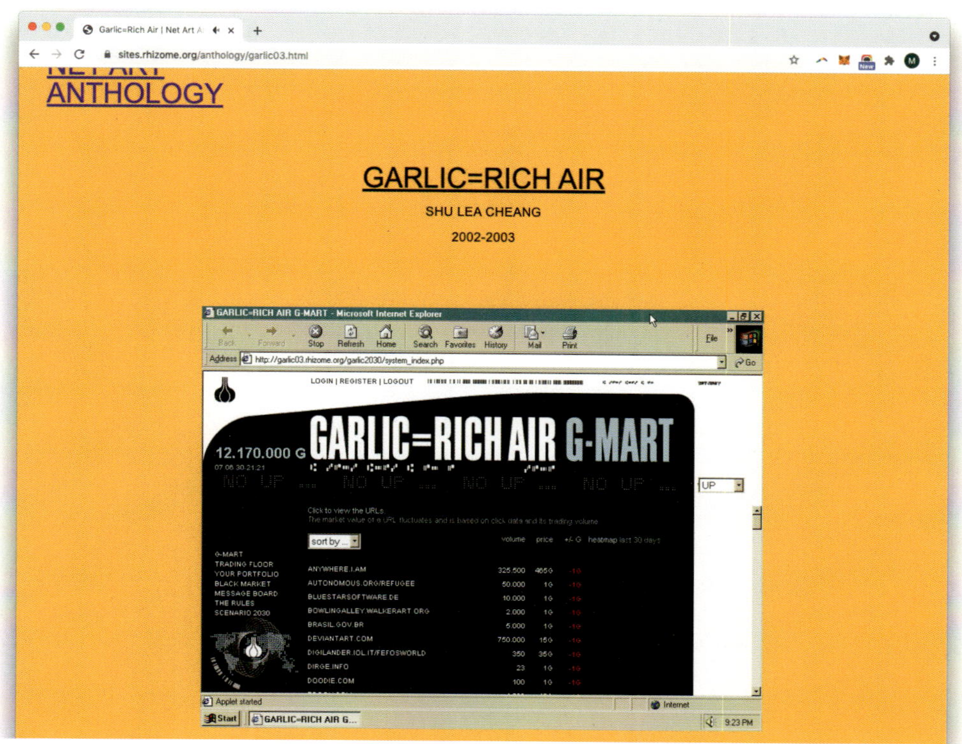

NET ART
ANTHOLOGY

GARLIC=RICH AIR

SHU LEA CHEANG

2002-2003

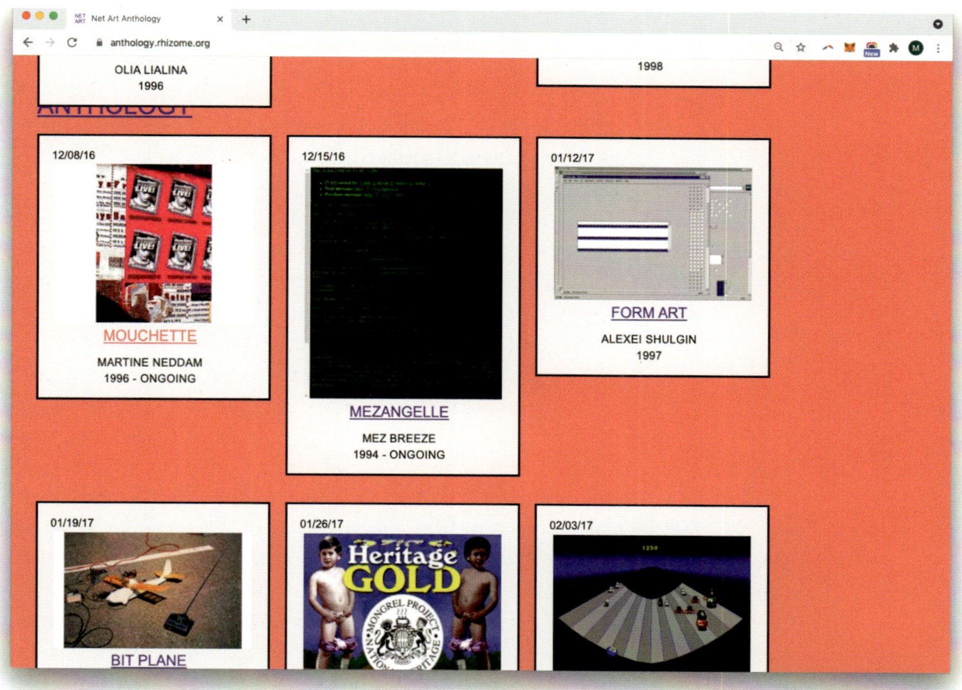

OLIA LIALINA
1996

1998

MOUCHETTE

MARTINE NEDDAM
1996 - ONGOING

MEZANGELLE

MEZ BREEZE
1994 - ONGOING

FORM ART

ALEXEI SHULGIN
1997

BIT PLANE

HERITAGE GOLD

presented as sold 'to a Chinese billionaire as a luxury private mansion'. The general feel of chaos and information overload also mirrors the day-to-day surreality of moving through the web, and indeed the everyday texture of life in current times – the extreme juxtapositions of content, cognitive dissonances and total saturation of commerce that characterises lives lived across multiple spaces, browser tabs and for-profit social platforms.

It may be, then, that 'online exhibition' is merely a symptom of the myriad overlapping crises facing contemporary art institutions at the present time. The global pandemic has served to exacerbate and bring into focus long-standing regressive social patterns and exclusions that existing systems and structures uphold. If one answer is to close things down, this is again something that artists and exhibition-makers have long experimented with; confronting the audience with obstructed spaces, such gestures have questioned our desires to encounter art as well as shifting attention to the (im)possibility of the exhibition by triggering more playful conceptual (with the idea of the exhibition) or material (with the concreteness of the exhibition space) engagements of the exhibition-form.[6] Another answer may lie in the demands of mutual care and social justice that a pandemic underlines – what if care for life was the institutional priority? To some extent, online exhibitions and their counterparts in the Zoom room or webinar might be seen as the failed realisations of earlier avant-gardist (tech-)utopias. But if, as these examples suggest, one's encounter with art was always one with the (im)possible, it is reasonable to say that online exhibitions have yet to happen.

Postscript, 2021

> *We must start afresh. To survive, we must return to all living things – including the biosphere – the space and energy they need. In its dank underbelly, modernity has been an interminable war on life. And it is far from over. One of the primary modes of this war, leading straight to the impoverishment of the world and to the desiccation of entire swathes of the planet, is the subjection to the digital. … In Africa especially, but in many places in the Global South, energy-intensive extraction, agricultural expansion, predatory sales of land and destruction of forests will continue unabated. The powering and cooling of computer chips and supercomputers depends on it. The purveying and supplying of the resources and energy necessary for the global computing infrastructure will require further restrictions on human mobility.[7]*

We wrote this short reflection in 2020 as two people trying to make sense of some of the claims that were being made about the exhibition in light of a rapid drive towards 'digitalisation'. Such observations are always marked with an indelible time-stamp, and Covid-19 only amplifies this. If little has changed between then and now, trying to engage with the ongoing shifts in the digital realm confronts us with the ungraspable speed and elusiveness of the current technological reformatting of human sapience. Art institutions have been opening and closing their doors intermittently; we asked ourselves, do we want the exhibition back? We felt anxious about the prospect of 'return' to an unsustainable 'normal'. We thought about issues of 'public' 'access' – 'public' as deployed ablenormativity, and 'access' as contained within neoliberal models of disability, as Khairani Barokka writes elsewhere in this publication. We considered the uneven geographies of the digital, its implication in the entrenchment of social divisions and border regimes. The text was published in two dominant 'global' languages (another way we might emphasise its extreme particularity) and addressed a situation dominated by those languages and the ontologies coded within them – the latter, the result of a field of questions currently undergoing drastic reconfigurations. We wondered about the intersection of language, technology and abstraction; thinking backwards to the historical complex of concrete poetry, cybernetics and early computer art; its interplay with variant forms of artistic abstraction; Cold War era geopolitics and the consolidation of the nation state through print capitalism. As these words are here remediated into the 'real' world in a new way, we may wish for their further transformation via multiple non-hegemonic and hybrid languages – translated, re-coded, creolised beyond recognition – and hope that a 'portal' towards a renewed set of relationships with the web of life may be one function of the 'online exhibition' to come.[8]

Notes

This text was originally commissioned by *Critique d'art* in 2020; see credits page in this publication for details. The authors would like to thank Sylvie Mokhtari and all at *Critique d'art*.

[1] The term 'IRL' – in real life – has been rightly called into question for the implication that 'real life' does not also take place online. An alternative is 'AFK' ('away from keyboard'), although this is also somewhat outdated given the wide use of non-keyboard-based devices.

[2] *Good Morning Mr. Orwell* was a broadcast shared between the US (WNET TV), Germany (Westdeutsche Fernsehen) and France (Pompidou Centre).

[3] One cannot, for instance, enter into the exhibitions or exit onto the street. 'Invisible wall' is a video gaming term: 'Invisible walls can create discrepancies between a game's systemic logic and its fictional logic, as a game's rules dictate that one cannot continue past the wall, while the fictional setting cannot explain why this is.' See https://en.wikipedia.org/wiki/Invisible_wall.

[4] See https://www.google.com/intl/en_uk/search/howsearchworks/mission/.

[5] See http://graphics.stanford.edu/projects/cityblock/.

[6] See the exhibition 'A Retrospective of Closed Exhibitions', 5 August–19 November 2016, Fri-Art/Fribourg Kunsthalle, curated by Mathieu Copeland.

[7] Achille Mbembe, 'The Universal Right to Breathe' (trans. Carolyn Shread), *Critical Inquiry*, vol.47, no.S2, 2021, available at https://www.journals.uchicago.edu/doi/full/10.1086/711437.

[8] See Arundhati Roy, 'The pandemic is a portal', *Financial Times*, 3 April 2020, https://www.ft.com/content/10d8f5e8-74eb-11ea-95fe-fcd274e920ca. With thanks to Charles Stankievech for his comments on the original text, and for invoking the '"online exhibition" to come'.

'Cities on the Move' in Public Space: A Journey Through the Archive

This visual essay traces routes through 'Cities on the Move' (1997–2000), drawing from the exhibition materials held by Asia Art Archive. 'Cities on the Move' was co-curated by Hou Hanru and Hans Ulrich Obrist to highlight the intersection of East and Southeast Asia's city cultures, as well as the region's urbanisation in the late-twentieth century. Involving more than 150 architects, artists, film-makers and designers, it has been hailed as a landmark event in contemporary exhibition-making as well as vilified for exotification and over-curation; with a strong involvement from architects, it attempted to recreate an ever-evolving city that occupied the white cube of different exhibition spaces.

These pages focus on the show's interventions in public spaces in the seven host cities: Vienna, New York, Bordeaux, Humlebæk, London, Bangkok and Helsinki. These pages are a response to an exhibition that has been more talked about, perhaps, than seen, with a history that is also a challenge to annotate and categorise (as its project archivists attest). This presentation does not attempt to offer a comprehensive view, but to open up a new set of perspectives on the project and invite further explorations.

Starting with some representative installation shots alongside the public 'entry points' and institutional hosts of the exhibition, we move outwards in different directions: exploring the journeys of particular works in public space as they would have been encountered by publics across different locations; following the pathways of tuk-tuk drivers and their passengers through various European cities; and, on the final pages, reaching a destination back in Bangkok, with billboards, moving-image works and performances. These pages explore the shifting meanings and interrelationships between artwork, exhibition, audience and place; for instance, we see Wang Du's *Alarm Tower* (1998–99) in front of its host institutions in London and Helsinki, as part of an opening parade in Bordeaux, as seafront public sculpture in Humlebæk or in deconstructed form in Bangkok.

Bangkok was the project's only Asian host city, and this was the only edition to take place without a core gallery presentation, appearing instead

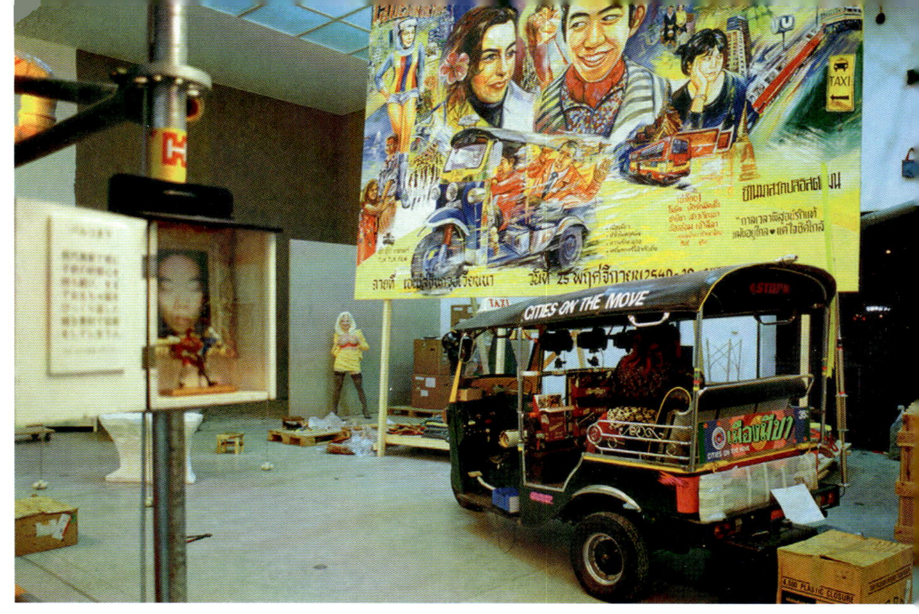

in multiple sites and public spaces across the city. The visual presentation offered here may be said to echo the Thai presentation's rationale in foregrounding moments beyond the core gallery presentations, as it looks across all the different editions of the show; it also draws from an *Exhibition Histories* publication on a very different Thai initiative, the independent art festivals known as 'Chiang Mai Social Installation' (1992–98). Indeed, the next few pages may be understood as a reimagining of the European and American editions of 'Cities on the Move' inspired by the method in play in Bangkok.

– Afterall *Exhibition Histories* and Asia Art Archive researchers

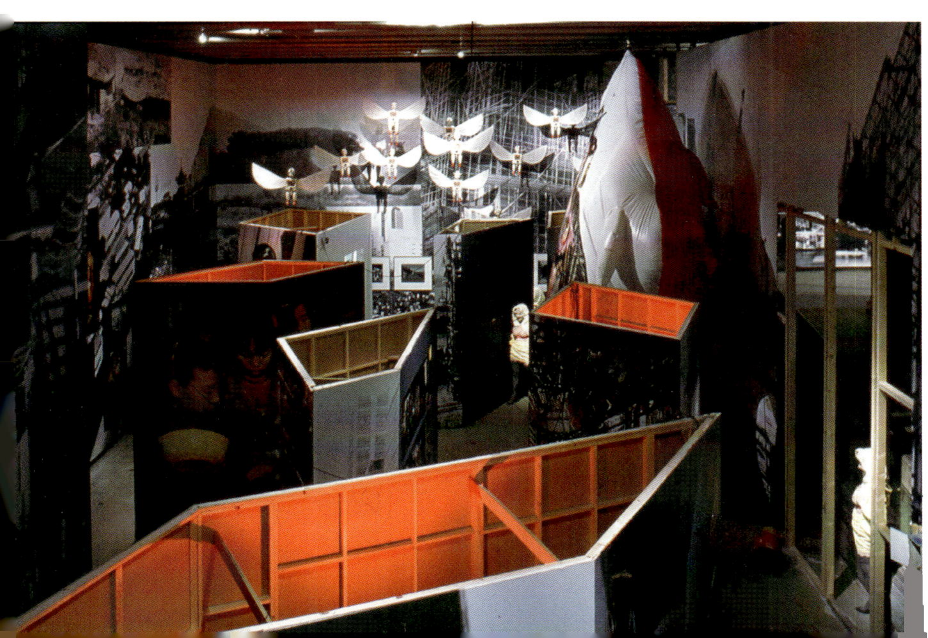

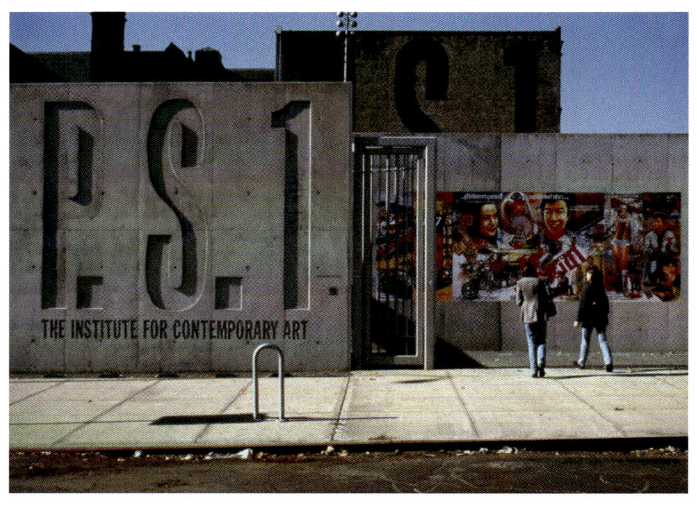
P.S.1
THE INSTITUTE FOR CONTEMPORARY ART

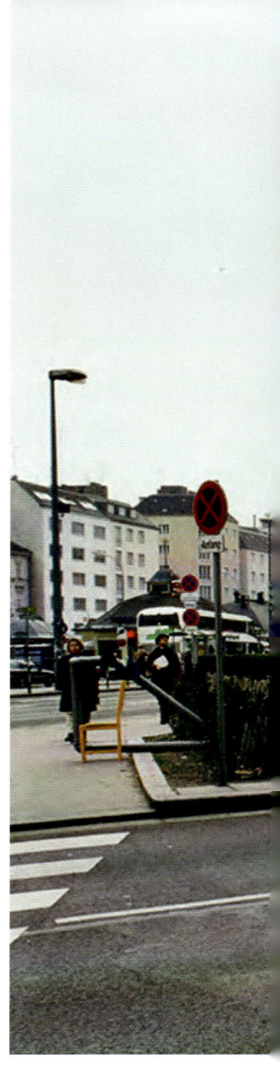

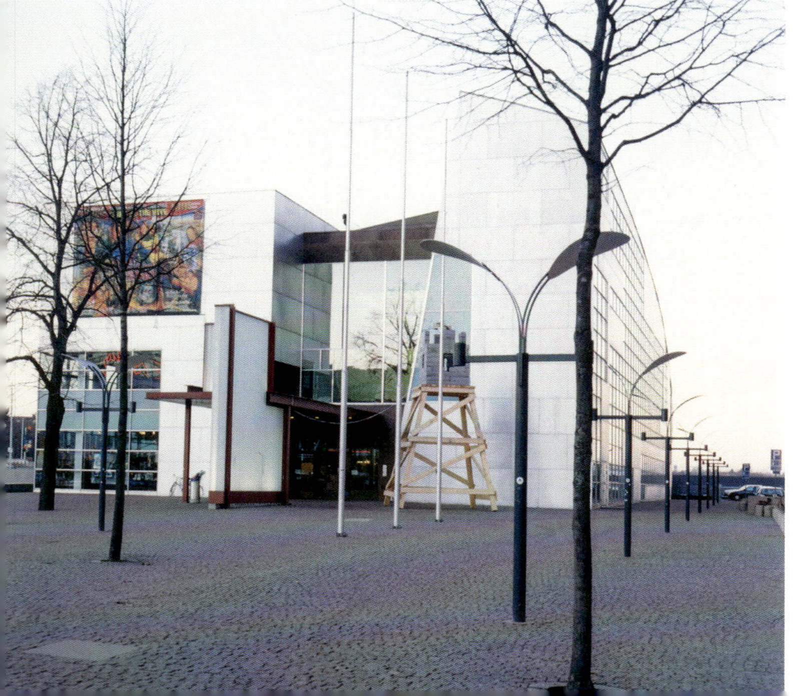

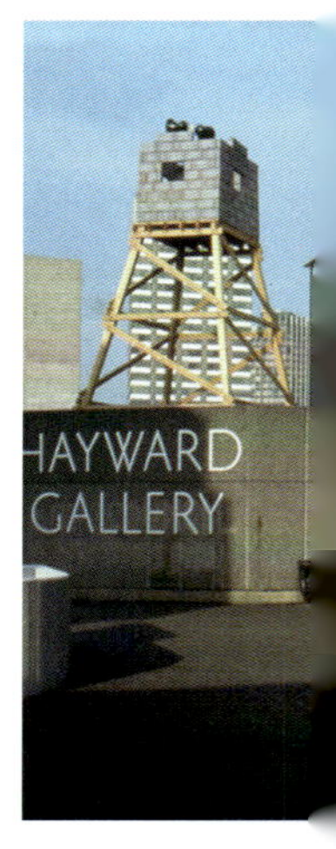
HAYWARD
GALLERY

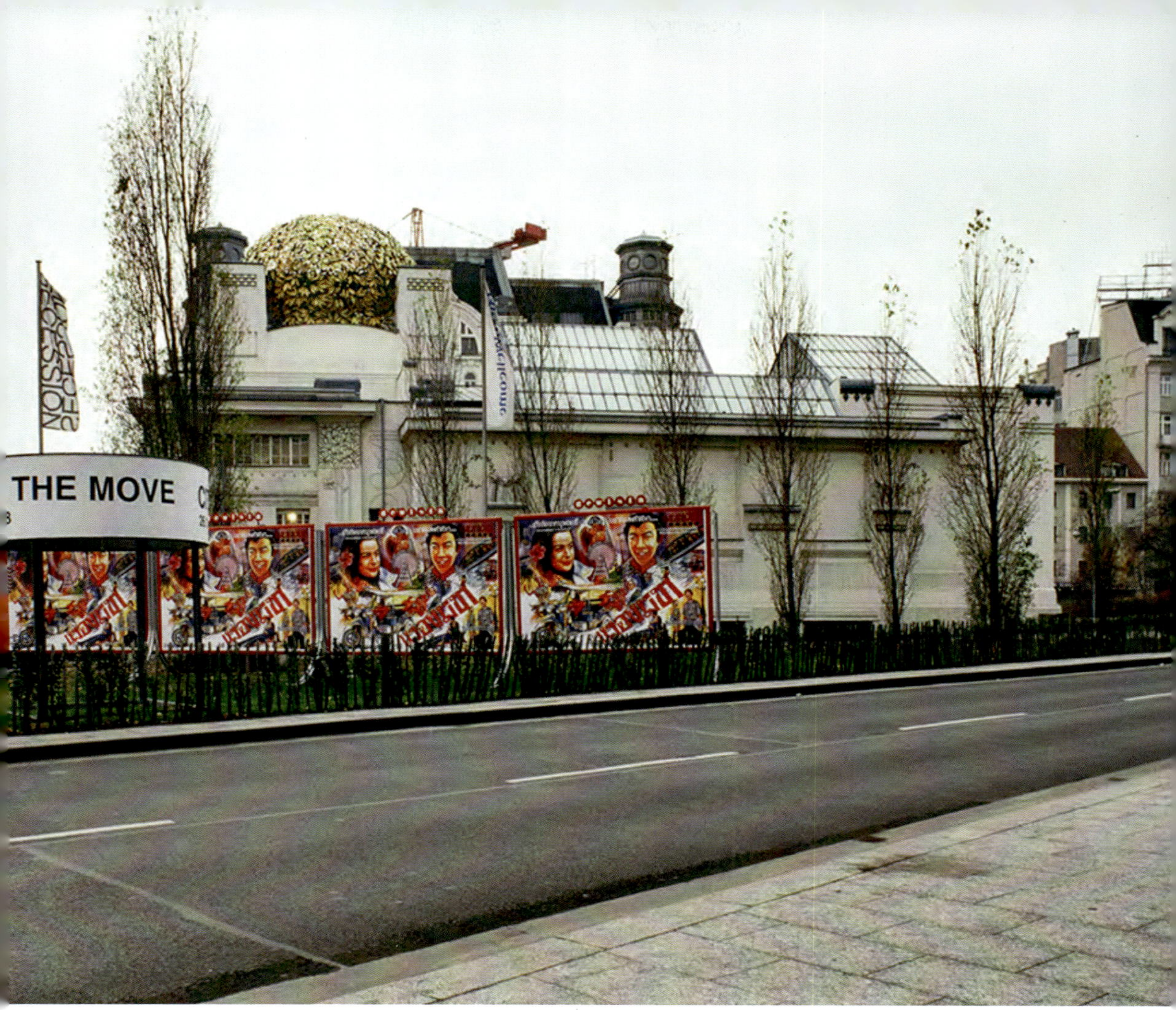

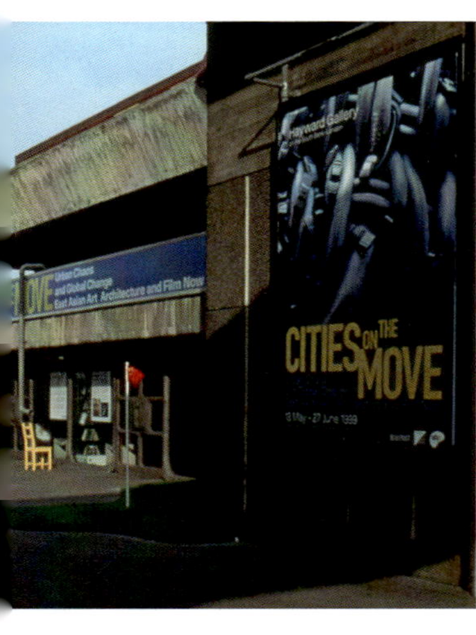
MOVE
Urban Chaos
and Global Change
East Asian Art, Architecture and Film Now
Hayward Gallery
CITIES ON THE MOVE
13 May - 27 June 1999

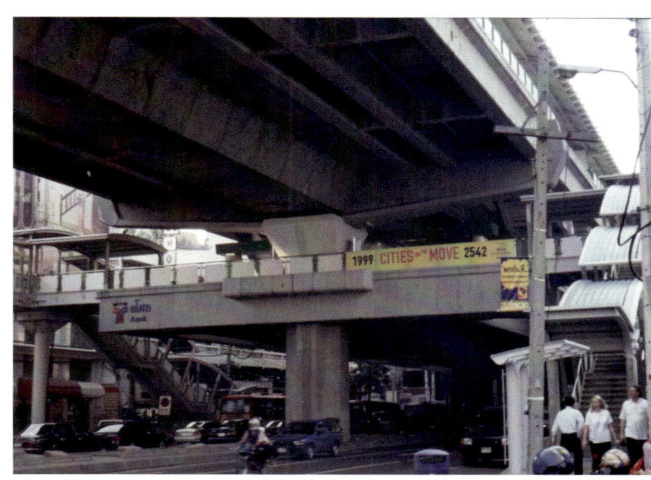
1999 CITIES ON THE MOVE 2542

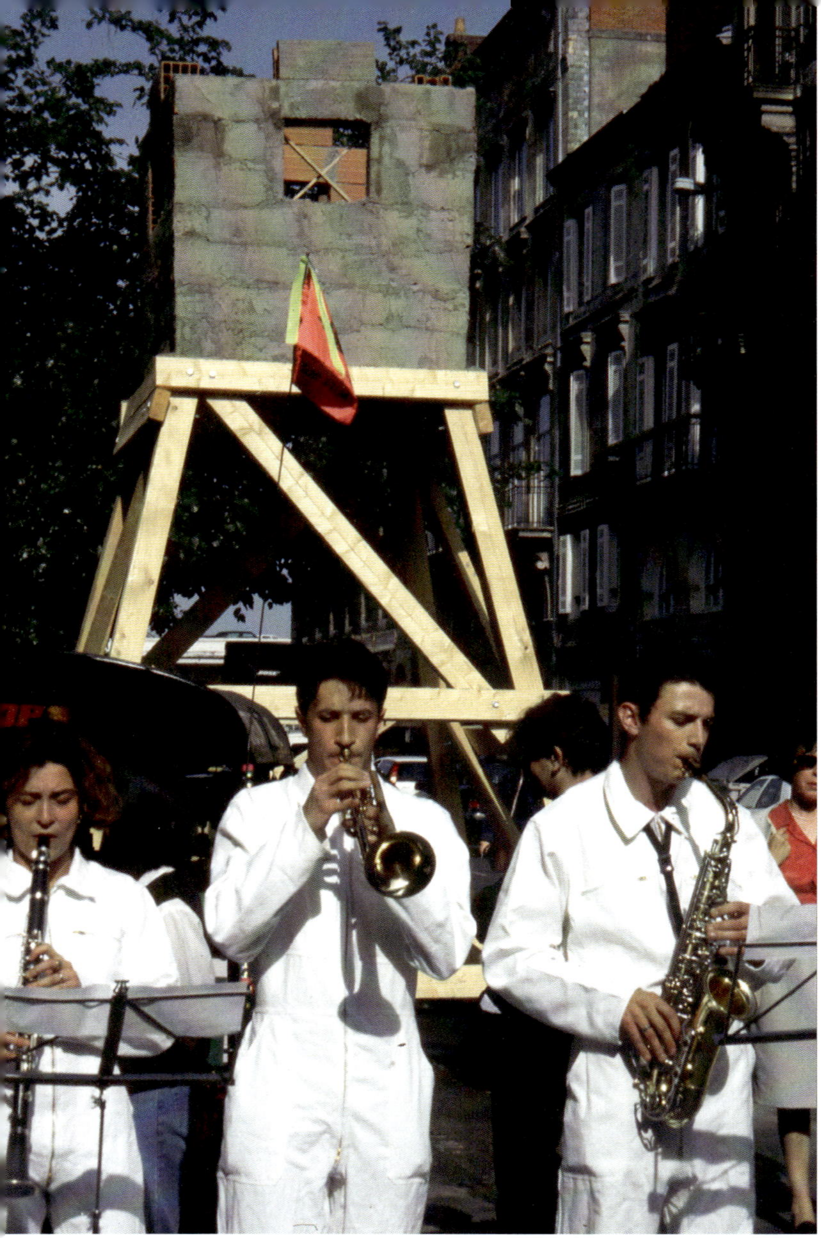

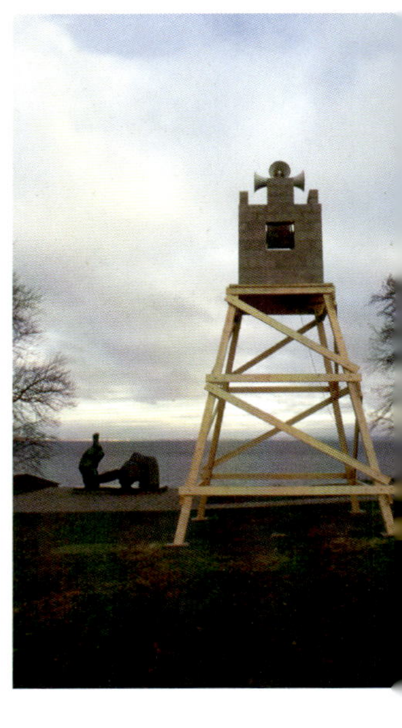

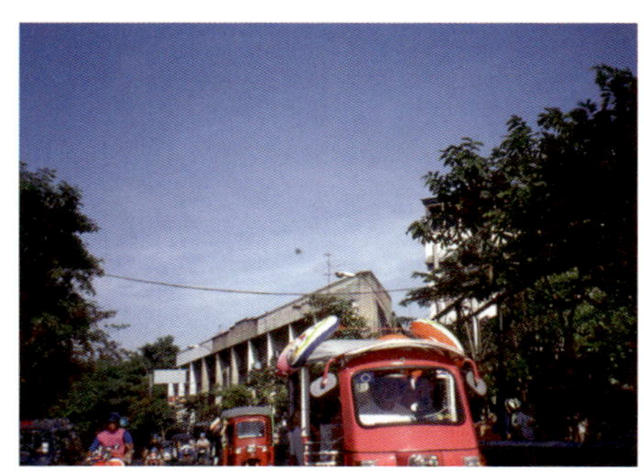

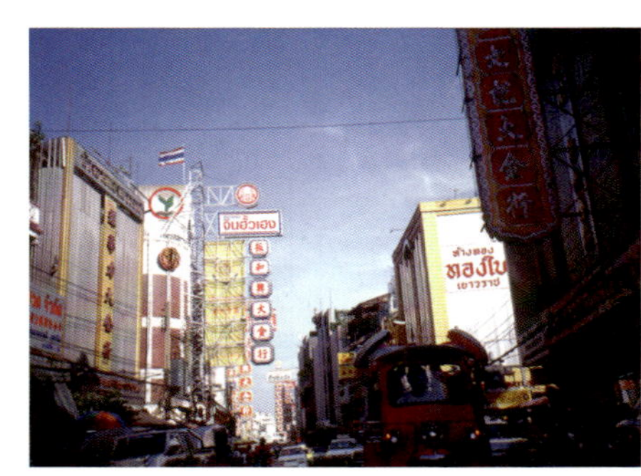

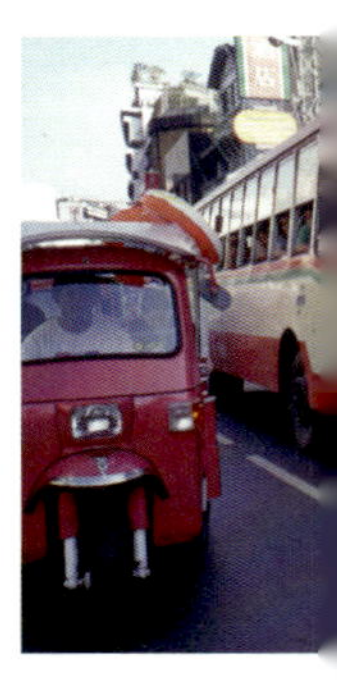

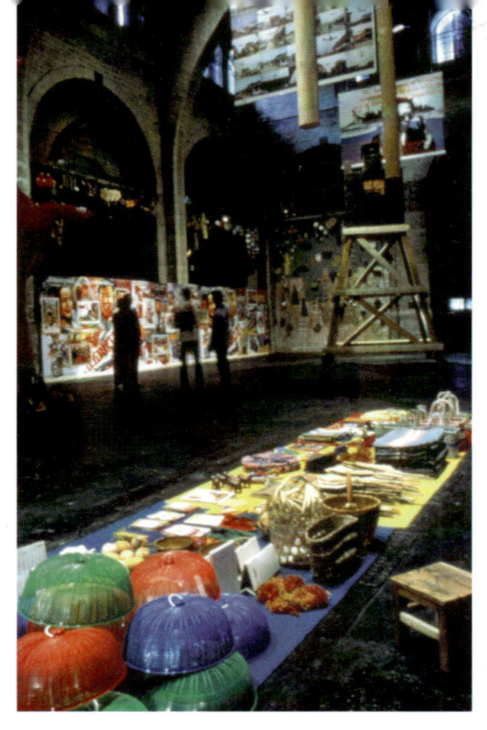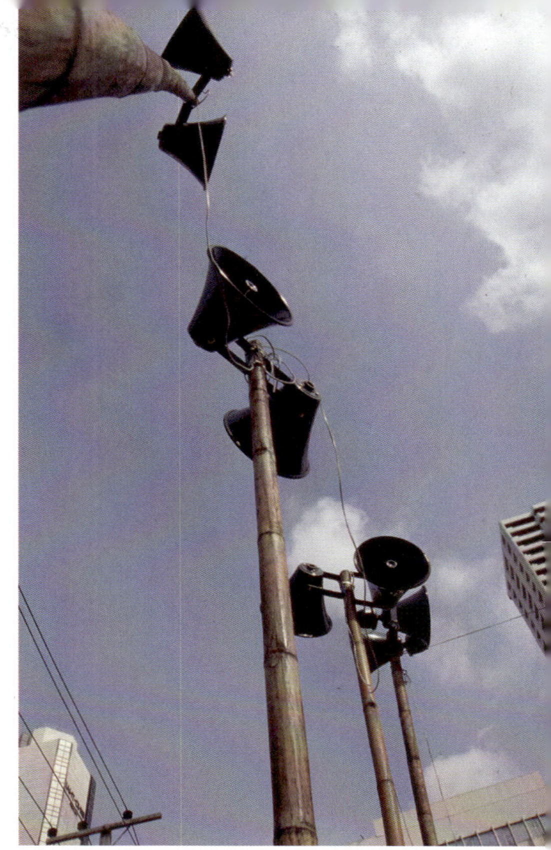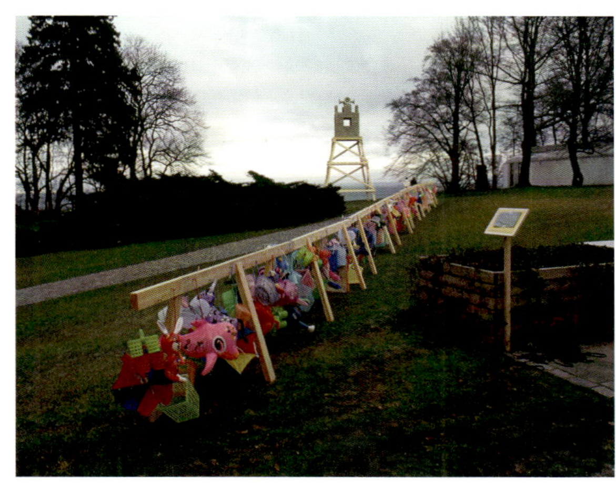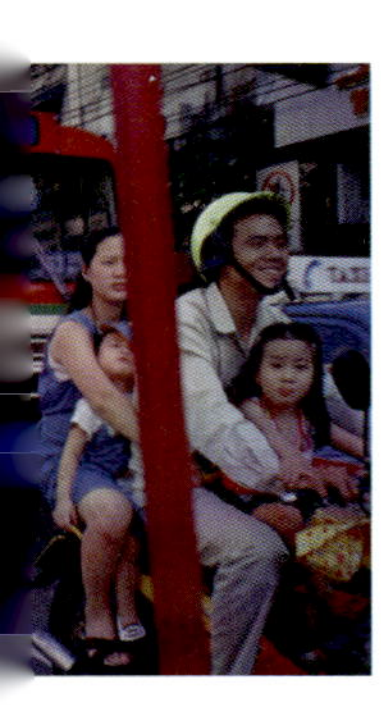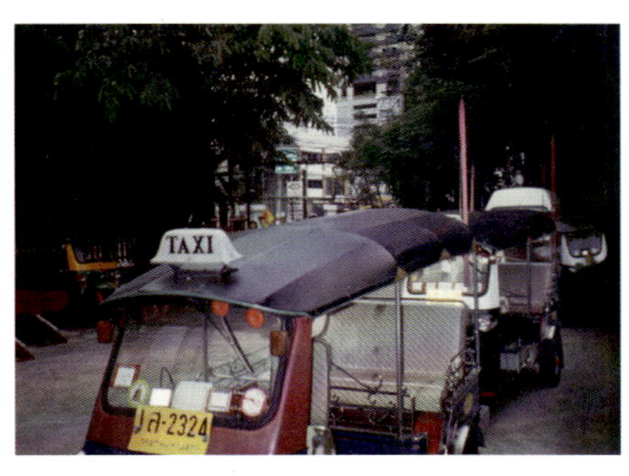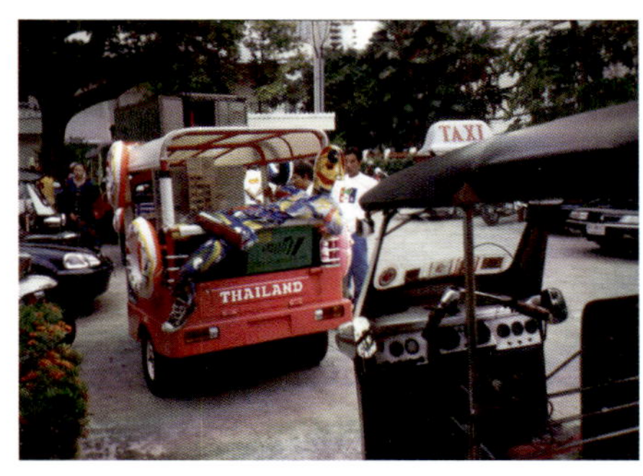

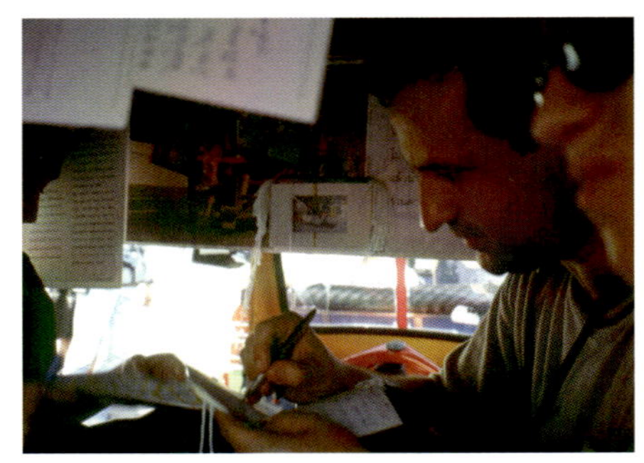
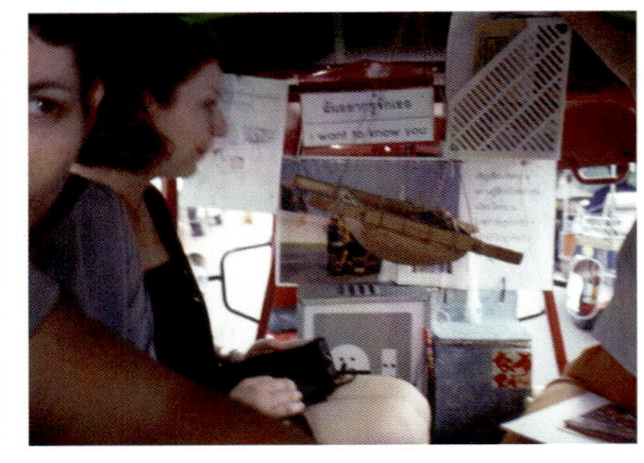
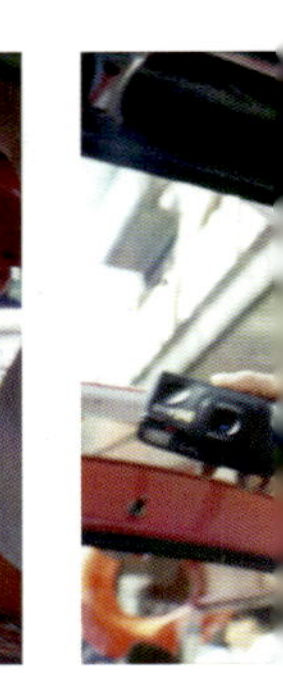
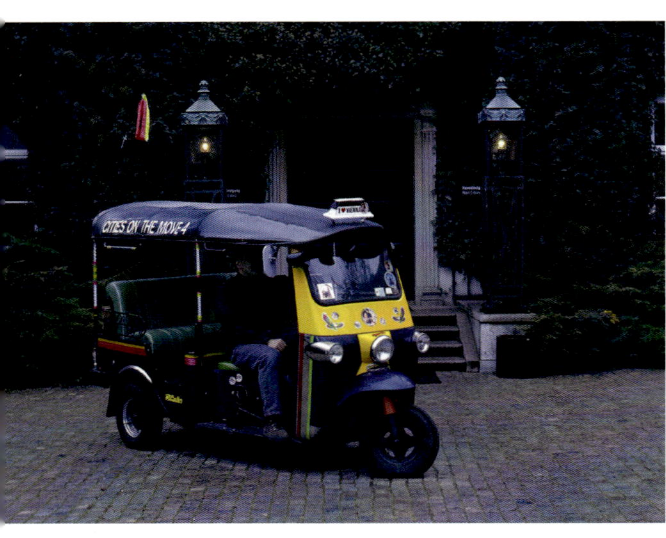

CITIES ON THE MOVE 4

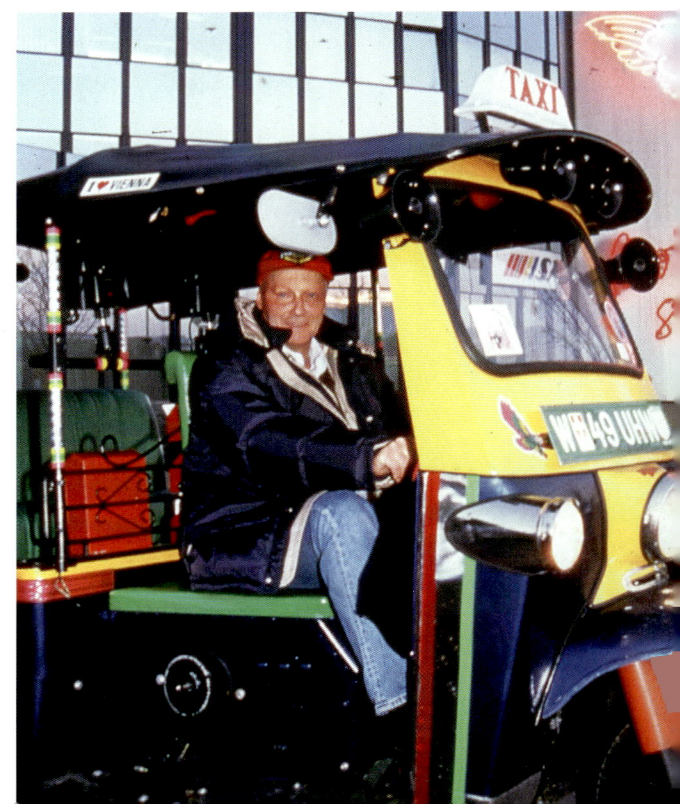

TAXI
I ♥ VIENNA

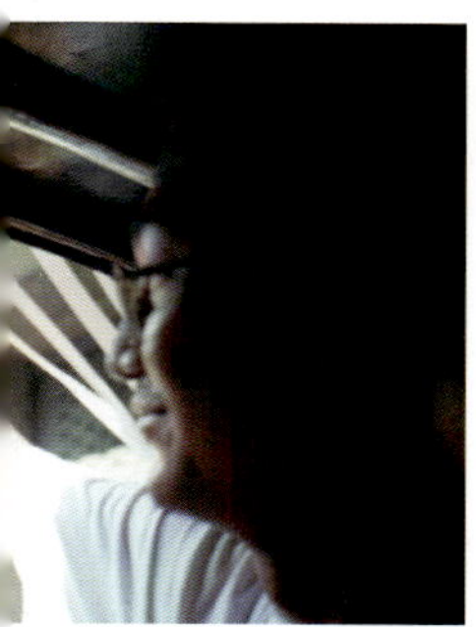
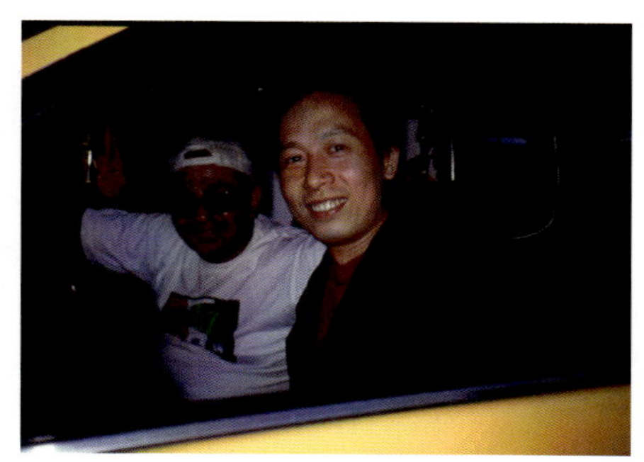
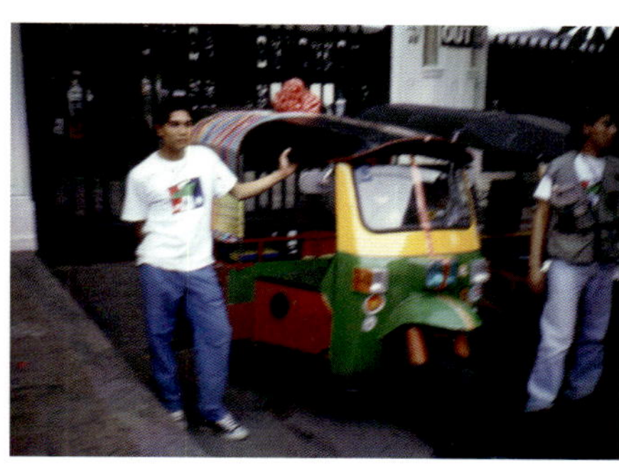

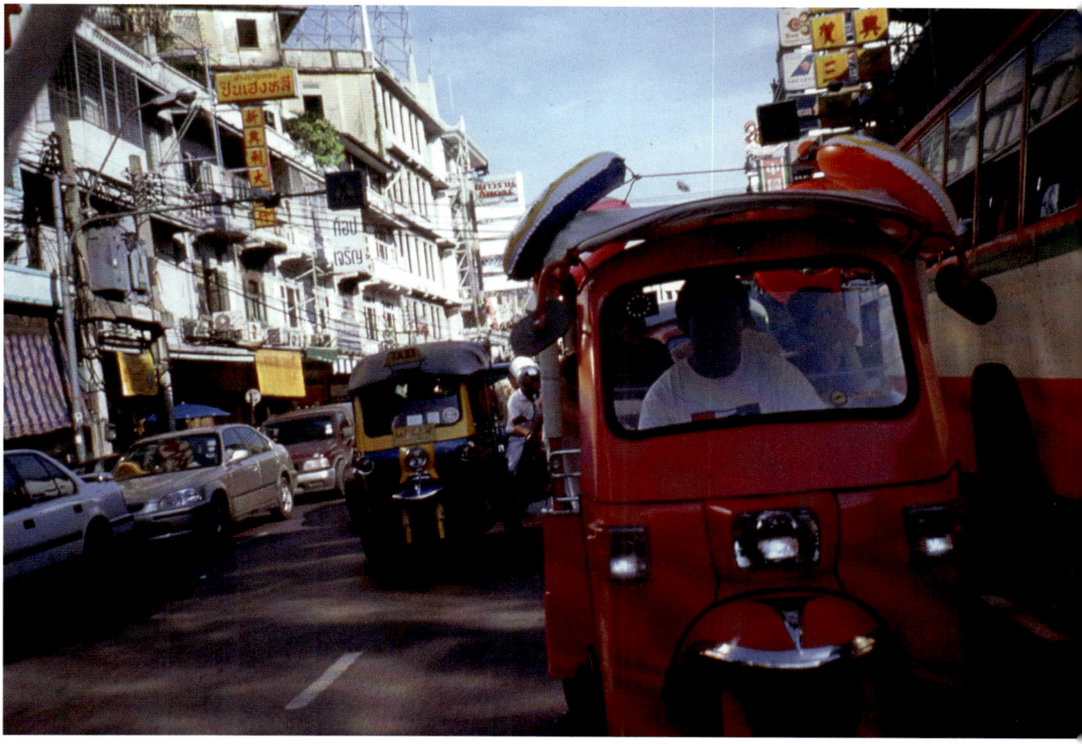

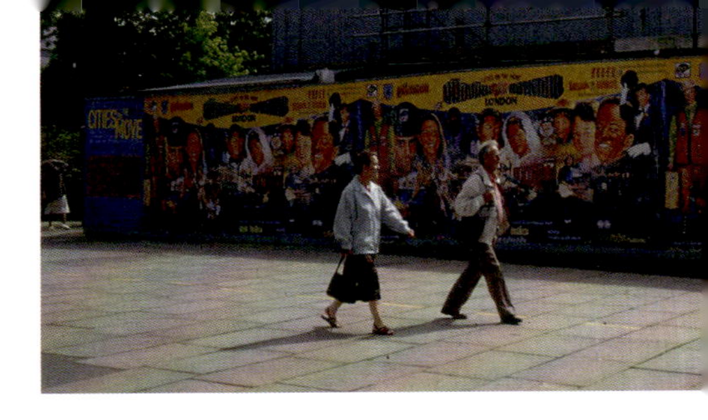

CITIES ON THE MOVE
LONDON

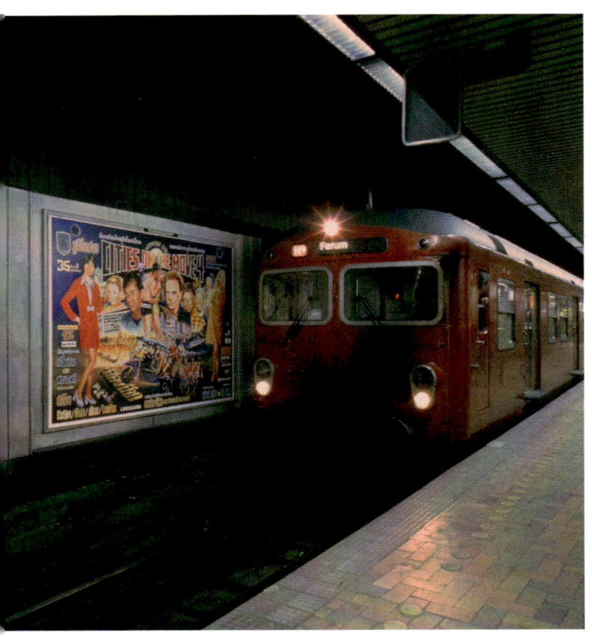

CITIES ON THE MOVE
Forum

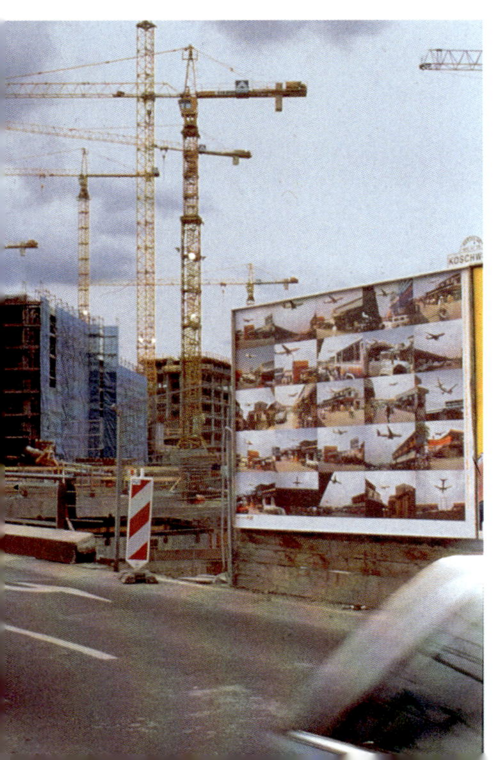

KOSCHW

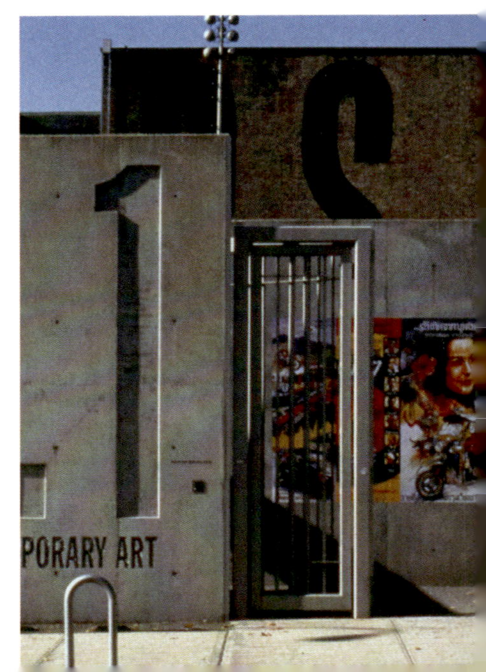

PORARY ART

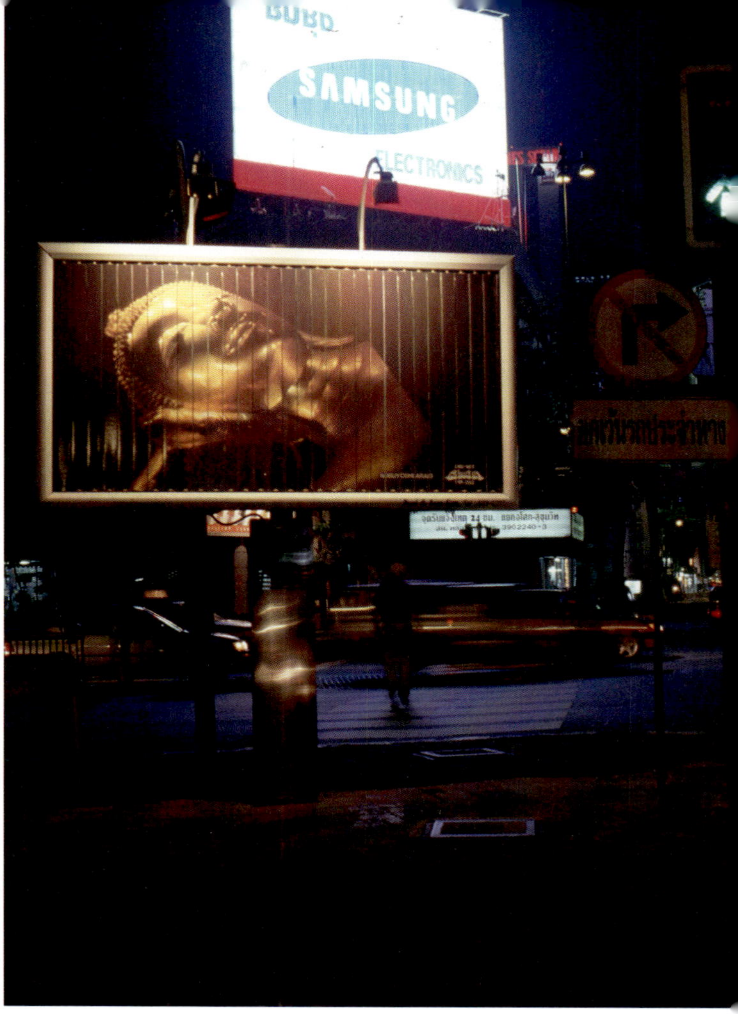

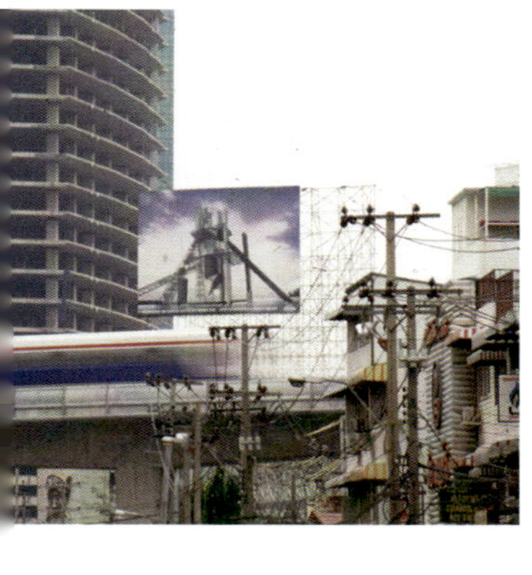

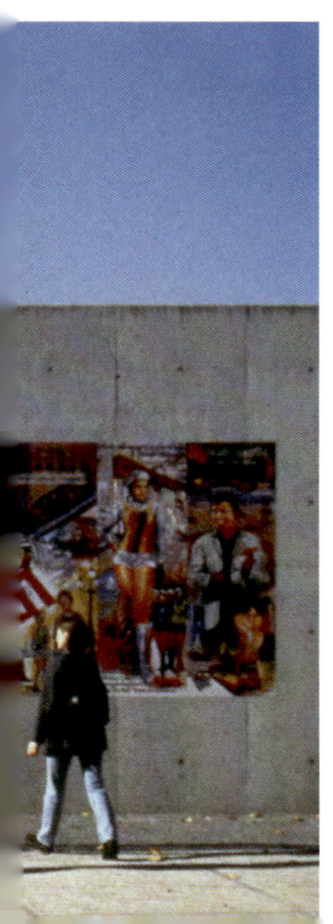

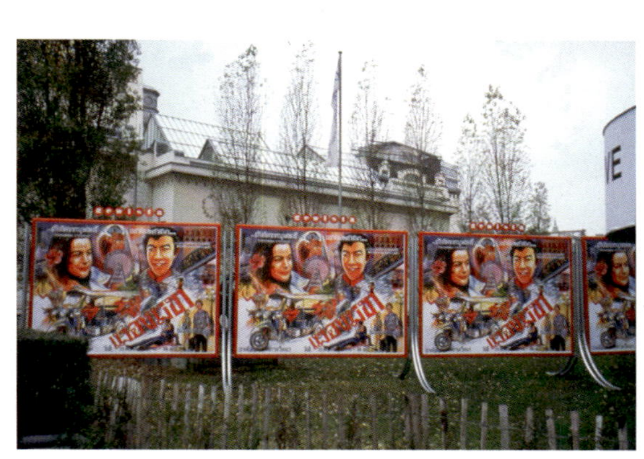

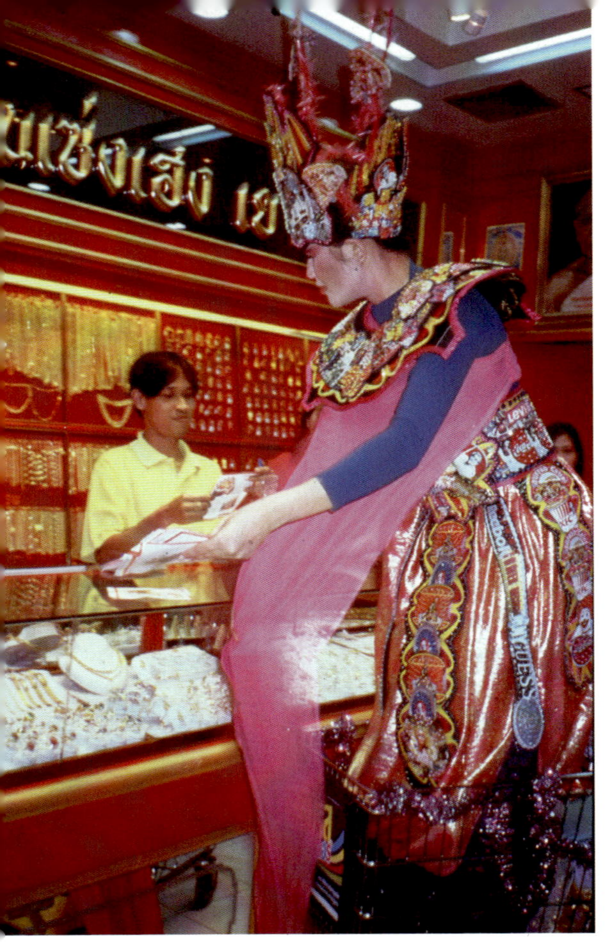
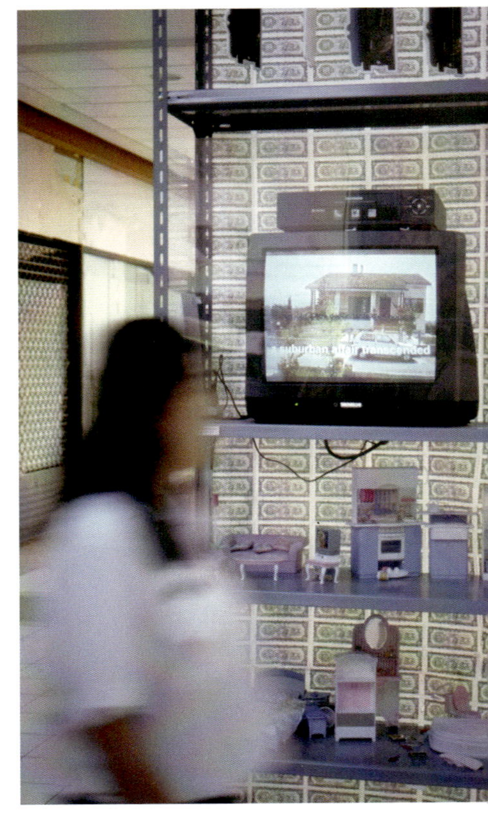
a suburban affair transcended
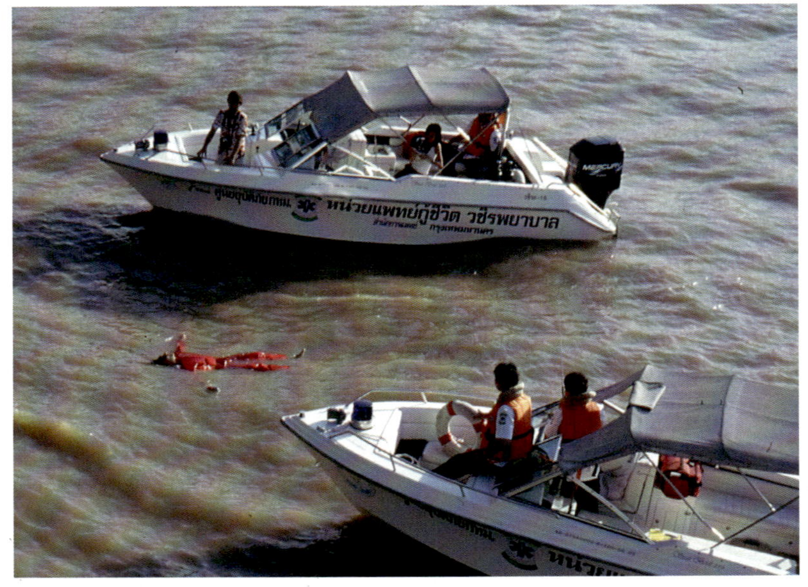

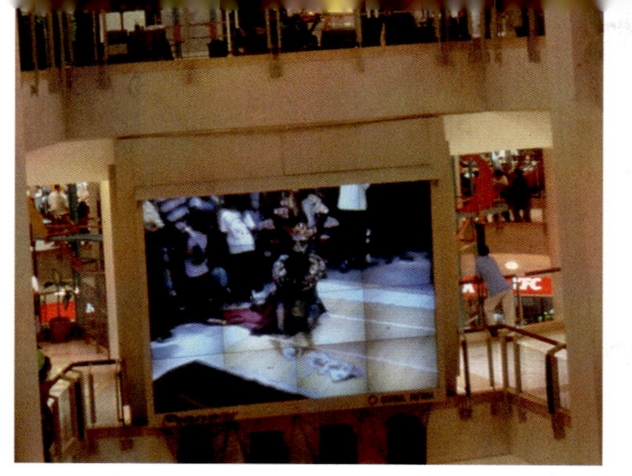
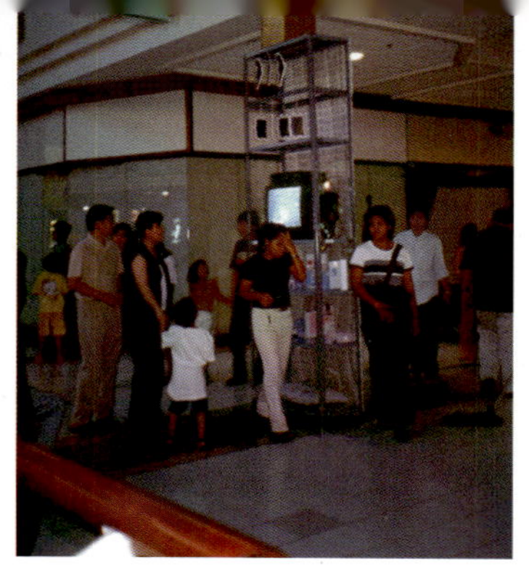

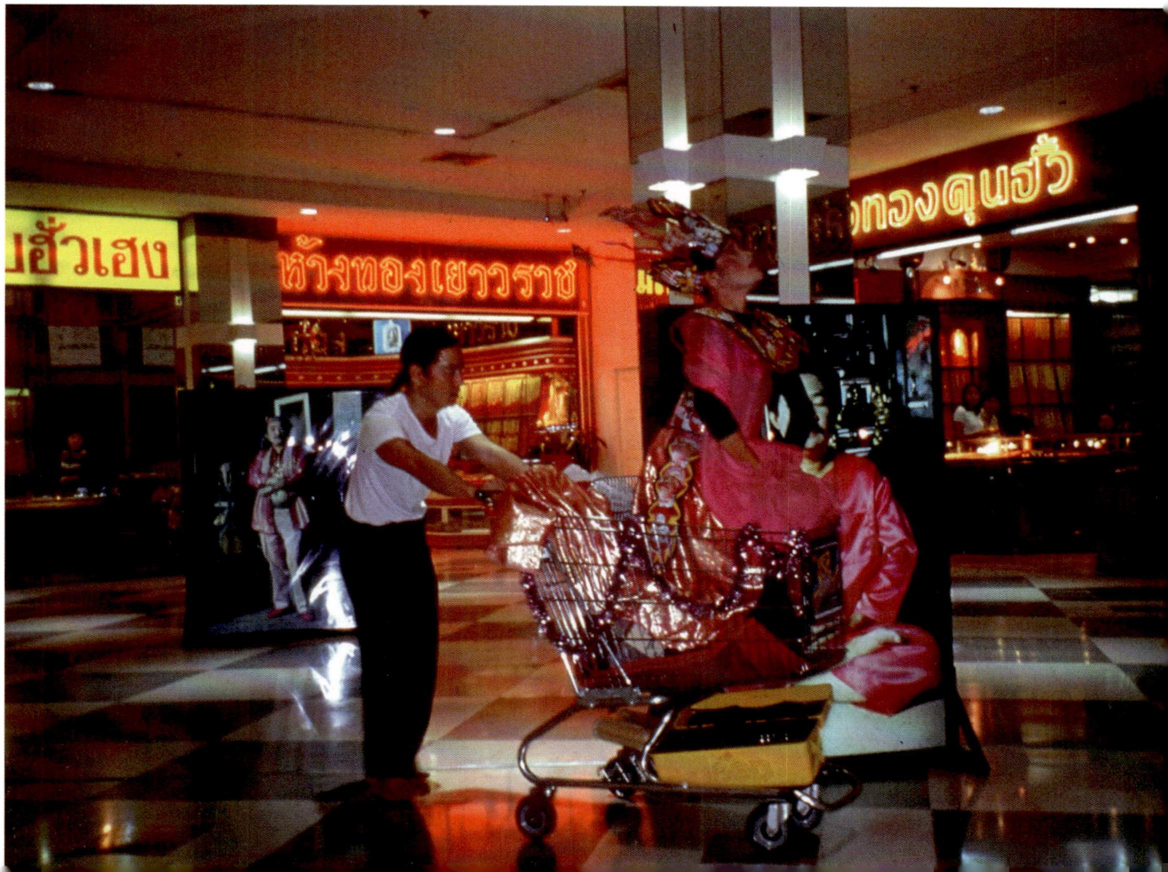

Potosí Principle: Following the Devil's Tail

Luiza Proença

Doing justice to the history of an exhibition can be a dangerous exercise, especially when the exhibition in question crosses diverse territories and world views. This is the case with 'The Potosí Principle: How Can We Sing the Lord's Song in a Strange Land?', curated by Alice Creischer, Andreas Siekmann and Max Jorge Hinderer Cruz and presented in 2010–11 in three different countries in Europe and South America: at the Museo Nacional Centro de Arte Reina Sofía (MNCARS), Madrid; Haus der Kulturen der Welt (HKW), Berlin; and the Museo Nacional de Arte (MNA) and the Museo Nacional de Etnografía y Folklore (MUSEF), La Paz. Its stories are multiplied by the range of documentation produced for the occasion and thereafter. It was documented at the time through a comprehensive catalogue – with research images, reports on the process, installation views, interviews with collaborators and complementary texts – and an independent 'process blog' maintained by the curators on Wordpress.[1] In addition, there is *Princípio Potosí Reverso*, a 'counter-catalogue' that emerged from the project, produced by Silvia Rivera Cusicanqui and El Colectivo (today, Colectivo Ch'ixi) to provide a deeper reading of the complexity of Andean cultural life and express a sense of dissidence towards the wider curatorial direction.[2]

More than an exhibition, 'The Potosí Principle' can be understood as a long-term project that risked a self-critical analysis of the functioning of art in the colonial-modern ideology, calling into question some fundamental principles of the Western political-philosophical tradition, such as justice and the law.[3] Initially called 'Inverted Modernity', the project relocated the origins of modernity from Europe to Bolivia, where, between the sixteenth and eighteenth centuries, huge amounts of silver were extracted from the mines of Potosí as part of a violent process of exploitation that propelled the growth of global capitalism. 'The Potosí Principle' argued that the mass production and circulation of images played a crucial role in the imposition of this system, spreading fear and terror in order to indoctrinate Andean peoples. To develop this analysis, the curatorial team commissioned around twenty artists, researchers and activists from different countries to establish a dialogue with 22 selected colonial paintings related to Potosí. The project was notable for extending its analysis to the perpetuation of neocolonial relationships of dominance and exploitation in current centres of economic power, implicating in turn the exhibitionary and institutional systems of contemporary art.

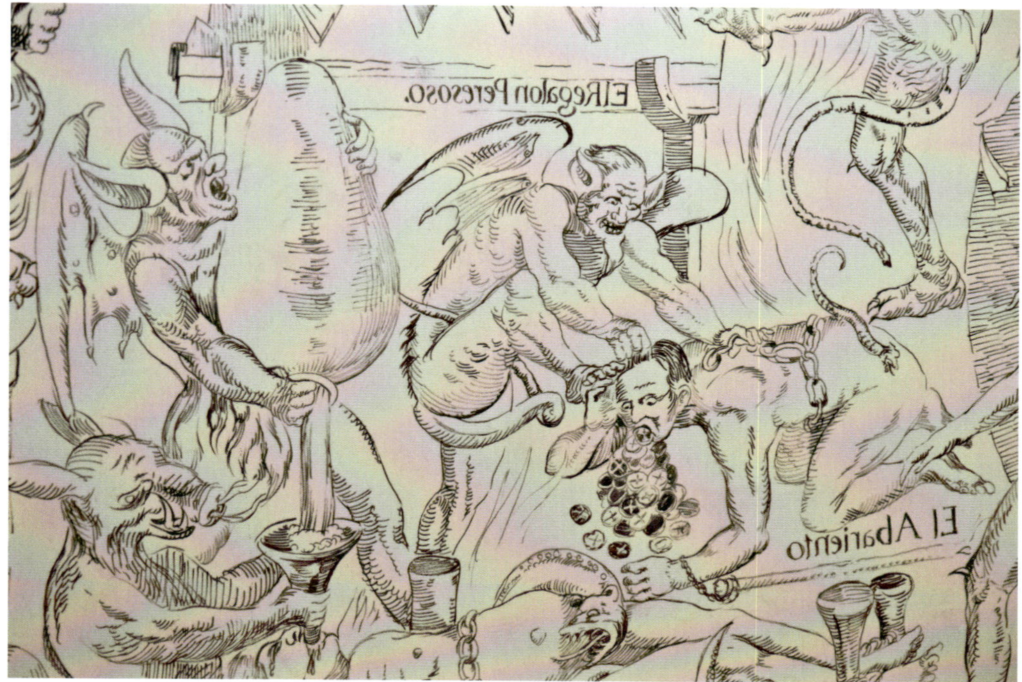

Detail of *Infierno*, 1739, reproduced by Quirin Bäumler, 2010. Photography: Sebastian Bolesch/Haus der Kulturen der Welt (HKW). Courtesy HKW

The 'principle' in the title is thus an allusion to the 'intense process of economic accumulation that could be considered the beginning of a global system of intricate material and symbolic flows: Modernity'.[4] The project resonates with Silvia Federici's account of the function of violence against women, peasantry and Amerindian populations as part of the 'primitive accumulation' at the origins of capitalism. As Federici argues, 'when feudal relations were already giving way to economic and political institutions typical of mercantile capitalism',[5] the number of women tried as witches reached its peak in Europe, while in the New World the notion of devil worship was a pretext for Spanish conquerors to subjugate and kill Amerindian peoples.

Borrowing from Félix Deleuze and Gilles Guattari's philosophy, for whom 'to think is always to follow the witch's flight' – a process that 'belong[s] to the order of dreams, of pathological processes, esoteric experiences, drunkenness and excess'[6] – this essay follows the snaking tail of the devil in thinking about a complex dynamic, of resistance to and complicity with diabolical forces, as developed in 'The Potosí Principle'.

The Devil and the Capitalist Infernal Alternatives

They come in many shapes. Creatures that are either red or greenish; half human, half animal; sometimes horned and tailed; with protruding ears and sharp teeth; beak-like noses, hooves and claws; the eyes red and wide; sometimes winged, other times covered in fur. There are approximately twenty such demonic figures depicted in the right half of *La Muerte* (*The Death*), a symmetrical composition painted in 1739: one side depicts the peaceful reality of

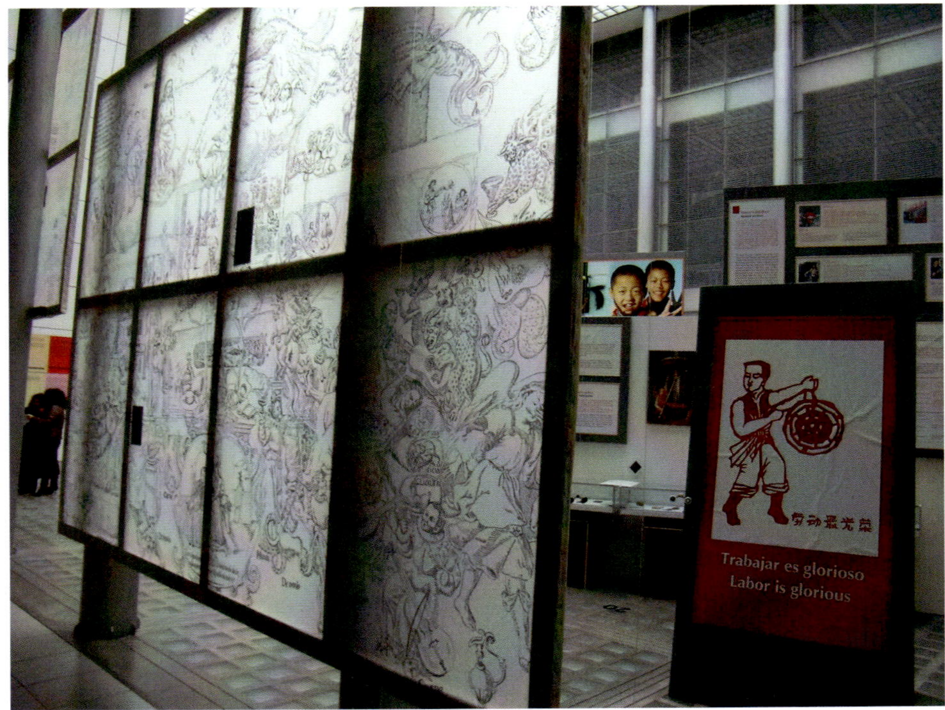

a 'good person' during its time on earth; the other shows the painful afterlife of sinners and heretics. In the middle, two skeletons stand atop an altar to present their judgement, sentencing the dying person to heaven or hell for eternity. The painting hangs in a church in Caquiaviri, a small Bolivian city where many indigenous people were recruited to work in Potosí's mines. *La Muerte* presents the dichotomies in which the Christian imaginary dwells: divine justice, which separates the world into good/heaven and evil/hell; and the opposition of human and nature, where humans are portrayed as virtuous whereas animals represent the seven deadly sins.[7] In the exhibition 'The Potosí Principle', a spectral image of *La Muerte* by the German artist Quirin Bäumler appeared as a tracing, in silver pencil on transparent plastic, alongside a tracing of *Infierno* (*Hell*), another one of a series of five *postrimerías* paintings in the Caquiaviri church that depict the torture, pain and terror inflicted by the devil in his domain.

Alongside the theme of the Last Judgment, *postrimerías* (pictorial representations about life after death) became common in South America in the seventeenth and eighteenth centuries, particularly in those churches designated for indigenous populations. Such images, whose iconography was transmitted from Europe through engravings, were understood as an important means of imposing the ethics and morals preached by the evangelists in the colonies.[8] In the case of *La Muerte*, with its iconography bearing similarities to the popular *ars moriendi* (art of dying) genre in Europe, references to Amerindian

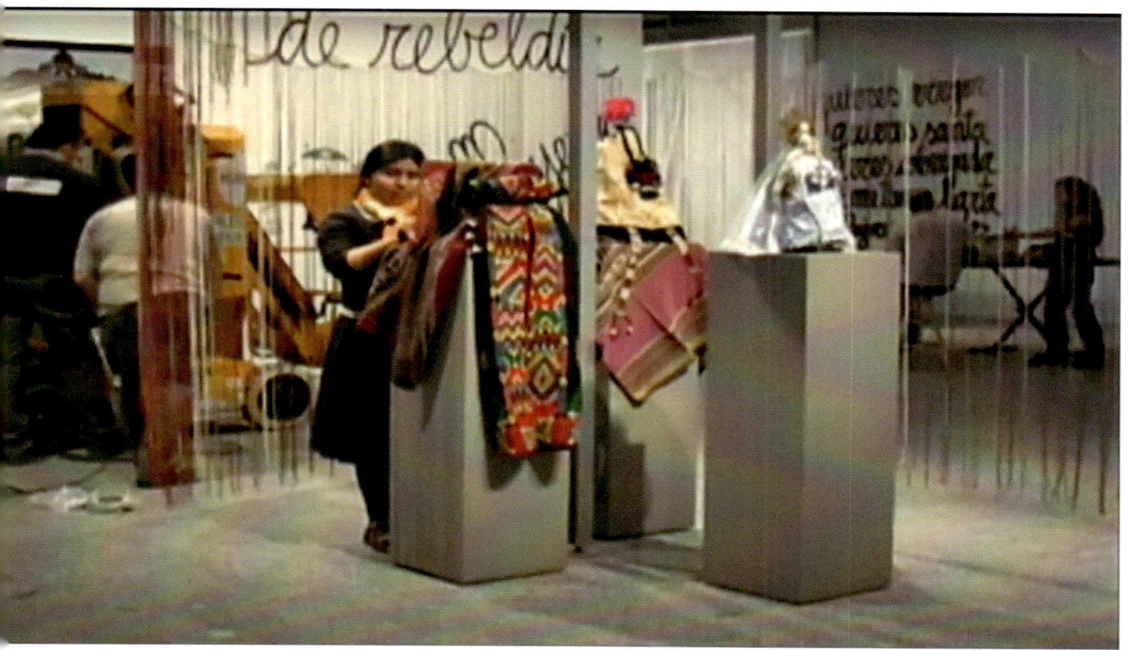

rituals – such as a demon flying with a ceremonial drinking vessel, or *kero*, in its hands – were included as part of the colonial campaign against indigenous religious practices.

As described by Michael Taussig, the introduction of the devil by the colonisers takes on the symbolic contours of the new relations of production and exchange, simultaneously destroying the meanings of local pre-capitalist practices, which they viewed as diabolical witchcraft, by establishing a 'space of death'.[9] In this account, the devil appears as mediator of the conflict between precolonial and capitalist economic systems. Addressing a similar contradiction, Isabelle Stengers and Philippe Pignarre define capitalism itself as 'a system of sorcery without sorcerers'; that is, 'a system operating in a world which judges that sorcery is only a simple "belief"'.[10] If the craft of the sorcerer is to activate multiple living forces, capitalism instead sentences everybody to accept its 'infernal alternatives', weakening the capacity of creation and resistance.

'The Potosí Principle' embodied this contradiction in the way it foregrounded the potential violence implied in its own curatorial practice. The exhibition had an open layout that visitors were invited to meander through, which encouraged the feeling of multiple perspectives, a contrast from the supposed neutrality of white walls and conventional exhibition dividers. Yet the logic of the exhibition suggested contradictory meanings: the open layout might also encourage the sensation of witnessing a narrative all at once, i.e. the totalising universalism of an idealised Enlightenment subject. Such ambivalence surfaced in the curatorial position:

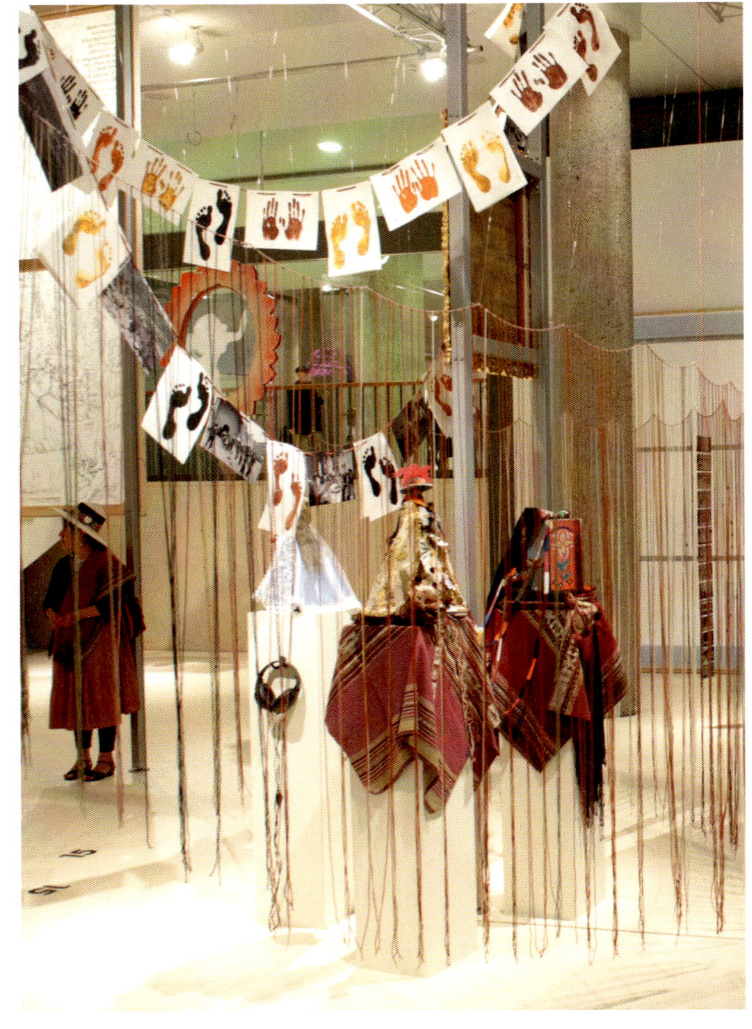

[T]he museum, too, gains a view of itself and acts like this spectral subject, enraptured by its existence, blind for its being a product, free from legitimation or the need for it. Have you noticed something? What we have been trying to do this entire time is to lead you and ourselves out of the belly of a fetish.[11]

The exhibition guide highlighted the lingering horrors of the art institution – in its structures, displays, hierarchies, divisions of labour, etc. – and its historical role in the colonial process – whether in Berlin, Madrid or La Paz.[12] The guide, and catalogue, informed us of the conflicts and negotiations experienced during the planning of the exhibition, as well as incidents such as loan refusals, making explicit the power relations between art institutions: many Bolivian communities feared that works on loan could be stolen by European museums, while the latter feared repatriation requests for the stolen artefacts in their holdings.

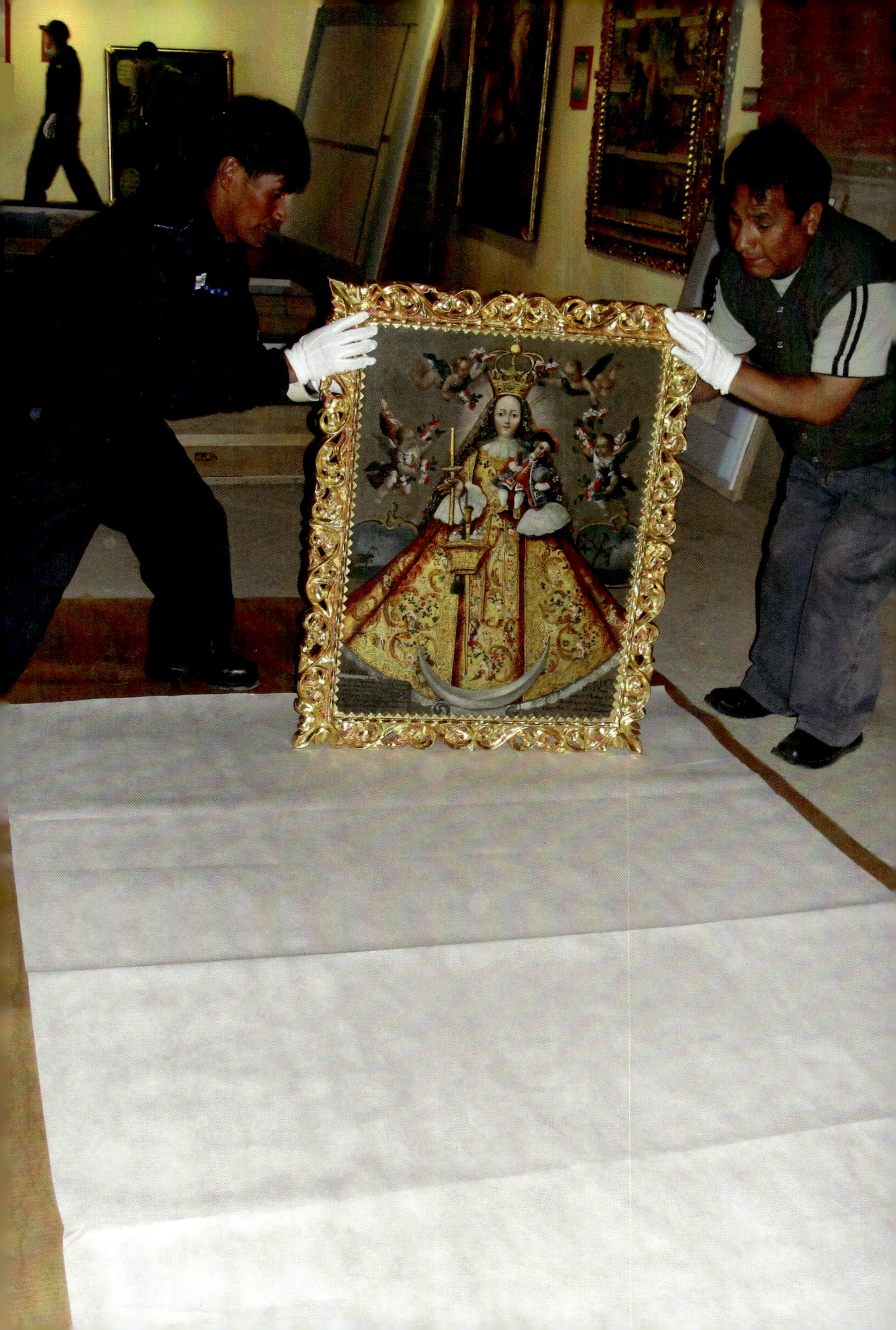

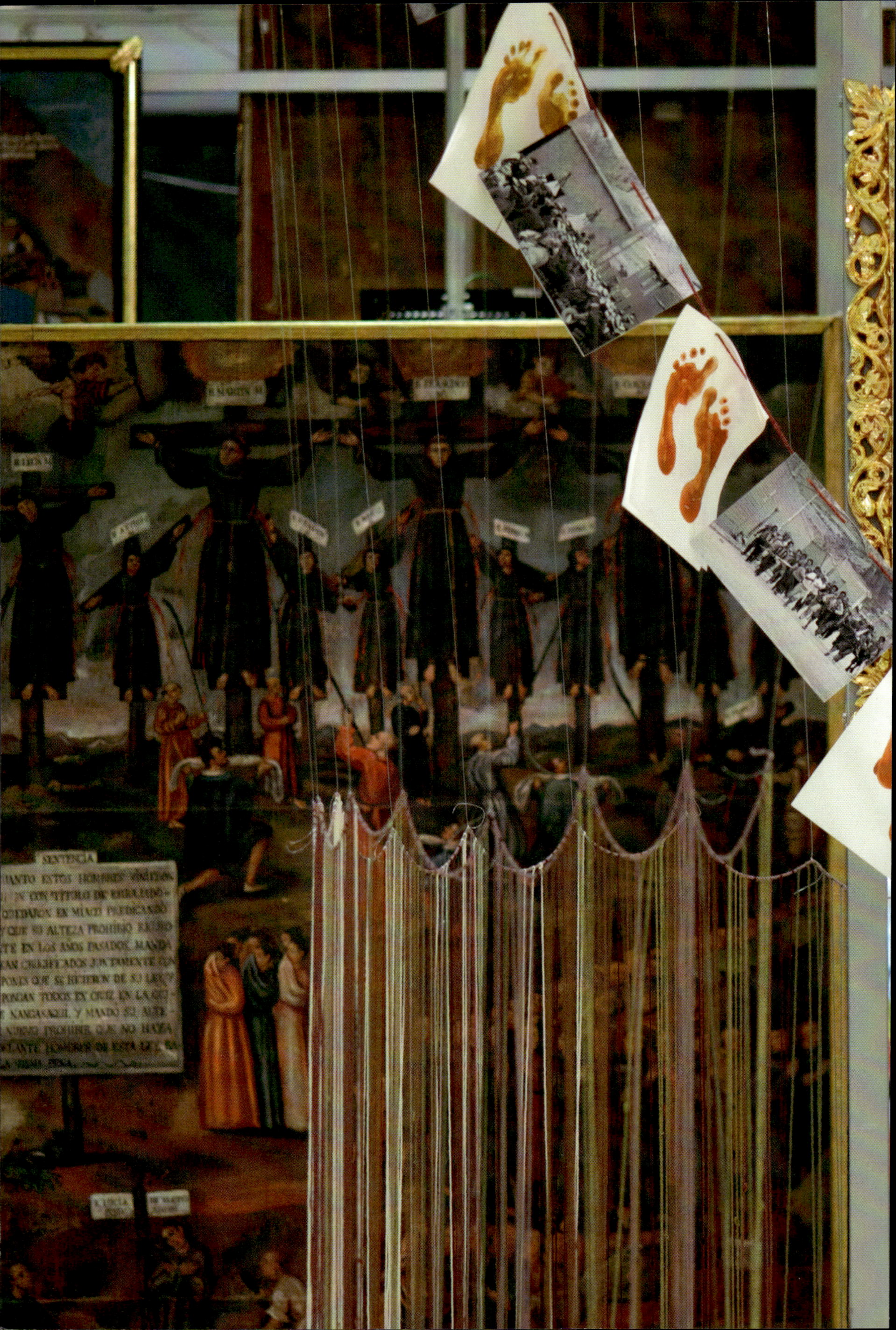

SENTENCIA
QUANTO ESTOS HOMBRES VINIERON
CON TITULO DE EMBAXADO-
QUEDARON EN MIACO PREDICANDO
Y QUE SU ALTEZA PROHIBIO RECIBO
TE EN LOS AÑOS PASADOS, MANDA
SEAN CRUCIFICADOS JUNTAMENTE CON
PONES QUE SE HICIERON DE SU LEY Y
MURAN TODOS EN CRUZ EN LA CIU-
DE NANGASAQUI, Y MANDO SU ALTE-
VANDO PROHIBE, QUE NO HAZA
DELANTE HOMBRES DE ESTA LEY, SO
LA MISMA PENA

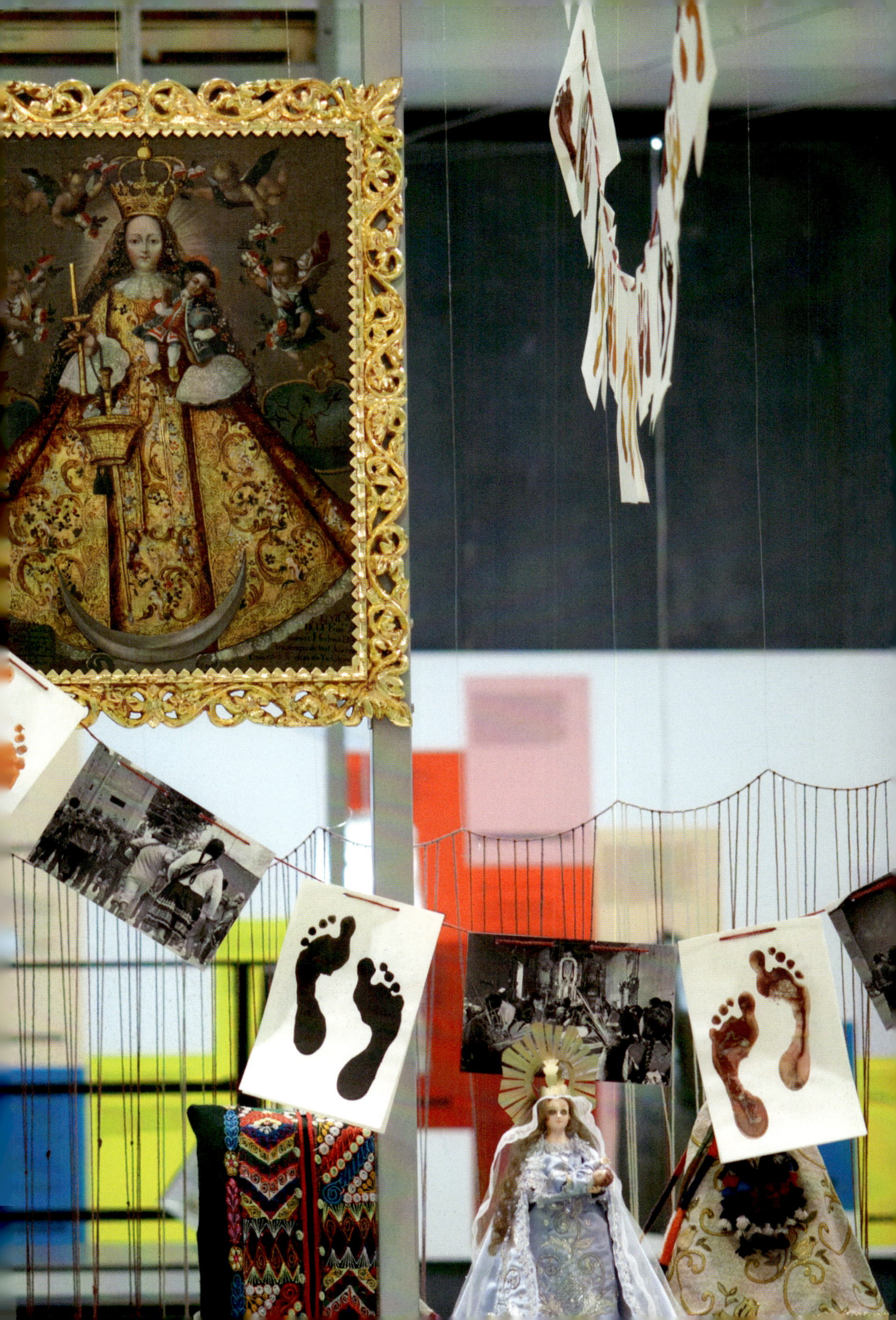

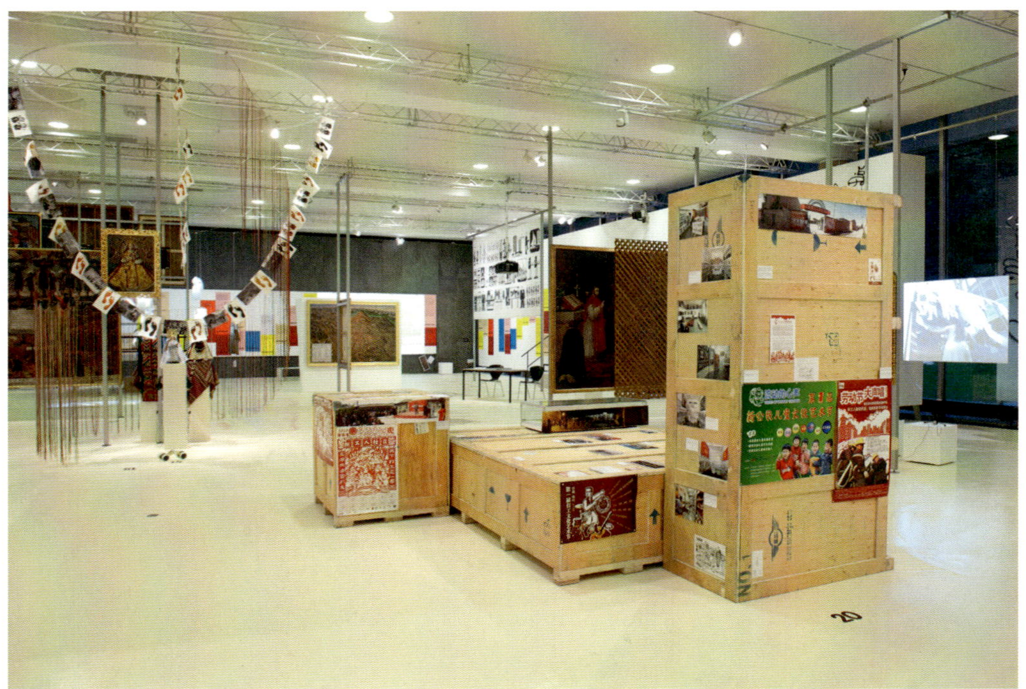

Paintings that were lent by communities in Bolivia were hung so that they did not touch the walls of the galleries, an aspect of the display that was very important to participating artist Elvira Espejo. This was a symbolic attempt at avoiding adherence to the dominant institutions, which also made it possible to see both sides of the artworks. Espejo, who is from the *ayllu* of Qaqachaca, said that throughout the exhibition one could experiment with other points of view in the same way that its artists and artworks enabled perspectives from different positions in the world: 'It is not to treat our community as if we were the only people on Earth.'[13] As they developed the project, the curators invited artists from cities they were interested in relating to Potosí, and these artists then invited others, extending and de-hierarchising the curatorship in a loose international network of shared affinities. We may imagine this curatorial effort in creating alliances and activating forces to overcome the horrors of colonial-capitalist trauma as a form of sorcery, casting spells from various places in a process of diabolical witchcraft. Meanwhile, the devil resurfaces as an immanent entity alongside other settler introductions to the Americas.

The Devil and Other Beings in Kinship

In Western Christian metaphysics, the devil may be seen as 'a bailiff' to reassert 'God as exclusive ruler' and to empty the world from 'competing influences'.[14] However, in the colonies, he was incorporated into Andean Amerindian imagery as a complex entity who could be domesticated or colluded with. In describing *La Muerte*, the exhibition guide briefly drew attention to an ambiguous scene in which a devil covers the mouth of an indigenous man apparently about to confess his supposed sins to a priest. For the catalogue, Max Jorge

156

Hinderer Cruz further developed this idea:

> [W]*hat in the foreground seems to be an allusion to the fault of the indigenous population regarding the Spanish Crown can also be read in another way: as shown by the adoration of El Tío (the Uncle) in the mines of Potosí, the devil, and the inhabitants of hell, should not necessarily be adversaries of the indigenous, but be assumed as an ally – according to the principle of the* pacha, *a deity who is in charge of maintaining the balance between 'giving to the earth' and 'taking from the earth' (also between life and death). Consequently, the painting contains an encrypted message that is invisible to the Christian point of view. This interpretation represents an invisible political subversion that escapes the hegemonic doctrine ('Don't say things that can be seen as sins!') and unites the indigenous community through the alternative principle of common understanding.*[15]

In the main chamber of almost every mine dug in the Andean mountains lies an anthropomorphic figure made of clay. It sits there, with erect phallus, horns, ears and pointy goatee; often it is surrounded by offerings such as cigarettes, coca leaves or alcoholic beverages. Considered as a god in the underworld of Cerro Rico de Potosí and other mines, this figure, El Tío, is a crossover between Supay, a Quechuan entity of the inner- and underworld forces (*ukhupacha*), and the Christian devil.[16] For the miners, El Tío is at the same time the boss, the foreman and a fellow miner with whom an intimate and mutually dependent relationship develops. This is expressed through such offerings as mentioned above, as well as in popular festivals where Christian-European and Andean ancestral traditions meld in coexistence through body language. Such festivals can be understood as events in which subjectivity disconnects from the notion of divine punishment towards other forms of existence, articulated through dances, costumes, chants and collectivity.[17] The objects and clothes produced for the festivals have agency – are active and thinking – and this context implies a different perspective on the very notion of labour than that of capitalist abstraction and alienation.

The work of Elvira Espejo evokes such reconfigurations of symbolic meaning, weaving a thick textile of space, language and subjectivity, and corresponding with Silvia Rivera Cusicanqui's idea of *ch'ixi*, a 'gray' or 'stained' dimension where contradictory practices and knowledge are juxtaposed.[18] *Camino de las Santas* (*Holy Path*), Espejo's installation in 'The Potosí Principle', dealt with the appropriative history of the Virgin of Candelaria, the most worshipped deity in the region, with origins that trace back to a statue of the Virgin Mary in Tenerife, one of the Canary Islands – a stopover on the route from Spain to Hispanic America – and which came to be associated with Pachamama, or Mother Earth, by the indigenous people of the Andes. In dialogue with a painting made by Luis Niño, a well-known eighteenth-century indigenous painter in Potosí, *Camino de las Santas* was comprised also of several photographs and objects taken from a festival associated with the Mama Candelaria (the Virgin) in Espejo's community of Qaqachaka. During the festival, dancers 'dressed in ragged clothes of red and green patchwork quilt, colours associated with the devil',[19] carry a wooden box wrapped in textiles containing a small

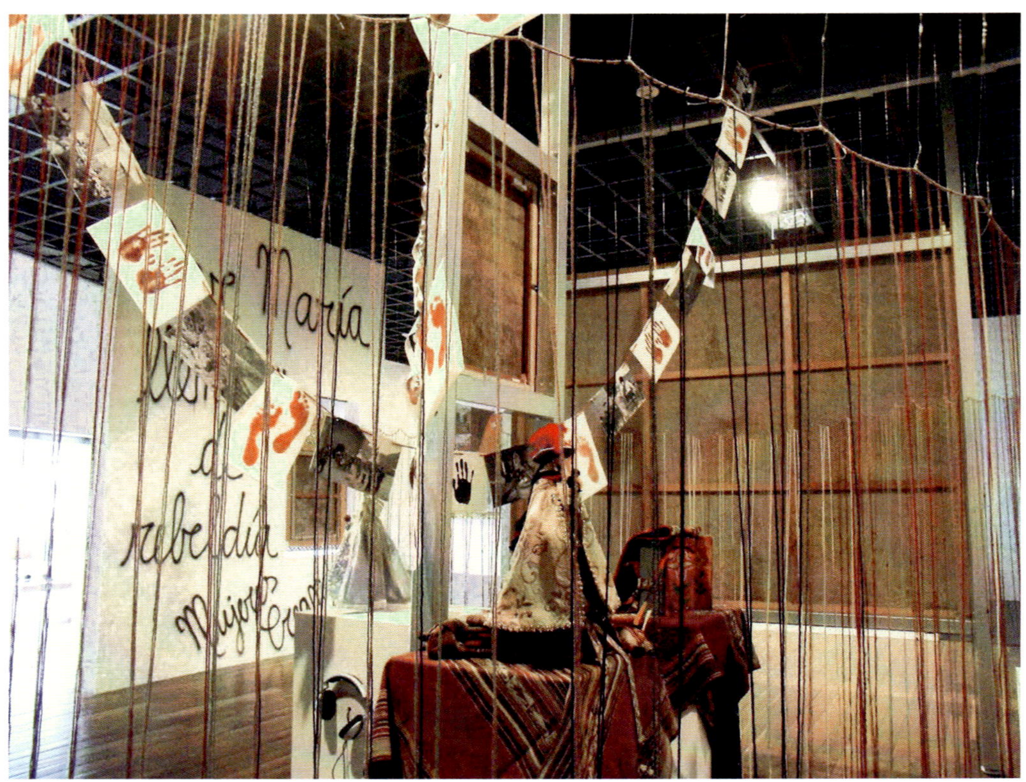

Installation view, 'The Potosí Principle', MUSEF, La Paz, 2011. Courtesy Alice Creischer and Andreas Siekmann

gold cross. The cross represents Tata Quri (the Golden Man), a powerful god/ devil from the mines of the mountain of Potosí, also strongly related to colonial Christianity. Tata Quri stands for mining and its environmental impact; therefore, it is seen as a monster making Mama Candelaria ill. 'For associating the mountain with their own bodies and for their predisposition to think history in bodily terms',[20] the women of Qaqachaka perform the action of wrapping the container box in order to tame Tata Quri. In *Camino de las Santas*, an audio device played a traditional chant, performed by Espejo herself: 'The year is over, and the penalties are over.'[21] A circle of threads spiralled down from the ceiling alluding to *khipus*, pre-Hispanic memotechnical instruments with ties to textile art. Made from wool or cotton, the knotted strings of *khipus* tell intertwined but undecipherable stories; some believe them to be related to accounting activities (suggesting a pre-capitalist economy with spiritual as well as material exchanges), while others consider them a form of writing. At the time of the exhibition, the largest collection of *khipus* in the world was at the Ethnologisches Museum Berlin, which refused to lend them for the presentation in Bolivia.[22]

By recovering *khipus* – included in the exhibition only as documentation, 'sadly un-symbolied and deprived of their epistemic density'[23] in German collections – Espejo's work played with the notion of connecting local pathways populated by dances and songs that recreate ancestral knowledges over the colonial territories raising this as a form of resistance to the space of death and terror. Much like the hidden information of *khipus*, not all elements of *Camino de las Santas* were fully accessible to everyone: even though it presented itself within the apparently common language of contemporary art installation, it did not accede to the aesthetic judgments of the Modern Subject. The devil in *La Muerte* may cover up the indigenous person's mouth to prevent him from being a victim of moral accusation, and perhaps also to resist the colonial attitude of wanting to understand and explain everything in the world, of being 'hungry to listen'.[24]

'The Potosí Principle' was one of the largest art exhibitions ever held in Bolivia, whose cultural institutions are not typically focussed on international contemporary art. *Camino de las Santas* was presented in the colonial building of MUSEF; two years later, Espejo would become MUSEF's director. As a nation-state institution, MUSEF's collection consists of archaeological, historical and ethnographic materials from Bolivian territory, which were presented through a historical narrative that suggested the stability of indigenous peoples at the expense of the dynamism of modern states.[25] Under the directorship of Espejo, MUSEF began to reverse the legacy of coloniality and violence by reorganising the collection in accordance with the materiality and processes of manufacturing for each 'object', and in collaboration with local communities with their own ways of knowing. Seen as subjects with political agency and social life, in recent displays the 'objects' do not nullify the stories that constitute them, resisting commodity fetishism. They are shown according to their own ontology: as living beings that interact with the world, able to animate the relationships between individuals or groups of people, creating networks of exchange.

When Espejo affirmed the importance of experimenting with different perspectives through 'The Potosí Principle', she also pointed in the direction of an art world beyond the inescapable, infernal and deeply divided one we currently inhabit; that is, in the direction of an art world where multiple ways of living, knowing and creating can coexist. Understanding exhibition-making as a collaborative process of interweaving connections, the curators were able to 'smell the smoke that demands we decide whether we are heirs to the witches or the witch hunters',[26] and they attempted to transform the art institution from a space of death and an agent of violence (as per Christian/European dualisms and devils) into an approach of negotiation, following El Tío and the mountains of the mines. Heretical exercises like this require the creation of dangerous alliances, a necessary risk in reclaiming politics as 'a relation of disagreement among worlds'.[27] There is no single formula in this – each institution or cultural agent needs to find their own way of breaking the capitalist spell. In these multiple forms of resistance, which can only take place underground, it may be necessary to descend into hell. The purpose is not mining, but a sort of archaeology to escape the horrifying frameworks of modern law and justice, and to reclaim art as witchcraft.

Notes

1 See Alice Creischer, Andreas Siekmann and Max Jorge Hinderer, *The Potosí Principle: How Can We Sing the Lord's Song in a Strange Land? Colonial Image Production in the Global Economy* (exh. cat.), Madrid: Museo Nacional Centro de Arte Reina Sofía (MNCARS), 2010 (a Spanish-language version was produced in Bolivia at the curators' initiative and followed by a second edition with new translations, published in Spain; unless noted, catalogue quotations in the present text are my translations from the latter Spanish-language edition); and Potosí Principle Process blog, available at potosiprincipleprocess.wordpress.com. At the time of writing, 'The Potosí Principle' is also being revisited for an archival presentation at HKW, as a continuation of the project as well as an exploration of its 'blind spots': 'Potosí Principle – Archive', HKW, 29 April–11 July 2021, hkw.de/en/programm/projekte/2021/potosi_prinzip_archiv/start.php.

2 See *Princípio Potosí Reverso*, Madrid: MNCARS, 2010. Silvia Rivera Cusicanqui, as a leading member of the Bolivian collective El Colectivo, was invited to be part of the curatorial team of 'Potosí Principle' and to produce, from local stories, a 'reverse' narrative about the colonial paintings to be displayed in the exhibition. El Colectivo, however, distrusted the analytical and non-representational aspect of the exhibition, and some disagreements involving the curators and MNCARS could not be resolved. According to Cusicanqui, the group decided to consult a coca leaf with Aymara healers who advised them to participate only through a book, because 'the only God [the other curators] know is science' (S.R. Cusicanqui, *Un mundo ch'ixi es posible. Ensayos desde um presente em crisis*, Buenos Aires: Tinta Limón, 2018, pp.58–59; translation mine). The collective's parallel contribution, invited by MNCARS director Manuel Borja-Villel as a way to mediate or perhaps provoke the dissidence, had the effect of dividing the project into two conflicting narratives, the European and the indigenous native, which has been the framework for some more recent critical appraisals of the project; yet, rather than cast 'judgement' or try to adjudicate between these two conflicting positions, my intention in the present text is to approach the project in terms of a more complex interrelation and multiplicity of narratives.

3 For instance, one of the four conceptual axes of the exhibition was titled 'There are human rights to have a right over humans', addressing the contradiction and the 'monstruous' facet of the modern universal rights as processes of subjectivation and subjugation between humans and non-humans.

4 Introductory text published on the exhibition map of MUSEF's exhibition, available at https://potosiprincipleprocess.wordpress.com/2011/02/11/fold-out-desplegable-mna-musef-la-paz/. Translation mine.

5 Silvia Federici, *Caliban and the Witch: Woman, the Body and the Primitive Accumulation*, New York: Autonomedia, 2004, p.166. The central axis of the exhibition 'The Potosí Principle' was titled 'There is a primitive accumulation that is merely so called'.

6 Gilles Deleuze and Félix Guattari, *What is Philosophy?* (trans. Hugh Tomlinson and Graham Burchell), New York: Columbia University Press, 1994, p.41.

7 In *La Muerte*, one can identify that the peacock is pride, the frog is greed, the goat is lust, the donkey is laziness, the jaguar is anger, the pig is gluttony and the sheep is envy. It is worth mentioning that witches and devils have always been associated with the goat, bestial behaviors and unbridled libido.

8 Many of these paintings in the Andes refer to a compendium by the Jesuit Eusebio of Nieremberg on life after death that became part of the editorial programme of the Plantin printing house in Antwerp and a missionary document for Jesuits in Latin America. Therefore, attached to the backs of several paintings in 'The Potosí Principle' were copies of original engravings that served as models for image production in the Andes. For an in-depth look at colonial paintings in the Andes, see Teresa Gisbert and Andrés Mesa, *Los grabados, el 'juicio final' y la idolatria andina en el mundo andino*, La Paz: GRISO-Universidad de Navarra / Fundación Visión Cultural, 2011.

9 While in *The Devil and Commodity Fetishism in South America* (Chapel Hill: The University of North Carolina Press, 1980) Michael Taussig describes the devil as a mediator after the introduction of the commodity fetishism by capitalist economy, in *Shamanism, Colonialism, and the Wild Man: A Study in Terror and Healing* (Chicago: The University of Chicago Press, 1986) he examines colonialism in South America through the culture of terror and the healing possibilities in shamanic practices or sorcery to subvert the terror.

10 Philippe Pignarre and Isabelle Stengers, *Capitalist Sorcery: Breaking the Spell*, London: Palgrave Macmillan, 2011.

11 A. Creischer, A. Siekmann and M.J. Hinderer Cruz, *The Potosí Principle, op. cit.*, p.131.

12 In the case of the host institutions in La Paz, founded as part of a nationalist project led by Bolivian urban elites in search of modernisation, this might be better understood in terms of the 'internal' processes of colonisation that ravage South America to this day. For a more complete approach to MUSEF's colonial and nationalist origins, see Juan Villanueva Criales, 'El Museo Nacional de Etnografía y Folklore (MUSEF) de Bolivia. Historia, esfuerzos y desafios', in *Global Turns. Descolonizacion y museos*, La Paz: Bonner Altamerica-Sammlung und Studien and Plural Editores, 2020.

[13] 'Colonialismo, modernidad, arte … Princípio Potosí', interview with Elvira Espejo and Maria Galindo for *Cambio*, Bolívia, 2011. Translation mine.

[14] S. Federici, *Caliban and the Witch*, *op. cit.*, p.203. Federici affirms that it also contributes to paving the way to new or modern science as a privileged source of knowledge.

[15] A. Creischer, A. Siekmann and M.J. Hinderer Cruz, *The Potosi Principle*, *op. cit.*, p.50.

[16] Pascale Asbi suggests that the term *tío*, literally 'uncle', has no specific origin, but accentuates the allusion to the family bond and kinship between miners and the devil. See P. Asbi, *Los ministros del diablo. El trabajo y sus representaciones en las minas de Potosí*, La Paz: IRD, Instituto de Investigacion para el DesarroUo; Embajada de Francia en Bolivia; IFEA, Instituto Francés de Estudios Andinos; Fundacion PIEB, 2005, p.100.

[17] It is interesting to highlight the *diablada* (dance of the devils), in which performers wear devil masks and suits to stage the confrontation of good and evil, bringing in elements from Andean indigenous cultures.

[18] According to Cusicanqui, the notion of *ch'ixi* dialogues with René Zavaleta Mercado's concept of *sociedad abigarrada* (roughly translated, 'motley society'). She first heard about the word *ch'ixi* from the Aymara artist Víctor Zapana, who described powerful *ch'ixi* beings that are many things at the same time.

[19] Denise Y. Arnold in collaboration with Elvira Espejo and Juan Dios Yapita, 'Wa'kas, objetos poderosos y la personificación de lo material en los Andes meridionales: pugnas de exégesis sobre la economía religiosa según las experiencias del género', in Lucila Bugallo and Mario Vilca (ed.), *Wa'kas, diablos y muertos. Alteridades significantes en el mundo andino*, San Salvador de Jujuy: Universidade de Jujuy, 2016. Translation mine.

[20] *Ibid.*, p.57.

[21] Translation mine. Espejo has told me that the chant, called *maraway tukusi* in Aymara, is sung by the community when a period of authority is over or when a saint travels from the workshop where it was made to a church; originally it was made for the *wa'kas*, sacred stones covered with textiles and taken to the hill.

[22] Today the collection is housed at the Humboldt Forum, a major institution housing nearly 20,000 artefacts, mostly from former European colonies, that opened in December 2020 in the reconstructed Berlin Palace. 'The Potosí Principle' catalogue included a text from the 2010 Anti-Humboldt congress organised by Alexandertechnik in Berlin against plans for the establishment of the institution; in the summer of 2020, the Coalition of Cultural Workers Against Humboldt Forum (CCWAH) was created with a logo co-designed by Creischer. 'While in other places in the world colonial monuments were being toppled, the reconstruction of the Berlin Palace was "crowned" with a golden cross', the collective wrote. See https://ccwah.info/.

[23] S.R. Cusicanqui, *Um mundo ch'ixi es possible*, *op. cit.*, p.60.

[24] Dylan Robison argues that European settlers, when they arrived in the Americas, were 'hungry' not only for minerals but for knowledge and information. See *Hungry Listening: Resonant Theory for Indigenous Sound Studies*, Minneapolis: University of Minnesota Press, 2020.

[25] Juan Villanueva Criales, 'El Museo Nacional de Etnografía y Folklore', *op. cit.*

[26] I. Stengers, 'Reclaiming Animism', *e-flux Journal*, no.36, July 2012.

[27] Marisol de la Cadena, 'Indigenous cosmopolitics in the Andes: Conceptual reflections beyond "politics"', *Cultural Anthropology*, vol.25, no.2, 2010, p.360.

Amo la montaña / I Love the Mountain

Silvia Rivera Cusicanqui

I'd like to begin with a few notes in order to clarify what I am doing in Ecuador and where these ideas come from. I am a practitioner of an intellectual craft I have christened Sociology of the Image.[1] At its root is my experience as a university student, when I discovered that sociology was the only discipline that could connect me with the political-creative work that I consider my authentic and inescapable vocation. I did not choose art, although as a girl (playing the 'game of the future') I would tell adults I would like to be a painter. I was as much in love with Impressionists, Expressionists, Cubists and religious painters as with the weavers and stonecutters and sculptors of my own land. One day I realised that the Van Gogh painting I loved came in various reproductions, each with colours lightly altered through technologies of mechanical reproduction, which led me to ruminate over what would have been the colour of the original. That experience, together with Che Guevara's assassination in Bolivia, which touched off the revolution in the universities, and the fact that various classmates had gone off to join the guerrillas of Teoponte, made me throw away my paintbrushes and dedicate myself fully to student politics until my frustration in that sphere left me hopeless. Oscar Eid – who went on to become the right-hand man of ex-leftist Jaime Paz, who, through his pact with ex-dictator Hugo Banzer, 'crossed rivers of blood' to gain the presidency – agitated in those far-off days with Mao's little red book, talking of the worker-peasant alliance. I asked myself if this character had ever even spoken with a flesh-and-blood peasant, apart from issuing commands, and decided to depart for Apolo, a Quechua-speaking region in the department of La Paz, and learn Quechua as an 'ignorant teacher' while my students learned Spanish. We learned together using a small bilingual textbook from the Summer Language Institute that I got from the Ministry of Education (nothing as sophisticated as *Les aventures de Télémaque*, as used by Joseph Jacotot[2]).

Later, upon my return from two exiles in countries that little by little became my own, I forced myself to forget Quechua in order to learn Aymara.[3] But I will not forget the lessons of life in that remote rural region of Bolivia, those lessons Che Guevara didn't have time to learn because he was tricked into the Eurocentric view that there is only *one* history that follows a path as straight as the Nevsky Prospect. Peasants in the Chaco region are said to remark that Che suffered from his asthma even though in their marches his guerrillas were

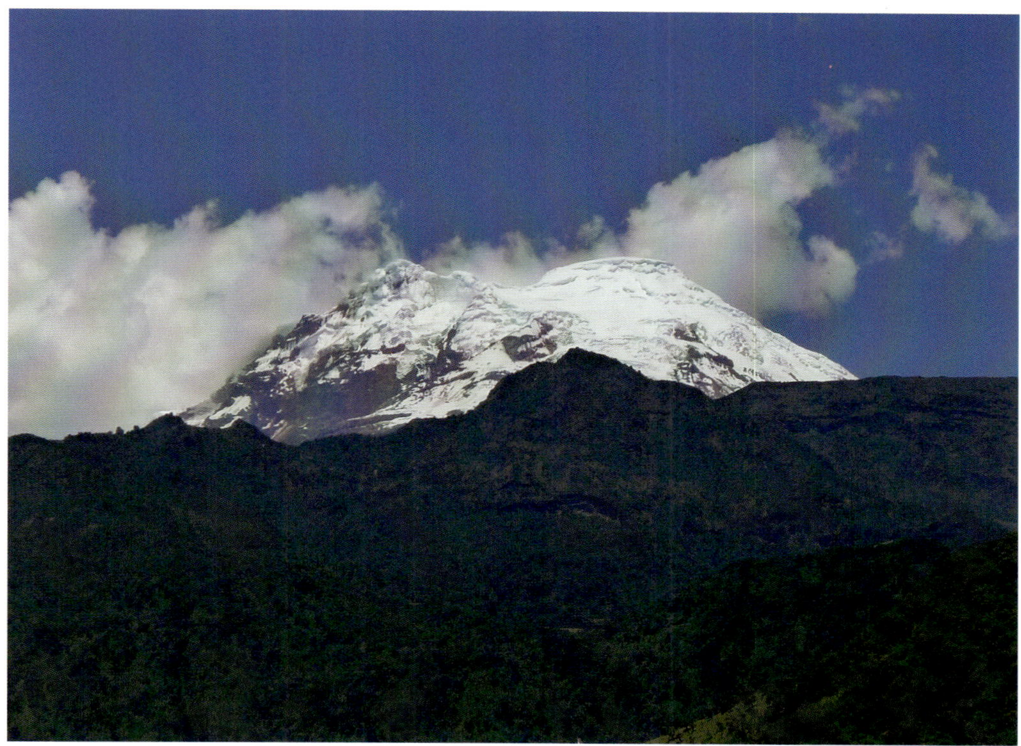

walking over the very plants that the women and healers of the region prized for their medicinal properties in curing respiratory problems like the ones that plagued our hero.[4]

What follows is an attempt to address such aporia of rational thought. I begin with three vignettes illustrating the daily acts I perform – in Ecuador or wherever I find myself – to decolonise my gaze and deconstruct the social text that underlies the everyday interactions in which I participate so that they might allow me to glimpse some allegories and memories.

1. Reminiscences at the crossroads of Papallacta

At three thousand metres above sea level, I begin to feel a great familiarity with the landscape, despite the profound humidity and fog. Of course, the Páramo Andes[5] also exist in my land, that narrow strip by which you cross from the Quimsa Cruz mountain range toward Punku, Unduavi and Chaku, and that quickly gives way to the opening of the depths of the Yungas valleys. However, it is strange that the *qiñwa* – which science has named *Polylepis* – can coexist with the *siwinqas, chillka* and ferns that are the plants at the head of the valley.[6] The *qiñwales*[7] I have seen in my land have beautiful warped trunks, but for the most part grow on the highlands and on the banks of Lake Titicaca, although my daughter Clea, who is a biologist, says that there are as many varieties as there are climate zones in the vertical landscape of the Andean cordillera. The biggest *qiñwa* forest I have ever seen was in the Stone City, in the

In Ecuador, the volcano Antisana seen from Papallacta, 2013. Photography: Libertad Gills. Courtesy the author

163

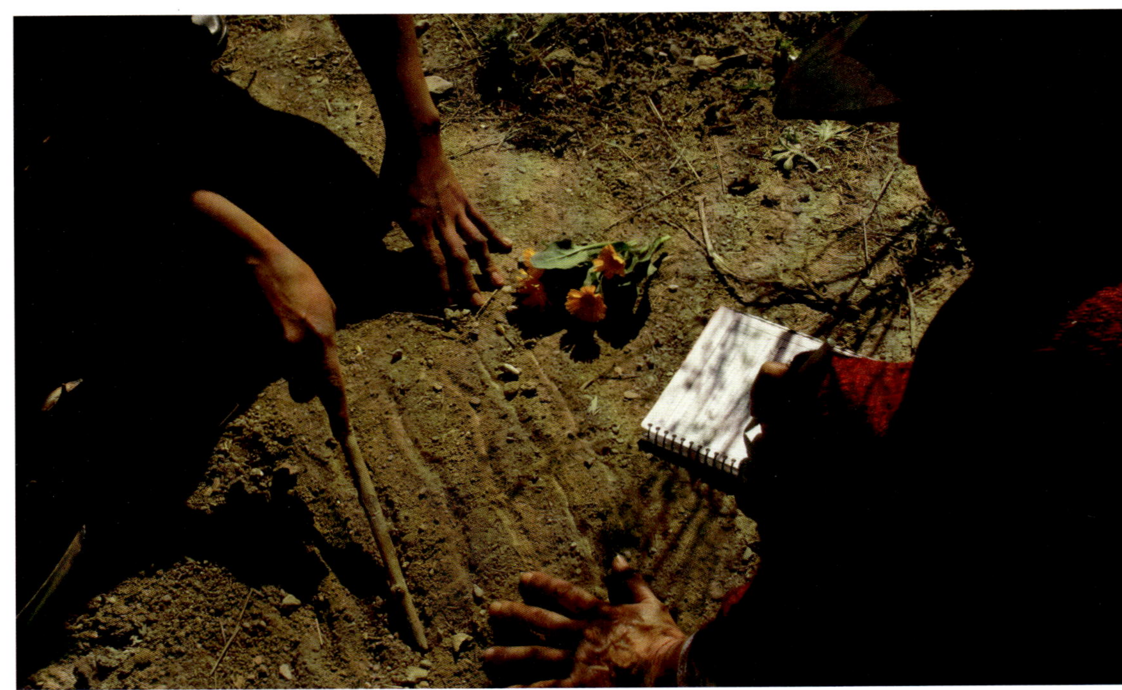

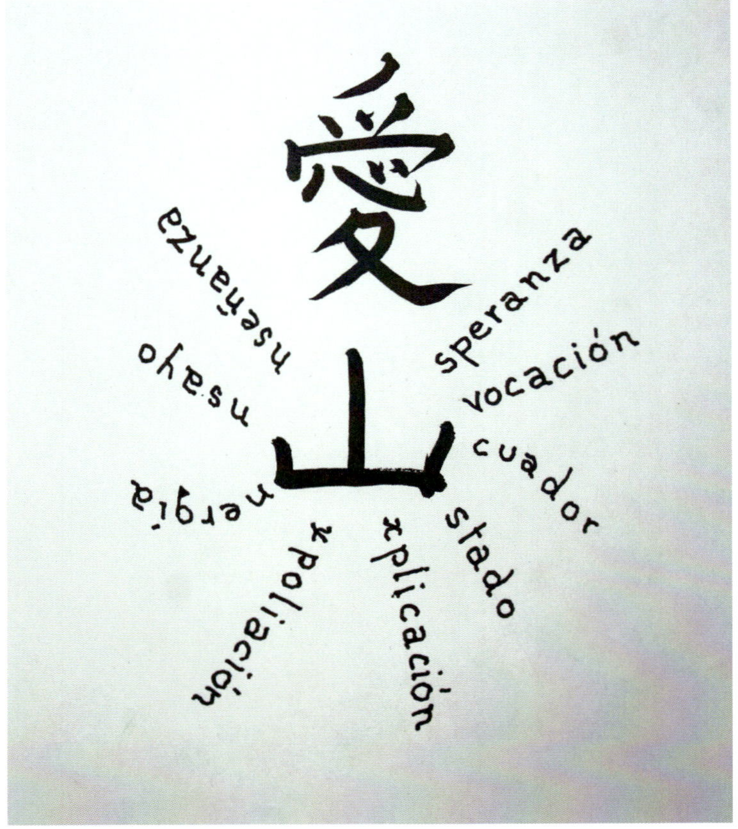

Tambo Colectivx,
reconstruction of a
lost photograph, 2015.
Photograph: Marco Arnez.
Courtesy the author

Calligraphy by Mamoru
Fujita, reconstruction of a
lost image. Photography:
Kilko Paz. Courtesy the
author

Pasa *ayllu* in the Pacajes province. In 1976, when Clea was four years old, we travelled around various spaces in that province: a community/*ayllu*,[8] a former hacienda, and the Corocoro mine. The labyrinthine formations of the Stone City were previously populated by immense *qiñwales* that now have nearly disappeared. It was there that those ancient trees (one of the few tree species native to the Altiplano) were threatened by the Corocoro copper fever, whose rapacity consumed enormous quantities of coal. To that region of sand and alpacas I went at 27 to figure out why my last name was Cusicanqui, a narcissistic question that was quickly replaced by encountering collective actions and original characters of a different order. There I learned of the long legal battle fought by the community member Eduardo Apaza, of Estación Campero, to keep the *qiñwa* forests from being snatched from his community by the invasion of mestizo coal traders that began with the arrival of the railroad.

The *qiñwa* I know has blood-red bark, which coats its trunk in layers like the skin of an onion. It is this layered bark that is a well-known remedy for kidney problems. I have sown *qiñwa* on my son Kilko's small piece of land in the Uni community, which was once a centre of the Quirwas of Oyune, facing the grand *mallku*[9] Illimani. I just learned in May 2015 that my little *qiñwa* tree was destroyed by the envy of a neighbour who did not respect the norms of the community.

To affirm the connection between the Páramo Andes and the Puna Andes (cf. Carl Troll), I have on my altar a small piece of *qiñwa* bark and two rocks I collected from the Papallacta *apachita*.[10] The *apu*[11] Antisana and the *apu* Imbabura (which can be seen only rarely) and the Illimani (which in this wintry season gleams like its name) will perhaps converse among themselves, illuminated by the *Cruz Chakana*.[12] When I return to Bolivia, the two sides of the pyramid (*apachita*) and the two macro structures of the Andes mountain range will thus be evoked in that microcosm that is my shrine to the dead, at once photo album and palimpsest of my travels over the planet.

2. Lessons in Anita's garden

Across from Imbabura, in the Angla community of the San Pablo parish in Otavalo, I found *aliq qura*: those weeds that are trod on daily in the country, and that are mixed into a tea to drink while fasting in order to prevent the illnesses and pains of the year ahead. On the lakeshores of Bolivia and Peru, they only drink this tea once a year, on Good Friday. It is the day on which Pachamama rejoices and unleashes all her powers of life and healing. It is the day on which Christ is in a tomb under the earth, nourishing it with his body/seed.

Anita Camuendo explained to me the name of each of the herbs we walked over to tour the garden: *Quwi qallu*, which the people of the region don't like because its roots are tough and tenacious; *Ino*, for tonsillitis; and *Felix Muju*, in infusion form for fever and in toasted-seed form for sinusitis.

The line she made in the dirt was a diagram of furrows where quinoa was interspersed with potatoes and corn with lupine (*tarwi* in Bolivia, *chocho* in

Ecuador). Her hands, worn from a life of farming and caring, joined mine, worn from writing, cooking and learning from the land, in the centre of a map where Anita taught me how to combine crops so that they protect each other from the *aliq qura* and from the hungry flies.

3. State Entanglements

A bizarre encounter in a high-altitude ecovillage, passing the Papallacta *apachita*. There it is cold and rainy when in Quito the sun shines, and there the stars all appear when on the other side of the mountain fog covers the city. In that landscape so conducive to meditation on geography, art and the sacred, Ecuador's ministry of culture organised a grand cultural diplomacy event: the visit of five artists from China for an 'exchange of experiences' with visual artists from Ecuador. To facilitate the encounter, the minister could think of nothing better than making an orientalist gesture whose geographical precision left much to be desired: he invited an artist who was a practitioner of Zen (a school of Buddhism whose cradle is in Japan) as well as Jungian psychology (anathema to the Communist Party, in China and everywhere else) to talk to the visitors in the name of Ecuadorian art. An extraordinary and beautiful woman, almost a century old, she perhaps was not aware of the power games in which she was involved. Nor did she realise how far the Chinese visitors were from the happenings of the Ecuadorian art scene. China is actually in the west of our gaze, if we consider the solar cycle, and we could also say it is now a symbolic and economic West for us. In this way, in honour of geography, we should speak of Europe as our Northeast. From where do we speak when we rant against 'Western culture'?

'They brought us as window dressing', the artist Sonia Rosales said to me, referring to a Cantinflas film that I don't remember having seen. When I jotted this down in my notebook, I noticed that an intelligence agent from the ministry was trying to read my writing with a sideways glance. Through it all, the axis of exchange seemed to centre on the photographs that would remain as a testimony to something that never occurred. We soon learned that effectively they had brought us as window dressing, because while the minister, his people and the Chinese artists posed for five or six photo and video cameras, the invited Ecuadorian artists – whom I joined accompanied by my student Edward Cooper – clustered around the pools of rocks, urged on by two corpulent guards, until finally the order was heard: 'Time to return to the meeting room.'

There the tone turned more pedagogical: 'Each one of you can ask five questions, which will be translated into Chinese and answered by the artists, who in turn will ask you five questions.' Sonia and I looked at each other and feigned a bit of smiling arithmetic: if each question lasted five minutes and the translation another five, we would have to be standing there talking nonsense for the next ten hours to complete the happy exchange. As soon as the minister left, paintbrushes and canvases took the place of words. Although one or two persisted in the fetishism of photos and autographs, many of us focussed on deciphering the writing that is at the same time drawing, bodily gesture and metaphorical potential of thought. With help from Sonia, who speaks Mandarin, I explained to a young artist with long hair and blue jeans that I wanted him to draw with his paintbrush the phrase that titles this essay. With an elegant calligraphy he wrote the characters *I love the Mountain* on a piece of bamboo paper. And to me the mountain looks like the letter E lying down, in whose axis the four fragments of this essay are articulated. In the *taypi*, or vertical space at the centre, I have intertwined Ecuador with the Energy of the cosmos, to give form to the dialectic without synthesis in which the *kupi* half, state and masculine, encounters/collides with the *chiqa* half, earthly and feminine.

Translated from Spanish by Molly Geidel.

Notes

[1] See my *Sociología de la imagen: Miradas ch'ixi desde la historia andina*, Buenos Aires: Tinta Limón, 2015. In the course I teach on Sociology of the Image I tend to participate in the final exam, presenting my own visual essay along with my students, not only as an exercise in dismantling 'pedagogical authority' (Pierre Bourdieu) but also to express what I have learned in each classroom situation and the larger landscape in which I teach my course. 'Amo la Montaña' was my final essay for the master's course in visual anthropology at FLACSO Ecuador, Quito in July–August 2010. I am grateful to the students on that course for the stimulating human and intellectual interaction we experienced on that occasion, and to Libertad Gills and Edward Cooper for their photographs. The essay was read fragment by fragment while I executed certain actions, dressed in white. I was accompanied by my yoga teacher supporting the performance. The stage was an empty classroom, with a small table in the centre on which were scattered some photographs in disorder, over a blue poster board. The element fire governed the first fragment: I wanted to conjure a misfortune that had just befallen me (the theft of my travel allowance and documents) and I burned a ten-dollar bill in a clay pot. The element of water dominated the second: while someone read it, I sat under the table and, in a lotus position, chanted an Aymara mantra, drinking in sips from a glass. To conclude the third fragment, everyone began to blow the photographs to represent the element air. Finally, upon uncovering the blue poster, the fourth fragment could be seen, sprinkled with lumps of soil. Since the original photos have been lost, I have reconstructed the images in the Situationist style, appealing to students, friends and my children, Clea and Kilko.

[2] See Jacques Rancière, *The Ignorant Schoolmaster: Five Lessons in Intellectual Emancipation* (1987, trans. Kristin Ross), Stanford, CA: Stanford University Press, 1991.

[3] These Andean languages share 30 per cent of the lexicon and have a similar pattern of suffixation, their similarity making them quite confusing.

[4] This story was told to me many years ago by the Chaco poet Jesús Urzagasti and is also recorded in his autobiographical novel *En el país del silencio* (La Paz: Hisbol, 1987).

[5] Refers to a variety of alpine tundra ecosystems, more commonly found in the northern Andes.

[6] *Siwingqa*: dragon fruit cactus (*cereus pitahaya*); *chillka*: medicinal shrub native to South America (*baccharis latifolio*).

[7] Castellanisation meaning a forest or group of *qiñwa* plants.

[8] The community grouping that comprises the basic element of Andean social organisation, composed of various subgroups.

[9] The summit of a mountain. Also refers to the condor, or an authority at various levels of Andean communities.

[10] The highest point of a road or hill, where we rest and perform a brief ritual to 'get rid of our exhaustion'.

[11] Sacred mountain.

[12] The southern cross.

II.
Artist/ Curator/ Other?

David Morris, Lucy Steeds and Charles Esche

What do we learn from 'the artist as curator'? The starting point for thinking about this section of the book was a consideration of how artists have experimented with the exhibition form, and of the convergent and divergent histories of politicised artist-organised exhibition projects that address systemic discrimination and exclusion. We quickly realised, however, that a majority of the texts included in this section do not feature any persons or groups who would easily identify as 'artists' in the classic singular modern(ist) sense. This is not to say that they do not often occupy this role or take on this function of 'artist', or indeed 'curator', particularly from the point of view of those organising, presenting or analysing their work, but it is to register a different set of priorities, roles and skill sets, where the traditional role of 'the artist' may not have the same resonance, meaning or position that it occupies in the Eurocentric hierarchies of knowledge (and attendant forms of violence) that shaped the modern world. Something similar may be said for the 'curator' role, and we might understand this difficulty in naming and categorising as a reflection of the complexities and contradictions within the modern-colonial construction of 'art'. In different ways, the essays that follow explore the multiplicity in such positions.

It is not uncommon to say that the roles of 'artist' and 'curator' are today highly interchangeable. This is sometimes traced back via certain lineages of art through the twentieth century, looking to historical moments in which these positions within the art system are seen to overlap. Stories of artists producing exhibitions are many and can be identified in various places worldwide across the last century and more. These examples cross over with another story, in which certain makers of exhibitions, since the 1960s, began to pioneer an approach to their gathering profession that absorbed a number of the functions that were traditionally associated with the figure of the artist. This has been compellingly recounted for Western Europe and Northern America as 'set[ting] the stage for the curatorial assumption of the artist's creative mantle' – with the figure of the 'contemporary art curator' emerging at the moment that collections management was abandoned in favour of exhibition-making for the 'new art'.[1] These histories provided a set of coordinates for discussions of the 'artist-as-curator' that emerged in the 2000s – discussions taking place in the context of a 'global' art field whose purview, from long-established centres in the West or Global North, was adamantly worldwide while challenged from new centres outside of their anchorage. In the prose on this subject written in the mid-2000s, the phenomena of the 'artist-curator' and 'curator-artist' are typically tracked back through activities in the North Atlantic art world during the 1960s–70s; these 'early' moments are often marked by conflicts between individuals within these circles, which we may understand in light of combative characteristics of the avant-garde tradition in which these events took place, with its particular fetishes for individualised authorship and 'who was "first"'.

The practices addressed in the following section were gathered according to a contrasting set of priorities – in particular, a sense of their potential for coming to terms with the complexity of these histories and how they may shape different futures. In short, we looked to essays and practices that felt adequate to the crises of the present moment. These crises are not new, of course, and we were drawn to examples that proceed from a deep sense of the entangled histories that have led up to this point.

This section features a predominance of collective practices. This did not happen by design on our part as editors, but it may reflect an instinct about the necessity for modes of art-making that escape Eurocentric/egocentric modes of subjectivity. Might we detect a similar slippage from 'artist' to 'curator' in terms of a loosening of the strictures of individualised authorship? Or are there better ways to understand the many organisational, creative and administrative acts of care that produce what we experience as art? Might such practices suggest other ways to escape the modern(ist) baggage of individualism, originality, authorship and ego? We wondered, in fact, if it might be more apt to speak of 'exhibitions without curators'? Or even 'art without artists'? This is not to deny the many agents and agencies that go into making art public, but to affirm their variety and multiplicity. We could take inspiration from the organisers of the Chiang Mai Social Installation (CMSI), a series of independent art festivals in northern Thailand during the 1990s, who in a 1995 text proposed the notion of 'culturalist' as an alternative to 'artist'. In the document in question, the group of artist-organisers identify themselves simply as a collective of friends.[2] CMSI's notion of the 'culturalist' is set up against individualism, egoism, professionalisation and authorship, emphasising a field of creative practice connected to daily life and not delimited by 'art'. The organisers' ambivalence extends to the role of the curator – participants would always insist that there was no curating involved, and they described their roles in various other ways, such as 'representative', 'filter', 'facilitator', 'teacher' or 'host of the party'.[3] Such attitudes and tendencies may be seen in other 1990s initiatives, in parts of Southeast Asia and beyond.[4]

The plural authorship of art is another commonplace observation – although the truth of this is rarely reflected in art's dominant economies or systems of valuation. The 'multiple authorship' shared by artists and curators, alongside the increasing overlap of activities and responsibilities taken on by these respective protagonists and the differing degrees of authorial autonomy implied, is a factor that has been used to explain the instability of or indistinction between the 'artist' and 'curator' roles.[5] Yet, the imbrication of these roles may also serve to entrench, rather than displace, the stubborn notion of individualised authorship. For instance, as our long-time *Exhibition Histories* comrade Yaiza Hernández Velázquez has pointed out with respect to Harald Szeemann's reconfiguration of the curator role in the 1960s–70s: 'What is striking is not that the exhibition should have become a medium at a time when anything and everything could claim the name of art; what is striking is the kind of artist Szeemann saw fit to revive', noting that 'the figure of the curator as romantic artist possessed of individual *Geist* rather than scholarly or technical knowledge was in many ways a throwback to the nineteenth century'.[6] As Hernández Velázquez argues, this provided a historical blueprint for 'the curatorial' and the figure of the itinerant, independent, 'emancipated' curator, 'who no longer had to speak in the name of the institution or to nationally held "collective values", but in the precise manner of a modern(ist) artist, deploy[ing] their individual voice to address the world at large'.

'The artist as curator' discourse during the early part of the twenty-first century may thus be understood as a response to material and cultural shifts emanating from the Global North or West at the time. Further, or in particular, as a coming-to-terms with the changing stakes of specific modern(ist) categories. These discussions coincided with the proliferation of academic programmes and the intensification of discourses related to curating and curatorial practice, and a number of publications dedicated to the topic would follow, perhaps most notably the series of essays under the title 'Artist as Curator' convened by Elena Filipovic from late 2013.[7] The *Exhibition Histories* project was an active participant in these discussions, with two symposia in 2012–13 organised under this very banner: while the first addressed the topic through the thematics of 'spaces', 'communities' and 'practice', the second, with the particular title 'Artist as Curator: Collaborative Practices', added questions of collective agency and was developed together with research students in the graduate programme in Exhibition Studies that we convene.[8] Putting this discursive moment into historical context is not to diminish or invalidate its concerns – and certainly we do not wish to suggest that its complex questions have been somehow resolved. As well as independent art festivals in northern Thailand, previous *Exhibition Histories* publications have focussed on artist-organised 'anti-shows' in Moscow during the 1980s,[9] and on an abstract, participatory 'exhibit' first staged by two artists and a critic for an art school in Newcastle upon Tyne in 1957.[10] We would agree that the ways that current understandings and functions of 'artist' and 'curator' have evolved continue to trouble traditional conceptions of exhibition-making. Yet the present section of this book attempts a different approach, a means perhaps of circumventing avant-garde antagonisms through envisaging reflections more appropriate to the practices and initiatives described in what follows.

The notion of interchangeability between 'artist' and 'curator' has uncomfortable echoes of the one-size-fits-all perspective of Western or First World 'globalism'. Rather than conforming to this apparent mode, the contributions to this section attend in different ways to the specificities of a range of practices and contexts. And although they do not concern themselves overmuch with a professional categorisation of roles, the texts gathered here articulate a number of specific dynamics, which might point to a different understanding of these positions. A certain kind of *materialism* may be said to animate the essays that follow; this includes a close attentiveness to the physicality and/or embodiedness of the practices themselves and the relations they form in public, complemented by careful readings of the material conditions of each situation and their respective historical-social-political realities. It is perhaps 'material' commitments of this kind that distinguish the approaches included in this section (and elsewhere in the book) from more generic modes of understanding, practicing and writing about the art of today and yesterday – seen in both art history and art criticism.

A moment from David Teh's writing on ruangrupa offers a concrete example of this manoeuvre. Teh notes that 'to profile ruangrupa is to describe an event: time-based, immediate and loosely structured; with a sense of purpose, yet more celebratory than agonistic', and which beckons 'a new regime of cultural production that is live, open-source and, above all, poly-vocal'.[11] By the prevailing standards of current writing about art, this alone would usually be considered enough – the text has already served its purpose to articulate, critically interrogate and/or celebrate the practice in question. Yet the text also goes a stage further: while noting the resonance of ruangrupa's practice with the artist-as-curator notion, it also emphasises the incompatibility of such a reading, an incompatibility that is illegible to the West-centric 'global' discourse, and which can only be understood by the contextual-historical particularity of artist-curatorship in Southeast Asia. Without attending to this particularity 'we run the risk of mistaking tactical moves for a strategic programme. And however appealing the image of their "contemporaneity", the group should first be seen in another light, a light in which modernity and nation still matter, and instrumentality is not (yet) the arch-enemy of art.' This meeting of Teh and ruangrupa – both of whom happen also to be long-standing interlocutors, collaborators and inspirations to our *Exhibition Histories* project – closes with a resonant notion of a different set of priorities, where 'the audience, rather than the work of art, may be the ultimate object of curatorial care.' Perhaps there is something in this that echoes through the practices that follow – rather than precious art objects, a dedication to life through art.

Connections between the practices discussed in this section are many. Although it would be unwise to apply unifying characteristics or categories, we may consider their resonances, entanglements and possible shared horizons. By and large, they relate to public manifestations in urban contexts, in major cities as various as Bangkok, Cape Town, Dakar, Hong Kong, Jakarta, Johannesburg, Kampala, Lagos and New York; and there are also examples from the hinterlands of China and rural Thailand. Activities range from being defiantly small-scale, low-key and 'local', to ambitiously expansive, with use of print and digital media to establish a wider discursive network. In some cases there may be an emphasis on shared 'process' – rather than objects and final outcomes – through workshops, discussions, publications and performances, and this may also include more traditionally 'material' practices of image- and object-making. In short, the practitioners here described gather widely from the many world-making possibilities of art, in largely collective undertakings, which might be understood in terms of what one contributor describes here as 'extended practice'.[12]

The present section therefore may be said to address the manifold 'other' practices, roles, proficiencies, strategies and tactics that have served to expand understandings of exhibition-making and to develop new possibilities for making art public.

Notes

[1] Bruce Altshuler, *The Avant-Garde in Exhibition: New Art in the 20th Century*, New York: Abrams, 1994, p.236.

[2] The document is reproduced in David Teh and David Morris (ed.), *Artist-to-Artist: Independent Art Festivals in Chiang Mai 1992–98*, London: Afterall Books, 2018, pp.138–41.

[3] See 'Oral Histories of Chiang Mai Social Installation', in *ibid.*, p.70.

[4] David Teh suggests the Baguio Arts Festival in the Philippines (begun in 1989) and The Artists Village in Singapore (established in 1988) as comparable regional platforms to CMSI. Their shared features include: energy and resources coming largely from artists and audiences rather than institutions; overlapping formal and thematic approaches, tending away from 'modern art' and towards interdisciplinarity, site specificity, social engagement, discursivity, performance and progressive political concerns; geographic positions away from their respective centres; and similar organisational structures that were initiated by artists (rather than curators, institutions or state actors) who eschewed 'authorial' or 'curatorial' roles. See D. Teh, 'Chiang Mai Social Installation in Historical Perspective', in *ibid.*, pp.12–47. Earlier 'artist-curator' 'pioneers' are addressed in Patrick Flores's *Past Peripheral: Curation in Southeast Asia*, Singapore: National University of Singapore Museum, 2008, though we may note the contrast between these charismatic individuals of the 1970s–80s and the more collective orientation of the above-mentioned initiatives during the 1990s.

[5] See Boris Groys, 'Multiple Authorship', in Barbara Vanderlinden and Elena Filipovic (ed.), *The Manifesta Decade: Debates on Contemporary Art Exhibitions and Biennials in Post-Wall Europe*, Cambridge, MA: MIT Press, 2005, pp.93–102; and Claire Bishop, 'What is a curator?', *Idea*, no.26, 2007, pp.12–21.

[6] Yaiza Hernández Velázquez, 'Imagining Curatorial Practice After 1972', in Paul O'Neill, Simon Sheikh, Lucy Steeds and Mick Wilson (ed.), *Curating After the Global: Roadmaps for the Present*, Cambridge, MA: MIT Press, 2019, p.257.

[7] See Elena Filipovic (ed.), *The Artist as Curator: An Anthology*, Milan: Mousse Publishing, 2017. Filipovic's essay on David Hammons from this collection, included in this volume, complements her book on another project through which Hammons engaged a public, see E. Filipovic, *David Hammons: Bliz-aard Ball Sale*, London: Afterall Books, 2017.

[8] The 2012 'Artist as Curator' symposium, convened by Charles Esche and Pablo Lafuente at Central Saint Martins, University of the Arts London (UAL), included presentations by Elena Crippa, Ekaterina Degot, Elena Filipovic, Alison Green, Ruth Noack, Willem de Rooij, Valerie Smith and David Teh. See https://www.afterall.org/article/afterall_artist-as-curator_symposium-videos-online. 'Artist as Curator: Collaborative Practices', convened by Elena Crippa, Ambra Gattiglia, Hyo Gyoung Jeon, Pablo Lafuente, Regina Souli and Yifei Wu, was held at the Whitechapel Gallery, London and included Clémentine Deliss, Liu Ding, Ines Doujak and Oliver Ressler. See https://afterall.org/article/artist-as-curator-collaborative-practices-symposium-videos-online.

[9] Margarita Tupitsyn, Victor Tupitsyn and D. Morris (ed.), *Anti-Shows: APTART 1982–84*, London: Afterall Books, 2017.

[10] See Elena Crippa and L. Steeds (ed.), *Exhibition, Design, Participation: 'an Exhibit' 1957 and Related Projects*, London: Afterall Books, 2016.

[11] D. Teh, 'Who Cares a Lot? ruangrupa as Curatorship', in this volume.

[12] Clémentine Deliss, 'Brothers in Arms: Laboratoire AGIT'art and Tenq in Dakar in the 1990s', in this volume.

David Hammons, *Untitled (Knobkerry)*, 1994

Elena Filipovic

As an artist I'm not aligned with the collectors or the dealers or the museums; I see them all as frauds.
– David Hammons[1]

An image comes to mind of a white, ideal space that, more than any single picture, may be the archetypal image of twentieth-century art; it clarifies itself through a process of historical inevitability usually attached to the art it contains. … Never was a space, designed to accommodate the prejudices and enhance the self-image of the upper middle classes, so efficiently codified.
– Brian O'Doherty[2]

David Hammons has made an art of making himself difficult to find.[3] He rejects most requests for interviews, largely dodges the inquiries of scholars, refuses to send out press releases or make artist statements. He doesn't have a website, and isn't officially represented by a gallery. He snubs most invitations to exhibit, and has eschewed retrospective surveys at any number of the venerable institutions interested in showing his work. Once he even went so far as to get a lawyer involved to make sure one prestigious museum *wouldn't* organise a retrospective devoted to him.[4] He declines, quite simply, to cooperate in the dissemination and promotion – the making widely visible – of an artistic 'oeuvre' of the type that artists are typically preoccupied with.[5]

Rather than trivial anecdotes of one artist's cagey behaviour, all of these accounts describe gestures that occupy the very core of Hammons's lifework. Arguably, these gestures *are* his lifework. Turning on its head the haunting line from Ralph Ellison's *Invisible Man* (1952), 'I am invisible, understand, simply because people refuse to see me',[6] Hammons's practice is based not on the habitual art world hope (and hype) for ultimate visibility and omnipresence, but the opposite: wilful obfuscation at the risk of obscurity. As a result, some of his most significant works have been unabashedly ephemeral, evanescent, unannounced, witnessed by only a few, uncollected (and uncollectable), recorded only occasionally, barely written about at the time (if at all), and evidenced only by a few photographs (if that). The artist's own crisp elucidation of his logic is as follows: 'To be invisible is more powerful than being visible.'[7] Because Hammons knows that to be Black in an art world as white as the walls of its museums, and in a United States where privilege and presence and whiteness go hand in hand, is to realise that visibility is something to mess with, to disavow.[8] Evasion, then, has become his operational strategy – an ethics, even – asserting 'fugitivity' (to use Fred Moten's term) as a form of resistance.[9]

This hasn't stopped him from forging a deeply influential – and undeniably material – body of work. From the late 1960s to the present, Hammons has powdered his drawings with Harlem dirt; attached deep-fried chicken wings by fishhooks to a friend's discarded Persian rug or to cheap costume jewellery; covered stones with 'nappy' hair and given them razor-cut hairstyles; lined telephone poles holding up impossibly high basketball hoops with thousands of bottle caps; hung barbecued ribs from wall sculptures made from greasy paper bags; and left upturned empty wine bottles on the branches of trees in vacant Harlem lots. He has also made 'drawings' from dust, organised exhibitions with little more than blue light, made and sold snowballs, and even spread rumours as art. His oeuvre, a mix of handcrafted and found elements, often from the street, has been so brazenly audacious as to sometimes barely be 'there' at all. And yet the resultant artworks are strangely charged, even witchy: at once modest, wonky, witty, and utterly commanding (that is their paradox).

Hammons's lexicon of ephemeral actions, funky materials, and self-consciously 'Black' readymades goes hand in hand with his self-construction as an elusive maverick. If his actions mine the street as both inspiration and stage, they also make a point of eschewing the whole art world machine: official announcements, bona fide institutional spaces, insider audiences. Instead, he has controlled the means of his distribution and taken his visibility into his own hands. Thus, to speak of Hammons's practice you might look not only at the artworks he has made, but also at the ways in which he has elected to present them, the operations he has organised around them, and even the actions he has orchestrated to conceal them – to make his work itself as evasive as he himself has been. Because, for Hammons, the artwork's power lies as much in what makes it visible (or invisible) as within the thing as such. He has said, 'It's not the art object itself. It's the daringness of the act, of presenting it, and the art object is the result … of empowering the object, as opposed to the object being powerful.'[10]

Hammons started off exhibiting his art in church basements or on pegboards in Jewish recreation centres, since 'they were the only places in Los Angeles that gave shows to black artists'. He was also 'showing around swimming pools, … putting art on trees' and finding still other unconventional sites: 'I've been in bars, showing in barbershops and cafés. I've done all that.'[11] In other words, he *made* his own exhibition context when more official options were not yet open to him. And this remained the case even once the art world began to take notice.

It is perhaps unsurprising that Hammons has never been fond of the so-called white cube – that white-walled, supposedly neutral blank slate of a space

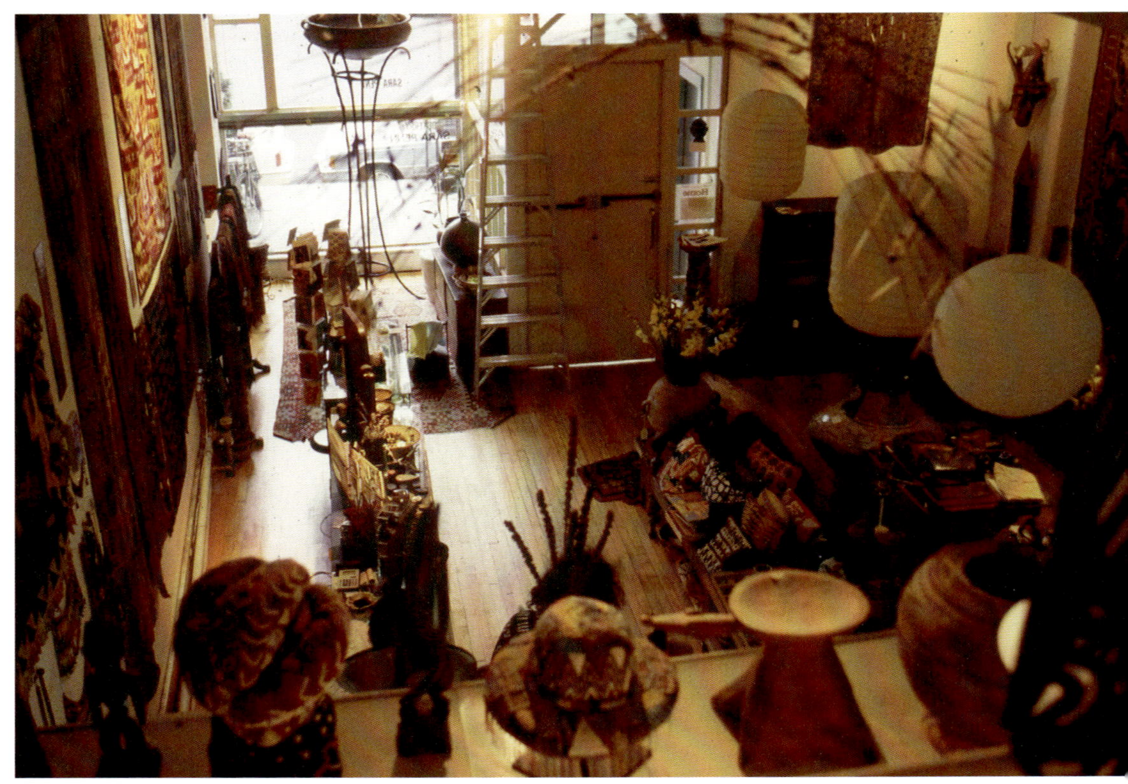

imposing a radical separateness between art and the outside world. One thing you can say about his most iconic and furtive work of art, *Bliz-aard Ball Sale* – a sale of snowballs on a wintry New York street corner in 1983 – is that it showed to what lengths he would go in order to avoid the white cube. Like Gustave Courbet's 1855 creation of a rogue pavilion just across the way from the official salon exposition in Paris, Hammons's carefully organised display of snowballs nearby the pristine white cubes of the burgeoning gallery scene was somewhere between a huckster's outdoor sales showroom and his own *salon des refusés*. However, if a kind of *salon des refusés* it was, then Hammons arranged it without having tried and failed to penetrate any official exhibition. He had, from the start, refused to accept not only the art world's conventional procedures and tidying sensibilities (its rules and paths to career building), but also the character of its spaces and the logics of its displays, once declaring:

> *Most of my things I can't exhibit because the situation isn't right. The reason for that is that no one is taking the shit seriously anymore. And the rooms are almost always wrong, too much plasterboard, too overlit, too shiny and too neat. Painting these rooms doesn't really help, that takes the sheen off but there's no spirit, they're still gallery spaces.*[12]

Like so many of Hammons's interventions, the force of his projects often lies not only in how cunningly they engage their contexts, but also in how diametrically opposed that context is to the conditions of the white cube with its in-built audience (think of *Pissed Off* and *Shoe Tree*, his ephemeral actions taken upon a Richard Serra sculpture in 1981, or his *Bottle Trees* and *Higher Goals*, equally precarious 'artworks' that occupied vacant Harlem lots between 1983 and 1986, not to mention *Bliz-aard Ball Sale* itself). That audience was just too busy 'looking at each other and each other's clothes and each other's haircuts', as Hammons famously observed.[13] Refusing to cater to such a public, and refusing as well to conceive of an exhibition as a neatly fixed and well-behaved display of auratic, authored things cut off from the world from which they were born, Hammons persistently pursued unconventional means and sites to show art. A perfect but little-known example is his 1994 self-initiated, untitled, unannounced exhibition at Knobkerry, a shop for African and Asian artefacts in the New York neighbourhood of Tribeca run by his friend Sara Penn.[14]

You could go to Penn's shop for Masai warrior necklaces or Japanese figurines, Moroccan kilim rugs or West African tribal masks. Hammons had known it for twenty years, regularly shopped there to find materials for his works, and admitted that for as long as he'd known the place, he had wanted to do an exhibition that would 'play off' its compendium of cultures.[15] His resultant orchestration – curation, really – of an exhibition of his artworks infiltrated the site's inventory with no indication, through presentation or signage, as to the differing status of each. As an outpost for precisely the kinds of ethnic folk objects the artist had often used as the basis for his own art, Knobkerry was a place where Hammons's art could effectively hide in plain sight.

Fittingly, the exhibition opened (according to one report) on that celebration day for trickster camouflage, Halloween (31 October 1994), and ran, with at least one date extension, for more than three months (through 15 February 1995). If it continued on after that is not certain.[16] There was no invitation, advertisement, press release, or opening event; and then, as now, rumour (and perhaps misinformation) about it is inseparable from the exhibition itself. From what photographic documents do exist of the show, it seems that some of the forms or constellations of objects may have changed; perhaps objects were even added along the way. At some point during its run, a small handwritten sign appeared discreetly on the floor telling visitors (if they noticed or cared): 'Works by David Hammons Now on Exhibit'. It was the only explicit mention in the shop that something out of the ordinary was going on. And for the duration of the artist-curated exhibition, few noticed in the art world. News of it passed mainly by word of mouth, and scattered mentions of it appeared in the press.[17] The show drew some insiders – a few eager collectors, a smattering of informed critics, a host of friends. But mostly it was visited by the small emporium's usual shoppers, who were there looking for the 'exotic' objects and ornaments that were Knobkerry's specialty.

'More than a dozen' works by Hammons ('more than fifteen' in another's estimation – it's interesting that no one could say for certain) were spread across the shop without calling attention to themselves, even to those looking for them.[18] They often combined Knobkerry's usual artefacts with the artist's

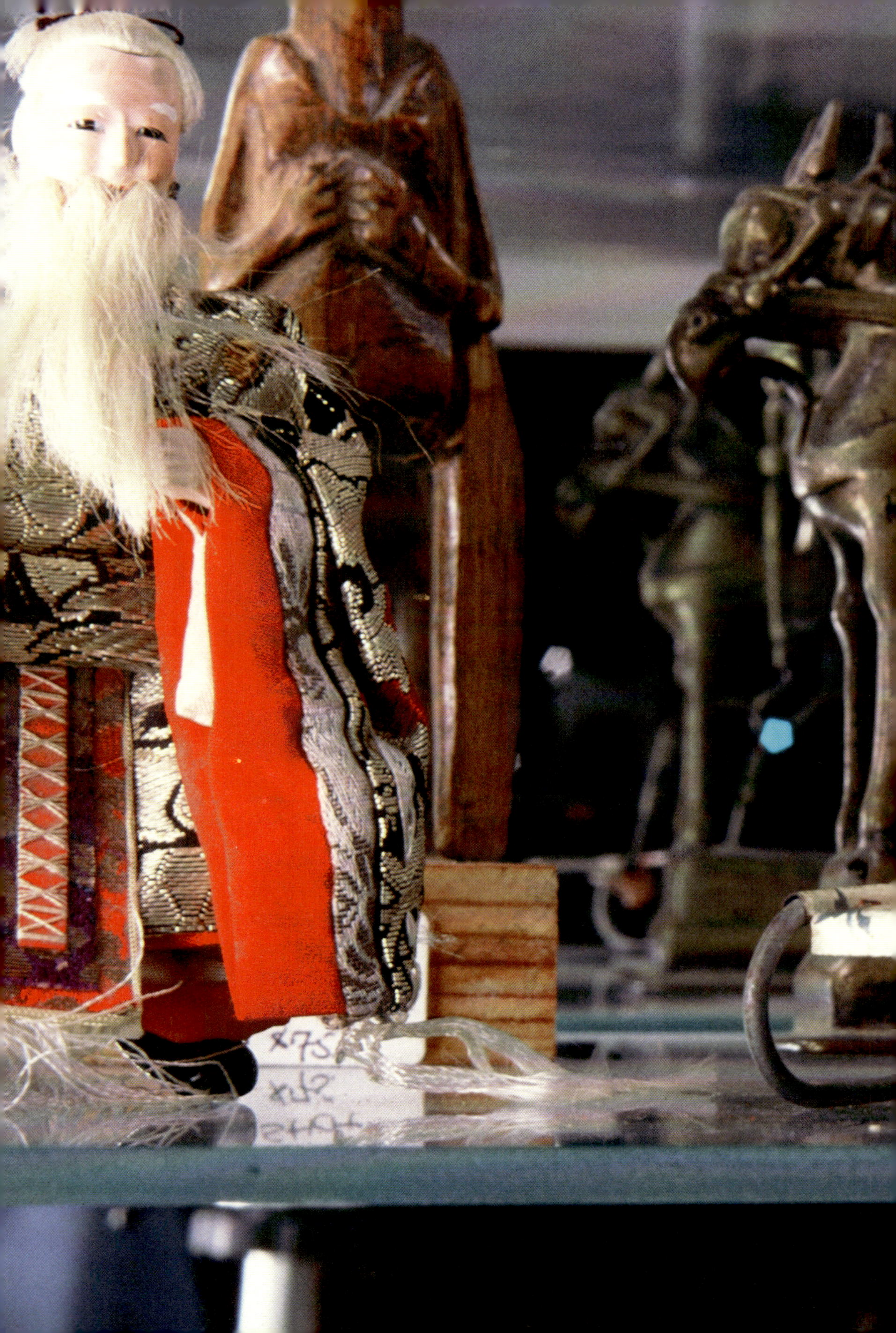

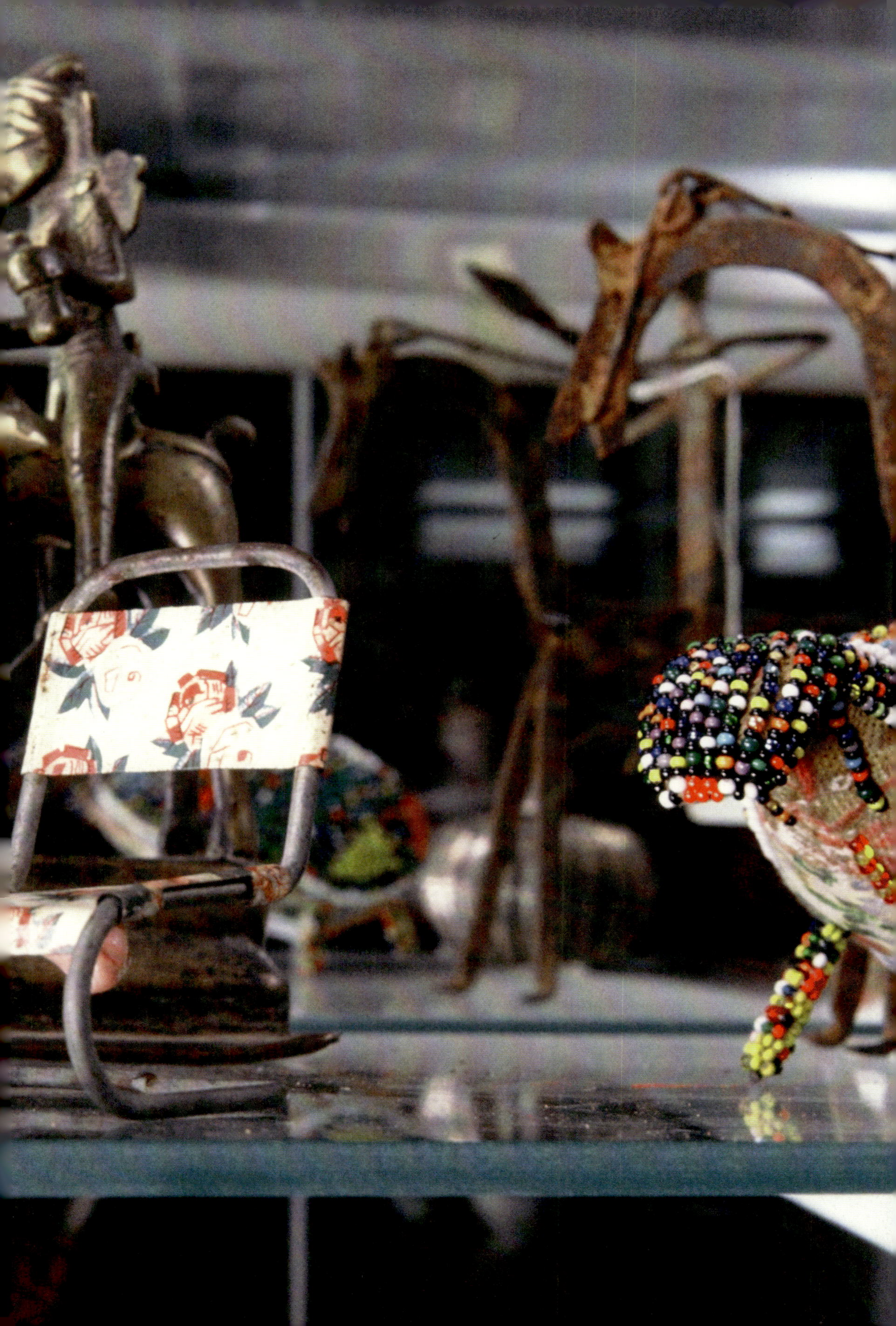

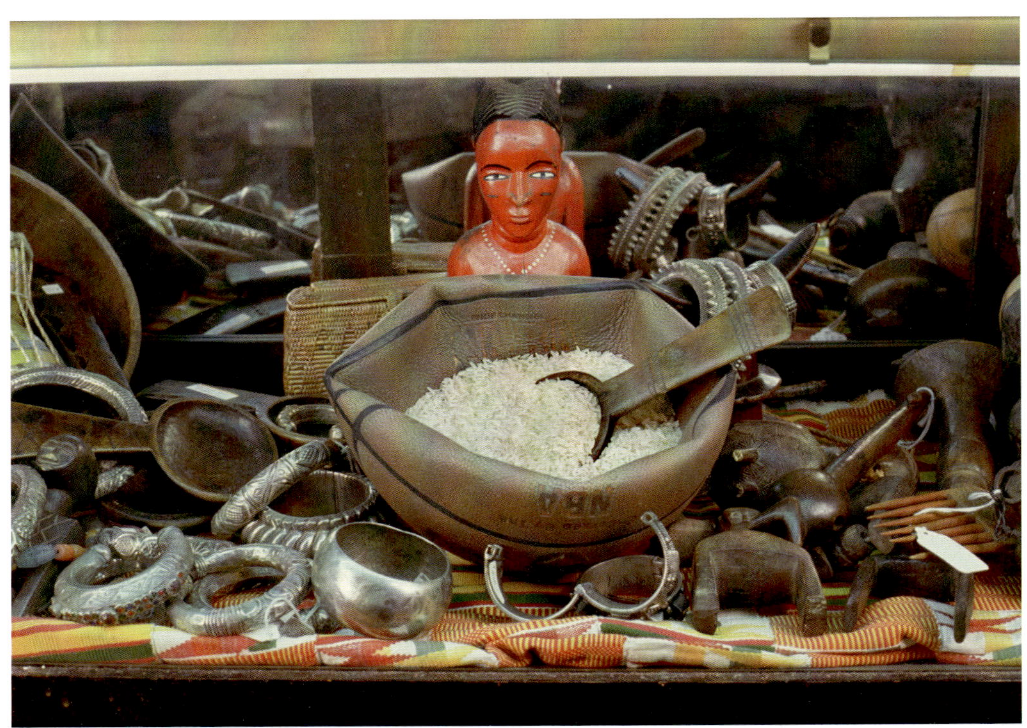

Installation view, untitled exhibition, Knobkerry, New York, 1994, with the entrance vitrine containing David Hammons's *Basketball Rice Bowl*. Photography: Erma Estwick. Copyright and courtesy Erma Estwick and David Hammons

material and semantic mainstays – from basketballs to tongue-in-cheek puns. All were for sale and none were behind glass or on pedestals or protected by stanchions; visitors could simply sift through the art while looking for something else. And although Hammons called upon a photographer friend, Erma Estwick, to document it and a handful of photographs remain, recorded facts are few and far between – including whether or not some of the unsold juxtapositions of items (temporarily considered artworks by Hammons during the show) resumed their previous status as mere merchandise afterward.[19]

An art of ferociously casual acts abounded, as did evidence of Hammons's truculent wit: black-eyed peas were strewn across the floor of a miniature Shinto temple (if the work had a title, no one seems to have taken note of it); a tangle of wire and cigarette butts was attached to the gold brocade of a seventeenth-century Buddhist monk's robe that had long been hanging on the shop's wall to become *Cigarette Chandelier* (unless otherwise noted, all works are from 1994); a deflated basketball served as a rice bowl positioned between ceremonial silver bracelets, Yoruba combs, and various wooden utensils in a vitrine near the cash register to become *Basketball Rice Bowl*; and on a wall hung *Marimba Ribs*, punning on the resemblance of the slab of meat and bones to the marimba, a xylophone-like percussion instrument developed in Central America by African slaves, and reminding viewers of the artist's early use of greasy food in his art (and, as Penn tells it, remaining just as unsellable).[20] The juxtapositions were often sardonic but also poignant, 'crossing', as noted by Roberta Smith (one of the few critics who wrote about the show at the time), 'racial, cultural and geographic boundaries, mixing old and new, high and low, East and West'.[21]

From a ceiling corner the artist suspended one of the only previously existing pieces in the show, *Flight Fantasy* from 1978, consisting of vinyl record fragments, hair, clay, plaster, feathers, bamboo, and coloured string, its bits of balled-up black hair and shards of 45rpm records swaying slightly with any movement of air in the shop; in an opening of an Asian armoire, positioned near Japanese dolls, the artist sat a decoy duck bandaged in surgical tape like a modern mummy, drolly called *Tape Duck*; and along one wall hung *Carpet Beater*, a kilim rug adorned with a grid of attached drumsticks (the kinds used on drums), creating a material and linguistic riff on Hammons's 1990 *Flying Carpet*, in which a grid of fried chicken wings had given that earlier carpet metaphoric flight. Hammons created two fountain works for the show, including a small wooden African mask with water pouring from its mouth into a bowl set below it, and a larger fountain in the entrance window comprised of a makeshift stand with a Chinese bronze bowl collecting water that spewed from the eyes and nose of an African mask plumed with white feathers and branches of cotton pods, appropriately called *Spitting Image*. But to describe the works as I have, or even to show the photographs taken of them, is to see them zeroed in on, almost out of their context, and thus to betray how furtively they actually occupied the space. Rather than there being art inside a shop, one must imagine a fully operational shop that slyly camouflaged an exhibition.[22]

It would not be the first or the last time Hammons 'curated'. Already in 1980, he conceived *Art across the Park*, an outdoor exhibition of ephemeral works shown in Central Park that continued for two iterations, after which the artist decided that its success and official offers to fund it made the project's continuance uninteresting, 'too institutionalised'.[23] And he has repeatedly curated exhibitions of his friends' works or inserted the works of other artists into his own or other exhibitions – whether an Agnes Martin drawing that he included without explanation in his 2010 solo exhibition at a London gallery, or, before that, in 2006, his orchestration of the inclusion of a work by Miles Davis in the Whitney Biennial.[24] But what he did at Knobkerry was considerably different. Here, his project was as much a reflection on the form of an 'art' exhibition as it was about the relationship of the artwork to the commodity, a questioning that has been central to a number of his other projects, from the 1983 *Bliz-aard Ball Sale* more than a decade before the Knobkerry show, to his 2004 *Sheep Raffle*, a full decade after it, to still other projects beyond.

Every Hammons artwork at Knobkerry was without a label and priced the same, no matter its size or seeming importance, as had been his snowballs when he peddled them on a street corner. But make no mistake, here the $25,000 price (no discounts given) was not that of a street seller: it was not a matter of democratising art but of rerouting its aesthetic sublimation.[25] And if some of the pieces may have more readily looked like art (or, let's say, like an artwork by Hammons), others – like a wad of gum stuck to the underside of a doll-size, flower-patterned lounge chair, a basketball improbably stuffed into a terracotta vase, or even toilet paper stacked into a pyramid – seemed even more slight or tenuous as 'works of art'. No one seems to have noted titles for these three, or whether after the show the gum was simply removed, the basketball extracted from its vessel, and the toilet paper returned to its regular place of use in the bathroom.

Hammons's gestures reversed the Duchampian act of bringing a store-bought thing into an exhibition space and proclaiming it to be art; here, he made the store into the exhibition, and made some of its usual stuff into his art. Objects might be deemed art by their maker, but – when unannounced, unpublicised, unlabelled, and merely infiltrated into an operating shop of artefacts or on the street among sellers of other commodities – they are decidedly untethered from the sorts of institutional, critical, and commercial collusions that otherwise aid in determining whether a spade is a spade, or an artwork an artwork. For an artist like Hammons, who has long observed those collusions, it was a way to integrate his art into a site of mercantilism – 'the real world', as he called it – and in so doing comment on the way people 'consume art'.[26]

The phenomenon of the artist as sales agent was not entirely new. But unlike Martha Rosler, for instance, who in 1973 had set up a monumental 'garage' sale and sold off her personal belongings in the museal confines of the University Art Gallery at the University of California, San Diego, Hammons did not take his sale into a gallery or museum. Instead he ensconced it in an operating shop, confusing his wares/works with regular commodities. In that way, his was an even more insidious approach, perhaps, than that of Claes Oldenburg, who in 1961 created *The Store* in an empty Lower East Side storefront. Oldenburg's display and sale of quasi-formless representations of cupcakes, ribeye steaks, and girdles was rooted in the premise that all art, no matter how recalcitrant, no matter how avant-gardist or daring, is recuperable.

For Hammons, the act was not innocent. In an art world that is predominantly white, the money that circulates within it is inextricably bound to issues of class and race. And although Hammons has had shifting views on the commodification of his art over the years, his interest by that point to 'take home as much money as possible' was a loaded one, a defiant statement of sorts.[28] As he explained:

> *It's possible to sell pieces for $100,000 that are the size of my palm. 'Cause this is a cultural statement that they have to address. Buying a small piece for $100,000 from a black artist, who just took two, um, pipe cleaners and put them together, you know, 'cause I'm interested in making that cultural statement towards the art world.*[29]

His embrace of commerce was thus as programmatic as his rejection of the white cube and general evasiveness in relation to a (normative, white) art world.

The Knobkerry show opened just a few weeks after *Time* magazine's triumphant cover declaration of a 'Black Renaissance'.[30] Blackness was suddenly a subject of US middle-class dinner-table discussion and Hammons, mentioned in the issue, was part of that discussion – maybe that's why he insisted all the more on going in the opposite direction, toward an infiltration that rendered

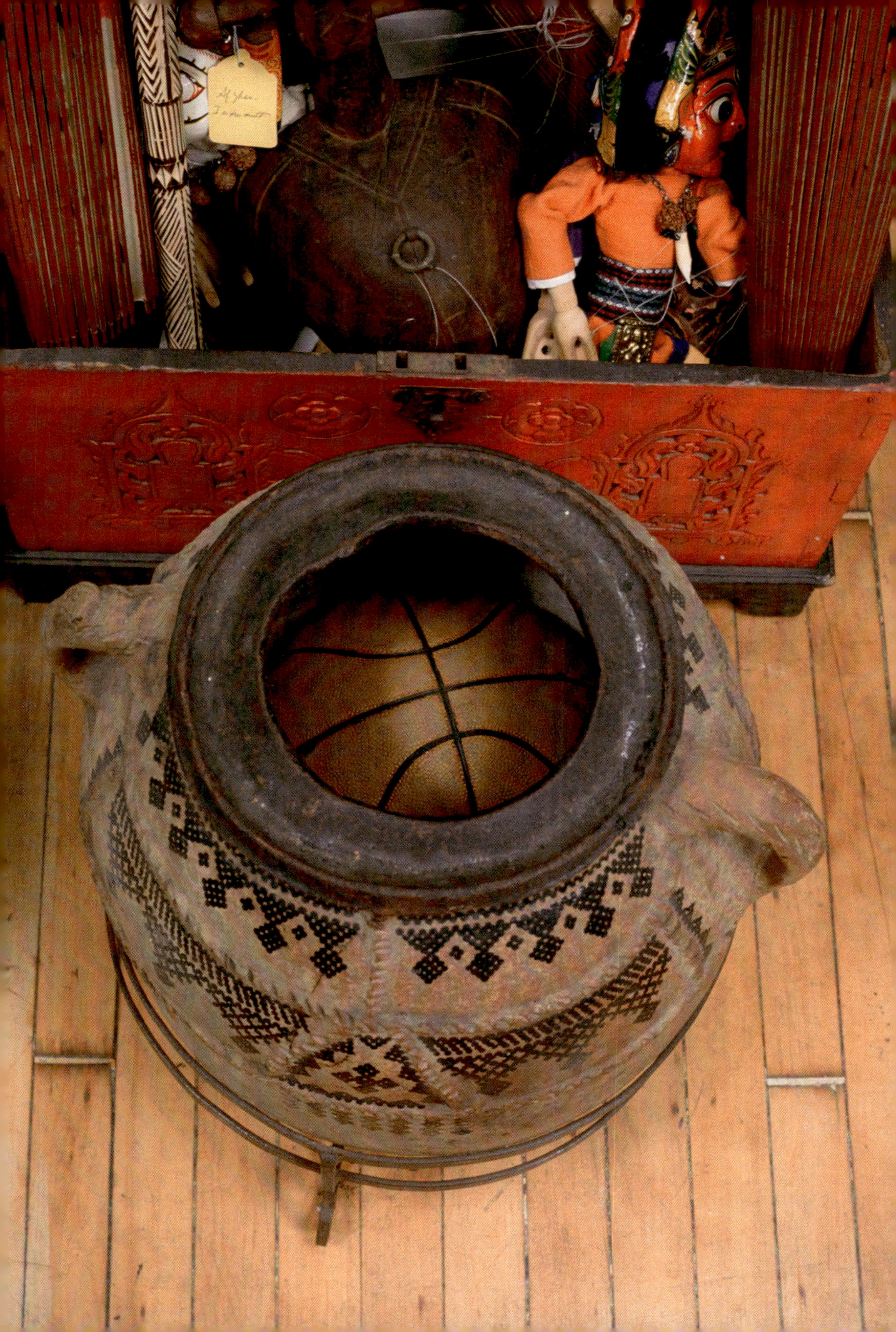

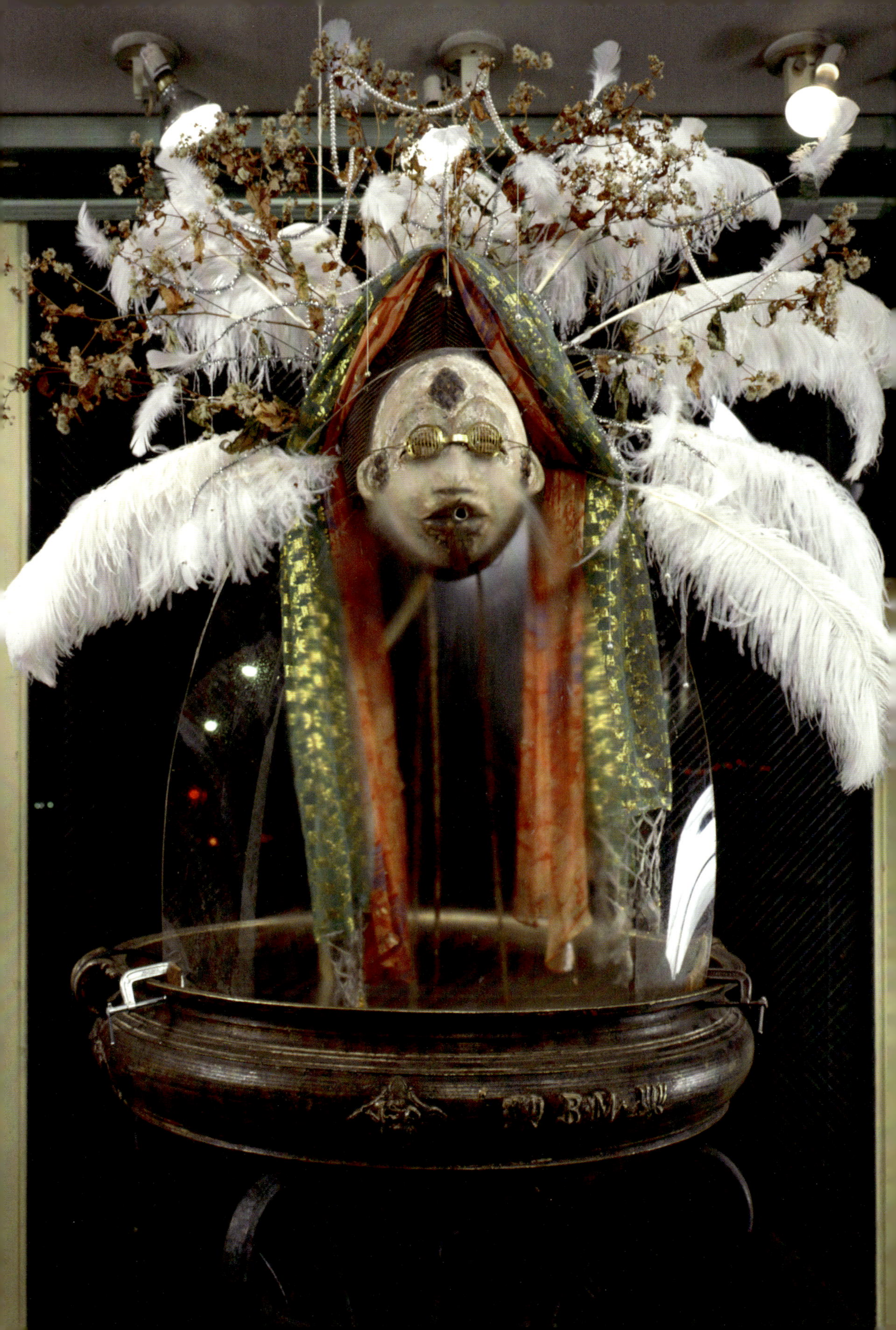

him nearly invisible. If you had asked him, though, he would tell you that his Knobkerry show was a guerrilla response to Thelma Golden's 'Black Male', a timely, controversial, and now landmark exhibition on identity politics shown concurrently at the Whitney Museum of American Art, New York.[31] A few of Hammons's pieces were included in Golden's show, incorporated into its biting inquiry regarding contemporary representations of race and masculinity, which is how Hammons knew about its concept and preparations before it opened to the public. He felt the Whitney show was, as he declared to a journalist without hiding his disapproval, 'a child's exhibition'. As a result, he conceived his near-simultaneous show of art tucked almost out of sight because he 'thought something should be in town that was much more subtle, the opposite of that'.[32] However deliberately provocative, and even perhaps ultimately unfair, his statements are revelatory. If Hammons staged his Knobkerry show specifically as a riposte to 'Black Male', it suggests that he believed that an inquiry into 'Blackness' could be more powerfully addressed through tongue-in-cheek juxtapositions of high and low, linguistic punning, and subterfuge that, first and foremost, began with a rejection of the white cube.[33]

This thinking was differently but no less powerfully articulated a decade later, in 2004, when Hammons conceived *Sheep Raffle* as a response to an invitation to take part in the United States' contribution to Dak'Art, the Biennial of Contemporary African Art in Dakar, Senegal. Refusing to display art in any of the exhibition venues, and indeed bypassing the jet-set biennial audience altogether, Hammons used his allocated budget to stage a free daily lottery of sheep for local residents. He organised the giveaway of a total of twelve sheep, two per day for six days. The event was staged at 4 p.m. each day at the busy intersection of two main avenues, where sheep are typically purchased or slaughtered to celebrate the local Festival of the Sacrifice (the Islamic holiday of Eid al-Adha). There, on a stage and accompanied by music and dancing, a master of ceremonies announced the rules and declared the daily winners. The event was promoted via billboards and radio jingles in French and Wolof, with raffle tickets distributed daily to locals eager for a chance to win a sheep. Recalling both *Bliz-aard Ball Sale* and the exhibition at Knobkerry, *Sheep Raffle* not only referenced the social rituals of the context, but was staged at a site where these types of events typically took place. Hammons modelled *Sheep Raffle* on other lotteries of products common for the area, and even accepted Maggi, the industrial soup bouillon and instant-noodle giant, as a sponsor, just like other local raffles did.

According to Hammons, he conceived *Sheep Raffle* because 'people in Dakar do not go to exhibitions. They think that the Dak'Art is for white people. ... At least with the sheep raffle, I'll give them something they can relate to.'[34] At an international contemporary art biennial, he effectively replaced the logic of aesthetic display with a display of a kind of transaction (the exchange of winning lottery tickets for animals that served as near-currency to locals). Exactly a decade after the exhibition at Knobkerry and more than two decades after *Bliz-aard Ball Sale*, he was trading in sheep as he had previously traded in African trinkets or snowballs. Raffle tickets circulated in place of money, and the corner of Avenue Bourguiba and Voie du Nord took the place of the Tribeca shop or

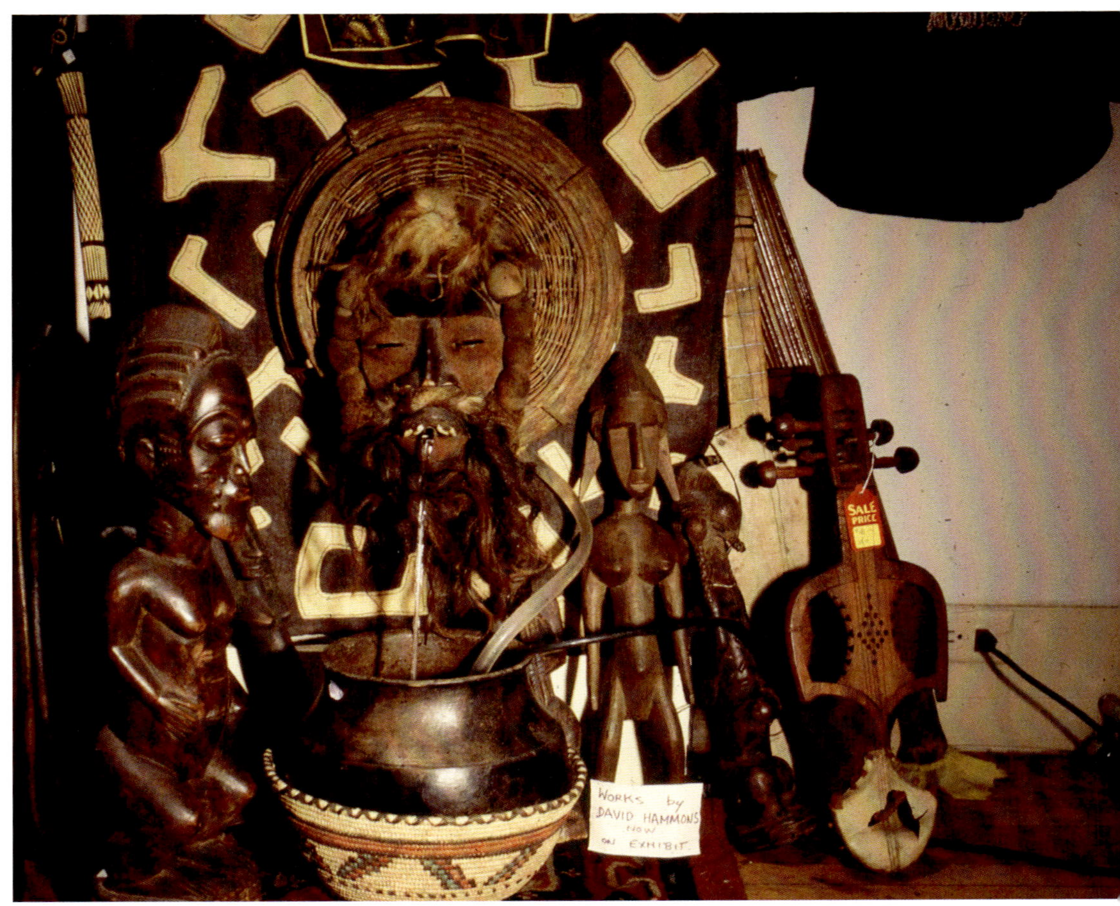

Installation view, untitled exhibition, Knobkerry, New York, 1994. Photography: Erma Estwick. Copyright and courtesy Erma Estwick and David Hammons

the corner of Cooper Square and Astor Place. His artwork was once again an event that left white cube exhibition spaces aside as it foregrounded the (economic) transactions and logic around which much of the art world revolves, indeed making a spectacular display of it: *Sheep Raffle* had, as one critic at the time astutely noted, 'few winners, many losers' and a 'questionable … multinational sponsor', Nestlé subsidiary Maggi, legitimising itself through it all.[35]

From his late 1960s and early 1970s grease and 'nappy' hair works to *Bliz-aard Ball Sale* to *Sheep Raffle*, with the Knobkerry exhibition as a remarkable example in between, Hammons's lifework has entailed, on the one hand, evading the institutions of art and their coolly antiseptic spaces and, on the other, revealing the power, race, class, and fiduciary dynamics that inflect them. Brian O'Doherty, in his 1976 trilogy of essays in *Artforum*, made abundantly clear that the white cube was not a neutral site, calling it nothing less than 'a social, financial, and intellectual snobbery which models (and at its worst parodies) our system of limited production, our modes of assigning value, our social habits at large'.[36] O'Doherty articulated this just as Hammons, in his own way, was showing up the white cube as an implicitly racialised space – its walls as

186

white as the culture it tacitly upholds. As Hammons himself would later say:

> *White walls are so difficult because everything is out of context. They don't give me any information. It's not the way my culture perceives the world. We would never build a shape like that or rooms that way. To us that's for mad people, you get put in them in the hospital. There is no other place I'd seen that kind of room until I came into the art world.*[37]

As a response to these spaces, he has often created disruptions literally aimed at their walls. Whether he defiles them with fried food or lice-strewn hair protruding from their floorboards or ceilings; whether he covers the museum's walls with the cheap stencilled wall patterns of Harlem tenement hallways or imprints them with dirt from a bounced basketball; whether he has guests at his first retrospective's opening play a pickup game of basketball in the middle of the exhibition; whether he empties a gallery of all signs of art and makes the white cube black and blue; or whether he leaves institutionalised spaces altogether to present his art on the street or in a shop or at a busy crossroads, the result is a practice that inserts dirt or grease or confusion or invisibility in order to clog 'the system'. It interferes with the machinery of the institution of art, all the better to make apparent how its cogs move and its gears engage. Because that machine, including its collectors, museums, curators, histories, and procedures of validation and value formation, was – and still is – a white machine. He shows that resistance to the institution of art need not be explosive; it can be light as dust and comprised of the particles of everyday existence that simply mar it from within. In so doing, he refuses to let reign unchecked the white cube and the 'prejudices and … self-image' (to repeat O'Doherty's words) of the society it is 'designed to accommodate'.[38]

Hammons once said: 'I always had to see their [white] reflections when I looked at Western Art. There is no information in there concerning my reference points. So my art had to be as black as their art is white.'[39] Perhaps the same could be said of his relationship to exhibition spaces. Maybe like writer Zora Neale Hurston, who declared that she felt 'most colored' when 'thrown up against a sharp white background', Hammons has treated the white cube and the conventional models of exhibition that typically feature within it as that 'sharp white background' against which he would make a lifework of responding.[40]

Notes

[1] Maurice Berger, 'Interview with David Hammons', *Art in America*, September 1990, p.80.

[2] Brian O'Doherty's trilogy of essays about the ideology of exhibition spaces, which appeared serially in *Artforum* in 1976, are now collected under the title *Inside the White Cube: Ideology of the Exhibition Space* (Berkeley: University of California Press, 2000), pp.14, 76.

[3] Parts of this essay are extracted from my book *David Hammons: Bliz-aard Ball Sale* (London: Afterall Books, 2017) and the nearly fifty interviews conducted in the oral history that forms its basis. As with that project, the importance of admitting the role of uncertainty and doubt – even as one attempts to contribute to the writing of history – lies at the centre of this essay.

[4] Hammons has never been afraid of being noncompliant. Recently, after learning that a New York

museum was planning a retrospective of his work, he took measures to ensure that the project would not happen while simultaneously allowing for two other exhibitions of his work (each billed as a 'retrospective', no less) to be organised: one at the opulent Upper East Side townhouse of Mnuchin Gallery, specialising in the secondary market and run by a former equity trader, and another at the undistinguished corporate collection headquarters in Athens of Greek shipping magnate George Economou, whose name bears etymological relation to 'economy'. None of the implications of each context would have been lost on Hammons, lover of wordplay that he is. Hammons might even have found these two venues appealing precisely *because* they defied expectation and made a spectacle of his interest in the functioning of the art market.

[5] And this was the case from the very start. The curator of Hammons's first institutional solo show, in 1974 at California State University, Los Angeles, recounts: 'The first thing David Hammons did, the day after I invited him to have a solo show, was to turn off his phone.' Josine Ianco-Starrels, 'Some Thoughts', in Connie Rogers Tilton and Lindsay Charlwood (ed.), *L.A. Object and David Hammons Body Prints*, New York: Tilton Gallery, 2011, pp.136–37.

[6] Quoted from the opening lines of Ralph Ellison's *Invisible Man*, a novel whose exploration of racism and perception in America offers a potent lens through which to read Hammons's construction of a fugitive stance.

[7] Hammons in conversation with the author, New York, 7 September 2009.

[8] The gaping discrepancy between the attention, monetary value, and reputation attributed to white versus minority artists and the institutions that supported each of them can't be emphasised enough. Well into the 1990s, when both Los Angeles and New York were racially and socially integrated, they were still astoundingly segregated professionally and institutionally – a reality that lingers today.

[9] Fred Moten has brilliantly articulated the potency of fugitivity across various texts, including 'The Case of Blackness', *Criticism*, vol.50, no.2, Spring 2008, pp.177–218.

[10] Interview no.1 with Papo Colo and Jeanette Ingberman in an unpublished typescript for a (never-published) catalogue by Exit Art, Fales Library and Special Collections, Exit Art Archives, p.12.

[11] Interview with Robert Storr, in *Yardbird Suite: Hammons 93* (exh. cat.), Williamstown, MA: Williams College Museum of Art, 1995, p.56.

[12] Kellie Jones, 'Interview with David Hammons', *Real Life Magazine*, no.16, Fall 1986, reprinted in K. Jones, *EyeMinded: Living and Writing Contemporary Art*, Durham, NC: Duke University Press, 2011, p.251.

[13] *Ibid.*, p.255.

[14] I gleaned many of the details of the Knobkerry exhibition from Sara Penn as well as Erma Estwick, whose photographs of the exhibition are among the few remaining traces of that ephemeral event.

[15] Amei Wallach, 'David Hammons' Secret Magic Show', *New York Newsday*, 23 December 1994.

[16] *Ibid.* Wallach mentions the start date as Halloween, putting the opening at 31 October 1994; it ran at least through 15 February 1995, according to a Knobkerry flyer with the handwritten addition: 'David Hammons show extended.'

[17] See A. Wallach, 'David Hammons' Secret Magic Show', *op. cit.*; Roberta Smith, 'The New, Irreverent Approach to Mounting Exhibitions', *New York Times*, 6 January 1995; and Coco Fusco and Christian Hale, 'Wreaking Havoc on the Signified', *frieze*, no.22, May 1995, pp.34–41.

[18] See *ibid.* and A. Wallach, 'David Hammons' Secret Magic Show', *op. cit.*

[19] On Hammons's ambiguous relationship to photography and documentation, see my *David Hammons: Bliz-aard Ball Sale, op. cit.*

[20] Sara Penn in conversation with the author, New York, 11 March 2014.

[21] R. Smith, 'The New, Irreverent Approach to Mounting Exhibitions', *op. cit.*

[22] Although very different, Fred Wilson's 1992 exhibition project *Mining the Museum* might usefully be discussed in relation to Hammons's Knobkerry exhibition. Wilson studied the items in the collection of the Maryland Historical Society and, by way of infiltration, exacted his own version of an existing display space and system when he presented repoussé-style silver vessels alongside slave shackles from the same period in a vitrine under the heading 'Metalwork 1793–1880', and ornate armchairs alongside a whipping post under the heading 'Cabinetmaking 1820–1960'. If Wilson's project was primarily about how race is lodged in the museological, Hammons's was primarily about how it is lodged in the fiduciary. On *Mining the Museum*, see Huey Copeland, *Bound to Appear: Art, Blackness, and the Site of Slavery in Multicultural America*, Chicago: University of Chicago Press, 2013, pp.25–62.

[23] Horace Brockington and Gylbert Coker acted as organisers of the project, although both attest that Hammons was its initiator and true curator. Brockington and Coker in conversation with the author, with the assistance of Alhena Katsof, New York, 4 August 2014 and 26 May 2014, respectively.

[24] See Philippe Vergne, 'Miles Away', in Michelle Piranio (ed.), *David Hammons Yves Klein / Yves Klein David Hammons*, Aspen, CO: Aspen Art Museum, 2014, p.105.

²⁵ Penn did not record the sales price and visitors' recollections vary, but one common refrain was that whatever the price, it was the same for every item. The Walker Art Center's records attest that they purchased *Flight Fantasy* (1978) in 1994 from Knobkerry for the sale price of $25,000, which suggests that it was the most probable sales price. For his part, A.C. Hudgins describes refusing, on Hammons's behalf, a discount to any potential buyer who asked. When one prominent collector insisted, it was suggested that he buy the work for $5,000 more than the sales price and apply a discount to that, effectively buying at the regular asking price. The collector declined. Conversation with A.C. Hudgins, 10 April 2017.

²⁶ Quoted in A. Wallach, 'David Hammons' Secret Magic Show', *op. cit.*

²⁷ Yve-Alain Bois, 'Ray Guns', in Y.-A. Bois and Rosalind E. Krauss (ed.), *Formless: A User's Guide*, Cambridge, MA: MIT Press, 1997, pp.173–76.

²⁸ K. Jones, 'Interview with David Hammons', *op. cit.*, p.253.

²⁹ Interview no.1 with Papo Colo and Jeanette Ingberman, *op. cit.*, p.11.

³⁰ The issue was subtitled, without irony, 'African-American Artists Are Truly Free at Last', with articles including Jack E. White, 'The Beauty of Black Art', and Henry Louis Gates, Jr, 'Black Creativity: On the Cutting Edge', *Time*, 10 October 1994, pp.66–73, 74–75.

³¹ See A. Wallach, 'David Hammons' Secret Magic Show', *op. cit.* 'Black Male' ran at the Whitney Museum of American Art from 10 November 1994 to 5 March 1995.

³² *Ibid.*

³³ Hammons likely thought that not much truly critical could come of an exhibition that didn't begin by refuting the site's white walls, corporate policies or institutional history of exclusion, least of all at the Whitney, since, as he declared in another context, 'Their relationship with black artists has been negative since Day 1.' Quoted in *ibid.*

³⁴ Quoted in Manthia Diawara, 'Dak'Art 2004 Sheep Raffle', in Salah M. Hassan and Cheryl Finley (ed.), *Diaspora, Memory, Place: David Hammons, Maria Magdalena Campos-Pons, Pamela Z*, Munich and London: Prestel, 2008, p.138.

³⁵ Iolanda Pensa, 'Art and Artists at Dak'Art 2004', *nafas*, http://u-in-u.com/nafas/articles/2004/dakart-2004/.

³⁶ Brian O'Doherty, *Inside the White Cube*, *op. cit.*, p.80.

³⁷ Interview with R. Storr, *Yardbird Suite*, *op. cit.*, p.30.

³⁸ *Ibid.*

³⁹ Quoted in Charlie Ahearn, '"Tragic Magic" Sparks Hammons Retrospective at P.S.1', *City Sun*, 16–22 January 1991, clipping in the MoMA PS1 archives, series I.A. 1583, 'David Hammons: Rousing the Rubble, 1969–1990 (16 December 1990–10 February 1991).

⁴⁰ Zora Neale Hurston, 'How It Feels to Be Colored Me', *The World Tomorrow*, May 1928, pp.215–16.

* This essay was originally written as a section of my book *David Hammons Bliz-aard Ball Sale* (London: Afterall, 2017), but was included only in parts for the final manuscript. It was subsequently published as a chapter in Elena Filipovic (ed.), *The Artist as Curator: An Anthology* (Milan and London: Mousse Publishing and König Books, 2017). For their help procuring images, precious memories, or other forms of support, the author thanks: Erma Estwick, Linda Goode Bryant, Carmen Hammons, David Hammons, A.C. Hudgins, Lauren Hudgins, Alhena Katsof, the late Sara Penn, Lois Plehn, Connie Tilton and the late Jack Tilton.

Brothers in Arms: Laboratoire AGIT'art and Tenq in Dakar in the 1990s

Clémentine Deliss

In the beginning, in the mid-1970s, the Laboratoire AGIT'art was a fluid, free group of men and women. There was no formal organisation, no president and secretary or proper membership system. Instead people were called to meet. These meetings would take the form of an atelier or a workshop. Originally, they were held behind closed doors. The first theatre workshops happened in 1974, at Cap Manuel, and then much later in the courtyard of Géerard Chenet, the Senegalese writer and dramaturge of Haitian origin. But they also took place in public locations such as the Musée Dynamique or on the stage of the Centre Culturel Français of Dakar.

Initially the Laboratoire AGIT'art was connected to an experimental theatre group called Les Tréteaux (literally, 'The Sawhorses', or 'The Trestles'), directed by the late Yussufa John. His troupe offered an antidote to the official productions presented at Dakar's Théâtre National Daniel Sorano, which centred around Aimé Césaire and other proponents of Négritude. A subsequent relationship brought theatre and the visual arts together with notions of madness, deviance and mendacity.

However, the specific interdisciplinary focus of the Laboratoire AGIT'Art, which soldered its alliance to the visual arts, actually originated with Tenq, the project space that I ran at the first Village des Arts, in the early 1980s. At the time, Tenq had revealed to us artists the correspondences that exist between all art forms. We had studios, ran workshops and set up a radio station, a kind of spoken magazine. When we were evicted from this space in 1983, we transferred our AGIT'Art workshops to Issa Samb's courtyard in the rue Jules Ferry in order to continue experimenting. From the start, the role of Issa Samb was not that of a visual artist but that of a philosopher, a writer and an agitator. Writing, and the question of the text, developed later on.

*Since ten years nothing more has taken place in the Laboratoire AGIT'art.
This is in great part because individuals have pushed to be recognised on their
own merits, and it is no longer about a group identity.*
– El Sy, 2013[1]

Artists' collectives often acquire mythical status despite the fact that they rarely remain intact over time. Misunderstandings and arguments together with purely circumstantial conditions can lead to bifurcations within what was once a shared ideal. The reason why one disavows a collective can be as banal as the wish to move on. It can also result from the mix of passion and enmity that constitutes any dynamic, experimental practice. Similarly, the narrative about a collective is likely to be recast according to whose participation is vocal at whichever moment in time. The following account is therefore subjective and inevitably partisan. It is rooted in my personal contact with artists, philosophers, writers and politicians-in-the-wings who lived and worked in Dakar in the 1990s. This includes the Laboratoire AGIT'art, of which I have been a member since 1995, and also the manifestations of Tenq[2] and Huit Facettes,[3] both important artist-run initiatives that, like the Laboratoire AGIT'art, were driven in great part by the curatorial work of Senegalese artist El Sy. At the time, my engagement with these collectives constituted a form of extended practice, beyond producing exhibitions.[4] Indeed, exhibiting these artists and their group projects was perhaps the least productive curatorial channel through which to mediate their practice. Instead, performances, workshops, think tanks and the publishing organ *Metronome*, first produced in Dakar in 1996, helped to convey both the specificity of our collaborations and the differentiated models of documentation that represented and communicated this work.[5]

It is helpful to remember that at the beginning of the 1990s very little information circulated on the state of contemporary art on the African continent. Apart from a few venues scattered around London, including the Africa Centre and the October Gallery, it was hard to actually see new work or locate recent catalogues and journals. There was *Third Text*, created in 1988 by Rasheed Araeen, which carried reviews and articles on mainly diasporic and postcolonial issues, and *Revue Noire*, the first edition of which was published in Paris in 1991. But magazines such as *Nka* (established in 1994) and *Chimurenga* (established much later, in 2002) did not yet exist. Further, the discourse around contemporary art practice and criticism in Africa rarely made the pages of the ethnographic or tribal arts periodicals, and pamphlets printed on the continent such as *The Eye* (based in Nigeria) were difficult to acquire.[6] The circulation of information was limited both outside and within the African continent itself. Artists working in Angola or South Africa were unlikely to be informed about their colleagues' practices in Senegal unless they travelled there to visit them. This insularity was compounded by francophone, anglophone and lusophone divides that not only produced spatial and linguistic handicaps but also redirected the flow of knowledge from the continent back to the former colonial base. There were no internet links, no websites, no emails and no Skype conversations, which, coupled with minimal funding to travel to the continent, meant that actually locating the nerve of a practice was not a straightforward procedure.

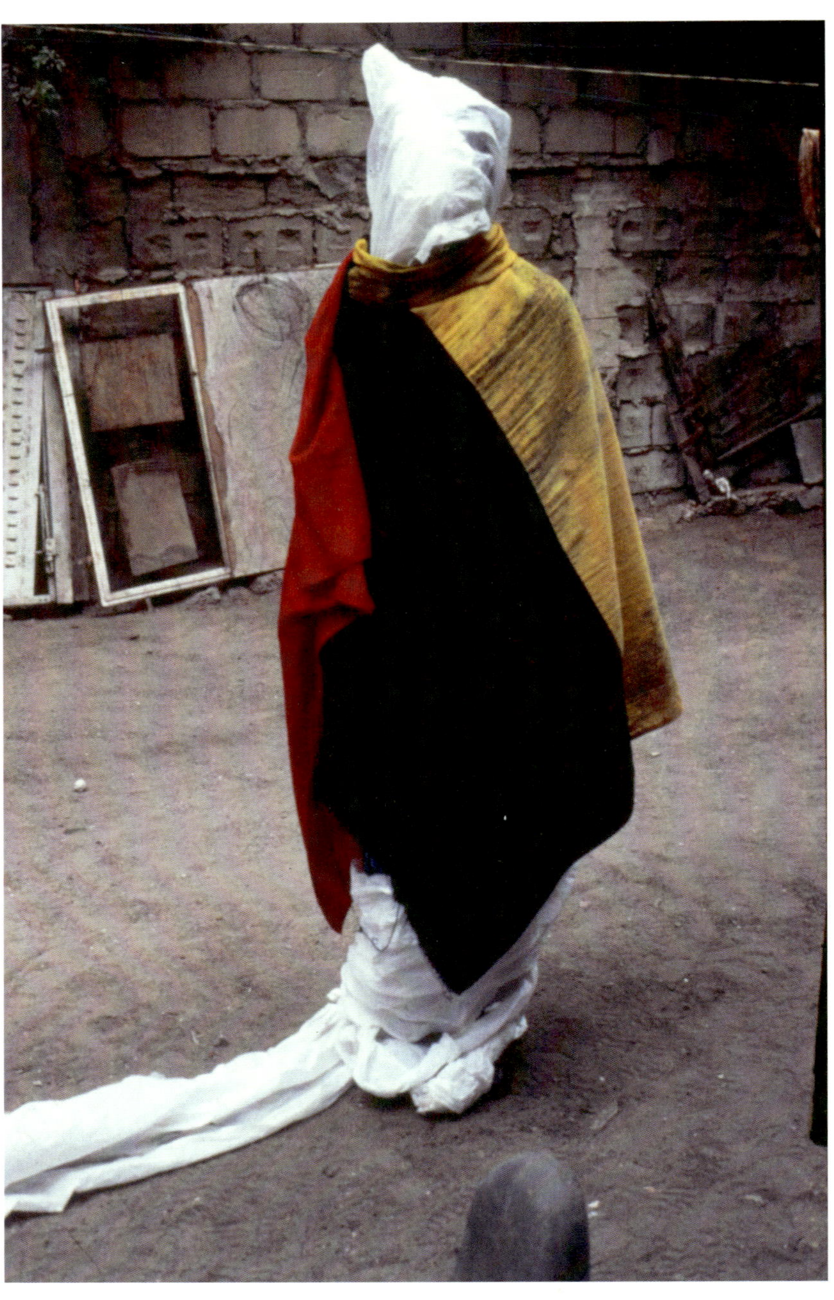

Performance of
the Laboratoire
AGIT'art,
Dakar, 1989.
Photography:
El Sy

Thanks to the trilingual anthology on Senegalese art edited by El Sy and the German educator Friedrich Axt, and published in 1989 by the Weltkulturen Museum in Frankfurt (which, in a strange turn of fate, I now direct [at the time of writing, 2014]). I could reference an indispensable mapping of the Dakar art scene, including critical texts and portraits of both individual artists and Senegalese arts institutions.[7] Under the direction of Josef Franz Thiel, the Weltkulturen Museum (formerly the Museum für Völkerkunde) had pioneered a shift in ethnographic collecting, acquiring near to 3,000 works by artists based in West, East, Central and Southern Africa over the course of several years, beginning in 1974. The anthology complemented the wide range of artworks that El Sy and Axt were commissioned to collect for the museum – probably making El Sy the only African artist and curator living on the continent to have been entrusted, in the mid-1980s, with the development of a new art collection for a museum in Europe.[8]

The debates around contemporary art from Africa that emerged in the late 1980s were heated. The large-scale exhibition 'Magiciens de la Terre' (1989), curated by Jean-Hubert Martin in Paris, spawned a new collecting fever for African art, focussed on non-academically trained artists.[9] On another tangent, *Revue Noire* began a comprehensive charting of artistic scenes on the African continent, and in 1992 featured a painting by El Sy on its cover.[10] If you knew where to look, the work of El Sy was of central importance, even though it emerged from a francophone rather than an anglophone alliance with the continent, which in early-1990s Europe was still significant. Although artists were engaging with a new global cartography, the former colonial connections remained steadfast: London and Paris divided the West African art scenes, just as their respective art academies had previously exported models of education based alternately on the British art school or the French Beaux Arts curriculum.[11] In addition to this informational divergence, polemics between so-called internationalist, scholarly informed artworks and a genre of self-taught, neo-traditionalist expression plagued discussion around new practices, setting up opposing camps and frustrating, rather than supporting, communication and exchange. As a curator, I was interested in experimenting with different platforms of mediation that would help to interconnect the strategies of artists working in diverse cities around the world. In 1991, I curated a seminar series on art criticism titled 'Making it real compared to what?' at the School of Oriental and African Studies (SOAS) in London. The discussions were based on pairings such as that of the late art critic and editor of *Artscribe* magazine Stuart Morgan with the Nigerian artist and academic Olu Oguibe, or the then-emerging artist Yinka Shonibare with the British collector and Triangle workshop initiator Robert Loder.[12]

I first met El Sy and Issa Samb in Dakar in March 1992, when I was doing research to develop a concept for 'africa95', a prospective arts festival spearheaded by the Royal Academy of Arts, to be held in Africa and the UK in 1995.[13] Our discussions took place in a courtyard in the centre of town and revolved around a fervent exchange of positions. It was clear that El Sy had experience in curating and was a respected artist and activist on the Senegalese scene. In the early 1980s, he had been behind the notorious artists' studio

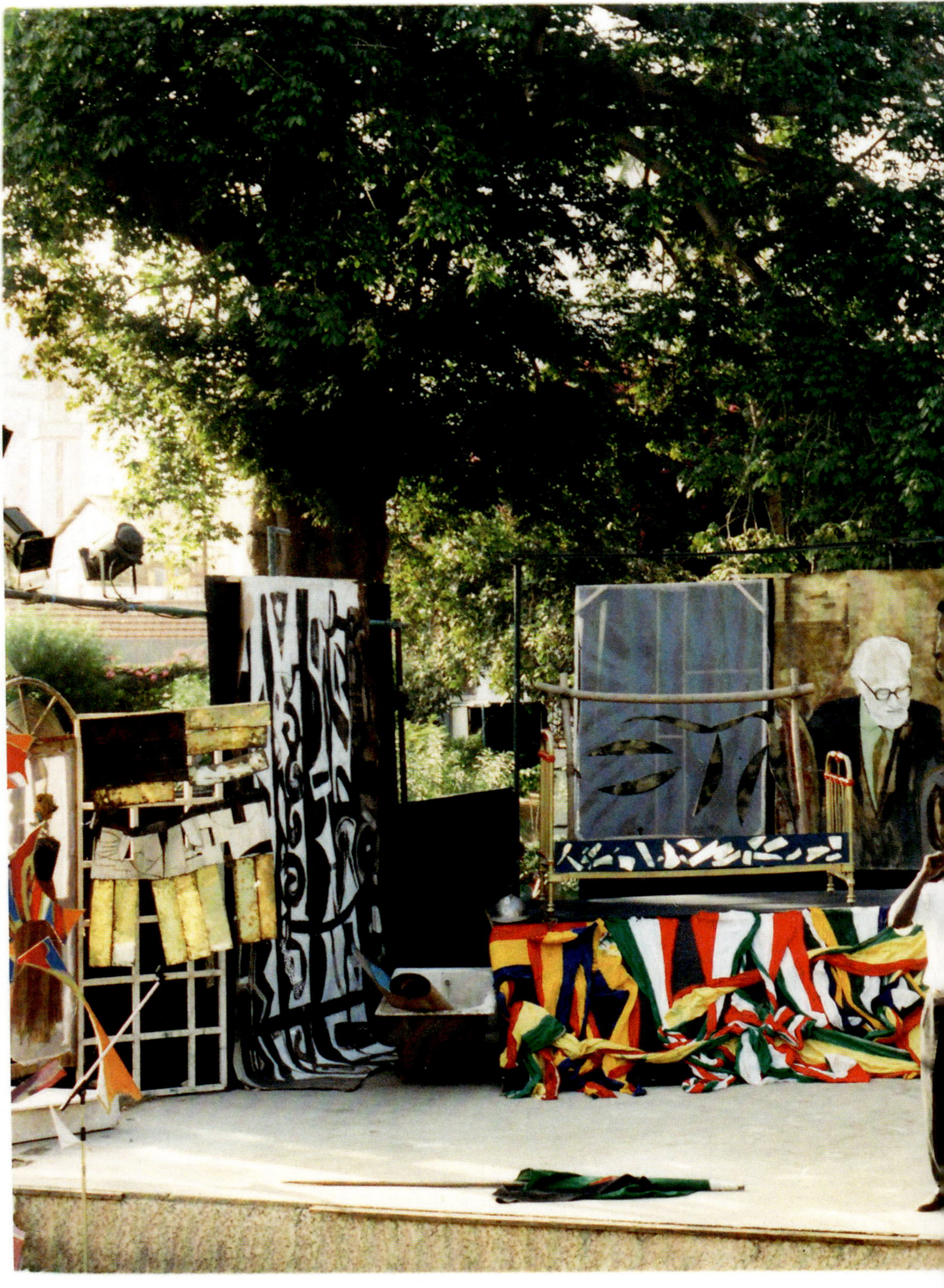

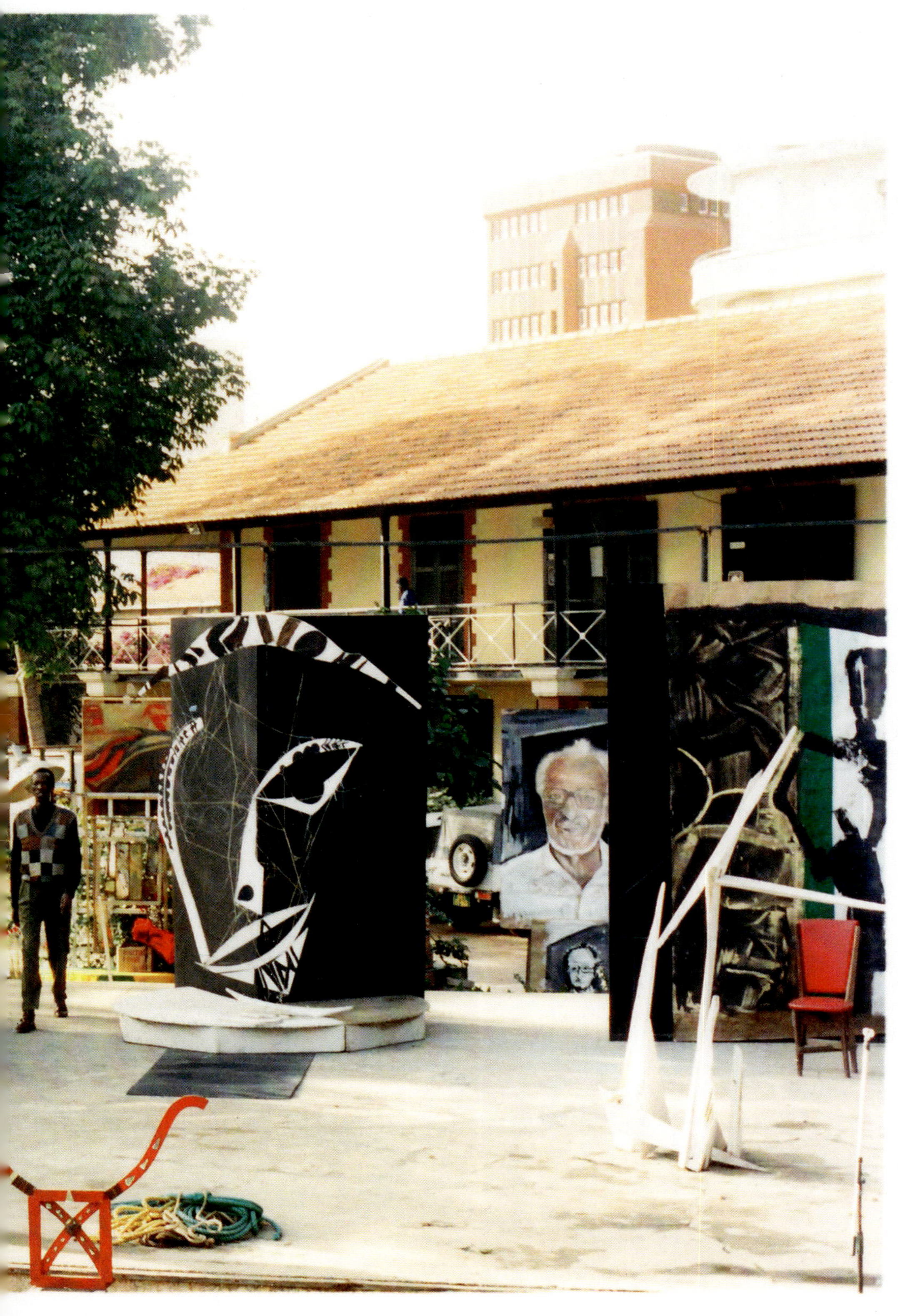

complex Village des Arts, located in a former army barracks on Dakar's seafront.[14] Until it was ambushed by the military in 1983, the Village des Arts, with its project space Tenq, run by El Sy and Ali Traoré, provided the main site of experimental development for around forty artists from different disciplines, including the Laboratoire AGIT'art, the Nouveau Toucan theatre troupe, musician Baaba Maal and the N'Guelewar Jazz Band de Banjul. El Sy was also known for his work as a painter: since 1979 he had quite literally used his feet to paint, and thereby kickstarted a defiant response to President Léopold Sédar Senghor's promotion in Dakar of the figuration associated with the mid-twentieth-century École de Paris.[15]

El Sy's work in the 1990s consisted of large-scale acrylic paintings on rice sacks. Both abstract and ornamental, these flexible, animated wall hangings offered a further riposte to the Gobelin-style tapestries that Senghor had put into production in the town of Thiés in the mid-1960s as part of his nation-building exercise. In contrast to the symbolic knighthood proffered to artists by the president, El Sy's references extended deep into the homesteads of Senegalese working-class families, whose consumption of foreign rice was symptomatic of the increasing growth of Asian-African trade routes. Collecting empty rice sacks from people's kitchens, he would stitch them together into two-by-three-metre-wide surfaces, which, once painted, could re-enter the homestead for the price of a full sack of grain. In some situations, they were nailed directly to buildings in the streets of Dakar, or exhibited in combination with tarred objects and oil paintings, suggesting a dynamic superimposition of structure, medium and façade. El Sy's performance-centred paintings, sometimes executed with his naked feet, generated a complex articulation between the body in movement and its immediate physical environment. In the late 1970s and early 80s, his exhibitions in Dakar were accompanied by actions in which images of paintings were projected onto the mummified frame of his body.

The dilapidated objects lying around the courtyard in which we first met also fascinated me. Their seemingly careless presentation not only contravened any notion of museological conservation but also suggested a defiance of the market – of being purchased as single artworks or recouped as part of an ethnographic collection. Hanging from strings or pinned to crumbling walls and covered with layers of sand, dirt and dead leaves, these heteroclite artefacts were in effect part of a wider web of interdisciplinary enquiry connected to the Laboratoire AGIT'art. They weren't the production of just one person, but the result of a dialogue between many, and had been used to punctuate a specific moment in collective and performative time. The incongruent character of this yard, located in Dakar's busy city centre and hidden behind an unassuming entrance, suggested something of an alchemical laboratory. Between the scattered matter, seemingly caught in a *caput mortuum* phase of degeneration, one could read quotations, aphorisms and traces of experimentation in chalk and charcoal script on black and white boards. A long table surrounded by chairs bore witness to daily meetings and impromptu sessions. Pamphlets and invitation cards, reminding one to attend diplomatic cocktails, literary readings or exhibition openings, lay together with notes scribbled on small pieces of paper by people who had passed by. All this together created an impression of choreographed chaos. I read in this scenario a deviant language of philological interpretation not dissimilar to the *bas-matérialisme* that Georges Bataille had evoked in his journal *Documents*.[16] In the entry for *poussière* (dust), Bataille acerbically points to the philosophical ramifications of rituals of domestic cleanliness that speak against impending death and the gradual decay of matter over time. To illustrate his text, he chose two photographs most probably taken in the Musée d'Ethnographie du Trocadéro in Paris, which feature several naked mannequins and various ethnographic artefacts, all covered in debris and dust.[17]

As our working relationship developed and I travelled to Dakar more frequently, I would take every opportunity to visit Issa Samb in the courtyard. I quickly learnt not to drop by in the early morning. Samb worked after dark, engaging in what might be best described as *le travail de la nuit*, or night work. Once dusk had fallen and the courtyard was pitch-black, he would leave, scaling the city streets in his long, flamboyant coat (designed by Oumou Sy) and coming into close contact with another group of citizens whose nocturnal existence informed his investigations into the metaphysics of time. Sometimes I would meet him by chance while out with El Sy, and we would go for drinks in one of the gaudy 'American bars' in town, or hang out at an international hotel, where we would be sure to meet Senegalese lawyers, bankers, politicians and traders, who more often than not were undisclosed members of the Laboratoire AGIT'art.[18] Dakar's city life, positioned around the central district of the Plateau, with its remarkable modernist architecture, was a hub for architects, artists, musicians and writers – the intelligentsia that had grown up under Senghorian cosmopolitanism. Samb, with his mercurial nature and ubiquitous presence at every high- or low-flying event in the city, was something of a *passeur*, who, like the jester or *fou du roi*, intercepted and mediated the changing moods in the polis. Neighbouring wars, transmigration, the devastation of natural resources, electoral fever, the poverty of the city or current cultural policy were all topics in the press and on the street that Issa Samb was passionate about. During my daily visits to the courtyard, I learnt an immense amount from him. He would ask me to write down as much as possible from our conversations and would listen carefully as I spoke to him about developments in my work. Other times we would sit and listen to the radio together, waiting for people to pass by. Samb's role in the Laboratoire AGIT'art was anchored around the yard in the rue Jules Ferry where, with a combination of eccentric philosophical and judiciary allure, he held court.

In London in September 1995, after working together for three years, El Sy and Issa Samb informed me that I had been co-opted into the Laboratoire AGIT'art. Their invitation to join the collective coincided with a high point in our collaboration: an unusual lecture held at the 'africa95' conference 'Mediums of Change', chaired by the late Stuart Hall, to which Issa Samb had been invited to speak about the visual arts of Africa. The night before the event, in classic AGIT'art methodology, he entrusted me with the task of typing, translating and editing his oral contribution, and delegated the visual dimension of the conference to El Sy. The next day, the three of us lined up onstage and Samb began speaking in Wolof, Senegal's national language, then abruptly switched

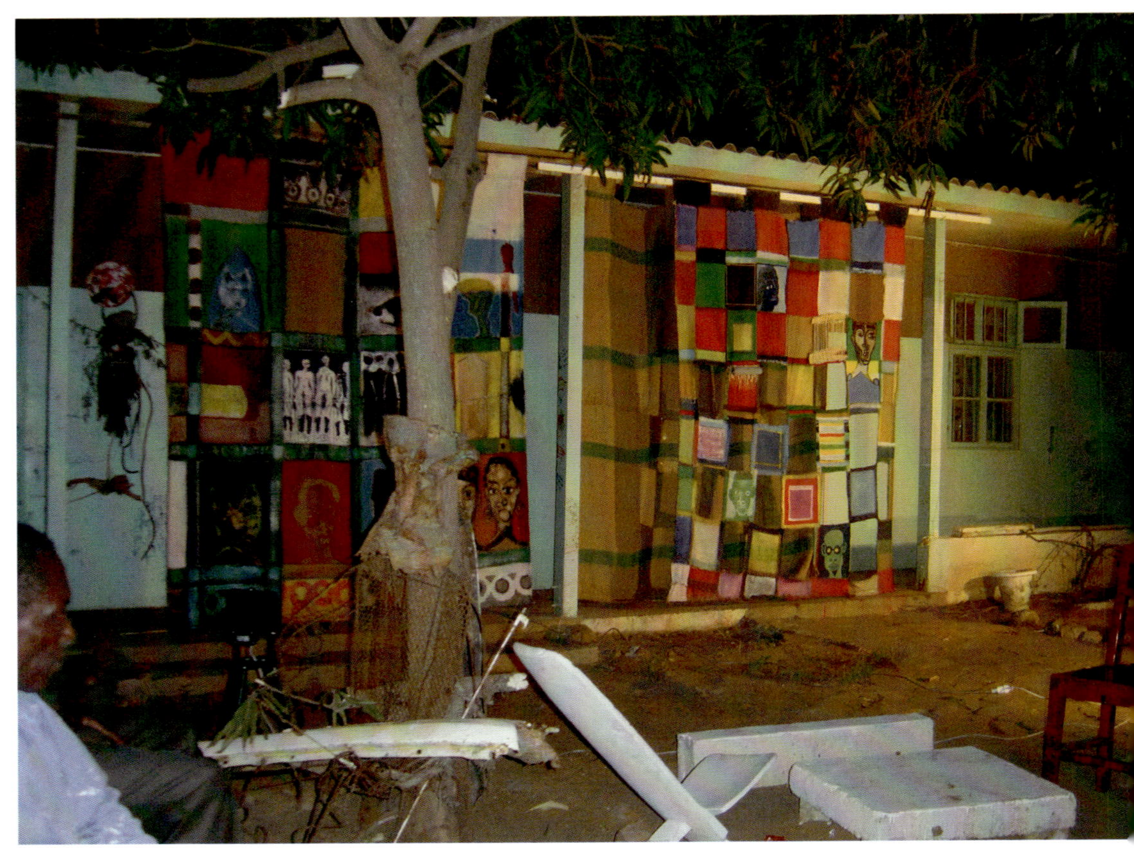

Paintings on rice sacks by El Sy, hanging outside his studio in the former Chinese camp, Dakar, 2004. Photography: Clémentine Deliss

into French. As soon as I sensed a pause in his speech, I would utter a rejoinder in English, reading out sections of the text that we had composed together:

> *If the Laboratoire AGIT'art has a love for time, it is not for the irrational and the spiritual. So don't talk here about race, don't mention Gobineau, Meiners, Darwin or Frobenius… The idea of the supremacy of race is to be excluded. And time goes by, like the red Mosel, like the red Thames, like the Ganges, like the Senegal. Time runs out, and the fascination with memory remains in the impossible amnesia between politics and despair, the wound on the body of painting. I'm sick of seeing drawings, of seeing objects, of seeing the past and of talking to myself about the present. Of which present are you talking about if not of presence itself? [...]*

> *The visual arts of Senegal are searching in the luminous outline of the mornings of market days. There one discovers that the museums store only one kind of knowledge, whose colours can only be grasped through an apparent immobility. At least in Senegal, the country I come from, one exists in the movement of colour at all moments of the day. In any case, in this country, painting could not be a goal in itself but simply a means to knowledge and therefore to transformation. If the dream is important, the real, the experienced is at stake.[19]*

Issa Samb and I continued alternating between languages while El Sy projected a kaleidoscope of slides that depicted everything from street scenes in Dakar to people, artworks and performances. Combined with the spoken word, the shower of disparate images created multiple layers of communication without ever proposing a clear position of authority or expertise. Samb had performed the antithesis of an art historical exegesis: a complex group action and lyrical discourse unexpected within the academic setting of the conference, and dismissed by many as sheer obfuscation.

'SOS Culture', the performance held two days earlier at the opening of 'Seven Stories about Modern Art in Africa', an exhibition I curated at the Whitechapel Art Gallery, London together with El Sy and four other curators from Africa, had proved equally unfathomable to the majority of those who witnessed it.[20] It contained key elements from previous actions by El Sy, such as an invocation of the past, a live mummification and a projection of photographs onto the human body. El Sy had designed a wooden stage at the foot of the stairs leading down to the Whitechapel's main gallery. Members of the public could sit on the steps, peep through the patchwork of punctured metal sheeting or stand tightly packed within the installation. Following a series of dirge-like exclamations, Issa Samb began to envelop El Sy with metres of white muslin, a practice that referenced both Muslim and Dogon burial rites. El Sy's sealed body stood upright on a NASA photograph of the world, which, within the context of the performance, communicated an archaic 'Afronautical'[21] figure. Using a slide projector to illuminate the stage, images were cast onto his swathed immobile body, while Samb stood nearby, reading out headlines from *Le Monde*. Members of the audience gathered close, attentive to the course of action but unsure of what to do. After citing various zones of conflict, from Chechnya to Casamance, in a mock-dictatorial tone, Samb began to unravel the bandages, before briefly placing a hangman's noose around his compatriot's neck. Having captured an unsuspecting member of the public, who was handed a metal apron and a disc to wear on his head, El Sy – now liberated – began to unroll a suspended painting of a cowrie shell, which dropped down like a translucent coloured screen. The performance ended thirty minutes later, when Samb, shouting, 'Alors, c'est de quelle Afrique qu'il s'agit?' ('So, which Africa are we talking about here?'), walked through another of El Sy's paintings, which acted as a permeable door into the neighbouring installation by Nigerian curator Chika Okeke.

Over the following years, El Sy and Issa Samb introduced me to numerous collaborators of the Laboratoire AGIT'art. As I understood it, the main quality of the group was its methodology: there were no exhibitions of the Laboratoire AGIT'Art; instead the heterogeneity and the complementary character of its members were reflected in the performances that they initiated together over the years. In the 1990s, these had become sporadic, even though daily discussions in the courtyard with impromptu visitors and members were a central part of the collective's activities. During my visits to Dakar I met and spent time with: the philosopher and critic As M'Bengue;[22] the actors Magaye Niang and Pap Oumar Diop dit Makéna; the latter's brother, the theatre director and actor Ablaye Dani Diop; the film-maker Djibril Diop Mambéty; the fashion designer Oumou Sy; the feminist and politician Marie-Angélique Savané; the architect Pierre Goudiaby; the arts organiser Mor Lyssa Bâ; the itinerant poet Thierno Seydou Sall; the sculptor Babacar Sadikh Traoré; the photographer Bouna Médoune Seye; the trader Abdou Bâ; the banker and collector Libasse Thiaw; and Mamadou Traoré Diop, author and advisor to the president.[23] Each person in the Laboratoire AGIT'Art held a particular role and responsibility, so that everyone's individual competence would always find its position within the group. The dramaturge Yussufa John, who later emigrated from Senegal to Martinique, was, until his untimely death in 1995, the 'Chef de l'atelier de théâtre' ('Head of the theatre studio'). His role appears to have been central to the creation of the collective in the mid-1970s, when performance and painting were first experimented with. When Issa Samb arrived at Heathrow Airport in the summer of 1995, unexpectedly dragging a two-metre-long bundle of rags through customs, he was effectively re-enacting Yussufa John's interment. This corpse-like sculpture subsequently became part of the installation curated by El Sy for 'Seven Stories', which included, together with four paintings by Souleymane Keita, numerous 'objects of performance' recuperated from the courtyard in Dakar and sent to London via more conventional routes.

In the Laboratoire AGIT'art, El Sy was 'Chef de l'atelier de peinture et de costume' ('Head of the painting and costume studio'), responsible for the *mise en espace*, or visual dramaturgy, of the projects the group was involved in. He created the visible parameters of the stage area, designed the costumes, engineered the lighting and also acted certain parts. Additional members took care of noise (*bruitage*), some wrote (like myself) and others were responsible for film and photography. The artist and film-maker Bouna Médoune Seye documented the courtyard and shot an important photographic series in 1994, titled *Les Trottoirs de Dakar* (*Dakar's Pavements*): startling black-and-white portraits of madmen and misfits who populated the city's streets.[24] Another key figure at the time was the poet Thierno Seydou Sall, who travelled to villages reciting biting parodies of contemporary politics, the pharmaceutical industry and the role of non-governmental organisations in Africa, and who was also involved in the Laboratoire AGIT'art's investigations into anti-psychiatry.

On various occasions, Issa Samb, El Sy and Thierno Seydou Sall spoke to me about their relationship to the former colonial psychiatric clinic of Fann, at Cheikh Anta Diop University in Dakar. El Sy, who had met Henri Collomb, the head psychiatrist and director of the clinic, was interested in the 'loss of the faculty to dupe' that he recognised in the patients. Appropriately, the workshops that the Laboratoire AGIT'Art conducted in the psychiatric unit in the 1980s were titled 'The Teaching of Deviance' and 'Premature Deviance and Loss of Consciousness'.[25] This crossover between art practice and experimental psychiatry connected to the collective's interests in performance, and also to their readings of Surrealism and the work of Antonin Artaud. Further, as a family member of the Tijani Sufi order, El Sy's practice engaged at times with a mysticism that might explain his attention to the dissociative intentionality of many psychiatric patients. Likewise, Issa Samb, who comes from the Lebou ethnic group centred on the shoreline of Dakar, is a practitioner of Ndeup, a traditional form of healing for individuals with psychic and social problems.

The relationship between Western notions of psychosis and Senegalese concepts of possession may well have provided an undercurrent to the structure of the performances produced by the Laboratoire AGIT'art.

Today it is hard to find written materials on or recordings of this early connection between the Laboratoire AGIT'art and the neurological and psychiatric research conducted at the university. However, transcriptions of interviews with Collomb, conducted by German author Hubert Fichte in the mid-1970s, suggest that Fann lay at the forefront of international debates about group therapies:

> *As doctors, we began to find out about traditional African and Islamic healing practices and I travelled all over Senegal and the neighbouring countries in order to visit traditional hospitals. [...] What I found so incredible were the social conditions within which these psychiatric patients lived. They were completely integrated in the everyday life of the village. They were not excluded or alienated. The therapist shared his daily life with them as if he had the same practical preoccupations and worries that they had. These impressions made me decide that in the Fann clinic in Dakar there would be no hierarchies between patients, carers and doctors. We take in many healthy people, too, family members of the sick, so that the sick person can get better by living together with healthy individuals. [...]*

> *Fann is a hospital that cares for those people who cannot be helped by the usual methods. These are individuals that we describe as existing in a state of transculturation. [...] We use a kind of group therapy, 'an ambient therapy' (thérapie d'ambience). [...] Sometimes, however, electroshock treatment satisfies the desire for an initiatory death, like a symbolic death, something that in traditional African societies precedes every new phase of transformation or development, and that can take place at the start of a psychiatric illness as much as it can signify the healing of it.[26]*

Unfortunately, Fichte does not appear to have met members of the Laboratoire AGIT'art, or if he did, I have not been able to trace any documentation of these meetings. However, his interviews at Fann, with their descriptions of group therapy, elucidate a tension between individual and collective identification that also characterised the Laboratoire AGIT'art. After a performance or a meeting took place, the group appeared to dissolve, leaving little trace of a physical communal presence beyond Issa Samb's courtyard, which acted as a depot for various objects left over from performances. What remained powerful was the act of verbal reiteration, a mnemonic referencing that recalled absent members. When I visited Dakar during the 1990s, several members were visible, even if many were no longer actively engaged in producing collective situations. Nevertheless, the former contributions of those who were absent, departed or deceased would invariably be called to mind by their colleagues through a process of repeated vocal referencing. An example of this unusual exercise of mnemonic restitution can even be found in a recent interview with Issa Samb, in which he invoked certain people he once knew, repeating their names, questioning where they might be and thereby reintroducing their pres-

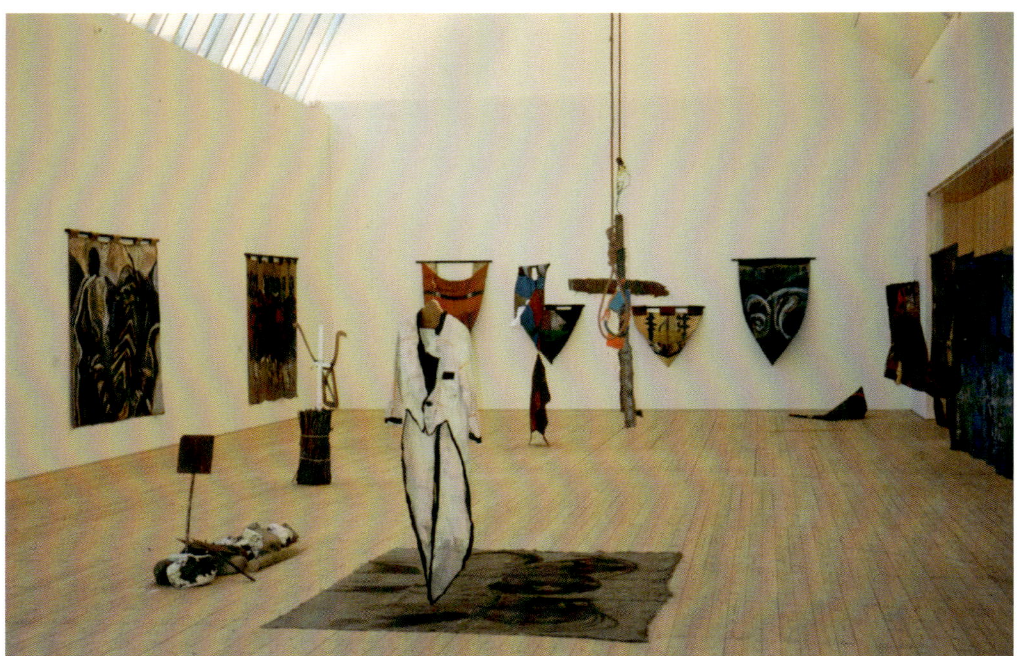

ence within a contemporary frame. Beyond this method of reiteration, which can prove baffling if you don't know who's who, Issa Samb doesn't explain the practice of the Laboratoire AGIT'art.

Throughout the 1990s, vigilance towards potential appropriation from the outside was a central concern for both El Sy and Issa Samb. Responding to Okwui Enwezor's investigations for the exhibition 'Global Conceptualism: Points of Origin, 1950s–1980s' (1999–2000), for example, Samb claimed to have travelled to Lagos with El Sy in 1977 in order to visit Fela Ransome Kuti's Kalakuta Republic.[27] This spurious statement was intended to support Enwezor's attempt to place Nigerian artists at the historical forefront of political activism and avant-gardist discourse in Africa, but it bore no relation to the truth. At the time, I interpreted this travesty as a form of communicational abstinence on the part of El Sy and Issa Samb, a tactic based on various tropes aligned to the dramatics of military communication: silence, disinformation, deferred response and abrupt action.[28] In a text published in *Metronome No.1* (1997), Samb partly divulges his interest in the manipulation of confusion. To do so, he employs the decoy of a fictive radio station to play out frictions between different players, who include an ex-politician turned art dealer and a voice, never identified, speaking on behalf of artists:

> *You see, rumour doesn't have a popular origin, it's one of the main weapons of power: it serves both to mould a feeble awareness and to divert the attention that might otherwise focus on the real – it's a roundabout way of preparing for events. Even better, a technique for overtaking them so as to change the course of time to one's advantage.*[29]

Laboratoire AGIT'art member Mamadou Traoré Diop once described Samb's trickster position to me as the posture of a 'contrabandiste d'idées',[30] a smuggler of ideas who slips between the higher echelons of Senegalese society and Dakar's twilight demi-monde. This theatrical persona is an aspect that Issa Samb has cultivated professionally, marking his career with a set of rarely overlapping realities and publics. Throughout the last twenty years, Samb has frequently left Dakar to work with the Marseille-based dramaturge Jean Michel Bruyère, with whom he also set up an organisation to rehabilitate street children.[31] He has acted in numerous stage productions directed by Bruyère and featured in his short films and videos. In turn, Bruyère has more than once been given free rein to reinstall the courtyard's environment. For the Dakar Biennale of 2004, the place was swept clean, works were strategically placed around the site and dead leaves were neatly piled along a labyrinthine route, which led to a cast-iron bed upon which a beggar-child slept.

If the state of the courtyard over the last forty years can be viewed as the developmental site of Samb's *Gesamtkunstwerk*, then the recent transposition of some of the objects into a gallery situation has effectively ruptured this extended time-based work with its subtle, alchemical decomposition.[32] His recent solo exhibitions at the Galérie Nationale d'Art, Dakar, in 2010, and the Office for Contemporary Art (OCA), Oslo, in 2013, have proved divisive within the collective. Several works, extricated from the courtyard and exhibited under his name, were effectively the results of group performances by the Laboratoire AGIT'art or productions from other workshops that were stored in the yard. Rather than include his colleagues in this recent re-contextualisation, Issa Samb has chosen to omit their presence and pursue a new, solo career as a visual artist.[33] This is not to imply that Samb has not always been an artist, but that his ascetic behaviour and his dialogical and political engagement have today veered towards a new field of individualised object production and commercialisation, which works in part to blot out his former brothers in arms.

Whilst Samb in the 1990s and early 2000s continued to hold court in his role of impulsive and volatile philosopher and agitator, El Sy's curatorial dedication to learning together and working together provided essential continuity to the sense of communality amongst artists in Dakar. In 1994, he reformulated the original Tenq of the early 1980s into an international workshop that he organised together with Anna Kindersley, Fodé Camara and a group of Senegalese artists in a former colonial secondary school in the northern town of Saint-Louis.[34] The two-week-long event also included the artists Johannes Phokela and Yinka Shonibare, whom El Sy had met in London. Two years later, Minister of Culture Abdoulaye Elimane Kane invited El Sy and me to take over an abandoned Chinese camp near Dakar's main airport, which became the location for a further version of Tenq as part of the Dakar Biennale in 1996, and subsequently became the new iteration of the Village des Arts.[35]

When El Sy and I took over the Chinese camp, there was running water but no electricity. Eleven barracks were subdivided into small sleeping chambers for five hundred workers, and, in addition to a large refectory and bathroom units, there was a press for producing bricks, stocks of ginseng and piles of maps and technical drawings, all in Mandarin. In the early 1980s, the Chinese government was commissioned by numerous West African states to design and build sports arenas in exchange for diplomatic support and trade privileges. The Chinese brought their own labourers to Senegal and built temporary housing for them in the suburbs of the city. Once the construction was completed, most of the Chinese left Senegal. Those who remained in Dakar moved out of the camp, and it remained uninhabited for over eight years. The camp had its own sophisticated system of irrigation and a profusion of mango trees, but it was rundown and needed cleaning up. Three weeks later, in May 1996, the new Tenq, understood once again as a point of artistic connection, opened the gates of the Chinese camp to the outside world. The flimsy dividing walls in the barracks had been knocked through and studios allocated to guest artists from Kenya, Zimbabwe, South Africa, Ivory Coast, Nigeria and the UK, who spent two weeks living and working together on-site. A gallery space was set up in the former canteen and a manifesto announcing the opening pasted onto the shed walls. 'Tenq 96' had an inflammable character, fighting for a new identity between the local history of artists' squats and government evictions on the one hand, and the demands for the high visibility and accelerated production that new internationalism commanded on the other. Although the occupation of the site was not intended to continue beyond the two-week session, El Sy and the core group never left the new Village des Arts and several artists have been based there ever since. This nearly untouchable situation has provided the city of Dakar with an arts infrastructure that remains one of the only initiatives related to the biennial to have survived throughout the years.

Both Tenq and, later, the group Huit Facettes, which operated from the rural village of Hamdallaye in southern Senegal, represented in the 1990s a form of infrastructural engineering initiated by artists. Although these projects originated from a local base, they mirrored the effects of the resurgent global economic situation of the mid-to-late 1990s. The Senegalese Ministry of Culture was sensitive to these artist-run strategies and often supported them, keen to connect to foreign agencies such as the British Council or Belgian NGOs. In terms of form and intentionality, these projects reflected other artist-led frameworks that were taking place elsewhere at the time, such as the Triangle workshops that brought artists together from different international localities,[36] or the early interventionism of the Danish group Superflex in Tanzania.[37]

In the 1990s, Tenq and Huit Facettes provided what many politicians were unable to at the time: they set up links between art and development politics; attempted to break down hierarchies within art practice; initiated space and structure for new work to be made; and relayed artistic positions across the African continent through the networking effects of international workshops. Such relations between artist and audience had been at the origin of the experimental Tenq of the 1980s, which effectively nurtured the Laboratoire AGIT'Art through its subversive methodology and underground politicisation.

In contrast to Tenq, the Laboratoire AGIT'art was less evident as a public collective; it practically cultivated autonomy from formalised cultural or social initiatives. In the mid-1990s, it was largely kept alive by the activities of El

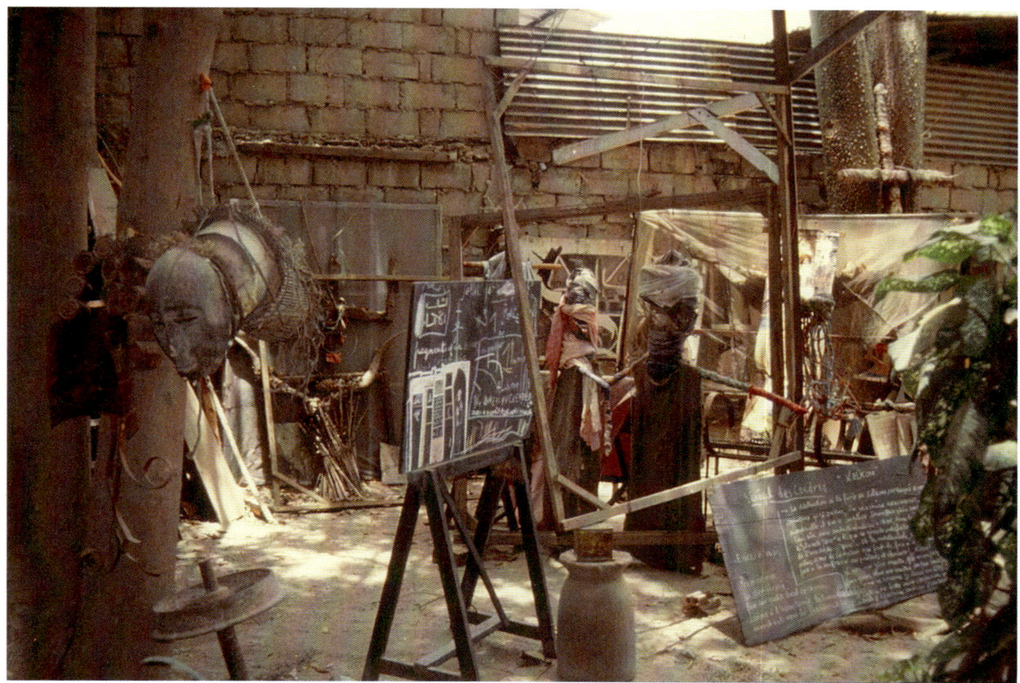

Sy, Issa Samb and myself. By the end of the millennium, the collective status of the group was at a low point. Attempts to reinvigorate it and convene several members at once for large-scale performances did take place, but the results were far from cohesive.[38] It appeared that the methodology of the Laboratoire AGIT'art was to remain the codified knowledge of a few people, and that, like all powerful artists' groups, it would be discussed with passion but rarely successfully reactivated.[39] As the years passed, the open-air office in the courtyard in the rue Jules Ferry increasingly resembled an old boys' debating chamber, where strategy would be discussed that was no longer connected to collective performances.

> *Micro-government. And again, or once more, as before, they meet. The lawyer, the economist, the philosopher, the film-maker, the curator. Everyday at 4 p.m., the majority of this micro-government convenes. And, repeating antecedents, emphasising solutions, naming the past, they discuss the breakdown of agriculture, the fate of farmers, the World Bank and its misfired attention and, underneath all of this, they seek parallels and wait for rain to fall, as if the parched land could only be rescued through the definition of actions.*[40]

Restive and controversial during its time, the Laboratoire AGIT'art's numerous collaborators were always cautious about divulging too many details about the way it operated. Instead the collective was founded on an ethos of initiate and interdisciplinary experimentation that was performed and exchanged through the different roles played by each of its protagonists. To break down this cryptic methodology into an art historical analysis for the benefit of today's global

View of objects of performance in the courtyard of Issa Samb, Dakar, 1992. Photography: Clémentine Deliss audience throws up many questions about the accelerated commodification of alternative theories of knowledge production and art practice. However legitimate it may seem to disseminate information on former artistic methodologies, this procedure raises many questions about the language employed to do so, the status of the document produced, the ownership of this material and, with it, the cannibalistic urge to accumulate the codes of other cultures as one's own. Before his death, film-maker Djibril Diop Mambéty warned El Sy and me of the dangers of vulgarising the Laboratoire AGIT'art and betraying the ethos behind its autonomy. El Sy's recent comment that the group no longer functions with the collective identity it once had reminds one of the dangers that exist today in romanticising former moments of creative conjunction between artists: 'The mummy has been buried. You can't exhume it now!'[41]

Notes

An earlier version of this essay was presented at the symposium 'Artist as Curator: Collective Practices', organised by MRes Art: Exhibition Studies, Central Saint Martins at the Whitechapel Gallery, London on 19 April 2013. Video recordings of the event are available at http://www.afterall.org/online/artist-as-curator-collaborative-practices-symposium-videos-online#.U2EoTce6AXw.

[1] El Sy in conversation with the author, November 2013. All quotes from El Sy are translated from French by the author.

[2] Tenq is Wolof for 'ankle joint', 'articulation' or 'connecting point', and translates in this context as 'Meetings between Artists and Audiences'. Tenq started as a gallery and project space, where El Sy and Ali Traoré organised experimental situations and exhibitions of artists' works between 1980 and 1983. It was later recast as an international workshop project, curated by El Sy and the Tenq group of artists in 1994 in Saint-Louis (as part of 'africa95') and in 1996 in Dakar (as part of the Dakar Biennale).

[3] Huit Facettes Interaction is the original name of this artists' grouping, but it is often abbreviated to Huit Facettes. Established in 1996, members included El Sy, Kan-Si (also known as Kane Sy), Fodé Camara, Cheikh Niass, Jean Marie Bruce, Abdoulaye Ndoye and Mor Lyssa Bâ. Their first event took place in 1996 and was called 'Les ateliers d'Hamdallaye' ('The Workshops of Hamdallaye'). The group worked with local craftspeople and developed alternative activities for the villagers during the winter season, initiating a specific relation between urban and rural aesthetic practices. The project was supported financially by a Belgian NGO and complemented by the investment of the artists themselves. Additional events organised by Huit Facettes include: 'Carrément pour la paix' ('Directly for Peace', 1997), 'Téléfood Dakar' (1998), the workshop 'Ici et maintenant' ('Here and Now', Joal-Fadiouth, 1998) and the performance-exhibition 'National Summit on Africa Washington DC' (2000). In 2002, the group took part in Documenta11 in Kassel.

[4] The following list details curatorial work I initiated between 1994 and 2003, which involved the participation of El Sy and Issa Samb as well as Fodé Camara, Kan-Si and other artists in Dakar: 'Tenq 94' (international workshop in Saint-Louis, as part of the 'africa95' festival, 1994); 'Seven Stories about Modern Art in Africa' (Whitechapel Art Gallery, London and Malmö Konsthall, 1995–96); 'Tenq 96' (Chinese village, Dakar Biennale, 1996); *Fama & Fortune Bulletin*, no.17 (1996); *Metronome* (1996–2007, of which no.0, 1, 3 and 7 include texts by Issa Samb and photographs by El Sy); 'Tempolabor: A Libertine Laboratory?' (a meeting behind closed doors with the participation of Issa Samb and Kan-Si, at Kunsthalle Basel and Kaskadenkondensator, Basel, which preceded the publication of *Metronome No.3 Tempolabor: A Libertine Laboratory?* (Basel) 1998); 'Bureau d'Esprit' (Michelangelo Pistoletto's Cittadellarte, Biella, 1999, with El Sy, as part of *Metronome No.4–5–6 Backwards Translation* (Edinburgh, Bordeaux, Frankfurt, Vienna, Biella) 1999); and 'The Timing of Transaction' (think tank that included Issa Samb and Abdou Bâ, co-produced by Arteleku/Consonni, Donostia-San Sebastián).

[5] For instance, in 1996 I was commissioned to create the seventeenth issue of *Fama & Fortune Bulletin*, published by Peter Pakesch and Johannes Schlebrügge in Vienna, and I used this platform to bring together conversations taking place in Dakar around the Laboratoire AGIT'Art and similar dialogues circulating around the work of the late Joshua Compston and the events of Factual Nonsense in London.

[6] For further information on local organs and periodicals, see Clémentine Deliss (ed.), *Seven Stories about Modern Art in Africa* (exh. cat.), Paris and London: Flammarion and Whitechapel Art Gallery, 1995.

[7] El Hadji Moussa Babacar Sy and Friedrich Axt (ed.), *Anthology of Contemporary Fine Arts in Senegal*, Frankfurt a.M.: Museum für Völkerkunde, 1989. The contributors include Léopold Sédar Senghor, Anne-Jean Bart, Issa Samb, Kalidou Sy, Ousmane Sow Huchard, Djibril Tamsir Niane, Ben Mouhamed Diop, Pierre Lods, Aissa Djionne, Sérigne N'Diaye, Friedrich Axt and El Sy.

[8] In 2015–16, the Weltkulturen Museum's exhibitions will focus on this seminal collection of African artworks produced prior to the 'global turn' of 1989.

[9] 'Magiciens de la Terre', Centre Georges Pompidou and the Grande Halle de La Villette, Paris, 18 May–14 August 1989. In the 1990s, the private collector Jean Pigozzi commissioned the curator André Magnin, who was responsible for the African selection of artists in 'Magiciens de la Terre', to create a comprehensive collection of works by artists from the African continent. Magnin's high purchasing power engendered heated debates at the time, and certain artists felt pushed to produce work that displayed signs of traditional aesthetic forms. See 'Contemporary African Art Collection by Jean Pigozzi', available at http://www.caacart.com.

10 See *Revue Noire*, no.7, Dakar, December 1992.

11 See C. Deliss (ed.), *Seven Stories, op. cit.*

12 The series also included presentations by curators and artists from the Black Arts movement, such as Sonia Boyce, Eddie Chambers and Rita Keegan. Gavin Jantjes and Sarah Wason presented their early concepts for Iniva, London, and artists such as Pitika Ntuli from Johannesburg connected the African continent to its London-based diaspora.

13 I was the artistic director of 'africa95' between 1992 and 1995. The festival took place over several months during 1995, with two workshops held in Africa the previous year: a visual arts workshop in Senegal curated by El Sy ('Tenq 94') and a dance workshop in Zimbabwe. 'africa95' was triggered by a team connected to the Royal Academy of Arts in London and ended up involving over sixty arts institutions in the UK.

14 According to El Sy, underground tunnels linked the former army barracks where the Village des Arts had its base to the sea, the main market and the presidential palace in the centre of town.

15 In the 1960s, Senghor invested 25 per cent of the Senegalese national budget on arts infrastructure: he commissioned the building of the Musée Dynamique, which André Malraux opened in 1966; created a music conservatory and an art school; and greatly supported the development of culture. This initiative was quashed by his successor, President Abdou Diouf, who, after coming to power in 1981, closed the Musée Dynamique and evicted the artists from the studio spaces in the Village des Arts.

16 Georges Bataille and Carl Einstein's *Documents*, published between 1929 and 1930, together with the ethnographic expedition Mission Dakar-Djibouti (1931–33), formed the material for my fieldwork in 1986 – not in Africa but in the library of the Musée de l'Homme in Paris. See C. Deliss, 'Exoticism and Eroticism: Representations of the Other in Early French Anthropology', unpublished doctoral thesis, London: University of London, 1988.

17 'Poussière', *Documents*, no.5, October 1929, p.278.

18 The relationship of higher echelons of political power, espionage and art practice suggested by the roles and methodology of the Laboratoire AGIT'Art is discussed in C. Deliss, 'The Parallax View', in *Metronome No.4–5–6 Backwards Translation* (Edinburgh, Bordeaux, Frankfurt, Vienna, Biella) 1999; reprinted in *Afterall*, issue 1, Autumn/Winter 2000, pp.53–58. During this time, there was a short-lived attempt to turn the courtyard into a restaurant, a transformation that provoked a period of 'anarchitecture' on the part of Samb, which I write about in C. Deliss, *Écran-Mémoire I: Lyrical Criticism Interaction, Laboratoire Agit-Art/Factual Nonsense, Fama & Fortune Bulletin*, no.17, 1996.

19 Issa Samb, 'Mediums of Change' (trans. C. Deliss), in *Metronome No.0* (Dakar) 1996. This publication also includes the manifesto of the Laboratoire AGIT'art, written in London in 1995.

20 'Seven Stories about Modern Art in Africa', Whitechapel Art Gallery, London, 27 September–26 November 1995, curated by C. Deliss together with El Sy, Chika Okeke, Salah Hassan, David Koloane and Wanjiku Nyachae. The exhibition travelled to Malmö Konsthall (27 January–17 March 1996).

21 El Sy in conversation with the author, February 2014.

22 As M'Bengue, fondly nicknamed 'Professeur Virgule' ('Professor Comma') because of his insistence on proper punctuation in the French language, wrote the manifesto for the Tenq workshop in 1996.

23 Sadly, several of these members have since passed away, including Djibril Diop Mambéty, Libasse Thiaw and Mamadou Traoré Diop. Other members at the time included the film-maker Johnson Traoré, the psychiatrist Aby Bâ and the theatre director Seyba Lamine Traoré. Mamadou Diouf, former director of CODESRIA in Dakar, is a long-time member of the Laboratoire AGIT'Art. Today he is the Leitner Family Professor of African Studies and the Director of the Institute for African Studies at Columbia University in New York.

24 Published as *Les Trottoirs de Dakar*, Paris: Éditions Revue Noire, 1994.

25 El Sy in conversation with the author, February 2014.

26 Hubert Fichte, *Psyche. Annäherung an die Geisteskranken in Afrika*, Frankfurt a.M.: Fischer Verlag, 1986, pp.20–21. Translation the author's.

27 'Global Conceptualism: Points of Origin, 1950s–1980s', Queens Museum of Art, New York, 28 April–29 August 1999; Walker Art Center, Minneapolis, 19 December 1999–5 March 2000; Miami Art Museum, 15 September–26 November 2000. See Philomena Mariani (ed.), *Global Conceptualism: Points of Origin, 1950s–1980s* (exh. cat.), New York: Queens Museum of Art, 1999. The exhibition was directed by Jane Farver, Luis Camnitzer and Rachel Weiss. They were joined by a team of eleven international curators, who provided specialist knowledge on specific geographic areas, among them Okwui Enwezor, who was responsible for the African continent.

28 See C. Deliss, 'The Parallax View', *op. cit.*

29 I. Samb, 'And this time that chases after us', in *Metronome No.1* (London) 1997, pp.50–53.

30 Mamadou Traoré Diop used this term during a workshop I organised called 'Magnetic Speech', held in Dakar in 2000.

31 The organisation Man Kenen Ki was run by Omar Sall and the late Moustafa N'Doye.

32 For an interview with Issa Samb and an elucidation of his quasi-animist and alchemical theoretical position, see Antje Majewski's film *La Coquille: Conversation entre Issa Samb et Antje Majewski* (2010). The text of her interview with Samb was reproduced in 'Object Atlas – Fieldwork in the Museum', curated by C. Deliss, Weltkulturen Museum, Frankfurt a.M., 25 January–16 September 2012.

33 Even the attempted reconstruction of the courtyard scenario for dOCUMENTA(13) in Kassel in 2012 failed to ignite the specific relational and methodological dynamic of the Laboratoire AGIT'art as a conceptual and physical meeting ground.

34 The core group of artists involved in the Tenq workshop in 1994 included El Sy, Fodé Camara, Souleymane Keita, Moustapha Dimé (deceased), Kan-Si, Guibril André Diop, Djibril N'Diaye, Khady Lette, Amédy Kré Mbaye (deceased), Jacob Yacouba (deceased), Musaa Baydi (deceased) and Pape Macoumba Seck. Guest participants included David Koloane and Sam Nhlengethwa (South Africa); Dasunye Shikongo (Namibia); Ndidi Dike (Nigeria); Atta Kwami (Ghana); Yacouba Touré (Ivory Coast, deceased); Flinto Chandia (Zambia); Agnes Nianghongo (Zimbabwe); Mohamed Kacimi (Morocco, deceased); Damy Théra (Mali); and Yinka Shonibare, Paul Clarkson, Anna Best and Clémentine Deliss (UK).

35 The core group of artists involved in the Tenq iteration in the Chinese camp (later Village des Arts) as part of the Dakar Biennale in 1996 included El Sy, Fodé Camara, Kan-Si, Guibril André Diop, Issa Samb, Mor Lyssa Bâ, Ass M'Bengue, Magaye Niang and myself. Guest participants included Assane Dionne (Senegal), Yacouba Touré (Ivory Coast, deceased), Juginder Lamba (Kenya/UK), Daniel Manyika (Zimbabwe), Chika Okeke (Nigeria) and Johannes Phokela (South Africa/UK).

36 Anna Kindersley, who organised the 1994 Tenq workshop together with El Sy, also assisted Robert Loder in disseminating the philosophy of the Triangle workshops, which had previously taken place in South Africa, Zimbabwe, Mozambique, Botswana and Zambia.

37 Norwegian artist Gardar Eide Einarsson explored this link in *Metronome No.4–5–6 Backwards Translation* (Vienna, Frankfurt, Bordeaux, Edinburgh, Biella) 1999. His conversation with the artist Kan-Si and Superflex was subsequently reproduced in the catalogue of Documenta11, where Huit Facettes presented work in 2002.

38 In 'Laboratorium' (various venues, Antwerp, 27 June–3 October 1999, curated by Hans Ulrich Obrist and Barbara Vanderlinden), for example, the group's work centred on the activities of the seminal anthropologist, physicist and politician Cheikh Anta Diop (1923–86), who ran the radiocarbon laboratory at the University of Dakar.

39 In 2003, I invited Issa Samb and Abdou Bâ to take part in a think tank called 'The Timing of Transaction' in Donostia-San Sebastián, which I curated together with Hinrich Sachs, Frank Larcade (Consonni) and Santi Eraso (Arteleku). The results of this week-long meeting, which included Catherine David, Maurizio Lazzarato, Manuel Borja-Villel, Adam Szymczyk, Charles Esche, Gardar Eide Einarsson, Christos Papoulias, Leire Vergara, Peio Aguirre and others, were never published.

40 C. Deliss, unpublished notes, August 2002.

41 El Sy in conversation with the author, February 2014.

Center for Historical Reenactments: Is the Tale Chasing its Own Tail?

Khwezi Gule

Over the last decade, writing, art-making, historicising, teaching, archiving and curating have been engaged in various acts of mutual cannibalism, disrupting the insularity of disciplines such as art history. This is also patent in the arena of what I would term 'memory work', referring to the myriad forms of institutional engagement with the past that take place in the public sphere, from memorials to public art projects and museums; all such edifices have developed discursive components, such as research projects, processes of public consultation, the recording of oral histories and event programming, in order to legitimise the public benefit of their enterprises. As a result, memory work has become highly specialised, highly lucrative, highly choreographed and highly policed. Mind you, this is taking place in a climate where, as far as the rhetoric goes, processes are open, transparent, participatory and democratic. In this knowledge economy, memory work exists partly as a strategy to privatise collective memory, and it serves in many instances to cement the authority of dominant voices. In the same way that the privileged global subject remains the Western white male in a world that is supposedly more plural and polyphonic, so too the white male artist remains the privileged subject in the post-apartheid art system of South Africa; indeed, a cursory look at public art projects realised there after 1994 reveals that most of them have been executed and commissioned by white male artists.

It is precisely at this moment that I think the notion of re-enactment put forward by the Johannesburg-based collective Center for Historical Reenactments (CHR) can be extremely useful. Rather than the kind of rehearsed spectacle designed for tourists in historic sites, the type of re-enactment at play in their work is one in which time is slowed down so that we can move through it a bit more deliberately.

PASS-AGES
CHR is [at the time of writing, 2015] made up of artist and academic Donna Kukama, artist Kemang Wa Lehulere and curator, educator and artist Gabi Ngcobo,[1] although participants and collaborators constantly move in and out

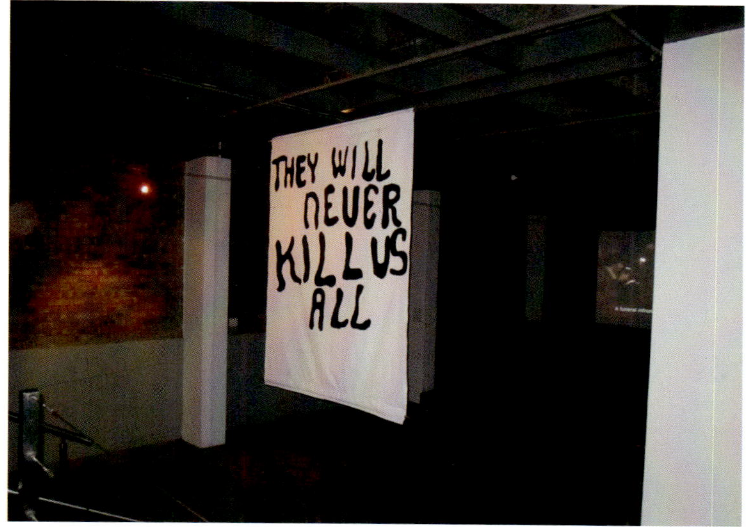

Center for Historical Reenactments, *Untitled (Banner)*, 2012. Installation view, 'Exuberance Project', Mandela Rhodes Gallery, Johannesburg, 2012. Courtesy the artists

Next Spread: Installation view, 'Center for Historical Reenactments: After-after Tears', New Museum, New York, 2013. Photograph: Jesse Untract-Oakner. Courtesy the artists

of projects, picking up CHR 'pollen' and depositing it in various localities internationally, so that ideas are able to further germinate in Berlin, New York, Dakar, Lyon and elsewhere in between. Indeed, while CHR critically engage with recent South African history, the narratives they study are not limited to a South African audience. Often involving a range of formats – whether publications, dialogues, performances or repurposed artworks and images – their projects provide different ways of accessing the histories invoked, and thus engage local as well as international audiences. This was already manifest in their inaugural project, 'PASS-AGES: References & footnotes' (2010), which was organised in collaboration with the Johannesburg Workshop in Theory and Criticism, a group that, like CHR, aims to speak to local concerns in ways that resonate with an international context, or as they put it, 'to contribute from the Southern Hemisphere to a reappraisal of theory and criticism in such a way as to think anew about a decentred world'.[2]

It goes without saying that the city carries memories; and not only the city, but landscape itself. Seeking to excavate these memories requires getting into the crevasses of received histories. Official histories leak, as bodies do. In the same way, memory exceeds the limitations of meaning or explanation. 'PASS-AGES' was a site-specific project attempting to deal with such excess insofar as it made visitors aware of the layers of history embodied in Johannesburg's former Pass Office, now a women's shelter run by a Christian organisation. The exhibition was housed in the disused basement of the shelter: a stark, concrete interior with fluorescent lights. There appeared to have been no attempt to convert the space into a neat white cube; the wooden cabinets that were used to display the exhibition material had the look of retro furniture. Everything exuded an oppressive state of being.

As you might recall, the passbook, or pass,[3] was not only a means of identification; it was an internal passport that identified Black Africans,

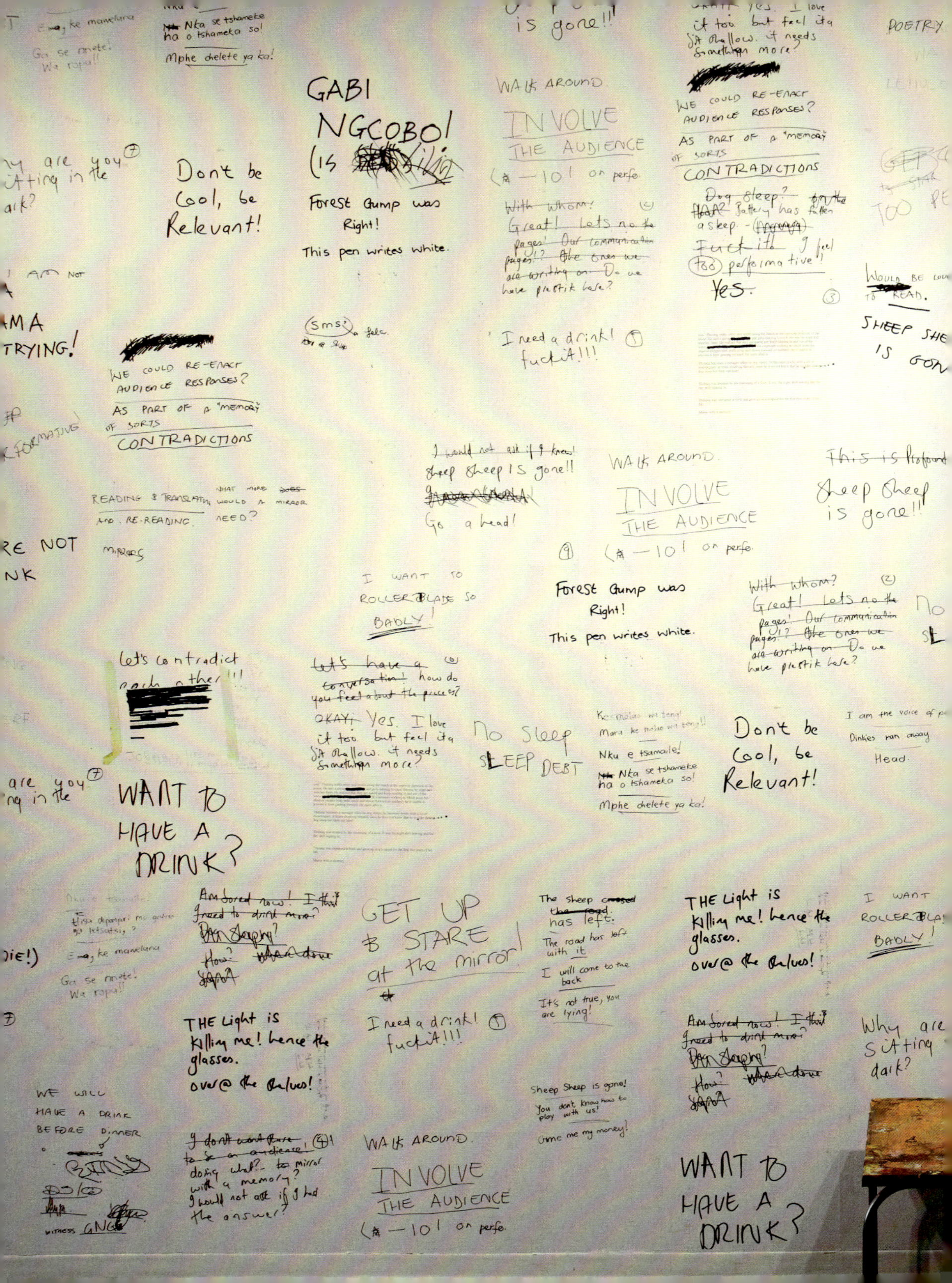

GABI NGCOBO! (is Brazilian)
Forest Gump was Right!
This pen writes white.
Dont be Cool, be Relevant!
Don't be Cool, be Relevant!
WALK AROUND
INVOLVE THE AUDIENCE
(A - 10' on perfo.
WE COULD RE-ENACT AUDIENCE RESPONSES?
AS PART OF A "memory" OF SORTS
CONTRADICTIONS
POETRY
Why are you sitting in the dark?
I AM NOT
I M A TRYING!
WE COULD RE-ENACT AUDIENCE RESPONSES?
AS PART OF A "memory" OF SORTS
CONTRADICTIONS
READING & TRANSLATING and RE-READING.
WHAT more does a mirror NEED?
WE ARE NOT MIRRORS
Let's contradict each other!!!
WANT TO HAVE A DRINK?
I want to ROLLERBLADE so BADLY!
Let's have a conversation! how do you feel about the process?
OKAY! Yes. I love it too but feel its Shallow. it needs Something more?
I need a drink! fuck it!!!
With Whom?
Great! Lets no the pages! Our communication pages!? Are ones we are writing on Do we have plastik base?
Forest Gump was Right!
This pen writes white.
No Sleep SLEEP DEBT
Nku e tsamaile!
Nka se tshameka ha o tshameka so!
Mphe chelete ya ka!
Don't be Cool, be Relevant!
I am the voice of p Dinkies ran away Head.
This is profound
Sheep Sheep is gone!!
Sheep Sheep IS gone!!
Go a head!
WALK AROUND.
INVOLVE THE AUDIENCE
(A - 10' on perfo.
GET UP & STARE at the mirror!
I need a drink! fuck it!!!
THE Light is killing me! hence the glasses. over@ the galues!
The sheep has left. The road has left with it I will come to the back It's not true, you are lying!
Sheep Sheep is gone! You don't know how to play with us! Gime me my money!
THE Light is killing me! hence the glasses. over@ the galues!
I want ROLLERBLADE BADLY!
Why are you sitting dark?
WE WILL HAVE A DRINK BEFORE DINNER
I don't want there to be an audience! doing what? to mirror with a memory? I would not ask if I had the answer!
WALK AROUND. INVOLVE THE AUDIENCE
(A - 10' on perfo.
WANT TO HAVE A DRINK?

YOU ARE NOT DRUNK

Why are you sitting in the dark?

I don't want there to be an audience doing what? - the mirror with a memory? I would not ask if I had the answer?

I am the voice of play!

I'm READING Dinkes ran away Head.

Don't be cool, be Relevant!

Why are you sitting in the dark?

This is profound!

Sheep Sheep is gone!!

I would not ask if I knew! Sheep Sheep IS gone!! Go a head!

BECAUSE I AM NOT DONNA KUKAMA OR DIE TRYING!

I would not ask if I knew! Sheep Sheep IS gone!! Go a head!

YOU ARE NOT DRUNK

I would not ask if I knew! Sheep Sheep IS gone!! Go a head!

Dog sleep? Battery has fallen asleep - Fuck it! I feel Too performative!! Yes.

(sms?)

GET UP & STARE at the mirror

GET UP TOO PERFORMATIVE

Sheep Sheep is gone! You don't know how to play with us! Gimme me my money!

WE COULD RE-ENACT AUDIENCE RESPONSES? AS PART OF A 'memoir' OF SORTS CONTRADICTIONS

KEMANG WA LEHULERE (KEMANG OR DIE!)

WE COULD RE-ENACT AUDIENCE RESPONSES? AS PART OF A 'memoir' OF SORTS CONTRADICTIONS

I WANT TO ROLLERBLADE SO BADLY!

No sleep SLEEP DE

Dog sleep? Battery has fallen asleep - Fuck it! I feel Too performative! Yes.

I would not ask if I knew! Sheep Sheep IS gone!! Go a head!

With whom! Great! Lets no the pages. Our communication Oi? Are once we are writing on. Do we have plastik here?

GET UP & STARE at the mirror

BECAUSE I AM NOT DONNA KUKAMA OR DIE TRYING!

Would be lovely to READ.

SHEEP SHEEP IS GONE!

GABI NGCOBO!

WALK AROUND. INVOLVE THE AUDIENCE

Am bored now! I think I need to drink more! Been sleeping?

GET UP TOO PERFORMATIVE

POETRY

YOU ARE NOT DRUNK

This is profound!

Sheep Sheep is gone!!

WE WILL a drink dinner

Let's have a conversation! how do you feel OKAY! it too Sit shallow. Something m

Would be lovely READ.

I am the Dinkes ra Head

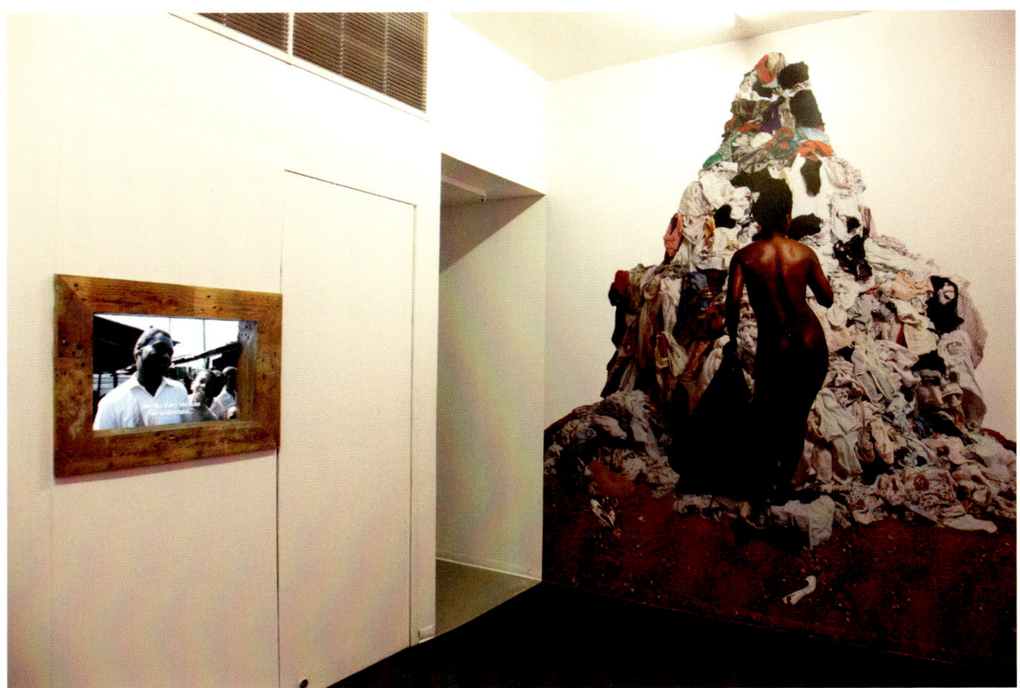

and as such was instrumental in the implementation of racial segregation laws such as the Population Registration Act or the Reservation of Separate Amenities Act, which sought to regulate the inflow of Black Africans into South Africa's urban centres.[4] Under apartheid, the pass was like a branding iron: it dictated where you could go, when and how; it designated your race and your future prospects in life. However, we must not forget that the idea of a pass was already present under British colonial rule, when Cape Town slaves needed a pass from their owner in order to travel from place to place.[5] The means of surveillance merely became more sophisticated and stringent under apartheid.

'PASS-AGES' invoked, then, the crowning achievement of both colonialism and apartheid: the institutionalisation of the idea of humans as chattel. From its establishment in 1954 until the ending of the pass system in 1986, the Pass Office was the very symbol of oppression. And yet, the old Pass Office is today on the cusp of a wave of urban regeneration, with the housing developments and office blocks around it being renovated or rebuilt. 'PASS-AGES' alerted me to the existence of this building, affording me a moment to reflect on an experience I had thought I was familiar with,[6] as well as bringing to mind the millions of souls that have criss-crossed its corridors – people whose lives were stolen by an impervious and indifferent bureaucracy. Had the exhibition taken place in a white cube, it would not have had nearly the impact that it did at the women's shelter: the bareness of the space spoke of a cold and impersonal past.

214

It was not only the history of passbooks that the project tried to bring back but also recent art history. One of the works invoked was Coco Fusco's 1997 performance *Rights of Passage*, in which she handed out passbooks to visitors to the 2nd Johannesburg Biennale in lieu of an entry ticket. The cover of Fusco's passbook was reproduced in a self-published newspaper that was distributed at 'PASS-AGES', which also included a conversation between Wa Lehulere and Ngcobo concerning the former's performance *uGuqul'ibhatyi* from 2008. For this work, which took place in the backyard of a house in Gugulethu,[7] Wa Lehulere dug up a hole and, in the process, discovered a cow's skeleton.[8] The performance is titled after the isiXhosa term for a turncoat, used to refer to Black Africans who altered their identity so as to be identified as 'coloured', since under the apartheid system so-called 'coloured people' held more privileges than Africans. The artist, significantly, used an Afro comb to dig the hole and to allude to the pencil test that officials used as a supposedly scientific way of classifying races: a pencil was inserted into the hair of the person being tested and, depending on the ease with which it moved through the hair, the test subject would be allocated to one racial group or the other.

By revisiting both an older and a more recent performance, CHR were suggesting that one needs to slow down the past as much as the present, and that by doing so one may illuminate unexpected connections between different historical moments. This layering of historical times was further complicated by another article published in the exhibition's newspaper, which raised questions about photographer Ernest Cole's motives for changing his last name (he was born Kole) and for 'passing' the test to be reclassified as coloured. In this way, the publication wove different narratives and creative forms together around the pass system.

They will never kill us all

For the exhibition 'Rise and Fall of Apartheid: Photography and the Bureaucracy of Everyday Life' (2012–13), CHR presented a banner reading 'they will never kill us all'.[9] The statement is borrowed from a sign in a 1985 photograph by Alf Kumalo, which was taken at a commemoration in Uitenhage, in the province of Eastern Cape, of the 1961 Sharpeville Massacre – a tragedy that resulted in the killing of 69 people after police opened fire against peaceful protesters demonstrating against pass laws.

Measuring nearly one and a half metres in length, made with simple linen and beautifully crafted in a way that belies the crudeness of the original protest sign, the careful stitching of black letters onto the white fabric lends the banner an appearance of understated nobility. The banner stood out as a singular object amongst the predominantly documentary photographs making up the exhibition (Kumalo's original photograph was reproduced in a book displayed as part of CHR's installation). Whereas most of the images in the exhibition bore witness to the might of the apartheid regime and the victimisation of Black South Africans, CHR's intervention presented a hopeful statement – one that sees freedom as a certainty. One could almost imagine the statement reading: 'Our victory is assured because they will never kill us all' – a fatalistic expression of defiance. The banner thus enjoins the viewer to

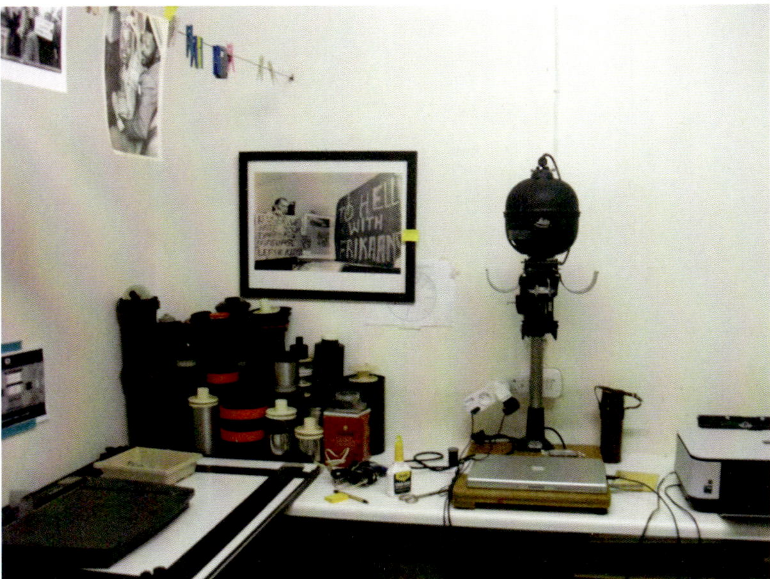

Center for
Historical
Reenactments,
Fr(agile), 2012,
darkroom
re-installation
at the Alf
Kumalo Museum,
Johannesburg.
Courtesy the
artists

focus on a particular moment within the overarching narrative, the moment when the victim demands to be heard. Clearly, the statement is addressed to 'us' and is about 'them', drawing attention away from the oppressor to galvanise the oppressed instead into resistance.

Bringing the past to bear on the present is perhaps the most important role that memory work and sites of memory should play. In CHR's work, this is seen as a continuous process: each manifestation and experiment generates material for the next. This same fragment of history, for example, was previously conjured up in 'The Exuberance Project' (2012), a weekend-long event in Cape Town,[10] and as part of a mural realised for the exhibition 'Center for Historical Reenactments: After-after Tears' (2013), at the New Museum in New York.[11]

In fact, the banner's genesis was a three-day residency that members of CHR undertook with museologist and LGBT activist Jabu Pereira at the Alf Kumalo Museum in Soweto, Johannesburg in early March 2012. Much of the work they did there involved cleaning and sorting out Kumalo's vast archive, which had been mostly neglected. At the end of the three days, the team held an 'open day' so that the results of their work could be seen. Clearly the space had not been set up as a museum; this 'open day' was not so much an exhibition as an opportunity to engage with the fragility of the archive. During the event, various objects were on display, including old cameras, books on Kumalo and piles of photographs, some cracked and bent. Titled *Fr(agile)*, the intervention pointed to both the vulnerability and resilience of the stories embodied in the museum's photographs and spools of film. Contradictory impulses are implicit in the attempts of CHR to rescue Kumalo's archive: on the one hand, preserving the life's work of one of South Africa's most import-

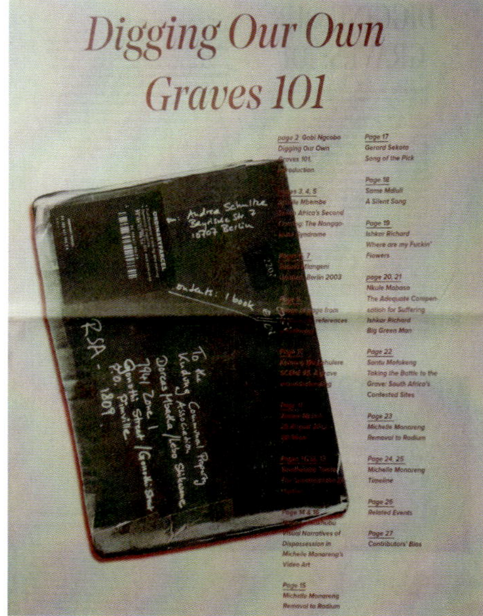

Cover of Center for Historical
Reenactments, *Digging Our Own
Graves 101*, published in 2014,
designed by Maziyar Pahlevan.
Courtesy the artists

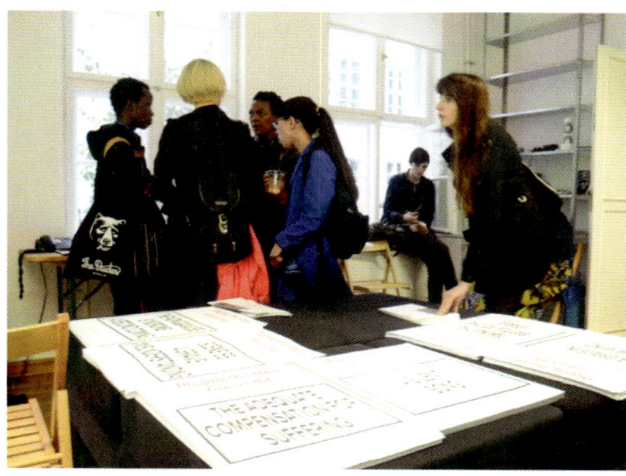

ant photojournalists; on the other, recognising that an institution can outlive the reasons for its founding.

Digging Our Own Graves 101

Clearly the shadow of death runs deep through the work of CHR, but so does the possibility of a second coming. Rather than seeing death as something to be resisted, CHR have often seen it as an ever-present possibility. On 12 December 2012, the collective staged an institutional 'suicide'. Playing on the notion of the end of times, the twelve-hour event – titled 'We are absolutely ending this' – consisted of lectures, presentations and performances to mark the conclusion of their occupancy of a space in August House, a building in downtown Johannesburg. If CHR are drawn to the idea of their own demise, it is perhaps because they seek to resuscitate the spirit of the Johannesburg Biennale, which was terminated after its second iteration in 1997.[12] Institutionally speaking, the Johannesburg Biennale has come to represent a failed institution and a spectre that haunts the South African art landscape. As Ngcobo has stated, it is a 'phantom limb': there is nostalgia for it, especially among those who did not witness it, as well as a desire to revive the discussion around some of the issues it raised, such as processes of migration and belonging.[13]

'After-after Tears' followed close on the heels of CHR's institutional suicide, suggesting that 'We are absolutely ending this' was rather an end of cycle. 'After tears' refers to a South African revelry ritual that takes place after a funeral, similar to a wake. For this project, which was part of their residency in the New Museum, CHR invited visitors to consider what happens after the dust settles. Involving a faux construction site, an artwork by Zanele Muholi, a screening of a film by Sandra Gross and Andrés Carvajal about two men who

Center for Historical Reenactments, *Digging Our Own Graves 101*, 2014, office at KW Institute for Contemporary Art, 8th Berlin Biennial. Photography: Michelle Monareng. Courtesy the artists dub pirated international films for live audiences in East Africa (*Flux: Veejays in Dar es Salaam*, 2010) and a discussion with Sohrab Mohebbi, Ngcobo and myself, 'After-after Tears' pointed to ways of remembering and commemoration, while also interrogating how an institution can occupy different spaces.

More than excavating, perhaps, CHR are concerned with exhumation, a practice with crucial historical connotations in post-apartheid South Africa. Many of the apartheid's victims were placed in unmarked graves; these were discovered years after the fall of the regime, and exhumations were essential to give the deceased proper burials with attendant rituals to allow the soul of the dead to rest in peace.

'Digging Our Own Graves 101' took place at the KW Institute for Contemporary Art in Berlin on the occasion of the 8th Berlin Biennale in 2014 and included talks with Ngcobo, Wa Lehulere, Michelle Monareng and Sinethemba Twalo, as well as the distribution of the newspaper *DOOG101*, which contained excerpts of essays by Nkule Mabaso, Nomusa Makhubu, Achille Mbembe, Same Mdluli and Sinethemba Twalo, amongst others, printed in a manner resembling roadside posters of newspaper headlines (a common sight in South Africa). Overall, the paper examined how the issue of land dispossession both predates and has survived the 1913 Natives Land Act that restricted the acquisition of land by Black South Africans. Mbembe's essay, for example, deals with acts of wilful self-destruction born out of desperation in the hope that sacrifice will miraculously yield abundance in the future – what has been termed the Nongqawuse Syndrome, after a Xhosa prophetess who predicted that if her people would slaughter their cattle and destroy crops, their ancestors would arise to bring about the destruction of the white man. (This call was heeded by hundreds of Xhosa people to catastrophic ends, leading to what is commonly known as the Cattle-Killing Movement of 1856–57.) The essay explores fatalism in contemporary South Africa and the faith placed in false prophets – in the political sense.

Refusing to be either pessimistic or depressingly hopeful, the publication, like CHR itself, follows the breadcrumbs of history wherever they may lead. The institutional and cultural matrix in which CHR operate includes state-sponsored memorials and commemorative events that are often billed as nation-building exercises and are supposed to act as cautionary tales concerning repeated crimes against humanity; such measures are intended to restore dignity to the dispossessed. However, recent events such as the xenophobic attacks on Black Africans and rampant gender violence clearly illustrate that this perspective is a fallacy.[14] They compound a fact that we already know: that public art and memorials do not necessarily foster civic pride. How, then, to mobilise history in such a way that it becomes a truly transformative exercise? Perhaps it is enough for now simply to tell stories as honestly as we can and as lyrically as we can rather than rushing too quickly to monumental and finite conclusions.

Notes

1 The US-based curator Sohrab Mohebbi is a former CHR member.

2 *PASS-AGES: References & footnotes* (self-published newspaper), Johannesburg: Center for Historical Reenactments and Johannesburg Workshop in Theory and Criticism, 2010, unpaginated.

3 The passbook was known by a number of names, including the vernacular *ipasi*. It was also referred to simply as a 'reference book' or sometimes as a 'dompass'. *Dom* is Afrikaans for stupid.

4 Although there were already many pieces of racial legislation prior to the 1950s, the National Party's election in 1948 accelerated the tightening of population control.

5 For more on the history of the pass, see 'Pass office is a place of shelter', *Joburg*, 30 July 2007, available at http://www.joburg.org.za/index.php?option=com_content&view=article&id=1420:pass-office-is-a-place-of-shelter&catid=127&Itemid=210.

6 When I was growing up, in the 1970s and early 80s, one was supposed to acquire a passbook upon turning sixteen, and so, paradoxically, it was also seen as a sign of having reached adulthood. Having a pass meant that you could seek employment and earn. It was a rite of passage, albeit one with undesirable connotations.

7 Gugulethu is the township in Cape Town, where Wa Lehulere grew up and later founded the collective Gugulective together with Unathi Sigenu.

8 The performance was staged as part of 'Scratching the Surface Vol.1', AVA Gallery, Cape Town, 4–22 August 2008, curated by Gabi Ngcobo and Mwenya Kabwe.

9 'Rise and Fall of Apartheid: Photography and the Bureaucracy of Everyday Life' was curated by Okwui Enwezor with Rory Bester and debuted at the International Center of Photography, New York (14 September 2012–6 June 2013). It travelled to Haus der Kunst, Munich (15 February–26 May 2013) and Museum Africa, Johannesburg (13 February 2014–30 April 2015).

10 'The Exuberance Project' took place at the University of Cape Town, where it was hosted by The Names We Give and the Gordon Institute for Performing and Creative Arts (GIPCA). It included a symposium, an exhibition and film screenings.

11 'Center for Historical Reenactments: After-after Tears', New Museum, New York, 22 May–7 July 2013.

12 The first iteration of the Johannesburg Biennale (28 February–30 April 1995) was curated by Lorna Ferguson; the second (12 October–12 December 1997), by Okwui Enwezor. The 1997 edition ended prematurely when the City of Johannesburg, which was supporting the exhibition, ran out of funds. In subsequent years the City did not offer funding for its continuation.

13 Gabi Ngcobo in conversation with the author, 20 December 2011.

14 Xenophobic violence reached unprecedented levels in May 2006, when more than sixty foreign nationals were killed in South African cities within the space of two weeks. South Africa also has very high levels of gender-based violence: gender activist Nhlanhla Mokoena has claimed that a woman is raped every 26 seconds in South Africa. See 'Rape Survivor Takes Long Walk to Raise Awareness', *eNews Channel Africa*, 13 October 2013, available at http://www.enca.com/south-africa/rape-survivor-takes-long-walk-raise-awareness.

Counter-Imaginaries: 'Women Artists on the Move', 'Second to None' and 'Like A Virgin...'

Serubiri Moses

In the past thirty years, contemporary African art has become more recognised through various international large-scale exhibitions, magazine articles and exhibition catalogues that repositioned African artists in a global dialogue. Notable among these are the biennials established on the continent during the 1990s in Bamako, Dakar and Johannesburg; magazines such as *Nka, Third Text* and *Revue Noire*; and catalogues for exhibitions such as 'The Short Century: Independence and Liberation Movements in Africa 1945–1994' and 'Seven Stories about Modern Art in Africa'.[1] Yet African women artists during the same period – their exhibitions, works and perspectives on modernity – have been critically and historically neglected. In this essay, I focus on three small-scale exhibitions organised by African women curators and artists: 'Women Artists on the Move', organised by Lilian Mary Nabulime at the Makerere University Art Gallery in Kampala in 1995; 'Second to None', curated by Gabi Ngcobo and Virginia MacKenny at the South African National Gallery in Cape Town in 2006; and 'Like A Virgin...', curated by Bisi Silva at the Center for Contemporary Art (CCA) in Lagos in 2009. Taken together, the divergent approaches of these three exhibitions, in Uganda, South Africa and Nigeria respectively, foreground a more complex history of the continent and challenge the assumptions of existing modernist histories and art academies in Africa.

I

According to which criteria do we define the importance of exhibitions? Is it according to the volume of press coverage and critical responses? According to their citation by artists and curators? According to formal or technical innovations? It is clear that 'Women Artists on the Move', and many exhibitions like it, are missing from historical accounts of contemporary African art in the 1990s.[2] Are we therefore to conclude that the only significant initiatives in African art, apart from a few mega-events such as the Dakar and Johannesburg biennials, were aforementioned exhibitions such as 'The Short Century' and 'Seven Stories' and their contributions to postcolonial debates

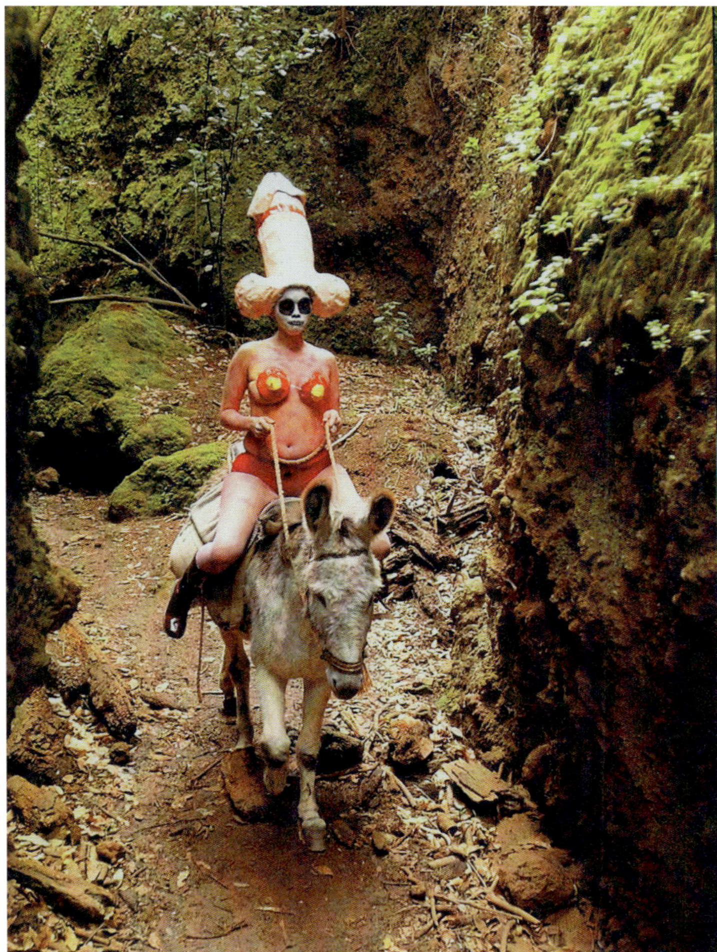

Tracey Rose, *The Prelude: Garden Path*, 2003, pigment inks on cotton rag paper, 73 × 49cm. Courtesy the artist and Dan Gunn Gallery, Berlin

from Europe and the United States? Or does a project such as 'Women Artists on the Move' – a collective of artists 'coming together as women', in which authorship is not centred within a singular curatorial mission, and which did not register in the international art press (headquartered in Euro-America) at the moment of its staging – suggest that we need a different criterion of importance?

'Women Artists on the Move' was held in the gallery space of Makerere University and featured works by Nabulime (the exhibition's primary organiser), Sylvia Katende, Rose Namubiru Kirumira, Margaret Nagawa and Maria Naita, amongst others. It was one of a number of all-women exhibitions taking place in East Africa in 1995,[3] and the exhibition may be seen in the context of emergent 1990s transnational feminism. Yet, in distinction to other female-centred initiatives from that year, 'Women Artists on the Move' was 'the first one for women artists that has been organised by a Ugandan woman for a women's cause', thus emphasising the explicit self-organising it

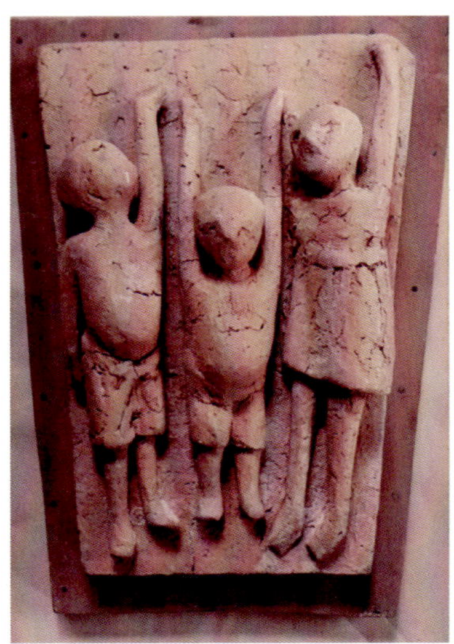

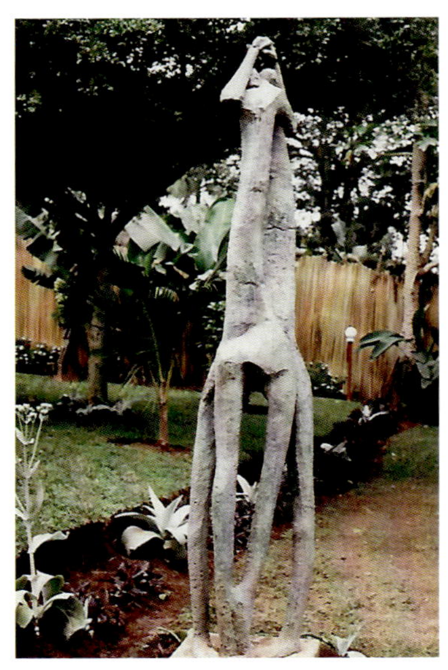

Selected works from 'Women Artists on the Move', Makerere University Art Gallery, Kampala, 1995. Clockwise from above, works by: Rose Kirumira; Silvia Katende; Venny Nakazibwe; Liliane Nabulime; Margaret Nagawa; Lydia Mugambi; Sarah Nakisanze. Courtesy Liliane Nabulime

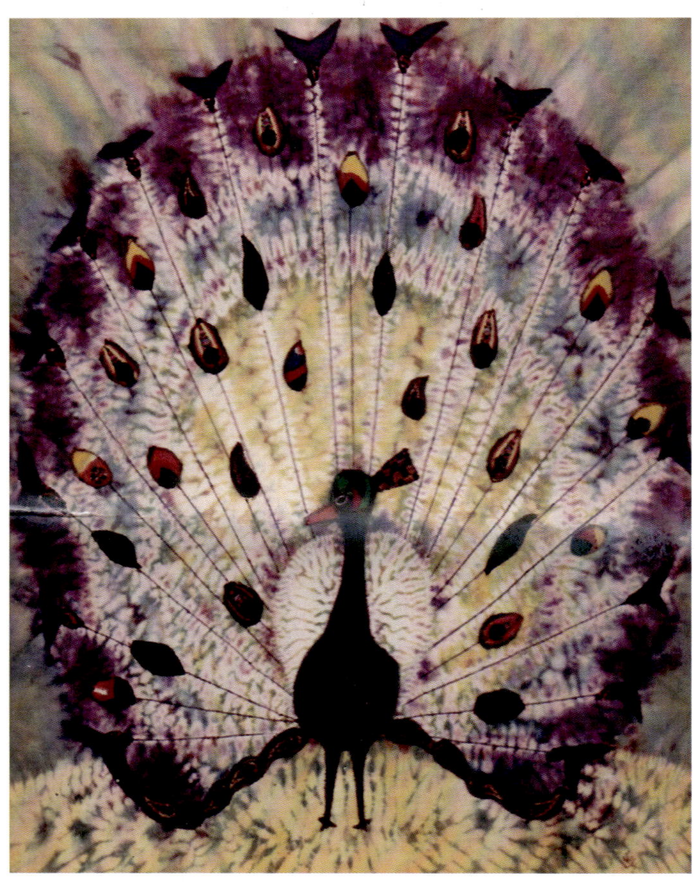

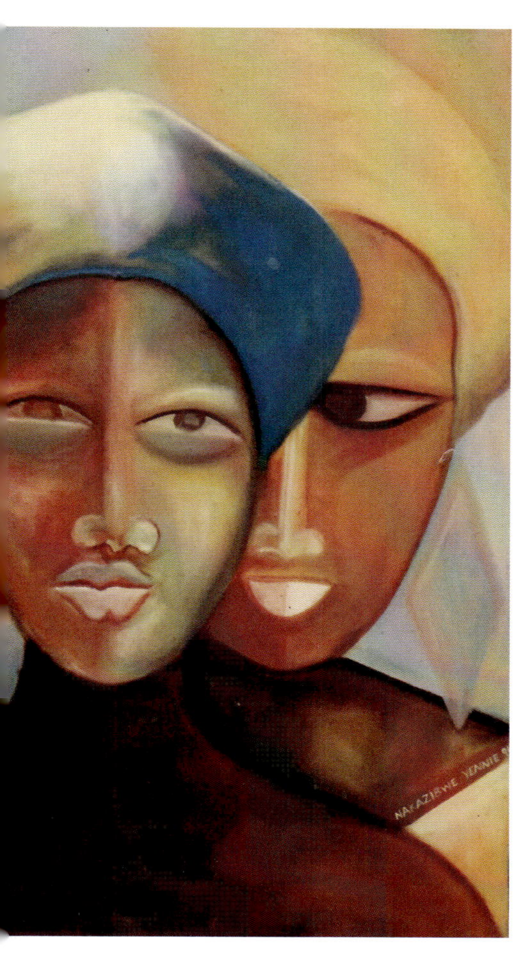

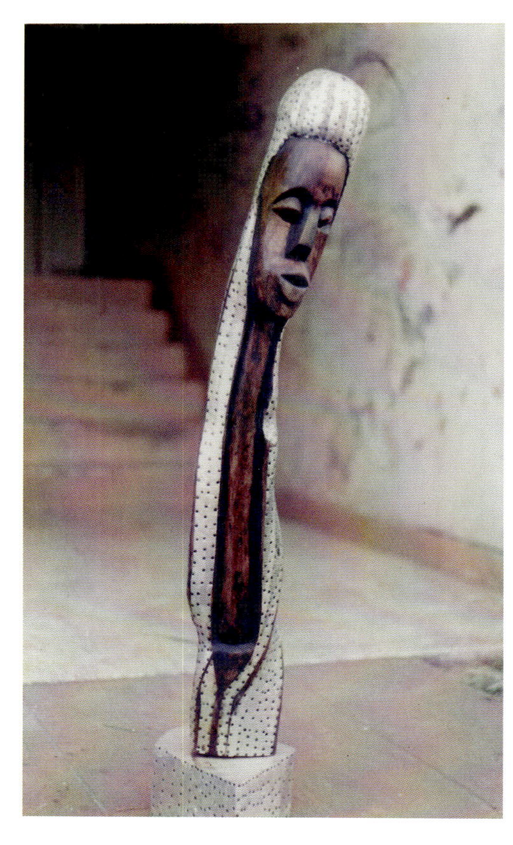

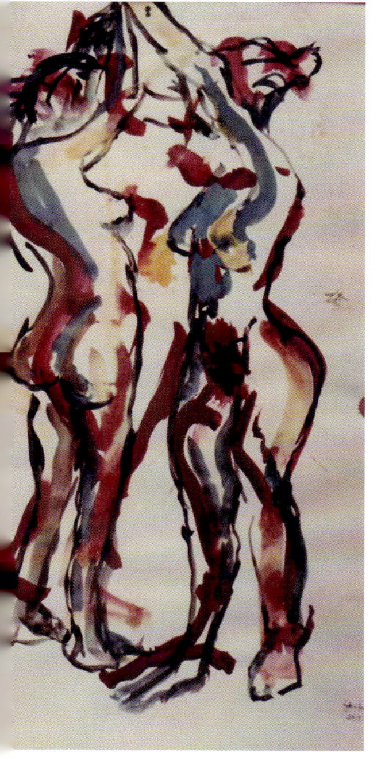

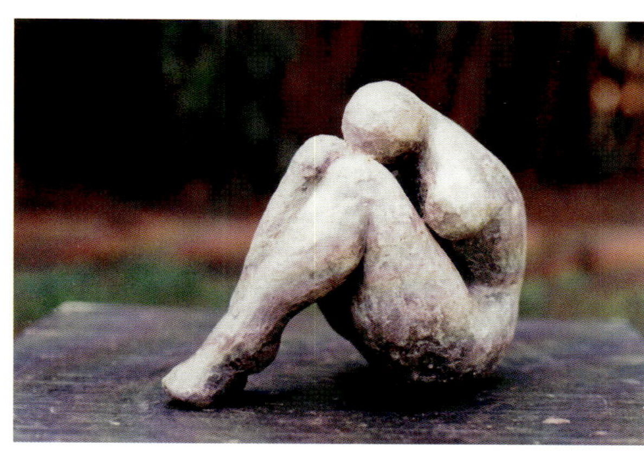

afforded Ugandan women artists and aligning it with projects of 'cultural' self-determination and emancipation.[4] As such, the curatorial thesis lay in the collaborative mutual development of exhibition-making through women-led collective organising. As participating artist Kirumira recalls, for Nabulime 'the experiences of women' were the explicit criteria and they specifically chose works 'that spoke to the audience as women artists'.[5]

The artists in 'Women Artists on the Move' were part of a 'second wave' of women artists to come out of Makerere University art school in the 1980s and 90s. An earlier generation, active since the 1960s, includes Rosemary Karuga, Theresa Musoke and Lydia Mugambi, to mention just a few practitioners who are still alive and exhibiting today.[6] Karuga made collages of tableaux and various scenes of daily life in Kenya; Musoke focussed on imaginative compositions of landscape and wildlife; and Mugambi is a notable painter. Mugambi and Musoke both studied in the US soon after Makerere, with the latter returning to East Africa in the 70s to teach at the University of Nairobi. The 'second wave' of Makerere women artists mostly joined the art school in the 80s and worked primarily in sculpture; although some, such as Venny Nakazibwe, Sarah Nakisanze and Josephine Mukasa, took up textile design and helped to usher in the school's efforts towards accommodating women artists in studying fashion.

'Women Artists on the Move' included sculpture, painting and textiles. In the catalogue, an untitled cement sculpture by Katende is described as 'expressive'[7] – not a reference to the European movement but rather to artistic strategies in depicting pain and trauma, borrowing from strategies by pioneering Makerere sculptor Francis Musangogwantamu (with whom Katende studied). For an earlier group of Makerere artists, expressiveness was connected to the memory of war in an East African context: most notably, the mobilisation of Ugandan subjects by the British colonial administration during the Second World War and events surrounding the Uganda-Tanzania War (1978–79) and Luwero War (1981–86). Elsewhere in the show, Nagawa's untitled clay sculpture showing a female figure curled up into herself recalls the influence of British artist Henry Moore, whose rounded sculptural abstraction was popular amongst Makerere-trained sculptors. By contrast, Nakisanze, perhaps one of the few artists at the time to focus on textile design, presented an untitled multicoloured tie-dye peacock textile. This trend of textile-based works had become popular during the wartime period in Uganda, as materials became scarce between 1979 and 1989. Artists were drawn to batik, and textiles, echoing the Indonesian technique, but infusing African tie-dye processes and designs.

The site of education itself, and the potential of African feminism(s) within this space, is a notable additional layer to the exhibition. The art school itself had been established by a woman, British educator and author Margaret Trowell, in 1937 – a fact noted in the catalogue, albeit without registering the complexity and ambivalence of this lineage.[8] Explicitly referencing the objectives of the 'Fourth World Conference on Women: Action for Equality, Development and Peace', a gathering in Beijing convened by the United

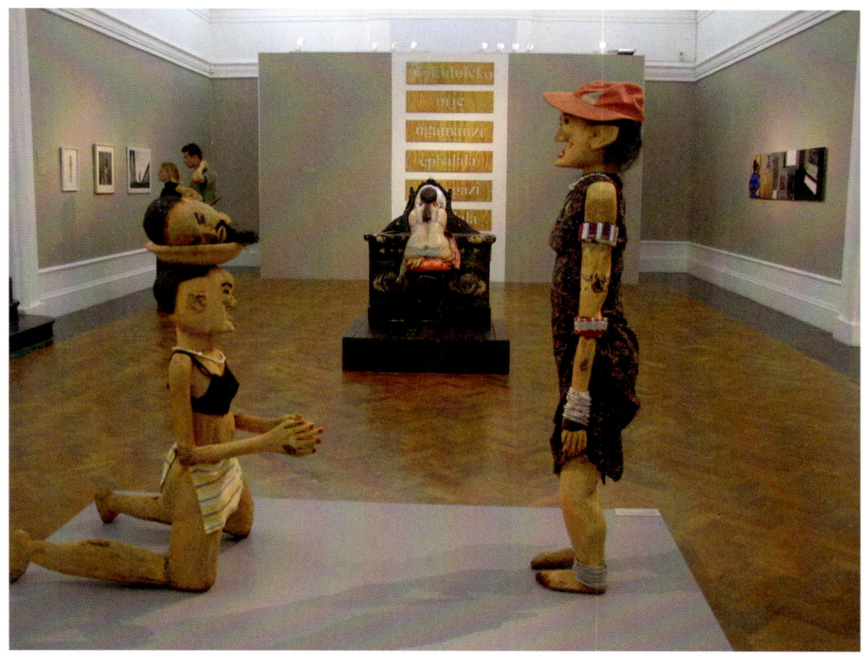

Nations that took place earlier in 1995, 'Women Artists on the Move' positioned itself in relation to the Beijing 'women in development' manifesto, which argued that economic development was not achievable without the full participation of women. While it is unclear to what extent the group was involved in Beijing, records indicate that participating artist Katende gave a conference paper on the art education of girls and that Kirumira attended a follow-up United Nations Plan for Action meeting in Manitoba, Canada.[9] Moreover, the experience of staging the exhibition within Makerere University solidified the visibility of women artists on the university campus, transforming the hitherto male-dominated space of art education.

Nabulime recalls that the exhibition attracted a generous press response, featured on the radio and in the daily newspapers.[10] Keturah Kamugasa's review in the national daily *New Vision* was glowing. Yet it provoked a more mixed and sometimes outraged response within the artistic community at large, something that Nabulime had not anticipated. The particular reasoning behind such reactions is not recorded, but a generalised backlash against the *visibility* of feminist artists in a small and male-dominated field would blight the success of women in art in subsequent years. And alongside these local problematics, the unevenness of global-local relations in the contemporary art field has led to an unfair imbalance in the historicisation of African women artists practising during the 1990s, a situation exacerbated by Uganda's weak economic position after the Luwero War and the fall of the Soviet Union, which dampened the enthusiasm of critics and collectors. The net result has been that small-scale shows on the continent are more-or-less forgotten, the smaller or artist-led institutions that host

Installation view, 'Second to None', South Africa National Gallery, Cape Town, 2006. Courtesy Gabi Ngcobo

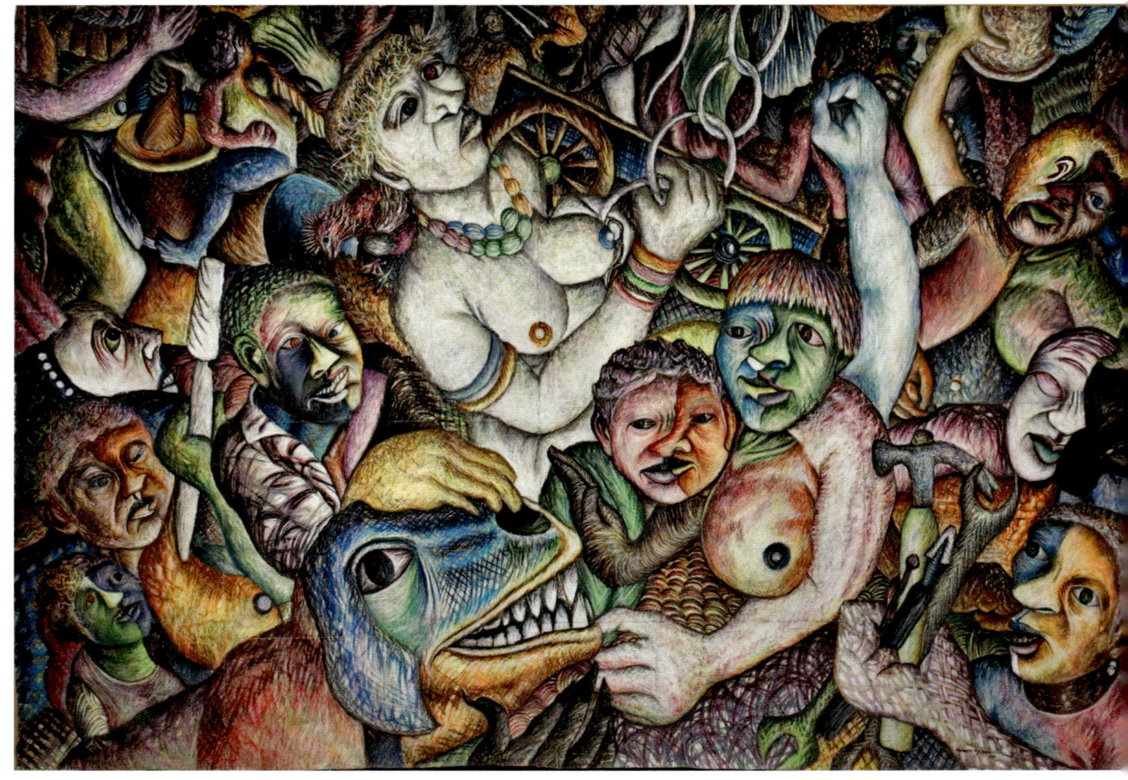

them are similarly historically neglected,[11] and, ultimately, critical attention is diverted from the important work being done within African feminist debates and practices.

II

The task of an African feminist art history, and of historicising African women artists, is one that forces us to reconsider how we analyse the legacy of pan-Africanism; this includes its treatment of women's bodies as purely illustrative of Africanist liberation ideology, or its relegating to the margins women student leaders and women intellectuals at the forefront of the establishment of political and cultural movements. Such a task would be to negotiate the complex battles between personal and collective memory and official national archives and records, and to accept neither the pathological nor ideological paradigms that have actively shaped the production of state-organised and even more radical social and political histories.[12]

'Second to None' (2006) is an example of an exhibition that foregrounds the political significance and 'power to action' of black women across history. Curated by Gabi Ngcobo and Virginia MacKenny, it drew from the under-acknowledged narrative(s) of black women in South African politics and their important contributions to social and political history. It took place on the fiftieth anniversary of the 1956 Women's March, organised by the African

National Congress Women's League, in which 20,000 women marched in protest of the South African government's 'pass laws' that required black South Africans to carry internal passports as part of the racist apartheid regime. Positioning itself explicitly in relation to this historical moment, the exhibition drew from the permanent collection of the South African National Gallery to convene a diverse range of works by women artists as a means to explore the role of gender and race in South Africa between 1960 and 1990 (which saw the lifting of bans on organisations such as the African National Congress and marked the beginning of the end of apartheid) and in the post-apartheid era. As its press release announced, the exhibition aimed to 'assert women's power to action' and to 'negotiate issues linked to individual and collective identity, race and gender'. Combining an explicit focus on race and gender with a non-identitarian approach (the artist list was neither only female nor only black[13]) 'Second to None' wrestled with an overdetermined framework of feminism laid out by white South African women historians, artists and curators.

As Sharlene Khan writes in an article on the state of curatorial and art historical work in South Africa that was published the same year as 'Second to None': 'White domination of the visual arts industry is overwhelming, the dominance of white females especially glaring.'[14] This shows how unusual it was for a black woman curator, Ngcobo, to be co-organising an exhibition at one of the country's leading museums in the nation's capital, Cape Town.[15] 'Second to None', the title chosen by Ngcobo, suggests a disavowal of male dominance – a reading supported by the official press materials (which reference 'women's power' in general rather than black women's power in particular). But a close reading of the curatorial argument as expressed in the exhibition itself suggests a stronger political charge: the disavowal of white female dominance, as in, black women are not second to white women.

At the forefront of the 1956 protest were the figures Albertina Sisulu, Winifred Madikizela Mandela and Adelaide Tambo, who were leaders of the African National Congress Women's League, a platform for black women's political action. It is important to underline here the political-racial dynamics of the 1956 march – it was an event organised by and for black women, in protest of a law that did not apply to white women. 'Second to None' thus builds a narrative that positions the key 1956 event, and by extension, black women's political organising, as the axis to rethink the progress made after 1994. Analogously, the 2006 show also sought to realign the position of black women within existing South African art histories: whereas black women appear as marginal in the histories of women in modern and contemporary South African art established by white women critics, 'Second to None' presented 'established' black South African women artists as equals to their white counterparts.

If the exhibition strategy was to build new narratives, foregrounding the contributions of black women in politics and art, it also suggested new lineages across different generations of black women artists. The show brought together 'established' first-generation black women modern artists, such as Helen

Mmakgabo Sebidi and Noria Mabasa; 'second wave' artists, including Tracey Rose and Berni Searle; and 'emerging' artists, like Keorapetse Mosimane and Zanele Muholi. Prominent amongst the exhibited works were Sebidi's iconic large-scale epic drawing *The Mother Holds the Sharp Side of the Knife* (1988–89), based on a Setswana proverb, and the bright colours of Rose's wallpaper work *Fucking Flowers* (2006), reminiscent of nineteenth-century Victorian paisley and print design, albeit with dripping white phalluses emerging from exotic-looking blossoms. Sensual, corporeal and sexual thematics continued into the third wave of black women artists in the show, with multiple works from Muholi's photographic series on menstruation, *Period II* (2005), and Mosimane's genderqueer portrait *Androgenia – A Beautiful Boy* (2004).

There are various examples of the shortcomings, distortions and misstatements of existing discourses around black women in South African art history. Often these arguments and accounts supporting modernism bear an implicit call for white and/or male dominance that negates any form of knowledge internal to black women. To give one example: beyond generally scientific notes on what girls learn from their grandmothers in rural South Africa, Sebidi's work was hardly taken seriously until her meeting with male artist John Koenakeefe Mohl in 1970.[16] A 2016 interview with Sebidi reveals how her work was deeply informed by the anxiety, violence and death of life in townships – aspects of the work particular to black South African life that had been negated in prior readings.[17] With reference to the historicisation of South African women artists, curator Nontobeko Ntombela has also sharply questioned categories such as 'primitive', 'uneducated' and 'first woman'; as part of her research on the artist Gladys Mgudlandlu for the 2009 exhibition 'A Fragile Archive' (which showed the work of Mgudlandlu and Valerie Desmore), Ntombela interrogates the popular myth that Mgudlandlu was the first black woman artist to exhibit in South Africa.[18] Such a project echoes the insistence of 'Second to None' on an unsettled and still unresolved record of black women in South Africa's official archive.

III

'Like A Virgin…' opened at the Centre for Contemporary Art (CCA), Lagos in early 2009. It presented photography by Zanele Muholi – who also participated in 'Second to None' – alongside the work of Nigerian artist Lucy Azubuike. It sought 'to highlight women's experiences, identities, their bodies and sexuality, in a manner yet to be explored in contemporary Nigerian art', with the exhibition's curator Bisi Silva stressing the experiences of women and their personal reflections.[19] Silva readily admits that Nigerian women artists have made works regarding womanhood for over thirty years – yet the exhibition's explicit focus on sexuality and the body was a means to counter dominant perspectives on black women's bodies centred on the male gaze and male pleasure. Both artists were in a position to offer critically astute and rigorous perspectives on sexuality, male violence and womanhood: Azubuike at the time was pursuing a postgraduate qualification in gender studies; and Muholi's earlier research on rape survivors had been published in the feminist South African journal *Agenda*.[20] Silva writes:

Lucy Azubuike, *Waiting to Excel*, 2005. Courtesy the artist

In an intransigent patriarchal society, in which sexism is prevalent, and in which homophobia is legalised, few if any artists have presented complex, provocative works on the body and sexuality the way Azubuike and Muholi are doing. Two young African women working on the continent, pushing boundaries, confronting taboos and challenging stereotypes, in essence expressing themselves in a way their predecessors have done before.

In Nigeria, recent debates on homosexuality have reintroduced British colonial-era moralism and homophobia, while adding to its moral 'obscenity' newer proposals against pornography that appeal to evangelical Christian morality. The Nigerian situation may be seen in connection with contemporaneous developments in Uganda, where a new anti-homosexuality bill was drafted in 2009, reinscribing the moralism of the British penal code, and going further by proposing a death penalty for those caught in the act. In Nigeria, sexuality has been defined in penal code laws according to which rape and homosexuality are respectively classified as gross indecency and obscenity. Morality in Nigeria, which is led by a federal government, is governed by a legal system, consisting of constitutional, religious and traditional laws. Nigerian federalism allows for states to implement their own laws. It is under this system that sharia law was instituted as criminal law in about twelve Northern Nigerian

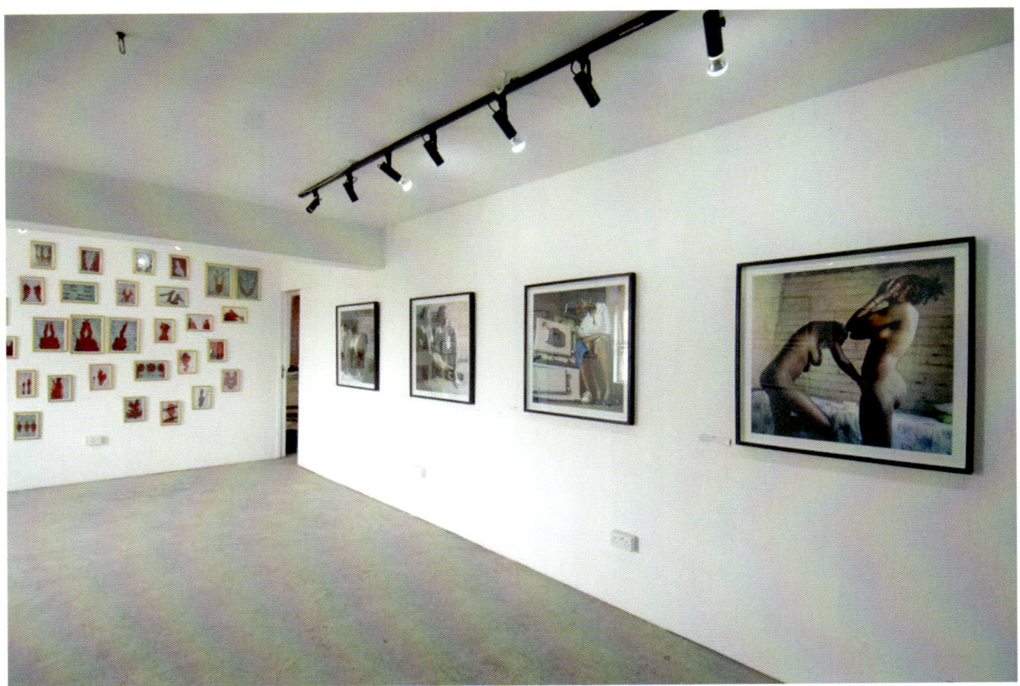

states in 2000.[21] The human rights scholar Vincent O. Nmehielle notes: 'The proclamation of the Islamic legal system led to a number of violent ethnic and religious rifts and communal disturbances in many states, resulting in enormous loss of lives.'[22] Some have argued that Islamic laws in the northern states, specifically those focussing on public morality, have led to 'the curtailment of women's activities, mobility and visibility'.[23]

This limitation certainly extends to the visual arts. In a recent interview, Silva mentioned that because of this development of public moral policing, the making of 'Like A Virgin...' posed a threat to both the curator and the art centre CCA. While Lagos State is not one in which sharia law applies to criminal matters, its symbolic location as Nigeria's economic capital cannot be overlooked when considering public-facing events. This intense set of political and moral circumstances divided the audience attending the exhibition. According to Silva, the guestbook was full of comments that reflected, on the one hand, praise, and on the other, disgust, including strong reactions to the spectacle of menstrual blood in Azubuike's *Menstruation Series* (2006).

Thus 'Like A Virgin...' bravely offered a queer feminist counterargument to public moral debates. It also opened up a critique of patriarchal tendencies within the apparently more progressive art world milieu. In her commissioned catalogue essay, 'Past Virginity: Women, Sexuality and Art', Christine Eyene confronts the leading Nigerian curators and art critics, Olu Oguibe and Okwui Enwezor, by challenging their understanding of the black female body, citing an 'African ideal' of decency and morality in descriptions that

230

mask a certain paternalism.[24] Eyene thus argues that the works in the exhibition, by betraying these idealistic and moralistic notions of the black woman's body in the gaze of Nigeria's male modern artists, both Muholi and Azubuike demean and confront the appropriation of African and black women's bodies within the modern canon.

IV

There is evidence, in all the exhibitions discussed, of a necessary confrontation with various acts of censorship, erasure and epistemic, ontological and physical violence. In the 2009 exhibition 'Like A Virgin…', Muholi and Azubuike confronted homophobia and a specific paternalistic gaze particular to African modernism, and Silva risked being caught in the post-Islamic Law Declaration violence that engulfed Nigeria in 1999 and beyond. The 2006 exhibition 'Second to None' confronted the erasure of black women in the South African historical archive by reconfiguring how a history of women's political action can be read from the perspective of a historic event organised primarily by black South African women. And in the 1995 exhibition 'Women Artists on the Move', there was an overall pushback against traditional paternalistic violence – in the form of denying women the right to education – by making visible women artists' contributions to the academic field.

The presence of African women curators in the space of either modern or contemporary art is also evidenced by all the exhibitions discussed. While the categories of 'first woman' are indeed problematic, we must account for the presence of African women curators within the larger local and international art field. Of the 1995 exhibition, Nabulime states that it was a first for a Ugandan woman to curate a group exhibition of Ugandan women artists, decrying the predominance of white, expatriate and philanthropic curators of African arts that had in previous decades dominated the field. This same point was felt in South Africa with the 2006 exhibition, in a context where the equality of black women artists within the art field had been neglected, if not denied. Then, similarly in Nigeria, while Silva was not the first Nigerian woman to curate group exhibitions devoted to women artists – earlier exhibitions organised by Afi Ekong are notable in this regard – her curatorial and institutional work countered the male-dominated Nigerian art field, which was filled with traditional paternalism and the exoticisation of black women. The three exhibitions that I've discussed present a number of important questions: How are we to fully realise feminist liberation without acknowledging the work of black African women? What potential does 'coming together as women' and communal value have in enabling the activities of African women artists in the arts sphere? How do we transform the flattening out of women's experiences as mere spectacle into a complex account of their personal and public lives? Each exhibition provides a critical basis for these complex questions, in order to show the potential of African feminist collectivity, and thus signifies what collective histories in the field of contemporary African art and exhibition history could look like.

This text is dedicated to the memory of Bisi Silva (1962–2019).

Notes

[1] 'The Short Century: Independence and Liberation Movements in Africa 1945–1994', curated by Okwui Enwezor, was first presented in 2001 at the Museum Villa Stuck, Munich and toured to Berlin, Chicago and New York. 'Seven Stories about Modern Art in Africa', curated by Clémentine Deliss, was at the Whitechapel Art Gallery, London in 1995.

[2] Amongst the better-known presentations of modern and contemporary African art from the 1950s until the 1990s are the cultural events held at the Mbari Club, Ibadan during the 1960s; 'Africa and Art: An Exhibition of Art in Africa Celebrating the Independence of Tanganyika', Margaret Trowell School of Fine Arts, Makerere University College, 1961; 'L'Art nègre: Sources, evolution, expansion' and 'Tendances et confrontations', Premier Festival mondial des artes nègres, Dakar, 1966; 'Contemporary African Art', Museum of African Art, Washington DC, 1974; the exhibitions at FESTAC '77: The 2nd World Festival of Black Arts and Culture, Lagos, 1977; 'Moderne Kunst in Afrika', Festival of World Cultures, Berlin, 1979, also presented as 'Art from Africa', Commonwealth Institute, London, 1981; 'Sanaa: Contemporary Art from East Africa', Commonwealth Institute, 1984; Cairo Biennale (since 1984); 'Tributaries: A View of Contemporary Southern African Art', Johannesburg, 1985; 'Magiciens de la Terre', Centre Georges Pompidou and Grande halle de La Villette, Paris, 1989; 'Africa Explores: 20th Century African Art', New Museum, New York, 1991; Dakar Biennale (since 1992); and the Johannesburg Biennale (since 1995).

[3] In the foreword to the catalogue, Kivubiro Tabawebbula notes the following 1995 exhibitions: '"Women Beyond Borders" … co-ordinated by Jony Waite and conceived to unite women artists around the world … an exhibition of Ugandan and Kenyan women to inaugurate the Museum Studio Centre, National Museum of Kenya organised by Wendy Karmali … "Artistically Speaking Women" at Gallery Cafe [in Kampala] and "Women Artists in Kenya" at the Gallery of Contemporary East African Art, National Museum of Kenya'. K. Tabawebbula, Foreword to *Women Artists on the Move* (exh. cat.), Kampala: Makerere Art Gallery, 1995, pp.2–3.

[4] *Ibid.*

[5] Rose Namubiru Kirumira in conversation with the author, September 2018.

[6] A handful of texts offer accounts of these artists. See, for example, Margaret Nagawa, 'The Challenges and Successes of Women Artists in Uganda', in Marion I. Arnold (ed.), *Art in Eastern Africa*, Dar es Salaam: Mkuki na Nyota, 2008, pp.151–73; and Sidney Kasfir, *Contemporary African Art*, London: Thames & Hudson, 2001, which also highlights a few East African women artists in the 1990s.

[7] Lilian Mary Nabulime, 'Katende Sylvia Nabiteeko', in *Women Artists on the Move, op. cit.*, pp.12–14.

[8] See Emma Wolukau-Wanambwa, 'Margaret Trowell's School of Art: A Case Study in Colonial Subject Formation', in Susanne Stemmler (ed.), *Wahrnehmung, Erfahrung, Experiment, Wissen Objektivität und Subjektivität in den Künsten und den Wissenschaften*, Berlin: Diaphanes, 2014, pp.101–22.

[9] See M. Nagawa, 'The Challenges and Successes of Women Artists in Uganda', *op. cit.*

[10] Interview with L. Nabulime by Nakisanze Segawa as research for this essay, Kampala, October 2018.

[11] Historical examples include Paa Ya Paa in Nairobi, run by Elimo Njau, and Mbari Mbayo Club, part of the Extra-Mural Studies programme in Ibadan, Nigeria; each was established during the 1960s.

[12] A recent research and exhibition initiative highlighting the position of women in liberation struggles is the multipart project 'Women on Aeroplanes', curated by Annett Busch, Marie-Hélène Gutberlet and Magda Lipska, and co-produced by Iwalewahaus, Universität Bayreut, in collaboration with Centre for Contemporary Art, Lagos; ifa Gallery Berlin; the Museum of Modern Art, Warsaw; The Showroom, London; and The Otolith Collective, London.

[13] The show included, for instance, black male artists such as Nicholas Hlobo and white artists such as Penny Siopis.

[14] Sharlene Khan, 'Doing it for Daddy', *Art South Africa*, vol.4, no.3, 2006, p.156.

[15] Ngcobo had been working at the museum since 2005, having been appointed as an assistant curator. Virginia MacKenny was a guest curator working at the Michaelis School of Fine Art, University of Cape Town.

[16] See M.I. Arnold, *Women and Art in South Africa*, Cape Town: David Philip, 1996. Furthermore, her practice is situated in a dichotomy of rural and urban life – yet without 'reason', the 'rural' can easily slip into the domain of barbarism and senselessness.

[17] See Gabi Ngcobo, Luciane Ramos-Silva and Thiago de Paula Souza, 'In Conversation with South-African painter Helen Sebidi', *Contemporary And (C&) América Latina*, 23 February 2018, available at http://amlatina.contemporaryand.com/editorial/south-african-painter-helen-sebidi/.

[18] Nontobeko Mabongi Ntombela, 'A fragile archive: Refiguring | Rethinking | Reimagining | Representing Gladys Mgudlandlu', unpublished master's thesis, Johannesburg: University of Witwatersrand, 2014.

[19] See http://www.ccalagos.org/archive/like-a-virgin/.

[20] See Zanele Muholi, 'Thinking through lesbian rape', *Agenda*, vol.18, no.61, 2004, pp.116–25.

[21] See Rasheed Oyewole Olaniyi, 'Hisbah and Sharia Law Enforcement in Metropolitan Kano', *Africa Today*, vol.57, no.4, 2011, pp.71–96.

[22] Vincent O. Nmehielle, 'Sharia law in the northern states of Nigeria: To implement or not to implement, the constitutionality is the question', *Human Rights Quarterly*, vol.26, no.3, 2004, pp.730–59.

[23] Fatima L. Adamu, 'Gender, Hisba and the Enforcement of Morality in Northern Nigeria', *Africa*, vol.78, no.1, 2008, pp.136–52.

[24] Christine Eyene, 'Past Virginity: Women, Sexuality and Art', in *Like A Virgin…* (exh. cat.), Lagos: Center for Contemporary Art, 2009.

Womanifesto

Bo Choy

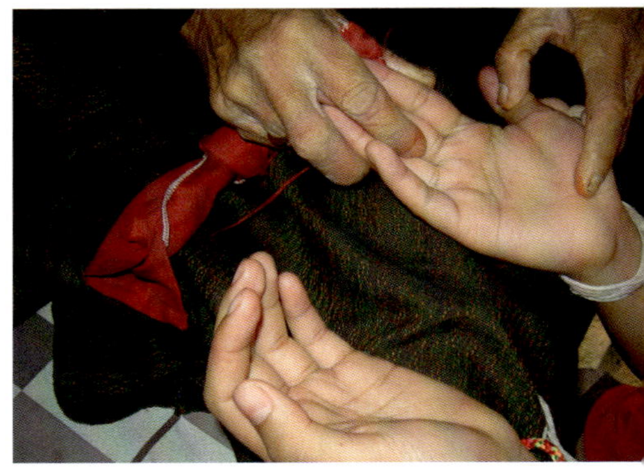

The Womanifesto archive is a treat for the mind's eye. I am drawn to the images of the workshops and residencies that took place at Boon Bandarm Farm, Northeast Thailand, in 2001 and 2008, which evoke yearnings for a cohabitation with nature on equal terms. A vision emerges where artists as humans become part of the land, working together co-operatively, sharing knowledge and skills and learning from one another. We see them gathering, not necessarily with the aim of making works of art but for the greater creative vision of a way of being together – for ideas to emerge and for the enrichment of each person's life through this collective endeavour.

With the context of the Fourth World Conference on Women in Beijing in 1995 very much in mind, Womanifesto's gatherings began in a series of exhibitions held in Bangkok, to foreground the work of woman artists. But after the first two editions, the artists realised that what they most enjoyed was just being together; this led to the vision of a more open-ended creative exchange with no specific exhibition outcome that could take place either online or offline.

At the time of writing, with the Covid-19 pandemic ongoing, this 'just being together' resonates particularly. The physicality of human touch, of bodies being in one space, here and now and with nature, the interrelation of the energies and vibrations of surrounding beings feels a long way from the amount of time currently spent in digital communion, mediated by screens and text messages. Yes, there is a spiritual dimension to this being-together; something magical maybe emerged from the weaves, the tie-dyes, the pottery and artefacts created from this gathering. A magic that may enchant younger generations of artists, including myself.

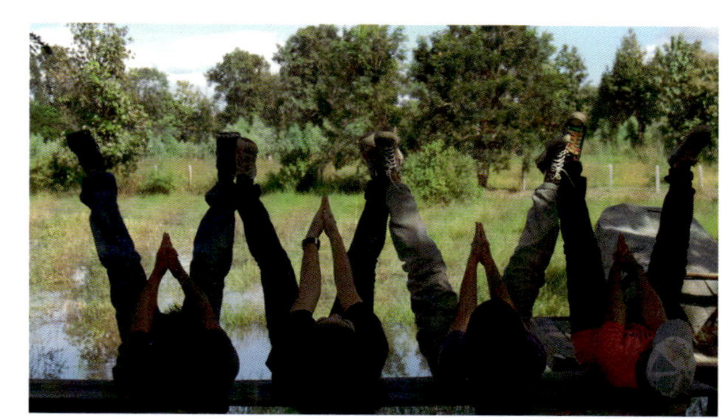

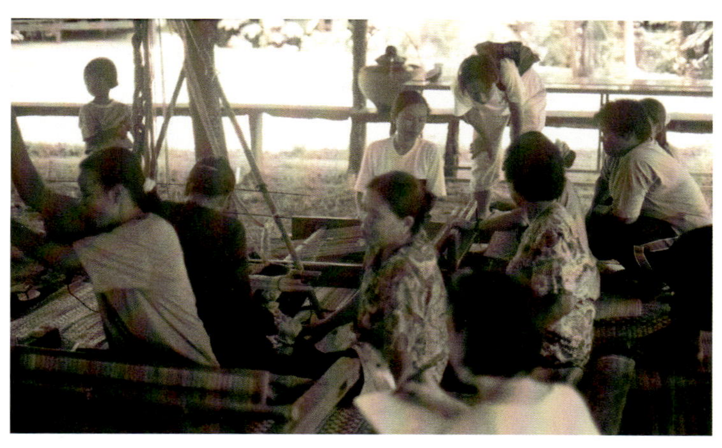

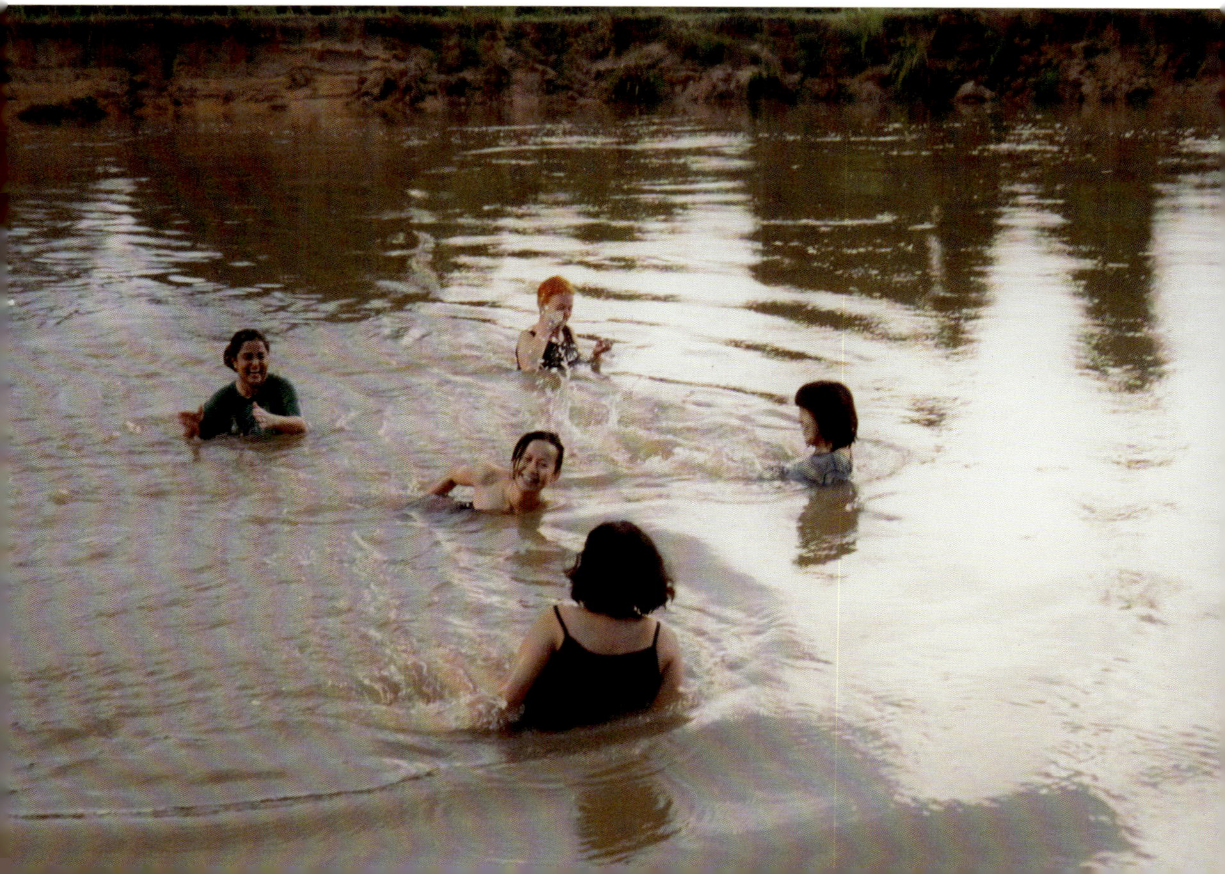

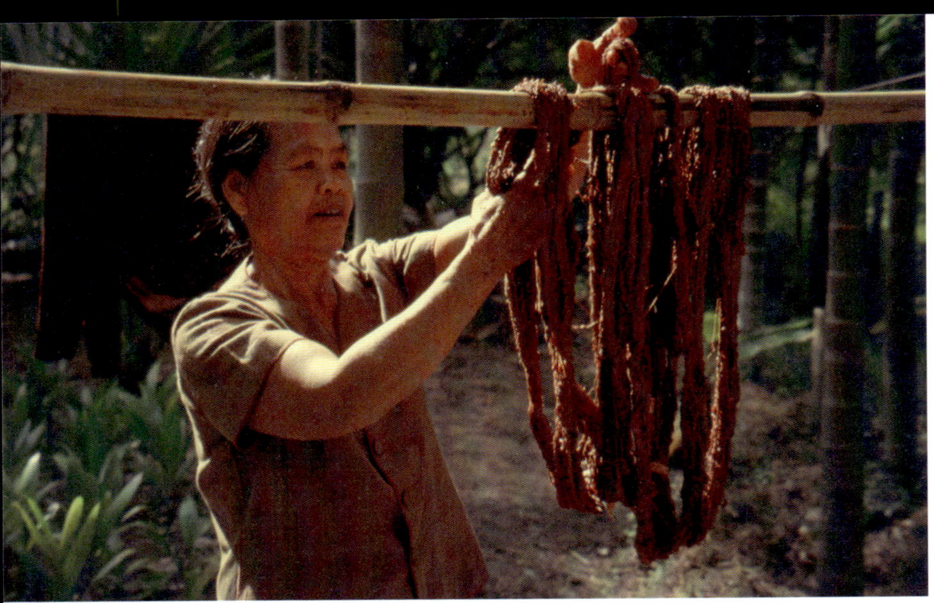

'It is because of the land; we are related to the land. This land can educate people'
– Pan Parahom (Mae Pan), 'Notes from the farm'.
Mae Pan has worked on the farm all her life with her family.

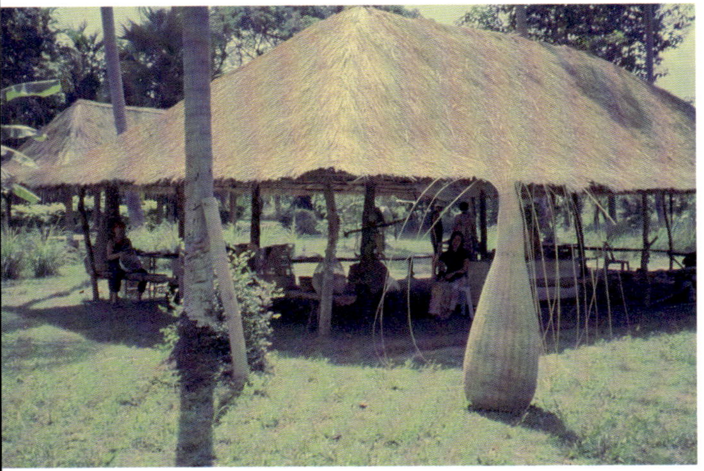

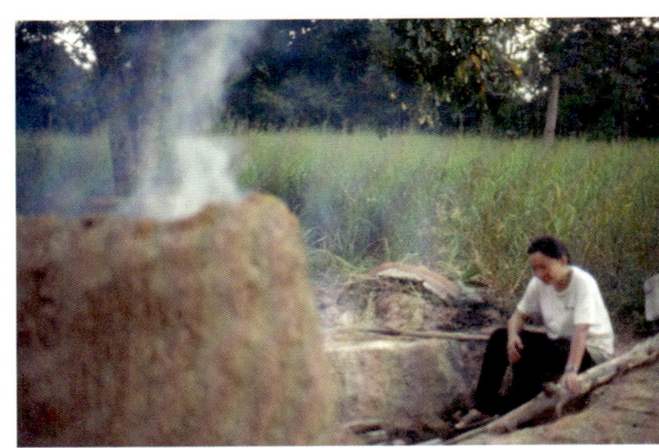

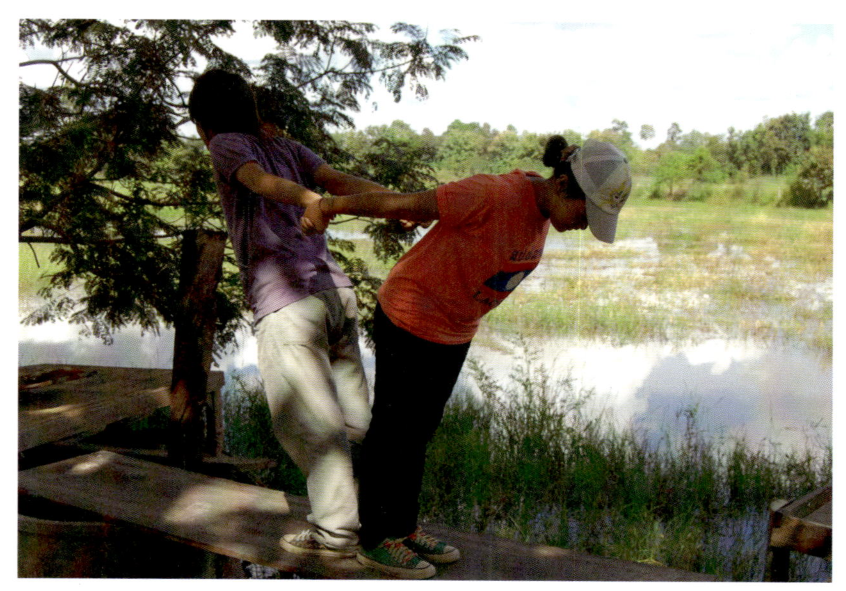

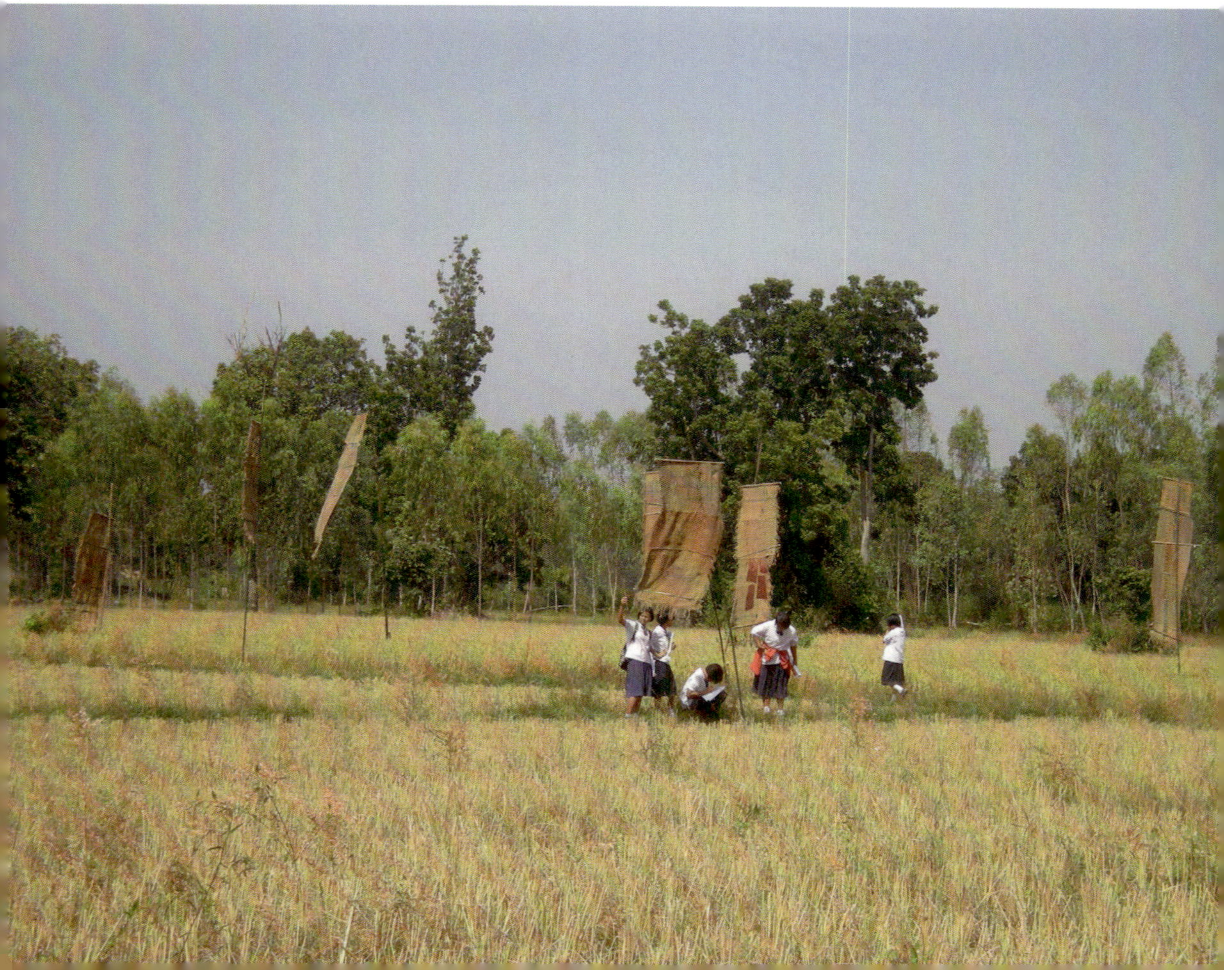

In a 'crit' with a group of art students in the week before writing this text, one of the group, Saya, said that simply by using the dichotomy 'human and nature' we are differentiating ourselves from nature. We are upholding this separation even at a linguistic-conceptual level. Perhaps it's our Ego and Self at play, always setting the boundaries between You and I, Us and Them. The participants at Womanifesto blurred this boundary by working with nature's technology – their own hands, bamboo for building a Spirit House, tree bark and plants for colour dyes, soil for the building of a kiln. Nature determined the artists' way. They accepted, embraced and nurtured the connection. Thich Nhat Hanh once said that 'your body belongs to your ancestors, your parents and future generations. It also belongs to society and to all the other living beings. The trees, the clouds, the soil and every living thing brought about the presence of your body.' The collective spirit at Womanifesto reminds that we are at one with all living beings. We are the trees, the fruits and the soil. We are nature.

It's not just the here and now – we also belong to past and future generations, and to the coming together of city dwellers and rural communities. The two iterations of Womanifesto ensured the handing down of knowledge through intergenerational, inter-land exchanges. The participants, of different ages, from different backgrounds, are like vessels, holding and transporting traditions, skills and practices, history and experiences; handed down, travelling onwards to their respective destinations to continue the passage. Xie Congyang describes elsewhere in this publication workshops and residency programmes in the Chinese hinterlands as ways for artists there to 'learn from the outside'. With Womanifesto, this direction of learning is reversed: turning our gazes away from the making and exhibiting circuit that artists can find themselves in, and the often-atomised existence of urban life, these images project a vision of collective living where art and creativity are grounded in the land and nature's technology.

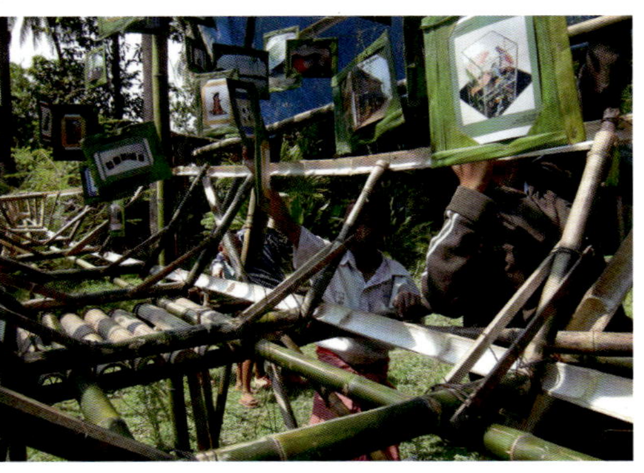

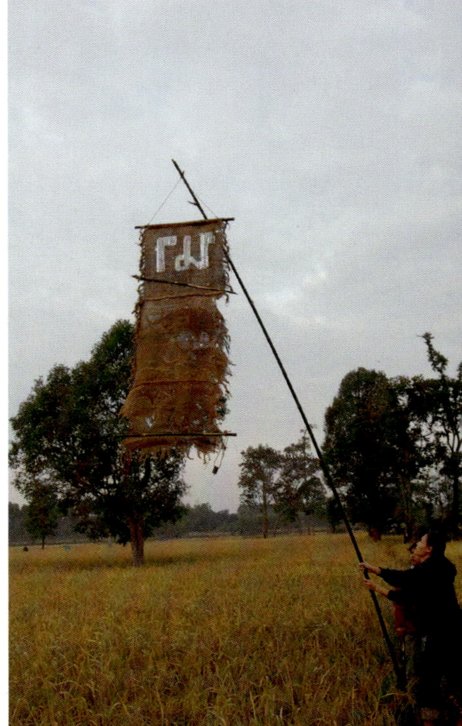

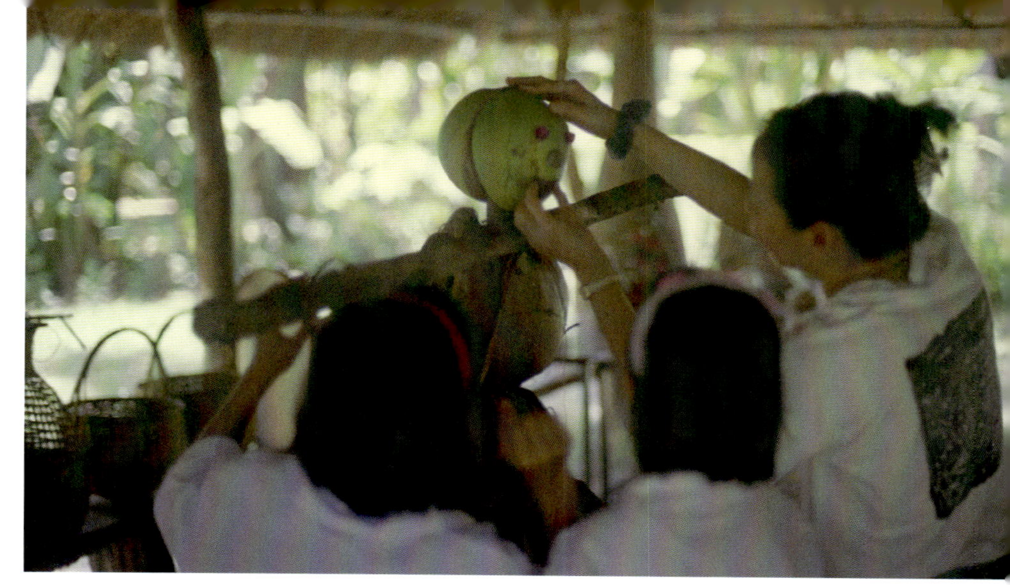

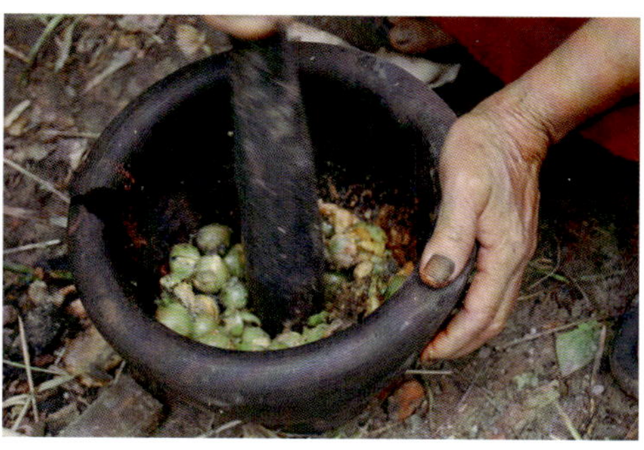

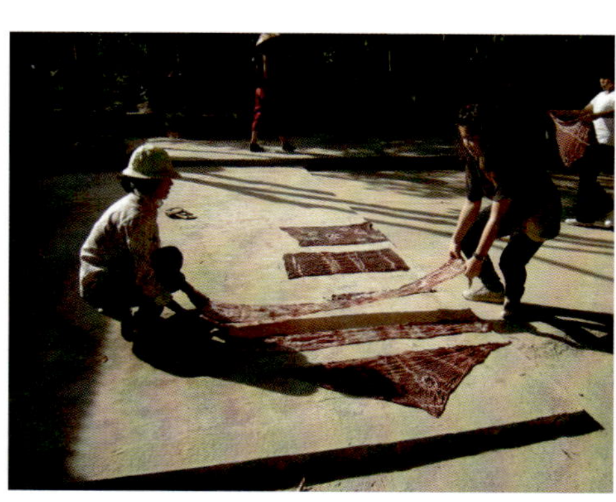

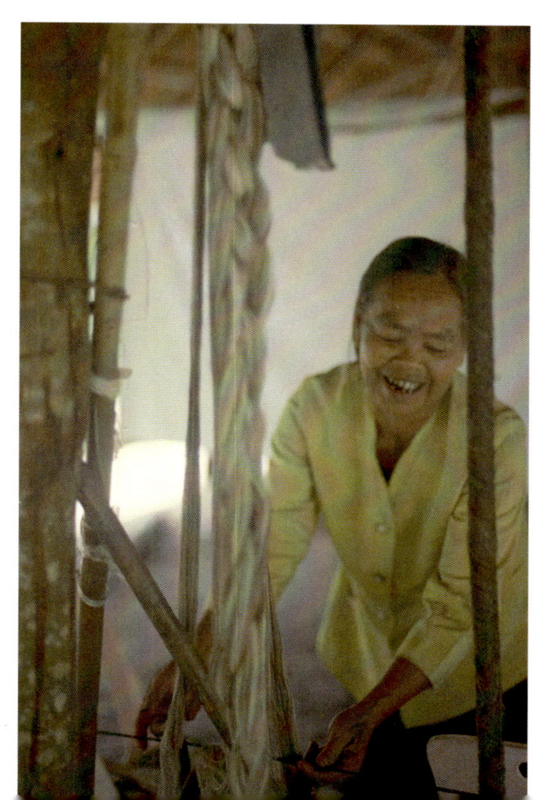

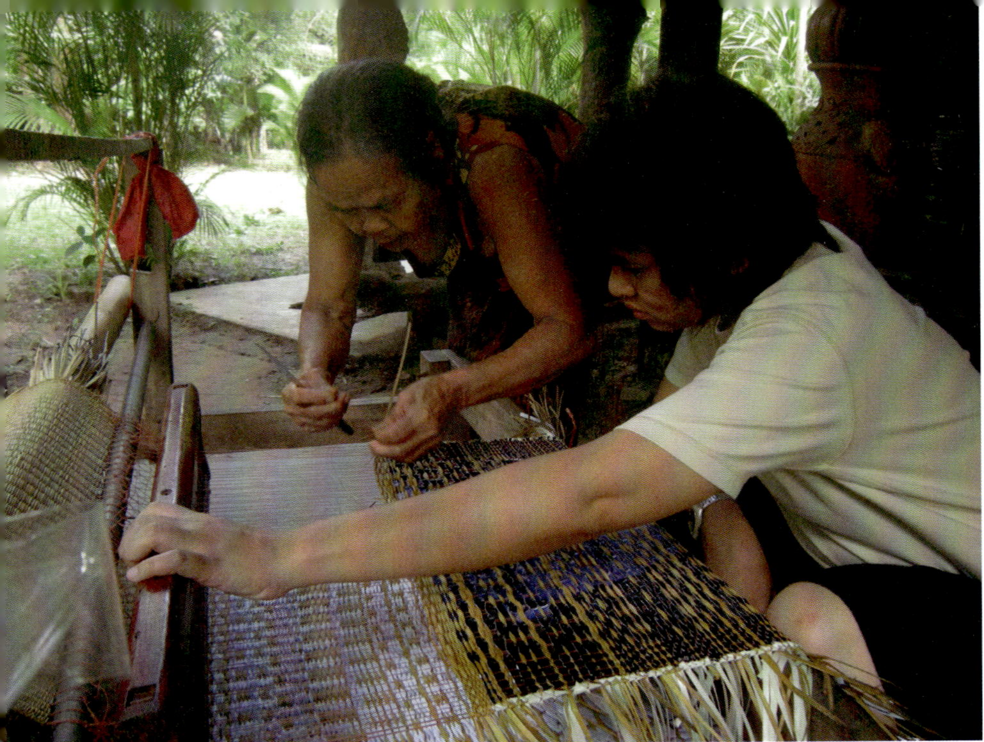

The technology with which Womanifesto works as a project is not confined to land and nature, working with whatever they could get their hands on at any moment in time. As one of the founders, Varsha Nair, has said, their way of working is to go with the flow. In 2003, one of the co-founders, Nitaya Ueareeworakul, became pregnant; to accommodate this, they decided to use email art as a format for their next 'gathering'. Each artist's email submission was designed into a single page to form a publication – *Procreation/Postcreation* – which culminated in a launch event where exhibitions, screenings, talks and performances took place. The next iteration of the project, the website 'No Man's Land' (2005–06), was a natural progression. Outside the mainstream gallery, biennale and residency circuit, Womanifesto endows a grounded DIY spirit of organising; it is as much about the friendships and bonds created and nurtured over the years as it is about making art public. It is this spirit that makes it unique and worthwhile.

With this spirit in mind, it makes me wonder if Womanifesto were to begin anew, what form would it take? What would it be called, who would consti-tute the 'we' and where would it take place? Much of what I have said is my own constructed memory from an archive, which evokes a series of questions in the now. How do we define 'togetherness' now? And how can we create and sustain support, proximity and a sense of 'magic' for self-identifying woman/non-binary artists across cultures in the post-pandemic world? Bodies in space, artefacts and screens aside, Womanifesto shows us that it is also the spirit inside us that keeps a bond alive.*

* For Womanifesto's founders, the spirit also continues: in 2021 they started 'GATHERINGS', in which each hosts a physical gathering of two to five artists in their respective locations – Udon Thani, Sydney, Berlin, Baroda, Basel and London. The process and outcomes are shared via their blog, http://blog.womanifesto.com.

240

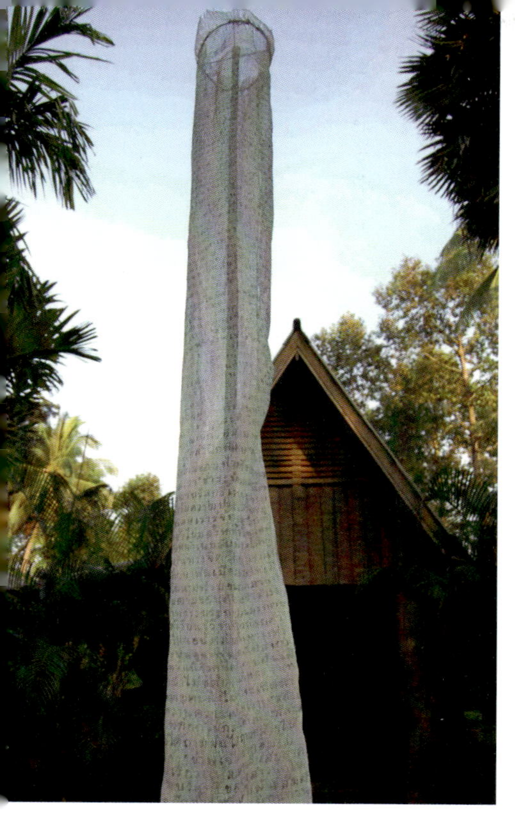
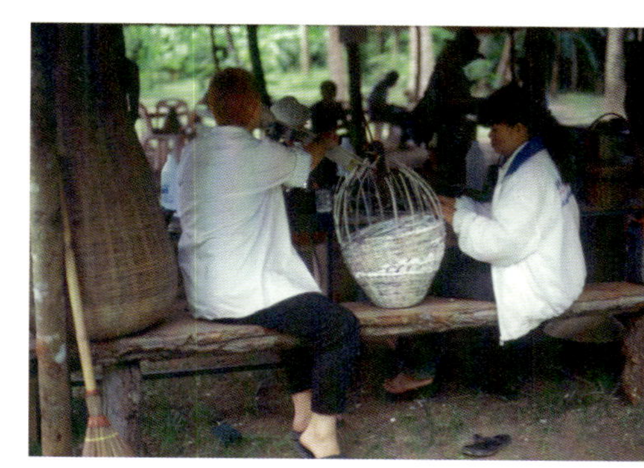
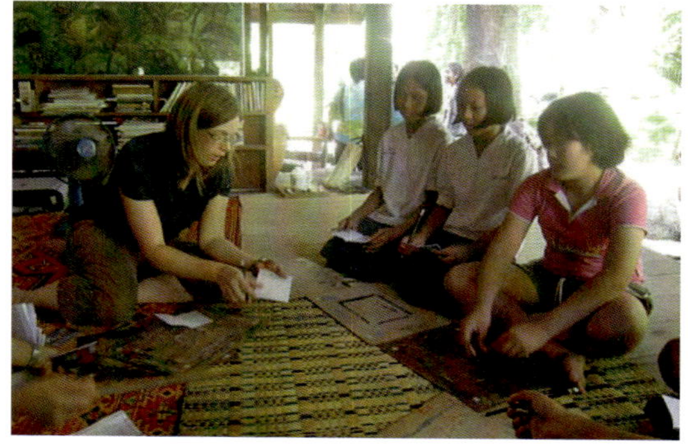
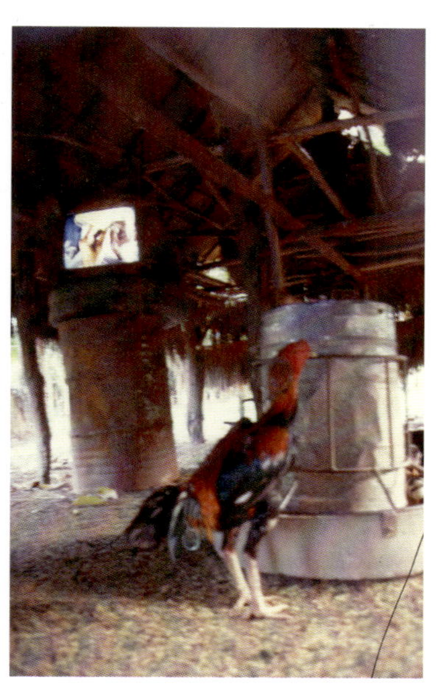
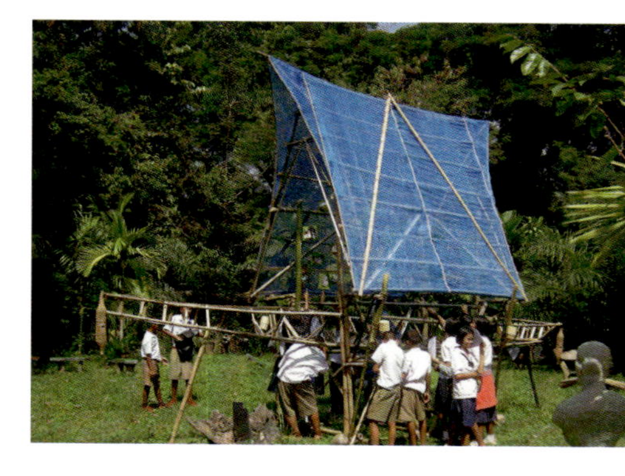
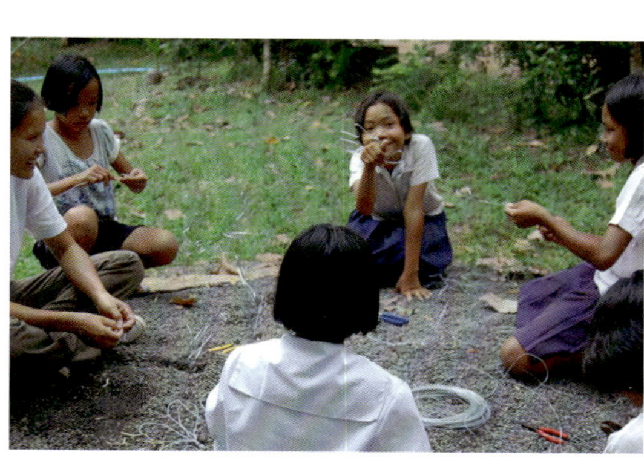

Fragmented Sites of Actions: Three Art Events in China's Hinterland, 1992–94

Xie Congyang

I

Throughout the 1990s, Chinese official art institutions prohibited the exhibition of contemporary art forms that were experimental in nature, which forced art practitioners to explore exhibition possibilities beyond regular venues. One consequence, as critic Liao Wen observed, was that 'flowers blossom[ed] outside the wall',[1] with artworks created in China leaving the country to be showcased in the West. While some practitioners in China endeavoured to improve the mainstream visibility of contemporary art by negotiating with official institutions, those who were carrying out more cutting-edge art experiments consciously chose to 'go underground', thus limiting their audience to a small circle of art professionals. Under various restrictions, more radical ideas of exhibition were put into practice. Some artists gave up displaying their work in physical spaces and instead presented documents – work plans, photographs, statements, etc. – by self-publishing and circulating booklets and zines.[2] This mode of 'exhibition' overcame geographic limitations and effectively connected highly localised practices of contemporary artists working across China.

What, then, were the 'sites' of exhibition where art and its public met? Who were the 'public(s)'? What exhibition-making strategies were developed, and why? These questions, particularly pertinent to Chinese art of the 1990s, become even more intriguing when we turn our eyes away from the art centres in the east and south coastal areas to instead look at China's vast hinterland. This essay will discuss three art events that took place in North and Northwest China: *The Funeral* (Lanzhou, Gansu Province, 1993), the *Village Project 1993* (Liulin County of Shanxi Province, 1992–93), and the serial events organised by the Central China Fire Stone Group (various locations in Henan Province, 1992–94). These projects speak to the complexities of 'located' practice within a 'global' art field and offer an alternative set of understandings of art and its publics.

242

The initiators and participants of these events had been engaged in avant-garde art activities in their own regions since the 1980s. Compared with artists working in China's major centres for art, such as Beijing, Shanghai and Guangzhou, the social support that these artists received was far more tenuous: provincial art schools were less supportive of students' art experiments; artists had fewer channels to access art information; and occasions for international cultural exchange were extremely scarce. In spite of these circumstances, in the 1980s active avant-garde art communities were formed in provincial capital cities in the hinterland, including Lanzhou, Xi'an and Taiyuan. Art publications such as *Fine Arts in China* played a vital role in the development of avant-garde art in these areas.[4] Headquartered in Beijing, the weekly newspaper was distributed nationwide, with its editors consolidating information on avant-garde art activities from all parts of China. Through *Fine Arts in China*, artists in the hinterland were not only able to learn about the latest art trends in China, they also had the opportunity to present their works and thoughts.

When *Fine Arts in China* was cancelled in 1989, artists in the hinterland lost a platform for publishing their work. During the 1990s, art writers, critics and publications that supported avant-garde art were absent in the hinterland. Meanwhile, elsewhere in China, art editors and critics were more and more actively engaged in exhibition-making, with the goal of building an infrastructure of contemporary art in China.[5] Through a series of seminal exhibitions held in China and the West, a few art trends became highly visible, in turn consolidating the power of critic-curators in the art scene.[6] The three events discussed here may be understood in relation to these changes. In the absence of art writers and curators in their own regions who could contextualise and evaluate the value of their work, artists in the hinterland had to organise themselves to articulate their artistic positions and negotiate artistic values with the larger art community in China.

II

The Funeral was co-organised by the artist group Lanzhou Art Army in protest of the First 1990s Biennial Art Fair in 1992.[7] With art critic Lü Peng as chief organiser, the fair sought to establish a domestic market for contemporary Chinese art, via a new (for China) mode of corporate-sponsored exhibition-making. Organisers imagined that a domestic art market would reduce artists' and critics' reliance on state institutions for their income, guaranteeing artistic freedom. Not all the participating artists were convinced. When the exhibition opened with an awards ceremony in Guangzhou in October 1992, suspicions around the fairness and transparency of the selection process immediately spread. The most extreme critics concluded that the art fair was a scam – that the awards were selected not based on the artworks' quality, but on personal relationships and backdoor financial exchanges.

Cheng Li, a self-taught artist based in Lanzhou, subscribed to this view. Cheng had not been awarded for his work in Guangzhou, and on his way back to Lanzhou he met with a few artists in Xi'an and Luoyang who held similar points of view. The artists decided to launch a series of events in their respective cities to voice their protest against the 'corruption' in the art circle.

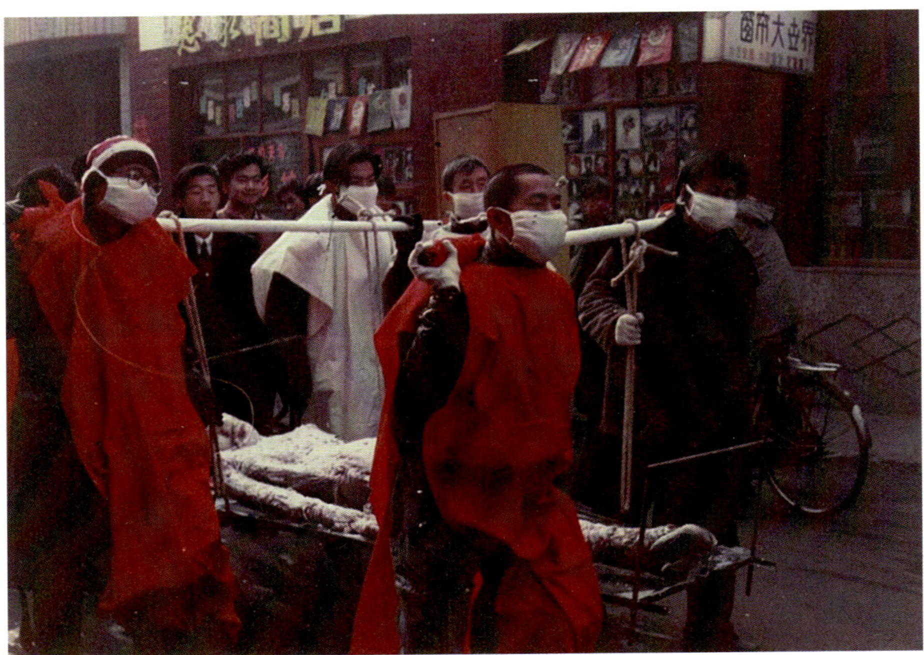

Members of Lanzhou Art Army marching on the street during *The Funeral*. Courtesy Cheng Li and Documenting Contemporary Art of Northwest China Archive at Asia Art Archive

Although the events in Xi'an and Luoyang failed to materialise, Cheng quickly mobilised a group of artists in Lanzhou to launch a protest action. Other key members of the group included Ma Yunfei, Yang Zhichao and Liu Xinhua, graduates from the Department of Fine Art at Northwest Normal University, a leading art education institution in Gansu Province. Calling themselves the Lanzhou Art Army, they presented *The Funeral* in January 1993.

The Funeral consisted of a series of symbolic actions commemorating the death of a fictional character, a middle-aged artist named Zhong Xiandai – meaning 'the finality of modernity' when read in Chinese – who quickly got rich from bribing art critics to sell his paintings and lived a life of extravagance. The story of Zhong was plotted in two fictions by Yang Zhichao, who depicted Zhong's luxurious life with ecstatic and sensational writing, evoking the shock that Chinese people experienced upon the sudden arrival of a world with overwhelming commodities. Cheng Li created several copies of brochures in which Yang's text was juxtaposed with reproductions of images found in fashion magazines, newspapers and other sources.

In early January 1993, the Lanzhou Art Army published death notices in a few newspapers in China, announcing that Zhong Xiandai had died on his way to selling paintings in the United States. They also distributed banners and posters of Zhong's funeral in the streets of Lanzhou. On 17 January, members of the Art Army, dressed in red paper uniforms that they had designed and made by hand, carried the fake dead body of Zhong and marched through the streets of Lanzhou, then gave a speech on the end of modern art in the playground of a middle school, where they burned Zhong's body.

244

Lanzhou Art Army used the death of Zhong as a critical allegory of the dim future of the artist who fails to resist the temptation of money. To communicate this message, they sent Zhong's death notice to artists, art critics and art publication editors across China, along with paper strips printed with the slogans 'Down with Art Dealers, Down with Publishing, Down with Bribery'.[8] After the march, Cheng Li produced several copies of scrapbooks containing documentation of *The Funeral* and sent them to art practitioners across China.

Although *The Funeral* comprised various forms of art practice including collage, graphic design, fiction and self-publishing, it is today remembered in art circles as an instance of performance art. On the other hand, the art circle perceived the event from the Art Army's outspoken opposition to the Guangzhou art fair, while its significance to local art communities in Lanzhou was neglected. In fact, apart from Cheng Li, none of the Art Army members submitted work to the biennial art fair, and their antagonism towards the art fair's organisers is ambiguous. Rather than protesting against the corruption of art, their commitment to the event may have been driven by the desire for a collective activity to motivate the creative energy of the small community of artists who were experiencing ongoing marginalisation in a society that privileged economic progress over the pursuit of art.

III

Initiating collective and aligned movement to reactivate the local art scene is a strategy shared by the Central China Fire Stone Group. The group was formed by Zhuang Hui, He Junan, Wang Hui and Cui Yanjun – all self-taught worker-artists in Luoyang city. Zhuang Hui, who remains active on the contemporary art scene today, was the central figure of the group. Prior to co-founding the Fire Stone Group, Zhuang had organised several experimental art activities. Departing from most of the self-organised group shows in China that brought together artists working in a particular city, Zhuang sought to organise aligned events that could connect artists nationwide. In 1992, he initiated 'Zhixing 92–417 Action' (translatable as 'Marching Straight Forward, 17 April 1992'), for which he proposed that artists in more than ten cities across China organise art activities in their respective locations as a united endeavour.

In a statement for the event, Zhuang targeted his criticism at art critics from a different perspective than that of *The Funeral*'s organisers.[9] What he opposed was the art circle's obsession with philosophical discussions and the tendency to base art practice on studying books and texts rather than on life experience (a tendency for which he held art critics largely responsible). Zhuang's discontent also derived from his experience of travelling extensively in the scarcely populated area of Northwest China during the early 1990s. Compared with the many fresh experiences he had during that journey, the endless theoretical discussions among his peers seemed boring and limited.

Criticising the art circle's 'cult for texts' (*wen ben qing jie*), the Fire Stone Group created a list of 'live materials' and 'live sites'. They also described their strategy as 'guerrilla war on the move'.[10] Departing from the concept of 'liveness', from

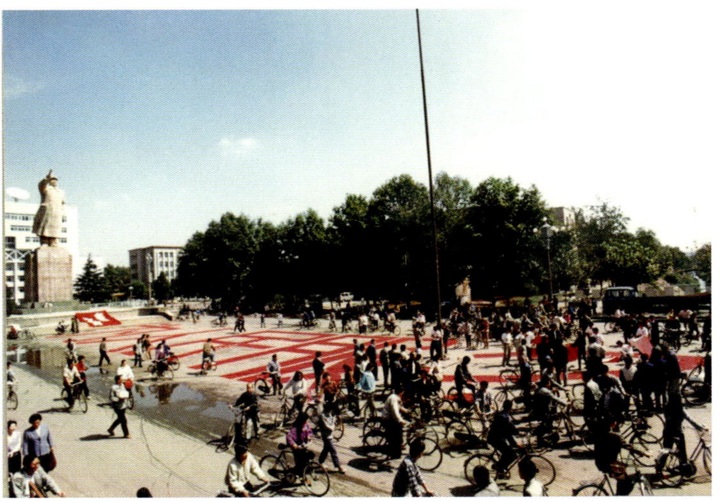

August to October 1992 the group organised several events in Luoyang and its suburbs, with the title 'Serving the People'. The slogan embodied the typical Maoist ideology that had been gradually abandoned since the late 1970s as China's younger generation began embracing individualism. The group recycled it to express opposition to art's tendency to become 'elite culture', losing its connection with the general public. In August, the group went to Foguang County, near Luoyang, to investigate peasants' education and economic conditions; they painted a huge 'Serving the People' slogan with white lime on a dam, and organised a film screening for local farmers. On 18 September, at Dongfanghong Square in Luoyang city, the group and their collaborators pasted red paper strips on the ground to form a large 'Serving the People' slogan on the ground in front of Mao Zedong's statue.

Zhuang's strategy of aligned action was maintained in the Fire Stone Group's activities. In March 1993, the group mailed the document 'Fire Stone Action Plan' to art practitioners across China. In another document that summarised the group's activities, the artists elaborated the significance of mail.[11] First, as a form of exhibition that breaks with convention, presenting work through the mail is a more effective way to communicate art. Second, applying mail as a method is ethical because it is economic. Given that so many Chinese people are still struggling in poverty, Chinese artists should be concerned with local reality, and those who are eager to catch up with the 'global art trend' should be ashamed. Third, for artists, using mail as a channel of self-publishing embodied a self-empowering spirit. According to the group, although the officially published art periodicals communicate the 'professional' opinions of art critics, they are institutionalised and static, incapable of capturing the latest movements and live spirits in the field. Thus, the group foregrounded the ephemerality, effectiveness and 'democratic' character of mail to express their attitude.

Another strategy of Fire Stone Group was to combine social investigation and long-distance tours with the art-making process. From May to June 1993, the

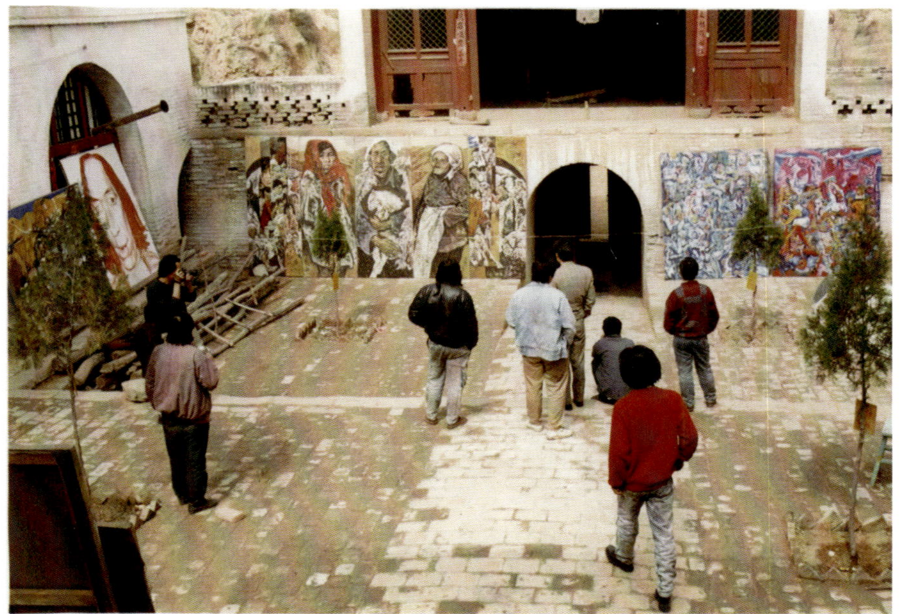

team members departed from Luoyang and rode bicycles in three directions. They investigated the natural, cultural, sociopolitical and economic conditions of the towns and countryside in Henan Province, improvising artworks that responded to these contexts along the way. To conclude the event, the group wrote: 'Through this movement, we further distanced ourselves from the narrow "Cult for Texts". In searching for a solution to conflicts in society, the group has deeply rooted its practice in the local context'.

IV

Making art relevant to a local context was also the motivation of *Village Project 1993*, an art event organised by about twenty artists, photographers and writers working in Taiyuan, Shanxi. From February to April 1993, the participants spent two months living in an old temple in Liulin County (250 kilometres from Taiyuan) while creating artworks in nearby rural areas.

Song Yongping, an artist born in Taiyuan, played a leading role in conceiving and organising the event. In 1984, Song went to Beijing to study film and television production for his job at the North China Radio and Television School. This learning experience greatly changed his view on art, as he realised that not only works of art but also the atmosphere, site and experience of a particular environment can be important in art.[12]

For *Village Project*, the site, atmosphere and experience were essential. At the very beginning, Song Yongping aimed to create an opportunity for artists living in the city to make artworks in a rural setting. Song explained that there were two reasons behind the emphasis on the countryside. First, at that time, most of the participants in *Village Project* were cultural workers of state-controlled

247

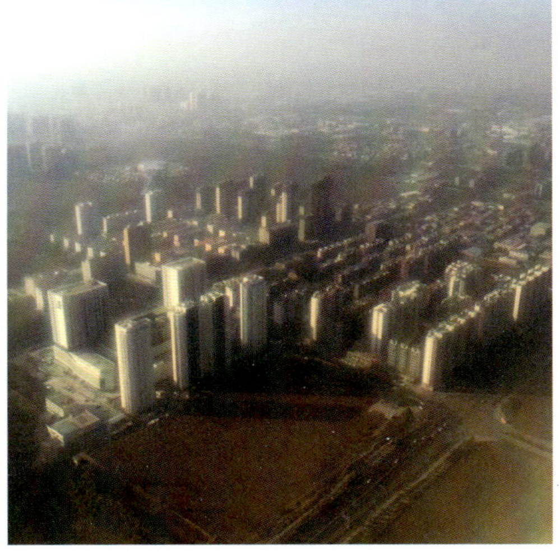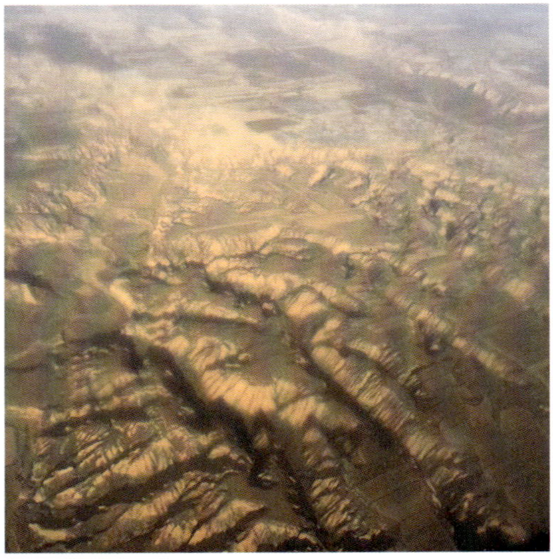

institutions. These young people generally felt discouraged under the political crackdown following the 4 June Incident in Beijing. Song Yongping believed that the countryside would help them escape the depressive atmosphere of their work units. In the countryside, they could breathe fresh air and get inspired by art.

More importantly, Song has always been impressed by the natural landscape of the rural area of Shanxi and the poor living conditions there. In the 1990s, contemporary art activities in China mainly took place in major cities, and many artworks responded to China's rapid urbanisation process. However, according to Song Yongping, the urbanisation of Taiyuan, where he lived, was far less prominent, and the city did not have any distinctive characteristics. On the contrary, the impoverished plains of yellow earth were the most special scenery of Shanxi.

Documents show that particular attention was paid to promoting the event through mass media, demonstrating the artists' ambition to gain recognition amongst the general public. The organisers actively contacted mainstream newspapers and journals to report on the event, they produced television documentaries, and local practitioners were invited to create theme songs and music videos. In fact, promotional work was the major expense covered by the funds raised.

Yet the story of *Village Project* told in these promotions does not fully reflect the event's significance. The experience of process was essential for *Village Project*, and more research is needed to account for participants' and observers' experiences.[13] Another deviation of narrative occurred when Song Yongping and his colleagues sought recognition from the artistic mainstream. To conclude the project, they rented gallery space in the National Art Museum of China, the country's most prestigious art venue, and another gallery space, affiliated to the *China Daily Newspaper* in Beijing, to hold an exhibition of artworks and documentation of *Village Project* for one week. A brief account of the exhibition was given in an essay published in *The New York Times Magazine*, which mainly focussed on the Chinese officials' censorship of the exhibition and a performance Song Yongping gave at the National Museum of Art as a reaction.[14] *Village Project* was thus taken as an example to illustrate the general antagonistic attitude towards the authority amongst Chinese contemporary artists in the early 1990s.

V

In conventional terms, these three art events may not appear successful. They did not gain much serious attention or produce a visible impact on the contemporary art scene in China, and few of the organisers maintained their practice long-term. As has been shown above, there were discrepancies between the art practices, the narratives that the artists used to describe them and the perception of these events within China's art circle. As the Lanzhou Art Army and participants in the *Village Project* repeatedly critiqued the deleterious effect of a market economy on art, the activating impulse that these events may have had for the local experimental artist group is obscured. Zhuang Hui, in reflecting upon the activities of the Fire Stone Group, regretfully expressed that while the initial intention of travelling was to guarantee the 'liveness' of art through confronting with less familiar environments, such purpose cannot be fulfilled because the eagerness to critique social reality and art world had led the artists to make preconceived judgements rather than making more insightful observations about life and society. [15]

Filling the gap between language and practice is also difficult due to the fact that these events were staged in parallel sites, with different agendas. One site was actual public space, the streets, factories and villages in the hinterland where the events took place; the other was 'virtual space', created by press materials, self-published newsletters and documents produced by the artists, which could potentially connect art practitioners across China. In their own regions, the artists organised the three events in response to the urgency of reactivating the local art scene through collective activities. In the larger art community that artists in the hinterland sought to communicate with, the three events reacted to the rise of art critic-curators and the prevailing tendencies that the art critic-curators promoted – the call to introduce a market economy to the art world, the 'conceptual turn' and the exclusive interest in urban subjects. The hinterland artists proposed alternative values and criteria for art. In this light, the emphasis on 'popularity' shared by the three art events should be regarded as primarily a gesture of symbolic resistance to the 'elites'. Although the willingness to engage with the general public in their own regions was genuine, their effectiveness in doing so remains ambiguous.

By the late 1990s increasing numbers of artists – including the key participants of these three events – would move from the hinterland to Beijing, as the development of art infrastructure became more and more uneven across China's different regions.[16] Lacking awareness of earlier art practices developed in their regions, a younger generation of artists who engaged with exhibition-making since 2000 in the hinterland, placed much value on connections to the 'outside', especially to the national art centres, as a source of learning and getting 'objective' feedback beyond their own tiny experimental art circles. This was the experience of Gao Yuan, artist and curator born in Xining, Qinghai Province. In 2015 he founded Xining Contemporary, an independent art space that hosts a residency programme for art practitioners worldwide and features the results at its gallery space. Recent years have seen art spaces such as Xining Contemporary take a role in forging new networks beyond the major cities, due to rising interest in China's more 'peripheral' historical and cultural contexts. While such developments generate new publics for exhibitions and experimental cultural experiments in the hinterland, the position of artists there remains a challenging one – demanding more sophisticated notions of place, of people, of criticality and of art.

Notes

[1] This phrase is the title of Liao's essay published in *Jie Dao* (Street), no.8–9, 1994, which reports on various 1993 exhibitions featuring contemporary Chinese artists on a global scale, including 'China Avant-Garde' in Berlin, the touring 'China's New Art, Post 1989' and the Venice Biennale. All translations mine unless otherwise noted.

[2] Examples include *45 Degree As A Reason* and *Agreed on the Date 26 November 1994 As A Reason*, two art projects initiated by Geng Jianyi, and the catalogue *Chinese Contemporary Artists' Agenda (1994)*, compiled by Wang Youshen.

[3] The research for this essay is based on primary materials related to the events as well as recent interviews conducted by the author with key participants. Major documents of the three events are held in Asia Art Archive's various research collections, including the Li Xianting Archive and the Documenting Contemporary Art of Northwest China Archive. On *The Funeral*, see https://aaa.org.hk/en/collections/search/archive/documenting-contemporary-art-of-northwest-china-lanzhou-1993-funeral; on *Village Project 1993*, see https://aaa.org.hk/en/collections/search/archive/li-xianting-archive-1993-village-project; on Central China Fire Stone Group, see https://aaa.org.hk/en/collections/search/archive/li-xianting-archive-zhuang-hui.

[4] For the significance of *Fine Arts in China* in the 1980s, see 'Conversation with Li Xianting', moderated by Anthony Yung at the symposium 'It Begins with A Story: Artists, Writers, and Periodicals in Asia', organised by Asia Art Archive at the University of Hong Kong, 11–13 January 2018, https://aaa.org.hk/en/programmes/programmes/it-begins-with-a-story-artists-writers-and-periodicals-in-asia/period/current-upcoming.

[5] Peggy Wang, 'Art Critics as Middle Men: Navigating State and Market in Contemporary Chinese Art, 1980s–1990s', *Art Journal*, vol.72, no.1, 2013, pp.6–19.

[6] These exhibitions included the touring 'China's New Art, Post 1989', curated by Li Xianting and Johnson Chang Tsongzung in 1993; 'The First 1990's Biennial Art Fair', with Lü Peng as chief organiser, in 1992; and the thematic exhibition 'Passage to the East', organised by Francesca Dal Lago at the 45th Venice Biennale in1993, among others.

[7] The fair had issued an open call to all Chinese artists, at home and abroad, and convened a group of leading art critics in China to form the jury committee and select award-winning works. It was announced that the Xishu Art Company, which funded the art fair, would purchase all the awarded works, so that the artists could be offered cash prizes. Each of the art critics received compensation for their work. For more details about the art fair, see Jane DeBevoise, *Between State and Market: Chinese Contemporary Art in the Post-Mao Era*, Leiden: Brill, 2014.

[8] Lanzhou Art Army's targeting of art publications can be explained by the coverage of the 1992 fair in *Jiangsu Pictorial*, one of the few art journals held in high esteem amongst the experimental art circle in China, which enthusiastically promoted the fair by publishing articles that emphasised the significance of the art market in several consecutive issues.

[9] In the statement, Zhuang wrote: 'Let our works be liberated from the hands of the "dead men" who have mastered academic theories, from the antique shops (museums) of old gentlemen and ladies and from various narrow circles.'

[10] In 'Central China Fire Stone Group In Action' [Zhong yuan huo shi zai xing dong], the artists

wrote: 'LIVE MATERIALS include movies, slogans, clothing, bicycles, language, signs, music, feelings, investigation, printing, mailing, etc. [...] LIVE SITES include significant places of Chinese revolution history [...], Cultural landscape [...], historical sites [...], social environment [...]. At the same time, public squares, factories, rural areas, construction sites, etc. are also suitable LIVE SITES for us. [...] From the study of materials to the transformation of art medium, the distinctive artistic language of the Fire Stone Group was invented: actions and events – we call it guerrilla war IN THE MOVE [...].' Reproduced in 'Bulletin of Art Experimental Village for Chinese Ordinary People (Special Issue)' [zhong guo ping min yi shu shi yan cun luo jian bao (zhuan hao)], a brochure self-published by Zhuang Hui.

[11] In 'Summary of Fire Stone Group's Activities 93 (92)', reproduced in *Bulletin of Art Experimental Village for Chinese Ordinary People (Special Issue)*, the group wrote: 'As a way of our activities, mailing not only shows great Liveness, but at the same time, as a carrier of intention, it abandons the usual state of existence of artwork (as exhibit, or as commodity). Upon its arrival at the recipient's side, it creates a continuous effect of an event [...]. In the poor land of China, when a group of gentlemen sit in their delicate tiny garden, contemplating the sophisticated works of Westerners, lamenting the primitive conditions of the Third World, and trying to catch up with the so-called "world trends", we are working with a new generation of Chinese youths in all fields today. In an extremely difficult environment, we spread our hot blood and work pragmatically. We try to make use of original materials, such as on-site investigations, movements, mailings, etc. to form our artistic language. We are continuously anticipating and practicing the prospects of Chinese art. The goal of the mailing activity in March 1993 was to search and connect with the ever-growing "national spirit" rooted in the scattered folk traditions. At the same time, we hope to make impacts upon the educated class who is controlling the newspapers, magazines, and news media. We, the Fire Stone Group, are the real gadflies at present times.'

[12] Interview with Song Yongping conducted by Asia Art Archive on 11 July 2009: http://www.china1980s.org/en/interview_detail.aspx?interview_id=93.

[13] For example, in reports published in *Shanxi Culture* magazine, several participants in *Village Project 1993* emphasised their perseverance in the poor living conditions of the countryside so as to express a critical attitude towards comfortable urban life and its consumerist culture. Yet questions of why the countryside was attractive in the first place, or how it inspired them – questions that were core concerns of the project – were not adequately addressed.

[14] See Andrew Solomon, 'Their Irony, Humor (and Art) Can Save China', *The New York Times Magazine*, 19 December 1993, available at http://andrewsolomon.com/articles/their-irony-humor-and-art-can-save-china/. The artist name Song Shuangsong in the text is a pseudonym of Song Yongping.

[15] See *Bulletin of Art Experimental Village for Chinese Ordinary People (Inaugurating Issue)* [zhong guo ping min shi yan cun luo jian bao (chuang kan hao)], and *China Battle Line 6* (Zhong guo zhan xian 6).

[16] Observing the impact that the centrality of Beijing had made on artists in the provinces, Beijing-based artist Song Dong organised 'Wildlife' in 1997, in which he invited 27 artists across China to create works in their own towns and then concentrated the documents of the works in a catalogue – a format that resonates with the proposals from the Central China Fire Stone Group. Interviewed by Wu Hung, Song Dong explained that '"Wildlife" rejected the notion of "centre" by initiating art projects in multiple places across the country.' See Wu Hung, *An Exhibition About Exhibitions: Displaying Experimental Art In the 1990s* [guan yu zhan lan de zhan lan: 90 nian dai de shi yan yi shu zhan shi], Beijing: China Nationality Photographic Art Publishing House, 2016.

On the Subject of *Object-act-ivities:* 1989 in Hong Kong

John Tain

It is no exaggeration to say that 1989 currently enjoys a privileged place in art history. Punctuated by the end of the Soviet Union and, with it, the Cold War; the fall of the Berlin Wall; and the invention of the World Wide Web, the year has been pegged by many as marking the beginning of the contemporary, of our present.[1] Afterall's *Exhibition Histories* project itself has underscored the year's special status through its designation of both the Bienal de la Habana and 'Magiciens de la Terre' as globally transformative events.[2] While both exhibitions did have an impact on developments in contemporary art in Asia, from the perspective of Asia, and China particularly, the year has a more ambiguous place: the crackdown in Tiananmen in June abruptly brought the democracy movement in China to a halt, resulting less in a start than an end.[3]

In Hong Kong, among the earliest of the responses to June Fourth was *Object-act-ivities* 東西遊戲, which took place over a week in mid-July.[4] Discussions for the interdisciplinary project began in March of that year between Choi Yan Chi 蔡仞姿, Leung Ping-kwan 梁秉鈞 (also known under his pen name, Yesi 也斯) and Yau Ching 游靜.[5] The exhibition at the Sheung Wan Civic Centre featured a number of surreal installations made by Choi out of deconstructed furniture and other ordinary objects, among them a rotating fan that inflated a large plastic bag attached to it and a heap of black feathers that moved around in a circle thanks to a motorised toy car.[6] Choi's pieces complemented poems by Yesi, several of which deal with everyday subjects such as 'Salad', 'Houseplant' or 'Furniture', which were recited and also printed in various formats, including on a wearable cardboard skirt. But the project took a different turn in the weeks after June. Photographs and photocopies on the walls prepared by Choi and Lau Ching-Ping 劉清平 displayed ambiguous figures. And Yesi's 'Still Life', clearly penned after Tiananmen, captures the anxious mood, plaintively asking 'Where have they all gone now?' as a refrain. Without ever naming them, it elegises those 'who dissuaded armed police with tears in eyes' and 'who fended off bullets meant for friends', who have been turned 'into the constant shadows by our sides', 'into the plants and furniture in our lives'.[7]

The palpable anxiety was perhaps most striking on the nights of 11, 14 and 15 July, when the landscape of installations became a set for ad hoc actions, as doc-

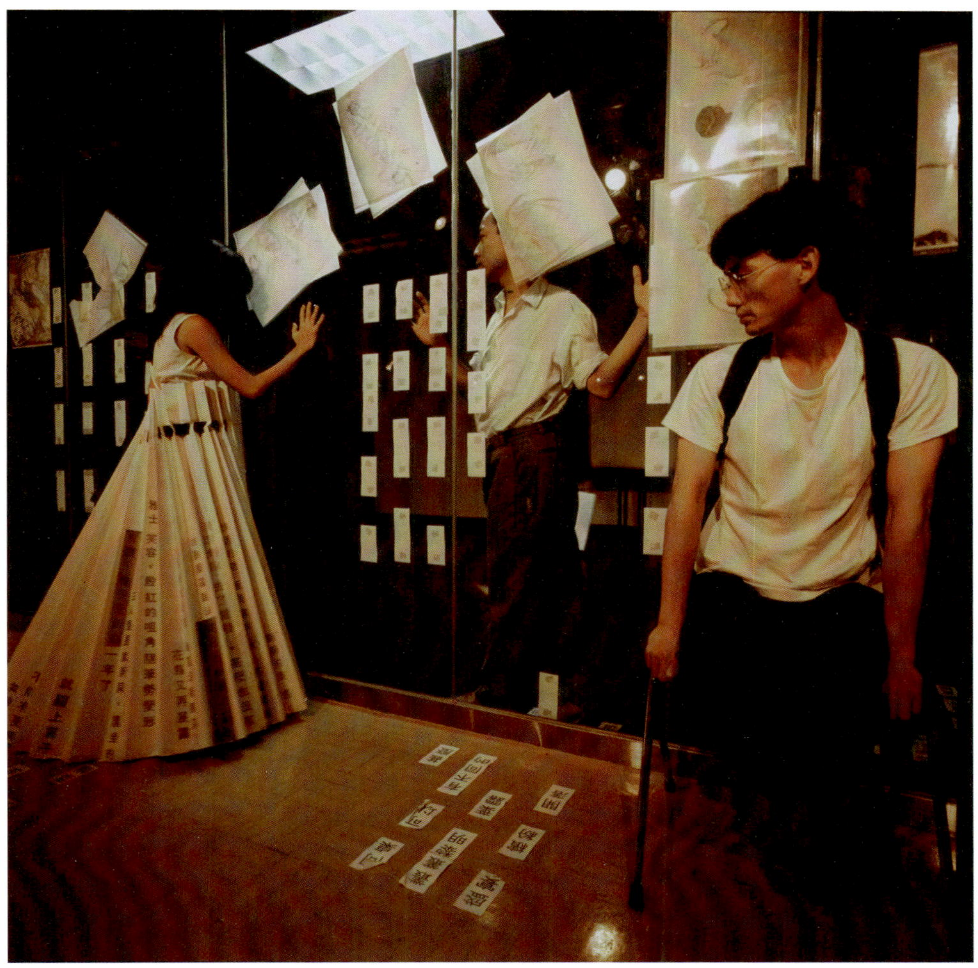

umented in a video of composite footage from the three days. One performer (Chen Ye 陳也) can be seen ceaselessly browsing a stack of newspapers planted before a static-filled TV, which eventually gets covered in red cloth.[8] Starker still is a figure wrapped head to toe in white cloth. The figure crawls into the space near the start of the event, only to be captured by another character, played by Yau Ching, who attaches it to a wall.[9] The figure breaks free and even manages to stand and walk through the space, but the interaction between the two haunts the whole of the event. That Yau Ching's character proceeds to tie up other parts of the space with straps, dividing some people and things, binding others, only underscores the fatalism of the bound figure.

Significantly, *Object-act-ivities*'s performances were not only impromptu, but also collective. Kung Chi Shing 龔志成, known for his work as part of 'the Box', filled the space with music and sound produced on a then-state-of-the-art Macintosh computer and an electric fiddle.[10] Mui Cheuk-yin 梅卓燕 and Chiang Afa 鄭志銳 interacted with each other and with Choi's installations,

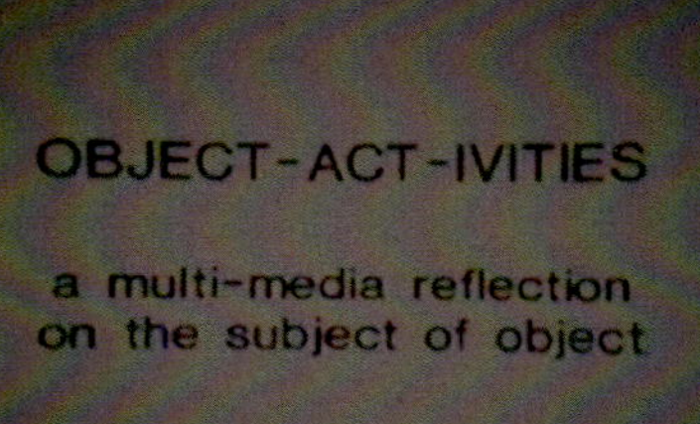
OBJECT-ACT-IVITIES

a multi-media reflection
on the subject of object
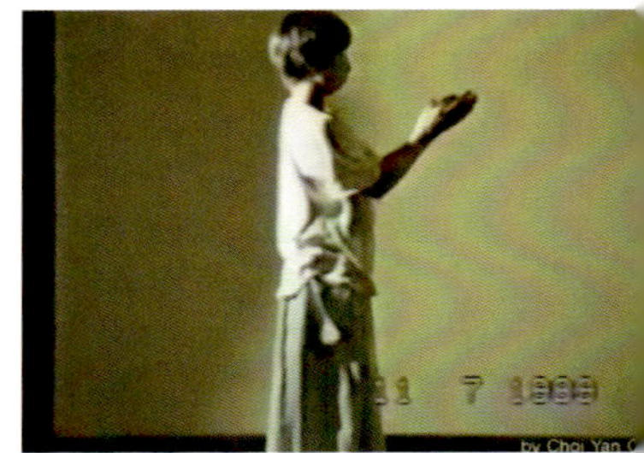
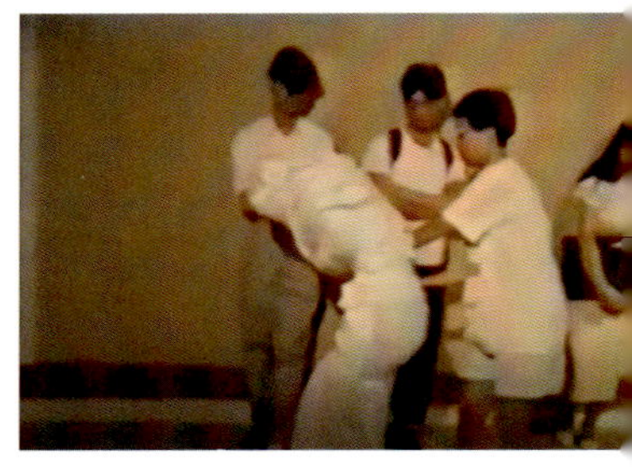
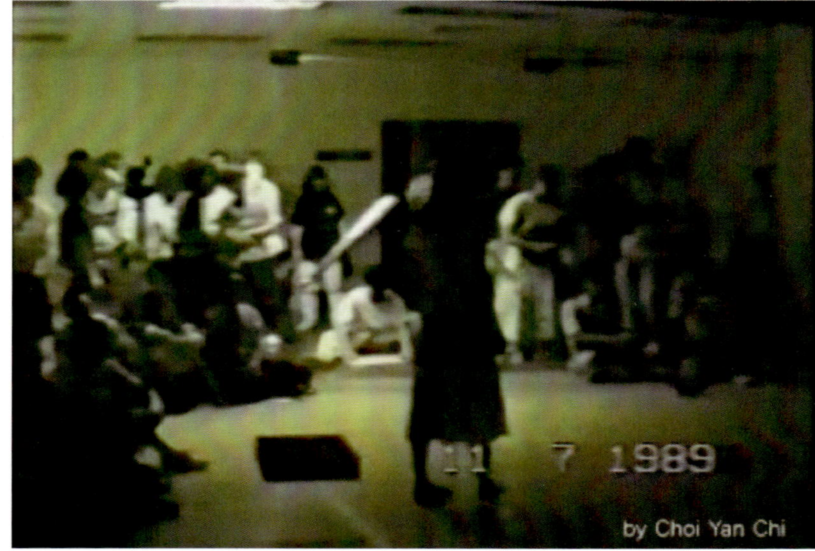
11 7 1989

by Choi Yan Chi
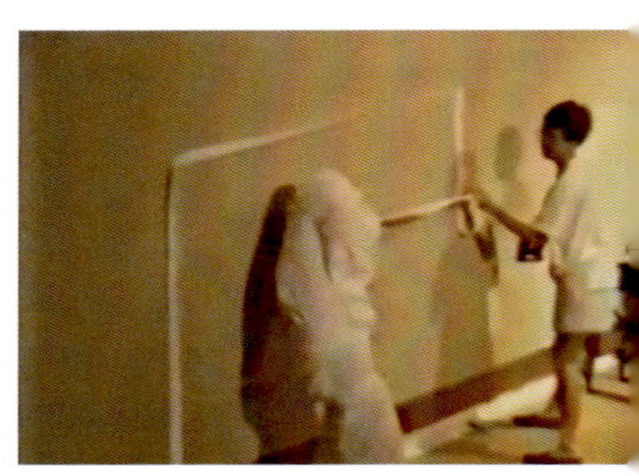
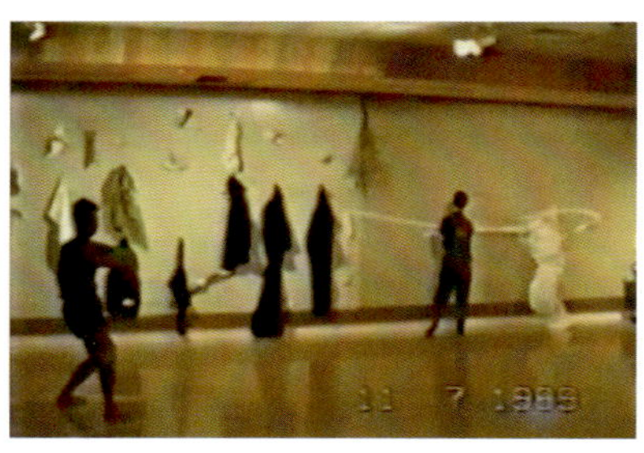
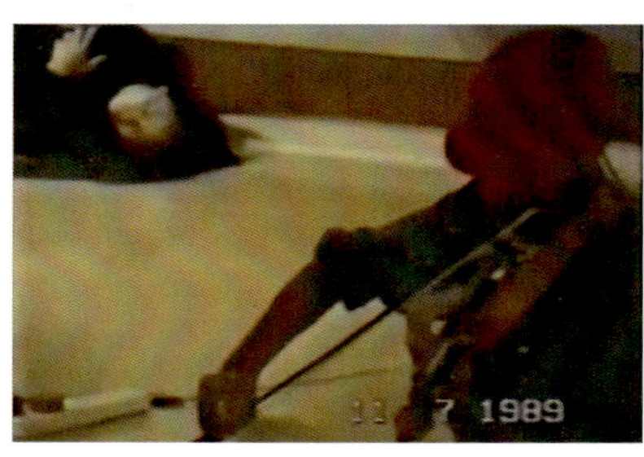
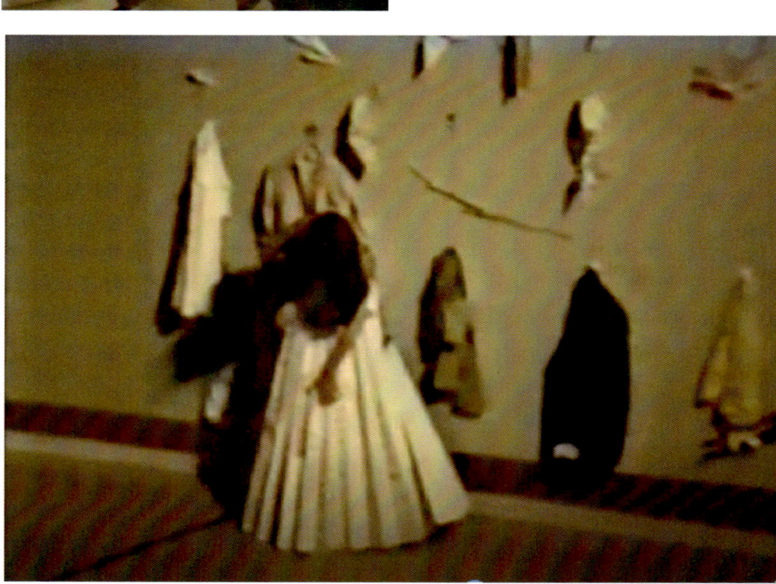
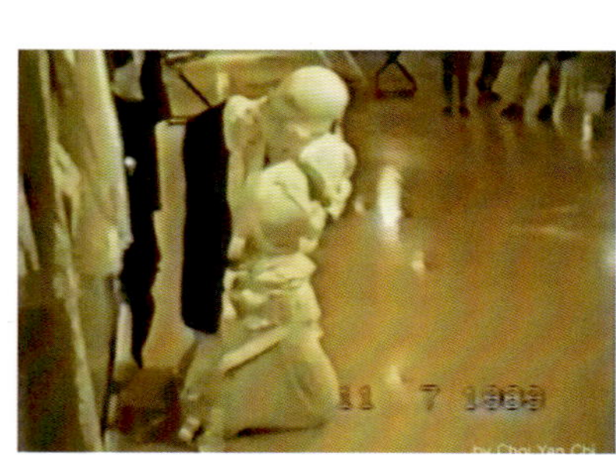

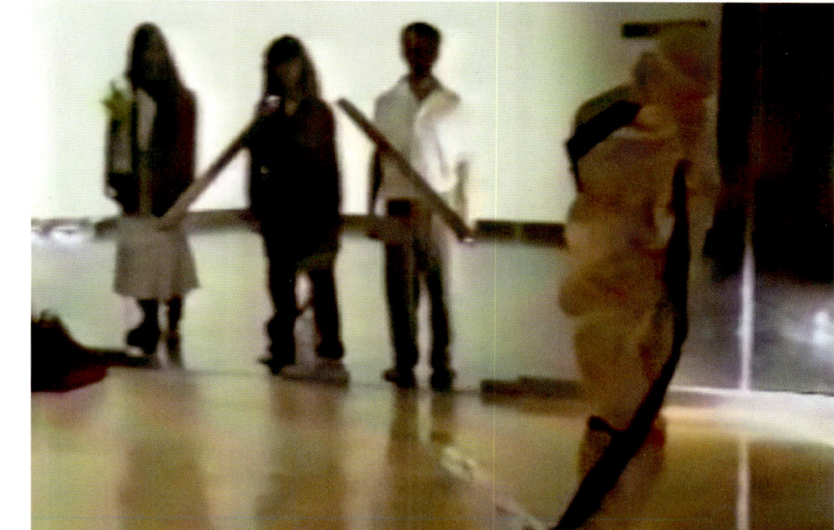

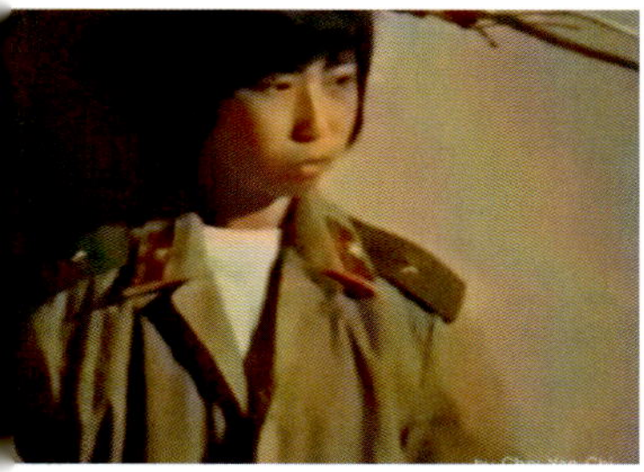

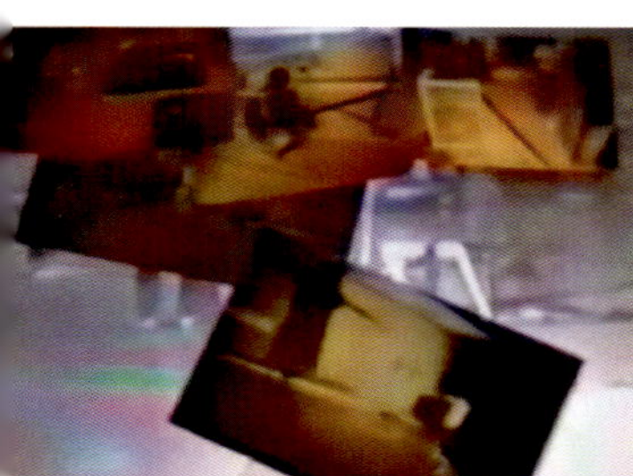

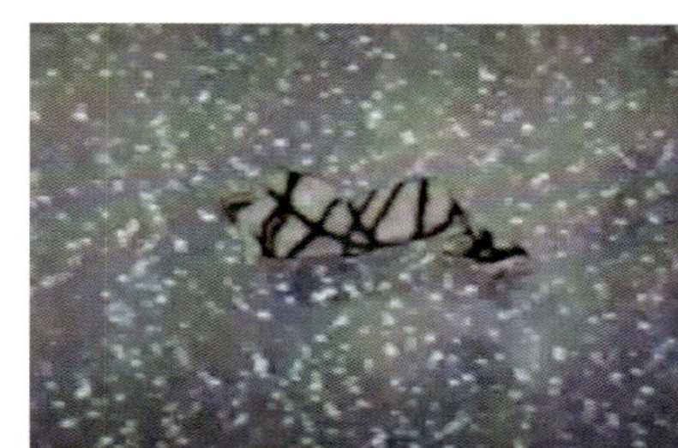

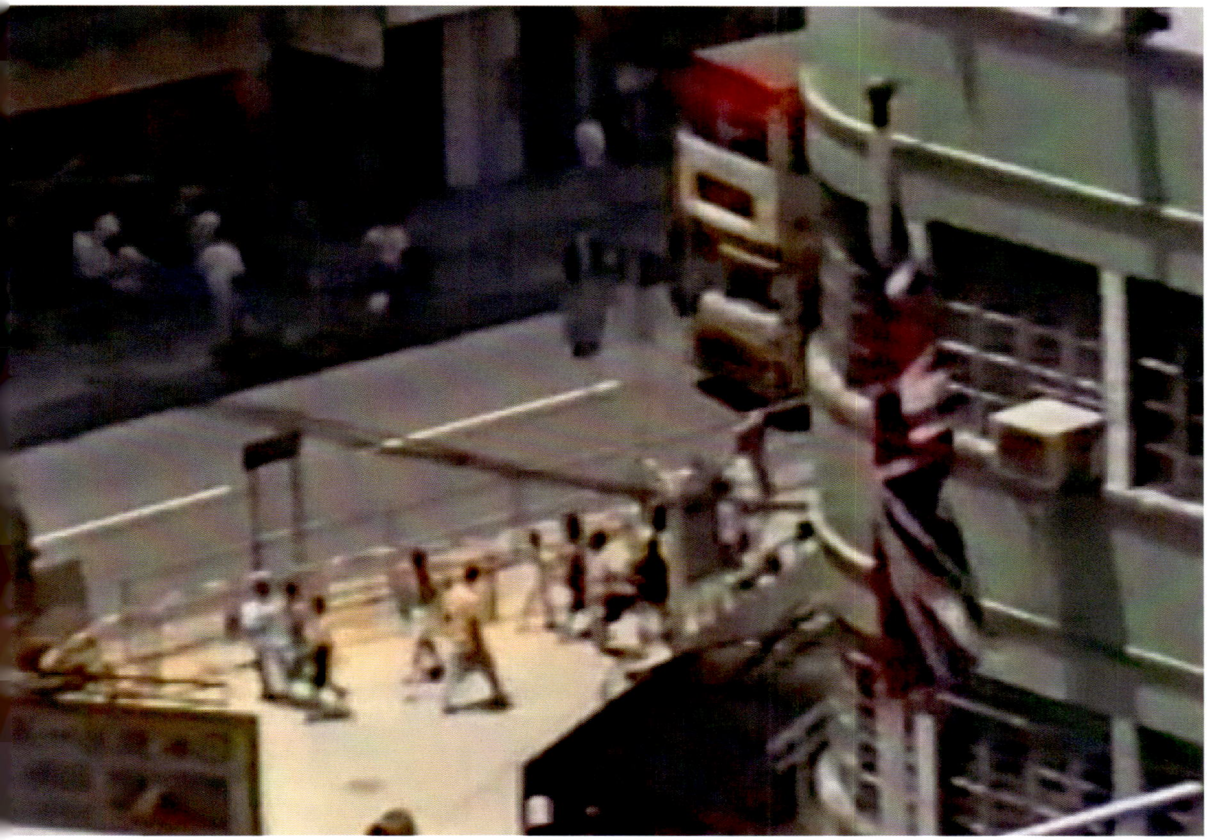

whilst dancer Ringo Chan Tak-cheong 陳德昌 danced in tai-chi-like movements in a circle. Emily Cheng Yee-chai 鄭綺釵, Winnie Fung Tak Kwan 馮德君 and Andy Ng Wai-shek 吳偉碩 (also known as 梵谷) engaged in physical theatre, as did Kwan Pun Leung 關本良, Chen Ye and Yau Ching. Not only did *Object-act-ivities* bring together visual art, poetry, music, dance and theater, but it also mixed performers with audience members, some of whom were inspired to join. Thus, Leung Man-tao 梁文道 and Lo Yin Shan 盧燕珊, who arrived as spectators, spontaneously contributed performances that engaged with the different objects in the space.

Even the video participates in this spontaneous game of things.[11] Toward the end, the documentary footage is suddenly replaced by a static-filled television, much like the one that was on display in the space, onto which is superimposed a black and white drawing of the bound figure, now recumbent, its white silhouette riven by black stripes.[12] The line between reality and media blurs further, with a hand appearing to interact with the performance, as when it covers the television with photographs of the performance. And while China is only obliquely evoked, most pointedly when one of the performers dons a Chinese PLA jacket hanging on the wardrobe wall, Great Britain is explicitly interpellated through a concluding shot of the area surrounding the Civic Centre, in which a British flag can be seen flying front and centre, the stripes of the Union Jack visually resonating with the black straps of the bound figure, which reappears before fading into snow.

The video's final images suggest that 1989 was less a rupture than part of a longer colonial history, one that also included 1984, when the Sino-British Joint Declaration confirmed China's reclaiming of sovereignty over Hong Kong, and 1997, when the actual handover took place. Indeed, that history remains a contemporary one, as Hong Kongers still live under the ever-evolving 'one country two systems'. But the actuality of *Object-act-ivities* also resided in the fact that its decentralised structure allowed its participants to act out, and in doing so to enact themselves as a collective subject. If it is a commonplace that the exhibition is where art encounters its public, in the case of *Object-act-ivities*, the public found its art, even made it there, and in doing so found itself.

靜物

本來有人坐在椅上
本來有人坐在桌旁
本來有人給一盆花澆水
本來有人從書本中抬起頭來

現在他們到哪兒去了？

那個隨著音樂起舞的人
那個喜歡吃麵條的人
那個愛喝白開水的人
那個戴頂帽子擋陽光的人

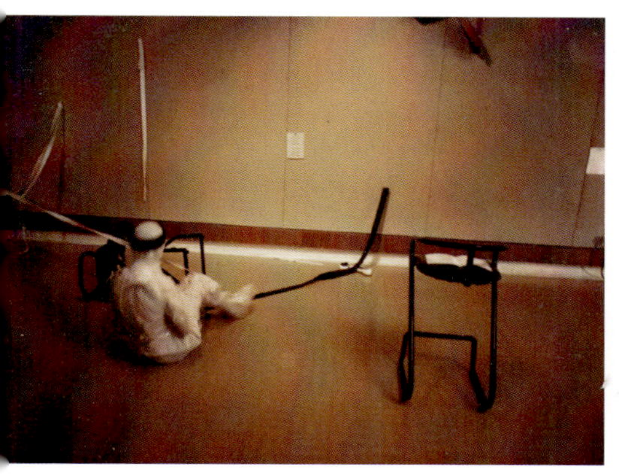

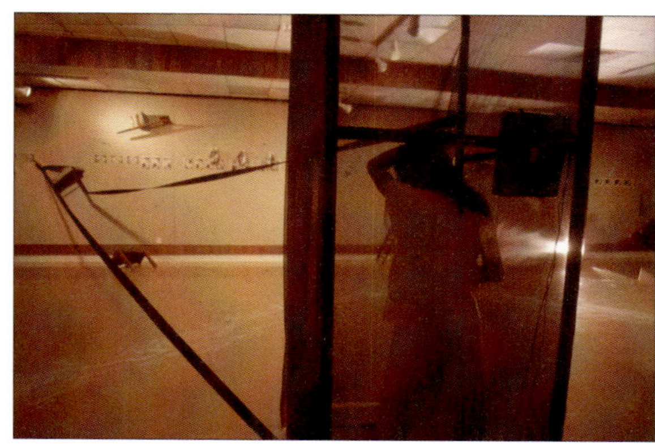

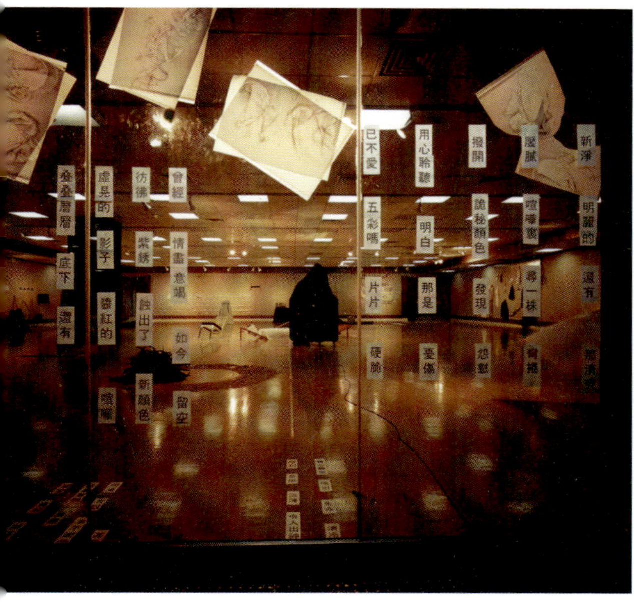

新淨
明麗的
還有
濃膩
喧嘩襄
撥開
詭秘顏色
發現
怨懟
用心聆聽
明白
那是
憂傷
已不愛
五彩嗎
片片
硬脆
曾經
情盡意竭
如今
留空
彷彿
紫綉
釀出了
新顏色
虛晃的
影子
蕃紅的
喧嘩
疊疊層層
底下
還有
將一株
荷捲

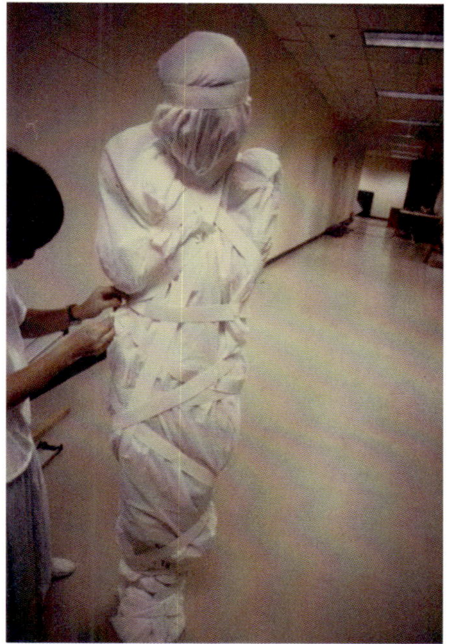

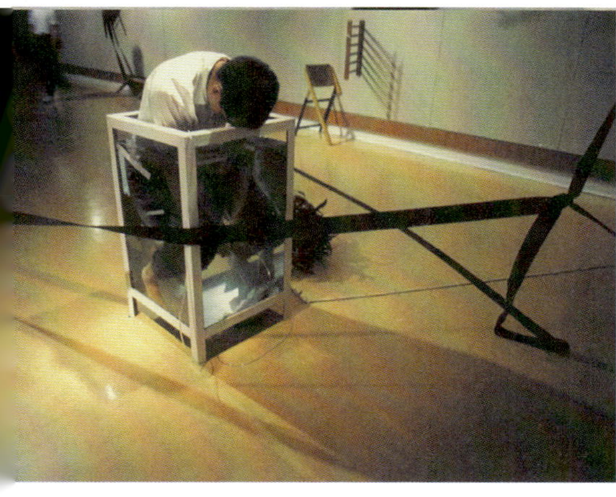

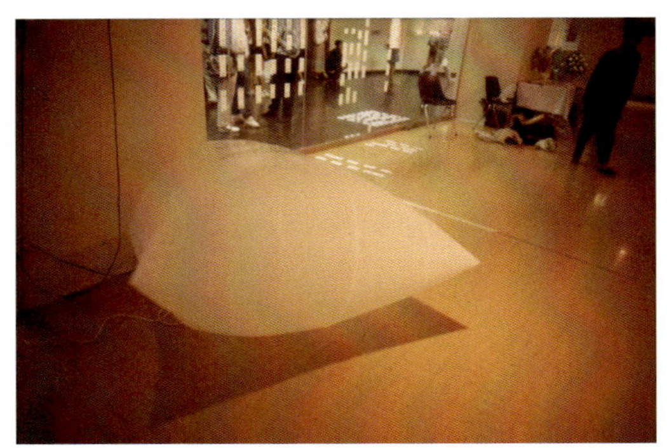

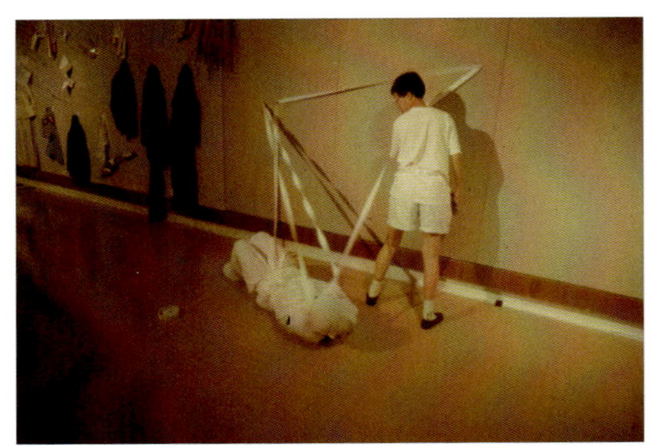

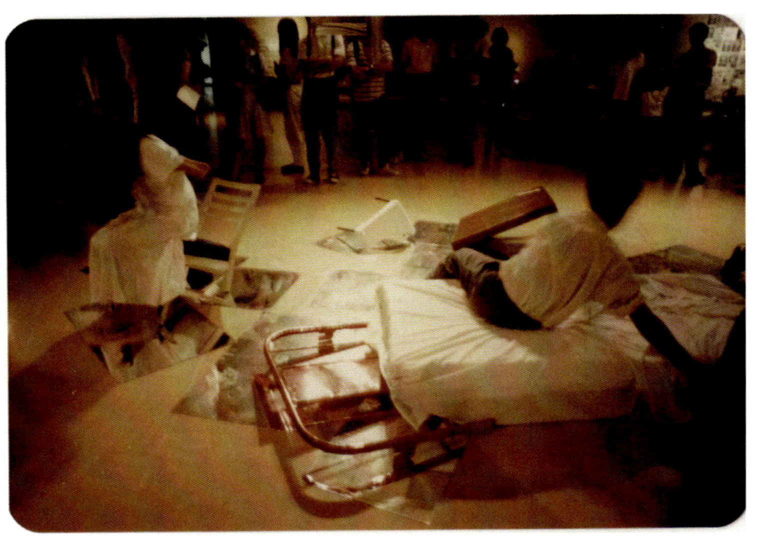

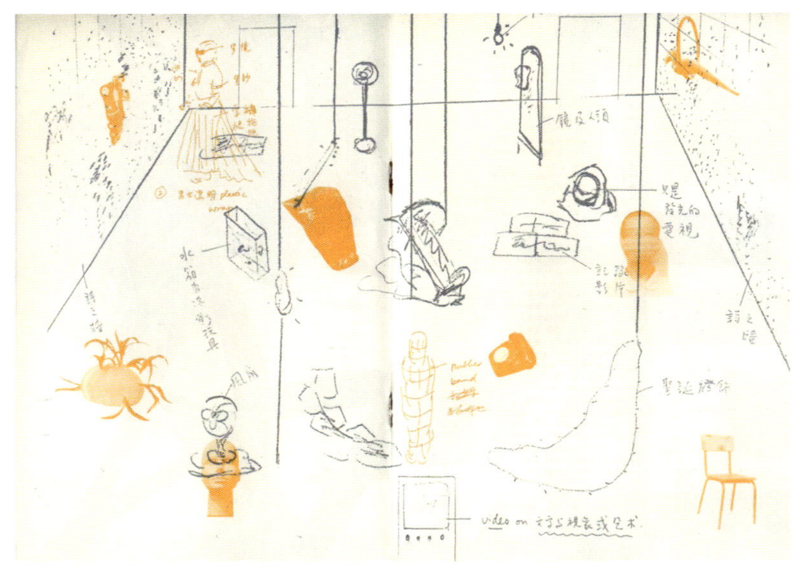

現在他們到哪兒去了？

是一個想與你好好說話的人
是一個與你緊緊挽著手的人
是一個想與你一起高聲歌唱
想與你一起仰望天空的人

現在他們到哪兒去了？

變成一個分水給陌生人喝的人
變成一個為信仰而停止進食的人
變成一個含著眼淚勸告武擎的人
變成一個為朋友擋去子彈的人

現在他們到哪兒去了？

輾成了碎片
撞成了彈孔
吹成了風砂
散成了灰塵

現在他們到哪兒去了？

變成了你我身畔永遠的影子
變成了我們每日的陽光和空氣
變成了生活裡的盆花和桌椅
變成了我們總在讀著的那本書

Still Life

At the beginning, there was someone sitting on the chair
At the beginning, there was someone sitting on the table
At the beginning, there was someone watering a plant
At the beginning, there was someone looking up from the books

Where have they all gone now?

The one who danced to the music
The one who liked eating noodles
The one who liked drinking plain water
The one who wore a hat to keep off the sun

Where have they all gone now?

Was someone who wanted to have a good talk with you
Was someone who wanted to hold your hand tight
Was someone who wanted to sing loud with you
to look at the sky together with you

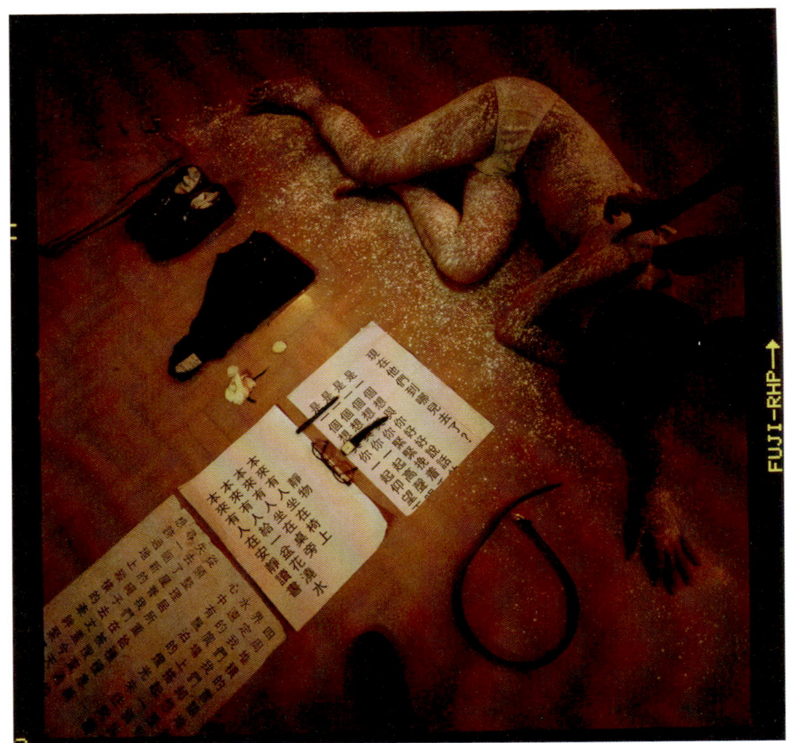

Where have they all gone now?

Turned into one who shared a drink of water with total strangers
Turned into one who went on hunger strike for what he believes in
Turned into one who dissuaded armed police with tears in eyes
Turned into one who fended off bullets meant for friends

Where have they all gone now?

Squashed to pieces
Riddled with bullets
Blown into sand
Scattered as dust

Where have they all gone now?

Turned into the constant shadows by our sides
Turned into the sun and air of our days
Turned into the plants and furniture in our lives
Turned into the book we read over and over again

– Leung Ping-kwan, 1989

Notes

¹ Publications that feature 1989 as a starting point include Alexander Dumbadze and Suzanne Hudson (ed.), *Contemporary Art: 1989 to the Present*, Oxford: Wiley-Blackwell, 2012; Hans Belting, Andreas Buddensieg and Peter Weibel (ed.), *The Global Contemporary and the Rise of New Art Worlds*, Cambridge, MA: MIT Press, 2013; and Kelly Grovier, *Art Since 1989*, London: Thames & Hudson, 2015.

² See Rachel Weiss et al., *Making Art Global (Part 1): The Third Havana Biennial 1989*, London: Afterall Books, 2011, and Lucy Steeds et al., *Making Art Global (Part 2): 'Magiciens de la Terre' 1989*, London: Afterall Books, 2013.

³ A consideration of the year's place in China can be found in Alexandra Munroe, Phil Tinari and Hou Hanru (ed.), *Art and China after 1989: Theater of the World*, New York: Guggenheim Museum, 2017.

⁴ A number of these events are discussed in Lo Yin Shan, '不能讓記憶沉睡:香港文化界八九六四記憶檔案' (Don't Let Memory Sleep: Hong Kong Cultural World's Memories of June Fourth) 陽光時務週刊 *iSun Affairs*, 30 May 2013, pp. 36–47, and '革命時刻, 藝術已失效?香港藝術家對六四的12種記憶' (At the moment of Revolution, did art give up? Twelve memories of Hong Kong Artists about 4 June) *The Initium* [online magazine], 30 May 2016, https://theinitium.com/article/20160530-culture-allremembering-64tiananmen/. A special word of thanks to Lo, who was also an original participant in *Object-act-ivities*, for answering questions and sharing photos, some of which are on view in the archive section she prepared for the exhibition 'New Horizons: Ways of Seeing Hong Kong Art in the 80s and 90s', curated by Janet Fong for the Hong Kong Museum of Art (2021). Since 1989, independently organised commemorative events were organized every 4 June in Hong Kong, until the police forbade gatherings in 2020 and 2021, citing the Covid-19 pandemic.

⁵ Information on *Object-act-ivities* can be found in Linda C. H. Lai (ed.), *[Re-]Fabrication: Choi Yan-chi's 30 Years, Paths of Inter-disciplinarity in Art*, Hong Kong: Para Site, 2006, especially pp.200–21, available at https://www.para-site.art/publications/refabrication-choi-yan-chis-30-years-paths-of-inter-disciplinarity-in-art/. The text also draws on the accounts of Choi Yan Chi, interviewed by the author, April 2021, and Ellen Pau 鮑靄倫, Yau Ching and Lau Ching-Ping, in correspondence with the author, May 2021.

⁶ Choi is credited with realising the first exhibition of installation art at the Hong Kong Art Centre in 1985. She also collaborated on a number of experimental theatre works, including 'Paintings by Choi Yan Chi and Works of Art in Dialogue with Poetry and Dance' (1986), with Yesi and choreographer Sunny Pang, and *As Slow as Possible* (1988), featuring Pang and others. See *[Re-]Fabrication*, *op. cit.*, pp.29–30, and Books Are Breathing: Choi Yan Chi Installation Series 1989–98, Hong Kong: Hong Kong Arts Development Council, 1999.

⁷ 'Still Life' is reproduced in Chinese and English in *[Re]Fabrication*, *op. cit.*, pp.206–07. Yesi was well-known for his interest in how ordinary objects related to identity. See C. T. Au, *The Hong Kong Modernism of Leung Ping-kwan*, Lanham: Lexington Books, 2020.

⁸ The record for the video, deposited at Asia Art Archive as part of the Out of Context collection, can be found at https://aaa.org.hk/en/collections/search/archive/out-of-context-research-project-personal-files-11433/object/event-documentation-of-object-act-ivities. Both Wong Chi Fai 黃志輝 and Ellen Pau worked on video for *Object-act-ities*, and Pau recalls there being more than one edit (conversation with the author, 25 May 2021).

⁹ On the first night of the performance, the mummy character was performed by Yau Ching, but then subsequently taken up by Kwan Pun Leung. Yau Ching then improvised the bondage.

¹⁰ The list of participants here is based on information found in *Books are Breathing*, *op. cit.*, n.p., supplemented by information in *[Re]Fabrication* and also Lo, 'At the moment of Revolution', *op. cit.*

¹¹ The subtitle for the video describes *Object-act-ivities* as a 'multimedia reflection on the subject of [the] object'. The Chinese title 東西遊戲 can be translated as 'game of things' or 'game of east and west'.

¹² As Pau noted, the emphasis on the thing-ness of the television screen itself can also be found in *Hong Kong: Only Something That Is About to Disappear Becomes an Image*, an anthology video prepared for the grassroots satellite network Deep Dish TV's series *…Will Be Televised: Video Documents from Asia, 1990*. Conversation with the author, 25 May 2021.

Who Cares a Lot? ruangrupa as Curatorship

David Teh

In 2011 Southeast Asia hosted two significant media art shows, both daring to juxtapose recent work from the region with seminal collections from the First World. In 'Video, an Art, a History 1965–2010', the Singapore Art Museum (SAM) tentatively aired its nascent Southeast Asian collection alongside a roving blockbuster from the Centre Pompidou in Paris. At the National Gallery of Indonesia (Galnas), the Jakarta artists' collective ruangrupa held the fifth instalment of their video art biennial, OK Video, featuring a curated selection from the catalogue of Electronic Arts Intermix in New York.[1] Both exhibitions were rare treats, featuring contemporary video works from Indonesia, Thailand and Vietnam, side by side with works by Western artists including Bill Viola, Dan Graham, VALIE EXPORT and Vito Acconci – the first time this canon had alighted on the region en masse. In both exhibitions worlds came together, but they were worlds apart.

I found myself wondering what it would be like if these two worlds were swapped, if SAM were to take over the ageing halls of Galnas, and ruangrupa the colonial nooks and crannies of SAM. For a start, we would see OK Video with fewer mosquitoes, and comfortable seats; with an injection of Singaporean efficiency, Galnas would get a much needed overhaul. SAM would meanwhile be unrecognisable, revived by a shot of the spontaneity and personality it lacks. Alas, it was wishful thinking. One can only dream of a day when the region's resources are effectively shared.

It could be objected that I am not comparing apples with apples. SAM is a well-funded public museum, with its own collection, but, like all of Singapore's institutions, it suffers from the overweening attentions of its bureaucratic parents. Galnas, meanwhile, is a criminally neglected child – a 'national' space for hire – and ruangrupa, while by now a de facto institution, is an autonomous artists' collective, with no collection and largely free from bureaucracy. Yet the comparison was telling: SAM baulked at the task of integrating their works (either spatially or intellectually) with the visiting ones, leaving Southeast Asia a peripheral plug-in for the touring Euro-American canon. At OK Video, the foreign material was not the main event; carefully

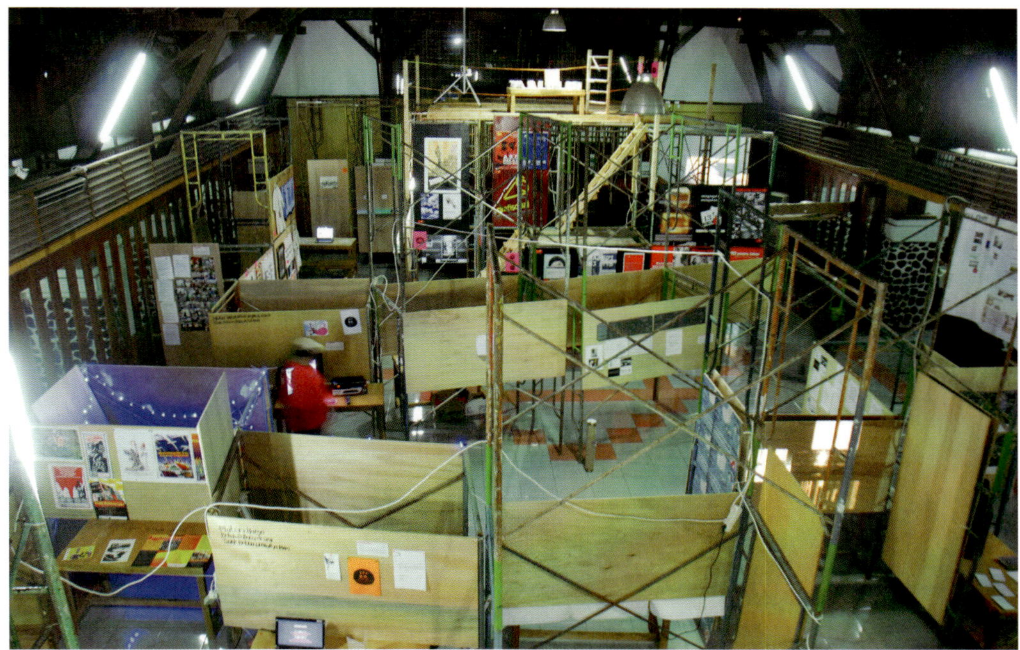

selected to feed and challenge Indonesia's thriving video communities, it was circumscribed architecturally in its own pavilion, but nested within a locally curated smorgasbord. The contrast was a stark demonstration of the raw value of curatorial vision, a value not proportional to budgets.

Context certainly helps. In Singapore's slick matrix of consumption, small curatorial fumbles will stick out like sore thumbs, while amidst the humming disorder of Jakarta – a city of some ten million souls, with a metropolitan population three times that – a little direction goes a long way. Yet the integration of local and international work was an important achievement, not least because the former draws upon, and critiques, the latter, but also because they are connected, whether consciously or unconsciously, through the history of the video medium itself, with shared formal parameters and shared referents in the world beyond the gallery. When it comes to exhibiting media art, it bears remembering that the museum itself is a medium, one to which a lot of media art is not native. The task of domesticating it is therefore fraught, especially in locations where institutions and curatorial practice are relatively young. So how is it that Jakarta, a chaotic mega-city with little infrastructure for contemporary art, has given rise to this sort of curatorial assuredness?

Site and Sound: Jakarta Calling (or, Karaoke as Method)

By far the most developed of Indonesia's 922 inhabited islands, Java is about half the size of the UK, with roughly twice the population. It dominates the national economy, and in creative industries increasingly casts a shadow over its richer neighbours. Of its three artistic hubs, Bandung and Yogyakarta (Jogja) are the established centres of learning and production. Jakarta has long been the business hub, with the most commercial galleries. Given its strong non-commercial agenda, ruangrupa might seem out of place in Jakarta – an hour's flight to the south-east, Jogja's cheap rents and slower pace make it an obvious base for collectives. But ruangrupa is bound to Jakarta in every sense: physically, spiritually and conceptually, it is through and through a creature of the capital. This speaks volumes about the group's significance and the unique path it has taken in Indonesia's current contemporary art boom.

The collective was founded in 2000 by a group of young artists in a city then devoid of platforms for contemporary practice and collaboration. Their workshops and exhibitions fast became magnets for artists, designers and re-searchers, eliciting broad-based community participation, distinguished by the group's knack for critical exploration of their urban surroundings. This urbanism has been their most consistent refrain. Though they have consis-tently worked with artists from elsewhere, ruangrupa has made a profound commitment to Jakarta as both site and subject, to its people as both audience and authors. Since day one the group has taken the city itself – a noisy engine room of commerce and administration, not traditionally seen as a font of culture – as the primary protagonist of an epic adventure in collective story-telling. Heuristic as their approach may be, it is not without a certain realism, focussed by an insistence upon the vitality of Jakarta's contemporary culture, as rooted not in some timeless past, but in a dense demographic and cultural stew of diverse and inextricable ingredients.

A pre-modern cosmopolitanism was forged here during the Srivijaya mari-time empire that dominated the Malay world until the thirteenth century. Sunda Kelapa, as Jakarta was then known, had already long been a melting pot of regional and diasporic trading communities when the Dutch arrived in 1619. Renamed Batavia, the city was colonised and modernised, then na-tionalised as Jakarta. It is now being globalised, but this doesn't mean homo-genisation – rapid economic growth has come with an equally rapid dilation of the public sphere, and for a porous organisation, the city's syncretic soil is fertile indeed. Such an environment puts a premium on openness, a trait ruangrupa exhibits inside and out. While the founders may worry that a new crop of decision-makers has been slow to emerge, a strong DIY ethos and a lack of hierarchy have been key to the group's sustainability. Their suburban headquarters in the south of the city boast a well-used exhibition space, but it's more like a clubhouse: always open, always peopled – a studio, a library, a research lab and a party venue, all in one. It would be lazy to call their collaborative house style 'inclusive'. Ruangrupa is shareware, their partnering indiscriminate – witness the soup of logos on their sponsor rolls. They tap ev-ery level of the institutional food chain, with a reach only possible in the last decade or so: from foreign NGOs and municipal and national governments, down to the humblest grassroots initiatives – a big tobacco company here, a national media network there, a small business around the corner.

According to Bandung-based curator Agung Hujatnikajennong, Indonesian contemporary art has seen two distinct phases. The first reflected civil so-ciety's atrophy under the authoritarian New Order (1965–98) of the coun-

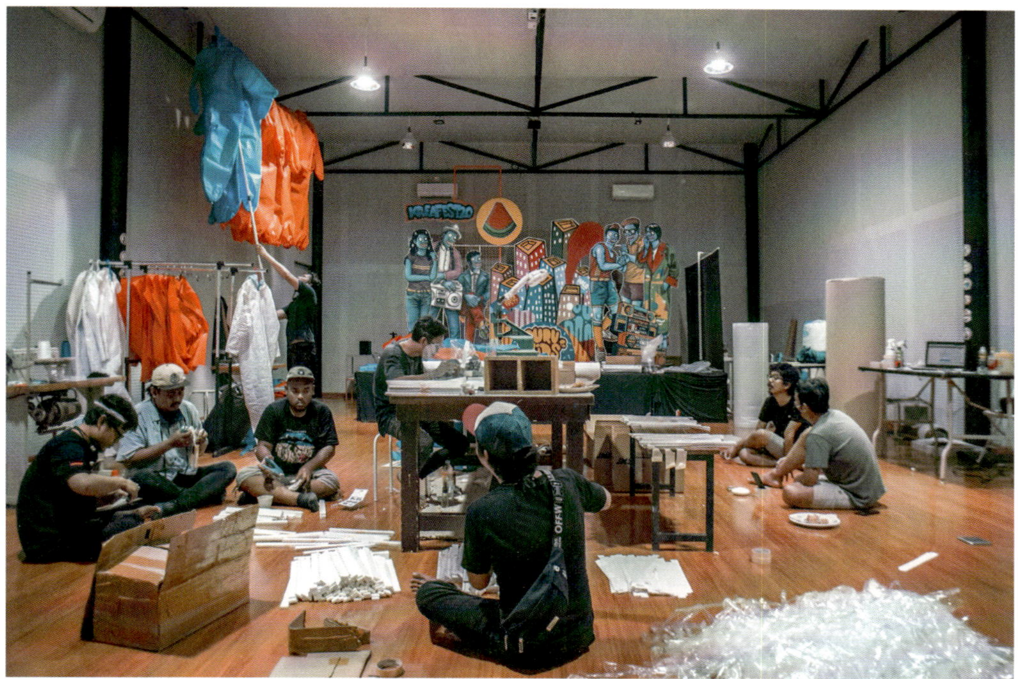

try's second president, Soeharto. The second, which is ongoing, reflects its flourishing and democratisation since the wave of popular disgust (*reformasi*) that finally unseated that regime amidst regional financial crisis in 1998.[2] In the earlier period, the social conscience that had long been a cornerstone of national aesthetics – modern art's *sine qua non* since the independence struggle against the Dutch – found expression in a figurative modernism still loosely social realist in its scope. Its story remained that of nationhood, of the people (as, or against, nation), seasoned here and there with the 'local' or the 'traditional'. Artists emerging since *reformasi*, however, are more playful and individualistic, enjoying the latitude of a liberalised public sphere, and the fruits of the country's steady rise in the global neoliberal pecking order. But while exemplary of this new generation, ruangrupa strives to retain something of the representational logic of the old.

The result is a remarkably stable compound of activism and populism. The group's early embrace of lo-fi copy cultures and digital and open publishing models dovetailed with a neo-Situationism that was de rigueur at the couch-surfing stratum of global art in the early 2000s. Since 2000, ruangrupa has published *Karbon*, a journal devoted to urban visual culture, which promotes criticism but also favours plain language. The biennial Jakarta 32°C, which they have organised since 2004, brings students' work into the museum under the group's curatorial umbrella, democratising the first steps to exhibition-making. Jakarta-based festivals like OK Video, meanwhile, become launch pads for nationwide tours and workshops, as did their tenth anniversary festivities in 2010, held under the project banner 'Decompression #10'.

In April 2020, the collective space at Gudskul, an alternative school initiated by ruangrupa and the collectives Grafis Huru Hara and Serrum, was turned into a mini-factory to produce face masks and hazmat suits for distribution to medical workers during the Covid-19 crisis. Courtesy the artists

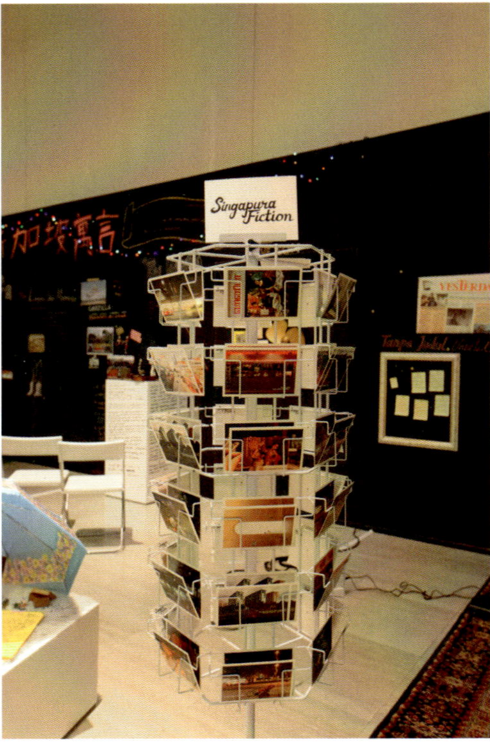

Singapore Fiction, 2011, installation with radio, documentation material, prints and video. Installation view, Singapore Biennale, 2011. Photography: Han. Courtesy the artists and Singapore Art Museum

And while in an earlier phase workshops were more hands-on and skills-based, as contemporary art production has flourished ruangrupa's educational focus has sharpened around the critical faculties of writing and curatorship. The collective's prodigious capacity for outreach makes for an unruly aesthetic, encompassing everything from punk and street cultures, through documentary and ethnographic research, to conceptual and process-oriented experiments. Binding it all together is a firm conviction that the participants are agents in a living social history, one that is fundamentally urban and modern.

To profile ruangrupa is to describe an event: time-based, immediate and loosely structured; with a sense of purpose, yet more celebratory than agonistic. If one had to choose a single medium to characterise it, that medium would be karaoke. Indonesians love to sing, and a rich musical patchwork is an ever-present accompaniment to daily life. The refrains of old folk songs segue into distinctive modern genres like the racy *dangdut*, a hybrid of Malay, Indo-Arabic and 1970s rock sounds. A vivid medley of subcultures jostles with local and global pop, especially in the streets, where chronic traffic jams create a captive audience for wandering *ngamen* (buskers). It is no accident that live music and a certain chaotic, mob-karaoke ritual have become trademarks of the ruangrupa experience. Indeed, this carnivalesque sonic profile betrays something of the group's curatorial programme – it is prophetic in the sense Jacques Attali reserved for *composition*, presaging a new regime of cultural production that is live, open-source and, above all, poly-vocal.[3]

In his compelling account of Javanese modernity, anthropologist John Pemberton describes an extraordinary process whereby the island's eighteenth-century aristocracy, whose role was rapidly becoming ceremonial, re-encoded the technologies and trappings of Dutch colonial might.[4] The once terrifying sound of cannon fire, for instance, came to announce official diplomatic correspondence, or to mark a royal birthday or wedding; a hybrid pageantry was improvised, retrofitted and elaborately codified. Pyrotechnics made for a spectacle of new order, distracting attention from the drastic defeat of the old. Pemberton also recalls how Soeharto, going through the motions of electoral democracy during the Cold War, took these vestiges of contest and refurbished them once again, as tradition, in the name of another 'new order'. Ruangrupa, we might say, represents the opposite aural evolution. It is a stethoscope held to the rattling yet still growing chest of the metropolis, amplifying the hum of a popular sovereignty – long suppressed by colonialism and authoritarianism – over the ceaseless urban din.

Ruangrupa as Curatorship?

In a recent essay on ruangrupa, art historian Thomas Berghuis takes up some topical vocabularies for lassoing contemporary art's vast diversity of practices and newly integrated territories.[5] With nods to Nicolas Bourriaud's relational aesthetics and Terry Smith's reckoning with contemporaneity, he casts the group in the uncertain light of 'the global', as a laboratory for an *art to come*. In the clamour of the Jakarta art world, many would say a breath of speculative air is just what the doctor ordered. But what is missing from this picture is a sense of the intense struggle – in this region, quite peculiar to Indonesia – over creative and intellectual labour. In this struggle the curatorial faculty is crucial, not only because curators are pivotal in capturing talent, but also because curatorial functions have long preoccupied many of the most talented. Some of ruangrupa's core members exemplify this bind, but they stand out for having maintained both their independence from the market and their standing with respect to the curatorial cartel that serves it. They are not the only collective to have thrived since *reformasi* – there are dozens – but their endurance and success, at home and abroad, prompts the question: has it perhaps been by appropriating the function of curatorship that this independence has been secured?

As a vocation, curatorship in Southeast Asia is tenuous. But in Indonesia, where a bullish market has the profession in its clutches, it is the craft that is tenuous, not the worker. One much sought-after Jogja painter makes enough from the sale of a single picture to buy a large house. Curators have not missed out on the bonanza. This newly struck professional mould, still setting, is guarded by a small band of entrenched tastemakers. In a country where an ample meal can be had street-side for a dollar, they are well rewarded – an anomaly in the region – especially a senior cohort whose number may be counted on one hand. But most of the throughput is handled by a younger generation who came of age during *reformasi*.

At worst, their job entails the perfunctory anointment of new product for the market. For some, the whole process may be done on a smartphone: syncing

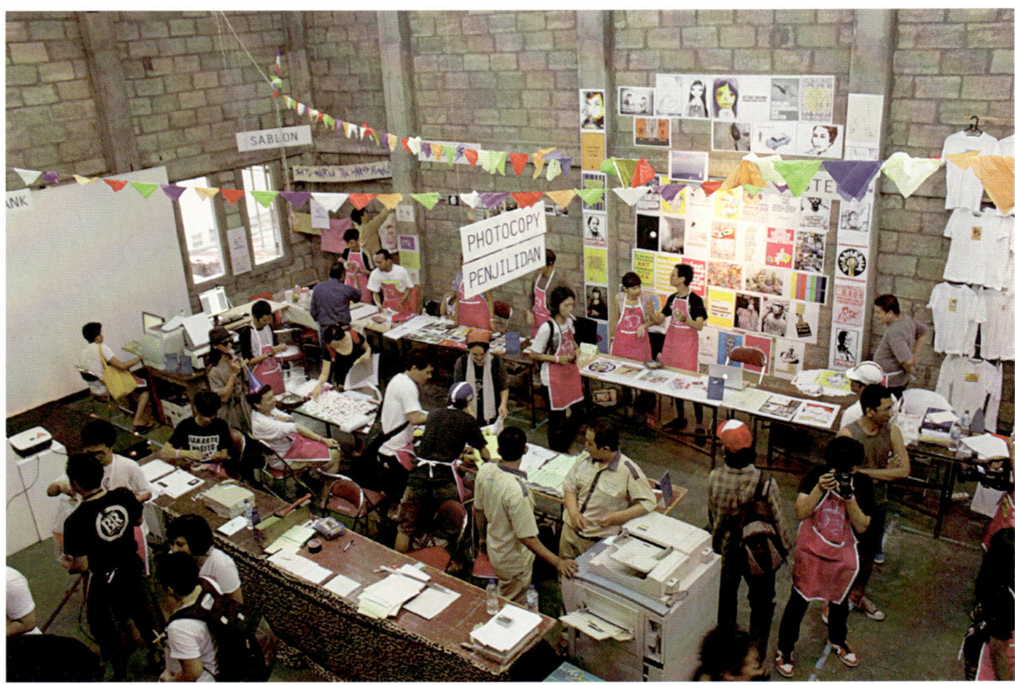

calendars, browsing and selecting images, cutting and pasting together a recycled curatorial 'essay', before parachuting into town for the opening reception. It's a well-oiled assembly line, by far the region's most efficient. The conscientious few will manage some conversation with the artist, maybe even write something new, but a backlog of shows leaves little time for research; the typical project-window lasts weeks, not months. It's a pity, for most were trained as artists and have a good grasp on matters of process; they speak persuasively of aesthetic currents, and artists' places within them. But for all their mobility, their horizons as curators are limited by a parochial market, and a lack of credible institutional systems of validation and power.

If Asian modern art history has seldom ventured beyond national framings, this is not without reason. Rarely the product of organic urban fermentation, modern art has more often been a state-sanctioned project. But the unravelling of the Cold War has set the stage for a new mode of circulation and a new currency for the visual – a currency now called the contemporary. Gaining new patrons and markets, artists have filtered out certain modernist strains, and spun what's left in the direction of international trends. But curatorship, by contrast – at least, curatorship as we *now* know it, unhinged from the collection that once grounded the role – has more or less had to invent itself from scratch. In the first proper regional study on the subject, Patrick Flores confirms that the role has always been the province of discursively inclined artists, and not defined around collections. He identifies pioneers such as Apinan Poshyananda (a Thai) and Jim Supangkat (an Indonesian), who plugged Southeast Asian art into international circuits in the 1990s, as the key midwives of this contemporary. Not incidentally, both were trained as artists; no less significantly, neither has ever taught curating, nor trained worthy successors. Entangled by bureaucratic and market strictures respectively, they seem to have accrued powers too precious to be handed down. Today's curators have inherited an invisible suit from these pathfinders, with little sense of professional continuity. And the corollary of this failure of professional memory is a failure to historicise exhibition-making *per se*. Ruangrupa and its collaborators stand out here for having kept alive a parallel world for historically informed – if not always art historically informed – ways of working.

Getting Modernity

I recently asked an Indonesian curator – trained and still practicing as an artist – what he thought of the curatorial studies programmes sprouting up around the world. If he were younger, where would he go to study this craft? His answer was revealing: 'The Netherlands. And Japan.' For an emerging leader from the global periphery, the prospect of acquiring curatorial expertise in emerging territories remains dim. And it is more than ironic that he should nominate both of his country's former colonial masters, both wealthy nations with developed infrastructures for art, both steady fonts of the aid that has helped shape professional horizons in Indonesia. The pairing also serves to dramatise a certain historical polarity, perhaps collapsing now, between two very different demographic orders, as the vanguard cosmopolitanism of the Netherlands shrinks into something more akin to Japan's insular nationalism. But my friend was answering, I suspected, with an eye on the past, not the future, which his explanation confirmed: 'Because these two places *really got modernity*.' The emphasis is his, and richly ambivalent – they 'got it' in the sense of understanding it, but perhaps also in the sense of *copping it*, of being on the receiving end of some painful but irrevocable gift. 'Getting' this most 'contemporary' métier would thus entail getting a certain modernity first. Clearly we were no longer talking about modern art, about this or that modernism, but about a *lived* modernity. The key knowledge for curating in Indonesia would be found where an antecedent modernity had taken root, whence Indonesia's own modernity was grafted.

Upon reflection, this insistence on a source modernity also runs counter to the romantic nomadism that still pervades the curatorial discourse of a would-be 'global' field.[7] Against the tide of this globalisation wades the stubborn figure of the modern nation – nation as product of modernity and modernity as the flagship product of nation – a structure that seems almost archaeological amidst the recent vogue for fallen utopias.[8] But decaying though it may be, this concrete modernity in Indonesia's cities is by no means the picturesque relic of a bygone internationalism. It is the everyday built environment, still being refurbished, still humming with life. Thus are Bandung's colonial bungalows repurposed as factory outlets. The weary framework of Jakarta's Taman Ismail Marzuki, a public facility for modern culture inaugurated in 1968, is the subject neither of fond portraits nor of ideological ghost stories – it still functions as a rare and valued piece of public infrastructure.[9]

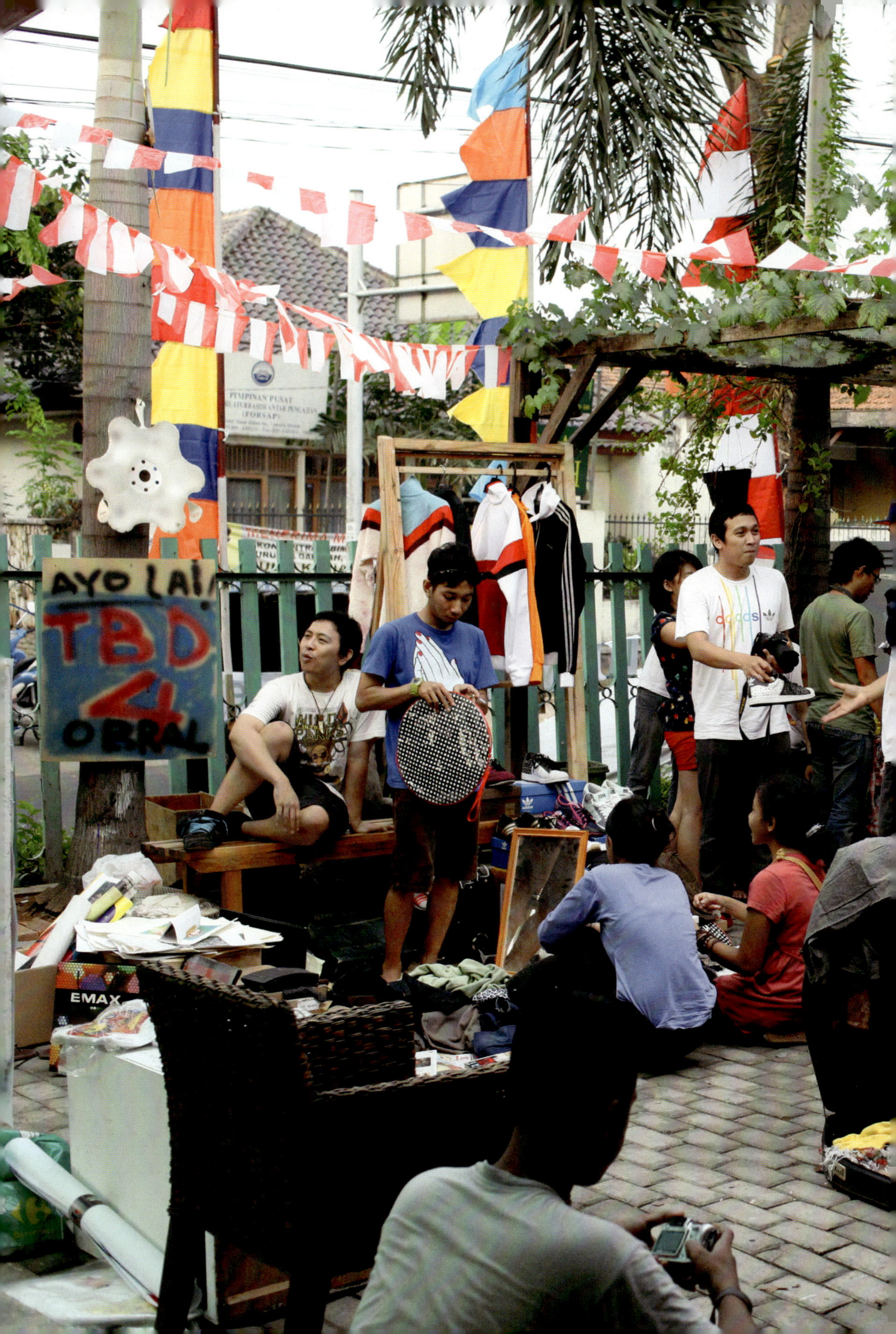

AYO LA!
TBD
4
OBRAL
PIMPINAN PUSAT
(FORSAP)

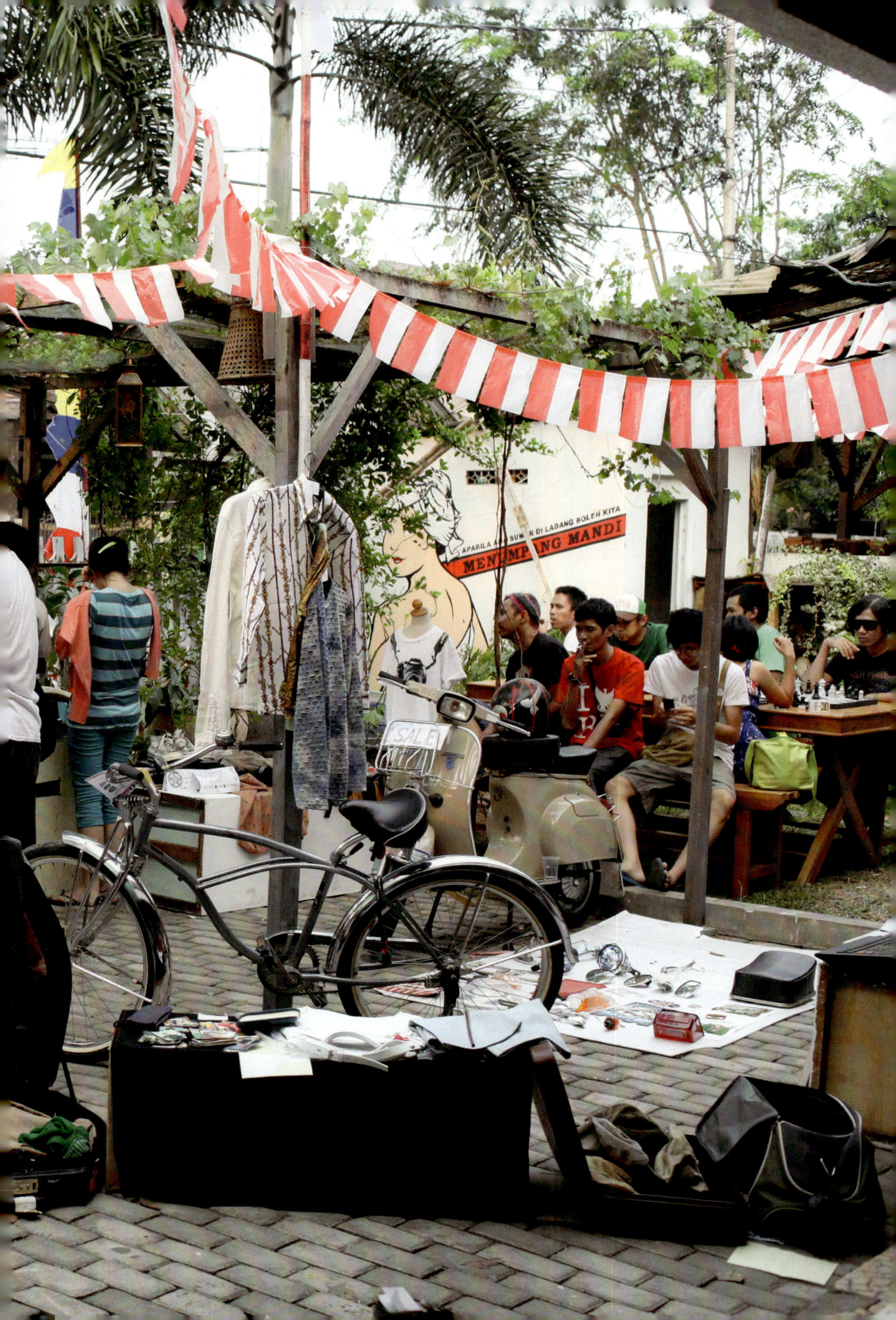
APABILA ADA SUMUR DI LADANG BOLEH KITA
MENUMPANG MANDI

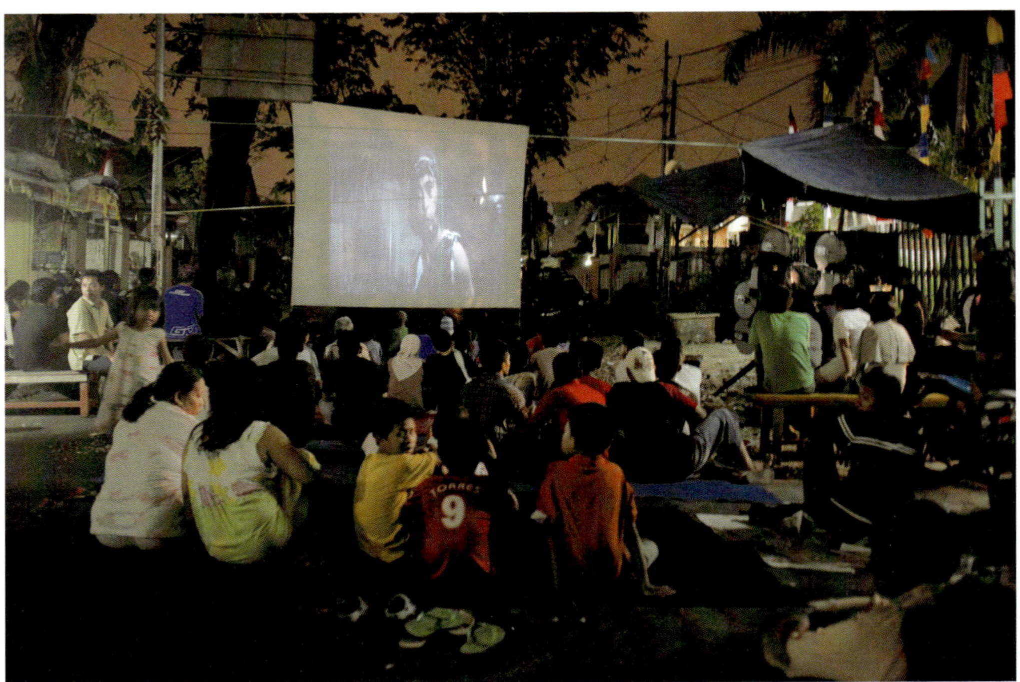

ruangrupa (ArtLab division), 'Lonely Market', Jakarta, 2009. Courtesy the artists

This unfinished modernity has done nothing to limit ruangrupa's contemporary currency. For the dematerialisation of art, too, is an incomplete project, and the 'relational' turn, far from transcending it, has only upped the ante. As the artwork becomes activity (participation, social engagement, conviviality) the market moves to outflank it, at once celebrating the ephemeral and unreified spirit of the work, whilst perfecting its titration into parallel currencies. As a collective exhibiting internationally, whose core activity is the production and dissemination of knowledge rather than things, ruangrupa is hardly immune. Indeed, the collective seems to exemplify that merger of artist and curator so often mooted in the ballooning discourse on exhibition-making. In a recent edition of *Manifesta Journal* devoted to this subject, positions are staked around Walter Benjamin's 1934 lecture 'The Author as Producer'. We can hardly doubt the enduring relevance of this text in the post-industrial world, where museum may be likened to factory, and the mere prospect of collectivisation, as John Roberts points out, no longer distinguishes artist from curator.[10] But these conditions are far from universal, and are by no means the manifest destiny of contemporary art in Asia. For Roberts, the curator unprepared to be an artist should step back into the wings and make way for those truly committed to thwarting art's instrumentalisation. Such a synthesis has the whiff of an undead Hegelianism about it: the 'artist-curator as producer' must finally take responsibility for his own philosophy of production, as Arthur Danto might have put it. But if anything, Southeast Asian artist-curatorship ought to be read against the grain of this *telos*. Even for the region's most conspicuous trailblazers (Apinan and Supangkat), the outcome was precisely the opposite: a renewed separation of roles.

However ruangrupa might seem to embody the disciplinary merger, then, in attributing to the group the form of a curatorship *to come*, with or without the italics, we run the risk of mistaking tactical moves for a strategic programme. And however appealing the image of their 'contemporaneity', the group should first be seen in another light, a light in which modernity and nation still matter, and instrumentality is not (yet) the arch-enemy of art; a light in which artists make artworks and curators curate, and it is possible to do both. Perhaps ruangrupa is more a *spirit* of curatorship – not limited to a single body, yet somehow tied to a place – that would defend the autonomy of artists, singular or plural, but not necessarily that of the artwork. For this spirit the audience, rather than the work of art, may be the ultimate object of curatorial care.

Notes

[1] 'Video, an Art, a History 1965–2010', co-curated by Christine van Assche and Patricia Levasseur de la Motte, Singapore Art Museum, 10 June–18 September 2011; and OK Video FLESH: 5th Jakarta International Video Festival, curated by Hafiz, Agung Hujatnikajennong, Farah Wardani, Mahardhika Yudha and Rizki Lazuardi, National Gallery of Indonesia, 6–17 October 2011.

[2] Agung Hujatnikajennong, 'Everything Melts onto the Screen: Video and Media Art in Indonesia', presentation at 'Video Vortex #7', Kedai Kebun Forum, Yogyakarta, July 2011. See also his 'The State and the Market: Two Decades of Indonesian Contemporary Art', in *Biennale Jogja XI – Equator #1* (exh. cat.), Yogyakarta: Yayasan Biennale Yogyakarta, 2011, pp.180–89.

[3] See Jacques Attali, *Noise: The Political Economy of Music* (trans. Brian Massumi), Minneapolis: University of Minnesota Press, 1985.

[4] See John Pemberton, *On the Subject of 'Java'*, Ithaca, NY: Cornell University Press, 1994.

[5] Thomas J. Berghuis, 'ruangrupa', *Third Text*, vol.25, no.4, 2011, pp.395–407.

[6] I would not be the first to observe that this nomadism is often a smokescreen for the industrial and economic transmigration it quite faithfully maps. See Pascal Gielen, 'Curating with Love, or a Plea for Inflexibility', *Manifesta Journal*, issue 10, 2010, pp.14–15.

[7] See, for example, Guy Tillim's *Avenue Patrice Lumumba* (2007–08), or Cyprien Gaillard's *Desniansky Raion* (2007). Louidgi Beltrame's film *Brasilia/Chandigarh* (2008) even made it to Singapore with the Pompidou show. The appeal of this genre is apparently universal, although it might be interesting to compare the respective geographies of production and consumption.

[8] The cultural centre was built on the site of a public park established by Raden Saleh, Indonesia's first modern artist, during the Dutch East Indies era. In using this space for exhibitions and concerts, ruangrupa continues a tradition of diverting art's resources towards the provision of public space. Patrick Flores deals specifically with the matter of incomplete modernities in 'The Curatorial Turn in Southeast Asia and the Afterlife of the Modern' (2008), in Melissa Chiu and Benjamin Genocchio (ed.), *Contemporary Art in Asia: A Critical Reader*, Cambridge, MA and London: MIT Press, 2011, pp.197–210.

[9] John Roberts, 'The Curator as Producer: Aesthetic Reason, Nonaesthetic Reason, and Infinite Ideation', *Manifesta Journal*, issue 10, 2010, pp.51–57. See also Hito Steyerl, 'Is a Museum a Factory?', *e-flux*, no.7, 2009, http://www.e-flux.com/journal/is-a-museum-a-factory/.

The Joy of Meta: On the Museum of American Art

Steven ten Thije

Meta-level is a position M defined in relation to P as an outside position that at the same time could recognise and even incorporate position P. Meta-position M recontextualises position P by assigning a new layer of meaning to P while not entirely forgetting its previous meaning. Constitutive notions that define position P cannot be constitutive notions for the position M.
– Walter Benjamin, 'On Meta', 2013[1]

For those of you who have never visited one of the venues or installations of the *Museum of American Art* or its 'affiliated' institutions – institutions with similar features, but who are not part of the *Museum* – please allow me to outline the basics. In a way the museum holds nothing out of the ordinary. It displays paintings and an occasional sculpture. All the works belong to the mainstream narrative of modern art. Only, what is on show is not limited to artworks alone, but also includes catalogues and other documents that relate to the history of the artworks on display. Sometimes an entire room is constructed to refer to important places in the formation of the narrative of modern art, such as the office of Alfred H. Barr, Jr, the first director of the Museum of Modern Art in New York (MoMA) – the institution that is implicit in the *Museum of American Art*'s name. In several of the installations there is also music playing: jazz or other light music of the early to mid-twentieth century. Almost everything on display is a copy, of either the original documents or the works themselves. These copies are made as oil paintings, drawings or plaster copies of the original sculptures, and none of them hide their second-hand nature. Even catalogue covers and pages are painted or drawn and exhibited on the wall. The quality of each copy is deliberately dilettantish and merely repeats the iconic features of the original, without paying much care to its material qualities. Finally, none of the installations or copies are attributed to an individual artist or curator; only the *Museum* itself is credited on the wall labels. The *Museum of American Art* exists anonymously, peopled by mundane characters such as technical assistants and caretakers. Searching for a commentator on the *Museum of American Art*, one will encounter a contemporary Walter Benjamin – a 'copy' of the one born in 1892 – who speaks not on behalf of the museum but as a friendly observer.

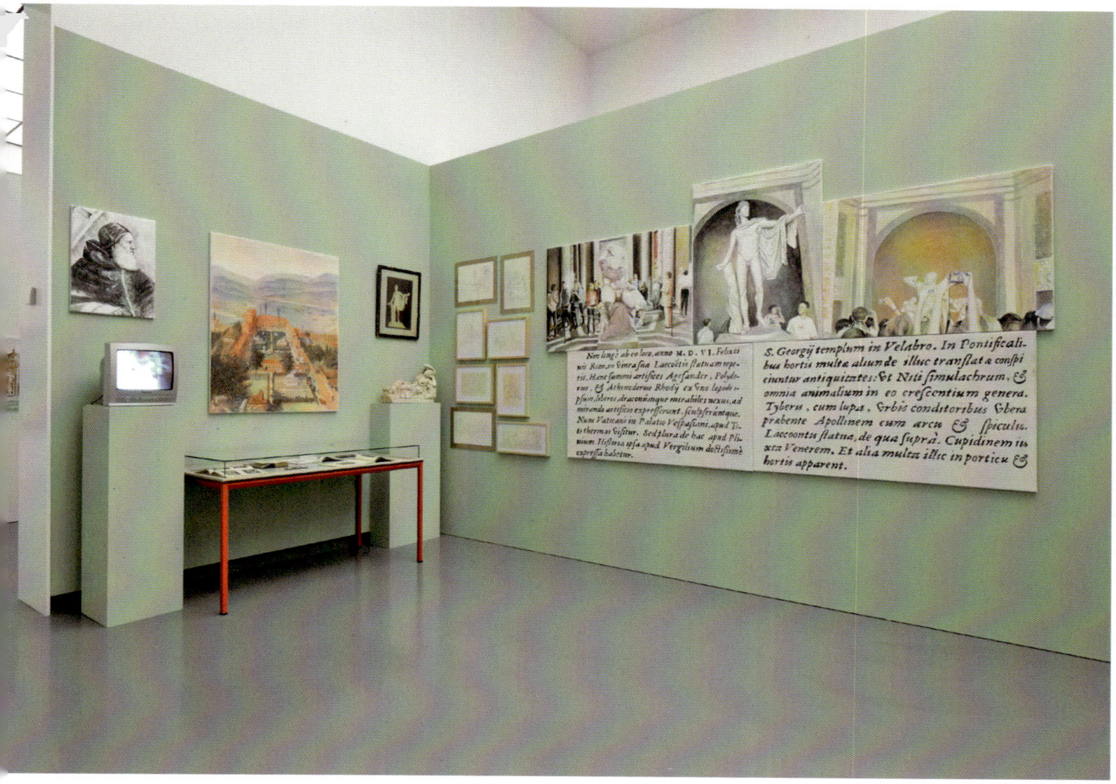

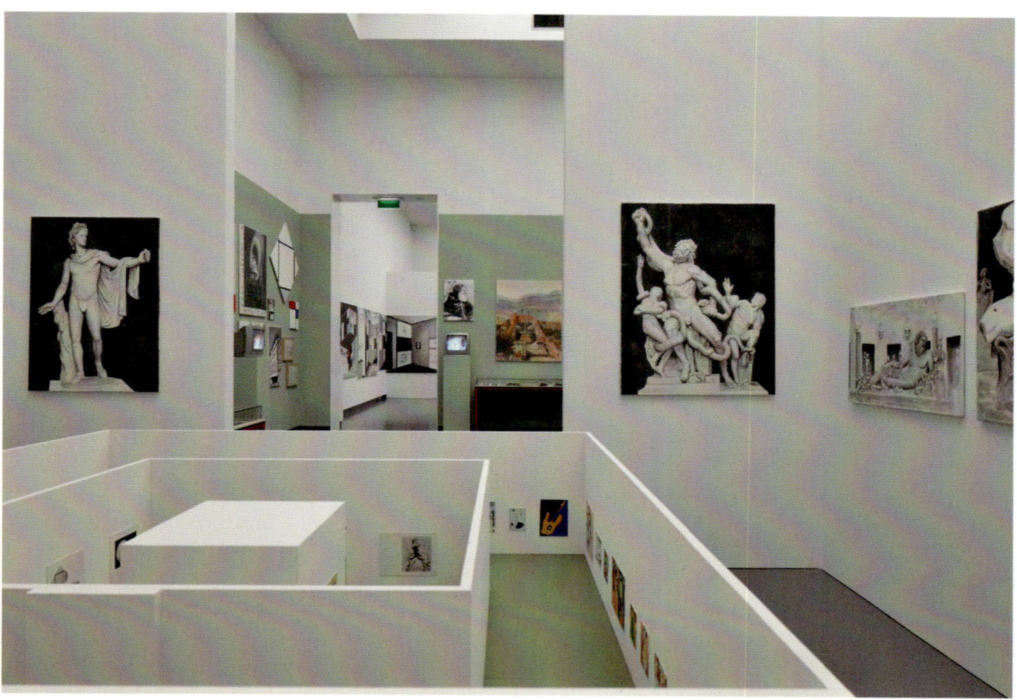

What is actually on display in the *Museum of American Art* is not the works themselves, but the story in which these works play a part. Often the display refers to the historical moments when these works entered into the story of modern art. The dilettantish copies thereby perform a precise role. They push the visitor away from contemplating the individual work as a masterpiece and invite him or her to reflect on the work in a specific situation instead. This is perhaps best illustrated by the fact that one of the most frequently copied artefacts in the displays of the *Museum of American Art* is not a work of art but the cover of the exhibition catalogue of MoMA's famous 1936 show 'Cubism and Abstract Art', which introduced European Cubism, post-Impressionism, Bauhaus and various forms of abstract avant-garde art to the US public. Moreover, 'Cubism and Abstract Art' is important to the *Museum of American Art* in that it essentially presented a schematic map of the history of modern art up until the very moment of the exhibition. This schema became, as a result of MoMA's fame after World War II, the blueprint for the narrative of modern art that came to dominate internationally. For the *Museum of American Art* the schema and the catalogue function as the most comprehensive documents in its explication of the notions of narrative and reproduction.

First of all, there is the narrative that unfolds via the display of the catalogue's cover and text, in which Alfred H. Barr, Jr – director of the museum at the time, curator of the exhibition and author of the catalogue – offers a bold story of abstract art that seamlessly ties together the various and sometimes even antithetical branches of abstract art in Europe. What is most spectacular about this gesture is the complete denial of what had been one of the key concepts of European art history: the national school. Barr writes: 'In general, movements confined in their influence to a single country have not been included.'[2] At the moment when Europe was on the verge of annihilating itself on the bases of nation and race, Barr, in deadpan observation, wipes the entire notion of national roots from the table. This neutrality towards nation or race is foundational for how the *Museum of American Art* understands Americanism in its title, namely as a synonym with 'international'. Articulated with great force within the catalogue *Cubism and Abstract Art*, it is this internationalism that the *Museum of American Art* particularly remembers and affirms.

The second crucial feature that marks the narrative of *Cubism and Abstract Art* is straightforward historicism. Following his observation on international influence, Barr states: 'In several cases the earlier and more creative years of a movement or individual have been emphasised at the expense of a later work which may be fine in quality but comparatively unimportant historically.'[3] Key to Barr's story is historical progression: the identification of unique and original events placed in chronological order. The importance of this progressive narrative was so powerful that it even seduced Barr to place a photographic reproduction at the beginning of the entire exhibition: Pablo Picasso's *Les Demoiselles d'Avignon* (1907). For Barr, the work was so central that it needed to be included regardless of the fact that he couldn't show the original. The *Museum of American Art*

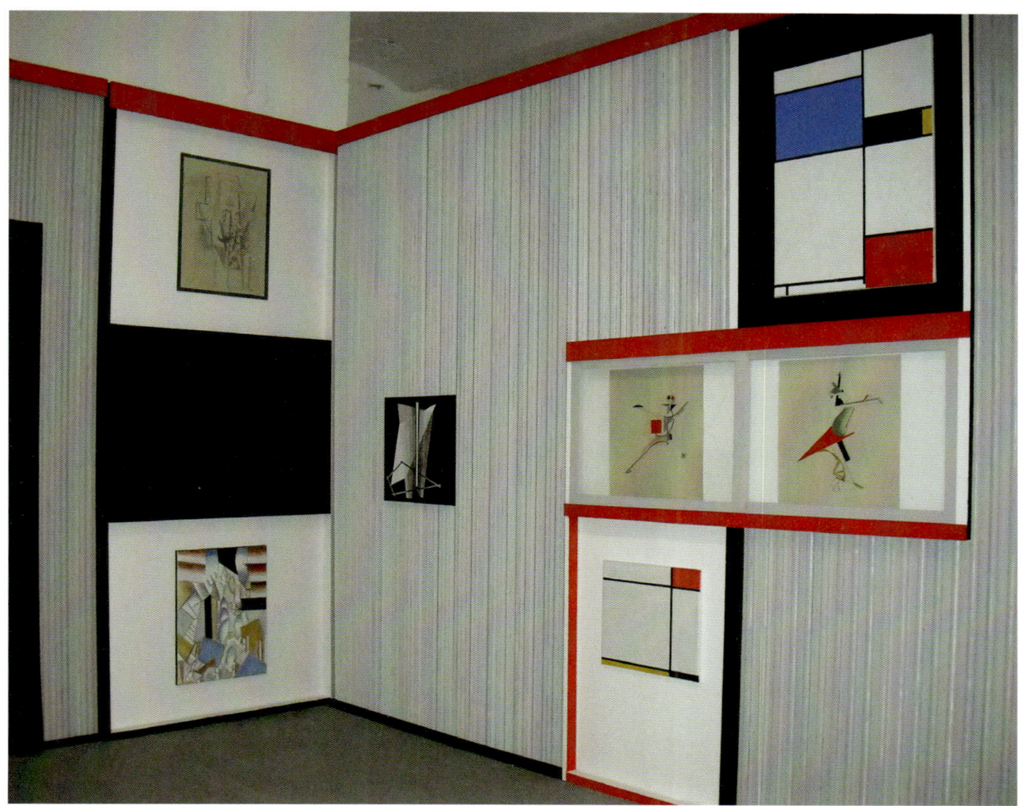

recalls this move in its own typical manner, with a hand-drawn copy of a photograph of the installation of this photograph, which one finds in several of its installations, or museum branches.

Next to the narrative and its structure, another element of *Cubism and Abstract Art* makes it a vital artefact for the *Museum of American Art*: the modern approach to the museum institution as developed by Barr and his staff. The catalogue became a landmark in the history of modern art not only for the merit of its content but also due to its successful dissemination by MoMA. The institution thereby benefitted in a tragic sense from the eclipse in Europe, which made MoMA in the post-War years the best equipped heir of the 1920s, the revolutionary decade of museum reform, especially in Germany.[4] Not only was MoMA a sanctuary for the advanced art that was banned throughout Europe during the 1940s, it also was the place where the most advanced thinking on the museum institution was maintained.

Within this context, Barr developed a remarkable and slightly antagonistic view on the museum. He drew simultaneously from the two poles of museological thinking that dominated the debate in the US and Europe in the early twentieth century. On the one hand, there were conservative aesthetes such as Wilhelm von Bode and his American counterpart Benjamin Ives Gilman,

277

who modernised the museum institution by placing much more emphasis on the aesthetic experience of the gallery visit. Instead of the nineteenth-century salon-style hang, which typically filled the gallery walls from floor to ceiling, Bode and Gilman promoted beautiful and legible installations that allowed visitors a more holistic viewing experience, presenting the entire room as a coherent display. On the other hand, there was the Bauhaus radicalism promoted in museological terms by Alexander Dorner, the director of the Landesmuseum in Hanover, who in some sense might be likened to the US librarian John Cotton Dana. While Dorner and Dana also broke with the salon-style hang, they further developed a line of thinking that let go completely of the notion of originality by transforming the museum into a library (Dana) or dissolving the category of art itself into a new type of aesthetic sensibility that manifested itself in Constructivism and Bauhaus design (Dorner). Barr brought these two sides together by keeping the notion of the masterpiece as the cornerstone of the museum enterprise, while also sharing in the idealism of modern culture's spread into new domains, such as photography, film and design, which he was familiar with and endeavoured to present in his museum. Indeed, Barr had no problem with collecting these nontraditional art forms and was pragmatic enough to use the most advanced marketing tools to spread the museum's perspective on modern art and even use copies to that end. MoMA started a vehement national and international publicity campaign, lending out exhibitions of reproductions and publishing a stunning amount of high-quality catalogues in volumes that flooded into world circulation.

The international branch of this museum enterprise, concentrated in the International Programme of Circulating Exhibitions, overtook Europe after its years of darkness (with indirect government support channelled through the CIA).[5] In the post-War years, MoMA promoted the notion of modern art beyond the idea of national schools – even if it was still firmly entrenched in a singular, universal historical narrative. The moment in which the MoMA/US model gained international dominance can symbolically be located in 1964, when, for the first time, a US artist, Robert Rauschenberg, was awarded the Golden Lion at the Venice Biennale (itself, ironically, the epitome of nation-state art history, with its theme-park garden of national pavilions).

The history of MoMA stands at the centre of the *Museum of American Art*'s research, which is consolidated in different collections at various venues.[6] One collection, for instance, presents one of Dorner's most famous Bauhaus-Constructivist experiments, El Lissitzky's *Abstract Cabinet* (1927–28), as one of the predecessors of MoMA.[7] The story of the International Programme of Circulating Exhibitions is central to the display of the *Museum of American Art* in Berlin, located in a residential flat in a classic GDR-high-rise building on what was originally named 'Stalinallee', now 'Frankfurter Allee', which is perhaps the institute's most comprehensive collection. There, the *Museum*'s Dorothy Miller Gallery shows the collection 'New American Painting', which combines pages from the catalogue of the 1958 exhibition of the same title (part of the International Programme of Circulating Exhibitions) with a mini-museum that shows the main narrative of 'Cubism and Abstract Art'.[8]

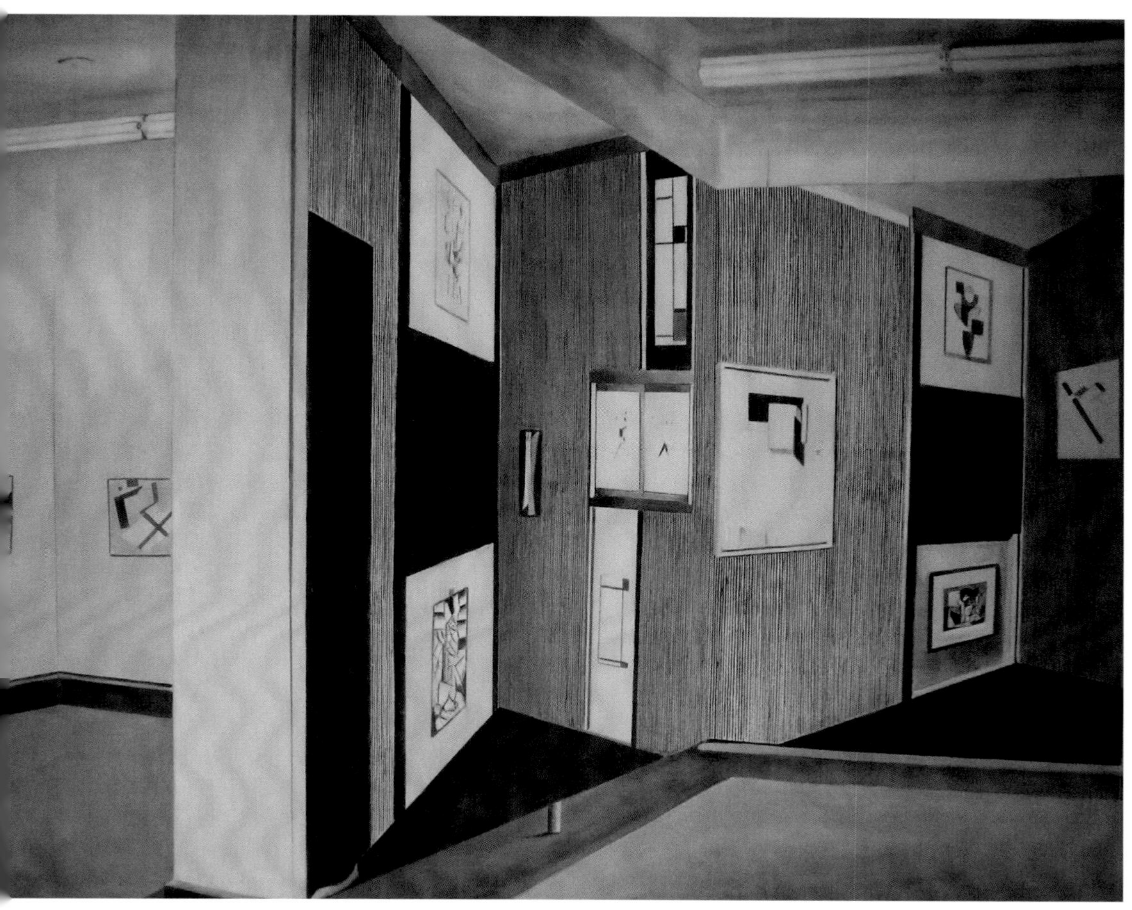

The *Museum of American Art* also presented the collection 'Americans 64', at the Venice Biennale in 2005, focussing on the moment when Rauschenberg received the Golden Lion. Affiliates of the *Museum of American Art* explore similar territory. In Belgrade, for instance, the *Kunsthistorisches Mausoleum (Art Historical Mausoleum*, 2003–ongoing) examines H.W. Janson's *History of Art* (1962), the leading art history textbook for years after its publication, as well as Herbert Read's *A Concise History of Modern Painting* (1959).[9] In New York, the recently closed *Salon de Fleurus* (1992–2013) presented a copy of Getrude Stein's Paris salon, where the young Barr perhaps encountered for the first time the combination of Picasso, Paul Cézanne and Henri Matisse that would form the opening chord for his own narrative on modern art.[10]

The displays of the *Museum of American Art* are rigorous and playful, just as it deals with its loaded topic in a manner both serious and humorous. It is a festival of going down the rabbit hole, where everything that is familiar turns into something strange. The question that is puzzling when walking through *Museum of American Art* displays is their seeming ambivalence about their subject. On the one hand, the use of dilettantish copies suggests a radical

Alexander Dorner, 'Die Zwanziger Jahre in Hannover', 2062 (Alexander Dorner, 'The Twenties in Hanover', 2062), acrylic on canvas, 150 × 200cm. Courtesy Museum of American Art, Berlin

Next spread: Installation view, 'The New American Painting' Dorothy Miller Gallery, Berlin, 2004. Courtesy Museum of American Art, Berlin

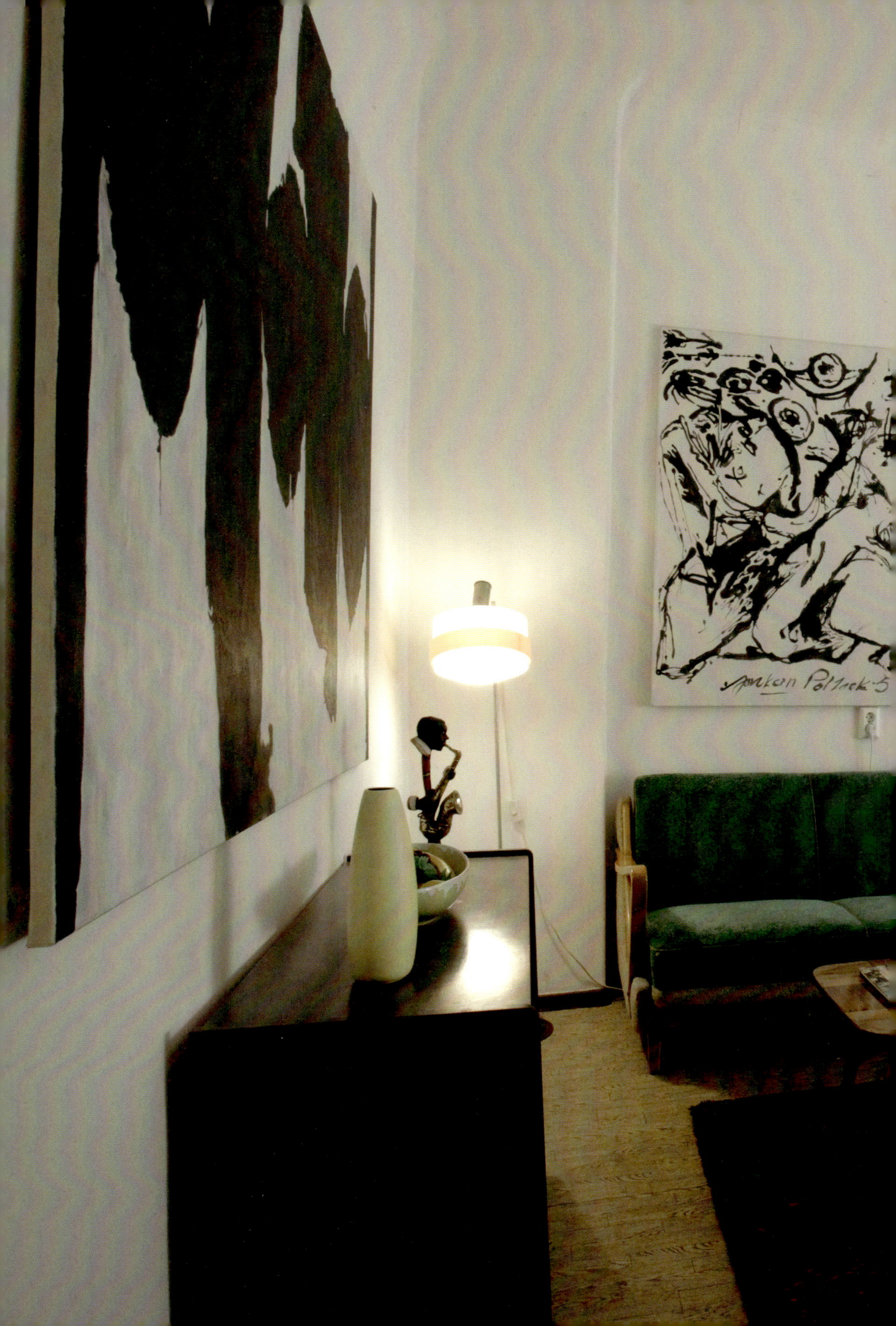

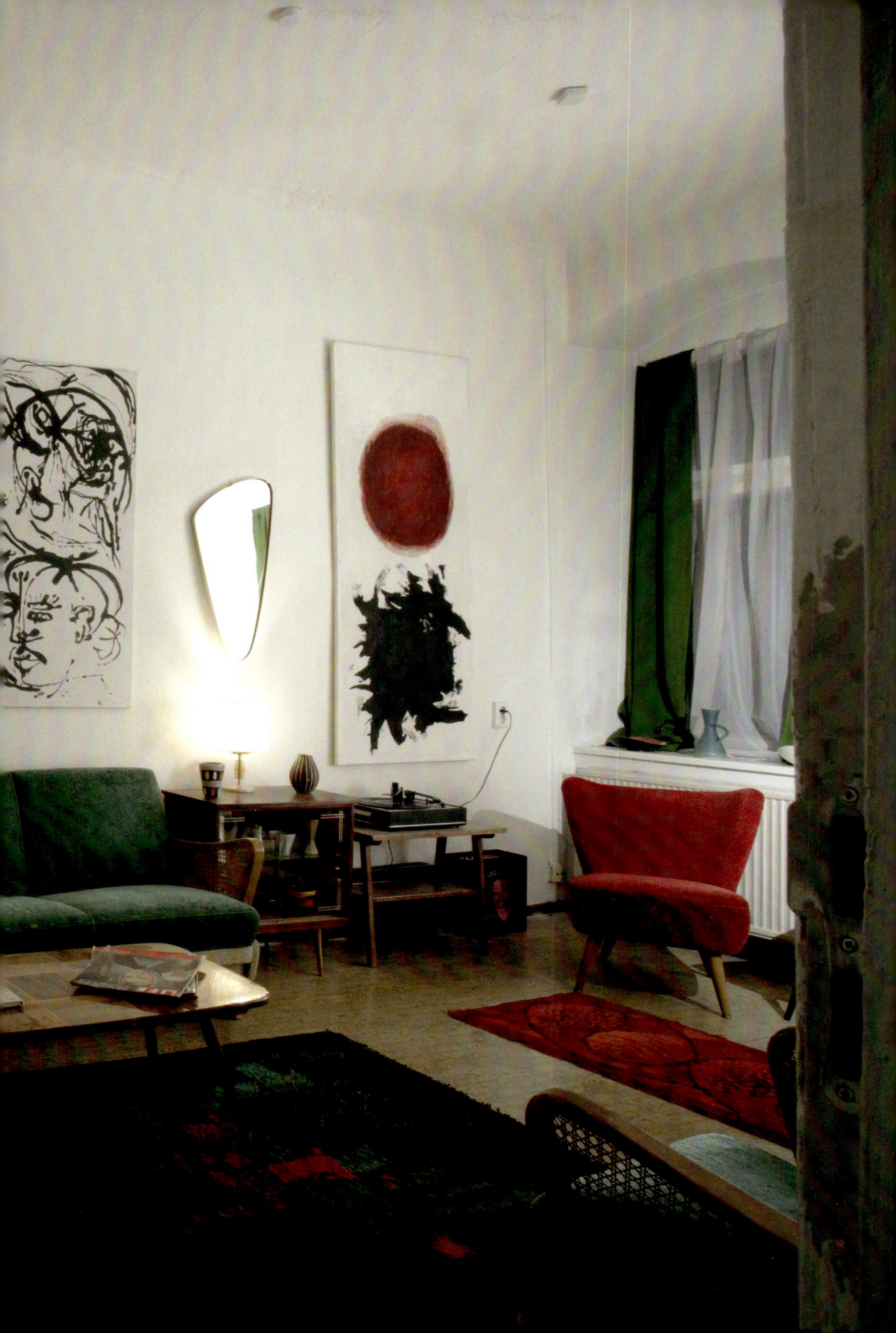

critique of the notions of uniqueness and originality that remain central to MoMA's narrative of modern art. On the other, there is an enormous delight and care in the reconstruction of that narrative, and a lack of cynicism in the way in which it celebrates MoMA's colonial dominance in the post-War period. If you ask a technical assistant of the *Museum of American Art* about Serge Guilbaut's famous study *How New York Stole the Idea of Modern Art* (1983)[11] or Eva Cockroft's influential research on the CIA's involvement in the International Programme of Circulating Exhibitions, he will shrug his shoulders and simply reply: 'Good for the CIA. At least they had good taste and knew what to choose.' How to reconcile the *Museum*'s simultaneous negation and affirmation of MoMA's story of modern art?

'Sites of Modernity' (2010), a collection belonging to the *Museum of Antiquities*, an affiliate of the *Museum of American Art* dealing with an exhibition of antique sculptures in the Vatican's Belvedere Gardens that was commissioned by Pope Julius II in 1502, is key to understanding the *Museum of American Art*'s position.[12] It presents an extreme example of what was accomplished in MoMA's 'Cubism and Abstract Art', contending that what started in the Vatican gardens was concluded four centuries later by a skinny US museum director who brought the story to its logical end: an independent, international history of modern art. Just as the 1502 display presented heathen religious sculptures from pre-Christian times in the most sacred institution of the Christian world, MoMA recontextualised (and arguably bastardised) all variations of conflicting abstract art, originally linked to nation states, in one uniform exhibition with a universalist narrative. In its display, the *Museum of Antiquities* investigates what is necessary for such a redefining of artworks to occur, both physically, in terms of exhibition display, and conceptually, in terms of the narrative being unfolded. What it lays out is the simultaneous invention of a notion of 'autonomous' art and of progressive historical development: the 1502 exhibition argued that its works were not so much representations of heathen gods, but rather exemplary works of art. They could acquire relevance in the Christian world, then, due to the fact that 'art' as an entity predated the Christian era. What is remarkable is that the logic of this argument not only applies to the ancient works of the Greeks and Romans, but it can also be projected into the future. If the concept of art predates the Christian world, why would it not survive it as well? Willingly or not, what Pope Julius II developed in mentally making space for the antique sculptures was a meta-position of historical progression that could incorporate the pre-Christian world, the Christian world and whatever world view might follow thereafter.

'Sites of Modernities' comprises elements from displays of the *Museum of American Art* alongside material from the Belvedere Gardens exhibition. In the middle of the first room, one finds a mini-MoMA that shows the narrative of 'Cubism and Abstract Art' in a scale model of an imagined square building with a perfectly geometric floor plan. The narrative of the exhibition is told within an outer corridor of the architecture model, which displays small copies of the paintings exhibited in 1936 as well as paintings of the catalogue pages and of installation views of the original exhibition. The exhibition walls surrounding the model display paintings of black-and-white photographs of the classical antique sculptures shown in the Belvedere Gardens, such as the Apollo Belvedere and the Laocoön Group. In the second room, on two opposite walls, the stories of MoMA and of the Belvedere installation are presented through more reproductions: of paintings of the Vatican gardens, Pope Julius II and Alfred H. Barr, Jr, as well as images of MoMA's building, the cover of *Cubism and Abstract Art* and much more; these are presented on a wall painted mint green, a colour reminiscent of the 1950s. Overall, the exhibition recalls a strange type of ethnographic or anthropological display, in which the history of MoMA is mirrored in the history of the Belvedere display.

But the exhibition's mirroring logic doesn't end in this clean, two-step development. With its anonymous copies, the display itself introduces a third perspective: a meta-position with respect to the autonomous, international history of art. While what is shown in the *Museum of Antiquities*, or in the *Museum of American Art* for that matter, might still look like art, or even function within the contemporary art world as such, it ceases to share many of the basic principles of uniqueness and originality that inform what is commonly identified as *art*. At first sight this might be considered a gesture of monumental irony; going deeper into the world of the *Museum of American Art*, however, the notion of irony disappears. The displays may be joyful, spectacular or even absurd, but they never suggest that they are not serious or that they only want to reaffirm, negatively and with a vengeance, the notions of authorship, identity, uniqueness and originality that form the foundation for the traditional historical narrative. Just like the Pope's sculpture garden, the anonymous and copying *Museum of American Art* is a Trojan Horse that, once allowed in, starts to overtake its surroundings.

Where, then, does this journey end? What logic overwrites MoMA's historicist method of placing unique events in a singular chronological sequence? The *Museum of American Art* itself expresses some humility in the face of these questions. If the *Museum* is anywhere it is at a threshold between an obsolete, historicist (art) world and a new world view being formed. What is clear to the *Museum of American Art* is that the defining features of the previous world will not be dominant in the next world. Where the historicist world was defined by linearity, progression, originality and uniqueness, our current world is defined by webs of relations, relativity and copies. What is at stake is therefore not only a transformation in art, but, more generally, a shift in how people relate to art and history. Instead of splitting the world between perceiving subjects and passive objects, the *Museum of American Art* knows no clean divide between who is watching and what is being watched. Subject and object become confused in copies of artworks and people that are both things and somethings or someones with agency.

What is the importance of such a realisation? To answer this question it is helpful to return to Walter Benjamin, the Frankfurt School writer who is the source for the contemporary Walter Benjamin associated with the *Museum*. His famous text on the copy, 'The Work of Art in the Age of Mechanical Reproduction' (1936), is as important to the *Museum of American Art* as the

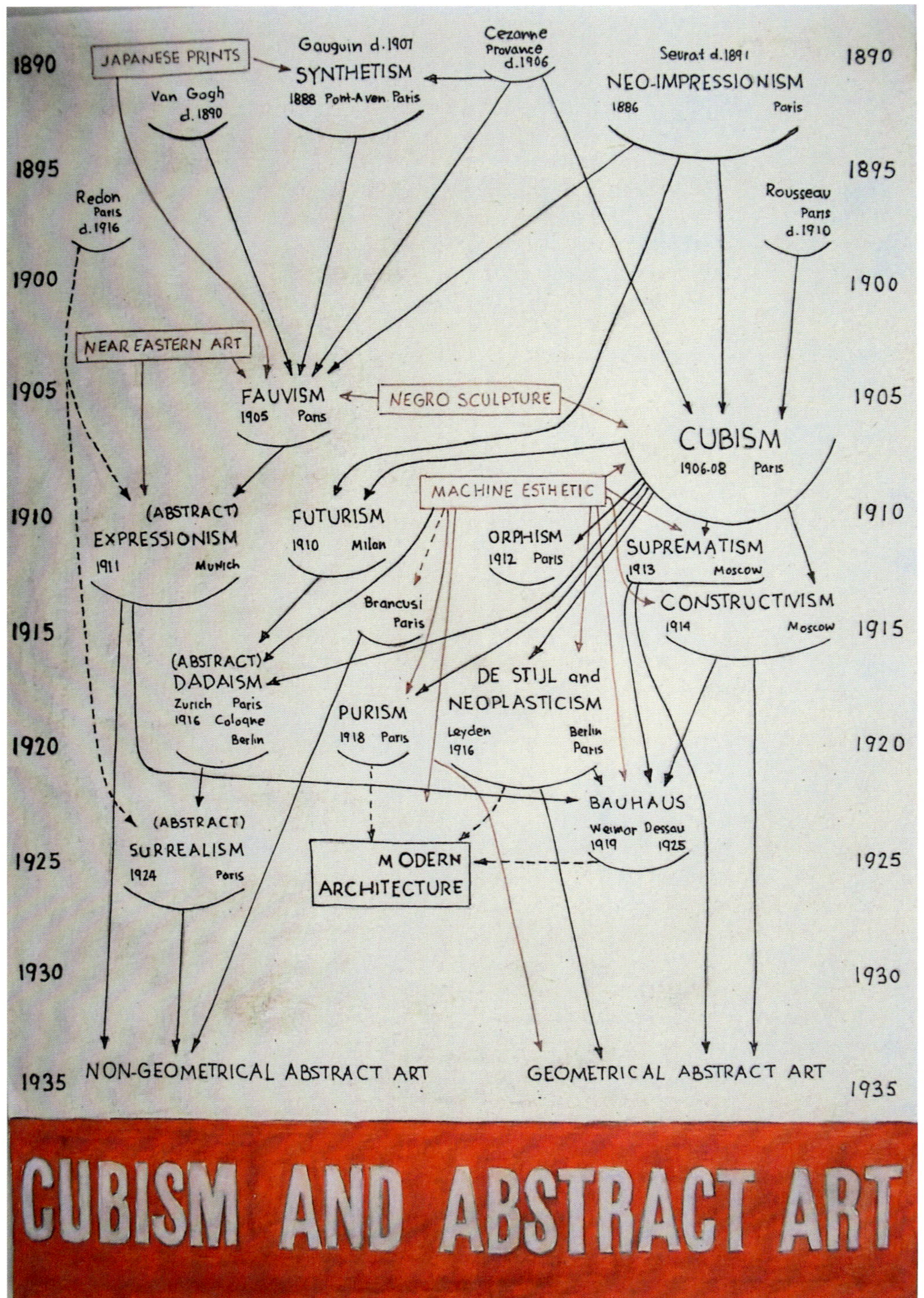

1890
JAPANESE PRINTS
Gauguin d.1907
Cezanne Provance d.1906
Seurat d.1891
1890
SYNTHETISM
1888 Pont-Aven Paris
NEO-IMPRESSIONISM
1886
Paris
Van Gogh d.1890
1895
Redon Paris d.1916
Rousseau Paris d.1910
1895
1900
NEAR EASTERN ART
1900
1905
FAUVISM
1905 Paris
NEGRO SCULPTURE
CUBISM
1906-08 Paris
1905
(ABSTRACT) EXPRESSIONISM
1911 Munich
FUTURISM
1910 Milan
MACHINE ESTHETIC
ORPHISM
1912 Paris
SUPREMATISM
1913 Moscow
1910
Brancusi Paris
CONSTRUCTIVISM
1914 Moscow
1915
(ABSTRACT) DADAISM
Zurich Paris 1916 Cologne Berlin
PURISM
1918 Paris
DE STIJL and NEOPLASTICISM
Leyden 1916
Berlin Paris
1920
(ABSTRACT) SURREALISM
1924 Paris
BAUHAUS
Weimar Dessau 1919 1925
1925
MODERN ARCHITECTURE
1930
1930
NON-GEOMETRICAL ABSTRACT ART
GEOMETRICAL ABSTRACT ART
1935
1935
CUBISM AND ABSTRACT ART

story of MoMA. Copying for the *Museum of American Art* is not done out of convenience or sheer possibility, but out of necessity and relevance. What is copied is that which has contemporary urgency. It is therefore no accident that the *Museum* started to remember the internationalism of the early MoMA right at the end of the 1990s, when in Europe, for the first time since World War II, nationalism had once again resulted in genocide, and when the US was slowly starting to translate its inclusive internationalism into an evermore problematic imperialism. Nor is it a coincidence that next to the *Museum of American Art* a Walter Benjamin started to appear in Belgrade in the 1980s to comment upon the *Museum*'s displays – the Frankfurt School Benjamin wrote his text on the copy under the dark spell of National Socialism. The first Benjamin argued in his endlessly cited text that the biggest danger of National Socialism was that it was trying to maintain a certain logic based on notions of identity and uniqueness combined with a Darwinian approach towards human evolution, or progressive historical development, in a world whose industrial and spiritual technology of reproduction was incompatible with that logic. In other words, Nazism pursued a historicist logic in a world that could no longer facilitate it. Benjamin showed that the consequences of modern technologies of reproduction such as photography and film were not subsumable into old familiar categories, and that we should be open to how they might suggest a whole new way of living and thinking.

With his famously proclaimed withering of aura, Benjamin noted that the tradition of art, which materialised in the cult of the original celebrated in museums, was on the cusp of change. Central to art's aura was the necessary divide between the viewer and the work, reinforced by the museum's 'don't touch' fetishisation of the original, with its religiously kept pedigree and its championing of the endless epistemological surplus of the original. The auratic conception of the artwork is epitomised in the common occurrence of being unable to articulate the experience of an artwork fully, making its meaning regress into the infinite plenitude of the unique event. In contrast, Benjamin imagined that the modern mass subject would engage with his or her surroundings as a playful critic. The appropriate attitude would not be silent contemplation but immersed distraction. Engrossed in a world of modern technology, the new subject would understand things through distracted and spontaneous assimilation; he or she would no longer be enchanted by the original but would critically engage in dialogue by appropriating the unreachable artwork (and more generally the world) through copies.

The nameless workers of the *Museum of American Art* can be seen as contemporary avatars of this mass subject that Benjamin recognised in the streets of Berlin, Paris and Moscow in the early decades of the twentieth century. They are no doubt generous avatars, open to sharing their special status as copies, or at least nameless characters, with whomever comes to visit the *Museum*. In Venice, for instance, a technical assistant of the *Museum* once told me that a visitor to the installation remarked to his partner: 'This is a type of *Meta-Kunst*.' It is to this nameless visitor that we owe the reading of the *Museum* as a meta-museum. 'Meta' here can be understood not only to allude to something that is 'self-referential', but, more importantly, to describe a subject-position that shares qualities with Benjamin's mass subject: a desire to come close to things and appropriate them in a copy. 'Meta' thus describes a position that literally takes up in itself the position in relation to which it is 'meta', but doesn't reflect upon it by means of distancing. It signals a mode of absorption that overcomes itself in a more Hegelian sense of the term. In this museum – perhaps contrary to what one would expect – the experience is not more difficult but more playful. Even if one is tempted, as I am in writing this text, to 'understand' the *Museum of American Art* as though one is a subject standing outside the institution and looking at it as an object, the more one delves into it the clearer it becomes that such an approach is in stark contradiction to what the *Museum* is. In the end, one is (or rather, I am) asked to let go of authorship – to give in to the frivolous joy of the mirror palace, with big-band jazz music playing, which makes one hum instead of frown.

Notes

[1] Walter Benjamin, 'On Meta', in *Walter Benjamin: Recent Writings 1986–2013*, Vancouver and Los Angeles: New Documents, 2013, p.193.

[2] Alfred H. Barr, Jr, *Cubism and Abstract Art* (1936, exh. cat.), New York: Museum of Modern Art, 1974, p.9.

[3] *Ibid.*

[4] See Alexis Joachimides, *Die Museumsreformbewegung in Deutschland und die Entstehung des modernen Museums 1880–1940*, Dresden: Verlag der Kunst, 2001.

[5] See Eva Cockcroft, 'Abstract Expressionism, Weapon of the Cold War', *Artforum*, vol.15, no.10, June 1974, pp.39–41.

[6] For the best overview of the *Museum*'s installations, see Inke Arns and W. Benjamin (ed.), *What Is Modern Art?* (exh. cat.), Berlin: Kunstlerhaus Bethanien, 2006.

[7] This installation was first shown in Alexander Dorner and El Lissitzky's 'Kabinett der Abstrakten – Original and Facsimile' ('Abstract Cabinet – Original and Facsimile') at Halle für Kunst Lüneburg (24 January–8 March 2009) and later exhibited at the Van Abbemuseum, Eindhoven as part of 'Museum Modules' (10 March–24 September 2010) and 'Time Machines Reloaded' (25 September 2010–30 January 2011).

[8] *The Museum of American Art Berlin* opened in 2004 at Frankfurter Allee 91, with appointments scheduled online.

[9] The installation has been on view in Belgrade on Braće Radovanovića 28 since 2003.

[10] *Salon de Fleurus* was located at 41 Spring Street in New York.

[11] Serge Guilbaut, *How New York Stole the Idea of Modern Art: Abstract Expressionism, Freedom and the Cold War* (trans. Arthur Goldhammer), Chicago and London: University of Chicago Press, 1983.

[12] The collection was also shown in 'Museum Modules' and 'Time Machines Reloaded' at the Van Abbemuseum, Eindhoven (see n.7).

The Artist as Director: 'Artist Organisations International' and Its Contradictions

Ekaterina Degot

In his famous 1935 lecture on the political position of Surrealism, delivered as the Second World War was fast approaching, André Breton stated that humanity lived 'in an era in which man belongs to himself less than ever, in which he is held responsible for the totality of his acts, no longer before a single conscience, his own, but before a collective conscience of all those who want to have no more to do with a monstrous system of slavery and hunger'.[1] One increasingly has this feeling today: as a 'monstrous system' continues to spread out into all layers of life, middle-class intellectuals and artists – to whom Breton was referring – are not just abandoned in their lonely precarity, but are also frequently held responsible (not least by themselves) for exactly this 'collective conscience'. Having interiorised the guilt of being socially isolated and deprived of togetherness, artists are beating themselves up over 'just' being individuals working in private; more than this, they are increasingly ashamed of 'just' being critical and reflexive, as these qualities now signify weakness and inability of action.

As today's cynical corporate capitalism supplants democratic politics for so many across the world, artists are now looking for democracy in unlikely places – namely, in art itself. On this territory, they are fighting structural inequalities propelled by the power of institutions and curators, with mixed results. But in trying to make 'righteous' art, might they be making themselves responsible for what they are, in reality, victims of? This question was on my mind as I sat on a stage at Hebbel am Ufer (HaU) in Berlin – the venue's stage and audience seating having been reversed for the occasion – for 'Artist Organisations International' ('AOI'), a congress of institutions and platforms organised by artists.[2]

The event was initiated by a theatre curator, dramatist and writer (Florian Malzacher), an activist-artist (Jonas Staal) and a visual arts and performance curator (Joanna Warsza); the twenty or so groups they brought together were

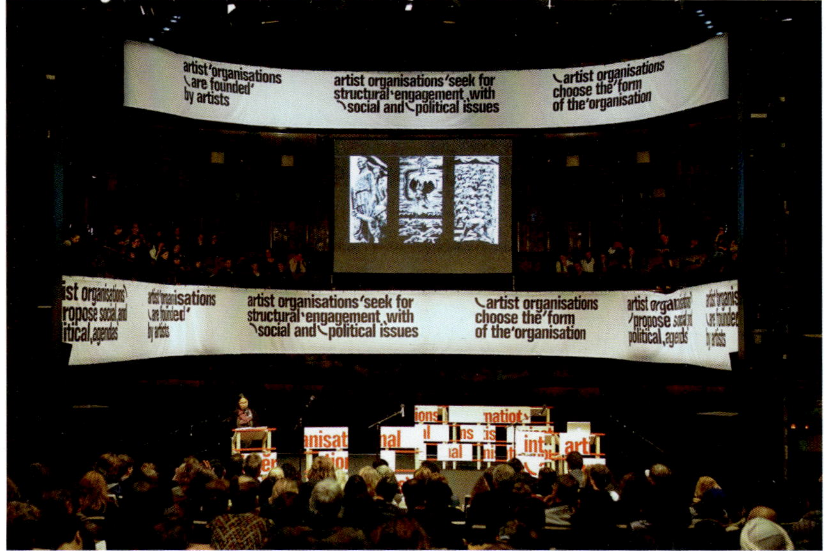

'Artist Organisations International', Hebbel am Ufer (HaU), Berlin, 10 January 2015. Photography: Lidia Rossner. Courtesy HaU, Florian Malzacher, Studio Jonas Staal and Joanna Warsza

a hotchpotch of different, often incompatible approaches and agendas. There were real political activists present (Concerned Artists of the Philippines, Gulf Labor), but also witty and ironic performance artists (Zentrum für Politische Schönheit). There were 'normal', if a bit informal, art institutions (Performing Arts Forum (PAF)) and there were 'official', though a bit unusual ambassadors of a political movement (Artist Association of Azavad). There were projects dictated by one artist's wild imagination that were later brought to reality by other people; some artists were ambivalent about this fulfilment of their dreams (Yael Bartana and the Jewish Renaissance Movement in Poland), while others welcomed this turn of events (Ahmet Öğüt and The Silent University). There were activists now in the midst of ecological downshifting (The Laboratory of Insurrectionary Imagination) as well as those at the height of a career climb towards the United Nations (Forensic Architecture). There were self-organised schools (Chto Delat's School of Engaged Art) alongside production companies hiding behind misleading names (Milo Rau's International Institute of Political Murder). There was a non-organisation about which little was known but which was already a vague object of certain political projections ('Artists of Rojava', present as a video only[3]), as well as a highly elaborate, extremely self-reflexive and ultra-controversial project (Institute for Human Activities, directed by Renzo Martens) that effectively questioned, if not castrated, exactly those kinds of political desires.

To call for such a congress was a timely move. If, until very recently, contemporary art could be seen as a religion of criticality, there is now a strong desire among curators and artists to stop the constant nagging of criticism, and to build a better reality instead. This reality is to be sustainable rather than temporary; tangible rather than imaginary; collective rather than individualist; indisputably 'good' rather than ambivalently subversive. In other words, such practices aim to create a discussion rather than an exhibition — or even better,

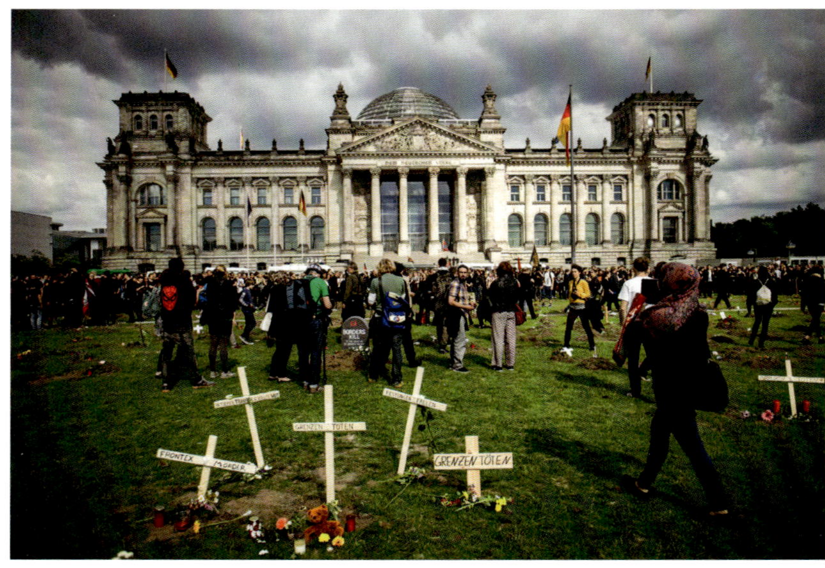

a school; better still, a commune, a political party or a bakery. Institutional critique is over; instead, the door is open to (re)construct the very thing that gives art scale, duration and – importantly – financial and organisational support: institutional activism.

There is an interesting moral undertone behind this activism. One increasingly hears that all art initiatives should be read and evaluated in a very basic, fundamental manner, in consideration of whether they do any good for society, or at least, whether they minimise harm (less transcontinental flights, less damage to the climate, less exploitation and inequality in working conditions). It is a question of the sustainable value art can produce, which, interestingly, seems to come more often from inside the art world than from outside it. And although critical observation and analysis is one obvious value that art has long produced, the current art scene seems to have lost unconditional faith in its force. Both the classical bourgeois institution of art (production of luxury commodities for individual consumption through the institution of collecting) and its cognitive-capitalist iteration (critical knowledge production for consumption through the institutions of exhibitions, biennials and, lately, artistic research) are perceived by many of their current practitioners as deeply and irrevocably flawed. Since critique itself is unsatisfactory, the 'original sin' of art is not to be dealt with through critical or self-critical practices, but only through repentance: one has to act. And indeed, it is not enough just to *act* 'good'; one must *be* 'good'. It is not an activist turn we are currently witnessing, perhaps, but an ontological one.

Should 'AOI' itself be understood as a project that operates along these lines? In other words, what were we part of, if we felt like taking part; what were we observing, if that is what we were doing there? The event was described as neither a conference nor a symposium, but nothing short of an *International* (in the revolutionary socialist sense of the word, or at least so I presumed); yet its status was something that even the organisers themselves obviously did not fully agree on. In his opening speech, Staal said he truly hoped it would not be 'one more thematic conference leading to the inevitable next', but a formative congress of artists who would no longer be betrayed by curators and institutions; who would proceed instead through self-organisation, 'regain[ing] control over the means of production, distribution and dissemination of the practice of art'. And yet, the very next speaker was a curator (invited, like myself, to moderate one of the panels), who did not hide the fact that everything at this event was 'very interesting' to him; he was there to research, to get an overview of a recent tendency of artists who defy research. Throughout the congress there were also complaints of being paired with groups who were not sufficiently activist or, at the other end of the scale, not sufficiently artistic, and while as an observer I was able to take intellectual pleasure in such quirky variety, there were people who felt insulted by exactly that. It was also clear that some attendees expected the literal inauguration of an 'organisation of artist organisations'; others simply took the title as a figure of speech. I can only suspect that the organisers anticipated that these conflicts and contradictions might work dialectically. And to a certain extent, they did.

The particular confusion between the regime of representation and critique understood as 'art' and the activist regime of 'real life' is something new. Whereas once upon a time the viewer who jumped onstage in order to save Desdemona was called naïve, naïvety is now rehabilitated as a revolutionary instrument; the activist turn insists on reconsidering any sort of art and reading it at face value. This shift should be distinguished from the historical avant-garde's claims of blurring the boundaries between art and life, since it was still under the rules of art's typical uselessness that avant-gardist 'art-life' works were to be judged. It is well known that Vladimir Tatlin's *Letatlin* (1929–31) did not, in fact, fly; and it is not by the body count that we assess the self-shooting scenarios of Chris Burden or Marina Abramović. Institutional-activist initiatives, by contrast, will hardly brag about their ineffectiveness. Here, we are finally out in the real world, bidding farewell to the arts and their cult of failure, and recognising initiatives by their fruit.

Here's an anecdote on the subject. Some years ago, at one of the many infamous court cases against artists in Russia, one gallerist made the familiar argument that art should not be interpreted literally.[4] The example he gave was Ilya Repin's huge and chilling *Ivan the Terrible and His Son Ivan on November 16, 1581* (1885), where the tsar is depicted just after killing his son. It would be naïve, the gallerist argued, to understand the painting as an appeal to murder. It is an artwork, not reality – not a pipe, in other words. Although all the traditions of modernism, the avant-gardes, even classical art might seem to support the gallerist's argument, he would have found much less understanding at 'AOI'. The representation of a murder scene, as artistic as it may be, nonetheless spreads uncontrollably into reality; the literal meaning cannot be excluded, and should perhaps even be the first to be considered. A pipe is a pipe after all, hence it is the right thing to 'call a pipe a pipe'. In fact, Repin would have agreed: *Ivan the Terrible* was painted as a political

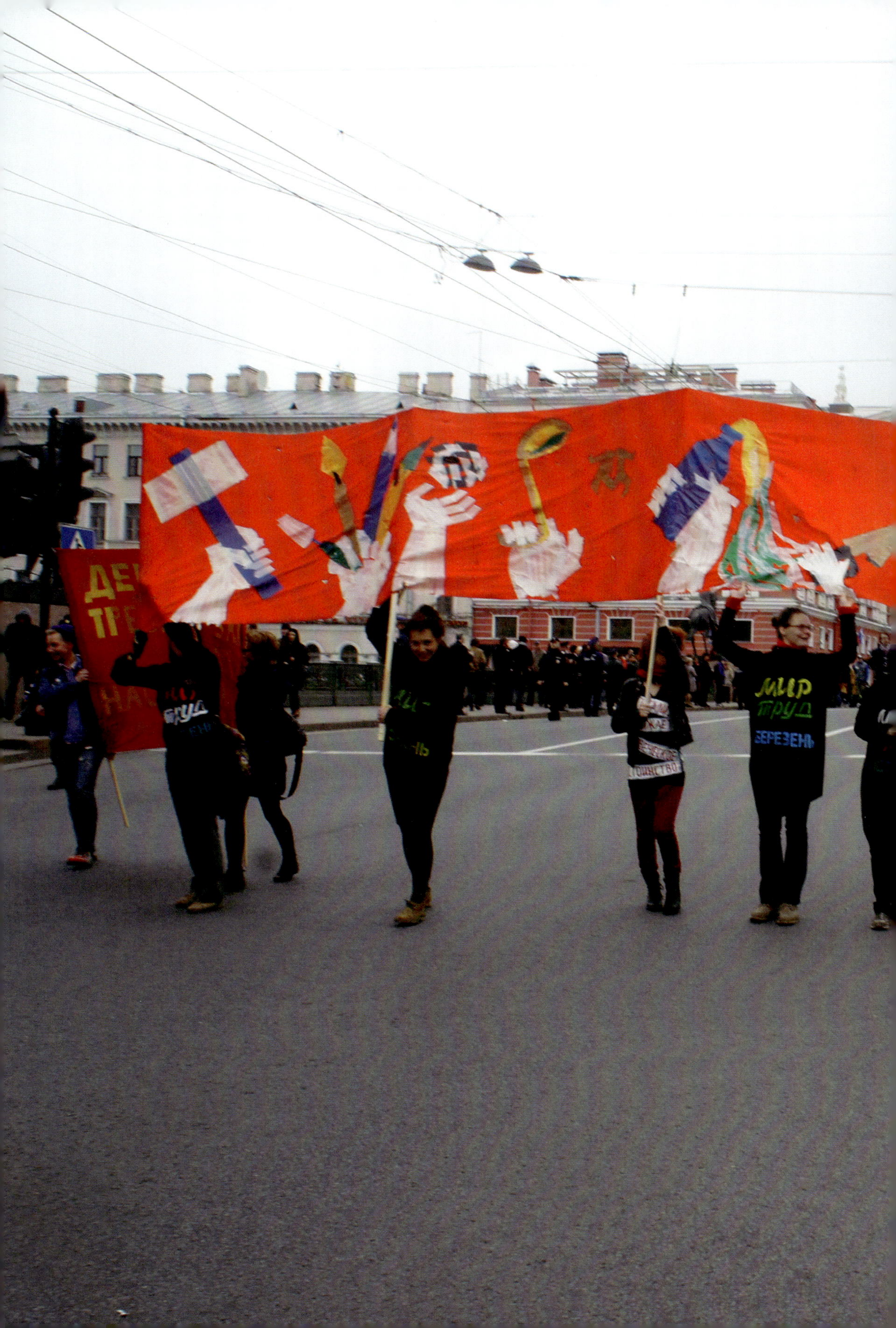
МИР
труд
БЕРЕЗЕНЬ

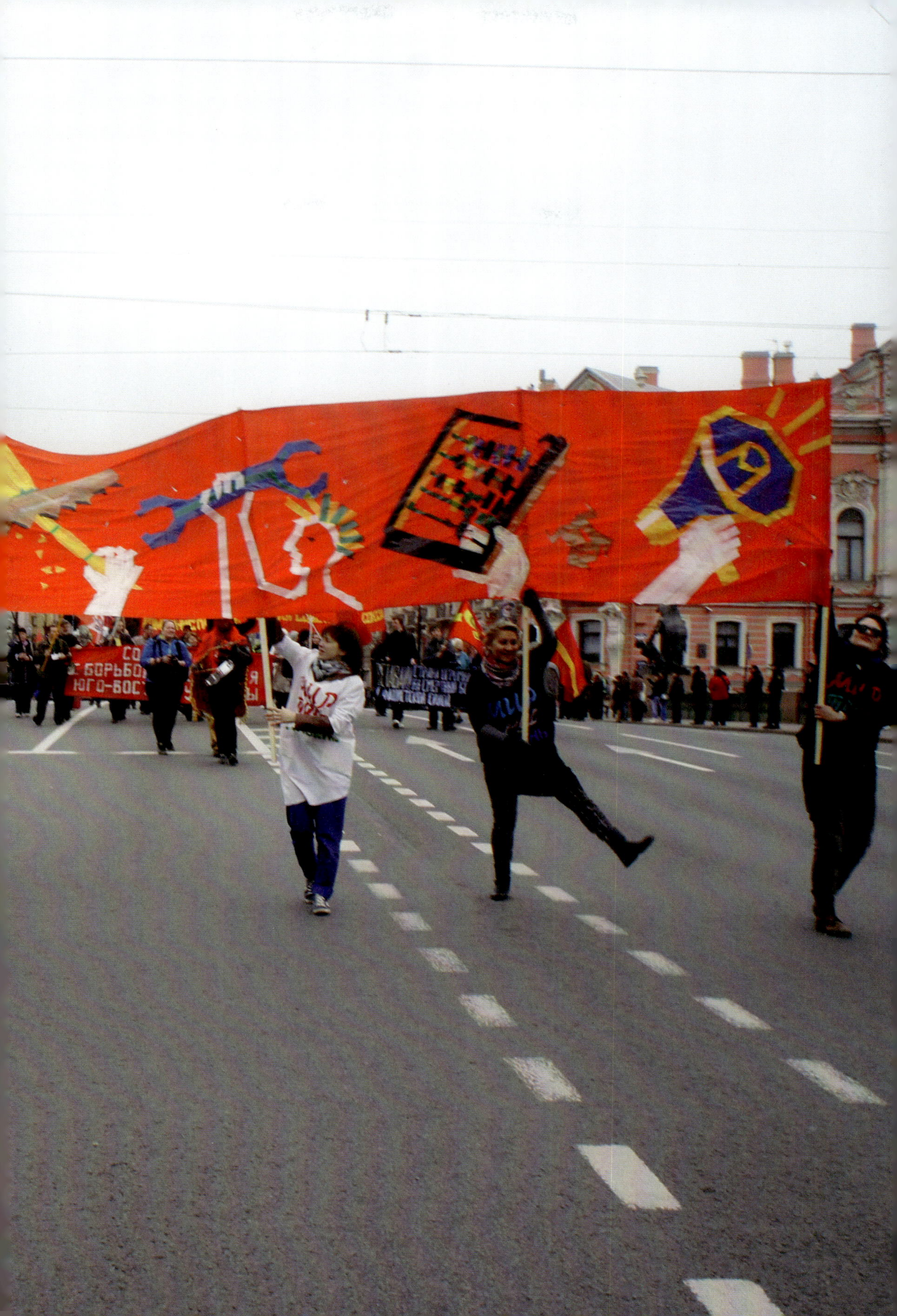

statement on the occasion of the terrorist assassination of Tsar Alexander II, its argument being that tsars were guilty of murder themselves, that violence breeds violence. The painting thus incorporates a dimension of real political action as part of its representational field.

'AOI' was similarly suspended between these two modes, and interestingly the mode of the 'real' (a political congress) required a larger infusion of art to support its claim than would have been expected within the mode of art-related critical research (a conference). There is something I call the 'hammer-and-sickle effect', which occurs when artists grow extremely sentimental about political one-liners and start to see them as 'good' in a moral, not just aesthetic, sense, using them to mark their identity and their territory. The inverted theatre at 'AOI' – (over-)designed in the brisk and vigorous style of Russian Constructivism – was indeed a one-liner. But between this strong design and the limp human figures who spoke in front of it, between the revolutionary mood of the set and the general depressive-as-usual tone of the presentations – between ideal and reality, if I may – there was an interesting gap, a telling disjuncture, so wide that it is impossible to bridge in one swoop (the sort of swift formal swoop that characterises so many of today's multimedia tours de force, performances and performance-lectures). I had expected that at least some of the organisations would be flamboyantly fictitious, but they all tended towards plain speech, without a performance-lecture in sight. And as the congress evolved into something slightly awkward, I found this disjointedness between actors and stage design stimulating and perversely enjoyable. The situation put me in mind of the 7th Berlin Biennale in 2012, curated by Artur Żmijewski (with Warsza as an associate curator), which was supposed to demonstrate the triumph of activist art, only to show its epic failure – but epic, nevertheless. At that moment, the defeat of activism seemed definitive; yet, in Beckettian style, it continues to 'fail better' again and again.

Regardless of whether the International of Artist Organisations will ever be inaugurated, it might make sense to take a closer look at this new tendency. It is often observed that in the previous regime of critical art, the role of the artist was strongly eclipsed by that of the curator, which increasingly led to artists either assuming this role themselves or excluding this figure in a self-organised, activist mode. Both paths generated interesting results, with the activist mode offering the more oppositional, anti-institutional approach. But what happens when this activism abandons its oppositional stance and reverses the paradigm, proposing institutional activism as the main mode of an avant-garde? Under these conditions, who are we finding in the curator's stead? Who are artists here competing or aligning themselves with, who are they gravitating towards, whose role are they taking on?

It is obvious to me that the answer to these questions is: the state. There always has been some longing for the state in the left-wing art scene, with its wariness of private money and private modes of production, with its insistence on identifying the artist as worker rather than entrepreneur. This attitude has been strongly reasserted recently by organisations such as W.A.G.E.:[5] artists are claiming the right of artist fees rather than relying on the vague promise

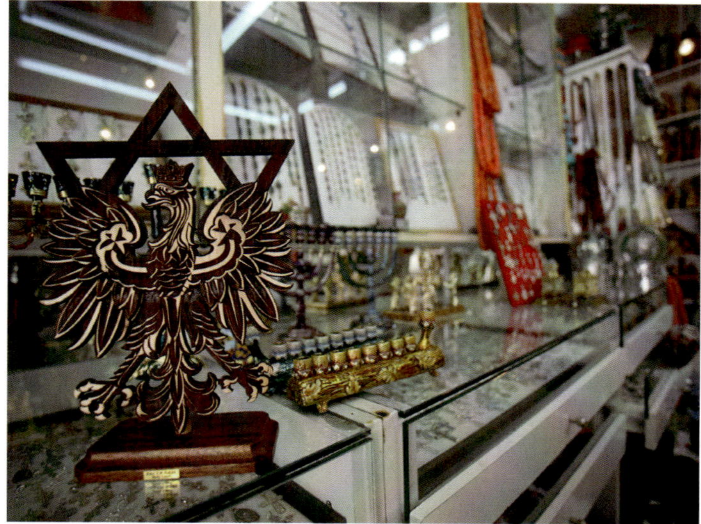

Yael Bartana,
*Das Symbol
der Bewegung
Jüdischer
Wiedergeburt in
Polen entdeckt
auf einem Markt /
The emblem
of the Jewish
Renaissance
Movement in
Poland seen
in a market*,
2011. Photo
© Nir Shaanani.
Courtesy the
artist and KW
Institute for
Contemporary
Art, Berlin

of the private market, which shows, of course, their awareness of their own precarity as well as highlighting the inequitable labour norms of the cultural field. Yet, it also suggests a potential willingness, or at a least lack of aversion, towards identifying as paid employees. The artist as a contract worker who is given a thematic frame that is oftentimes ideological and political – this is not the 'free', 'independent' artist. And so, just as they finally dealt with curators, artists may look forward to a time when they might cut state or state-like organisations out of the loop entirely by assuming their functions and then giving this frame to others. Today, the state is becoming the horizon of artists' ambitions.

This situation recalls the dilemma, according to Breton, that the contemporary artist was facing in 1935 (with reference to Karl Marx's famous eleventh thesis on Feuerbach[6]): 'The very urgency of the task of changing the world, such as it appears to us, commonly leads people to believe that all available means ought to be enlisted in its service, that the pursuit of all other intellectual tasks should be postponed.'[7] Breton himself is clearly on the side of discursive practice that 'raises awareness', that works on the conscience (this is the core of Marxism to him), but he also admits this is because he resides in the West, where artists 'live in open conflict with the immediate world', a world *without an alibi*. His Russian comrades in the USSR can permit themselves to be, as he puts it, 'witnessing and participating' as they are building a completely new world.[8]

It is Breton's path, not the path of the Russian comrades, that Western academic Marxism has taken in the aftermath of 1968 – the path of individualism, criticism and constant reminders that the world around us has no alibi. Since this aftermath remains traumatic, it is no surprise that today's artists express their dissatisfaction by shifting towards collectivism and action. In something that could be described as a desperate act of regression, artists appear to be returning to the mid-century in order to correct historical mistakes – the type of the state they are longing for, and compete with through their artistic NGOs, is obviously the welfare state. Importantly, this was a time when artistic freedom seemed unshakable, and when the avant-garde, despite its unpopularity, still benefited from the political climate of the Cold War – this art represented the 'free world' (something not really on the table anymore). In the same desire to reconstruct the Cold War ideological balance, artists often flirt with the re-enactment of the missing Soviet Union that worked as a counterweight to the Western system: they recreate their 'imaginary communism' under whose conditions they can 'witness' (the return of realist practices, in drawing as well as documentary film this time, is another tendency that is clearly in the air) and 'participate'.[9] But it is not just participation that is on the agenda now, it is also its bureaucratisation – not just 'imaginary communism', but something closer to 'really existing socialism'. Needless to say, this idea of the Soviet Union as the realm of collectivism, solidarity and state support is totally fictitious; after 1968 (which, in this part of the world, was about the collapse of the Prague Spring), self-reflection, criticism, despair and extreme individualism were dominating the social landscape to a much greater extent, it seems to me, than in the West.

In any case, the idea of artists' organisations seems to be rooted in all sorts of deep leftist traumas. In a recent conversation with Peter Engelmann, Alain Badiou claimed that 'the defeat of the Paris Commune gradually led most revolutionary militants to embrace the idea that a well-structured party was necessary, that representation was necessary'.[10] This desire to compete with the state machine brought violence into the picture – the left's fascination with violence is no secret, of course – but the catastrophic fortunes of really existing communist states in the last century has no doubt indelibly marked the left's collective psyche. (Perhaps all the more so for not being immediately apparent to Western intellectuals who, as Badiou has noted, once greeted this violence with great optimism.) In the Constructivist environment of 'AOI', it was difficult not to compare the congress with the leftist congresses of artists and writers during the 1930s. The USSR Union of Artists was inaugurated in 1932 as an open and participatory group of like-minded cultural producers as well as a platform for the representation of different artists' collectives and individuals, an instrument of assistance for their work and life. It was almost an artists' state. But even before it was appropriated by the real Stalinist state (which would happen a couple of years after its founding), it revealed a dimension of violence and exclusion: discussions led to expulsions and *Berufsverbots*, non-aligned members were not tolerated and political intransigence overtook artistic radicalism. When Staal claimed that 'institutions should adapt their ethical stances to those of artists', I shivered slightly, imagining the fate of artists who would not agree to be a monolithic group with a unanimous idea of moral standards. I also wondered what the relation of a union of artists who have organisations might be to other artists who are not protected by those initiatives. Should an International of Artist Organisations come about, could any artist turn to it for help, or only members? Would it offer a hierarchical relationship? A representational model? A relation of exclusion?

Or perhaps these concerns are just my Soviet paranoia. Maybe organisational artistic initiatives are a way of pragmatic survival for artists in the world of creative capitalism, where the traditional art market is not supporting them anymore, or only marginally, but art is invited to infiltrate every zone of life. It is a step similar to the move towards institutionalised 'artistic research' in academia, which, for years now, has been formalising and bureaucratising the existing inclination of contemporary artists towards processing information, documenting and archiving. In the same way that artists feel economically and socially safer by becoming university professors, they may feel safer in many different ways by becoming directors, or even honorary directors, of organisations, platforms or obscure institutes, and this tells us something about the world we are living in: among other things, that art is now much more welcome in the capitalist system than it was at the time of Breton. He had to defend the role of art in society, citing Leon Trotsky's claim of the human right 'not only to bread but to poetry'.[10] Whatever good or bad poetry can do now, it seems to come in larger supply than bread.

Notes

[1] André Breton, 'Political Position of Today's Art' (1935), *Manifestoes of Surrealism* (trans. Richard Seaver and Helen R. Lane), Ann Arbor: University of Michigan Press / Ann Arbor Paperbacks, 1972, pp.212–33.

[2] 'Artist Organisations International', Hebbel am Ufer, Berlin, 9–11 January 2015. Except where noted, quotations in this article are taken from video documentation of the event, available at http://www.artistorganisationsinternational.org.

[3] The video, which can be seen at http://www.artistorganisationsinternational.org, features footage and interviews from the region and focusses more on the political project of Rojava than any organisation of artists as such. The video was co-produced by the New World Academy, an academy established by Jonas Staal and BAK, Utrecht in 2013, and connected to the New World Summit, also founded by Staal, in 2012, which is 'dedicated to providing "alternative parliaments" hosting organisations that currently find themselves excluded from democracy'. See http://newworldsummit.eu/about/.

[4] The gallerist in question was Marat Guelman, who posted about the case on his blog on 26 August 2012. See http://snob.ru/profile/5167/blog/page/2?perPage=25.

[5] W.A.G.E. (Working Artists and the Greater Economy) is a 'New York–based activist organisation focussed on regulating the payment of artist fees by non-profit art institutions'. See http://www.wageforwork.com.

[6] 'Philosophers have only interpreted the world, in various ways; the point is to change it.' Karl Marx, 'Theses on Feuerbach' (1845, trans. W. Lough), in *Karl Marx and Frederick Engels Selected Works*, vol.1, Moscow: Progress Publishers, 1969, pp.13–15; available at https://www.marxists.org/archive/marx/works/1845/theses/theses.htm.

[7] A. Breton, 'Political Position of Today's Art', *op. cit.*, p.223.

[8] *Ibid.*, p.216.

[9] Claire Bishop has been critically addressing what she calls 'the social turn' for a decade now, and her diagnosis of the discursive criteria of socially engaged art as being 'drawn from a tacit analogy between anti-capitalism and the Christian "good soul"' is still relevant. See C. Bishop, *Artificial Hells: Participatory Art and the Politics of Spectatorship*, London: Verso, 2012, pp.39–40.

[10] Alain Badiou and Peter Engelmann, *Philosophy and the Idea of Communism* (trans. Susan Spitzer), Cambridge: Polity Press, 2015, p.85.

[11] Leon Trotsky, 'To the Memory of Sergei Essenin' (1926), as cited by A. Breton in 'Political Position of Today's Art', *op. cit.*, p.228.

III.
Institutional Histories?

David Morris, Charles Esche and Lucy Steeds

Questions of instituting have always shaped the *Exhibition Histories* project. Through an approach grounded in the material conditions of exhibition – a materialism in several senses of the word[1] – the importance of attending more closely to the 'slower', longer or more concerted histories of institutions has come to the fore. This final section of the book imbricates the field of exhibition histories explicitly with that of art institutions.[2] It presents a number of texts that seek to explore how exhibitions connect with – or develop into – longer-term projects, and how recurring events, instituent practices and institutional formation allow for a more sustainable approach to art becoming public, or to nurturing publics for art. It also seeks to interrogate and de-naturalise dominant assumptions around notions of 'public' that are invested in false notions of universality and discriminate on grounds of disability, race, gender and sexuality as part of a wider condition of ongoing colonial violence, as Khairani Barokka argues in these pages.[3] This underlines the need to combine concrete critical scrutiny of established institutions with careful investigation of the possibilities raised by more speculative and propositional practices.

Rather than fixing and defining terms, we hope to preserve an openness towards what the study of institutions might mean in different places and at different times.[4] Our wish is that small- and large-scale, local, national and international claims of relevance and modes of funding do not play a determining role in which institutions might be worthy of study. Our premise is that all are potentially worthy. The perspectives that follow are assembled and offered in the spirit of what Tonika Sealy Thompson and Stefano Harney here describe as 'reading together', grounded in what they describe as Afro-Asian intellectual projects:

> *Reading together, silently or aloud, belongs with dancing together, cooking together, drinking together, watching movies together, building and cultivating together – and making together. Rather than understanding making as the result of successful social reproduction, we practise it as a temporary emanation, a stepping out without stepping away, where art remains part of the life-giving arts, not a superior comment on them or achievement based on their reproductive support.[5]*

Consistent with the earlier parts of this book, we look back as far as the early 1990s. In the contributions to this section, we again move across a number of historical and geographical lineages. In parts of Latin America, for instance, the concept of the 'integral museum', developed in the 1970s, drove new methodologies in museology prompting a proliferation of community museums by the 1990s. An institution such as the Museo Comunitario del Valle de Xico, established in 1996, saw its founding mission as the preservation of the heritage of the local community, which has expanded to include defending the land and water rights of indigenous peoples in the area against neoliberal extractivism.[6] Also in the 1990s, understandings of 'institutional critique' – which may be traced back to Europe and the United States around 1968; complemented and challenged by contemporaneous practices in Latin America – were usurped by manifold approaches to the institution as a more complex platform, understood by those connected with it as an ambivalent space with potential for both allyship and instrumentalisation. Artists, curators and others began to play around with the status of the institution, forming their own organisations and initiatives – both real and fictional – working with and against the demands of museums and art centres depending on what they saw as possible in given situations.[7] Across the present book we see disparate examples of this in operation in Bangkok, Berlin, Dakar, Dhaka, Jakarta, Johannesburg, Lisbon, the Visayas islands and elsewhere.

Most notable in the context of Western and Central Europe of the 1990s, perhaps, was the rise of curators schooled in institutional critique taking up directorships in various cities and seeking to test out the limits of what came to be called 'institutionality', typically under the banner of 'New Institutionalism'. Such museums and art centres were managed on the basis that the programme, relations with various publics and forms of commissioning and collecting could be looked at as a whole and understood within a particular curatorial or artistic framework. Some related concerns fed the establishment of the Institute for International Visual Arts (Iniva) in London at this time, which moreover refused the privileging of European or US practice as a basis for convening publics. The shifting fortunes of institutions over the years are reflected in this anthology's essay analysing Iniva at a moment of crisis a few years ago now.[8] The organisation's recent renewal, as a post-academy research agency, gives us hope.

As the essays in this section attest, institutional dynamics are best understood without recourse to hierarchies drawn up on the basis of scale, size, media attention or longevity. The binary understandings on which those criteria typically rely ('major' versus small-scale; establishment versus artist-run; public versus private; independent versus state-run, to name a few) are not always useful in looking for how institutional invention or responsiveness takes shape. The institutions described here may be better approached in terms of their *inter*dependence.[9] The following texts address diverse efforts and all should invoke any number of interrelations with other organisations and agencies. What might be seen in many ways as typical of the arts institution hailed as 'major' under neoliberalism – for instance, the Museum of Art, Architecture and Technology (MAAT) in Lisbon, which is described by Ana Teixeira Pinto as part of a familiar complex of real-estate speculation, city branding, 'starchitecture' and gentrification – is also anachronistic in certain respects. Pinto argues that one of the most curious features of this art-led gentrification is its occurrence in a place without a particularly well established art scene, and that this may be a symbol of what 'contemporary art' is at present.[10] The wider situation she describes is characterised by the sheer variety of institutions that participate in 'contemporary art', across a range of sizes, funding structures and agendas.[11]

A focus on institutional histories also foregrounds certain processes and practices that are crucial to the narratives of art that museums and related organisations shape and uphold. Bureaucratic and administrative matters do not always make for the most edifying or eye-catching aspects of institutional life, but they are fundamental to the reproduction of the same. Pursuing a more radical approach to museology may benefit from understanding these mechanisms. Consider, for example, the implications of exhibition-making on the acquisitions strategies of modern art (and 'other') museums. The *Exhibition Histories* project has addressed this in various ways, for instance in published research on the 1989 exhibitions 'Magiciens de la Terre' and 'The Other Story: Afro-Asian Artists in Post-War Britain', which have had complex legacies in France and Britain respectively, both in terms of the collection versus destruction of the artworks exhibited and regarding display versus storage, or indeed de-accessioning, post acquisition.[12] What determines whether an artwork ends up in the Musée national d'art modern or the Musée national des Arts d'Afrique et d'Océanie (turned Quai Branly), in France, or, in the UK, in Tate's collections of modern and contemporary art, the V&A Museum or the British Museum? The many years that it took Rasheed Araeen, curator of 'The Other Story', to intervene in the politics of national-canon formation reflect the stubborn entrenchment of racism and other forms of exclusion in the British establishment, as well as the slow, uneven and not-always-forwards progress of institutional transformation – but also the necessity for strength and perseverance given the steady urgency of this work.

A national collection may be understood as a kind of social-cultural archive, a set of 'images' and objectified imaginings of life in common; this underlines its significance for social reproduction. In this sense, such collections are repositories of history, but also of shared futures. The changing status of collections and archives themselves in recent decades, alongside dynamics of marketisation, enclosure and extractivism, reflect that 'Imperial citizenship needs a past. The role of institutions such as archives and museums in the "preservation" of the past is the effect of a vast enterprise of destruction conducted at the expense of and as a substitute for destroyed worlds.' Ariella Aïsha Azoulay suggests 'unlearning' and 'rewinding' as ways

> *to insist on the existence of different patterns and incommensurable modal-*
> *ities of citizenship experienced prior to colonisation by different groups and*
> *peoples who shared their worlds as cocitizens of different sorts in the societies*
> *in which they lived. Such a movement is to embrace the incommensurability*
> *as a common ground upon which imperial citizenship cannot be assumed to*
> *embody the invariable model against which other modalities are evaluated.*[13]

The necessity of a plurality and multiplicity of institutional models leads on to questions of institution-building and the development of institutional networks. *Exhibition Histories* publications on biennials in São Paulo and Havana, for example, have developed an understanding of these two long-standing national institutions given historical perspectives; understanding their genesis and development in relation to nation-state diplomacy, 'soft power' and the geo-political eras in which they emerged. The second book in the *Exhibition Histories* series addressed the Bienal de la Habana's founding ambition to establish a transnational network of practices across what is now known as the Global South in the context of 1980s Cold War geo-political binarism.[14] At the other end of this era is the establishment of the Bienal de São Paulo in the

1950s as the second-oldest international biennial, after Venice – an initiative driven by Brazilian elite and industrialist ambitions to assert the nation's position as allied to the US and as leading Latin America. Lisette Lagnado has highlighted the 1998 edition's significance in establishing an understanding of modernity particular to the Brazilian context, as well as the under-recognised efforts made by that edition to establish links with loaning institutions in other parts of the world as a basis for future exhibitions.[15]

In a recent account of 'obstacles to exhibition history', David Teh highlights another set of problems with the supposedly universal applicability of traditional constructions of 'the public institution'. With particular reference to Southeast Asia, he notes that exhibitions in the region are produced by very different power relations from those found in the West, or Global North. Noting important structural differences, amongst them authoritarianism, censorship and self-censorship, he writes that 'the First-World notion of an independent public institution, subject to bureaucratic review yet operating at arm's length from government, is an exotic one in Southeast Asia.'[16] Over the time span this book covers, institutional actors have seen their places of work and production become more flexible, fungible and fragile as a result of privatisation and globalisation, with a concomitant re-emergence of reactionary populist and authoritarian forms of governance. The project of historicising and contextualising institutions therefore needs to construct frameworks of analysis that are sensitive to the different political and material circumstances that prevail in particular places and times; where 'art' is understood as a product of these relationships and conditions of possibility. The need to do so stems from a recognition that the presumption of stable civic institutions, and the public sphere presumptions on which the Western museum is based, do not reflect current realities, especially at a moment when neoliberalism has thoroughly eroded what were presumed to be 'eternal' institutions in the West – just as art's 'authentic' and 'eternal' status has for even longer been called into question.

In current times of generalised uncertainty, the necessity of understanding historically what makes an institution sustainable – and what makes one insecure – seems increasingly pressing. There is newfound precarity for public institutions in the historic West, or newly defined Global North, through the impoverishments of neoliberalism; and there is some newfound ingenuity by way of response. There is also a collectivised learning to live with and through loss. Gabi Ngcobo has described the short-lived Johannesburg Biennale as a 'phantom limb' in the imaginary of the art scenes of South Africa.[17] The Center for Historical Reenactments (CHR), the collective formed by Ngcobo and others, may be understood in some respects as an outgrowth of this institution's absence after its second edition in 1997, even while CHR was then carefully killed off by its protagonists.[18] Compare the winding up of Chiang Mai Social Installation (CMSI), an artist-led series of festivals in Northern Thailand during the mid 1990s, which some of the organisers suggest needed to be dissolved precisely in order to avoid looming institutionalism.[19] Yet we'd like to consider simultaneously the initiative VIVA ExCon, which is discussed here by Võ Hồng Chương-Đài as following a singular path through the decades of its existence since 1990.[20] Both CMSI and VIVA ExCon complicate any norms that might be summarised in the name of 'Asian biennialisation' in the 1990s.[21]

CMSI, VIVA ExCon and CHR each approach the zone of the institutional field that is sometimes tagged with terms such as 'artist-led', 'self-organised', 'instituent' or 'para-institutional'. The activities of APTART in Moscow during the 1980s,[22] or the projects of Mujeres Creando (in this section) or ruangrupa (in the previous section), might also be understood in such terms. Again, it is important to avoid falling into binaries around, for instance, 'official' versus 'unofficial' practices, curatorial versus artistic agency or 'proper-' versus 'para-institutions'. In our understanding, institutionality is a matter of degree along different dimensions or – better – of orientation. It is also worth bearing in mind that ruangrupa and Mujeres Creando, for instance, provide services within their localities that exceed what might be expected or considered the norm for cultural organisations.[23] The selection of texts in what follows seeks to open out the ways in which various popular binaries – including those already mentioned, also top-down versus ground-up, bureaucratic versus artistic – may be dynamised, or indeed dynamited, to enrich the potentials of institutionality through and around art for publics.

Asked to reflect on art's exhibition histories, Brook Andrew has written: 'To be antagonistic towards histories of imperialism, through an exhibition, involves a dismantling of the institution itself.'[24] This provides inspiration for how we may understand past exhibitions and the organisations that have supported them, within and against the entanglements of imperial history. However, challenging imperialism in what we do surely involves an unlearning of the imperial dynamic of European thought and the very words we then use. Writing in the context of a recent edition of the Bienal de São Paulo, Denise Ferreira da Silva has asked us to contemplate 'the dissolution of the grip of the Understanding and the releasing of The World to the imagination'. What would institutional histories, emerging from exhibition histories, on this basis, then be? Perhaps a response to sociality as nurtured through and around art, where sociality is reimagined, after Ferreira da Silva, 'in such a way that attending to difference does not presuppose *separability*, *determinacy* and *sequentiality*, the three ontological pillars the sustain modern thought.'[25] If we have already put into question 'art', 'history' and 'exhibition' (in the overall introduction to this book) with more destabilising of 'the public' and 'the institution' (in this section introduction), let us now move to 'understanding', 'world', 'space' and 'time'. Perhaps, by thinking about institutions together with exhibitions in this way, through and with sociality, we can re-entangle ourselves otherwise. The following texts are offered by way of invitation.

Notes

1 As elaborated in the earlier section introductions, 'Making Art Global?' and 'Artist/Curator/Other?' in this volume, and also in the overall introduction to this book.

2 Yaiza Hernández Velázquez opens this section with a critical analysis of the intellectual and institutional forces that have produced such an imbrication, as well as of its potential for more radical reformulations. See Y. Hernández Velázquez, 'Who Needs Exhibition Studies?', in this volume.

3 Khairani Barokka, '"Public" and "Access": Genealogies of Theft, Community, Violence and Pedagogies', in this volume.

4 Zdenka Badovinac suggests that the definition of the art institution is itself flexible and that 'distinguishing institutions and organisations facilitates discussion of the relationship between them, examining the different contribution each makes to social change'. See Z. Badovinac, 'My Post-Catastrophic Glossary', in this volume. We use both terms rather indiscriminately here, following many of the assembled authors, because art institutions remain the most common collective term of address for museums, exhibition spaces, artists' initiatives and the rest of the non-commercial art infrastructure.

5 Tonika Sealy Thompson and Stefano Harney, 'Ground Provisions', in this volume.

6 See Genaro Amaro Altamirano in conversation with Ana Bilbao, 'Museo Comunitario del Valle de Xico: A Community's Trench of Struggle', in this volume. See also Y. Hernández Velázquez, 'Imagining Curatorial Practice After 1972', in Paul O'Neill, Simon Sheikh, Lucy Steeds and Mick Wilson (ed.), *Curating After the Global: Roadmaps for the Present*, Cambridge, MA: MIT Press, 2019.

7 An analysis of artist-led organisations gathered as part of 'Artists Organisations International' in Berlin in 2015 is given in Ekaterina Degot, 'The Artist as Director: "Artist Organisations International" and its Contradictions', in this volume.

8 See Eddie Chambers, 'Iniva: Everything Crash', in this volume.

9 Small scale organisations can and do work together to raise their voices and those of their publics, of course. To this end, for example, Afterall was one of the founding partners of Common Practice in London in 2009. Research emerging from this ongoing initiative can be consulted online: https://www.commonpractice.org.uk/research-papers/.

10 See Ana Teixeira Pinto, 'The Art of Gentrification: The Lisbon Version', in this volume.

11 It is worth noting that this ecosystem is structured in part through the exclusion of Afro-Portuguese voices from the privileged *lugar de fala* (place of speech). See Carlos Garrido Castellano and Jerssi Esperança Restino Paulo, 'Unapologetic Soundings of Afro-Portuguese Creativity', *Afterall*, issue 47, Spring/Summer 2019, pp.127–35.

12 See the contribution of Lucy Steeds to *Making Art Global (Part 2): 'Magiciens de la Terre' 1989*, London: Afterall, 2013, pp.85–88; and her essay 'Retelling "The Other Story" – or What Now?', 2018, available at https://www.afterall.org/exhibition/the-other-story/retelling-the-other-story-or-what-now/.

13 Ariella Aïsha Azoulay, *Potential History: Unlearning Imperialism*, London: Verso, 2019, p.19.

14 See Rachel Weiss et al., *Making Art Global (Part 1): The Third Havana Biennial 1989*, London: Afterall Books, 2011.

15 See Lisette Lagnado, 'Anthropophagy as Cultural Strategy: The 24th Bienal de São Paulo', in Pablo Lafuente and L. Lagnado (ed.), *Cultural Anthropophagy: The 24th Bienal de São Paulo 1998*, London: Afterall Books, 2016.

16 David Teh, 'Obstacles to Exhibition History: Institutions, Curatorship and the Undead Nation-State', in P. O'Neill, L. Steeds and M. Wilson (ed.), *The Curatorial Conundrum: What to Study? What to Research? What to Practice?*, Cambridge, MA: MIT Press, 2016.

17 Gabi Ngcobo, speaking at 'New Institutionalisation & Neoliberal Frameworks: Shall We Stop Producing Altogether?', 27 February 2021, part of the South South Think Tank hosted by Elvira Dyangani Ose for The Showroom, London.

18 See Khwezi Gule, 'Center for Historical Reenactments: Is the Tale Chasing its Own Tail?', in this volume.

19 See 'Oral Histories of Chiang Mai Social Installation', in David Teh and David Morris (ed.), *Artist-to-Artist: Independent Art Festivals in Chiang Mai 1992–98*, London: Afterall Books, 2018, pp.75–85.

20 Chương-Đài Võ, 'VIVA ExCon: Itinerant Indeterminacy', in this volume.

21 See Charles Green and Anthony Gardner, '1989: Asian Biennalization', in *Biennials, Triennials and Documenta: The Exhibitions that Created Contemporary Art*, Hoboken, NJ: Wiley-Blackwell, 2016.

22 See Margarita Tupitsyn, Victor Tupitsyn and David Morris (ed.), *Anti-Shows: APTART 1982–84*, London: Afterall Books, 2017.

23 For instance, Mujeres Creando's artistic-political interventions are developed from La Virgen de los Deseos (Our Lady of Desires), their shared house in La Paz, which has taken on the func-

tions of creche, café, restaurant, library, grocery and pharmacy, as well as providing legal aid and social programmes. See 'To the Last Consequences: Mujeres Creando in Conversation with Max Jorge Hinderer Cruz and Pablo Lafuente', *Afterall*, issue 46, Autumn/Winter 2018, pp.55–65; and Mujeres Creando, 'La creatividad es un instrumento de lucha y el cambio social un hecho creativo (Creativity Is an Instrument of Struggle, and Social Change a Creative Act)', in this volume. As another example, in the midst of the Covid-19 pandemic in 2020, ruangrupa (who are discussed in David Teh, 'Who Cares a Lot? ruangrupa as Curatorship', in this volume) turned their operations towards the manufacturing of personal protective equipment for medical use.

[24] Brook Andrew in response to Saloni Mathur, 'Why Exhibition Histories?', *British Art Studies*, no.13, https://doi.org/10.17658/issn.2058-5462/issue-13/conversation.

[25] Denise Ferreira da Silva, 'On Difference Without Separability', in *32a São Paulo Art Biennial: 'Live Uncertainly'* (exh. cat.), São Paulo: Fundação Bienal de São Paulo, 2016, p.64.

Who Needs 'Exhibition Studies'?

Yaiza Hernández Velázquez

If there is, indeed, something we can call 'Exhibition Studies', it is institutionally weak and fairly circumscribed. Most often 'exhibition studies' crops up as a welcome support for other, more vocational courses. This is the case, for example, in the Exhibition and Curatorial Studies department at the School of the Art Institute of Chicago, the Museums and Exhibition Studies MA at the University of Illinois at Chicago or the MA Exhibition Studies at Liverpool John Moores University, which are all primarily focussed on exhibitions of contemporary art. The course I used to lead at Central Saint Martins in London, a Master of Research in Exhibition Studies, is the only one, to my knowledge, that specialises in studying the exhibition as both a historical and philosophical problem, without a component of curatorial praxis tied to it. I hasten to add, however, that this is not meant as an endorsement – to be 'the only one' is hardly something to be proud of if there is no need for one to exist at all. While I continue to teach exhibition studies and necessarily contribute in that way to shaping this field, this text responds to some of my concerns about the way it is 'shaping up'.

The appeal to the exhibition as a field of 'studies' – in a manner inaugurated by 'area studies' and popularised by countless other thematically constructed scholarly discourses such as 'cultural studies', 'gender studies', 'animal studies'… – already implicitly suggests a critical refusal of disciplinarity, or at the very least, an ability to function across disciplinary borders.[1] However, given that the most direct disciplinary restraints to the study of exhibitions would have historically come not just from Art History, but perhaps most directly from either Museum *Studies* or Curatorial *Studies*, the will to further 'undiscipline' this knowledge seems paradoxically entangled with a desire for further disciplinary differentiation. As such, it is a move that demands some scrutiny – in what follows, it is the negotiation of these borders that is scrutinised.

The first problem is, of course, the elusive nature of what 'an exhibition' is. If (as we tried to think of them at Central Saint Martins) exhibitions are moments when 'art' meets its 'publics' and we remain conscious, on the one hand, of the problematic history of how 'art' and 'publics' have been constructed in relation to power, and on the other, of their continuing resistance to being easily subsumed under such categorial constructions, then the question remains recalcitrantly unsolvable. An 'exhibition studies' that starts from that question commits itself to ongoing critical speculation on it. But even if we accept a working, 'common sense' definition of the exhibition, the difficulty does not go away. Exhibitions are resistant to scholarly research and retrospective appraisal. They are short-lived, taking place in particular locations, and when they travel they inevitably transform themselves as they do so. If the 'experience' of an exhibition is an essential part of what they are, accounting for multiple, shifting experiences after the fact is a thankless, impossible task.[2]

Taking recourse to formal analysis is made difficult by the fact that they are hard to document faithfully. Moreover, they have for the most part been scarcely and erratically documented, and only the recent surge of interest in them is starting to change this habit.[3] It is therefore not surprising that until quite recently most writing on exhibitions was carried out by critics rather than art historians. Indeed, the very genre of art criticism emerges as the appropriate kind of response to public art exhibitions. But to the extent to which the 'exhibitionary complex' – the ensemble of disciplines and techniques of display that simultaneously ordered objects for public inspection and the public that inspected them – remained as an unscrutinised background, criticism continued to pay much less attention to the exhibition form than to individual artworks.[4] It is perhaps fitting, then, that it is to Lawrence Alloway – who thought of criticism as 'short-term art history'[5] – that we owe one of the earliest works that can be retrospectively claimed for this emerging field, *From Salon to Goldfish Bowl*, his history of the Venice Biennale published in 1968.[6] There, he offers a compelling justification for studying exhibitions:

> *We tend to relate* [artworks] *to humanism rather than to the competitive area of fairs and shows. … Our preference has been for works of art as symbols of permanence rather than as complex structures subject to numerous interpretations. However, art is physically and conceptually mobile, which means that it can be seen in various contexts. As it is subject to the communications network of our time, physically and in terms of reproductive processes, some of art's talismanic solidity is reduced by the increase in connectivity. A work that was executed for a chapel and stays there, can be connected with fewer art works and environments than a work that is movable. … There are many studies of artists, schools of art, media and iconography, but not much has been written on the distribution of art. The groups that artists formed in the past to organise their own profession have been thoroughly investigated, but their more recent means of contact with an increasingly large public have been less discussed. The tendency is to study the work of art as an object, rather than as part of a communications system.[7]*

Instead of art history's traditional focus on the circumstances that surrounded the work's production, Alloway argues for approaching the artwork through its variable and defining encounters with its publics.[8] This is in line with Alloway's view of art as a network existing within a wider 'communications system',[9] but significantly for our purposes, it also makes clear that studying the exhibition is important or interesting because it allows us to expand outwards from the artwork, to think of art as something *other, or more than* an (art) object. And it is this broadening of the scope that seems to necessitate a transgressing of disciplinary borders.

However, much has changed since Alloway published his pioneering work in 1968. In the wake of the proliferation of academic courses on curating in the 1990s, the study of exhibitions has received an unprecedented amount of attention. The majority of significant art historical works that existed until then were clustered around the nineteenth century, the time of the emergence of public exhibiting institutions.[10] Museological writing, while more abundant, paid scant attention to specifically artistic exhibitions, and the most critical strands associated with new or critical museologies had tended to turn their gaze outside the museum altogether.[11] To the above, we could add the genre of books aimed at illustrating techniques of display that often situated themselves within architecture or design, casually straddling the line between the commercial and scholarly applications.[12] Within this context, the publication in 1976 of Brian O'Doherty's *Inside the White Cube* constitutes a watershed moment, problematising the 'exhibitionary complex' of contemporary art institutions – the novelty of this intervention justifies its enduring appeal.[13]

But as the *authorial* profile of curators has grown in step with academisation, so has interest in the exhibition.[14] Understood in itself as an artistic medium, the exhibition has increasingly become the focus of contemporary art criticism, occasionally at the expense of individual artworks. Monographs on exhibitions are now routine. Important early works like Bruce Altshuler's *The Avant Garde in Exhibition* (1994) and Mary Anne Staniszewski's *The Power of Display* (1998) opened the way for art historical studies either of a sweeping nature, like Isabel Tejeda's *El montaje expositivo como traducción* (2006) and Charlotte Klonk's *Spaces of Experience* (2009), or centred on particular authors, periods or institutions, such as Kristina Wilson's *The Modern Eye* (2009).[15] As a genre it has proved appealing enough to accommodate the publication of coffee table anthologies.[16] Early anthologies like *Visual Display* (1995) and *Thinking About Exhibitions* (1996) also opened the way for more theoretical reflections on the exhibition form.[17] Despite my necessary bias, I think it is fair to suggest that the *Exhibition Histories* series produced by my colleagues at Afterall constitutes the more sustained effort to navigate the line between attention to the social and historical character of particular exhibitions and theoretical reflection that remains less wedded to *art* history. This proliferation of literature has been accompanied by a steady stream of research projects, articles, PhD theses, conferences, symposia… And to all of the above we need to add a growing interest on the part of institutions in revisiting their exhibitions archives and, in some fortunate cases, making them more widely available, a tendency that has developed in tandem to the ongoing enthusiasm for reconstructing or re-staging exhibitions.

But however abundant these publications might be, they are also heterogeneous enough to suggest tensions within this emerging field of 'studies', even if for the most part they have remained implicit. Indeed, the broadening of focus that Alloway advocates has not survived this boom in the literature. In this way, for example, in the introduction to the influential volume *Thinking About Exhibitions*, mentioned above, the editors explicitly distance themselves from museological concerns, making the case for an exhibition-specific study on the following basis:

> *The literature relating to museums tends to minimize instances of protest and scandal and often isolates the implications of the architectural or spatial surround. The discourse also ignores the increasingly varied sites and forms for constructing, experiencing and understanding exhibitions outside museums. A tendency to stress the seemingly fixed characteristics of permanent displays has deflected attention from the ever-growing number and diversity of temporary exhibitions and the structural and historical relationships of these more ephemeral events to long-term displays.*[18]

Hence, the exhibition here does not offer a zooming out from the art object, but a zooming in from the museum. But, moreover, if discourse about the museum tends to minimize instances of 'protest and scandal', we are encouraged to read the temporary exhibition as precisely the site of those instances. The temporary show is portrayed as more socially transgressive (scandal) and politically active (protest), than the museum can afford to be. The exhibition is diverse and ephemeral, erecting, as it were, its own site; the museum display is fixed, permanent and rigidly constrained by its architectural setting. Here, as it is often the case, language vacillates between the metaphorical and the literal use, so that architectural attributes can be said to stand for, say, political ones. These subtle premises inform a great deal of writing on exhibitions, and by extension, on exhibition-makers, those freelance or independent curators whose freedom or independence is – needless to say – not guaranteed by their subcontracted condition. This simultaneous dismissal of museological concerns coupled with the vindication of the curator as a figure singularly capable of 'escaping' the institution from within has been nothing if not ambiguous, resembling as it does, an earlier Greenbergian trope about the avant-garde escaping bourgeois society. Amongst other things, it has allowed for the socially transgressive and politically active aims of the so-called New Museology, which aimed at the wholesale transformation of the institution, to be largely obliterated from the curriculum of courses on curatorial studies.

Hence, before we turn to them, I would like to think of their earlier precedents, courses in museology, which were motivated not just by a desire to establish 'professional standards', but, quite often, by a desire to question and break with institutional conventions. The earlier debates over the need to differentiate between museography – as pertaining to technical and practical skills necessary for museum work – and museology – which took the institution of the museum itself as an object of study and critical reflection – revealed this need to depart from the mere transmission of current ways of working. As early as the 1920s, but with renewed impetus after the Second World War, it was proposed that the training of museum professionals should take place not in the museum itself, where the methods, habits and policies of a particular institution would become naturalised, weakening the students' institutional imagination, but in the university, where a theoretical approach that allowed for more speculative reflection on the institution could be complemented by occasional placements and visits to different professional settings.[19]

While the work of Georges Henri Rivière in Paris is most often associated with this desire to renew museum practice, these proposals had gathered initial force not in the metropolitan centres of Europe or North American, but in Latin America and Eastern Europe.[20] The Facultad de Filosofía y Letras of the Universidad de Buenos Aires offered courses in museology from 1923, quickly followed by similar ones in Rio de Janeiro, as early as 1938. The influential school of Brno (Czechoslovakia) established a chair in museology as early as 1922. This is not a moot point, as part of the need to rethink the museum came from the sense that an institution designed in Europe in the nineteenth century did not meet the needs of communities elsewhere and that the mere propagation of this model was not compatible with wider decolonial projects.[21]

And yet, since 1969, Georges Henri Rivère and Yvonne Oddon at the Paris offices of the International Council of Museums (ICOM) had been tasked with devising a standard curriculum for museum professionals with the intention that UNESCO would eventually be able to support a network of training centres distributed worldwide, a project only fragmentarily realised.[22] By 1966, the split between museography and museology would be taken to have been sublimated by the establishment at Leicester University in Great Britain of the School of 'Museum Studies'. This new model of training reinforced the idea that improving the work of museums demanded not just a refinement of techniques and methods, but a theoretical understanding of the institution itself, a reflection on the aims and stakes of the museum. This meant that, going beyond their particular disciplinary specialisations (from biology to history or contemporary art), museum workers were required to educate themselves on *every aspect* of a museum institution. Significantly, this was felt to be a more pressing need as more institutional roles within the museum became differentiated and specialised. Geoffrey Lewis, then director of the School of Museum Studies at Leicester, writes in 1987:

> *Should museum studies training now embrace all the various specialisms involved as well as the many disciplines traditionally associated with museums? Or should training compartmentalize the many specialisms comprising museum work rather than embrace the whole operation? Museum work is team work and, to provide cohesion within the museum as an institution, its members should know and understand not only their own role but that of their colleagues as well. The same argument also applies to the cohesiveness of the museum professional at large. There is a distinct body of knowledge relation to the museum phenomenon and museum practitioners, whatever their role, need to be aware of this theory and develop their practice accordingly.*[23]

It is remarkable then, that by the early 1990s contemporary art curators were sidestepping these aims to establish an entirely different training route.[24] Indeed, 'curatorial studies' is a bit of a misnomer: almost without exception courses in 'curatorial studies' refer not to curatorial training tout court – that would have been the earlier mission of 'museum studies' – but to the training of *contemporary art* curators. There is a pervading sense that in establishing these courses what was at play was not so much an explicit opposition to museum studies as a certain obliviousness to it. In this way, for example, the curatorial course at the École du MAGASIN, established in 1987, describes the rationale for its foundation as follows:

> [The École du MAGASIN] *provided the institutional setting of an art centre for a new type of pedagogical program, one that was aware of the nascent schools of thought linked to contemporary curating. Up until that time there were few such programmes regarding contemporary curating in general. In France for example, there was no official field of study on the subject – curating could be learned only by experience.*[25]

What they call 'contemporary curating in general' refers more precisely to the curating of contemporary art. Indeed, they go on to cite Harald Szeemann as the model of curator they were aiming to form, making no mention of available museological routes to training, which in France at that time would have included at least the long-established École du Louvre.[26] This sense that museum studies did not respond to the needs of contemporary art curators was not unique to Grenoble. Describing the genesis of the 'MA Visual Arts Administration: Curating and Commissioning Contemporary Art' at the Royal College of Art, London, its first director, Teresa Gleadowe, has similarly explained that it was jointly funded by the RCA and the Arts Council of Great Britain in order to 'fill a perceived gap in the training of curators of contemporary art', drawing from the experiences of the curatorial pathway of the Whitney Independent Study Program in New York and, indeed, L'Ecole du MAGASIN in Grenoble.[27]

Since then, courses in contemporary art curating have become ubiquitous, obscuring the question of their necessity. However, their epistemic specificity is far from settled.[28] If there is a virtue to them, it might reside, precisely, in their stubborn resistance to 'settle', with emphasis often put on learning a broadly conceived 'critical theory' alongside more practical work, which often includes the collective staging of an exhibition. In this way, for example, the fairly typical example of the Royal College of Art course – now renamed as an MA in 'Curating Contemporary Art' (banished from the title is any mention of 'administration') – includes at the time of writing seven different units in its curriculum. Alongside a core course for the whole of the School of Arts and Humanities (which provides a broadly conceived humanities syllabus), students are offered Critical and Historical Studies, Curatorial Thinking, Curatorial Practice, Research in Practice, a Graduate Project (which normally consist of a collectively staged exhibition) and an Independent Research Project or dissertation. By keeping the units so loosely defined, enough flexibility is given to accommodate both changes over time and diversities of approach to practice; running through it is an emphasis on 'theory', which is not always or primarily a 'theory of curating'. Within Great Britain, this is a curriculum that resembles most closely of all those of studio-based Fine Art courses.

Indeed, the genealogy of the new curator has been recurrently constructed on the basis of a growing affinity to artistic practice. The question of whether curators are artists or artists can be curators is quite possibly over-represented in the literature. All the more so if we take into account that in the wake of conceptual art the question has long been settled: anything and everything (including, of course, an exhibition) can be art (at least in principle).[29] Quite often the emergence of the contemporary art curator – understood as a 'new' figure that breaks both with any reliance on museum studies and with older professional conventions – is explained as the result of 'catching up' with artistic practice in general and an internalisation of so-called 'institutional critique' in particular.[30] Understood in this way, critical curatorial practice has emerged as a canon in the making that, like the institution it critiques, is largely male and largely based in the Global North, allowing for a mode of (self-)historicisation based on direct transmission and influence that can appear myopically self-referential and circumscribed. This is a problem not just because the process of canonisation itself was part of what institutional critique sought to challenge,[31] but because it serves to establish an artificial binary between artists and museum workers, with critique circulating only in one direction and curators being able to navigate that divide only after establishing a phantasmatic 'autonomous zone' within the institution. Gone is also the commitment to a holistic understanding of the institution.[32]

I would like to return now to our initial question. If, as Alloway suggested, we should be thinking of art beyond the limits of the art *object*, that is to say, we should be thinking of art *in* exhibition, coming into being as it encounters its successive publics and connects with wider networks, then the danger is that by turning the exhibition into the art object itself those limits are merely reinstituted at a different level. An Exhibition Studies that is conceived as ancillary to Curatorial Studies is most at risk of falling into this trap.[33] The bad habits of the old art history can come back through the back door, with the curator slotting seamlessly in the space vacated by the Romantic artist and a power-blind canonicity safely restored to its former glory. This is particularly dangerous given the already canonising nature of exhibitions themselves. Despite the fact that, as we like to tell our students at Central Saint Martins, Exhibition Studies is a 'global native' (which is really just a fancy way of saying that it comes into play after postcolonial studies) this has hardly been reflected in the writing of this field.[34]

In this way, for example, Bruce Altshuler's highly informative and lavishly illustrated two-volume anthology *Exhibitions that Made Art History* (2008 and 2013) includes a total of 49 exhibitions, all but four having taken place in Europe or the United States, a proportion that is barely more balanced in Jens Hoffmann's equally lavish *Show Time* (2014).[35] Understood in this way, Exhibition Studies turns into a subgenre of traditional art history, so that, leaving dominant art historical narratives untouched, scholarly attention is paid to those exhibitions that, indeed, *made* Art History as we know it. Art historical methodologies are left intact and Art History is expanded by furnishing it with a subhistory of 'innovative exhibitions' and maverick curators that reinforce an extant sense of what constituted 'the new' and 'genius' at any given point.[36] If this is what Exhibition Studies can bring to the field, I am not sure that there is indeed any need for it.

Despite all this, I would not, or not yet, write off the value of Exhibition Studies. But we need to get rid of any desire for a 'common sense' understanding of what an exhibition is. What we take to be common sense is most often aimed at maintaining the status quo, an Exhibition Studies that is truly a 'global native' is not compatible with that aim.[37] In the early 1970s, museum workers from the Global South refused to accept common-sensical notions of the museum, promoting an exercise in institutional imagination that transformed the range of what was possible, allowing for other kinds of museum to be conceived, even if not always realised.[38] The Exhibition Studies I have tried to defend is not indifferent to this history but understands itself in transgenerational and transdisciplinary alliance with it. It starts from the idea that there is nothing self-evident about exhibitions. They are not necessarily organised by museums and galleries with a curator in charge, with an opening and a closing date, some artworks, wall labels, maybe a catalogue or even a public programme of events. *Exhibitions* are moments when *art* meets its *publics*. A mode of inquiry that focusses on this encounter while disregarding common-sensical notions of all three terms is urgently needed, the question of where it finds its disciplinary home remains open, but that is what I have in mind when doing Exhibition Studies.

Notes

1 On the proliferation of 'studies' and their relation to 'discipline', see the special issue of *Revue d'anthropologie des connaissances*, 'Les *Studies* à l'étude', vol.11, no.3, 2017.

2 In this respect, I find much to agree with in Brandon Taylor's somewhat ungenerous review of Charlotte Klonk's *Spaces of Experience: Art Gallery Interiors from 1800 to 2000* (New Haven: Yale University Press, 2009), which attempted to achieve such a feat, see 'Here, Too, Confusion Reigned', *Oxford Art Journal*, vol.33, no.2, 2010, pp.249–52.

3 See W. Grasskamp, 'To be continued: Periodic Exhibitions (*documenta*, for Example)', *Landmark Exhibitions*, *Tate Papers*, no.12, Autumn, 2009, available at https://www.tate.org.uk/research/publications/tate-papers/12/to-be-continued-periodic-exhibitions-documenta-for-example as well as the study *Folding the Exhibition*, Barcelona: Museu d'Art Contemporani de Barcelona (MACBA), 2014, https://www.macba.cat/en/essay-folding-the-exhibition.

4 See Thomas Crow, *Painters and Public Life in Eighteenth Century Paris*, New Haven and London: Yale University Press, 1985. I use 'exhibitionary complex' in the sense developed by Tony Bennett, *The Birth of the Museum*, Oxford: Routledge, 1995.

5 James L. Reinish, 'An Interview with Lawrence Alloway', *Studio International*, vol.186, no.958, September 1973, p.63.

6 Lawrence Alloway, *The Venice Biennale 1895–1968: From Salon to Goldfish Bowl*, New York: Graphic Society, 1968.

7 *Ibid.*, pp.14–15. It is worth noting how Alloway's account goes against the grain of another, more nostalgic tradition that spans from Quatrèmere de Quincy via Paul Valéry to some contemporary defences of site-specificity for which art's 'mobility' always entails some kind of a loss (of its 'proper' home, of its roots, of its social links, etc.).

8 This was, of course, an aim shared by the social history of art, a somewhat different case for it is made convincingly in Donald Preziosi, 'The Question of Art History', *Critical Inquiry*, vol.18, no.2, Winter 1992, pp.363–86.

9 See also L. Alloway, 'Art and the Communications Network', *Canadian Art*, no.100, January 1966.

10 The work of Martha Ward, Patricia Mainardi, Stephen Bann, T.J. Clark and Timothy Mitchell merit a special mention in this respect.

11 The anthology edited by Ivan Karp and Steven D. Lavine, *Exhibiting Cultures: The Poetics and Politics of Museum Display* (Washington DC: Smithsonian Institution, 1991) merits special mention.

12 George Nelson's *Display* (New York: Whitney Publications, 1953) is perhaps the clearest example here, but the genre is much larger (if not always as brilliant). On the waning attention to this genre, see Martin Beck, 'The Exhibition and the Display', in Lucy Steeds (ed.), *Exhibition*, Cambridge, MA: MIT Press, 2014, pp.27–33.

13 See B. O'Doherty, *Inside the White Cube: The Ideology of the Gallery Space* (San Francisco: Lapis Press, 1986). The essays that compose the book had been published by Artforum ten years earlier, in 1976.

14 On the shift from curator to author, see N. Heinich and M. Pollack, 'From Museum Curator to Exhibition Auteur: Inventing a singular position', in Reesa Greenberg, Bruce W. Ferguson, and Sandy Nairne (ed.), *Thinking About Exhibitions*, London: Routledge, 1996, pp.231–50.

15 Bruce Altshuler, *The Avant Garde in Exhibition: New Art in the 20th Century*, New York: Abrams, 1994; Mary Anne Staniszewski, *The Power of Display: A History of Exhibition Installations at the Museum of Modern Art*, Cambridge, MA: MIT Press, 1998; Isabel Tejeda, *El montaje expositivo como traducción. Fidelidades, traiciones y hallazgos en el arte conemporáneo desde los años 70*, Madrid: Trama, 2006; C. Klonk, *Spaces of Experience, op. cit.*; and Kristina Wilson, *The Modern Eye: Stieglitz, MoMA, and the Art of the Exhibition 1925–1934*, New Haven: Yale University Press, 2009.

16 B. Altshuler, *Exhibitions that Made Art History*, vol. 1 and 2, London: Phaidon Press, 2008 and 2013; and Jens Hoffmann (ed.), *Show Time: The 50 Most Influential Exhibitions of Contemporary Art*, New York: Thames & Hudson, 2014.

17 Lynne Cooke and Peter Wollen (ed.), *Visual Display: Culture Beyond Appearances*, Seattle: Bay Press, 1995; R. Greenberg, B.W. Ferguson and S. Nairne (ed.), *Thinking About Exhibitions, op. cit.*. More recent contributions in this line include L. Steeds (ed.), *Exhibition, op. cit.*, and James Voorhies, *Beyond Objecthood: The Exhibition as a Critical Form since 1968*, Cambridge, MA: MIT Press, 2017.

18 R. Greenberg, B.W. Ferguson and S. Nairne (ed.), *Thinking About Exhibitions, op. cit.*, p.2.

19 See J.P. Lorente, 'The development of museum studies in universities: from technical training to critical museology', in *Museum Management and Curatorship*, vol.27, no.3, 2012, pp.237–52; H.G. Rodeck, 'The Role of the University in Education Towards Museum Careers', Curator, vol.4, no.1, 1961; L. Teather, 'Professionalization and the Museum', in M.S. Schapiro and L.W. Kemp (ed.), *The Museum: A Reference Guide*, Greenwood, NJ: Greenwood Press, 1990, pp.299–328, and the special issue on 'Staff Training' of *Museum International*, no.156, vol.39, issue 4, 1987.

20 See J.P. Lorente, *op. cit.* Georges Henri Rivière, then director of ICOM, devised and delivered the *Cours de muséologie générale contemporaine* to postgraduate students at the Paris I and Paris IV universities from 1970. See G.H. Rivière, *La museología*, Madrid: Akal, 1993.

21 The Roundtable of Santiago de Chile in 1972 was a key moment in this respect. See *Round Table on the Role of Museums in Today's Latin America*, Santiago de Chile, 30 May 1972, translated and reprinted as 'Basic Principles of the Integral Museum', *Museum International, Special Issue Key Ideas in Museums and Heritage (1949–2004)*, vol.66, issues 1–4, 2014, pp.175–82.

22 The first draft of the curriculum was ready by 1971 and discussed at the ICOM general assembly in Grenoble. See P.J. Boylan, 'Museum training: A central concern of ICOM for forty years', *Museum*, no.156, vol.34, issue 4, 1987, pp.225–30.

23 G. Lewis, 'Editorial: Why train museum staff?', *Museum*, no.156, vol.34, issue 4, 1987, p.220. I do not mean to suggest here that these aims were fully realised.

24 It is from the end of the 1980 that curatorial courses began to proliferate. To list but a few by year of foundation: MAGASIN-CNAC, Grenoble (1987); Bard College, Annandale-on-Hudson (1990); Royal College of Art, London (1992); De Appel Foundation, Amsterdam (1994); Goldsmiths College, London (1996); CCAC Wattis Institute, San Francisco (1999); Columbia University and the Whitney Museum of American Art, New York (2002). While the geography of these courses has now expanded, their blueprint was very much a Northern Europe-US affair.

25 'École du MAGASIN: Curatorial training program', undated brochure, p.2.

26 The École du Louvre was set up in 1882 and by the late 1980s it had expanded its remit from practical and managerial concerns to include more museological-theoretical teaching, extending to contemporary art. For this, Georges Henri Rivière's famous *Cours de muséologie générale contemporaine* at the Université de Paris I between 1971 to 1982, established with the support of UNESCO, was instrumental in extending this focus. See Dominique Poulot, 'The French Museology', in D. Poulot and I. Stankovic (ed.), *Discussing Heritage and Museums: Crossing Paths of France and Serbia*, Paris: Website of HiCSA, October 2017, pp.7–30.

27 Teresa Gleadowe, 'Curating in a Changing Climate', in *Curating in the 21st Century* (ed. Gavid Wade), Walsall: The New Art Gallery, 2000, p.29.

[28] A good sense of this is given in L. Markopoulos (ed.), *Great Expectations: Prospects for the Future of Curatorial Education*, London: Koenig Books, 2016; and Paul O'Neill, L. Steeds and Mick Wilson (ed.), *The Curatorial Conundrum: What to Study? What to Research? What to Practice?*, Cambridge, MA: MIT Press, 2016.

[29] This is not to say that paying attention to exhibitions curated by artists or to exhibitions qua artworks cannot render brilliant insights, as attested by the volumes by Elena Filipovic (ed.), *The Artist as Curator*, Milan: Mousse Publishing, 2017; and Alison Green, *When Artists Curate*, London: Reaktion Books, 2018.

[30] See, for example, J. Hoffmann, 'The Curatorialization of Institutional Critique', in *Institutional Critique and After* (ed. John C. Welchman), Zurich: JRP|Ringier, 2006, and Paul O'Neill, *The Culture of Curating and the Curating of Culture(s)*, Cambridge, MA: MIT Press, 2012.

[31] See Gerald Raunig and Gene Ray, 'Preface', in G. Raunig and G. Ray (ed.), *Art and Contemporary Critical Practice: Reinventing Institutional Critique*, London: MayFly Books, 2009, p.xv.

[32] This can have convoluted effects, like the current wave of interest in thematising 'pedagogy' at a curatorial level, most often without any lasting effects or direct agency by educational departments. This retreat to the thematic level is sharply described in J. Graham, V. Graziano and S. Kelly, 'The Educational Turn in Art: Rewriting the Hidden Curriculum', *Performance Research*, vol.21, no.6, 2016, pp.29–35.

[33] This has been an ongoing concern and subject of many conversations at Central Saint Martins and, indeed, my colleague Lucy Steeds has written about this danger elsewhere in terms that I largely share. See L. Steeds, 'What is the Future of Exhibition Histories? Or Towards Art in Terms of its Becoming Public', in P. O'Neill, L. Steeds and M. Wilson (ed.), *The Curatorial Conundrum, op. cit.*, pp. 16–25.

[34] Catalina L. Imizcoz, who graduated from the course in 2016 has published an amended version of her dissertation that focusses precisely on this issue, see 'Extending the Study of Exhibitions across Geographies', *Caiana*, vol.1, issue 10, 2017, http://caiana.caia.org.ar/template/caiana.php?pag=articles/article_1.php&obj=257&vol=10.

[35] See B. Altshuler, *Exhibitions that Made Art History, op. cit.*, 2008 and 2013 and J. Hoffmann, *Show Time, op. cit.*, 2014.

[36] See B. Altshuler, 'A Canon of Exhibitions', *Manifesta Journal*, no.11, 2011. Responding to Michael Brenson's dismissal of 'Magiciens de la Terre' (1989) on the basis of the lack of 'quality' of its contents, Altshuler suggest that the exhibition as a whole, rather than its contents, can provide the standard of 'quality' leaving untroubled the need for a hierarchical judgment of 'quality'. A precise response to this position is offered in the same issue of the journal by Simon Sheikh: 'On the Standard of Standards, or Curating and Canonization', *ibid*.

[37] The problem with 'common sense' is elucidated in Errol Lawrence, 'Just Plain Common Sense: The Roots of Racism', in Centre for Contemporary Cultural Studies, *The Empire Strikes Back. Race and Racism in 70s Britain*, London: Routledge, 1982, pp.47–94.

[38] The 1972 ICOM roundtable in Santiago de Chile is a watershed moment in this respect. I have written elsewhere about the obliteration of this history from curatorial studies, see Yaiza Hernández Velázquez, 'Imagining Curatorial Practice after 1972', in *Curating after the Global: Roadmaps for the Present* (ed. P. O'Neill, L. Steeds and M. Wilson) Cambridge, MA: MIT Press, 2019.

The Art of Gentrification: The Lisbon Version

Ana Teixeira Pinto

On 7 August 2017, CNN published an advertorial about Lisbon titled 'The new Berlin?' To push the narrative that 'austerity helped Lisbon's creatives to succeed', the piece deployed pictures of the Museum of Art, Architecture and Technology (MAAT), a waterfront building in Lisbon designed by architect Amanda Levete's firm AL_A, which upon construction quickly became a fixture of in-flight magazines.[1] To be fair, the MAAT photographs well, rather better than it actually looks. In reality it feels cramped and crooked, and its function feels closer to a city branding initiative than a cultural institution: the wave-like shape ties old chauvinist tropes (Portugal as a nation of naval explorers), leisure fantasies (sea, sand and sun) and dynamic imagery (economic recovery) into the type of iconic landmark so appealing to PR-speak. The article reinforced this impression by advertising the city's cheap rents to 'creatives' priced out of London. Seen from Berlin, where I am based, what is happening to Lisbon feels depressingly familiar.

As I land in Oporto, my taxi driver tells me he cannot afford to retire, his pension is too meagre. After 45 years as an industrial worker he took to driving, the only available job he could find. He usually takes the night shift. His story also rings familiar: I heard it often from drivers in Berlin, whose GDR (German Democratic Republic) pensions all but evaporated after reunification.[2] Needless to say, the socialisation of losses goes hand in hand with the privatisation of gains – aka space to be had on the cheap for those from abroad. In opening a direct conduit between contemporary art and gentrification, the MAAT is, in Lisbon, the first of its kind. This is not because the museum's mission statement is in any way exceptional – from Oslo to Bilbao, contemporary art is routinely recruited to boost real-estate speculation – but rather because Portugal has entered the global markets at an exceptionally belated stage.

From Colonial Power to Quasi-Colony

Portugal did not experience modernity, modernism or modernisation. Under a fascist regime until 1974, the country leapt directly into postmodernity: unlike Italian or Spanish fascism, which invested heavily in modernisation, Portuguese fascism was anti-modern, ruralist and insular.[3] From 1961 onwards,

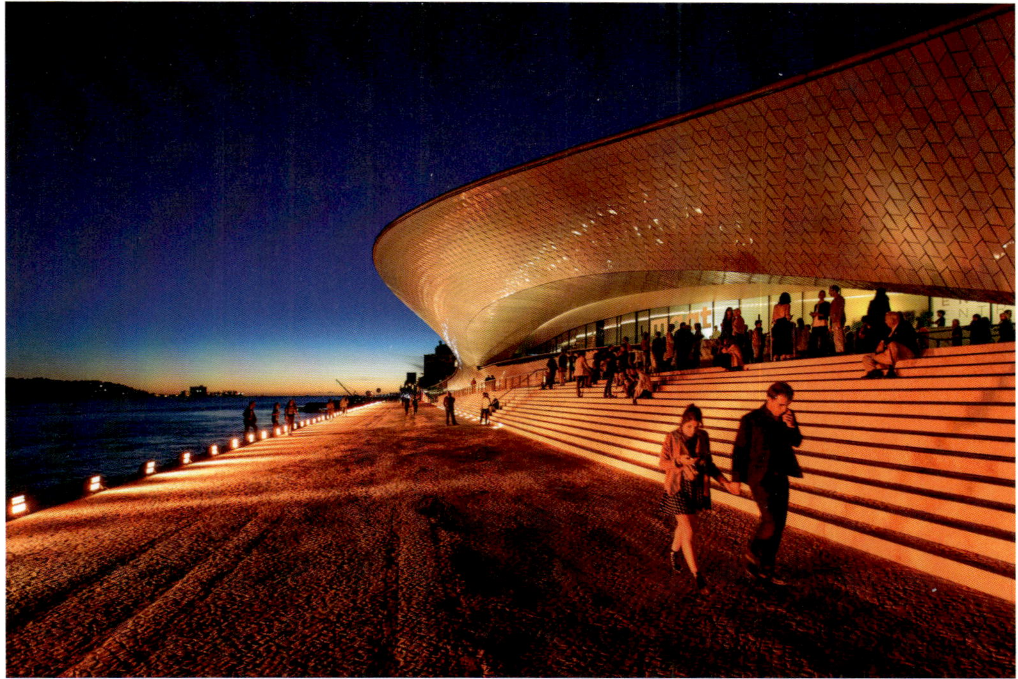

Portugal found itself fighting a costly war with its African colonies – Angola, Mozambique and Guinea-Bissau – which by the 1970s had become unsustainable. Five families alone controlled the extraction industry in the colonies, and their economic activities were key to both Portugal's isolationist policies and the dictatorship's domestic survival. This situation pitted the regime against its increasingly disgruntled military, in a feud which ultimately lead to its downfall with the Carnation Revolution in 1974.[4]

After the transition towards democracy, Portugal joined the European Union in 1986, but its deep structural problems were never solved. They were, rather, masked by the EU's consolidation programmes, which were mostly channelled towards infrastructure. This period, from the mid-1990s to the mid-2000s, was the only moment in the country's history when immigration exceeded exodus, largely due to demand in the construction sector. It was also during this time that two of the biggest contemporary art venues in Lisbon were built – the Foundation Centro Cultural de Belém (CCB) and the Culturgest (1993) – and the now defunct Institute of Contemporary Art (IAC) was founded (1997). Though the country tried hard to appeal to investors and tourists, in the late 1990s low-cost carriers exploded, rendering 'exotic' destinations inexpensive. The efforts to internationalise Portugal's art scene also bore scant fruit, partially due to institutional ineptitude, partially due to circumstance. Whilst Eastern European conceptualism soared in the art markets, the Portuguese presence in international venues was slight. By 2005 the urban landscape was peppered with white elephants: the already mentioned CCB, Expo '98 and the several stadiums built for Euro 2004.[5] While Berlin was 'poor but sexy', Lisbon was chintzy but stale.

Museum of Art, Architecture and Technology (MAAT), Lisbon, 2016. Photography: Paulo Coelho. Courtesy EDP Foundation Lisbon and MAAT

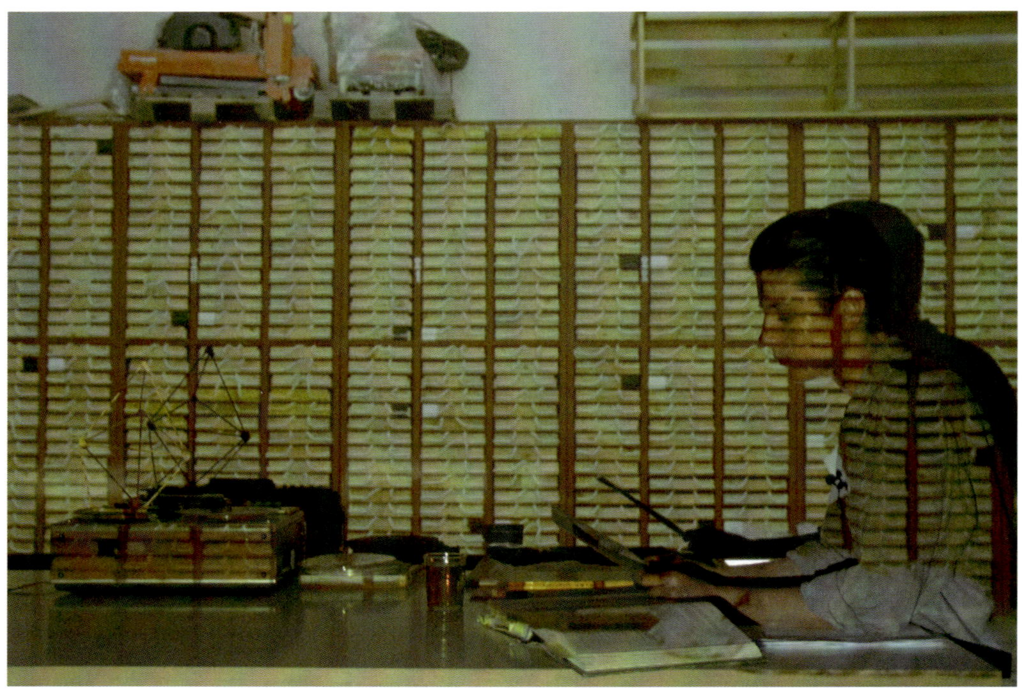

To compound the problem, the apparent growth was misleading. Rather than endless prosperity, the highways the EU built brought cheaper agricultural produce and low-cost goods. The economy shrunk in inverse proportion to German export growth. From 2005 onwards, the country was in a recession. In 2008, the financial crash hit, and what began as a private debt crisis, driven by deregulation, swiftly morphed into a chauvinist narrative, about the industrious north and lazy southerners, predicated on the 'figuring of scarcity' (of resources) as 'excess' (of debt, of profligacy).[6] When the market collapsed, the Portuguese economy contracted and tax revenues went down while the deficit went up. Portugal was pressured to protect its financial sector, which in practice meant nationalising bad debt at the behest of the EU, to avoid contagion, and in the same breath Portugal had to start repaying loans to the bond markets, provided on short-term contracts when the financial sector was in full swing. In 2011, to prevent a situation of insolvency, the newly elected social democrat centre-right party (PSD), under the leadership of Pedro Passos Coelho, requested a 78 billion euro bailout. The result was disastrous for the Portuguese population: the austerity measures, aimed at deficit reduction, were heavily geared towards the downsizing of the welfare state – for example, slashing education, unemployment and health benefits; freezing state pensions and salaries; and massive privatisation programmes – whilst aiming to introduce greater labour flexibility, via wage-repression, regardless of whether workers would be able to live on the resulting incomes. In spite of the sufferance exacted, the adjustment programme was equally damaging to the Portuguese GDP, leading to a spiral of economic decline as public sector contraction led to further falls in aggregate demand, shrinking the economy as a whole. Unsurprisingly, the country voted against austerity in the subsequent election, and a left-wing coalition formed by the socialists (PS), communists (PCP), greens (PEV) and the New Left (BE) secured a majority in parliament. The process was not devoid of polemics, however: the Portuguese president refused to recognise the result of the election. In his view, an anti-austerity platform could not be allowed to govern, as this would send 'false signals to financial institutions, investors and markets'.[7] For almost two months, from 4 October until 24 November 2015, Portugal had, de facto, no government,[8] until the coalition government – widely derided as *geringonça* (jerry-built) – finally took office.

The two years that followed became known as the 'Portuguese miracle'. I have no wish to be cynical about these accomplishments; the new government did manage to reverse the most punitive policies while propping up growth, and in Portugal the relief is palpable. That said, 'anti-austerity' is hyperbolic, the coalition's policies are best described as 'austerity-light'. The economic recovery is tied to, and contingent upon, the explosion of an utterly deregulated tourism industry, which is swiftly turning the country into a manufactured pseudo-folkish monoculture.

MAAT was to succeed where the CCB formerly failed by virtue of the intersecting vectors of several crises: the immiseration, caused by imposed austerity, led to a surge of 'crisis investment opportunities'. Whereas in the 1990s the world was expanding, now it is contracting. The political instability in Europe's immediate vicinity (Egypt, Turkey and Tunisia) and the fear of terror attacks dented tourism to North Africa and the Middle East, making Portugal a safer holiday option. The former government's fiscal policies engineered a population replacement by actively courting affluent retirees and liberal professionals with a ten-year income tax exemption. While this triggered a realty boom in the historical centres of Lisbon and Oporto, the young and jobless were nudged to leave (in officialese: Europe's younger generation must be prepared to 'commute' in search of work). Last but not least, the recovery has a seedy underbelly. Under the Golden Visa programme, any non-EU citizen who invests 350,000 euros in real estate obtains a residency permit with minimal caveats: the property cannot be resold before five years have passed and the purchaser must remain in Portugal for a minimum of seven days.

Decolonising Aesthetics

Artist Filipa César scrutinised this policy in her eponymous video installation *Golden Visa or the Disposing of the Discredited* (2014), which ties the sale of residency permits to the granting of mining permits to the Canadian corporation Colt Resources to prospect for gold in southern Portugal.[9] The colour gold (Golden Visa, gold rush) functions as an analogue for capital, in contradistinction to the blackness of the mined soil, and black as a signifier for everything that is devalued or degraded. In the project's title, 'Disposing of the Discredited' is a quote from French philosopher Michel Feher, according to whom the granting, and by extension the refusal, of credit functions as a necropolitical tool, typically deployed to manage the undesirable population surplus in Europe (migrants, the unemployed, Roma minorities). As César's film *Mined Soil* (2012–14) sustains, there is a hidden racial dimension, which ties the structural racism that was born in chattel slavery to a colonial matrix, whose operations can be mapped onto current political events, like the sovereign debt crisis. The area where Colt Resources now operates was once studied by Amílcar Cabral, an agronomist – who would later become one of the leaders of the Guinean independence movement until his assassination in 1973 – whose project of nation-building César contrasts with the neo-imperial chastising of 'failed states'.

César's preoccupations are echoed by Pedro Barateiro, whose video essay *The Current Situation* (2015) conflates parasitic and financial contagions by juxtaposing two unrelated events: an anti-austerity demonstration in front of the Portuguese parliament, and the felling of the last palm trees that once stood at the entrance to the Príncipe Real gardens, infested by red weevils. As the chainsaw is revving up, the roar of the crowd merges with its rattle, creating a single, strident sound wave. The deafening buzz could be construed as the soundtrack to globalisation as the process through which 'cheap natures' (labour power or natural resources) are torn from their surroundings and dragged into the global markets.[10]

Both César, who is based in Berlin, and Barateiro, are rather exceptions to the national norm when it comes to their subjects and formats of choice. Political or institutional critique, in Portugal, has rarely departed from the satirical, and as a rule contemporary art has embraced poetry rather than theory. Akin to Berlin-based Grada Kilomba or New York–based Pedro Neves Marques and Mariana Silva, they are also among the few who have addressed the imbrications of economy, race and empire. Neves Marques recently edited *The Forest and The School: Where to Sit at the Dinner Table?* (2016), the first wide-ranging anthology about *antropofagia* in English, and he has been working through this concept as the way in which colonised cultures appropriate the symbols of the colonisers into their own cultural idioms.[11] Kilomba is an Afro-Portuguese artist and writer whose performance works recount the experience of colonisation from the perspective of those hurt. In spite of having a thriving international career, her work was shown for the first time in 2017 in Portugal, in two solo shows: one at Galeria Avenida da India, in a project initiated by João Mourão and curated by Gabi Ngcobo, and another curated by Inês Grosso at MAAT.

It is not coincidental that Kilomba, César and Neves Marques are based abroad. Portugal remains disinclined to address its colonial legacy or to acknowledge its pervasive institutional racism. Minorities are notoriously absent from public discourse, in spite of their immense contribution to public life. The refusal to engage with, or atone for, past atrocities, is coterminous with the refusal to redress present grievances. To say Portuguese culture has yet to be decolonised is a euphemism: Portugal romanticises its age of imperial expansion as a glorious, heroic epoch and wallows in nostalgia for its lost grandeur. Mainstream culture typically portrays the colonial relation as orderly and harmonious, if not outright civilising.

In October 2017, to give but one recent example, a statue of Padre António Vieira, a Jesuit priest – commissioned by the Santa Casa da Misericórdia, a

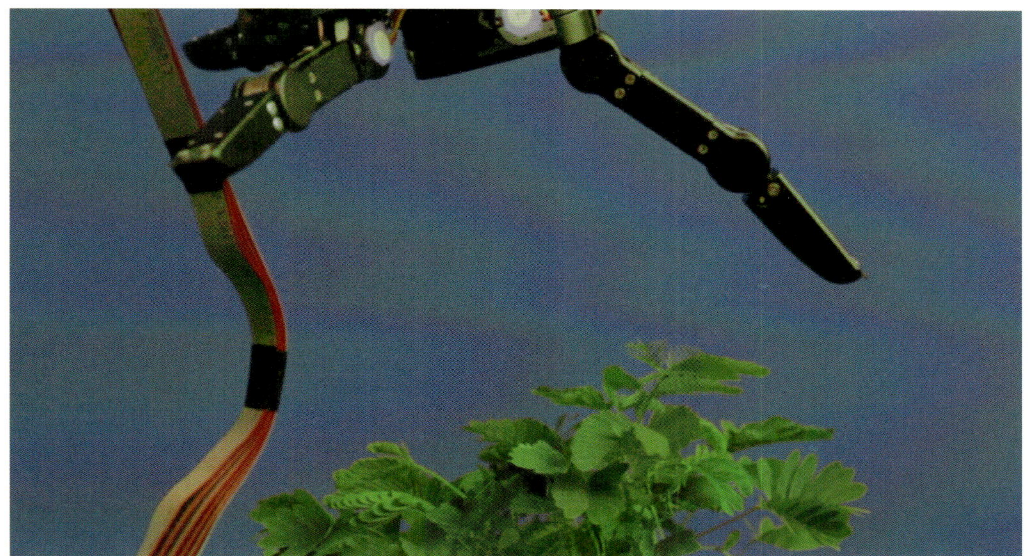

Catholic lay brotherhood, to be installed in the historic centre of Lisbon —
triggered a protest by SOS Racismo and the activist group Descolonizando.[12]
Whatever one thinks about Vieira's complex legacy (the Jesuits were not
abolitionists and though Vieira advocated liberating Brazilian Indians he
supported the trade and enslavement of Africans), the statue, representing
Vieira surrounded by naked Indian children, one of whom kneels at his feet,
is a grotesque monument to Western supremacy. Descolonizando intended to
stage a performance qua demonstration in front of the recently unveiled effigy,
but their event was thwarted by extremists waving Portuguese flags.[13] Even
if one could find dissenting voices in academia and some lone voices in the
media – like Mamadou Ba, a writer and activist, or Carla Fernandes, a journalist who runs the audioblog Rádio AfroLis, or the platform Buala, an invaluable
publishing site for postcolonial studies in the Portuguese language – the vast
majority of the Portuguese literati fell over each other in the rush to heap scorn
on the activists, rather than disown the far right.[14]

Though it would be tempting to see the growing interest in Afro-Portuguese
voices – still vastly absent from the contemporary art scene – as signalling
a changing sensibility, one could also note that their increasing institutional presence is coextensive with the surge of Angolan investment in the
Portuguese economy (1.53 billion euros in 2014).[15] Similarly, ARCO Lisboa,
the Portuguese leg of ARCO Madrid, which was inaugurated in 2016, could
be described as an attempt to court Angolan wealth as well as the affluent
newcomers who benefited from the Golden Visa scheme.[16]

Idle Institutions: Art as Financial Asset
The impact of these developments is by no means positive. As Mourão and
Luís Silva, who run the non-profit Kunsthalle Lissabon, noted last time we
spoke, the net effect is a changed relation to urban space: an empty or derelict

Pedro Neves
Marques, *The
Pudic Relation
Between Machine
and Plant*, 2016,
video, 2min
30sec. Courtesy
the artist

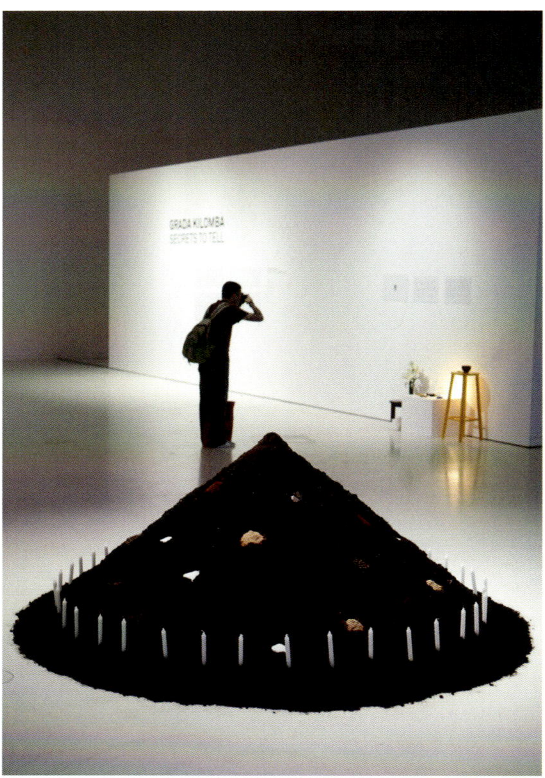

View of the exhibition
'Grada Kilomba'
('Secrets to Tell'), MAAT,
2017. Photography: Bruno
Lopes. Courtesy EDP
Foundation

building will no longer be made available to a non-profit or artist-run space; landed property is now a profitable commodity, and both the city hall and private proprietors want to monetise rather than socialise. The Kunsthalle Lissabon opened their first exhibition space in 2009, in a vacant building, which the debt-stricken Banco Espírito Santo (BES) had permitted artists to make use of, located on Lisbon's main avenue, Avenida da Liberdade. From 2009 to 2015, the Kunsthalle Lissabon ran a programme based on solo exhibitions, inviting emerging artists who in spite of very solid careers were mostly unknown to the Portuguese audience.[17] Downstairs, inside a former barbershop, curator Margarida Mendes hosted The Barber Shop, a programme combining artist residencies with a conference series focussing on experimental film, cybernetics and philosophy. The upper floors were occupied by artist studios and by the collective Parkour, devoted to exhibiting a younger generation. The same informal networks that energised the Kunsthalle Lissabon extended to other projects emerging at roughly the same time, like Oporto, a screening programme devoted to experimental film, where one can delight in unknown gems of independent film-making. The liveliness of the alternative scene was palpable in these spaces, but it never managed to galvanise the city's institutions, which remained trapped in their own parochialisms.[18]

The institutional landscape in Lisbon is generic, marred by mismanagement, corruption, neglect and political opportunism. As a rule, curators and museum directors are political appointees who serve at the behest of the political hierarchy, and hence can be removed arbitrarily. This scenario ensures an absolute lack of institutional continuity. Though there have been notable exceptions, such as Miguel Wandschneider's programme for Culturgest, which had a carefully crafted identity,[19] or the programme curated by Liliana Coutinho for the Maria Matos Theatre, examples of mercurial management abound. In 2005, Delfim Sardo resigned from a short-lived stint as director of exhibitions in the CCB due to budget cuts. In 2009, Pedro Lapa was removed from the directorship of the Museu do Chiado in a polemic decision, contested by the art scene, after successfully lobbying for the expansion of the museum's curricula and facilities. The same museum lost a second director when David Santos resigned over the erratic behaviour of his superiors in 2015.[20] The official opening of the museum's new venue was overshadowed by an artist-led demonstration protesting the government's cultural policy. Also in 2015, António Pinto Ribeiro resigned from the Gulbenkian Foundation due to executive overreach, and Isabel Carlos rescinded her contract as director of the Centro de Arte Moderna (CAM) following Gulbenkian's decision to merge the CAM with its ancient and modern art museum. In 2006, after languishing without funding or a proper programme for years, the CCB was officially converted into the Museu Coleção Berardo (MCB), an arrangement similar to the one found between the Friedrich Christian Flick collection and the Hamburger Bahnhof in Berlin. This trajectory – from political vanity project to a private investor's vanity museum – perfectly illustrates the economic transition, which defines the pre- and post-crisis, from bloated public works to the private/public partnership scheme. In 2017, in yet another idiosyncratic decision, the MCB did not renew the contract of its director of exhibitions, leaving the museum to be run as a private fiefdom.

On a wider economic scale, the entanglements between finance and contemporary art are mired in opacity. Joe Berardo owes the Caixa Geral de Depósitos CGD (a Portuguese state-owned bank) something close to one billion euros.[21] Technically speaking, the collection is no longer his – the creditors have requested that his assets be mortgaged – but there is no political will to tackle the situation. Another failed bank, the BPN, nationalised in 2008 at a cost of 1.8 billion euros (the tip of what the press called the greatest financial crime ever in Portuguese history) had among its assets 85 paintings by Joan Miró, the sale of which was halted by the auctioneer Christie's after the opposition parties applied for a court injunction.[22] The bankruptcy of another nebulous financial entity, Privado Holdings, also left its Ellipse Foundation Contemporary Art Collection in juridical limbo, literally withering away in a warehouse on the outskirts of Lisbon. The perplexing nature of these processes, and of political management in general, contributes to a spawning graveyard of failed institutions, totally disconnected from the artist-run scene. To make matters worse, the stunted career paths of an older generation led to an unspoken belief in seniority, the apex of which is the Venice pavilion – younger artists are supposed to wait their turn rather than 'cut the line',[23] a policy which results in the notable absence of the best internationally known names, like Leonor Antunes, César, Barateiro, Neves Marques or Silva from the official selection. The

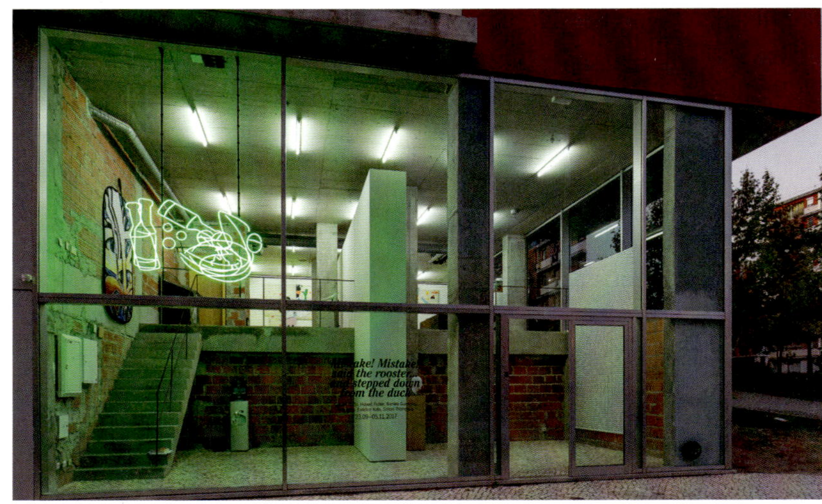

Installation view, 'Mistake! Mistake! said the rooster… and stepped down from the duck', Lumiar Cité, Lisbon, 2017. Photography: DMF. Courtesy Maumaus / Lumiar Cité, Lisbon

effects of this generational discord can also be felt in the lack of open avenues that would allow a younger generation of curators and programmers to transit into the institutional scene.

The Serralves Museum, in Oporto, remains the only internationally renowned Portuguese institution, and its newly appointed director, João Ribas, who was formerly the curator of the List Visual Arts Center at the Massachusetts Institute of Technology (MIT), from 2009 to 2013, is one of the few examples of Portuguese returning rather than leaving Portugal. The only Portuguese curator to favour the essay-exhibition model, Ribas served as the deputy director at Serralves, under Suzanne Cotter, and curated 'Under the Clouds: From Paranoia to the Digital Sublime' (2015)[24] and, more recently, the 4th Ural Industrial Biennial of Contemporary Art (2017). Serralves is also the sole Portuguese institution to consistently select its director via an international open call, in a process that was only recently mirrored by the Gulbenkian Foundation, when Penelope Curtis, former director of Tate Britain, was appointed director. Though international open calls are a welcome development, in both cases the selection process was supervised by the recruitment consultants Liz Amos Associates,[25] which in practice leaves the two biggest Portuguese institutions under the management of the same (heavily Anglo-Saxon) network.

Non-Profits and Artist-Run Spaces

Non-profits such as the already mentioned Kunsthalle Lissabon, Oporto or Hangar have been occupying the overall void of content. Hangar is a residency and exhibition space that fosters transdisciplinary exchanges and public engagement, with a particular emphasis on postcolonialism and the Afro-Portuguese scene.[26] These more recent projects have been accompanied by the somewhat older Galeria Zé dos Bois, a cultural centre created in 1994 and invested in music, performance and contemporary art, and by Maumaus. Maumaus is an independent study programme and artist residency that has played a major, albeit informal, role in the internationalisation of the

Portuguese art scene, by, for instance, introducing a whole generation of artists, film-makers and theorists to the local audience (Harun Farocki, Diedrich Diederichsen and René Green amongst them) and by shaping the path of a younger generation of artists whose trajectories would radically change the spirit of the city's art scene (such as Pedro Barateiro, Francisco Vidal or Bruno Leitão, who went on to found Hangar after working with curator Jürgen Bock in the Lumiar Cité space).

The study programme was founded in 1992 by Bock and now has an ancillary exhibition space (mentioned above) called Lumiar Cité. The exhibition programme began in 2005, in Lumiar, after the school was offered a space in an unusual location close to the outskirts of the city, in an area populated by a multicultural working class. Like Maumaus, Lumiar Citá has a strong emphasis on institutional critique and postcolonial studies. It has shown work by artists such as Green, Farocki and Antje Ehmann, Manthia Diawara and Allan Sekula (all long-time collaborators of Bock). Works by younger generations of artists including Francisco Vidal or Gabriel Abrantes have also been shown.[27]

But however professional these spaces may prove to be, their condition remains precarious: they are mostly funded by the DGARTES, Direção Geral das Artes (Directorate-General for the Arts), the public institute that came to replace the IAC, or by the Gulbenkian Foundation, and must reapply every two years. After the building on Avenida da Liberdade was sold to investors, The Barber Shop closed, and Mendes left Portugal to join the curatorial team of the 11th Gwangju Biennale. She is now developing a public programme for CA2M, Centro de Arte Dos de Mayo in Madrid. The Kunsthalle Lissabon had to relocate to the post-industrial area of Xabregas; and Sintaxe, another small non-profit space, is said to be closing due to lack of funding.

In a process comparable to what happened in Berlin, as the non-profits get marginalised or displaced, a new bevy of commercial galleries is in the process of opening storefronts in Lisbon and a growing number of international artists are moving to the city. The welcome effect of this uptick, according to local artists, is the destabilisation of the country's stale hierarchies. The unwelcome effect, however, is felt in spiralling rents and overall real-estate pressure.

It remains somewhat puzzling that a country that never had a strong contemporary art scene could witness contemporary art–led gentrification. But that probably says more about what contemporary art is, at present, than about what Portugal became. In the last three decades, the socio-economic space within which contemporary art circulates has been thoroughly imbricated with speculative finance and gentrification, instituting social and economic dynamics that run counter to the political aspirations of most artists. And yet, as Andrew Stefan Weiner argues, the field hasn't been able to think through the contradictions between what it purports to do and what it inadvertently does.[28] It only compounds the problem that its models and modes of global circulation are particularly ill-suited for this task.

Notes

[1] Mairi Mackay, 'The new Berlin? How austerity helped Lisbon's creatives to succeed', CNN, 7 August 2017, http://edition.cnn.com/style/article/lisbon-cultural-scene/index.html.

[2] Wolfgang Schäuble, who as head of the Treuhand (Trusted Hand) presided over the fire sale of the former East German public companies, is now the German finance minister in charge of the troika's asset stripping. For an in-depth view of the Treuhand's policies, see Dirk Laabs, 'Why is Germany so rough on Greece? Look back 25 years', *The Guardian*, 17 July 2015, https://www.theguardian.com/commentisfree/2015/jul/17/germany-greece-wolfgang-schauble-bailout.

[3] 'Orgulhosamente sós' ('Proudly alone') was the regime's motto; poverty was a state policy. In the 1970s, about 36 per cent of Portuguese households lacked electricity, 53 per cent running water and 42 per cent proper plumbing. Child labour was widespread, vast urban areas were occupied by slums and illiteracy ranged over 30 per cent. By the time the regime fell, over two million Portuguese people had emigrated to France, Luxembourg, Belgium or Germany to escape hunger and unemployment. See Luís Graça, *O Período de 1926–1974: A Modernização Bloqueada. 3.1. Nacionalismo e Corporativismo (1926–1958)*, Lisbon: Universidade Nova de Lisboa, 1999.

[4] The Carnation Revolution started as a military coup in Lisbon, on 25 April 1974, and resulted in the overthrow of the regime of the Estado Novo. The movement was supported by a popular campaign leading to the withdrawal of Portugal from its colonies in Africa.

[5] 1998 Lisbon World Exposition. The Euro 2004 failed to find an audience, nationally as well as internationally.

[6] Denise Ferreira da Silva, 'Unpayable Debt: Reading Scenes of Value against the Arrow of Time', in *The documenta 14 Reader* (ed. Quinn Latimer and Adam Szymczyk), New York and London: Prestel, 2017, p.89.

[7] Ambrose Evans-Pritchard, 'Eurozone crosses rubicon as Portugal's anti-euro Left banned from power', *The Telegraph*, 23 October 2015, http://www.telegraph.co.uk/finance/economics/11949701/AEP-Eurozone-crosses-Rubicon-as-Portugals-anti-euro-Left-banned-from-power.html.

[8] Fortunately the president did not hold the institutional power to dissolve the parliament since his mandate was too close to its terminus.

[9] Two years after the film was shot, Colt Resources folded and its executives absconded, leaving behind unpaid wages and contaminated soil.

[10] Jason W. Moore, *Capitalism in the Web of Life: Ecology and the Accumulation of Capital*, London: Verso, 2015, p.2.

[11] Together with Mariana Silva, Neves Marques runs Inhabitants, an online channel for experimental video. See http://inhabitants-tv.org/.

[12] Descolonizando is a collective comprised of artists, academics and activists, which is informally connected to the campaign #decolonizethisplace. Their intention was not so much to protest the figure of Vieira but rather the narrative of the 'benign' colonist.

[13] Descolonizando had secured a permit for the event, the extremists had not, but the police refused to intervene nonetheless.

[14] See http://www.buala.org.

[15] See Paul Ames, 'Portugal is becoming an Angolan financial colony', *Politico*, 8 April 2015, available at https://www.politico.eu/article/angola-portugal-investment-economy/.

[16] The 'Golden Visas' have raised 1.39 billion euros since 2012. Chinese investors make up over three quarters of the 2,290 visa recipients to date. Other nationalities include Brazilians, Russians, South Africans and Angolans.

[17] For example, Amalia Pica, Mariana Castillo Deball, Iman Issa, Jonathas de Andrade and Marwa Arsanios.

[18] Oporto has been run by multimedia artist Alexandre Estrela since 2007, from his own studio located on a former merchant sailors' union perched atop Santa Catarina's hilltop. The project never managed to galvanise the institutional scene, which remained trapped in its own parochialisms.

[19] Under his tenure as curator for contemporary art from 2005 to 2016, Culturgest exhibited artists such as Asier Mendizabal, Jos de Gruyter, Harald Thys, Jean-Luc Moulène and Dorota Jurczak.

[21] The controversy revolved around the collection of the Secretaria de Estado da Cultura (SEC), first promised to the museum, then suddenly moved to Serralves. The collection comprises 85 paintings by Joan Miró, which were formerly owned by the BPN, a bank whose immense debt was nationalised in 2008.

[21] The loan was contentious if not outright illegal. But unlike other figures implicated in the financial crash (the former Portuguese Prime Minister, José Socrates, or the founder of BES, Ricardo Salgado), Berardo was never indicted.

[22] See Peter Wise, 'Christie's pulls Miró auction after Portuguese protests', *Financial Times*, 4 February 2014, https://www.ft.com/content/277c59a8-8dce-11e3-ba55-00144feab7de.

²³ The notable exception was the choice of João Maria Gusmão and Pedro Paiva, in 2009.

²⁴ The exhibition described the metaphoric trajectory that computer networks undertook, from ominous, life-annihilating military technology to ubiquitous, life-style gadgetry via the emblem of the 'cloud', once a deadly radioactive gas, now an ethereal data-saturated ecosystem.

²⁵ Liz Amos Associates is a headhunting firm based in London whose clients include Frieze, Lisson Gallery and the Tate consortium, as well as Serralves and Gulbenkian in Portugal.

²⁶ The space is run by Mónica de Miranda and Bruno Leitão.

²⁷ In September 2017, Lumiar Cité opened the exhibition 'Mistake! Mistake! said the rooster… and stepped down from the duck', a collaboration with the project Hubert Fichte: Love and Ethnology (2017–19), conceived by Diedrich Diederichsen and Anselm Franke for the Goethe-Institut and Haus der Kulturen der Welt (HKW) in Berlin.

²⁸ Andrew Stefan Weiner, 'The Art of the Possible: With and Against Documenta 14', The Biennial Foundation, 14 August 2017, http://www.biennialfoundation.org/2017/08/art-possible-documenta-14/.

'Public' and 'Access': Genealogies of Theft, Community, Violence and Pedagogies

Khairani Barokka

Two years ago, during an arts festival in London, my Indonesian peers and I received invitations to an evening event to see artefacts stolen from Indonesia. For one night only. A colleague and I agreed: we would rather not respond to this assumption that gratitude and cocktail wear were due for being given the chance to see, in person, artefacts that our communities had been robbed of. These goods had been 'made public', were part of Empire's 'public goods'. And at that time, we were unwilling to be participants in the curators' notions of 'making public', 'giving access to', as moral good. The invitation so deftly reinscribed the violence of stolen property, dismissing our fraught feelings around these artefacts and where they are kept.

As a disabled and chronically ill artist, notions of 'public' and 'access' are always at the forefront of my mind. This piece grapples with, and is an introduction to further work on, how these two terms are deployed in art publics as pluriversal, fluid configurations often circumscribed to specific remits within neoliberal arts industry structures. There is a need to explore how 'public' and 'access' contain multiple meanings, at times simultaneously, that are marked by colonial, capitalist pasts and presents. They may be understood as always hyperlocally situated, within multiple conceptions of the 'global'.

Specifically, here I touch on:

> 1) 'public' as deployed ablenormativity, and 'access' as contained within neoliberal models of disability;
> 2) genealogies of theft and genealogies of community that exist simultaneously and are framed differently within those terms;
> 3) ongoing colonial violence as always part and parcel of 'public', including this obscuring of genealogies of theft, genealogies of community, the ablenormativities of 'public', as well as that word's relationship to 'access';

4) the right of refusal within neoliberal narratives of 'public' and 'access', and how 'public' and 'access' may try to exist outside of these narratives.

For us disabled art workers, similar misgivings to the ones my Indonesian colleague and I had in the aforementioned incident arise when an exhibition is 'public' but inaccessible (and this doesn't, of course, just mean making areas step-free, but comprises many policies to cater to as many bodyminds' access as possible). In both cases, there is the sense of knowing how skewed 'making public' can be, the phrase's partiality and how invested that phrase is in false notions of universality.

'Public' and 'access' are both virtue signals, yet there is rarely an acknowledgement by arts institutions of how 'making public art accessible' highlights the circumscribed and discriminatory scope that supposedly public art had before. Never have I read an example of apologia with regards to making 'public art' 'accessible' when it wasn't before. There is scarcely, in non-disabled and non-D/deaf media, an acknowledgement of how ablenormative 'public' actually is, overwhelmingly, in arts institutions. How violent.

As an artist who has been literally physically injured in and by arts institutions innumerable times, and who has written about some of these incidents, it remains astonishing that art institutions are not thought of by some as places of violence. Violence which is 'public'.

An exercise that can be applied to any arts institution is to unpack the dynamics between the phraseology of these two terms within it: 'making public' and 'accessibility'. These terms are bandied around within the same institutions without ever acknowledging the separation between the former and the latter, and specifically that the former indicates 'non-disabled public' and the latter 'disabled and D/deaf people too', as add-on. As violence and discrimination. Or that 'public' is bound within nation-state.

As ableism is too often defined through the most privileged of lenses, I call on Talila Lewis's working definition of the term:

> *A system that places value on people's bodies and minds based on societally constructed ideas of normalcy, intelligence and excellence. These constructed ideas of normalcy, intelligence and excellence are deeply rooted in anti-Blackness, eugenics and capitalism.*
>
> *This form of systemic oppression leads to people and society determining who is valuable and worthy based on people's appearance and/or their ability to satisfactorily produce, excel and 'behave'.*
>
> *You do not have to be disabled to experience ableism.*[1]

To this definition I would add: These constructed ideas are also rooted in colonialities, anti-indigeneities, anti-pluriversalities. Ableism defined as such is why 'making art public' is overwhelmingly synonymised with 'non-disabled, speaking, hearing publics'. And how capital flows and border politics that continually make and remake conceptions of 'disability' have formed – and expose – the contours of 'public accessibility' along fraught, colonial lines.

Ever-present as undercurrent in the imperialist present: the painful knowledge that others have been made disabled to serve hegemonic political interests, whether in Palestine or in Indonesia, and thus placed in an othered category in which their likelihood for welfare is even more diminished. This is the thesis of Jasbir Puar's book *The Right to Maim* (2017).[2] There is thus, by virtue of colonial capital flows – such as the ties of donors to weapons manufacturing, militarism and environmental violences – a perpetuation of colonial violence and trauma in 'public' acts within fine arts industries. Here I refer to Western colonialism as well as other forms of violence organised around nation-state formations, such as colonialisms within Indonesia perpetrated against Papuans.

Thus, a public arts exhibit that is accessible to those within nation-state boundaries whose bodyminds are privileged is also a deeply ableist one – in the sense of operating within stratified geo-politics that maim and kill and disable and rob from the disabled, especially in countries affected by Western imperialism.

There are, within configurations in arts institutions of 'public' and 'access', genealogies of theft and genealogies of community that exist simultaneously and are framed in various ways. Due to the aforementioned complicity we all have in colonial capitalism, ongoing colonial violence is always part of the 'public', including an obscuring of genealogies of theft and of community by virtue of the ablenormativities of 'public' as well as that word's relationship to 'access'.

A public higher arts institution in the UK has different usages of 'public' across its various campuses and entities, which are used in different emotional pedagogies of 'public'. The 'public' in 'public institution' does not mean that art school tuition is non-existent; there is a price to entry. Thus 'public' is already limited to those who can afford it, or to those lucky few who undergo competition for rare scholarships, and borders of nation-state citizenship and residency laws. In a society marked by racial, ableist, cisheteropatriarchal capitalism, that 'public' is circumscribed along lines of race, what Wendy Trevino calls the 'cruel fiction' of it, as well as according to Western allocations of sexuality and gender identities, to work with Maria Lugones's decolonial framework of imposed gender categories as inherently colonial, and along lines of normativity for certain bodyminds.[3] The inaccessibility of spaces, events and procedures within a public university has caused multiple violences over the years to those who attempt access – ongoing physical and emotional distress.

There are different emotional pedagogies, emotional conditioning systems, that create narratives around 'public' and 'access', as per Sara Ahmed's *The Cultural Politics of Emotion* (2004) – we are conditioned to think kindly of 'public' in the case of 'public exhibition' or 'public gallery' and to be alarmed at phrases like 'public controversy', often employed in media outlets that do not outright name the violences of racism, ableism, sexism, etc. within capitalism that may be involved.[4]

A revealing question: Which parts of a 'public' exhibition or institution are public? Complaint forms? Donor information, lender information? Employee conversations? Though obvious, in laying out an institution's blueprint for what is *presented* as public, and *how*, we may lay bare the ways in which public relations schemata architect affect and undisrupted capital flows.

Genealogies of theft within colonial arts institutions, and genealogies of community, shape these usages of 'public'. Artefacts, wealth and the continuity of lifeways were thieved from colonised communities and became the loot of 'the public', those claiming citizenry and/or residency in the thieving nation-state. Organisations engaging with stolen artefacts, or even subjects of arts regimes as we all are, are interwoven with genealogies of theft and of community.

The relationship of 'public' and 'access' to multivariable notions of 'theft' and 'community' are vastly varied within different arts institutional and extra-institutional contexts. 'Theft' of course has a negative connotation, while 'community' tends to be used more often as a positive connotation in arts settings; the complexity of relationships between these terms in one entity is a concept to bear in mind.

As I wrote in 'Caption in Red Thread: D/deaf and/or Disabled Histories in the African, Asian and Afro-Caribbean Art in Britain Archive', there are innumerable potential narratives present in arts archives and artefacts, particularly in colonial archives, that have had to operate stealthily to avoid detection by violent forces, under suppression from above.[5] Thus we are all embroiled in genealogies, histories, that we may well never be aware of, particularly when in close proximity, adjacency and complicity in white supremacist colonial capitalism.

In the words of Eve Tuck and K. Wayne Yang,

> *Decolonization brings about the repatriation of Indigenous land and life; it is not a metaphor for other things we want to do to improve our societies and schools. [...] The metaphorization of decolonization makes possible a set of evasions, or 'settler moves to innocence', that problematically attempt to reconcile settler guilt and complicity, and rescue settler futurity.*[6]

'Making a collection public' is also rooted in such moves to innocence. Public art exhibitions, public institutions and public property are all, in a world marked indelibly by colonialism, built on genealogies of theft. 'Public land' in the context of stolen Indigenous lands, whether in Indonesia or the United States, is thieved land, even when packaged and sold as a 'national park' or 'heritage site'.

Making a collection that was previously private into a public good – for instance, a donor gifting previously owned historical artefacts to a museum –

overwhelmingly does not come with an apologia for having withheld these, but is instead a move to innocence on the part of the donor. Making art more accessible to a certain public, and making art 'public', virtually never comes with apologia. Furthermore, 'public' is still circumscribed by the logics of neoliberal arts institutions operating within nation-state formations. What came before 'making public'? Ownership, legalities, the histories and colonial frameworks of private art. It is bound up in violence, including the disablement of body-minds and, as I term myself and others in my spiritual community, soulbodies.

'Public' with regards to governmental arts bodies, in particular, is caught in the thorns of localised histories of violence. This is felt keenly in my own context, of having grown up in the repressive, capitalist authoritarianism of President Soeharto's New Order. Traumatised through art itself, from around the tender age of eight – with, for instance, the hyperviolent film *Pengkhianatan G30S/ PKI* (1984). The film falsely recreates the supposed Communist uprising, erasing the genocide of likely millions of people under false pretences; it was regularly shown in schools and television stations. As children we went on school field trips to memorials supporting such false notions of history, scarring myself and three generations of Indonesians. We continue to live in a world where we and/or people we know have been violated or traumatised or made missing or gone by the repercussions of the New Order – a dictatorial regime installed by the CIA and its allies.

Jakarta Biennale 2021 programme director Farah Wardani recently wrote, in an online text also distributed to colleagues in the arts:

> *After experiencing a repressive regime for three decades – an experience shared by many of us – its survivors have gotten used to taking care of themselves, minding their own business, cooperating with various non-governmental entities, be it locally, nationally or even internationally. Therefore, it makes sense that many of us working in the arts, in academia or in any scene really, who managed to survive such regimes, have never felt the need to work with the government nor its institutions. Many of us have become our own self-made institutions and have carved out their own ways of doing things.*[7]

Reading this resonated deeply with me, and this last part is key: 'self-made institutions'.

An example of bottom-up institutions in Indonesia that arose, self-made, outside of governmental 'publics' is Jatiwangi Art Factory (JAF) in West Java. Created by artists who left the city of Bandung for a less frenetic pace, and with intentions to create a village-based artistic collective that truly included all, Jatiwangi is an example I look to in terms of relational ethics and a participatory manifestation of 'public'. Resident artists, both local and international, are required to do projects in partnership with the local community; not in any savior sense, but as co-artists. All in the village are asked to be invested, as residents temporary or long-term, in the aliveness of the place, against neoliberal encroachment in the form of unchecked 'development'.

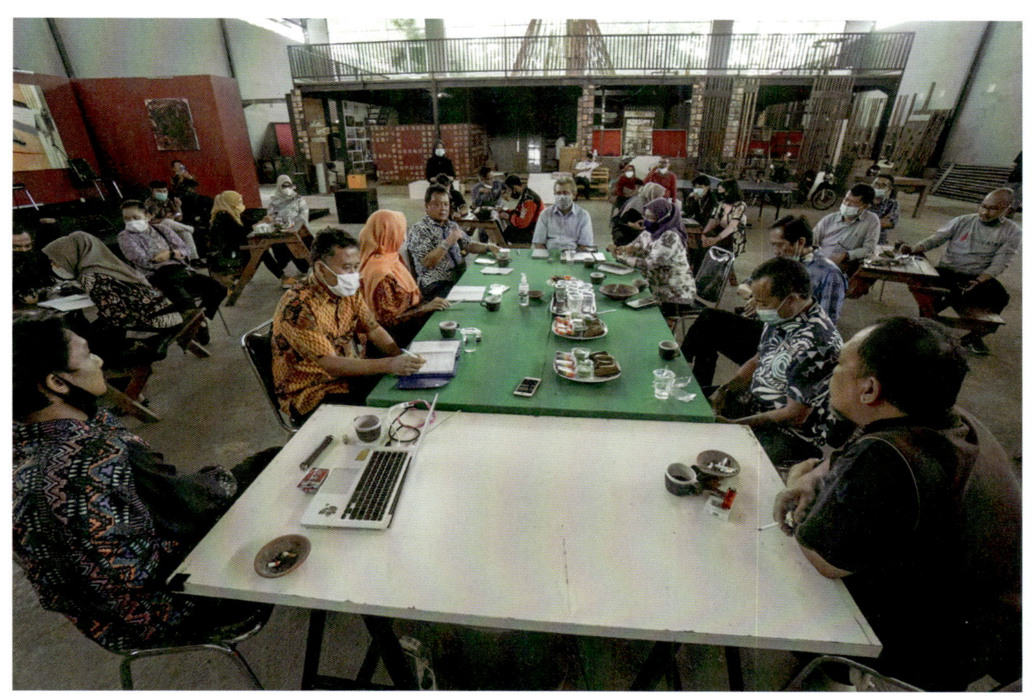

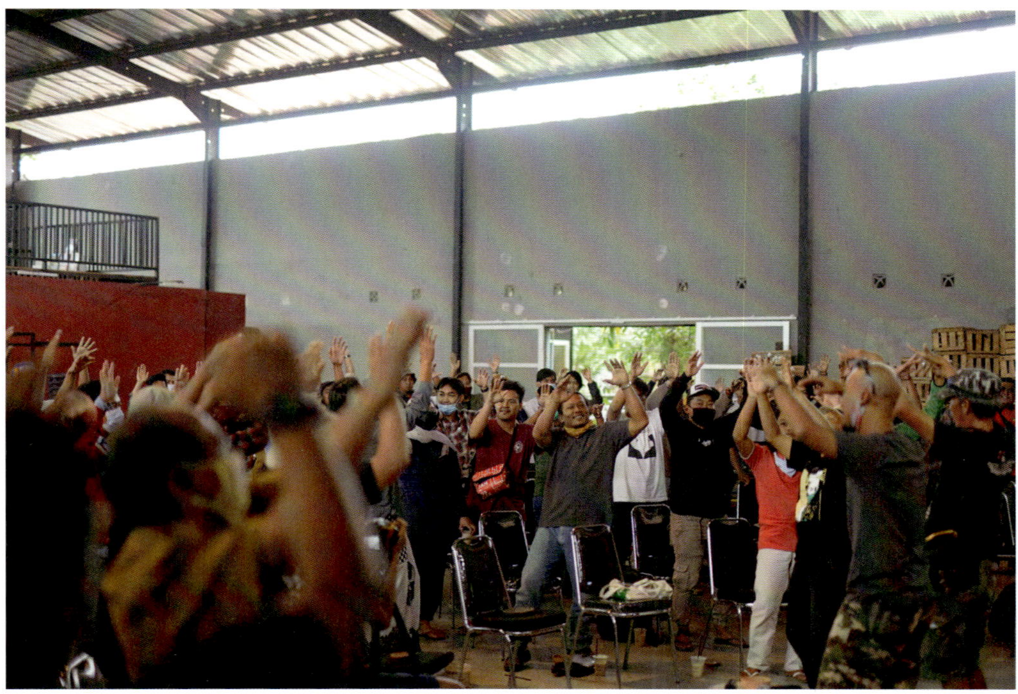

I had the opportunity to be an artist-in-residence during their 2012 Village Video Festival, creating with new media artist Krisna Murti the participatory performance installation *Samudra Keram* (in which locals' improvised vocal contributions were part of my performance on a giant bed of sand, onto which oceanic images were projected) and teaching poetry-filmmaking at a local primary school. When Krisna and I arrived at the train station near the village, I was surprised that we were met by a convoy of police cars and escorted to the residency inside those police cars by officers including the local police chief. The latter, I discovered, wanted to be a video artist, and he along with other village residents participated in Krisna's lecture on new media art with intensive discussions on ethics and the image, fakery in a digital age and whether there could even be an ethical role of law enforcement within such circumstances.[8]

There are a plethora of artistic communities in Indonesia, in formations such as JAF, and in other manifestations. It is a land with over 700 languages and as many cultures, over 17,000 islands, and vast histories of artistic creation in the face of government repression and colonial exploitation. Communities that are already public because the public created them, rather than having art 'made public' to them – they create art that is inherently public.

Yet outsiders looking in with colonial mentalities will erase these formations' existence, regarding art in the Indonesian archipelago as terra nullius. This is particularly the case for those formations existing outside neoliberal spheres and capital flows. Farah Wardani writes:

> *Some even cling to the typical 'foreign' claim that we do not have an art infrastructure. Yet, things have always happened. There have always been festivals, exhibitions, shows, performances, programs, etc. How can we say that there is no infrastructure?*[9]

Within the landscape of multiple 'publics' exists the right of refusal. There is the right of refusal to exist within colonial narratives, or for a trans artist to be identified with their deadname, or for a public to engage with colonial infrastructures. There is the right to acknowledge the many publics around the world that have been created as always inherently public, and increasingly (though not nearly fast or prevalent enough) with the drive for more accessibility, in a truer sense – an anticolonial, anti-imperialist sense. From the bottom up.

A relevant descriptive quote by Yoshi Fajar Kresno Murti from the brilliant book *Arsipelago* (2014), on Indonesian community archiving practices:

> *And, that is how it should be: indonesianness is formed not from an abstract concept of national(ism) hegemony, but built from small efforts and ideas arising from everywhere through the practical, everyday realities – complex and full of injustices – of its peoples.*[10]

We honour these already-publics, whether or not we are aware of each. We honour these forms of access.

Notes

1 Talila Lewis (@talilalewis), Twitter, 14 March 2019, 8.58 a.m., available at https://twitter.com/talilalewis/status/1106223049119055873.

2 Jasbir K. Puar, *The Right to Maim: Debility, Capacity, Disability*, Durham, NC: Duke University Press, 2017.

3 Wendy Trevino, *Cruel Fiction*, Oakland, CA: Commune Editions, 2018; and María Lugones, 'Toward a Decolonial Feminism', *Hypatia*, vol.25, no.4, 2010, pp.742–59.

4 Sara Ahmed, *The Cultural Politics of Emotion*, New York: Routledge, 2004.

5 Khairani Barokka, 'Caption in Red Thread: D/deaf and Disabled Narratives in the African-Caribbean, Asian and African Art in Britain Archive', University of the Arts London, 2021, available at https://www.arts.ac.uk/ual-decolonising-arts-institute/projects/decolonising-archives-research-residencies.

6 Eve Tuck and K. Wayne Yang, 'Decolonization is not a metaphor', *Decolonization: Indigeneity, Education & Society*, vol.1, no.1, 2012, p.1.

7 Farah Wardani, '[Letter] Notes from the Programme Director', Jakarta Biennale 2021 blog, https://blog.jakartabiennale.id/?p=703.

8 When I was in residence at Jatiwangi, I still had difficulty communicating my access needs as a chronically ill woman who at that time did not have access to the medicines that would eventually lessen episodes of extreme pain. There was hesitancy at articulating how in pain and in danger of pain I constantly was. Now, still in touch with the artist-organisers from JAF, I know better how to communicate my needs, to ensure that a repeat experience would be accessible and kinder. It occurs to me that feeling safe enough to declare access needs is a fundamental tenet of truly accessible art spaces and groups. Access also means safety – feeling safe declaring one's access needs.

9 F. Wardani, '[Letter] Notes from the Programme Director', *op. cit.*

10 See F. Wardani and Yoshi Fajar Kresno Murti (ed.), *Arsipelago: Kerja Arsip & Pengarsipan Seni Budaya di Indonesia*, Yogyakarta: Indonesian Visual Art Archive (IVAA), 2014, p.xii. Translation mine.

Museo Comunitario del Valle de Xico: A Community's Trench of Struggle

Genaro Amaro Altamirano

Ana Bilbao

In 1971, during the tenth General Assembly of the International Council of Museums (ICOM) in Grenoble, France, speakers from African and Latin American countries agreed that non-European peoples had specific cultural needs. The Western museum model, a colonial legacy, did not seem to sufficiently respond to this specificity.[1] The speakers raised the urgency of developing museum models that adapted to local needs independently from the European model.[2] The following year (May 1972), ICOM organised the Round Table of Santiago in Chile, where there was a debate on the role of the museum in the Latin American context. Representatives of different museums on the continent took part in interdisciplinary forums, discussing the work museums needed to do to improve what they offered to the less privileged members of their communities.[3] The concept of the 'integral museum' emerged from the scrutiny of the role of such institutions in rural, technological, scientific, ecological and educational contexts. This refocussing towards the 'integral museum' recognised that the museum must be at the service of the community, which must participate in articulating bridges between its historical past, its natural and cultural environment, and its current national reality.[4] This was reflected in adjustments that implied the creation of new methodologies for large museums and the creation of spaces of different scales and with distinctive regional missions. In Mexico, this process is now known as the Nueva Museología Mexicana (New Mexican Museology), and this context gave rise to Mexico's community museums. These spaces proliferated between the mid-1980s and 90s as the INAH (National Institute of Anthropology and History) inaugurated a support programme for them in collaboration with the SEP (Ministry of Public Education), arguing that communities could take over the management of their heritage.[5] From the beginning, community museums were defined as spaces created by the active participation of local populations, and their programming was meant to directly address peoples' own interests and needs.[6]

The Museo Comunitario del Valle de Xico opened its doors in the State of Mexico in 1996. The safeguarding of indigenous peoples' environmental and land rights resulted from an initial struggle to defend the cultural heritage of the locality. Here, Genaro Amaro Altamirano, traditional chronicler and coordinator of the Xico museum, talks about the social-ecological context that gave life to this space, as well as the changes, achievements and challenges that the museum has faced since its founding.

Ana Bilbao: Genaro, could you tell us about the context in which the Museo Comunitario del Valle de Xico began? For example, about the social struggles, and in particular its relationship to community land and water rights?

Genaro Amaro Altamirano: What is now the Chalco Solidaridad Valley, an urban settlement on the outskirts of Mexico City, emerged in the 1980s. The environmental conditions were difficult since the terrain was almost a desert moor. In the dry season, a layer of salty soil gave way to dust, and in the rainy season, loose soil gave way to mud that spread everywhere. There were no utilities – no drinking water, sewerage, sidewalks, decent public transportation, electricity, schools, markets, etc. This resulted in people actively taking part in social mobilisations to fight for essential services. People self-organised, often with the support of local political parties, to address social struggles, sometimes peacefully, but on some occasions violently, as was the case with the struggle for the control of Route 100, a public transportation system that was run by a militant union. Under these circumstances, as a group of neighbours concerned about the systematic destruction of the site's archaeological heritage by urban development works – we saw the remains of vessels and pre-Hispanic objects broken, destroyed by the hasty manner in which the work was being conducted – we called the public to form a social organisation in order to create the Museo Comunitario del Valle de Xico. Seventeen people attended the initial call, almost all participants from social organisations who saw the creation of a museum as an opportunity to provide a new form of community organisation for the people of the Chalco Valley.

The original people of the region, faced with a human avalanche because of the excessive population growth of Mexico City, began fighting for their rights to the land and water of the region. They formed the Amecameca River Basin Commission and 'La Compañía' under the auspices of researchers from the Autonomous Metropolitan University, with whom they created a water plan for the region. This is how the museum's activities began supporting and accompanying the native peoples in their struggle to conserve their lands and avoid the dispossession of their waters. Above all, the struggle focussed

337

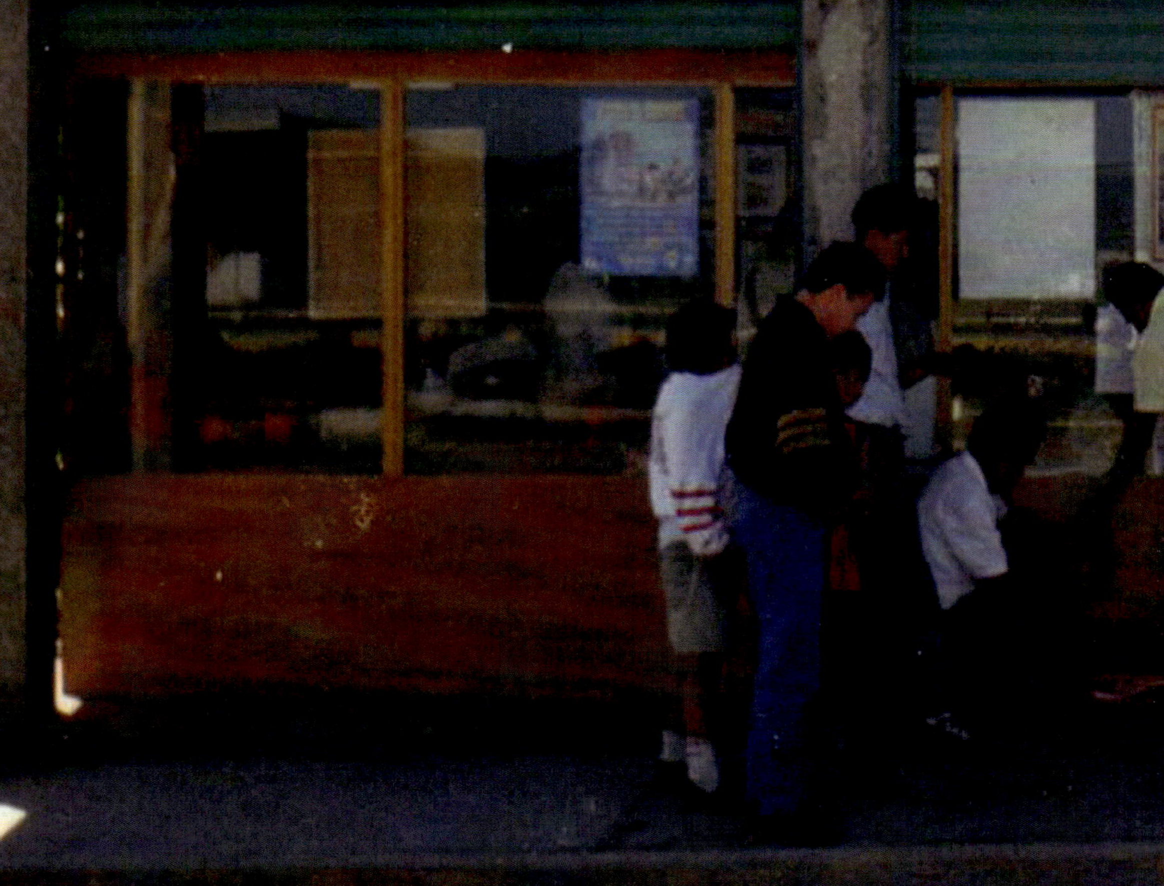

MUSEO COMUNITARIO DEL

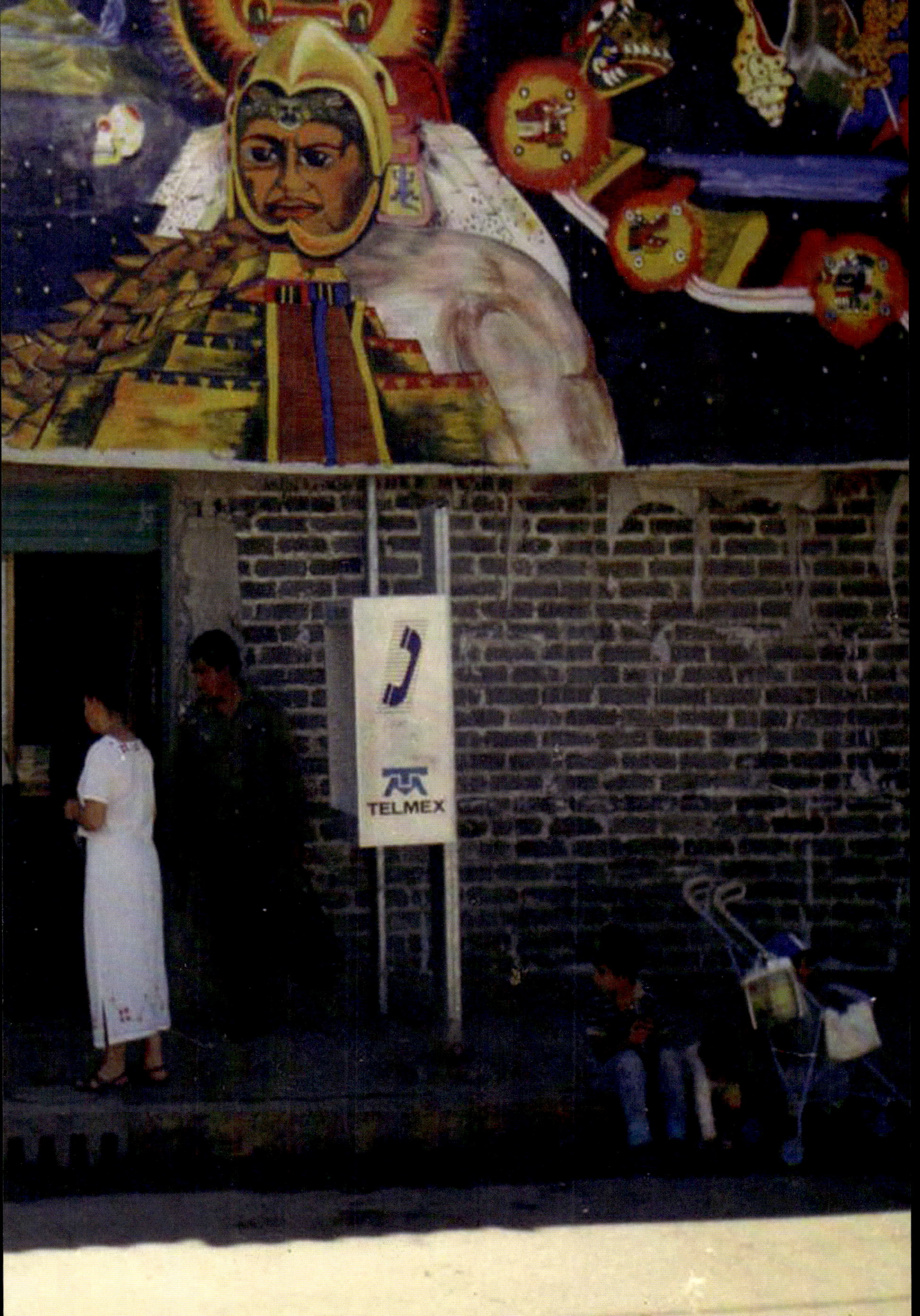

TELMEX

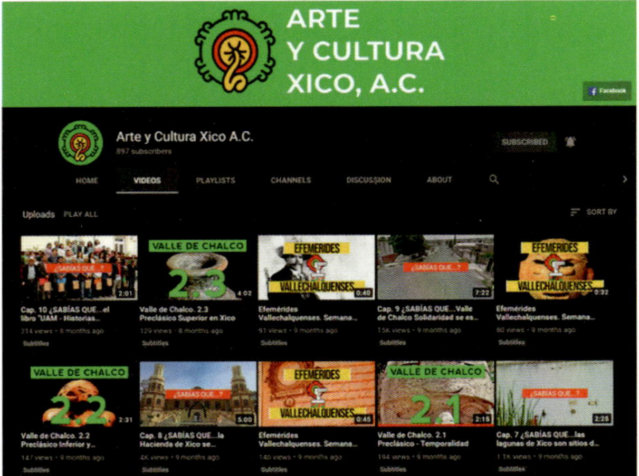

Museo Comunitario del Valle de Xico YouTube page, 2021, at https://www.youtube.com/c/ArteyCulturaXicoAC/

on the resurgence of Lake Chalco due to the over-exploitation of the aquifer mantle, which caused differentiated land subsidence – a depression of forty centimetres per year, which, with time, became twelve metres, forming a land concavity where the river and rainwater are held. Thus, Lake Chalco now occupies the space it once had. This presents the opportunity to recover part of the natural environment from before the lake dried up, a natural environment altered and destroyed by human intervention. (Íñigo Noriega Lasso, owner of the Xico hacienda, carried out the drying up of Lake Chalco at the beginning of the twentieth century.)

AB: One of the monumental tasks that the museum has carried out has been its dialogue with the local community about three related issues: land rights, environmental rights and heritage. How relevant are these themes for the museum programme today, a quarter century later?

GAA: Throughout these years that the community museum has existed, we have learned to feel and understand the great social problems the community experiences, both the native peoples and the new neighbourhoods. The knowledge of social and cultural dynamics within the community allows us to develop participation strategies based on their needs. I believe the most heartfelt problems our population suffers, and on which the museum can exert an influence, concern land and water, the right of the population to access local and national culture, and the creation of a sense of identity based on the historical knowledge of the site. Above all, this last aspect – generating a sense of identity and belonging to the place where one lives – is important because the inhabitants come from different parts of the country. The new generations of dwellers, especially those who came here as children or were born here, develop feelings for and a rootedness in the physical space upon learning about local history and fusing it with daily cultural dynamics.

AB: You use a very interesting concept, which is that of 'museum as a trench'. Could you elaborate a bit on your thinking in relation to this concept?

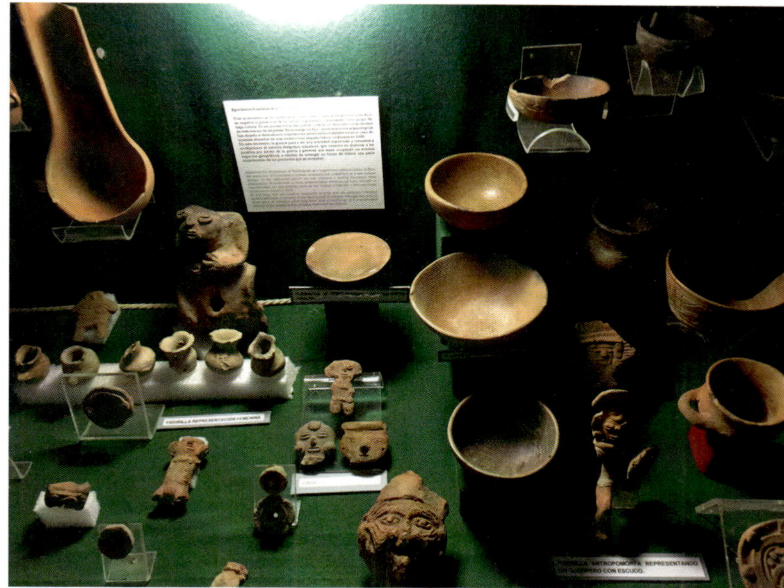

Museo Comunitario
del Valle de Xico,
c.2013/16. Courtesy
Pablo Lafuente and
Michelle Sommer

GAA: As I have said, most people who answered the call of creating the community museum were part of local organisations struggling to find solutions to the demand for public services. When we built the project to create the Museo Comunitario del Valle de Xico, we analysed the possibility of creating a community organisation to better fight for the social objectives we aspired to.

In my case, I had a taste for writing and for the history of Mexico and the world. I considered the museum as a trench from which to develop my taste for writing and history, and that is why I became a chronicler of the museum, 'the one who preserves history' – this is how my personal skills are at the service of the museum in continuing the struggle against poverty and marginalisation in our community.

AB: The last time we spoke, the museum was in a very different situation. Currently it is closed, in part because of the Covid-19 pandemic. But the museum had in fact closed earlier…

GAA: The museum worked with the community on various projects that gave it recognition and a good reputation with various government bodies and social organisations in the area. As time passed, municipal authorities were tempted to appropriate the museum. We had installed the museum in a space that belongs to the municipal authority, the Xico hacienda, and every three years, with a change in administration, we have had to renegotiate our permanence in that space. In 2010, municipal authorities attempted to strip us of the museum for the first time. They placed tarpaulins on the museum's asbestos ceiling, damaging it and causing water leaks. We realised the risk for the archaeological collections – the water could damage them – so we moved the display cases to an additional space. When municipal authorities saw that we

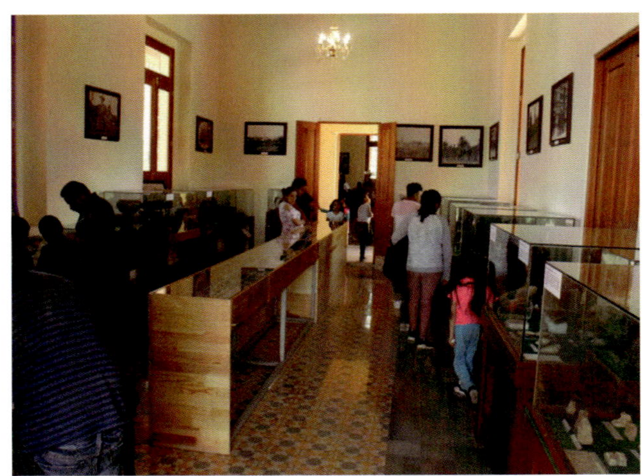

From top: Visitors
to the Museo
Comunitario del
Valle de Xico,
January 2019;
municipal police
closing access
to the museum,
11 February
2019; meeting
with cooperative
members, Tláhuac,
2013. Courtesy
Museo Comunitario
del Valle de Xico

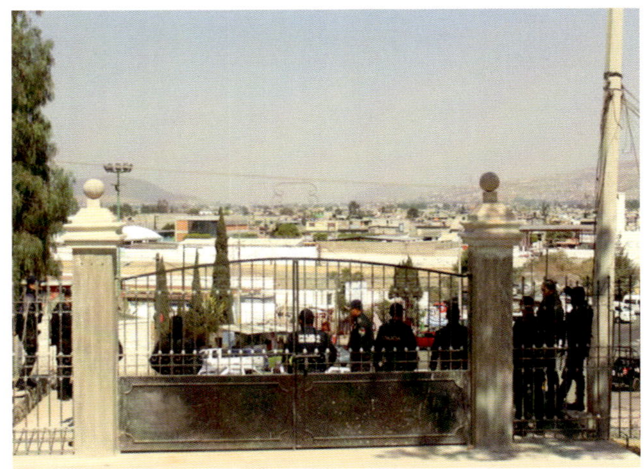

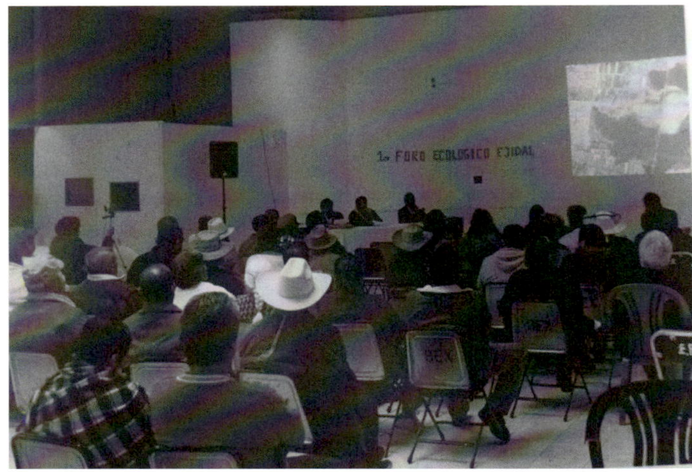

were moving the showcases, they must have assumed that we were leaving the premises for good, and they closed the building's doors with chains and padlocks. The federal authorities of the National Institute of Anthropology and History had to intervene to allow our access to the premises. We had all the required documentation to operate as a museum, and we agreed to make improvements to the space with a concrete roof. This work took eight months to complete while the museum continued to function provisionally in the space.

We had signed the last loan for the museum space with the municipal government in 2016, and it expired on 31 December 2018. In 2019, when the new authorities took office, our task was to arrange a new loan for the museum. They thought the museum belonged to the municipality and that they could intervene in its operation – they did not know that comrade Juan Manuel Rodríguez Neri was the director of the museum, nor that my position was municipal chronicler. They pretended that by paying out some colleagues, the museum would pass under their administration. Obviously, the colleagues did not allow such an outrageous move, and through various communications sent to municipal authorities, we made them aware of our capacity as Auxiliary Body of the National Institute of Anthropology and History and of our autonomy from municipal authorities.

The Culture Council of Chalco Valley was planning an event in the Xico hacienda, and the authorities verbally denied permission in order to close the museum facilities on 11 February 2019. It is important to note that the Culture Council was an organisation with which the community museum collaborated, but it was the Culture Council and not the community museum that requested the event. After the museum's closure, they tried to get the National Institute of Anthropology and History to give them recognition and a concession to use the collections so that they could open and manage the museum. However, the federal authority did not make any concessions because our legal situation with INAH was in order and we were the legal administrators of the collections. Faced with the impossibility of taking over the museum, they opted to keep it closed to the public, arguing that it was being restored. So, since February 2019 the Xico hacienda and the museum have remained closed.

AB: A fundamental aspect of the community museum is the networks and relationships formed to serve the community. As you have said many times, physical space is secondary to that commitment. With the political complications and the pandemic, what are the strategies and methods that the museum has designed to continue listening to the community's needs in the absence of physical space?

GAA: Since the museum's closure in 2019, we have made complaints and efforts to reopen, but we've found ourselves without access to the museum premises. We've had to adopt strategies to continue pursuing our aim of disseminating the history of the region – that is how we intensified the presentations of 'Taller de Historia Xico. Ayer y hoy, Imágenes desde la Infancia' ('The Xico History Workshop: Yesterday and today, Childhood Images') amongst the groups of the municipality's schools. During those first months, we toured the schools presenting that workshop, until the pandemic caused the schools to close. Soon, a proposal to use digital media to bring information to the public arose amongst some colleagues, although the actual target was students. Thus, we developed a series of informative capsules about local history and current problems and uploaded them to the internet every eight days, hoping to influence the Vallechalquense population. We promoted three different series: first, 'Efemérides Vallechalquenses' (Vallechalquense Anniversaries), which recalled characters and important events related to the municipality's history; second, 'Sabías qué…' ('Did you know that…'), for which we devised capsules with relevant and little-known events of the municipality; and third, the site's chronology, going through all the stages of the site's history. To confirm the impact of the capsules, we noted the number of subscribers on our social media and continuously corresponded with workshop teachers for feedback. Thus, we put into practice one of the museum's guidelines: to be a living museum interrelated with the community beyond the framework of the museum walls. To date, we have had great acceptance amongst the public.

AB: What can other institutions – not only artistic – learn from the major challenges and achievements of the Museo Comunitario del Valle de Xico?

GAA: Well, I think there are several aspects to highlight about the museum's experience. The first is that the museum arose through the initiative of the community itself, with the purpose of playing a role in local cultural dynamics – a museum of the community for the community. The second aspect is that we can generate series of actions from the community's perspective to generate income, and this can solve the need for economic resources through the participation of community members who offer their collaboration for the good of the project – bricklayers, electricians, plumbers, instructors of various art workshops and, above all, museum custodians. Third, it is important to take care in working with young people to guarantee the generational renewal of the museum. This starts with involving them in the museum's activities regardless of age or gender, because the museum belongs to the community and will continue to do so for as long as it appropriates the museum's space. The fourth aspect to consider is that the museum is a means for the community to participate in the enquiry to appropriate and preserve the cultural and ecological heritage for which it was created. Unlike government and private museums that base their educational work on the value of objects' aesthetic qualities, the community museum must see in its museum objects the opportunity to recreate the daily life of communities. It is in this day-to-day life that peoples' aspirations and desires can best be appreciated. It must be very clear that participation and coexistence with authorities are sometimes very complex matters, full of controversy, which should lead to the generation of strategies outside of political interests – but without neglecting the possibility of working with the authorities because, if working without the government is good, working with the government and with all social actors should be better.

Translated from Spanish by Ana S. González Rueda.

Notes

[1] During the colonial era, cabinets of curiosities – historical predecessors of the European public museum – were imported to Latin America. The colonial legacy comprises not only the adoption of this museum concept but also its historical trajectory. The first space of this nature in the 'new world' was installed in downtown Mexico City in 1790. The so-called 'first cabinet of natural history' was open to the public and had a collection of local flora and fauna as well as scientific instruments.

[2] Hugues de Varine, 'The Origins of the New Museology Concept and of the Ecomuseum Word and Concept in the 1960s and the 1970s', in *Communication and Exploration*, Trentino: Trentino Cultura, 2005, p.53.

[3] See Mario Teruggi, 'The Round Table of Santiago (Chile)', *Museum International*, vol.53, no.4, 2001, pp.15–18.

[4] Miguel Ángel Azócar M, 'A Treinta y Cinco Años de La Mesa Rendonda de Santiago', available at http://www.patrimoniocultural.gob.cl/dinamicas/DocAdjunto_991.pdf.

[5] Natalia Ramírez, 'Museos comunitarios mexicanos: entre espejismos teóricos y autonomías in-exploradas', *Archivo Churubusco*, no.1, 2016, https://archivochurubusco.encrym.edu.mx/n1letras3.html.

[6] *Ibid.*

'Struggle as Culture': The Museum of Solidarity

María Berríos

Can a museum be a weapon? What follows is the story of how a small-scale early-1970s counter-information campaign to defend the Chilean 'revolution without arms' against a transnational imperialist smear campaign materialised into an experimental museum, based on the principle that art and politics are intrinsically inseparable.[1] Initially simply a 'beautiful and generous' *idea* of a museum free and open to all, and against the geo-political monopoly of art by the interests of the capitalist metropolis, the 'museum of solidarity' – self-proclaimed as such before the existence of a collection or a building to house it (the latter came only decades later) – would indeed become an important organ for resistance.

The museum in question, the Museo de la Solidaridad (Museum of Solidarity), was founded in 1971. Conceived as a collection 'for the people, by the people' to support the emancipatory struggles of the Third World, at the time of the military coup on 11 September 1973 – only two years after the project was born – it comprised over 700 artworks, and continued to grow during its itinerant existence as an 'international museum of resistance'. The present text will focus on how the project emerged and the urgencies it tried to address at the time – what it *built on* and what it *destroyed* – by following the Museum as a collective and internationalist experiment in art and politics strongly grounded in the revolutionary struggle that had been taking shape for some time in Chile.

Concentrating on how the project emerged means stepping aside from a prevailing emphasis on the value of its collection – the outstanding individualised works of art it contains – to instead focus on the Museum of Solidarity as an expanded collaborative work, wherein artists and artworks become key elements of a community of agitators and organisers that materialised as a seemingly utopian experiment in museography. Looking into its origins – the becoming of a museum, and the foundations set by the local workings of art and revolution before it – enables an understanding of the radical differences between its collection and other prestigious Latin American modern art collections. What it came out of and how it came to life makes very clear

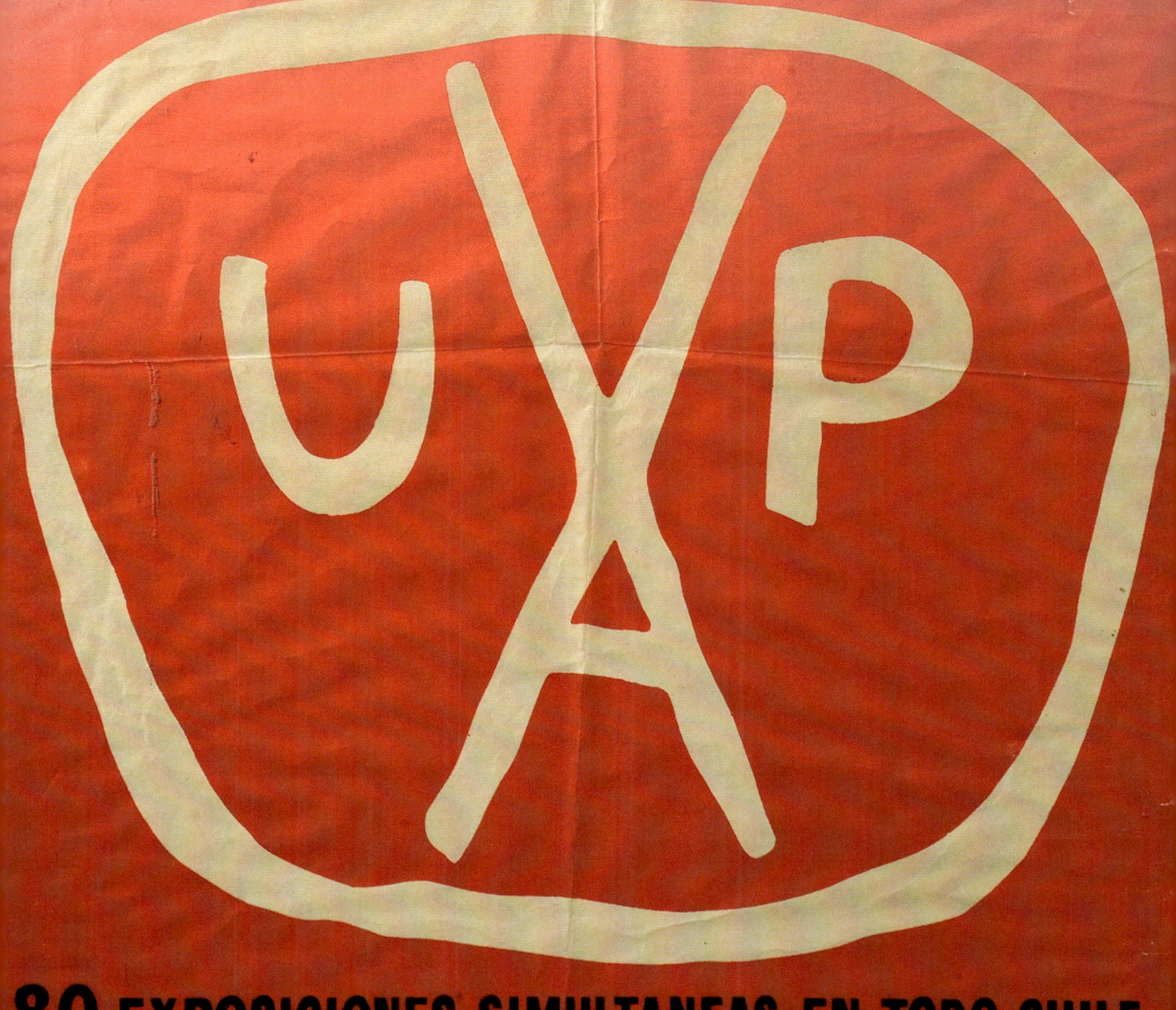

EL PUEBLO TIENE
ARTE CON ALLENDE
UP
80 EXPOSICIONES SIMULTANEAS EN TODO CHILE
DE LOS ARTISTAS DE LA U.P.
DEL 12 AL 22 DE AGOSTO 1970

how and why the Museum of Solidarity Salvador Allende is an operation of a fundamentally different nature and aim.[1]

Art and the 'Revolution Without Arms'

After the triumph of the Unidad Popular (Popular Unity) candidate Salvador Allende in the 1970 Chilean presidential election, a nation few people could locate on a map suddenly began to appear in mainstream international media as a dangerous threat to the 'free democracy' of capitalist imperialism. The media's portrayal was part of a deliberate scare campaign to effectively impede Allende from coming to power: because he only had a relative majority, according to Chilean law he would have to be ratified in Congress. His national and international opponents saw a window of opportunity to stop Allende from occupying the presidential seat. Simultaneously, Chile attracted progressives from around the world, especially heterodox, non-aligned leftists. In the context of the disenchantment that followed after 1968, Chile's 'revolution without arms' was viewed as an inspiration and a source of new hope (as Cuba had been in the previous decade).

One of the trademarks of Popular Unity in general, and of Allende's presidential campaigns in particular, was the pivotal role of culture and cultural workers. Never before or since has a Chilean candidate had such enthusiastic support across an immense portion of the artistic community. The active participation of cultural workers – not as advertising agents but through their own artistic practices – was considered a main asset in what had been an otherwise severely underfunded presidential campaign. The magnitude and force of the diverse artistic knowledge the 'artists with Allende' provided was the one clear advantage the Popular Unity campaign had against its opponents, the centre and right-wing candidates (who were well funded and backed by the United States Central Intelligence Agency[4]) and the corporate media. The electoral triumph of Popular Unity was recognised with the ratification of Allende's presidency by Congress on 26 October 1970. At that time, it is fair to say that artists were not only extremely invested in politics, but already experimenting and reflecting on how art and politics could together contribute to the revolutionary struggle. The project of the Museum of Solidarity can be traced to the principles developed through art workers' practices.

One of the first art exhibitions to take place after the election was 'Homenaje al triunfo del pueblo' ('Homage to the Triumph of the People'), which involved the participation of over 200 artists from Uruguay, Argentina and Chile.[4] Organised by the Instituto de Arte Latinoamericano (Latin American Art Institute, IAL), it opened at the Museo de Arte Contemporáneo (Contemporary Art Museum) on 4 November 1970 – the same day Allende was sworn in as president. The catalogue's opening statement reads:

> *More than an exhibition in the traditional sense, 'Homage to the Triumph of the People' is a manifesto of visual artists. The show does not intend to define a style but simply to assert Chilean and foreign artists' militant position, total support and contribution to the construction of a new society.*[5]

Allende's presidential campaign had already used art and the exhibition form as modes of political action through the itinerant exhibition 'El pueblo tiene arte con Allende' ('The People Have Art with Allende'). Organised by the Comité de Artistas Plásticos de la Unidad Popular (Committee of Visual Artists of Popular Unity), it consisted of a set of thirty silkscreens simultaneously exhibited in eighty different locations throughout Chile on 12 August 1970, just weeks before the election. The stylistically heterogeneous prints – abstract compositions, reinterpretations of folk art, agitpop and more lyrical figurative images – could be purchased at a price affordable to the common worker. In Santiago, the show was installed inside a circus tent behind the Museo Nacional de Bellas Artes (National Fine Arts Museum). The same prints were exhibited around the globe and donated to institutions in Cuba, Colombia, Peru and the German Democratic Republic, in line with the internationalist approach of their notions of art and revolution. The 'catalogue', consisting of a single sheet of paper, states:

> *This show, which will be seen by many thousands of Chileans of all social and cultural conditions, is an expression of our fervent desire that art cease to be about unique objects to be purchased by the wealthy, the exclusive privilege of a few. We emphatically reject this buy-out/sell-out of art.*
>
> *The cruel conditions that we are subjected to by the capitalist regime denigrate our role as artists, which is, at the same time, used to divide people into first- and second-class citizens. We believe that due to its social nature, art must be within the reach of everyone. …*
>
> *We want to make an art that can bear testimony to the struggles and realities of the people, a free art that does not allow itself to be colonised. An art that is rebellious and new. A courageous art that cannot be bought off.*[6]

In January 1971, two months after Allende initiated his mandate, a similar set of prints travelled as part of the 'El tren popular de la cultura' ('The Popular Culture Train'), for which over fifty artists travelled around Chile for forty days. 'The Popular Culture Train' was a revised version of other train wagons and rickety buses turned into itinerant culture platforms used in Allende's previous campaigns.[7] It travelled to remote localities, where artists performed live theatre, dance and music; screened films on a portable canvas; presented makeshift exhibitions; and produced in situ silkscreen prints. Loosely inspired by the 'pedagogical missions' and 'popular museums' of the Second Spanish Republic as well as the Soviet 'agit-trains', 'The Popular Culture Train' travelled the country focussing on isolated populations and shaping their presentations, most notably their theatre performances, through encounters with locals.[8] The convoy was often the first contact people had with art, cinema and live performance, and in many places the train was awaited with great anticipation, greeted by entire towns dressed in their Sunday best and cheering.[9] Many participating artists described it as a life-changing experience, and it was a great success in terms of shattering the general assumption that 'high art' cannot not be popular.

Operation Truth

The more precise origin of the Museum of Solidarity lies in the radical communications campaign 'Operación verdad' ('Operation Truth'), an international counter-information strategy to defend the revolution from reactionary attacks by the national and international press. According to one of its instigators, Renzo Rossellini, an Italian cinema producer and communications consultant for Popular Unity living in Santiago at the time:

> *Operation Truth was a cultural and political necessity, we had to explain to the planet that a revolutionary experience without arms and within democratic elections was occurring in Chile, something that had never before occurred on planet earth, a revolutionary anti-imperialist process. Operation Truth had as its main objective to show the world what the Chile that Popular Unity had to govern looked like.*[10]

The dirty 'rumour' campaign against Popular Unity and Allende was the front of an escalating communications war and took place in an already violent climate that included political assassination and economic sabotage from a heavily financed and extreme right backed by the United States.[11] The reactionary communications offensive became so belligerent that from the very beginning of his mandate Allende felt forced to dedicate relevant portions of almost every presidential speech to refuting the false information published daily by the right-wing-dominated press. This situation, together with the distorted portrayal of Chile by the international press as an authoritarian communist regime, made it imperative for the government to find a way to fight back. Rossellini and Augusto Olivares, press director of Televisión Nacional during the Popular Unity era, organised the counter-strategy that would become Operation Truth; they involved other important close collaborators of Allende, including the Uruguayan film producer Danilo Trelles, personal friend and communications advisor to the president.[12] They knew their communications counter-attack had to take place in a scenario outside the mainstream media, for the limited economic resources of Popular Unity meant they did not have a chance against the combined multinational press magnates (represented by the Associated Press and the Inter American Press Association). So they opted for a more personalised strategy, based on real and potential political friendships and solidarity.

The Chilean Operation Truth stood out from other 'truth campaigns' because it was not based on notions of 'objectivity' – despite the obvious aim of denouncing malicious rumours and correcting outright lies.[13] While the right-wing media insisted on its political 'neutrality' journalism, Operation Truth was an attempt at sharing and opening up the subjective, lived experience of the revolution.[14] On the international front, it took advantage of international curiosity about the 'Chilean model' (it did not take much convincing for people to agree to make the trip), and brought journalists, intellectuals, artists and activists together in informal meetings and wanderings – insisting that theirs should not become an exclusively 'official' programme (which was partially offered through press conferences with Popular Unity ministers and the president himself). Operation Truth was launched as an open invitation

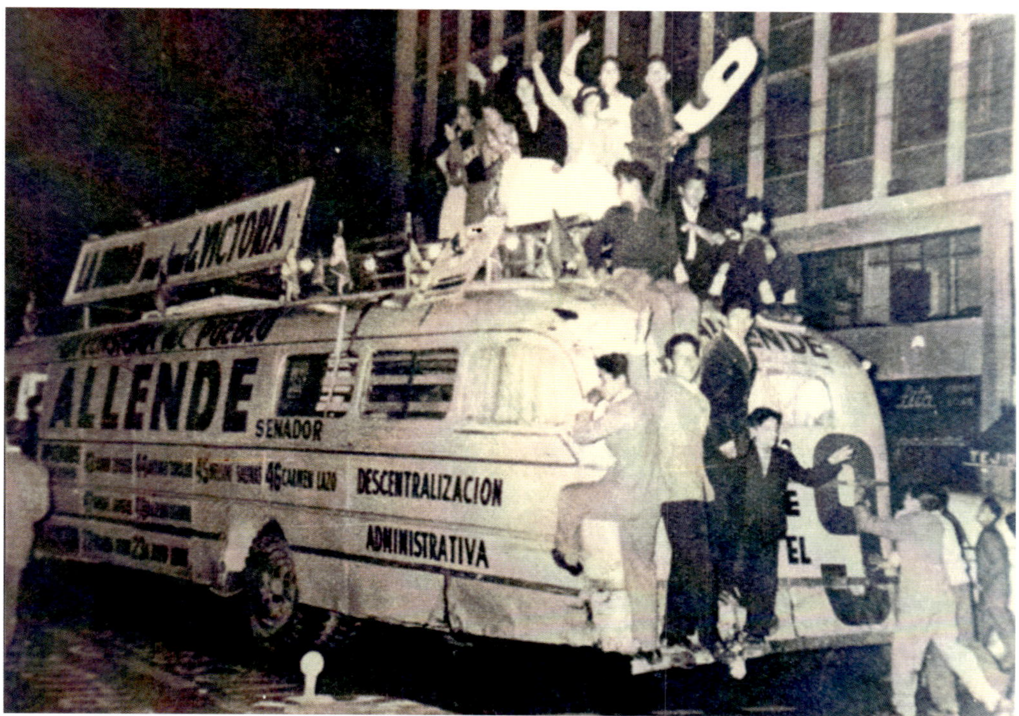

to international guests – potential friends of the revolution – to visit Chile to observe, enter into dialogue with and experience the revolution on their own terms.

> *We dispensed with detailed programmes that are overwhelming for guests. The idea is to give the foreigners free rein. Let them explore the country devoid of obstacles or guides of overbearing amiability.*[15]

For an international 'event' in April 1971, over fifty guests arrived in Santiago, amongst them artists, musicians, film-makers, playwrights, left Christian Democrats, poets, priests, anti-fascist activists, politicians and journalists.[16] The guests were provided with information regarding activities they were invited to join, including meetings of the workers' union and peasant co-ops as well as visits to copper and coal mines and student political assemblies.[17] They were also encouraged to explore on their own and even urged by the president himself to meet with representatives of the opposition.[18] There was no protocol or expected outcome, although the devisers of Operation Truth hoped that first-hand contact with the revolutionary process would touch and motivate people to become a part of the struggle in whatever way they saw fit.

Museum of Solidarity

One of the most exceptional and unexpected long-term outcomes of this meeting would be the Museum of Solidarity. It is said that the idea of a museum emerged during Operation Truth, in a relaxed conversation between

Campaign bus for Salvador Allende's 1961 campaign for the senate seat of Valparaiso and Aconcagua. Courtesy Fundación Salvador Allende, Santiago de Chile

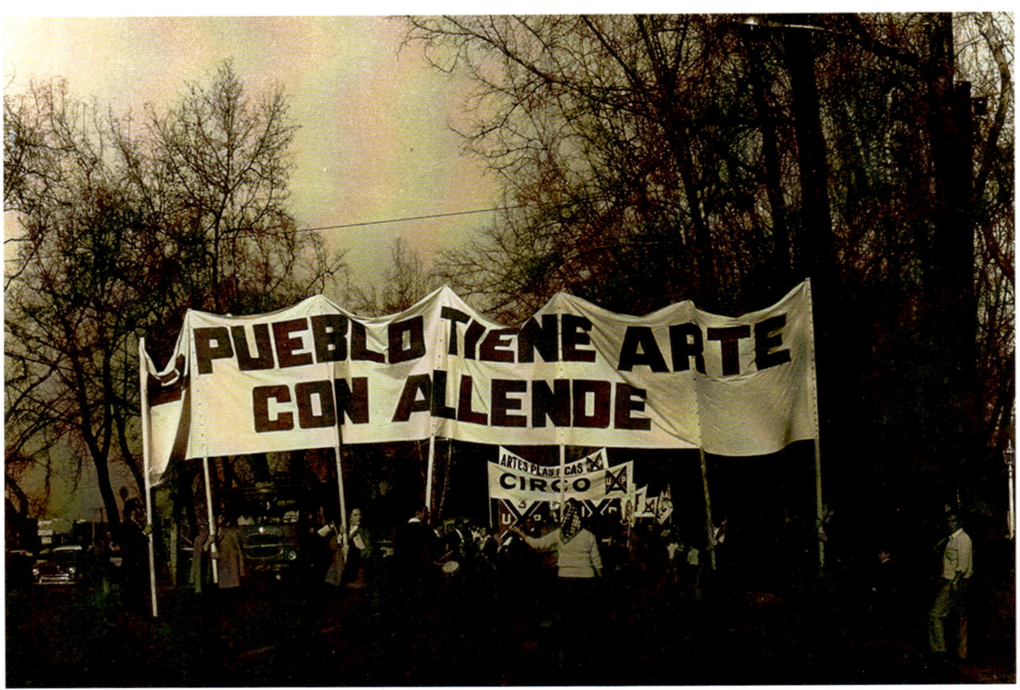

Luis Poirot, *Acto Cultural: El pueblo tiene arte con Allende, Campaña presidencial de Salvador Allende (Cultural Action: The People Have Art with Allende, Salvador Allende's Presidential Election Campaign)*, 1969, silver-gelatin print, 32.5 × 48.4cm. Courtesy the artist

friends in a hotel room. Other versions say it was while the small group strolled through downtown Santiago. But all accounts coincide in one of the guests, José María Moreno Galván, a Spanish communist and art critic who discussed with local artist friends the possibility of an international museum made up of artists' donations as a way that international artists could contribute to the Chilean revolutionary struggle.[19] Instantly his friend José Balmes, a Catalan painter living in Chile, urged that the idea be proposed to the president. Fellow guests of Operation Truth supported the motion, and some later became important contributors. Allende himself wrote a personal letter to Moreno Galván soon after Operation Truth, asking him to please 'accelerate the museum project' to be ready to open for the third edition of the United Nations Conference for Trade and Development (UNCTAD), which Chile would host in less than a year's time.[20] Most supporters were aware that the likelihood of a museum based in sheer solidarity with the aim of having a collection substantial enough to exhibit within ten months (and all of this for 'free') was close to impossible. Yet their enthusiasm for the Chilean 'revolution without arms' somehow convinced them it could be done.

Immediately the project began to take shape in Chile. The Latin American Art Institute (IAL), which had been actively supporting the Committee of Visual Artists of Popular Unity (involved in some way in all the aforementioned exhibitions), became the local headquarters of the project and put its modest team, which included María Eugenia Zamudio (coordinator), Carmen Waugh (public relations) and Virginia Vidal (press agent), to work on promoting the future museum.[21] The IAL was a small yet ambitious organisation led by Miguel Rojas-Mix, who was linked to the arts faculty of the University of Chile, directed at the time by José Balmes and later by Pedro Miras. It was decided that an organ for the promotion and development of the project was needed and also that it should have exclusively international members; thus the Comité Internacional de Solidaridad Artística (International Committee of Artistic Solidarity, CISAC) was founded.[22] The exiled Brazilian art critic Mário Pedrosa, also a member of the IAL, was asked to preside,[23] while Danilo Trelles, one of the organisers of Operation Truth, was named secretary. By November 1971, a considerable body of artworks had already been donated or committed to the future museum. CISAC released a three-page document, 'Declaración Necesaria' ('Necessary Declaration'), consisting of five points that more or less stated:

1. The artists who had donated artworks did not do so in isolation, but as a 'community, deeply devoted to the ideal of a society that is more just, free and human than that which prevails in most of the world'.

2. Artists have historically been involved in supporting diverse emancipatory movements; socialism is a natural and fundamental position for artists who today feel that the work they produce is being degraded by its commodification in capitalist society.

3. Artists call for widespread access to their artworks and 'cannot be indifferent to their works being monopolised for the aesthetic pleasure of those privileged collectors able to purchase them'; they reject the confinement of their works to 'the rich countries of the north-western hemisphere and their metropolis'. On the contrary, they demand their 'works be made profusely available to the large underprivileged areas of the Third World. Chile and its revolution against oppression represent that world.'

4. The gift of artworks to the people of Chile 'does not obey political partisanships or sectarianisms', but is 'political in the highest sense of the word; in a fundamentally ethical, humanist and libertarian sense'.

5. The CISAC has 'clumsily tried to translate to words what the artists simply do through their actions: with artworks'.[24]

The declaration put the donating artists and their artworks at the forefront and recognised their solidarity as political action. Simultaneously, it provided an outline of the principles guiding the museum underway – a museum that openly denounced how the art system and its segregating institutions of concentrated wealth ultimately degraded art and artists. In this sense, the Museum of Solidarity was born as a museum against museums, an anti-museum: the basic notions of the proposed museum were an assault on existing art museums, especially the prestigious and admired institutions of the metropolis; it questioned their geo-political monopoly by calling out the absolute incompatibility of their social function and the principles of the artworks (and artists) in their care. Following this logic, the Museum of Solidarity initiated a motion that would attempt to 'reclaim' Pablo Picasso's

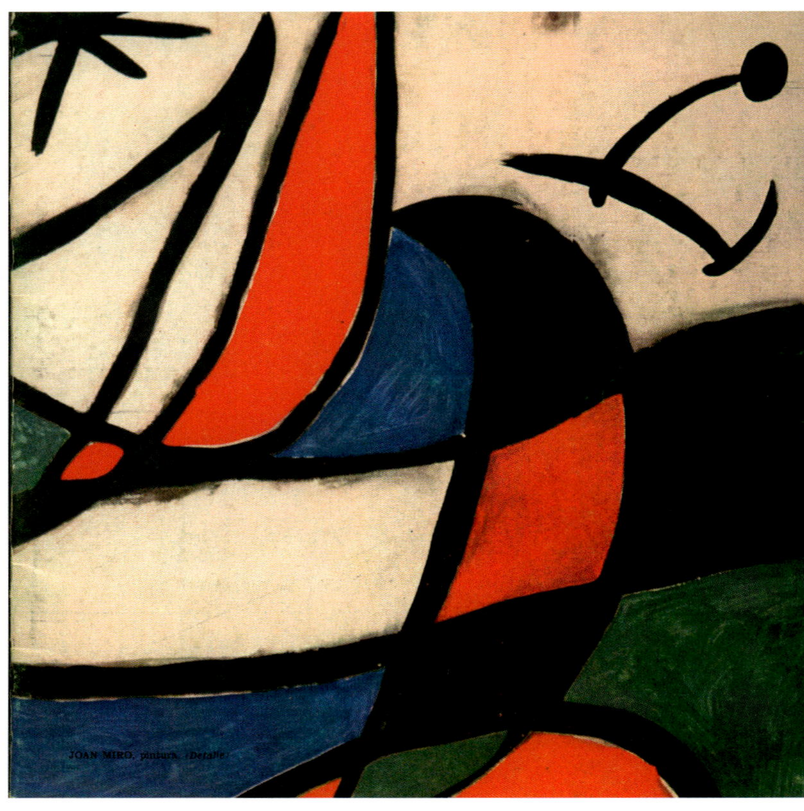

Cover and inside pages of the catalogue for the first exhibition of the Museo de la Solidaridad collection, 1972. Courtesy Museo de la Solidaridad Salvador Allende, Santiago de Chile

museo de la solidaridad chile

DONACION DE LOS ARTISTAS DEL MUNDO AL GOBIERNO POPULAR DE CHILE.

COMITE INTERNACIONAL
DE SOLIDARIDAD ARTISTICA CON CHILE

INSTITUTO DE ARTE LATINOAMERICANO
UNIVERSIDAD DE CHILE
1972

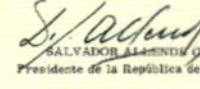

TO THE ARTISTS OF THE WORLD

On behalf to the people and the Government of Chi
wish to convey my heartfelt gratitude to the artists
have donated works that will be the basis for the fu
Museum of Solidarity. This is, no doubt, an unique ev
which begins a new type of relationship between the cre
of art and the people. Indeed, Chile's Museum of Solida
which later will be housed in the UNCTAD III buil
will be the first one where the highest expressions of
temporary painting and sculpture will be brought to
great masses of the people thanks to the will of the ar
themselves.

I feel especially touched by this noble form of contribu
to the transformation process that Chile has put in me
to affirm her sovereignty, mobilize her resources
accelerate the material and spiritual development of
people. This is the proper framework for advancing on
road to Socialism which the people have chosen with
awareness of their destiny.

The artists of the world have cleary understood the
found significance of this Chilean style of liberation an
an action without precedent in cultural history, have f
decided to make a gift of this magnificent assemblag
masterpieces, for the enjoyment of citizens of a re
country who otherwise would hardly have access to t
In addition to a deep gratitude, how could I not feel
we have assumed a solemn obligation towards them
those who give us their support, a commitment to res
to their solidarity?

This commitment, which we make with full confid
in the strength of our people and the support of
friends, is to persevere without dismay in the process b
after the democratic victory of the Popular Unity,
esentially is also aimed at the entrance of the ma
the people, in conditions of dignity, into the realn
culture.

The Museum of Solidarity and the friendship of the a
represented here are already one of the best fruits re
in our endeavour towards national liberation.

I also wish to thank the members of the Internati
Committee of Artistic Solidarity with Chile, who have t
care of coordinating and executing the task of assem
and bringing to Chile the works of the world artists.

SALVADOR ALLENDE G.
Presidente de la República de

COMITE INTERNACIONAL DE SOLIDARIDAD ARTISTICA CON CHILE

LOUIS ARAGON:
Poeta, Director de "Letras Francesas".
JEAN LEYMARIE:
Director del Museo de Arte Moderno de París.
GIULIO CARLO ARGAN:
Ex Presidente de la Asociación Internacional de Críticos de Arte.
E. DE WILDE:
Director del Museo de Arte de Amsterdam.
DORE ASHTON:
Crítico de arte norteamericano.
RAFAEL ALBERTI:
Poeta español.
SENADOR CARLO LEVI:
Pintor y escritor italiano.
JOSE MARIA MORENO GALVAN:
Crítico de arte español.
ALDO PELLEGRINI:
Escritor y crítico de arte argentino.
JULIUSZ STARZYNSKI:
Profesor y crítico de arte de Polonia.
MARIANO RODRIGUEZ:
Pintor, subdirector de la "Casa de las Américas".
MARIO PEDROSA:
Vicepresidente de la Asociación Internacional de Críticos de Arte.
DANILO TRELLES:
Cineasta, consultor del Departamento de Bellas Artes de la UNESCO.

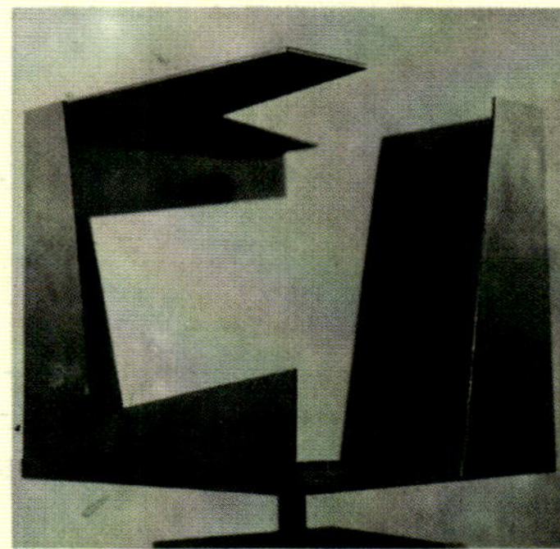

Colaboraron en el diseño gráfico el compañero Raúl Wilton, del Depto. de Tipografía de la Empresa Editora Nacional Quimantú, Luis Araneda y José Moreno, del Instituto de Arte Latinoamericano, U. de Chile.

AUX ARTISTES DU MONDE

nom du peup'e et du Governement du Chili, je désire
primer ma gratitude aux artistes qui ont offert leurs
uvres pour constituer la base du futur Musée de la
lidarité. C'est là, sans conteste, un évènement excep-
nnel qui inaugure un type de relations inedit entre
ateur et spectateur de l'oeuvre artistique. En effet, le
sée de la Solidarité, du Chili, qui sera plus tard logé
ns le bâtiment où se tient la Conférence de la CNUCEP
, sera le premier, dans un pays du Tiers du Monde, à
ttre à portée des grandes masses populaires les mani-
tations les plus hautes des arts visuels, et ce par la
onté des artistes eux-mêmes.

suis particulièrement touché par cette noble forme de
tribution au processus de transformation que le Chili a
cé afin d'affirmer sa souveraineté, mobiliser ses ressour-
, et accélérer le development matériel et spirituel de
peuple. Ce sont là les conditions pour progresser jus-
'au Socialisme pour lequel le peuple a opté dans la pleine
science de son destin.

artistes du monde ont su interpréter ce profond senti-
ent de l'esprit de lutte du Chili pour la libération natio-
le et, par un geste sans précédent dans les annales cul-
elles, ils on décidé d'offrir spontanément cette mag-
ique collection de chefs-d'oeuvre pour la délection des
oyens d'un pays lointain qui, autrement, n'auraient pu
e difficilement y acceder. Comment ne pas sentir qu'en
tre de notre émotion et de notre reconnaissance nous
ons contracté avec eux et avec tous ceux qui les suivent
solennel engagement, l'obligation de correspondre à cette
anifestation de solidarité?

engagement que nous assumons avec une absolue con-
nce en la force de notre peuple et l'appui que nous
portent nos amis, est de persévérer sans fléchir dans la
he que nous avons entreprise avec le triomphe civique
l'Union Populaire, qui est essentiellement destiné aussi
ncorporer avec dignité l'homme-peuple dans le domaine
la culture. Le Musée de la Solidarité et l'amitié des
tistes ici representés constituent déjà un des fruits les
s purs de notre effort de libération nationale.

s remerciements vont aussi aux membres du Comité
ternational de Solidarité Artistique avec le Chili, qui ont
s à leur charge la tâche généreuse de coordiner et d'or-
niser la tâche de faire parvenir à notre terre les oeuvres
s artistes du monde.

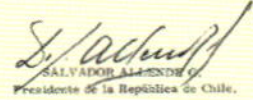

SALVADOR ALLENDE
Presidente de la República de Chile.

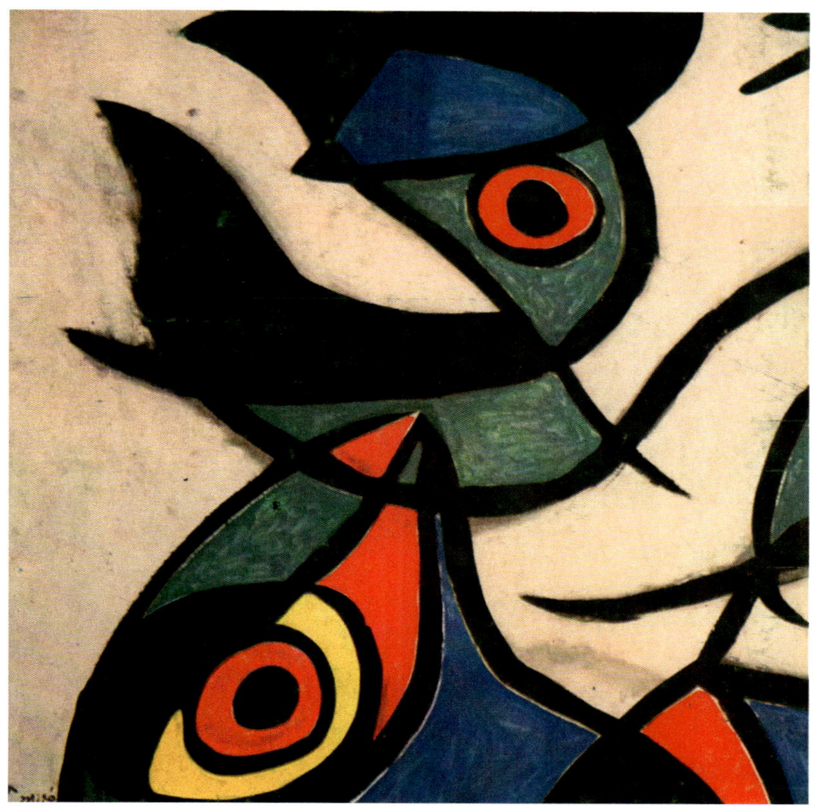

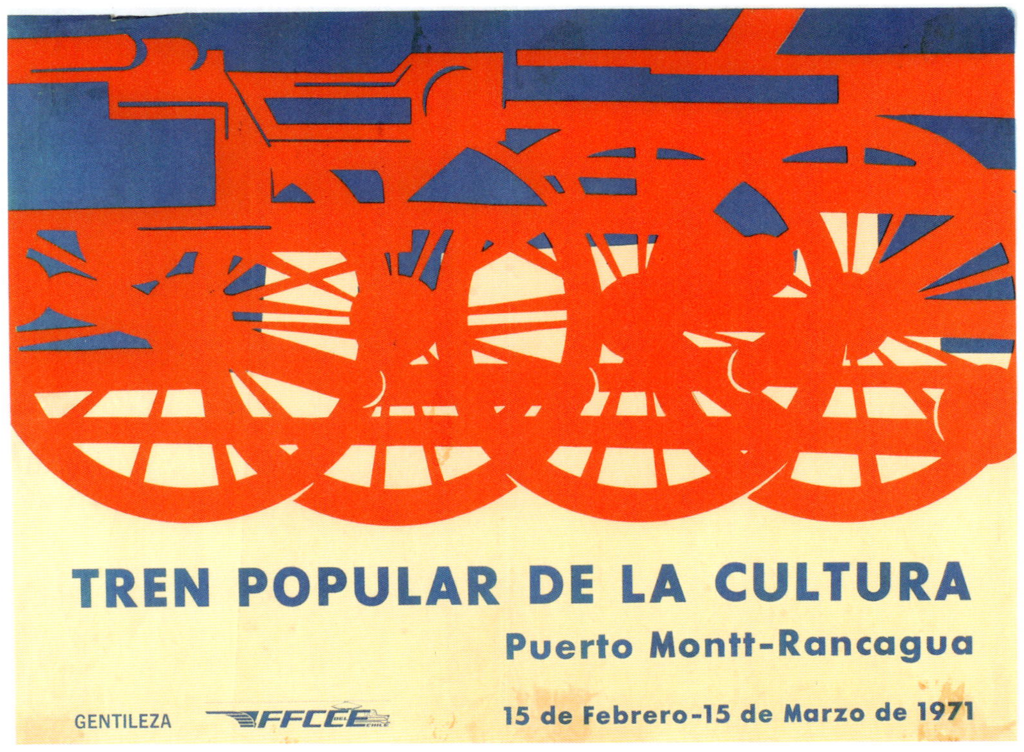

Talleres gráficos FF. CC del Estado de Chile, poster for 'El tren popular de la cultura' ('The Popular Culture Train'), 1971, offset lithograph, 69 × 53.5cm. Courtesy Fundación Salvador Allende, Santiago de Chile

Guernica (1937): they argued that the Museum of Modern Art in New York, positioned in the centre of 'history's most prominent producer of guernicas', was unfit to be its custodian. They wrote a letter explaining their reasoning and offering to relocate the painting to the Museum of Solidarity, where it could be 'honoured and housed decently'.[25] As Pedrosa would note in a letter to another CISAC member, 'art and politics are today inseparable'.[26]

In the intense two years that followed the initial motion for the Museum of Solidarity, the project continued to develop and certain ideas were further clarified. Although it was considered strategic and fundamental to include 'first-category artists with firm political positions',[27] the non-partisanship they insisted on can be observed in the group of works that came together during those brief first years. The collection is unique in its heterogeneity and in the way it quite literally embodies a slice of time and no specific style (although great care was taken in reviewing the kind of works received through the donation process).[28] A commitment to changing the world inevitably involved a conception of art as change, so in this sense there was a natural affinity with modern art reflected in the collection. But, as correspondences between CISAC members attest, they – and particularly Pedrosa – considered it crucial to also incorporate 'experimental artists': 'new artists, non-artists, anti-artists and their "non-objects"'.[29] The Museum itself should become an open, permeable space involving artists through their own 'experiences' and research. It was planned that contemporary artists should travel and spend

356

some time in the country – as they had done in Operation Truth – so that they might gain familiarity with the revolution on their own terms without particular outcomes in mind (although discussions about in situ works were already taking place).[30]

While the donations were made to the 'people of Chile', it is impossible to know if the Museum of Solidarity could have become the popular museum it wanted to be. Despite much effort, including the direct involvement of the president, during the rule of Popular Unity the Museum of Solidarity never managed to secure a building. It was to be a museum without walls for almost twenty years. The museum was to be open and free to all, and there were plans for parts of the collection to be itinerant, moving to different locations, factories, mines and rural or remote areas. 'The Popular Culture Train' was evoked in the attempt to have a first iteration of these exhibits in a copper mine in the north.[31] Three large exhibitions managed to open: one in the Contemporary Art Museum; the others simultaneously in that museum and in the building that had been constructed to host UNCTAD. The latter building was to become the home of the Museum of Solidarity, until it was realised that the architecture was not fit to house an art collection. For a short period of time after UNCTAD took place in Chile, the building became an active and popular cultural centre, and it was in this context that the exhibition taking place was interrupted by the military coup. There remains little documentation of these exhibitions, with the exception of their mention in correspondences, some scant glimpses in press coverage, and a modest first catalogue (full of embarrassing typos, as one CISAC member complained). At the time of writing, almost no surviving images have been found.

Nonetheless, that any of it existed, especially the Museum of Solidarity itself, is already an incredible exception. Even under ideal circumstances, it goes against all odds that a museum without funding could manage a first exhibition within a year of its founding and acquire a significant collection of over 700 artworks in little more than two years. Pedrosa responded to Dore Ashton's understandable frustration with the misspelt names in the 1972 catalogue by explaining that it was all pulled off under conditions of extreme precariousness. It was explained to another CISAC member that 'currently in Chile everything is done without funding and in an improvised way'.[32] These conditions gave a new sense to Pedrosa's definition of art as the 'experimental exercise of freedom', applicable to the new museum in the making. During those first two years, the artworks would arrive at the IAL through the Chilean embassies, frequently in diplomatic 'pouches', their registration consisting of a handwritten line in a small notebook. Some works arrived just in time for scheduled exhibitions; it is said that an early icon of the Museum, a cockerel by Joan Miró, was still wet when it was hung in the opening show on the 17 May 1972. All of this took place in an increasingly tense and complicated political context that Pedrosa himself described as an unarmed civil war. In this setting, the Museum was a work not only of solidarity but also of militant audacity on behalf of all involved. It represented the 'beautiful chaos'[33] that had overtaken many spheres of daily life in the times of Popular Unity.

Disappearance and Exile

The project was cut short, as was the political experiment of Popular Unity, with the 11 September 1973 military coup – roughly two and a half years after the idea for the museum was first uttered. Its collection comprised art then valued at 8 million US dollars, an amount that surpassed the direct investment made by Richard Nixon's regime to destabilise Chile within the same period of time. Amongst the first images to come out of Chile under military power were those of house raids and book burnings; for example, young military cadets were portrayed on French television scorching books including literature on Cubism. (Apparently some kind of link to Cuba was suspected – books in shades of red suffered a similar fate.) The material destruction of all things even remotely linked to Popular Unity and leftist culture was immense. All of those involved with the Museum were forced into exile shortly after the coup; despite several attempts to recover the works in the years after, including a plan to temporarily house the museum in Mexico, the fate of the collection was uncertain for decades.

The project was reborn as a museum in exile in 1975, as the International Museum of Resistance Salvador Allende (MIRSA, in its Spanish acronym).[34] The people that had been involved with the Museum of Solidarity in Chile began to collect new works and continued to do so over the course of the dictatorship. The spirit of the Museum materialised through this new nomadic existence: artworks accumulated in people's homes and borrowed institutional storage spaces, and different fragments of the growing collection were shown in all kinds of venues during the seventeen years of military rule, from festivals to international solidarity events. Murals and large-scale paintings were often produced in situ by one of the several nomenclatures of the international anti-fascist painters brigades, made up of Chilean and Latin American artists-in-exile and their European collaborators.[35] This continued existence of the Museum – its second life – was supported by the widespread surge of solidarity for those displaced by the repressive dictatorial regimes of Latin America in the 1970s. National Committees for the Museum were created in Cuba, Spain, France and Mexico, in which prominent intellectuals took part, pooling efforts to rebuild the collection. As a museum-in-exile, the project remained a campaign, but with a new cause: the plight of Chile under military rule.[36]

Despite the military's attempt to erase any trace of Popular Unity, the collection that had been amassed by the Museum of Solidarity survived. Apparently this was because the ideologues of the dictatorship were afraid that were it to be destroyed, it would have turned into an international campaign against them[37] – a chilling fact given their lack of consideration for human life. If Operation Truth had failed to halt the offensive against the revolution, the fact that the artworks of the Museum of Solidarity in and of themselves were something to be feared is not an insignificant detail. It was only after the end of the dictatorship that the museum-in-exile and its disappeared collection came to form what is today the Museo de la Solidaridad Salvador Allende (Museum of Solidarity Salvador Allende, as of 1991). Its first director was Carmen Waugh, a relentless advocate of the Museum in all its stages, who stored much of the collection in stuffed closets during her exile, from Italy to Spain to Nicaragua. Waugh led the political and legal struggle to reclaim the disappeared initial collection that had been stashed in different bureaucratic corners of state patrimony, some of which was only passed over to the Museum of Solidarity in 2017.

The Museum of Solidarity itself was born as an act of struggle – a cultural response to a political urgency. Initially part of a strategy of radical communication, it turned the very notion of a museum on its head. 'Mediation' as it is understood today (conventionally: socialising, learning with and making a collection public) is not something that emerged as a necessity after the Museum of Solidarity's collection was assembled – it was a basic condition of its founding. In the process emerged an unprecedented experimental institution for art and politics, an international utopian 'museum', born in a small country in the south that had initiated an equally unprecedented revolutionary transformation.

Notes

[1] This essay is adapted from a paper given at the Museu de Arte de São Paulo (São Paulo Museum of Art, MASP) on 15 April 2016, commissioned by Luiza Proença. I am deeply grateful to those whose rigorous work and research made my own research possible: Carla Macchiavello; Carla Miranda; and Claudia Zaldívar, current director of the Solidarity Museum, whose team includes Federico Brega, María José Lamaitre and Caroll Yasky. Special thanks to Virginia Vidal, agitator for the cause since the early 1970s, and a secret protagonist of this story.

[2] A conventional hanging of the Museum's 'key' modern works can be hard to distinguish from that at any prestigious modern Latin American art collection.

[3] Allende's rivals in the 1964 and 1970 elections received substantial financial 'covert' support from the CIA. Anti-Allende propaganda was spread through press articles, editorials, radio spots, pamphlets and posters. In 1964, these famously depicted child soldiers and tanks sieging the government house, thereby equating an Allende presidency to a militarised communist dictatorship. Regarding the 1964 triumph of the centre-right candidate Eduardo Frei Montalva, the US Select Committee reported: 'The CIA regards the anti-communist scare campaign as the most effective activity undertaken by the US on behalf of the Christian Democratic candidate.' In 1970, right-wing candidate Jorge Alessandri received CIA funding through *El Mercurio* and its director, Agustín Edwards. See Frank Church and John Tower, 'Covert Action in Chile 1963–1973, Staff Report of the Select Committee to Study Governmental Operations with Respect to Intelligence Activities, United States, 94th Congress, 18 September 1975', US Government Printing Offices, 1975. See also Seymour Hersh, 'The Price of Power: Kissinger, Nixon, and Chile', *The Atlantic Monthly*, vol.250, no.6, December 1982, pp.31–58.

[4] Amongst them, the Argentineans León Ferrari, Marta Peluffo and Luis Felipe Noé; the Uruguayans Luis Arbondo and Jorge Nieto; and the Chileans José Balmes, Juan Dávila and Luz Donoso. Many of the artists in the exhibition later donated works to the Museum of Solidarity.

[5] *Homenaje al triunfo del pueblo* (exh. cat), Santiago de Chile: Instituto de Extension de Artes Plásticas, Universidad de Chile, 1970. Unless otherwise specified, all translations and emphases are my own.

[6] *El pueblo tiene arte con Allende* (leaflet/catalogue), Santiago: Impresora Horizonte, 1970.

[7] Joris Ivens's 1964 film *Le train de la victoire* (*The Victory Train*) is a beautiful document of that year's campaign. There was no train in the 1970 campaign; a small plane transported Allende through the country, but the campaign rallies did rely heavily on the cultural participation that had developed in previous campaigns. Marcelo Casals describes how the 1970 campaign perfected the 'use of culture for the massification of the message'. See Marcelo Casals Araya, *El alba de una revolución: La izquierda y el proceso de construcción estratégica de la 'Via chilena al socialismo' 1956–1970*, Santiago de Chile: LOM Ediciones, 2010, p.119. For a detailed account of

'El bus de la victoria' (1961), see Orzen Nikola Agnic Krstulovic, *Allende, El hombre y el político: Memorias de un secretario privado*, Santiago de Chile: RIL Editores, 2008.

[8] According to the testimonies of participants and artists as well as people who encountered the train at the time, from Carolina Espinosa's documentary film *El tren popular de la cultura* (2010).

[9] Virginia Vidal was the only journalist who joined the trip to cover the event at the time. She provides a compelling testimony in V. Vidal, 'El tren popular de la cultura', *El Siglo*, January 2009, p.24. A parallel project was the 'Tren de la salud' ('Health Train'), with travelling doctors, dentists and nurses. It has been said that Allende's use and identification with the train system was one of the reasons the dictatorship made such efforts to dismantle the railroad circuit in Chile – despite the relevance, necessity and geographical logic of the railroad in a problematically centralised country that is basically a long narrow strip of land.

[10] Renzo Rossellini, email correspondence, January–February 2016. Rossellini's involvement in Operation Truth continued his commitment to creating collaborative networks for revolutionary struggle: he was involved in the creation of Free Radios in Italy and later in Afghanistan; he also set up the San Diego Cinematográfica, an important hub for the Third World Cinema Committee (1973–74) and a point of intercontinental encounter between committed film-makers, especially Middle Eastern and Latin American.

[11] The assassination of General René Schneider on 22 October 1970 was the most well-known attempt to impede Allende from being ratified by the Congress. An interesting document in this regard is Cuban director Santiago Alvarez's short film *Cómo, porqué y para qué se mata a un general* (1971). For a detailed account of US involvement, see S. Hersh, 'The Price of Power', *op. cit.*

[12] Trelles had much experience in creating networks of political and cultural solidarity. He made an immense contribution to bring together politically committed Latin American film-makers in the 1950s, while living in Uruguay. He set the foundations for what became the Third World Cinematheque, in addition to his work on the regionally relevant publication *Marcha*.

[13] It is improbable that those involved in designing the Chilean Operation Truth were unaware of the Cuban Operation Truth, but the latter is, probably intentionally, never mentioned as a reference. It took place on 21 January 1959, shortly after the triumph of the revolution, and consisted of a day-long meeting of international journalists with Fidel Castro, who offered his counter-views to the international portrayal of Cuba in the media.

[14] Internally Operation Truth called for journalists to defend the revolution by getting involved in work with the people, not only in witnessing the everyday trials and struggles of shanty town dwellers and workers, but also by collaborating with them in the creation of popular 'correspondents', at the same time investigating and denouncing the thinly veiled interests involved in the 'objective' journalism of the reactionary media and their power connections. A major milestone on the local front was the Primera Asamblea de Periodistas de Izquierda (First Assembly of Leftist Journalists), where thorough analyses of the economic and political connections of the national press were presented and collective working strategies devised. See *Punto Final*, no.129, April 1971.

[15] 'El abre lata necesario', *Revista Ahora*, 27 March 1971, p.5. This description was by the person in charge of receiving the guests, named in the article only as the 'Coordinator of the First Assembly of Leftist Journalists'.

[16] There is contradictory information about the dates, characteristics and guests of this event. I have based my data on primary sources such as a document handed out to guests and press during the event, in addition to information provided by people who attended or were involved in the organisation of Operation Truth, such as Renzo Rossellini and José Antonio Gurriarán. Other participants included Pedro Altares, Carlos Castilla del Pino, Corrado Corghi, Alberto Fillipi, Moreno Galván, Mario Gaviria, Marcella Glisenti, Claude Julien, Giorgio La Pira, Catherine Lamour, Carlo Levi, Gilles Martinet, François Mitterrand, Alfonso Sastre, Mikis Theodorakis and Father David Turoldo.

[17] 'Operación verdad. Programa del 19 al 24 de abril, 1971', Florence: Fondazione Giorgio La Pira, n.d.

[18] See José Antonio Gurriarán, *Caerá Allende?*, Barcelona: Dopesa, 1973, p.16.

[19] The conflicting stories, involving varying dates and people, respond more to the vertiginous temporality of Popular Unity rather than claims of authorship. The project was developed collectively from the beginning and all those involved were deeply invested in its conceptualisation and realisation. See Moreno Galván, document B.1.b0020; as well as recorded interviews with José Balmes, Miguel Rojas Mix, Archivo Museo de la Solidaridad Salvador Allende, Santiago (MSSA Archive).

[20] Thanks to Carolina Olmedo Carrasco for sharing with me a transcription of this letter, currently at the Archivo José María Moreno Galván, Centro de Documentación, Museo Nacional Centro de Reina Sofía, Madrid.

[21] When the museum became the International Resistance Museum, Carmen Waugh – in exile – shared her flat in Madrid with around 300 works she had helped bring together. After the dictatorship, she became a director of the Solidarity Museum (1991–2005).

[22] The official committee members were Rafael Alberti, Louis Aragón, Giulio Carlo Argan, Dore Ashton, Eduard de Wilde, Carlo Levi (who was a part of Operation Truth), Jean Leymarie, José María Moreno Galván, Aldo Pellegrini (a prominent Argentinian critic living in Chile at the time and also part of the IAL staff), Mariano Rodríguez and Juliusz Starzynski. In 1972, Harald Szeeman and Sir Roland Penrose would also contribute.

[23] Pedrosa arrived in Chile in October 1970, as part of a growing population of Brazilians in exile that included Paulo Freire amongst many others. This was after spending three months in the Chilean consulate in Rio de Janeiro, waiting for asylum after having fled the 'preventive' prison ordered by the dictatorial regime in Brazil. In Chile, he was invited by Rojas-Mix to form part of the IAL. I thank Bel Pedrosa for providing me with this information.

[24] 'Declaración Necesaria del Comité Internacional de Solidaridad Artistica por Chile, noviembre 1971' (facsimile), in Claudia Zaldívar (ed.), *40 años Museo de la Solidaridad por Chile: fraternidad, arte y política, 1971–1973*, Santiago de Chile: Museo de la Solidaridad Salvador Allende, 2013, pp.15–17. Apart from the statements within quotation marks, the extract here paraphrases the original.

[25] What remains is a draft of a letter to Picasso, as well as detailed notes on how to transport *Guernica* safely to Santiago. See 'Proyecto de carta a Picasso', July 1972, MSSA Archive. A similar logic was exercised by the Art Workers' Coalition in the 1970 action involving *Guernica* as a counterpoint to the explicit anti-Vietnam war poster *And Babies* (1969). On the latter, see Julia Bryan-Wilson, *Art Workers: Radical Practice in the Vietnam War Era*, Berkeley: University of California Press, 2009.

[26] Letter to Dore Ashton, June 1972. Quoted in Carla Macchiavelo, 'Una bandera es una trama', in Claudia Zaldívar (ed.), *40 años Museo de la Solidaridad por Chile, op. cit.*, p.41.

[27] M. Pedrosa, letter to D. Ashton, 9 January 1972, MSSA Archive.

[28] Dore Ashton quite bluntly affirmed that she did not accept 'minor works': they had to be relevant works and this frequently meant studio visits and continued conversations. Pedrosa's correspondence is clearly just as careful and attentive to detail in relation to the discussions around the works to be donated. See the interview with Ashton in C. Zaldívar (ed.), *40 años Museo de la Solidaridad por Chile, op. cit.*

[29] M. Pedrosa, letter to Hélio Oiticica, 9 June 1972, MSSA Archive.

[30] These discussions are attested to in much of Mário Pedrosa's correspondence at the time, where he mentions a proposal to Ferreira Gular to install his 'poema enterrado' (buried poem) as well as an invitation to Hélio Oiticica to realise an 'experiencia' on the future site of the Museum. See MSSA Archive. Regarding Pedrosa's role and vision for the Museum of Solidarity, see María Berríos, 'Por el futuro artístico del mundo', in Gabriel Pérez Barreiro and Michelle Sommer (ed.), *Mário Pedrosa. De la naturaleza afectiva de la forma*, Madrid: Museo Nacional Centro de Reina Sofía, 2017, pp.86–101.

[31] The plans for an exhibition in the El Teniente copper mine, which had just been expropriated for nationalisation by the US company Kennecott, were highly advanced, but there are no traces of it ever taking place. It is probable that such an exhibition was impeded by the urgent situation that arose due to the right-wing-supported strike in the mine, initiated in late April 1972, with devastating economic consequences for the government.

[32] M. Pedrosa, letter to Eduard de Wilde, 10 January 1972, MSSA Archive.

[33] 'Beautiful chaos' is what Ernani Maria Fiori believed a learning institution should be. Fiori was, like Pedrosa, a Brazilian exile in Chile. He was briefly vice chancellor of the Catholic University in Santiago, the first after the implementation of the 1967 University Reform. Quoted in Carla Rivera, 'La construcción de un campo de saber', doctoral thesis in history, Pontificia Universidad Católica de Chile.

[34] Regarding this period, which surpasses the aims and limits of this essay, see Caroll Yasky and Claudia Zaldívar (ed.), *Museo Internacional de la Resistencia Salvador Allende, MIRSA 1975–1990*, Santiago de Chile: Museo de la Solidaridad Salvador Allende, 2016.

[35] The Chileans involved include José Balmes, Gracia Barrios and Guillermo Nuñez, amongst others. They were mainly active between 1974–78. See J. Balmes, 'Las brigadas muralistas en europa', in Eduardo Castillo (ed.), *Puño y letra: movimiento social y comunicación gráfica en Chile*, Santiago de Chile: Ocho Libros, 2006, p.144.

[36] To a lesser degree, it was also used as a fundraising campaign for the resistance to the dictatorship. This aspect was more polemical, as it was not clear to which specific organisations the monies raised should be given. Also, many artists and some of the organisers were not in agreement about artworks being sold. In any case, the donators usually specified if they allowed the works to be sold.

[37] According to testimonies of former cultural 'officials' of the dictatorship. See Claudia Zaldívar, 'Museo de la Solidaridad', thesis in art history, University of Chile, 1992.

La creatividad es un instrumento de lucha y el cambio social un hecho creativo

(Creativity Is an Instrument of Struggle, and Social Change a Creative Act)[1]

Mujeres Creando

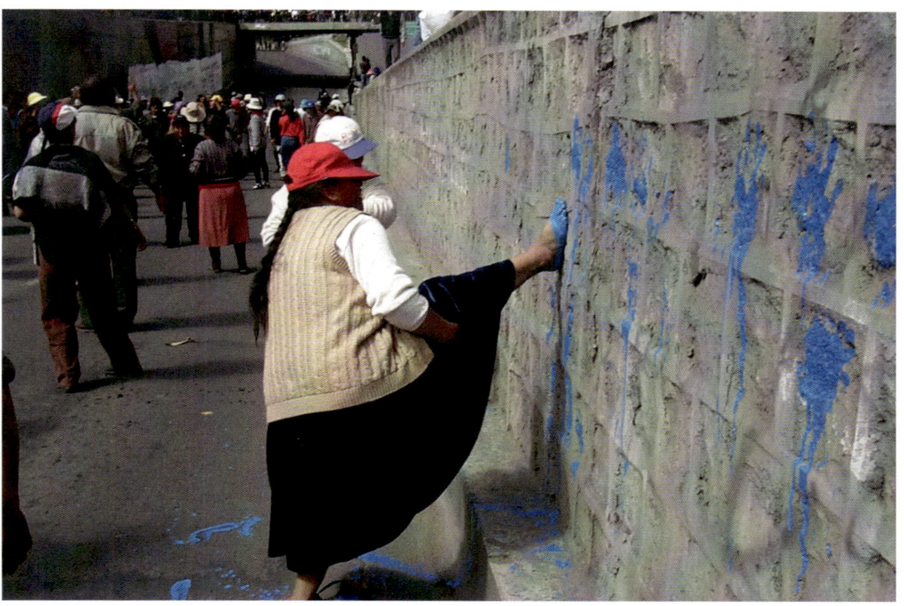

Concepto: Un feminismo desde los pies
(A Feminism from the Feet)

¿Quién les ha dicho que el feminismo es un producto europeo nacido en el contexto del Estado moderno y transportado desde el patrón y visión eurocéntrica a ser reproducido por las mujeres del sur del mundo?

No hay un feminismo, sino muchos feminismos. No nos sentimos conectadas con las luchas de las sufragistas de principios del siglo veinte, ni con las que enunciaron los derechos de las mujeres en el contexto de la Revolución Francesa. Nuestro feminismo nace de una memoria remota propia anti-colonial y anti-racista. Entendemos el feminismo como un fenómeno planetario presente en todas las culturas y latitudes del mundo con genealogías propias y dispares. El feminismo es la desobediencia personal o colectiva a los mandatos patriarcales presentes en todas las sociedades del mundo a partir de las luchas históricas de todos los pueblos. Por eso, el feminismo está conectado con las luchas anti-esclavistas y anti-coloniales.

Who told you that feminism is a European product that emerged in the context of the modern state? Who told you that feminism was imported from the patriarchal Eurocentric vision to be reproduced by women from the South?

There is not one feminism, there are many feminisms. We don't feel connected with the struggles of the suffragettes at the beginning of the twentieth century, or with those who spoke of women's rights in the context of the French Revolution. Our feminism is born from our own ancient memory: anti-colonial and anti-racist. We understand feminism as a planetary phenomenon present in all cultures and latitudes of the world, with particular and diverging genealogies.

Feminism is a personal or collective disobedience with respect to patriarchal mandates, present in all societies in the world, and in the historical struggles of all people. This is why feminism is connected with anti-slavery and anti-colonial struggles.[2]

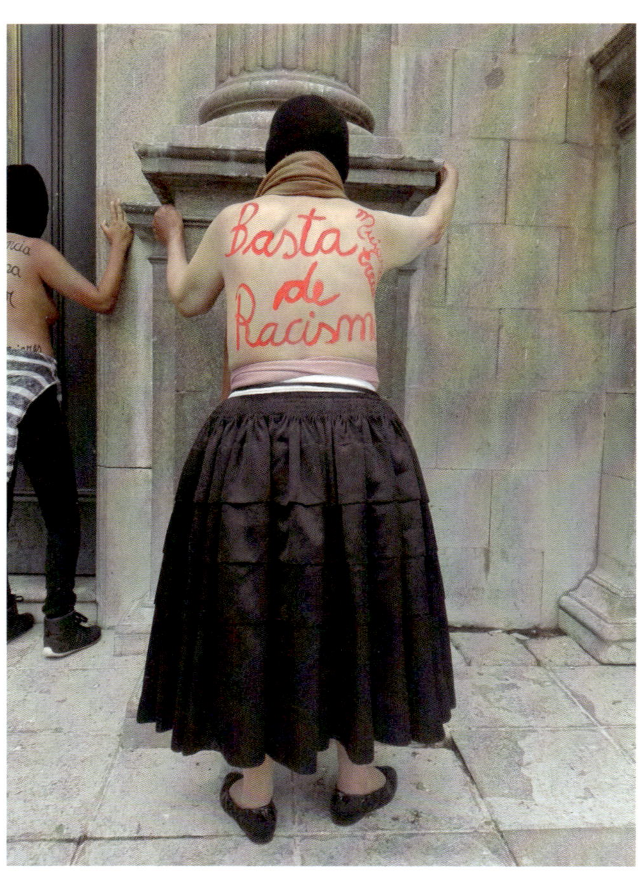

Concepto: Un feminismo desde las calles
(A Feminism from the Streets)

Nosotras consideramos la calle el lugar central de la historia y de la política, es por ello que hemos hecho de la calle nuestro centro de actividad. No se trata de una performance que toma la calle como escenario ocasional, sino de entender la calle en las sociedades latinoamericanas como el único foro de deliberación democrática que tiene la sociedad para expresarse. Se trata de asumir la cantidad de estrategias históricas que se desarrollan en la calle como medio de subsistencia, como lugar de expresión por una infinidad de sectores sociales como son las vendedoras ambulantes, como son las pordioseras o las locas, como son las innumerables marchas que pueblan nuestras ciudades como parte de su actividad vital.

We think of the street as a central place in history and politics. This is why we have made the street the centre for our activities. It is not about performances that use the street as an occasional stage, but about understanding how the street in Latin American societies is the only forum for democratic deliberation. It is about assuming the amount of historical strategies that develop in the street as a means for subsistence. The street is a space for expression reclaimed by an infinity of social agents, such as street vendors, beggars and the insane, or for the innumerable marches that inhabit our cities and are part of their vital activity.[3]

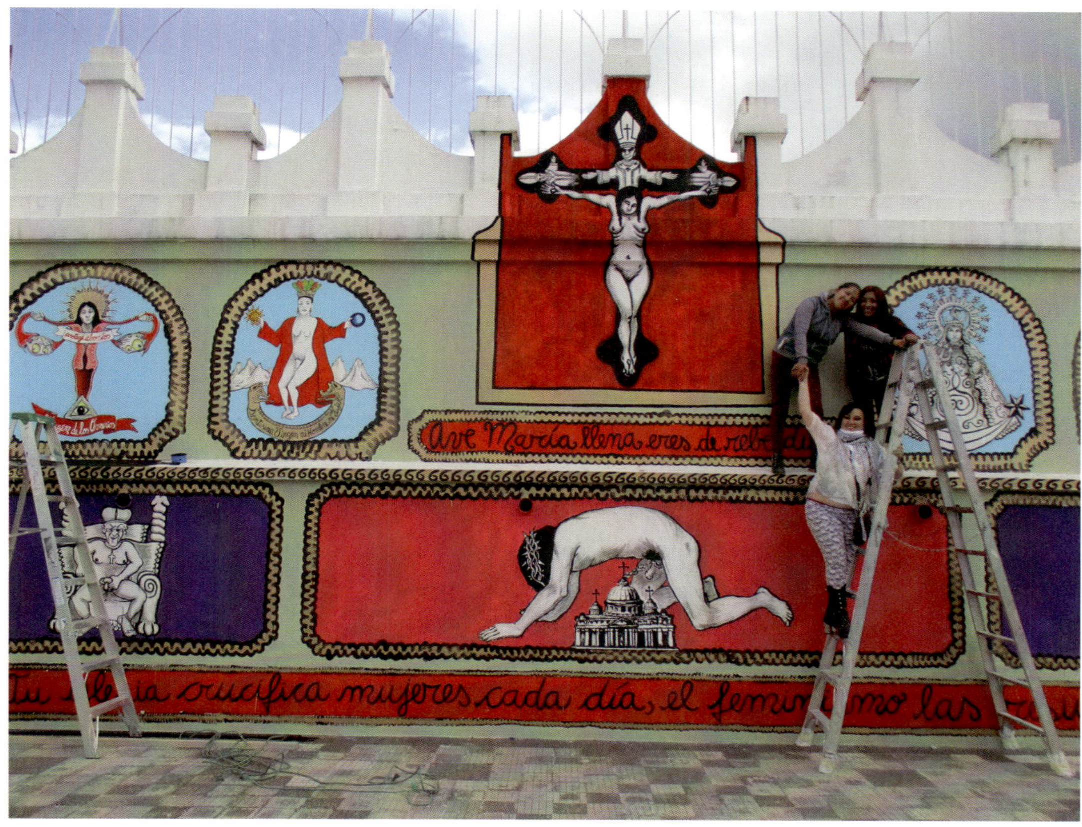

Concepto: Un feminismo desde la creatividad
(A Feminism from Creativity)

Cuando planteamos un feminismo desde la creatividad no es que nos estemos refiriendo al errado concepto de querer cambiar el mundo desde el arte. Ni somos tan ingenuas, ni en lo absoluto creemos que se puede hablar del arte sin tomar una postura crítica frente al sistema dentro del cual están insertos los museos y las galerías, la historia oficial del arte, y el control del concepto de arte por parte de las elites y hegemonías políticas de todos los tiempos. Lo que nos interesa, y en lo que nosotras trabajamos, es en la creación de lenguajes de lucha, en la necesidad de repensar cada palabra, de entender el mismo campo del lenguaje y la poética como campos fundamentales de lucha.

When we propose a feminism that stems from creativity, we do not refer to the mistaken idea of wanting to change the world with art. We are not that naïve, and we certainly don't think that it is possible to talk about art without taking a critical position towards the system in which museums, galleries and official art histories are inserted, a system that has allowed for elite and political hegemonies to control the very concept of art. Instead, we are interested and we work towards the creation of vocabularies of struggle, bearing in mind the necessity of rethinking every word and of understanding the very field of language and poetics as fundamental fields for struggle.[4]

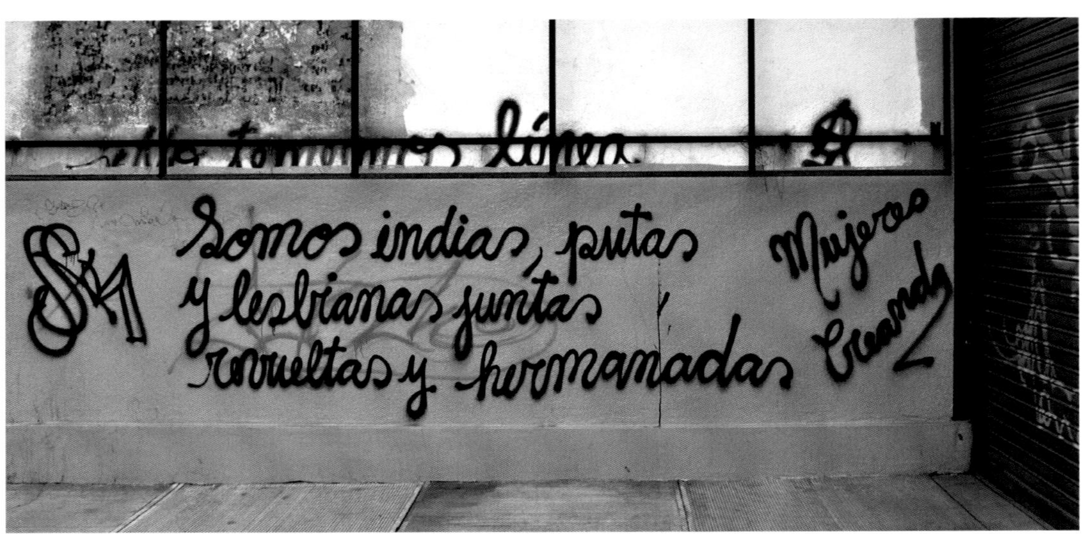

Concepto: Un feminism no identitario
(A Non-Identitarian Feminism)

Creemos que uno de los errores que han cometido muchos feminismos es partir de un sujeto amorfo como son 'las mujeres en general', un sujeto que no existe como tal y que como universo, es complejo y está atravesado por contradicciones históricas fundamentales como son las de clase, social, cultura, color de piel, generación, opción sexual, relación con la maternidad, etc. Esto de entender el feminismo desde las mujeres en general ha simplificado las luchas feministas y las ha empobrecido.

Nosotras partimos de un sujeto poético, metafórico, heterogéneo que lo enunciamos como indias, putas y lesbianas; juntas, revueltas y hermanadas. A partir de allí entendemos el feminismo como la construcción de un sujeto heterogéneo que tiene como punto de partida las mujeres de 'abajo', las señaladas, las perseguidas, las tatuadas. Se trata de un sujeto conformado por alianzas entre quienes está prohibido establecer alianzas, entre quienes está prohibido mirarse. Alianzas insólitas son las que nos permiten entender la profundidad de las luchas y las profundas conexiones entre luchas.

We believe that one mistake made by various feminisms comes from starting from the amorphous subject 'women in general'. This subject doesn't exist as such, it is a complex universe traversed by fundamental historical contradictions including social class, culture, skin colour, generation, sexual orientations and relations to maternity, among others. Understanding feminism from the perspective of 'women in general' has simplified and impoverished feminist struggles. We start from a poetic, metaphorical, heterogeneous subject that we enunciate as indigenous, whores and lesbians; together, mixed in sisterhood. This is how we understand feminism, as the construction of a heterogeneous subject that takes as its starting point the women 'from below', those who are stigmatised, prosecuted, marked. It is a subject constituted through alliances between those for whom alliances are forbidden, those who are forbidden to look at each other – unusual alliances that allow us to understand the depth of the different struggles and the deep connections between them.[5]

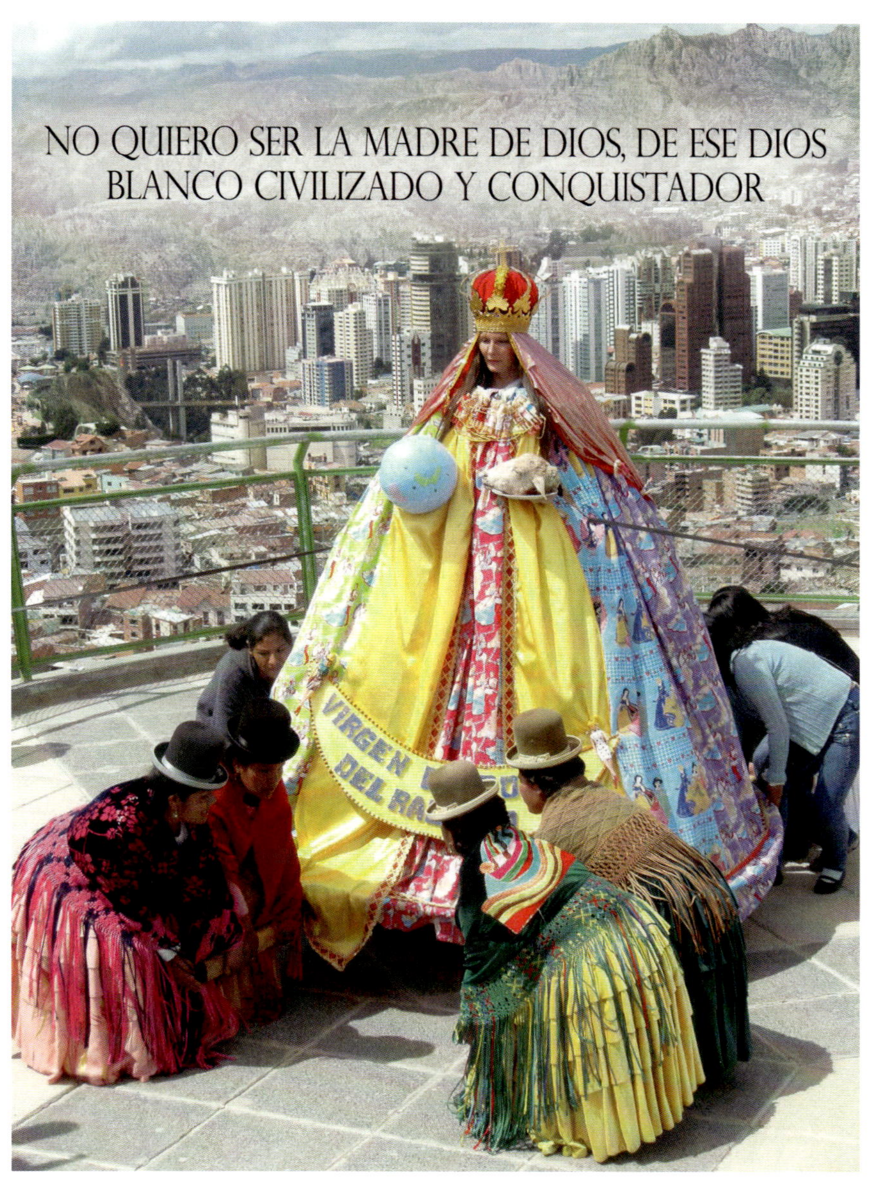

Concepto: No se puede descolonizar sin despatrialiarcalizar
(There is no Decolonisation without Depatriarchalisation)[6]
La descolonización como proceso político fundamental no es posible sin entender que la matriz colonial del pensamiento es, además, una matriz patriarcal. Por lo tanto, es imposible hablar de descolonización sin entender que éste
es un proceso también de despatriarcalisation.

*Decolonisation as a fundamental political process is not possible without understanding that the colonial matrix of thought is also a patriarchal one. This is why
it is impossible to talk about decolonisation without understanding that it is also
a process of depatriarchalisation.*[7]

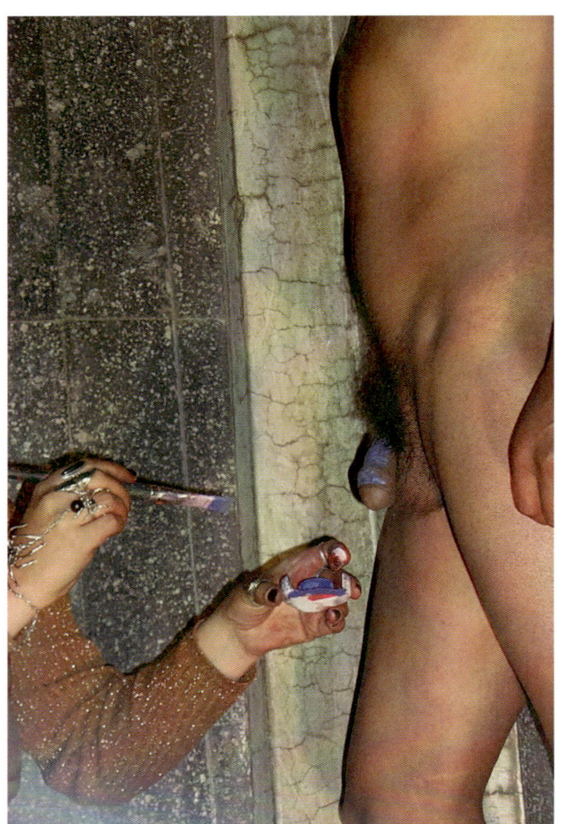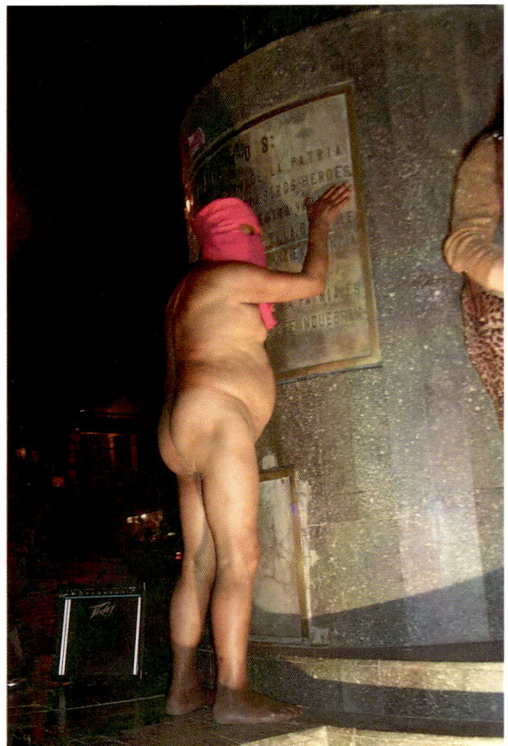

Concepto: Un feminismo desde la interpelación a la historia
(A Feminism from Interpellation to History)

No tenemos nada mejor que hacer con nuestras vidas que esta lucha feminista que consume lo mejor de nuestras energías y lo más profundo de nuestros sueños. Para nosotras no es una cuestión de pasatiempo, no es una reunión quincenal, no es una marcha a la que vamos una vez al año a gritar contra el patriarcado. La nuestra es una lucha cotidiana donde vamos tejiendo subversiones pequeñas que se convierten en trascendentes por su constancia, por su terquedad y por su capacidad de construir una plataforma donde la lucha sea nuestra venganza de felicidad. Como dice uno de nuestros graffitis: NUESTRA VENGANZA ES SER FELICES.

We don't have anything better to do with our lives than this feminist struggle that consumes the best of our energies and our deepest dreams. For us, this is not a pastime, it is not a fortnightly meeting, it is not a protest that we attend once a year to shout against patriarchy. Ours is a continuous struggle where we weave small subversions that turn transcendental because of their constancy, their stubbornness and their capacity to build a platform in which our struggle becomes a revenge through happiness. As one of our graffiti says: OUR REVENGE IS BEING HAPPY.[8]

Notes

[1] All of these photographs represent the actions, struggles and interventions of the Bolivian collective Mujeres Creando over twenty years. The texts in this insert are authored by group member María Galindo, and they describe the political practices and the feminist agenda of the collective. For more information, please visit www.mujerescreando.org and www.radiodeseo.com.

[2] This picture corresponds to a street action in which we wanted to denounce how hundreds of thousands of women obtain microcredits from banks. These microcredits change the women's identities from 'unemployed' to 'indebted'. They sign these contracts with their fingerprints since they don't know how to read, thus they can't understand the terms and conditions of the unpayable debts they acquire. La Paz, Bolivia, 2001.

[3] Intervention in the central square of one of the most feudal and conservative cities in the country, Santa Cruz de la Sierra. Putting the body at the centre of our struggle is a constitutive element of our practices. Ciudad de Santa Cruz, 2011.

[4] Esther Argollo, Danitza Luna and María Galindo in front of a fragment of the *Milagroso altar blasfemo* (*Miraculous Blasphemous Altar*). The *Milagroso altar blasfemo* is the work by Mujeres Creando that has faced the most censorship attempts in recent times. Quito, Ecuador, 2017.

[5] Since its inception in 1992, Mujeres Creando has used graffiti as an instrument of struggle, painting in four cities in Bolivia for twenty years. Mujeres Creando has turned its graffiti into a powerful mechanism to communicate with society.

[6] Translation of the text in the image: 'I Don't Want to be the Mother of God, of that White, Civilised and Colonising God'.

[7] Still from *La Virgen Barbie* (*The Virgin Barbie*), a short film presented by María Galindo as part of the exhibition 'Principio Potosí', Museo Nacional Centro de Arte Reina Sofía (MNCARS), Madrid, 2010.

[8] Stills from a short film about the character of *la puta* (the whore) in the series *Mamá No Me Lo Dijo* (*Mama Didn't Tell Me*, 2004). The Bolivian State took us to court us for the 'obscene acts' presented in this film.

VIVA ExCon: Itinerant Indeterminacy

Võ Hồng Chương-Đài

When the Covid-19 pandemic upended the order of the world, reluctant curators and directors had to postpone one biennale after another, into the unknown. One of the few events of scale that went ahead in 2020 was VIVA ExCon (Visayas Islands Visual Arts Exhibition and Conference), though it, too, shifted gears – moving online and opening its three-day conference without an exhibition. A month later, a much longer conference akin to a bimonthly seminar unfolded with talks and conversations. The usually invisible work of studio visits, research and brainstorming became a possible exhibition rooted in the contours of location. Each Saturday morning, artists shared their responses to the theme of 'Kalibutan: The World in Mind', as curators and coordinators conveyed the cultural and physical geographies of their region. There were sessions about practical skills and needs: art materials, a mobile relief kitchen, residencies, the art market, museum standards. The mix was eclectic, a constellation of art-making, activism and culture research – a community surveying its terrain.

VIVA ExCon does not fit easily into 'global' exhibition histories or accounts of the post-1989 contemporary art world.[1] Its first priority was and remains the local: artists in the Visayas archipelago, one of the three main geographic and administrative divisions of the Philippines (the other two being Luzon, to the north, and Mindanao, to the south). Until recently flight paths went through Manila, with few direct routes between neighbouring islands; travel within the Visayas – six large islands and hundreds of islets – meant a rough, day-long journey by bus, ferry and bus. That centripetal infrastructure is but one manifestation of the country's political and cultural powerhouse.

VIVA ExCon changed that dynamic: artists organised themselves and called on the new national government's outreach to cultural institutions in the provinces following the ouster of Ferdinand Marcos in 1986. The two halves of the biennale's name – exhibition and conference – continue to draw participants and audiences with disparate aesthetic, intellectual and political affiliations, cutting across generations and class lines.

Every edition has received national support, starting with the Cultural Center of the Philippines (CCP) for the first three editions, and thereafter more substantial funding from the National Commission for Culture and the Arts

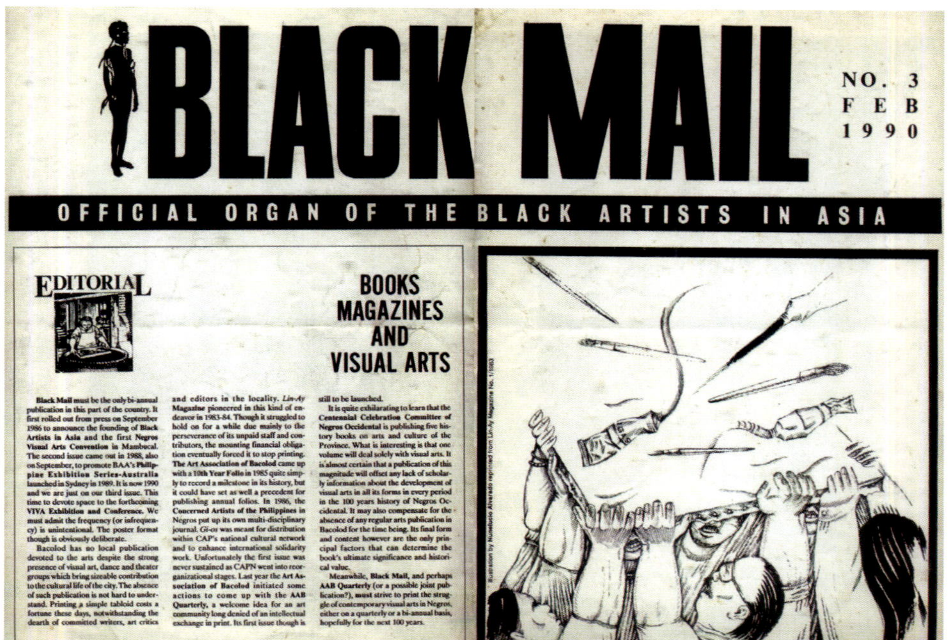

EDITORIAL

BOOKS MAGAZINES AND VISUAL ARTS

Black Mail must be the only bi-annual publication in this part of the country. It first rolled out from press on September 1986 to announce the founding of **Black Artists in Asia** and the first **Negros Visual Arts Convention** in Mambucal. The second issue came out in 1988, also on September, to promote BAA's **Philippine Exhibition Series-Australia** launched in Sydney in 1989. It is now 1990 and we are just on our third issue. This time to devote space to the forthcoming **VIVA Exhibition and Conference.** We must admit the frequency (or infrequency) is unintentional. The poster format though is obviously deliberate.

Bacolod has no local publication devoted to the arts despite the strong presence of visual art, dance and theater groups which bring sizeable contribution to the cultural life of the city. The absence of such publication is not hard to understand. Printing a simple tabloid costs a fortune these days, notwithstanding the dearth of committed writers, art critics and editors in the locality. *Lin-Ay Magazine* pioneered in this kind of endeavor in 1983-84. Though it struggled to hold on for a while due mainly to the perseverance of its unpaid staff and contributors, the mounting financial obligation eventually forced it to stop printing. **The Art Association of Bacolod** came up with a **10th Year Folio** in 1985 quite simply to record a milestone in its history, but it could have set as well a precedent for publishing annual folios. In 1986, the **Concerned Artists of the Philippines** in Negros put up its own multi-disciplinary journal. *Gi-ot* was meant for distribution within CAP's national cultural network and to enhance international solidarity work. Unfortunately the first issue was never sustained as CAPN went into reorganizational stages. Last year the **Art Association of Bacolod** initiated some actions to come up with the **AAB Quarterly,** a welcome idea for an art community long denied of an intellectual exchange in print. Its first issue though is still to be launched.

It is quite exhilarating to learn that the **Centennial Celebration Committee of Negros Occidental** is publishing five history books on arts and culture of the Province. What is interesting is that one volume will deal solely with visual arts. It is almost certain that a publication of this magnitude will offset any lack of scholarly information about the development of visual arts in all its forms in every period in the 100 years history of Negros Occidental. It may also compensate for the absence of any regular arts publication in Bacolod for the time being. Its final form and content however are the only principal factors that can determine the book's ultimate significance and historical value.

Meanwhile, **Black Mail,** and perhaps **AAB Quarterly** (or a possible joint publication?), must strive to print the struggle of contemporary visual arts in Negros, either on a quarterly or a bi-annual basis, hopefully for the next 100 years.

(NCCA). It is common now for each edition's host to augment that support with in-kind and monetary commitments from their local and regional governments and foreign institutions. Though the total budgets are modest compared to that of many biennales around the world, the base of support across the Visayas is steadfast and proud – having struggled through significant tests of will and vision.

Black Artists in Asia

VIVA ExCon comes out of a turbulent history shaped by the region's semi-feudal economy and knotty relations with the national centre. Marcos's dictatorship (1965–86) brought wide swathes of the working class and middle class together for massive demonstrations. The national democratic movement gave cohesion to an unlikely mix of groups, including artists at the national and regional levels. In the Visayas, students at La Consolacion College's School of Architecture and Fine Arts in Bacolod City joined the coalition through Pamilya Pintura, a group founded in 1980 by former political detainee Nunelucio Alvarado along with Felixberto Solmayor, Oscar Moises and Perry Argel. Three years later, film-maker Lino Brocka founded Concerned Artists of the Philippines (CAP) in Manila, with writers, artists, film-makers and other cultural workers.

CAP Negros opened later that year when Brocka visited Bacolod, the capital of Negros Occidental Province; the regional chapter opposed both the Marcos dictatorship and the semi-feudal system that structured society throughout the Visayas. A powerful oligarchy has ruled the islands since Spanish colonial times, maintaining as common practice *tiempos muertos*, the 'dead season'

Black Mail: Official Organ of the Black Artists in Asia, no.3, February 1990, edited by Norberto Roldan, produced by BAA Atelier with assistance from Philippine-Australia Church Conference and Bayanihan ng mga Pilipino sa New South Wales. Courtesy Green Papaya Art Projects

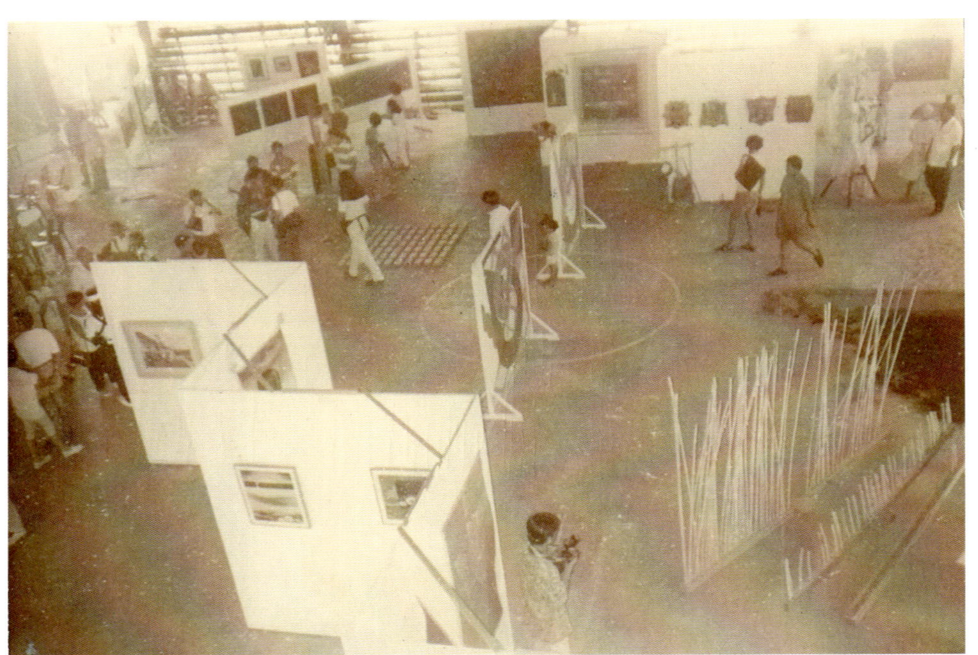

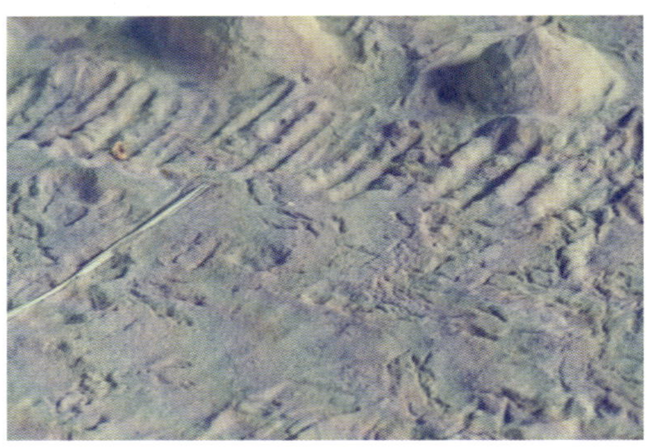

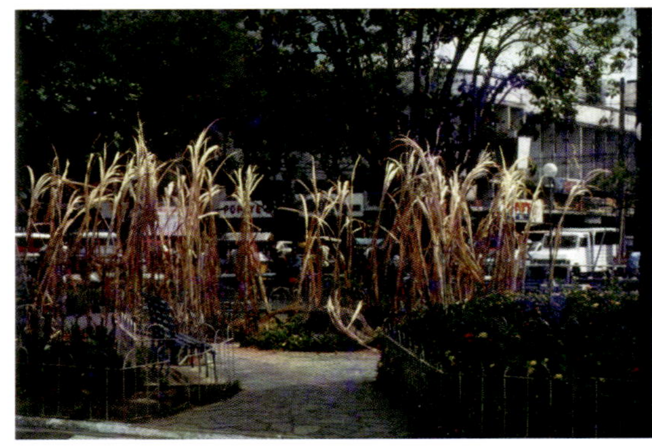

Top: Installation
view of VIVA ExCon,
Bacolod, 1992,
showing works by
Tsunetaka Komatsu,
Hitomi Utami,
Charlie Co and Willy
Magtibay. Courtesy
Maria Lourdes
Nening Villanueva

Above and right:
documentation of
VIVA ExCon, Bacolod,
1992, including work
by Hitomi Utami
(right). Courtesy
Green Papaya Art
Projects

372

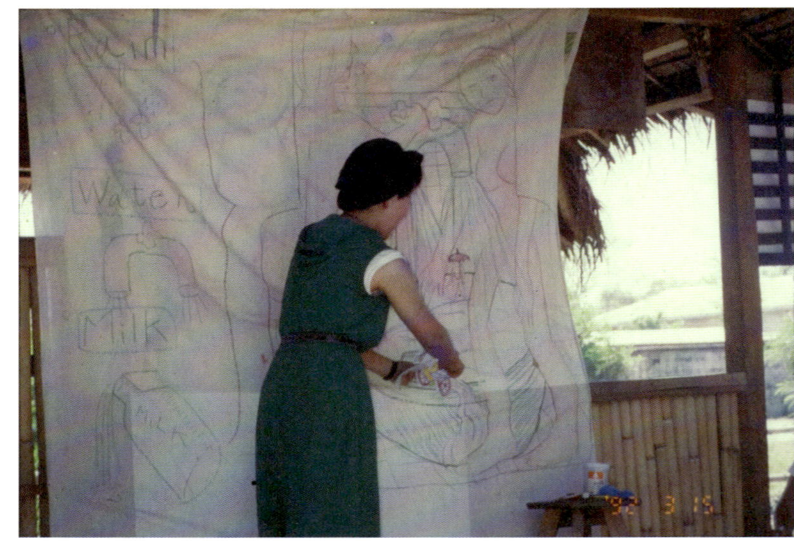

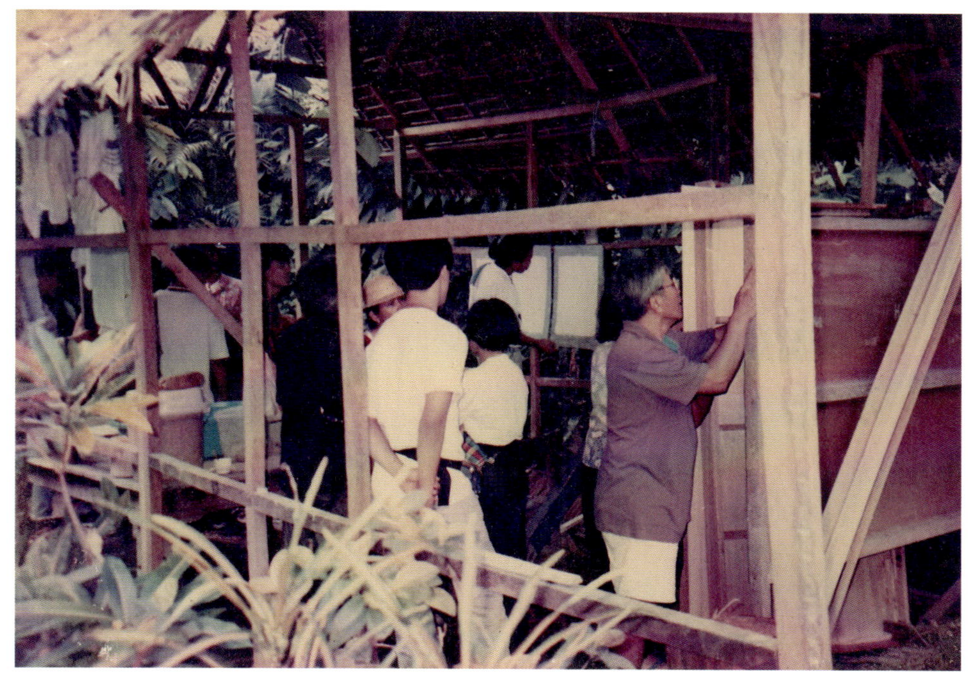

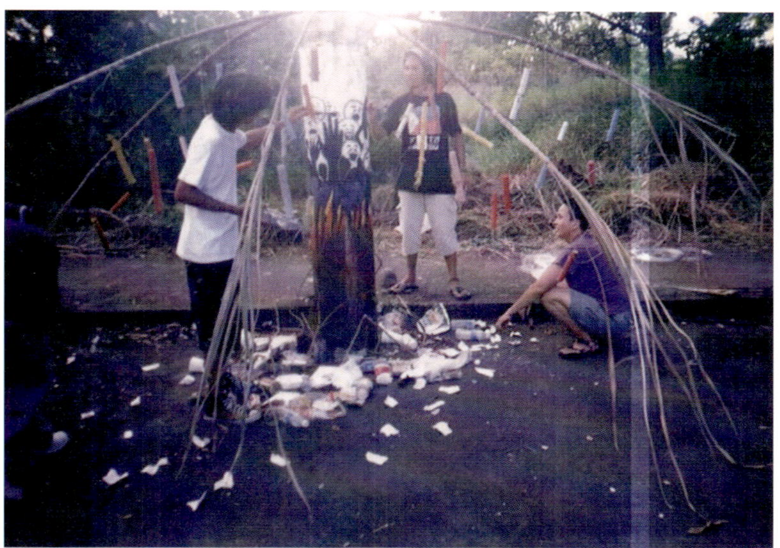

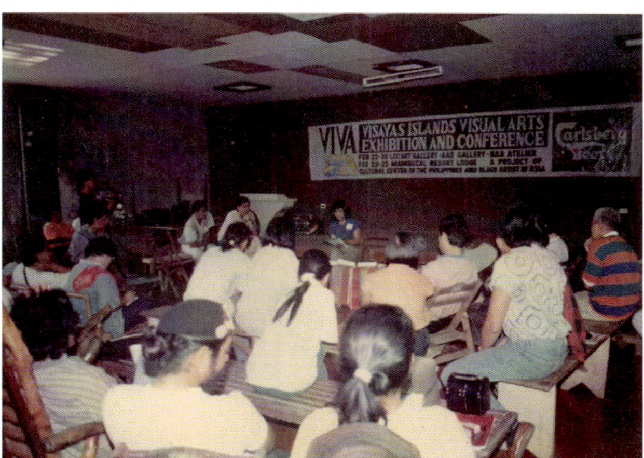

From top:
Participating artists
including PG Zoluaga,
Charlie Co, Milton
Dionzon and Bobi
Valenzuela installing
their works at VIVA
ExCon, Dumaguete,
1994; Dante Enage
and Glenn Lumantao
participating in the
delegates' collab-
orative installation
on the theme of
'Purgatoryo' at VIVA
ExCon, Bacolod,
2004; and VIVA
ExCon conference
documentation,
Bacolod, 1990, with
Dea Doromal, Tommy
Haffala, Tess Ariola,
Roy Veneracion and
Nito Teves. Courtesy
Green Papaya Art
Projects (upper two
images) and Maria
Lourdes Nening
Villanueva (left)

during which the local peasants who work on plantations are not paid for two months. They borrow money to support themselves during this time, then spend the next season paying off the debt. This perpetual cycle keeps many in de facto servitude to the land-owning class. From 1983 until the end of the Marcos regime, CAP Negros organised campaigns and rallies for political democracy and economic justice, calling on artists to create streamers, banners, murals and street theatre.[2]

The intense struggles of the 1970s and 80s were not without risks. The pervasiveness of state and military surveillance prompted the CAP Negros leadership to establish safety protocols to safeguard activists. M. Cecilia Locsin Nava and Norberto Roldan led the chapter as chair and co-chair, while Roldan chaired the visual arts section. He was a cultural leader and activist identified with the leftist movement, and his work put his life in danger. Upon advice from his brother, he temporarily left Bacolod for Sydney in 1987.[3] After Marcos's fall in 1986,[4] the CCP announced a new cultural policy shaped by 'Filipinisation', 'democratisation' and 'decentralisation'.[5] Former First Lady Imelda Marcos had supported the building of the CCP as the regime's jewel in the crown – a brutalist stage for classical and modern art forms that catered to international diplomatic circles. In contrast, the new artistic director Nicanor Tiongson decentralised the coffers by funding outreach programmes and initiatives outside Metropolitan Manila.

An atmosphere of promise and optimism saw the formation of groups such as Black Artists of Asia (BAA)[6] in Bacolod and BANAAG (Center for the Popularisation of Visayan People's Culture) on the island of Cebu. BANAAG itself was an offshoot of PETA (Philippine Educational Theater Association), a model for theatres of the oppressed in Asia. Before he went into temporary exile, Roldan wrote BAA's manifesto, which was much more explicit than the CCP's post-1986 policy of promoting 'democratisation'. With echoes of Mao's talks at the 1942 Yenan Forum, the BAA platform equated 'Filipinisation' with 'use of local and indigenous materials and forms'; called for 'contribut[ing] creative and technological resources to the socio-economic activities of the community'; and advocated 'a unified national consciousness, regional identity and affinity'. BAA's name asserts an affiliation with racialised and colonised subjects, referring specifically to the dark-skinned indigenous inhabitants of the Visayas whom the Spanish nearly decimated. However, BAA's choice of the colour 'black' was also an affirmation of the artists' desire for non-alignment and a move away from direct political action.[7] These amalgamations of the local, the national and global, embodied in the group's name and manifesto, would play out in overlapping and conflicting aspirations for VIVA ExCon.

BAA started with sixteen members, but usually is associated with four in particular: Roldan, Alvarado, Charlie Co and Dennis Ascalon. They had earlier joined Pamilya Pintura and struggled alongside each other during the Marcos years, working on group exhibitions and eventually this much larger endeavour. Soon after its founding, BAA convened the First Negros Visual Arts Conference. Roldan had hoped to follow up by collaborating with BANAAG to host the First Visayas Consultation Conference on the Visual Arts in 1986.[8]

This vision would not materialise until he returned from self-exile, consulting with close friends and colleagues as well as BAA members to launch VIVA ExCon in 1990.

An earlier festival gave the Visayan artists inspiration. Santiago Bose had founded the Baguio Arts Guild in 1987, which remarkably put the Baguio Arts Festival and northern Luzon on the international map within a few years. Roldan recalls fondly his close friendship with Bose, each man pledging to support the other and his ambitions for their provinces. 'I discussed VIVA with colleagues in the Visayas, and also extensively with Bobi Valenzuela, Manny Chaves and Santiago Bose,' says Roldan. 'Baguio Arts Guild started a few years before VIVA and instantly became an international sensation for artists elsewhere. When we were about to launch VIVA, I spoke to Santi and he said it's our [Bagiuo artists'] turn to support Bacolod [BAA's base]. The entire Baguio Arts Guild landed in Bacolod and we weren't even prepared for hosting them. I hosted twelve of them in my house. Ben Cab[rera] was a part of this.'[9] Manila-based artists such as Brenda Fajardo joined them, making the first edition at La Consolacion College, the base for Pamilya Pintura, a reunion of sorts for the nationally and internationally minted names of the Philippine contemporary art scenes.

There had been previous initiatives in the Visayas, to name a few: Masskara Festival, founded in 1980 on Bacolod; Maki-Isa Negros: Festival of People's Culture in 1984; and Hublag: The Ilonggo Arts Festival, on Iloilo from 1988 to 1994. Roldan and Ely Santiago had consulted Defensor and Hubon Madya-as, the artist group he founded, about the possibility of VIVA ExCon. With Hublag's network on Panay Island, BAA was able to bring those artists on board.[10] Charismatic male artists and curators led the early days of such artist groups, festivals and platforms. The Baguio Arts Guild and the Baguio Arts Festival (1987–2002) had Bose, Kidlat Tahimik and BenCab while BAA has had Roldan and Co. This concentration of energy has opened to broader, grassroots and multi-centred leadership and resources.

Roldan pushed for the 1992 VIVA ExCon to grow beyond the Visayas, notably with a group of nine visual artists and drummers from Japan including Tatsuo Inagaki, Teresa Kobayashi and Akatsuki Harada. 'There was no internet at that time. There wasn't funding for artists to go abroad to have exposure. The only way for local artists to get exposed and to hear what their counterparts were doing was to bring in the international', says Roldan.[11] The camaraderie and collaborations would lead Bose, Ascalon, Co, Roldan, Roberto Villanueva and Lilibeth La'O to participate in the Lake Naguri Open Air Exhibition in Japan later that year. The exchanges left strong and cherished memories, as was clear from Inagaki's recollections during a panel at the 2018 VIVA ExCon. In 1993, Alvarado, Bose and Villanueva would be invited to participate in the First Asia Pacific Triennial of Contemporary Art (APT) in Sydney, a much larger stage that brought prestige and sales.

But there was unease: many of the artists from the Visayas felt overshadowed by their peers from Baguio, Manila and Japan. The 1994 VIVA

ExCon edition almost did not happen due to uncertainty about whether to go forward along with a last-minute scramble of logistics. Roldan had moved to Manila in 1993, and the other BAA members were not as active, leaving Co and Ascalon to organise, which they felt ill-equipped to do. Manila-based artists Fajardo, Imelda Cajipe-Endaya and Elmar Ingles attended in their capacity as NCCA representatives, leading intense, closed-door workshops where the Visayan artists asked themselves whether they wanted VIVA ExCon to continue and for whom. Co and Ascalon led the BAA affirmation, but VIVA ExCon would serve the Visayas – showing only artists living in or from the Visayas.[12]

Camaraderie and inter-island world

Certain editions of international biennales are known for their artistic directors and curators, whether for their crystallisation or miscalculation of an idea. VIVA ExCon, too, has had curators: Bobi Valenzuela, co-founder of the pioneering, Manila-based Hiraya Gallery, cautioned against indiscriminately displaying whatever comes through the door. The art critic Ruben Ramas Cañete curated the 2008 and 2010 editions in Cebu, renaming VIVA ExCon as the Visayas Biennale without plenary approval and introducing an art fair and awards, avowedly to make the event appeal to an international audience. Both of these components have been discontinued, and the 2012 delegates voted to retain VIVA ExCon's founding name instead of adopting the internationally legible tag of 'biennale'. Roldan led Green Papaya Art Projects as the curatorial team for the 2018 edition, creating a conversation between the biennale's early history through artists such as Bose at the Civic Center; 'Story House', curated by Inagaki; group exhibitions of younger artists at Panublion Museum and People's Park; and a community archive display of memorabilia, photographs, posters and documents. Art historian Patrick Flores curated the 2012 edition, in Dumaguete; the 2014 edition, in Bacolod; the 2016 edition, in Iloilo; and the 2020 edition, which may or may not take physical form in Bacolod by the middle of 2021.

While the curators have left their mark, it is the wide base of the organising that testifies to VIVA ExCon's relevance for its audience. That human infrastructure comprises artists, cultural workers and volunteers who put in the long hours and pass on their knowledge to future hosts. Having attended the 1990 and 1992 editions while still in college, two decades later Babbu Wenceslao and Yvette Malahay-Kim, members of the teaching faculty at Foundation University and Silliman University, respectively, prepared for the 2012 edition by consulting with previous artist-organisers Co, Manny Montelibano, Dennis Montera, Paul Pfeiffer and Maria Taniguchi. With Flores as curator and students as part of their crew, they brought the biennale to their campuses as well as the Jorge B. Vargas Museum in Manila (Vargas was a son of Negros Occidental).[13] Such overlaps of function and duties regenerate enthusiasm throughout the community, making the biennale a learning and lived experience beyond the event itself.

For artists and students travelling to the host city, the trip once involved exhausting bus rides over mountains and ferries across seas. But they pushed

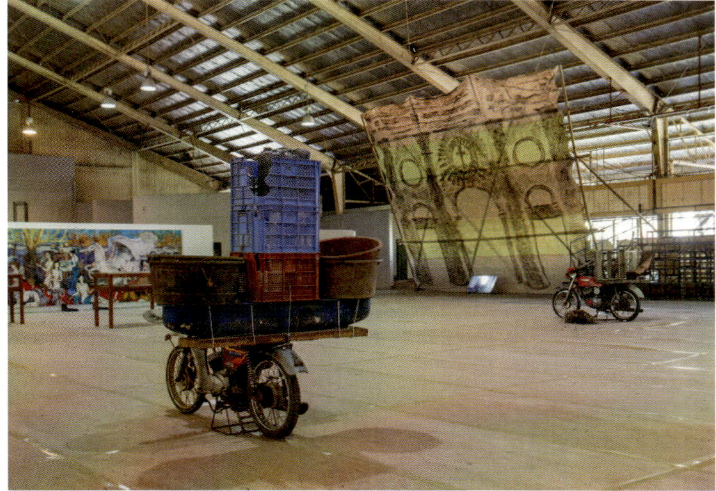

Installation view, 'Bisan Tubig Di Magbalon (Don't Even Bring Water)', Civic Center, Roxas City, Capiz, as part of VIVA ExCon Capiz, 2018. Works by Kitty Taniguchi, VIVA ExCon Community Archives Project, SKYLAB (Jonard Villarde, Ania Shane Martinez, Mercy Audencia and Santiago Alvarez) and KLMTW (Ronyel Compra, Wyndelle Remonde, Greys Lockheart). Photography: Kiko Nuñez. Courtesy VIVA ExCon Capiz 2018

on with the excitement of seeing friends and meeting new faces from other islands. They continue to come from high schools and colleges, they come from the world of theatre, music and film. The enthusiasm and camaraderie spur interest beyond the white walls, and have led to new art schools in Dumaguete, Bacolod and Cebu.[14]

Exhibitions are usually the most important component of biennales that follow the Euro-American model, but the discursive is critical at VIVA ExCon. The conference is decidedly regional in focus, exemplified by what organisers call the 'island reports', when delegates share updates on their arts communities: new and still-running spaces and institutions, artists and their fields, funding sources and working relationships with local governments. The workshops are popular and often cited in post-conference commentary, as artists and other guests talk about art awareness in their communities, financial resources, new media and processes, arts criticism, exhibition opportunities and issues of intangible heritage. The conversations raised by the panels and lectures ebb and flow into social gatherings, sponsored meals, performances and late-night drinks. The promise of sociality creates anticipation for each biennale, and when it comes, it renews friendships and expectations for the next edition.

Not easily assimilable
One of the biennale's unique characteristics is its itineracy. The 1992 delegates agreed that aspiring hosts could bid for the next edition and campaign to win, by majority vote, on the last day of the conference.[15] BAA has been critical at the onset, but other hosts have included Cristina Taniguchi's Mariyah Gallery, Dumaguete; the artist group Hubon Madya-as, Iloilo; Pusod, Cebu; Kasikasi, Leyte; and Datu Sikatuna Guild of Arts, Bohol. The itineracy more than once has led to tense situations, most notably when a local politician hijacked the 2006 edition in Samar, inviting artists to a public lunch in the park with the military surrounding them.[16] The 1994 delegates had put in place an executive committee to help hosts pass the baton. That effort evolved

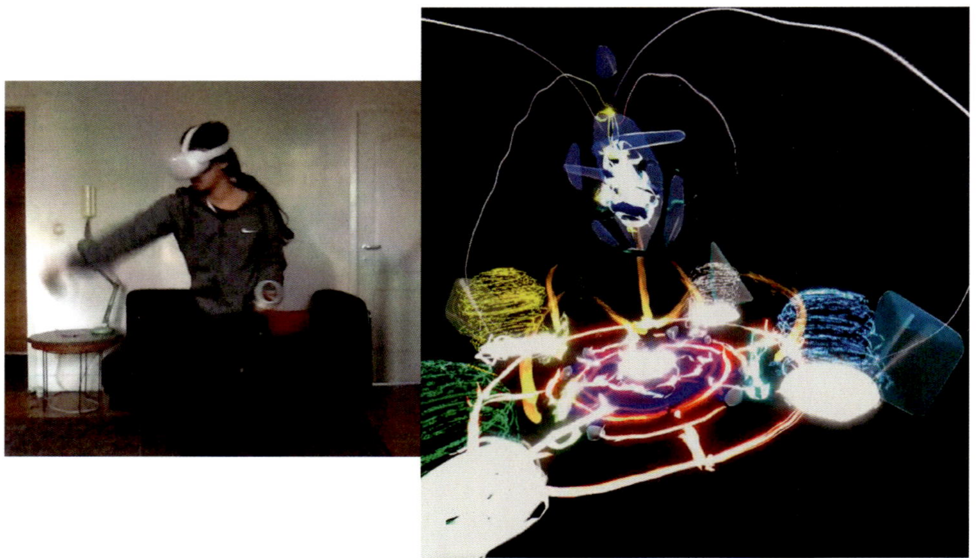

into the VIVA Association two years later, which did not last long due to the difficulties of maintaining a single office and coordinating people.[17] Instead, a different model took hold from the ground up: 'a council of "elders"/"organisers"' advising the next host and rallying their fellow islanders to participate and contribute.[18]

These relationships, nurtured over decades in the archipelago, make VIVA ExCon unique in the Asia Pacific region, if not further afield. A short-lived festival held from 1992–98, Chiang Mai Social Installation, was meant to break the institutional grip of the Bangkok School, but the festival dissolved with strained resources and clashing visions, even as it attracted more and more international artists and visitors. The large biennales in the Asia Pacific region that burst onto the international stage in the 1990s – such as the Asia Pacific Triennial in 1993, Gwangju Biennale in 1995 and Fukuoka Asian Art Triennale in 1999 – serve museum collections and an international audience.

VIVA ExCon is not opposed to the outside world, but it is less tied to the international. 'It's a mixed bag that's less confined to the grammar of the contemporary or the conceptual. It's partly indifferent to the market and being critical of the institution', observes Flores, as he curates the 2020–21 edition. 'Here it's rock n roll. We don't want to streamline it. It's not how it's wired. There are interventions within that might speak to those issues, rooted in particular experiences.'[19]

A combination of rootedness and itineracy has made VIVA ExCon remain relevant to its core audience – the artists, curators, art critics, students, faculty and organisers of the Visayas. The constant change of host organisations and locations has bred chaos and confusion, but it has also led to a decentralisation of energy and leadership that renew themselves whenever and wherever

378

the biennale travels. Each host brings their community's excitement, dynamic and momentum to the ties of the inter-island, creating a biennale shaped by the vocabularies, forms and lived experiences of the local communities who constitute and transform it.

Notes

1 This article uses archival material found in the Bobi Valenzuela Archive at Lopez Museum; Terminal Reports submitted to the National Commission for Culture and the Arts (NCCA); and research and interviews conducted for *VIVA ExCon, 1990–2016: The Community Archives Project*, a forthcoming publication(hereafter abbreviated as *Community Archives*) initiated by VIVA ExCon 2018 artistic director Norberto 'Peewee' Roldan for that edition of the biennale. For *Community Archives*, Iris Ferrer and Mayumi Hirano worked with Lesley-Anne Cao, Merv Espina and Touki Roldan to interview people and document VIVA ExCon's history. The pages cited in this article are based on a book draft that Ferrer shared with the author in March 2021. Many of the news articles reprinted in the book can be found in the Bobi Valenzuela Archive and the Terminal Reports for NCCA. Some of the materials are available online through Green Papaya Art Projects Archive, Asia Art Archive. I would like to thank the research team and community members who shared their materials and stories. I also would like to thank Roldan and Patrick Flores for their reflections and insights.

2 For a history of VIVA ExCon, see Ma. Ceclia Locsin-Nava (ed.), *ViVA EXCON 1990–1996: The Contemporary Visual Arts Movement in the Visayas*, Manila: National Commission for Culture and the Arts, 1998. See also Georgina Luisa Olivares Jocson, 'The Impact of Black Arts in Asia on the Contemporary Art of Negros Occidental and the Visayas Region, and on a Wider Scale, The Contemporary Art Narrative in the Philippines', master's thesis, LASALLE College of the Arts, Singapore, 2012.

3 Norberto Roldan, interviewed by the author, 24 March 2021.

4 Known also as the People Power Revolution, the EDSA Uprising refers to the massive demonstrations that took place along Epifanio de los Santos Avenue in Metro Manila.

5 *Black Mail*, no.1, September 1986, p.1.

6 *Ibid.* and *Black Mail*, no.3, February 1990. BAA was originally named Black Artists of Asia, but changed its name to Black Artists in Asia in 1990, in response to criticism that BAA does not represent artists of Asia.

7 Black Artists of Asia manifesto, 1986.

8 *Black Mail*, no.1, September 1986, and no.3, February 1990, p.3.

9 N. Roldan, interviewed by the author, 24 March 2021. See also 'Striking Affinities: On the Magician, Santiago Bose', panel with Roldan, Kawayan de Guia and Alfredo and Isabel Aquilizan, moderated by Patrick Flores, Silverlens Galleries, Makati, Metropolitan Manila, 15 April 2021, available at https://www.youtube.com/watch?v=o20tli1r7Ps.

10 Interview with PG Zoluaga, *Community Archives, op. cit.*, pp.57–60.

11 N. Roldan, interviewed by the author, 24 March 2021.

12 See NCCA terminal report on VIVA ExCon III.

13 Yvette Malahay-Kim, interviewed in *Community Archives, op. cit.*, pp.126–29.

14 PG Zoluaga, interviewed in *Community Archives*, p.60; and P. Flores, interviewed by the author, 12 April 2021. On the importance of friendship and camaraderie nurtured by VIVA ExCon, see Antonio Alunan Wenceslao, 'Recalling the Fourth VIVA', in *Community Archives, op. cit.*, pp.44–56. Butch Dalisay remembers the 2016 edition in 'The Southern Lights Shine Brightly', *Penman, Philippine Star*, 28 November 2016, reprinted in *Community Archives, op. cit.*, pp.152–55.

15 Estela Ocampo Fernandez and Raymund L. Fernandez, interviewed in *Community Archives, op. cit.*, p.68.

16 'Roundtable Conversation with Charlie Co, Dennis Ascalon, Manny Montelibano, Ann Legaspi-Co, Milton Dionson, Iris Ferrer and Mayumi Hirano', *Community Archives, op. cit.*, pp.167–68.

17 PG Zoluaga, interviewed in *Community Archives, op. cit.*, pp.57–60. See also NCCA terminal reports on VIVA ExCon III and IV.

18 E.O. Fernandez and R.L. Fernandez, interviewed in *Community Archives, op. cit.*, p.70.

19 P. Flores, interviewed by the author, 15 April 2021.

What was Chobi Mela and what happens next?

A project by Naeem Mohaiemen for Chobi Mela IX; timeline drawings by King Kortobbyo (Suborna Morsheada, Mehedi Hasan, Md Khairul Alam Shada, Pijush Talukder, Rakib Anwar); curated by Tanzim Wahab and Munem Wasif; coordinated by Sayed Asif Mahmud; photography by Pranabesh Das and Debashish Chakrabarty; research by Habiba Nowrose; based on information provided by Shahidul Alam, ASM Rezaur Rahman, Rahnuma Ahmed, Munira Murshed Munni, Mirza Taslima, Taslima Akhter and others.

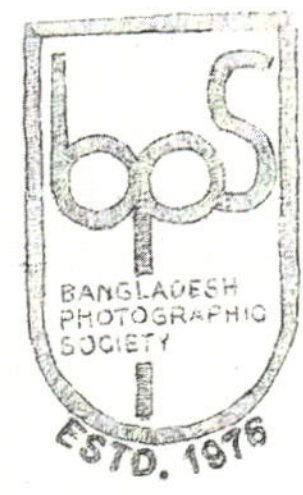

SHAHIDUL ALAM
STEPS DOWN FROM
LEADERSHIP OF BPS
(BANGLADESH
PHOTOGRAPHIC
SOCIETY)

1989

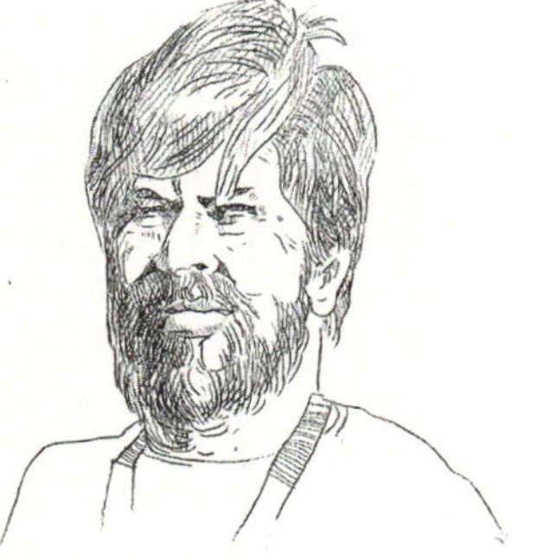

ALAM
ESTABLISHES
DRIK PICTURE
LIBRARY

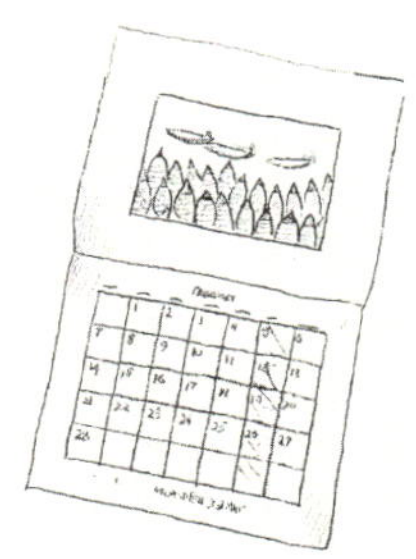

DRIK
LAUNCHES ANNUAL
CALENDAR
FEATURING
BANGLADESHI
PHOTOGRAPHERS

1990

BANGLADESH
PHOTOGRAPHIC
INSTITUTE
ESTABLISHED

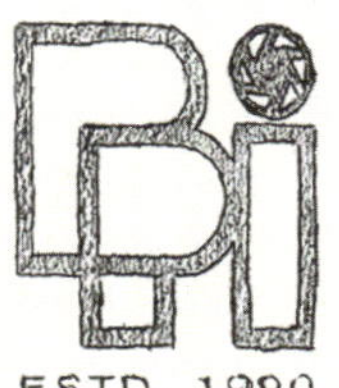

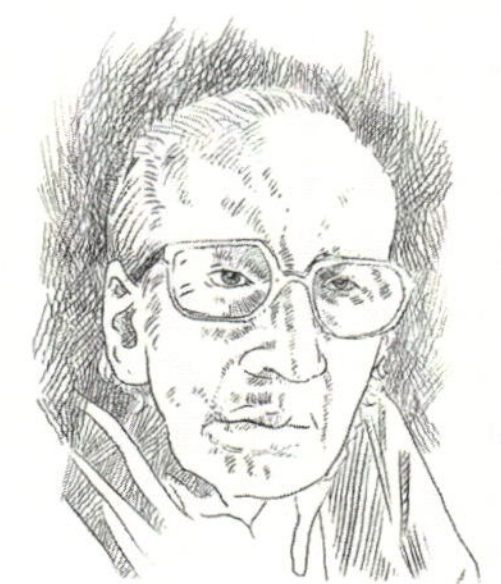

1991

NEW YORK TIMES
RUNS PHOTO
SPREAD OF
BANGLADESHI
PHOTOGRAPHERS

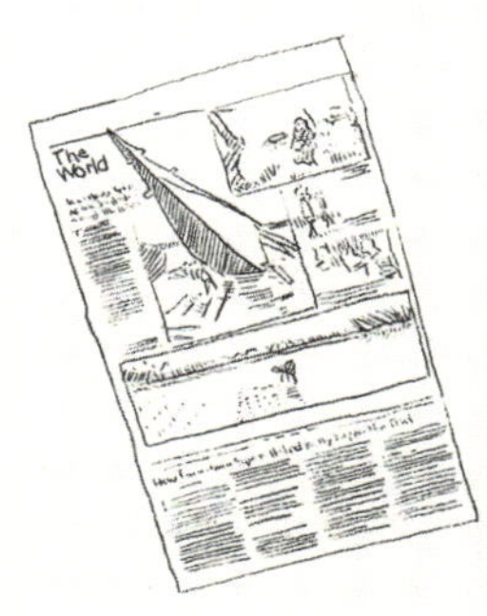

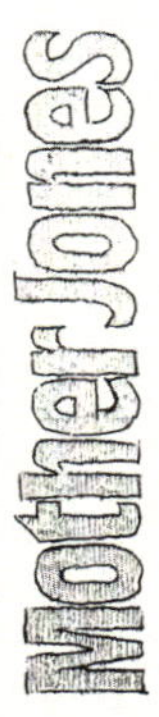

DRIK SETS UP
LINK WITH
MOTHER JONES
MAGAZINE

19 92

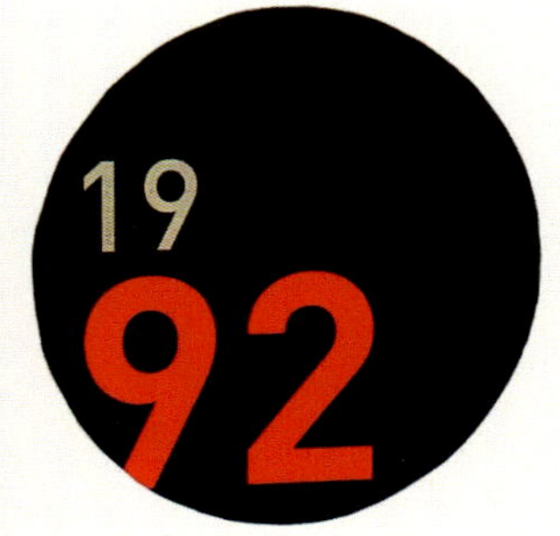

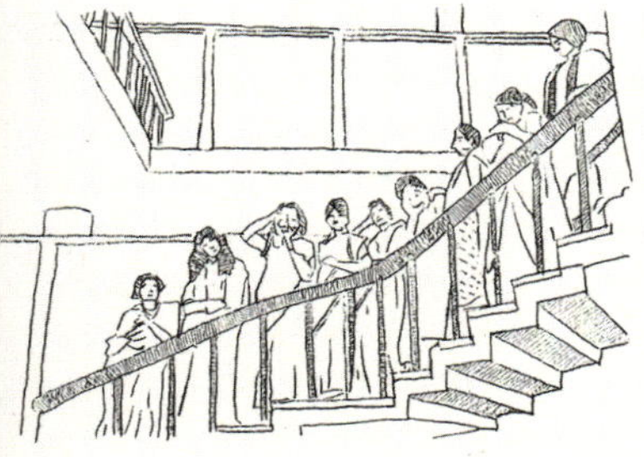

WOMEN'S
PHOTO COLLECTIVE
ONNO CHOKHE DEKHA
HAS GROUP SHOW AT
SHILPAKALA ACADEMY

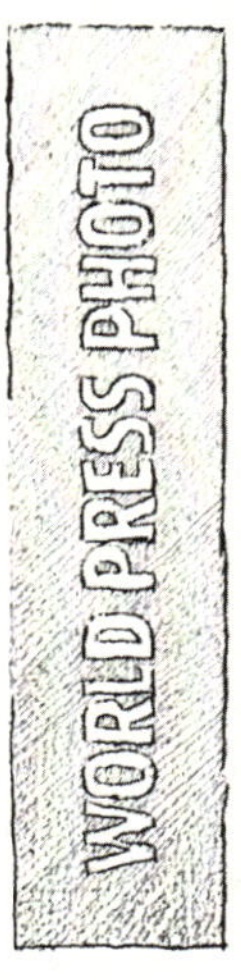

WORLD
PRESS
PHOTO
COMES TO
BANGLADESH

19 93

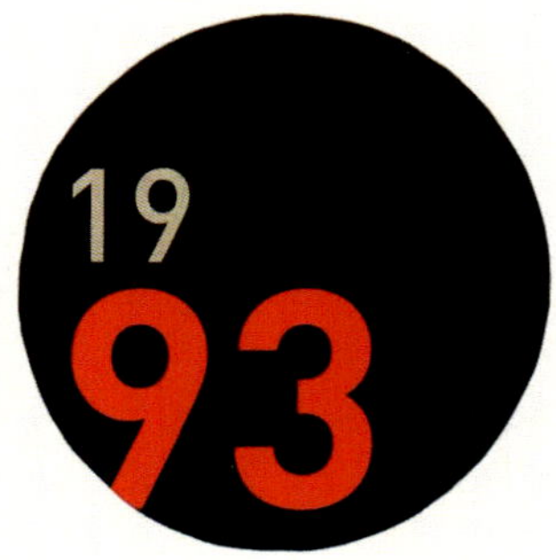

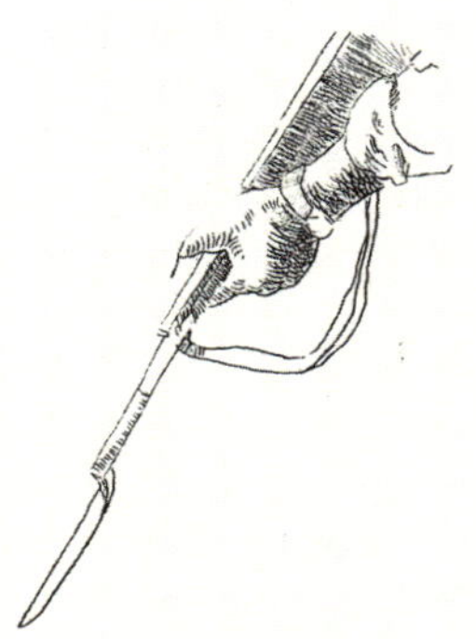

RASHID TALUKDER
1971 PHOTO OF
BAYONETTING IN
PALTAN PUBLISHED
FOR FIRST TIME

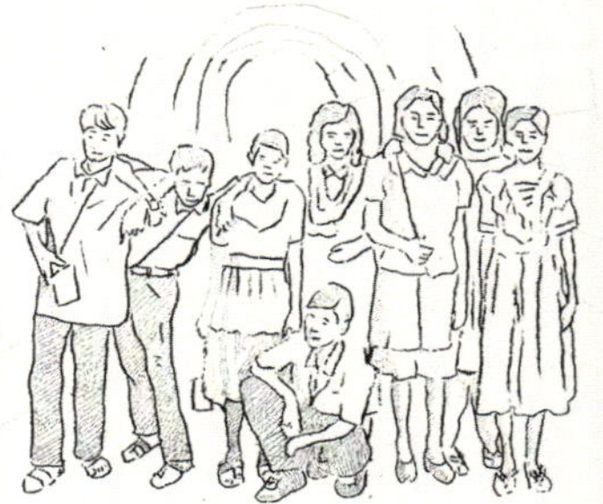

DRIK LAUNCHES
OUT OF FOCUS
CHILDREN'S PHOTO
GROUP

19 94

DRIK
LAUNCHES
EMAIL SERVICE
IN BANGLADESH

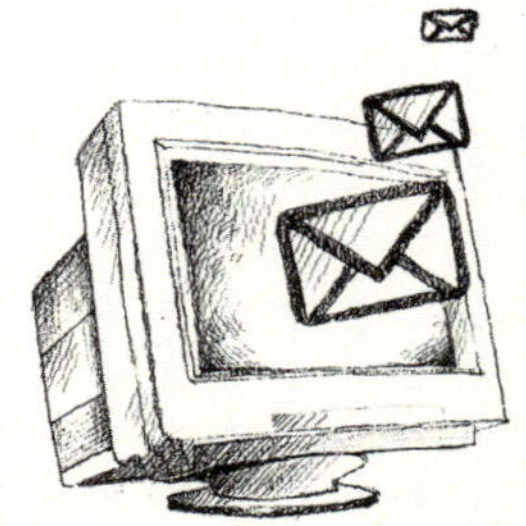

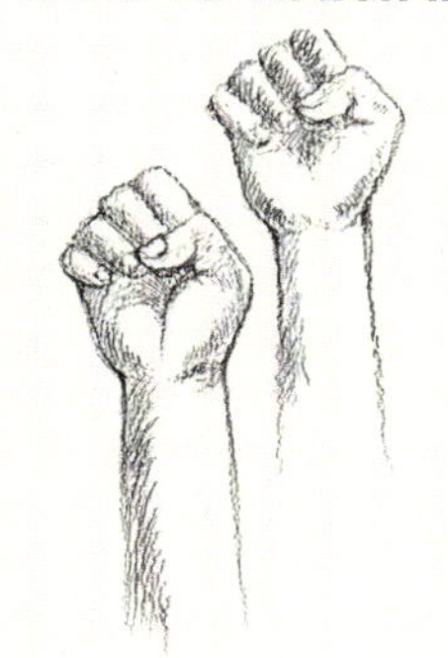

DRIK'S FIRST
DHAKA PHOTO
FESTIVAL
CANCELLED
DUE TO HARTAL

19 95

MAP PHOTO
AGENCY
FOUNDED

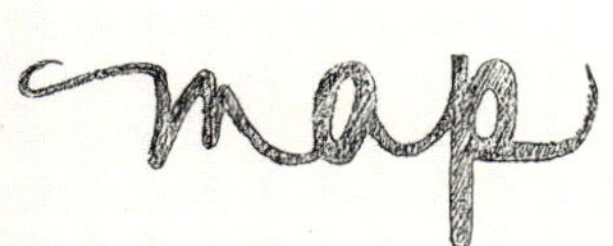

DRIK CALENDAR
OF 1971 PHOTOS
RELEASED ON
WAR'S 25TH
ANNIVERSARY

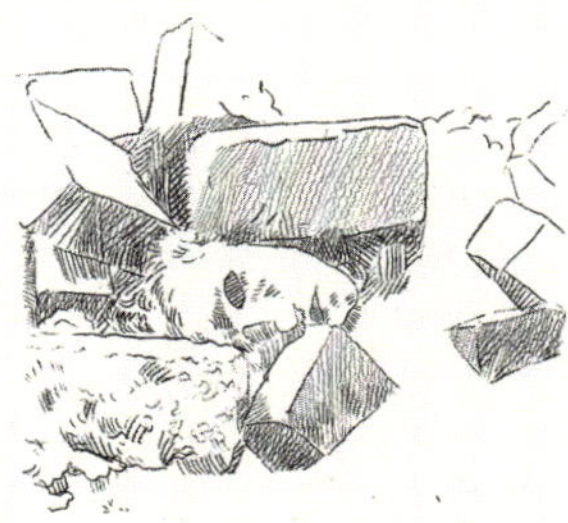

19 96

INTERNET COMES
TO BANGLADESH AT
10 TAKA PER MINUTE

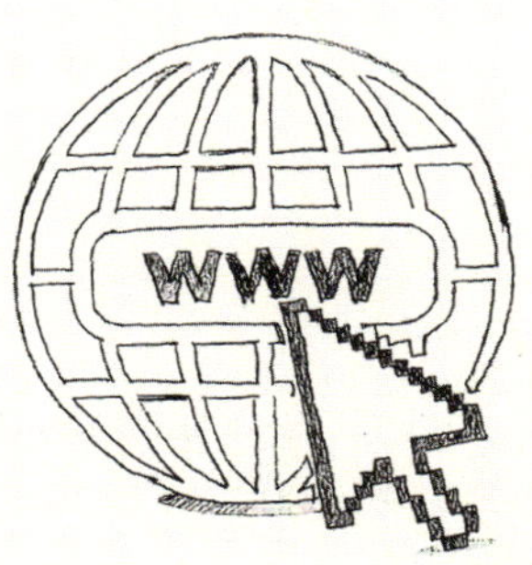

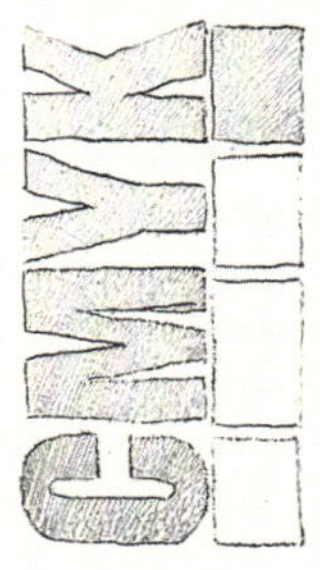

DRIK
CALENDAR
PRINTED IN
FULL COLOR
FOR FIRST TIME

19 97

BANGLADESH
POPULATION
REACHES
124 MILLION

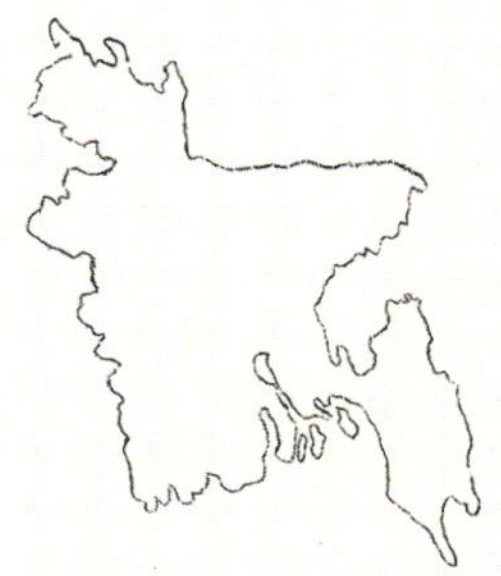

DRIK'S
PATHSHALA
SCHOOL
BEGINS
CLASSES

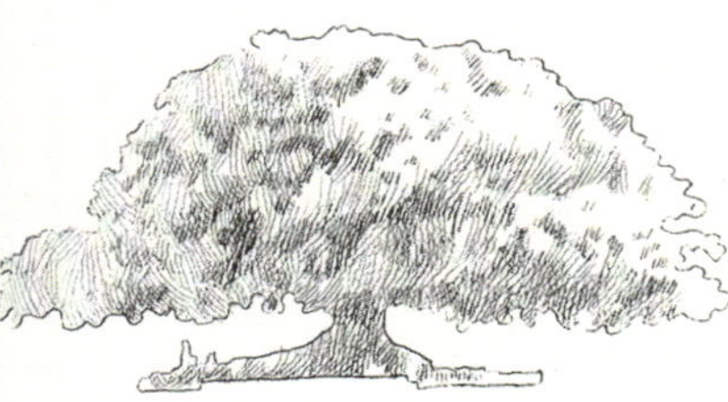

19
98

FIRST DRIK
CALENDAR TO
LOOK AT
FAMILY LIFE

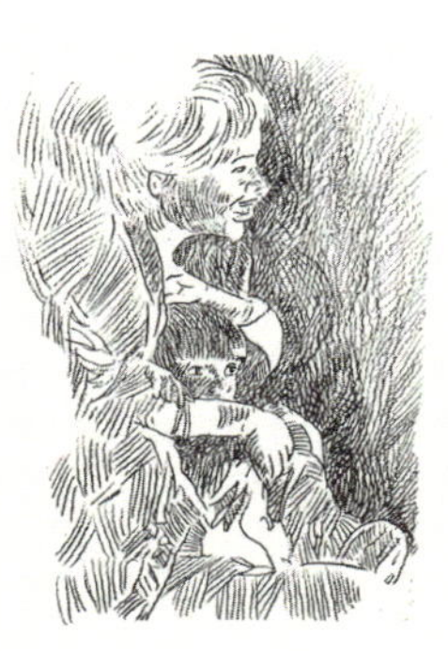

DAILY STAR
NEWSPAPER
SETS UP VIRTUAL
PICTURE DESK

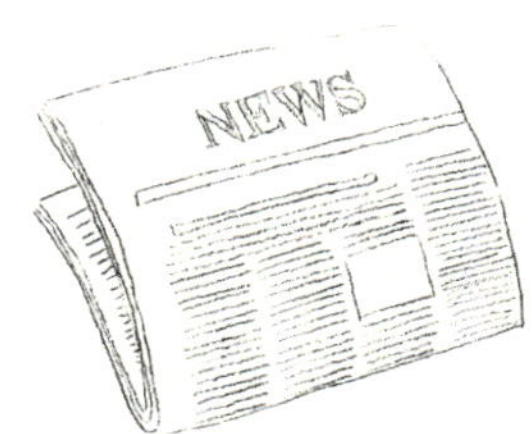

19
99

'POSITIVE LIVES' IS
FIRST DRIK CALENDAR
FEATURING GAY MEN

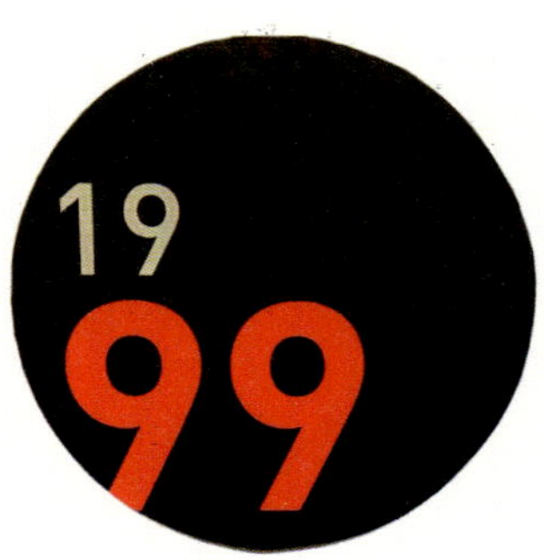

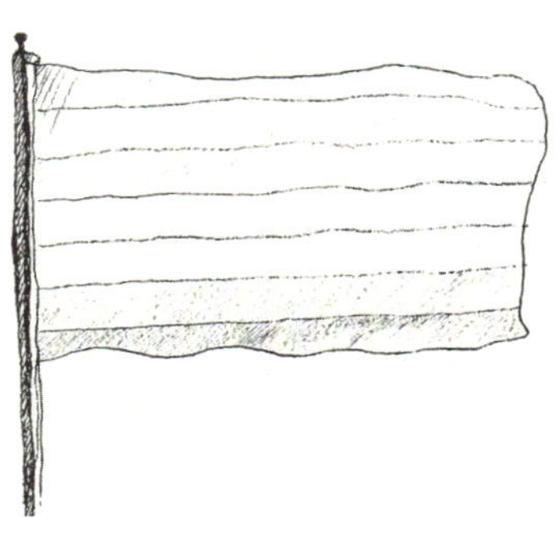

'NOSHTA NARI'
IS FIRST DRIK
CALENDAR
FEATURING
SEX WORKERS

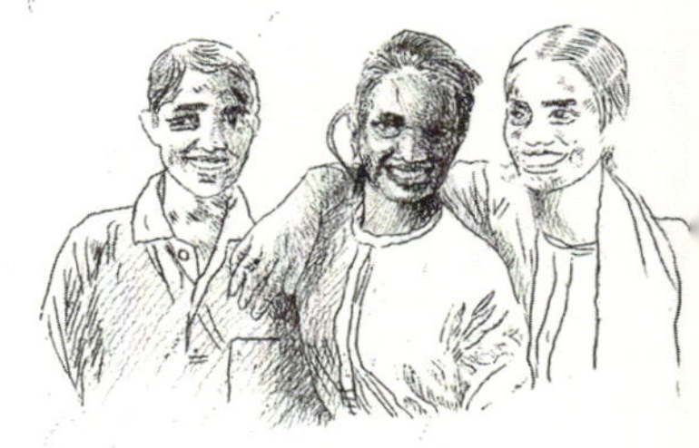

CM I
20
00

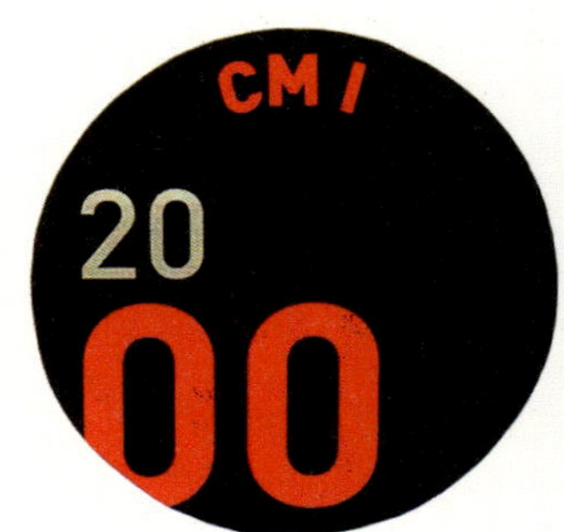

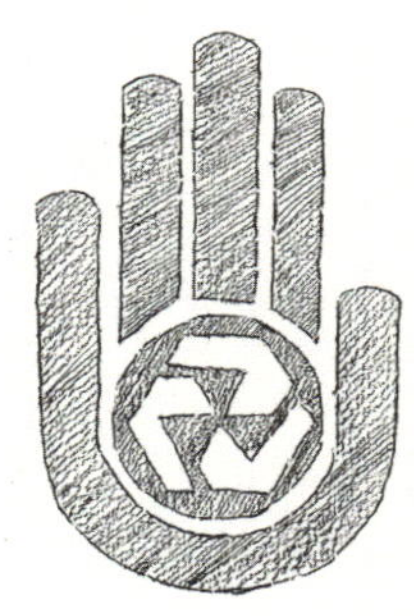

BENGAL
GALLERY
OPENS

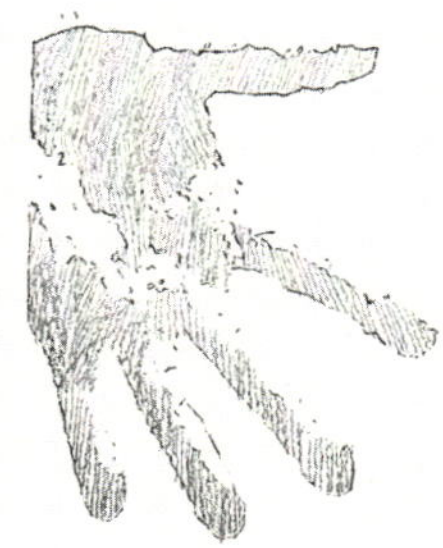

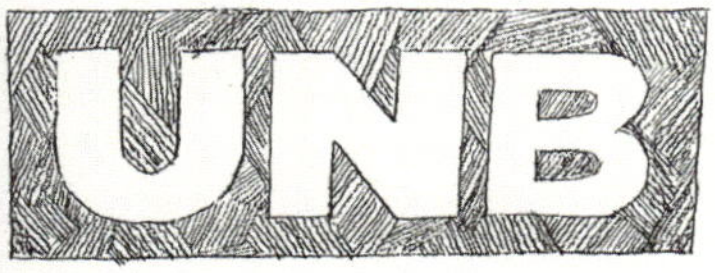

BRITTO
ARTS TRUST
COLLECTIVE OF
ARTISTS FORMED

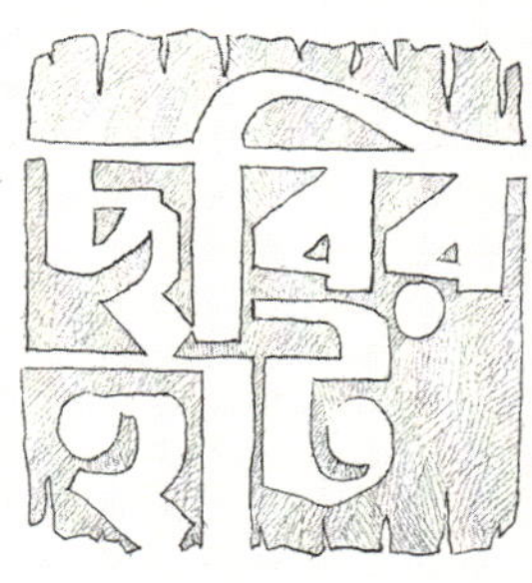

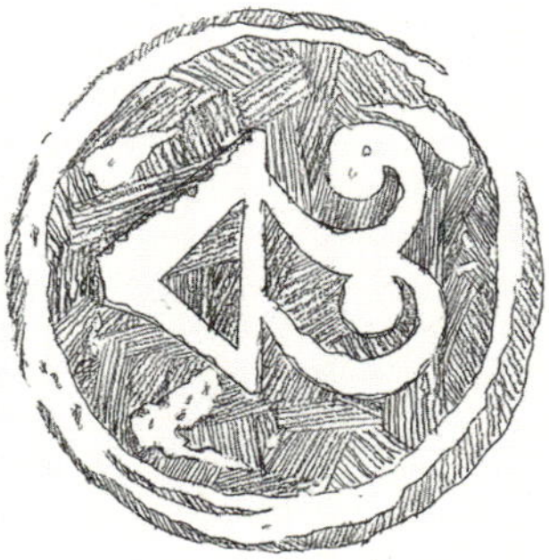

CHOBIR HAAT
OPEN AIR ART
MARKET OPENS
NEAR CHARUKALA

20 01

20 03

UNITED NEWS
BANGLADESH
AND DRIK
CO-PUBLISH
BOOK ON
BANGLADESH
HERITAGE

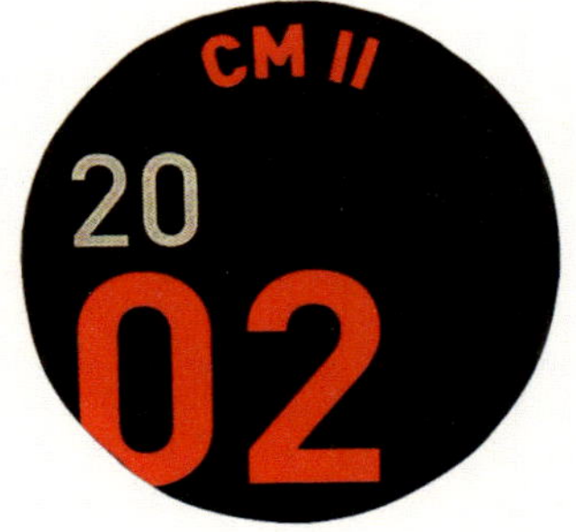

20 02

FIRST BANGLA
ANTHROPOLOGY
TEXTBOOK EDITED
BY DRIK'S
RAHNUMA AHMED &
MANOSH CHOWDHURY

BLACKBERRY
LAUNCHES
SMARTPHONE

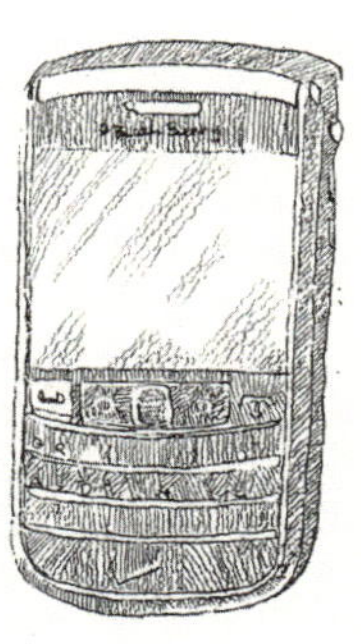

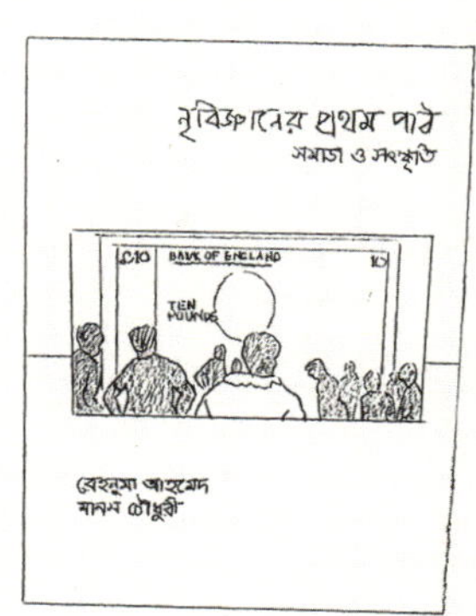

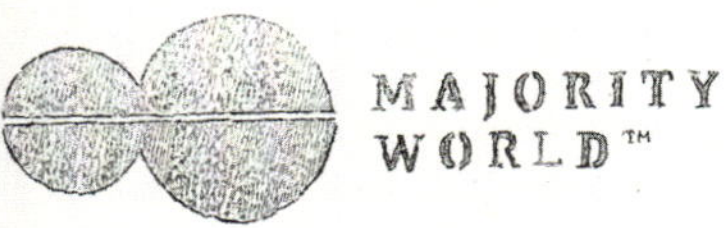

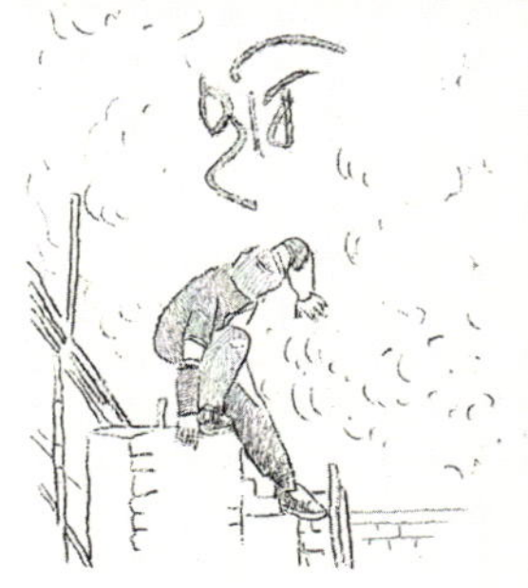

**DRIK LAUNCHES
MAJORITY WORLD
PHOTO AGENCY**

**DHAKA PRESS
PHOTOGRAPHERS
START USING
DIGITAL SLR
CAMERAS**

**DRIK PUBLISHES
FIRST BOOK IN
BENGALI ON
PHOTOJOURNALISM
BY AZIZUR RAHIM PEU**

**CM III
20
04**

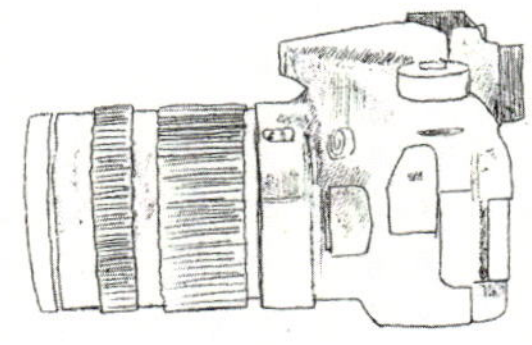

**CM IV
20
06**

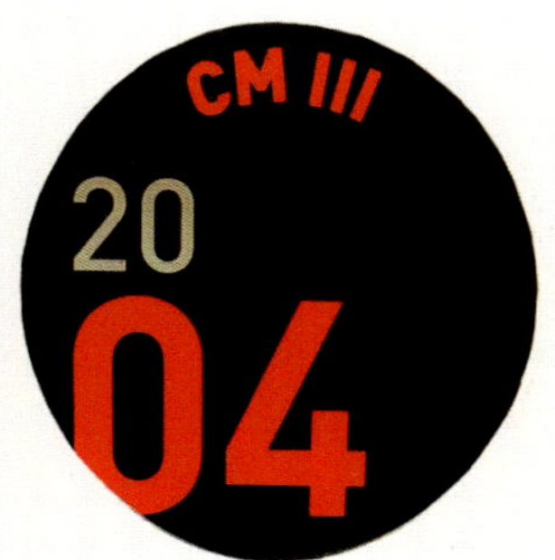

**20
05**

**KONICA-MINOLTA
CLOSE DOWN**

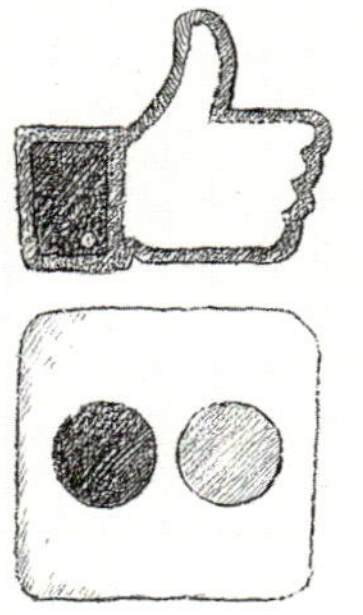

**YOUTUBE
LAUNCHES**

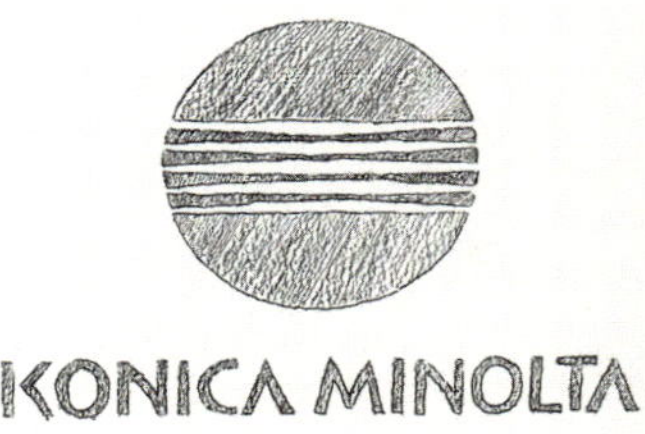

**FACEBOOK AND
FLICKR LAUNCH**

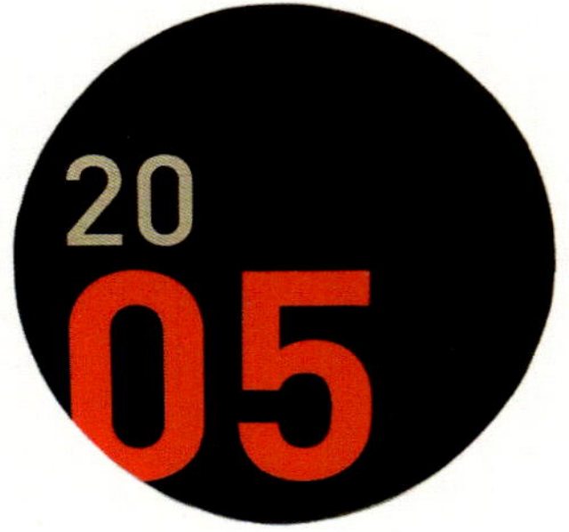

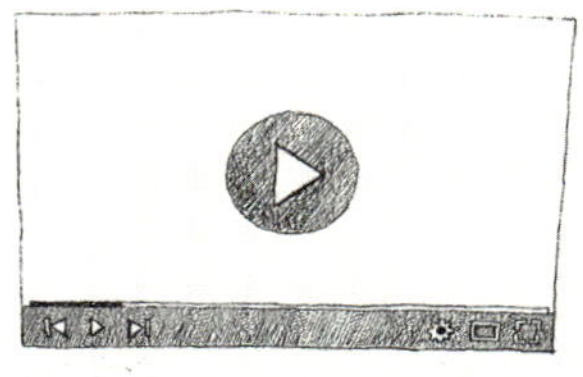

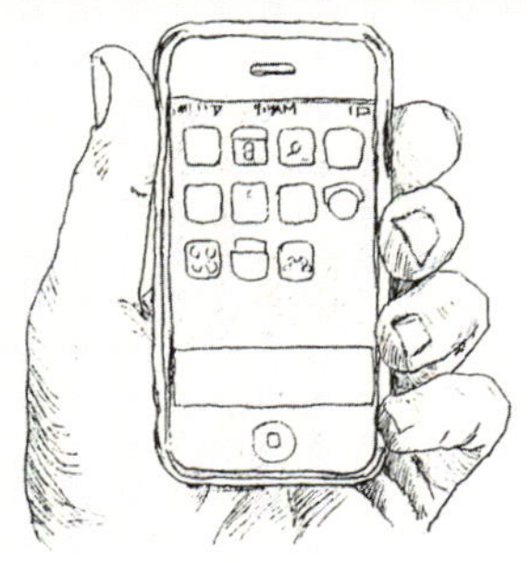

APPLE
LAUNCHES
iPHONE WITH
2.0 MEGAPIXEL
CAMERA

20 07

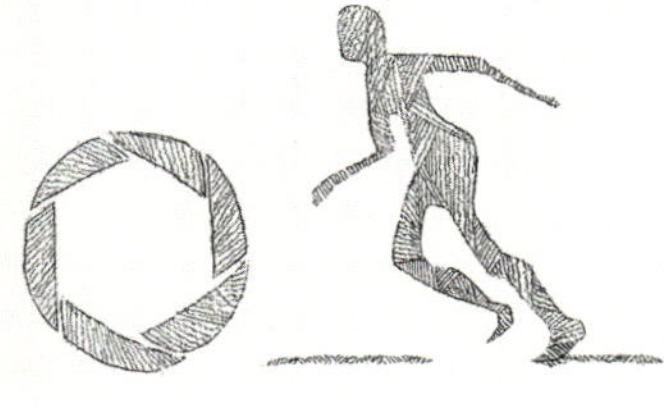

ONLINE
PHOTOGRAPHY
CLUB TTL (THROUGH
THE LENSE)
ESTABLISHED

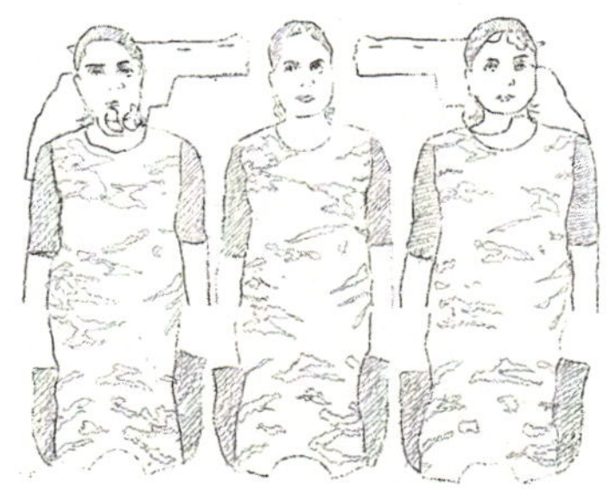

BRITTO
ORGANIZES
'OFF THE BEATEN PATH'
EXHIBITION

20 08

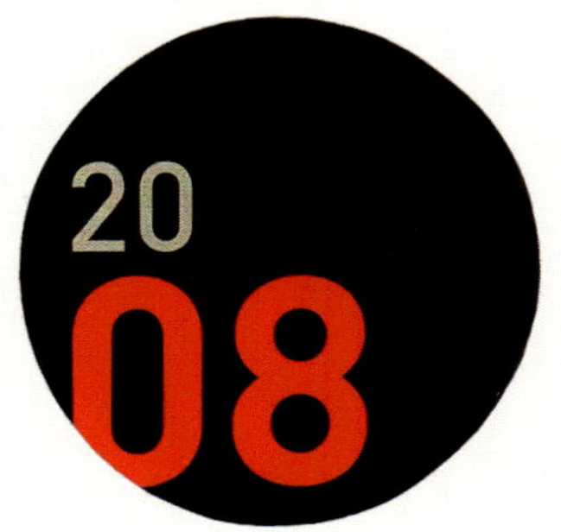

NOKIA
CAMERAPHONE
OVERTAKES
KODAK DIGITAL
CAMERA SALES

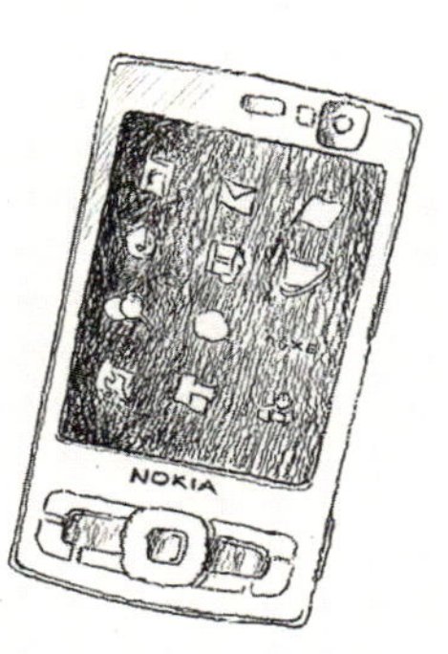

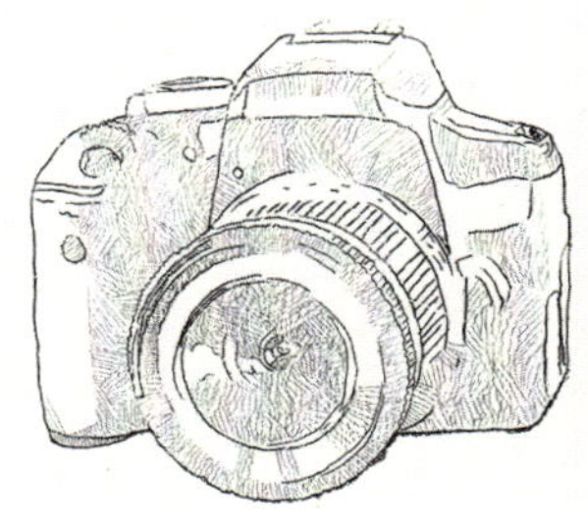

CM V

20 09

KUNDA DIXIT
PUBLISHES
NEPAL BOOKS
AT CHOBI MELA

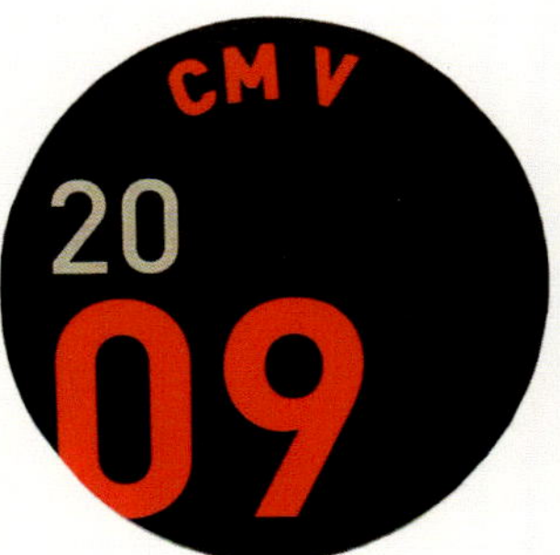

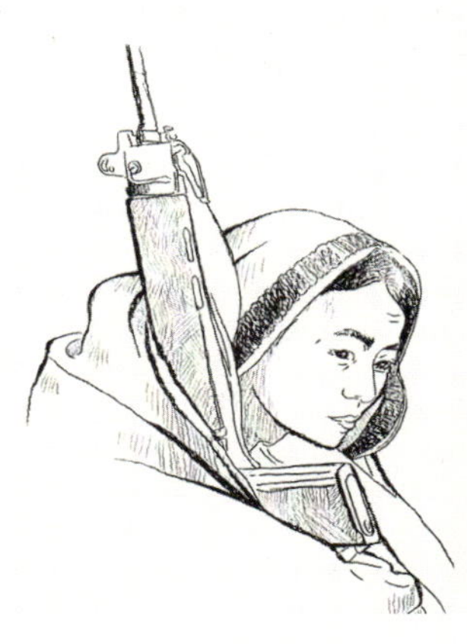

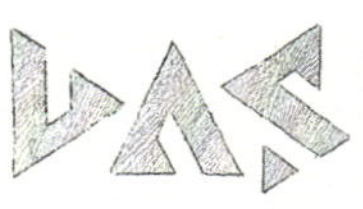
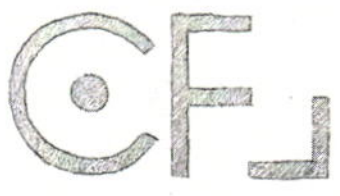

DHAKA ART
CENTER OPENS

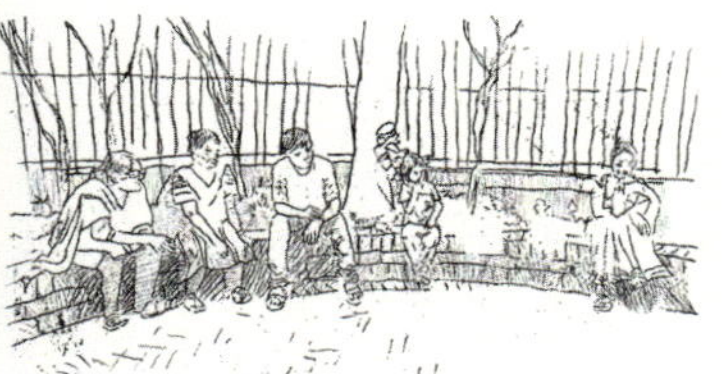

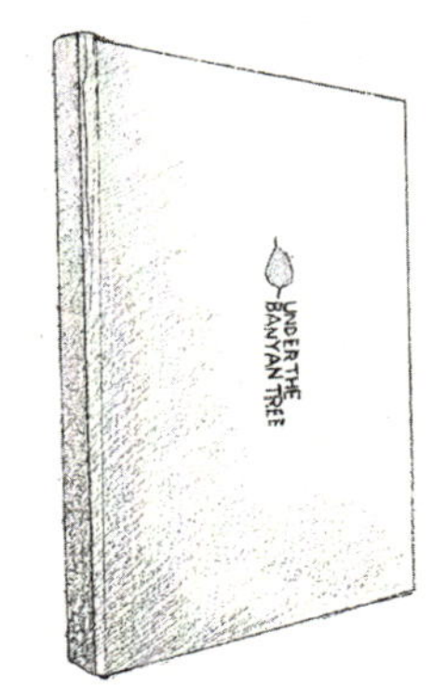

DHAKA ART SUMMIT,
COUNTER FOTO
SCHOOL,
AND
KAMRA JOURNAL
BEGINS

20 10

PATHSHALA
PUBLISHES
'UNDER THE
BANYAN TREE'

20 12

INSTAGRAM
LAUNCHES

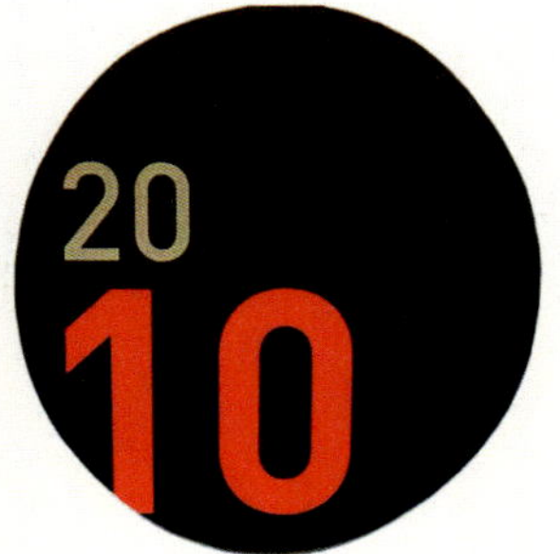

CM VI

20 11

Kodak

FACEBOOK
BECOMES
LARGEST
ONLINE
PHOTO HOST

KODAK
CLOSES
CAMERA
BUSINESS

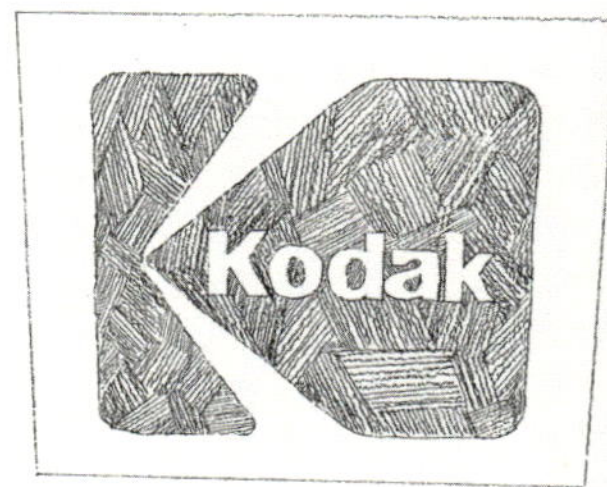

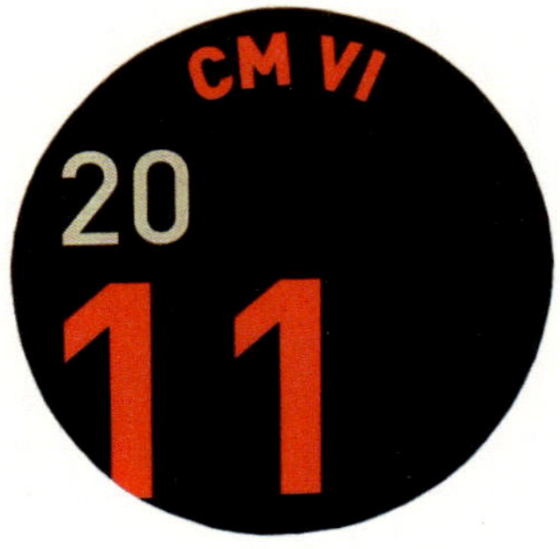

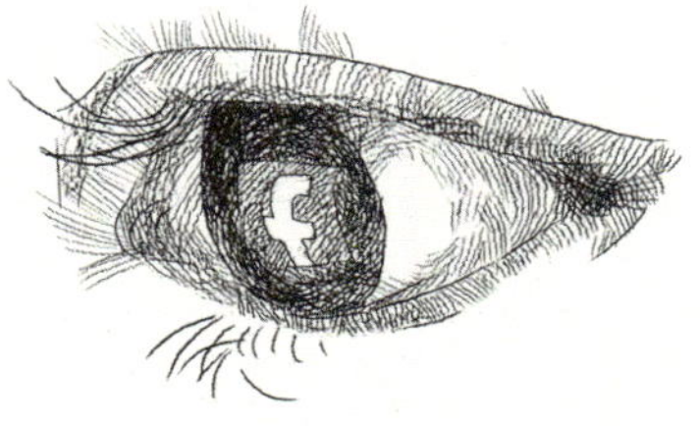

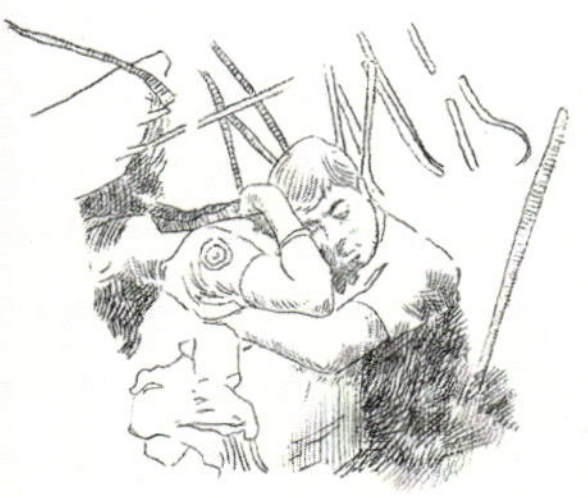

TASLIMA AKHTER'S 'LAST EMBRACE' BECOMES ICONIC IMAGE OF GARMENTS FACTORY TRAGEDY

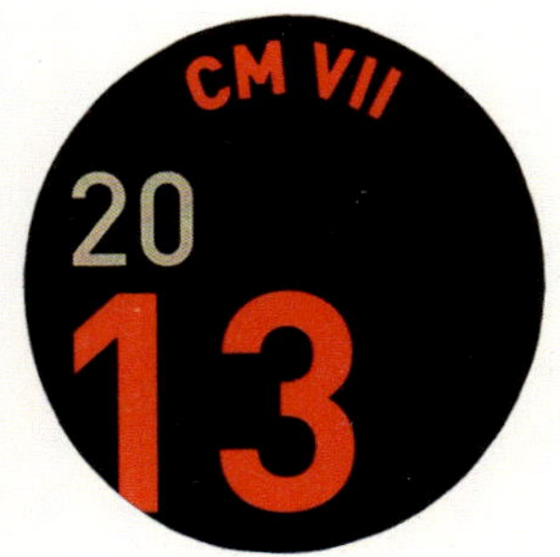

CM VII

20
13

NOKTA PUBLISHES TRANSLATION OF SUSAN SONTAG'S 'ON PHOTOGRAPHY'

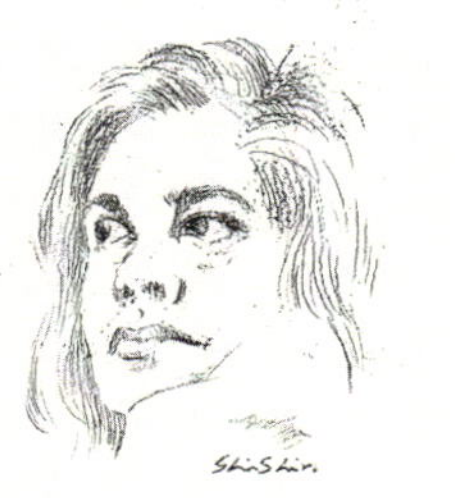

'1134' EXHIBITION ON GARMENTS INDUSTRY TRAGEDY OPENS

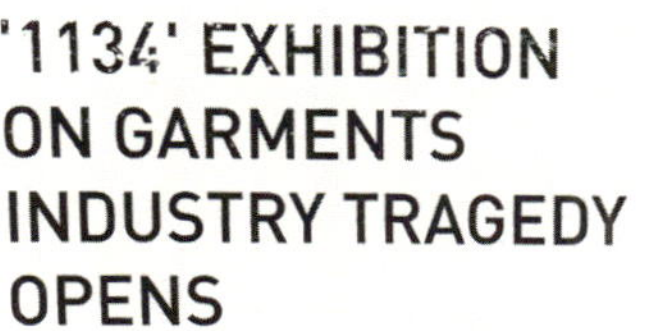

20
14

PATHSHALA LAUNCHES INTERNATIONAL PHOTOGRAPHY COURSE

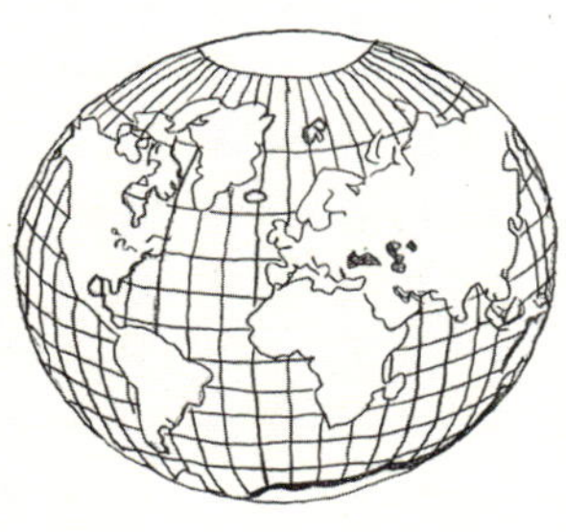

FIRST WEDDING PHOTOGRAPHY CONFERENCE HELD

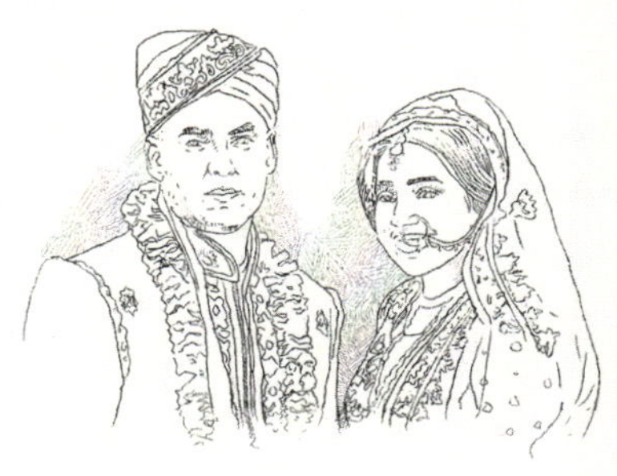

CM VIII

20
15

DHAKA ART CENTER CLOSES AND ABDUR RAZZAQ FOUNDATION OPENS IN SAME BUILDING

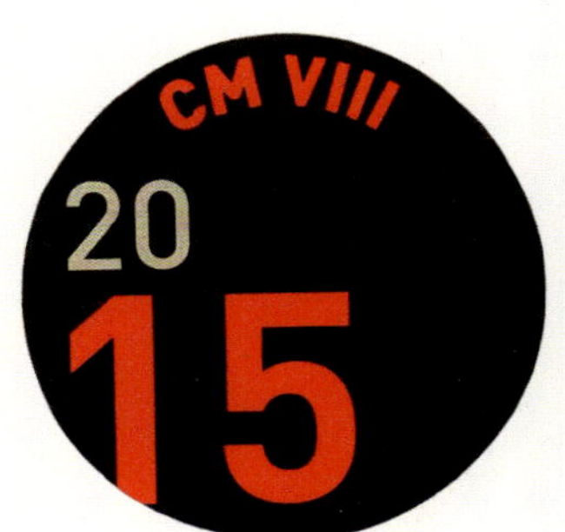

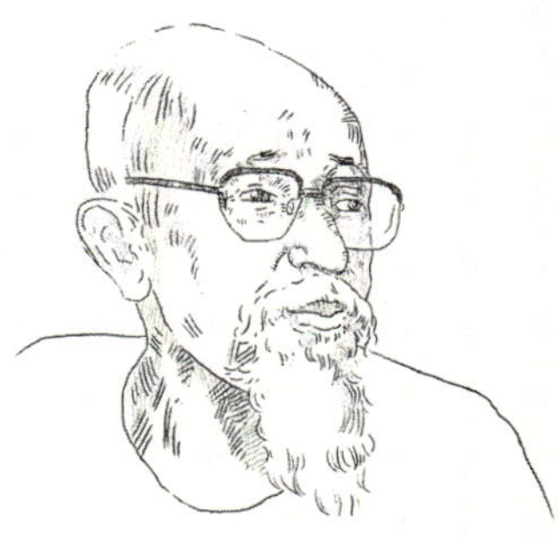

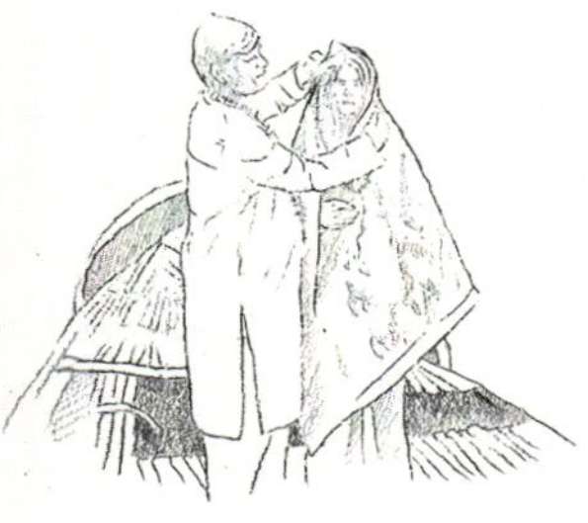

COUNTER FOTO
OPENS 'FREEDOM'
EXHIBITION

20 16

APPLE
LAUNCHES
IPHONE 7 WITH
DUAL CAMERA

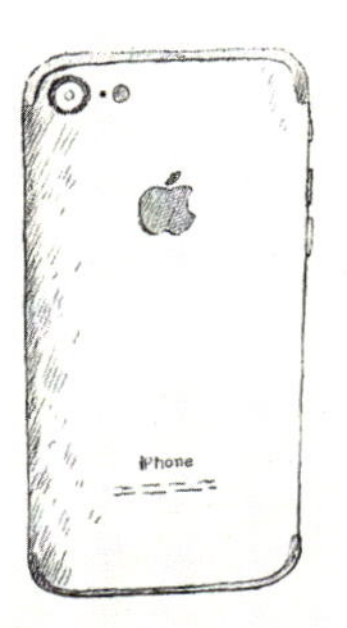

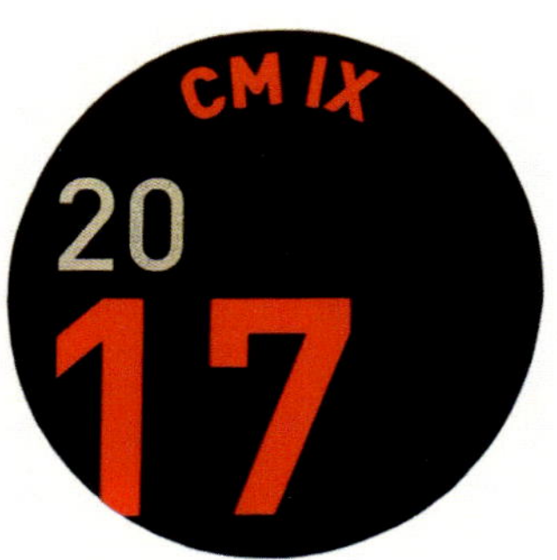

200TH BATCH
OF BASIC
PHOTOGRAPHY
COURSE AT
PATHSHALA

CM IX
20 17

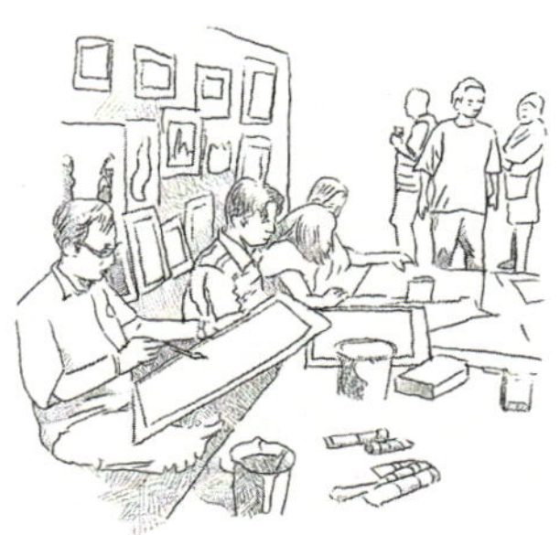

CHOBIR HAAT
FACES PRESSURE
FROM AUTHORITIES
TO CLOSE DOWN

DIGITAL SECURITY
ACT PASSED WITH
WIDE POWER TO
PROSECUTE ONLINE
IMAGE AND TEXT

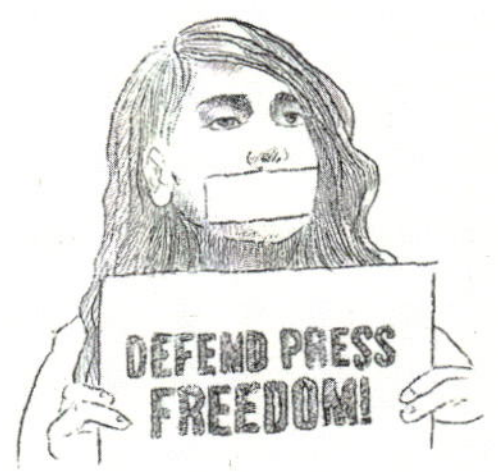

20 18

SHAHIDUL ALAM
JAILED FOR 107 DAYS
FOR HIS ONLINE
REPORTING ON
STUDENT PROTESTS

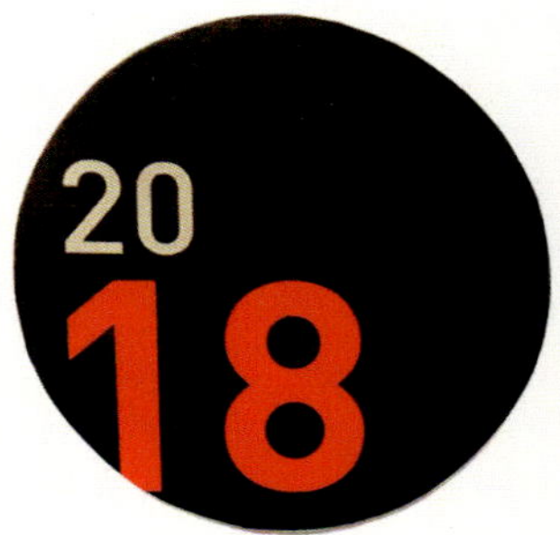

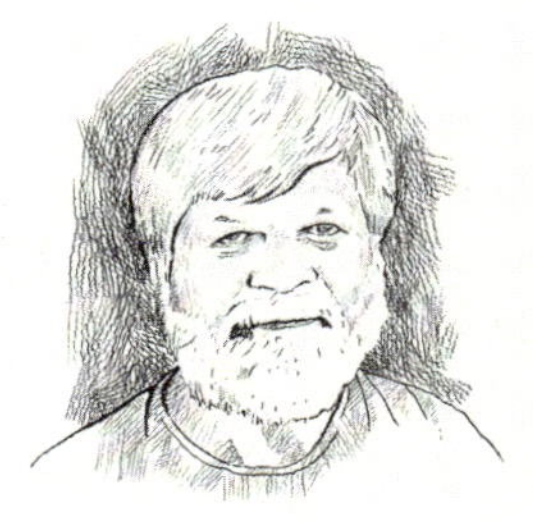

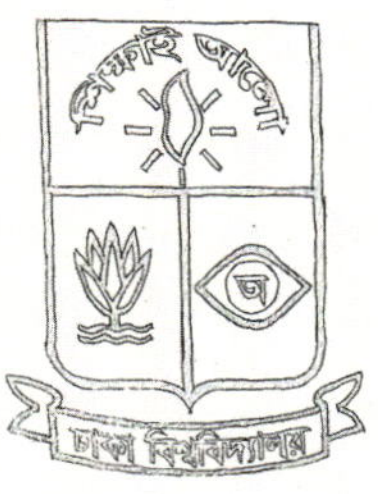

PATHSHALA BEGINS CLASSES UNDER DHAKA UNIVERSITY GRANTING BA DEGREES

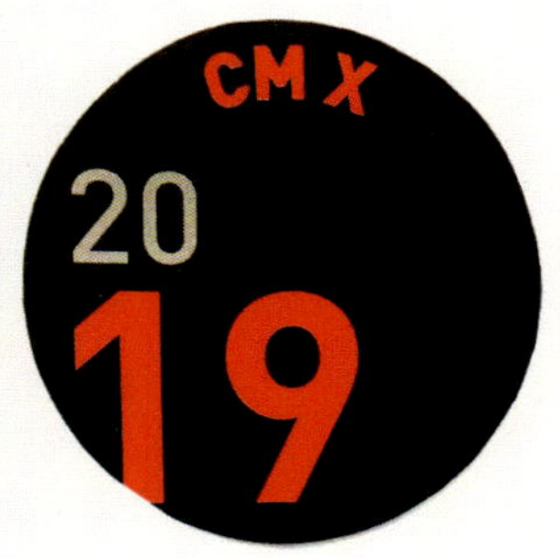

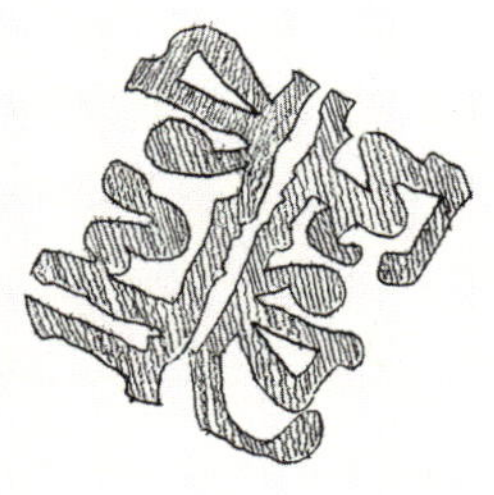

KALAKENDRA (CO-FOUNDED BY MEMBERS OF DHAKA ART CENTER) ENTERS FOURTH YEAR

Eighteen years is a long time, measured by tectonic changes in what is expected, accepted, or challenged in photography. Steve McCurry's *Afghan Girl* (1984) might still be taken today, but the audience would immediately raise sharp questions. The subject of the western gaze is no longer 'willing', and is shooting back, with camera and pedagogy. Chobi Mela (CM) played a role in all this, creating a Global South photography context over two decades. As Asia's first photography biennial, it had a regional ripple effect, inspiring affinity groups in Nepal, India, China and elsewhere. While Western photographers were challenged on ethics and methods, Chobi Mela also faced evolution and rupture. If you compare images from CM I (2000) and CM IX (2017), the early years carry a fever of fighting inequality through the camera. By the second decade, works had also turned towards autobiography, abstraction and surrealism. In the year of CM III (2006), Pedro Meyer wrote: 'Everyone is a photographer these days.' Four years later, in 2010, he asked: 'Are too many people taking photographs?' A decade on, both questions are settled facts – we live in a world shaped by technologies that made everyone a photographer.

Iniva: Everything Crash[1]

Eddie Chambers

It is now well known that the Institute of International Visual Arts – one of Arts Council England's flagship initiatives, more commonly known by its acronym, Iniva – has [in 2015] become become mired in a protracted and seemingly fatal combination of budgetary, structural and, perhaps most importantly, ideological difficulties.[2] Details of Iniva's problems make for uncomfortable reading, though, sadly, arts initiatives launched with much fanfare and running into chronic difficulties relatively shortly thereafter are indeed a now-familiar occurrence. This text has as its concern Iniva's ideological framing and the ways in which the tensions, contradictions and flaws that lay behind its stated agenda of 'internationalism' have come to be exposed like open wounds or compound fractures.

Iniva's origins in the early 1990s can be traced back to the pronounced emergence of Black British artists in 1980s Britain. (For the purposes of this text, 'Black British artists' is taken to refer to British-born, British-raised or British-based artists whose backgrounds lie in the continents and regions of Africa, Asia and the Caribbean.) The 1980s were, relatively speaking, years of unprecedented activity for Black artists in Britain. Previous decades, going back to the 1960s, had seen a number of important visual arts contributions at certain, mostly London-based galleries by artists who had come to Britain in the early to mid-twentieth century, often from countries belonging to the former British Empire. These included Grabowski Gallery (1959–75), which was attached to a pharmacy on Sloane Avenue in Chelsea and showed artists such as Frank Bowling and Aubrey Williams in solo exhibitions and, equally importantly, in mixed group shows, particularly in the early 1960s. Elsewhere in London, other pioneering spaces – including Gallery One (1953–63), founded by poet and dealer Victor Musgrave; New Vision Centre (1956–66), co-founded and directed by South African painter Denis Bowen; and Signals (1964–66), co-founded by Filipino artist David Medalla – opened their doors to Commonwealth and other international artists and were instrumental in setting up global networks of artistic exchange.

The 1980s, however, produced a new generation of artists, for the most part British-born; the majority were, or were to become, art school graduates. As such, they presented themselves as an intriguing and confident new presence within the art scene, manifested in a number of group exhibitions held throughout Britain. The earliest exhibitions signalling this new presence were initiated by art students such as Keith Piper and, in time, Marlene

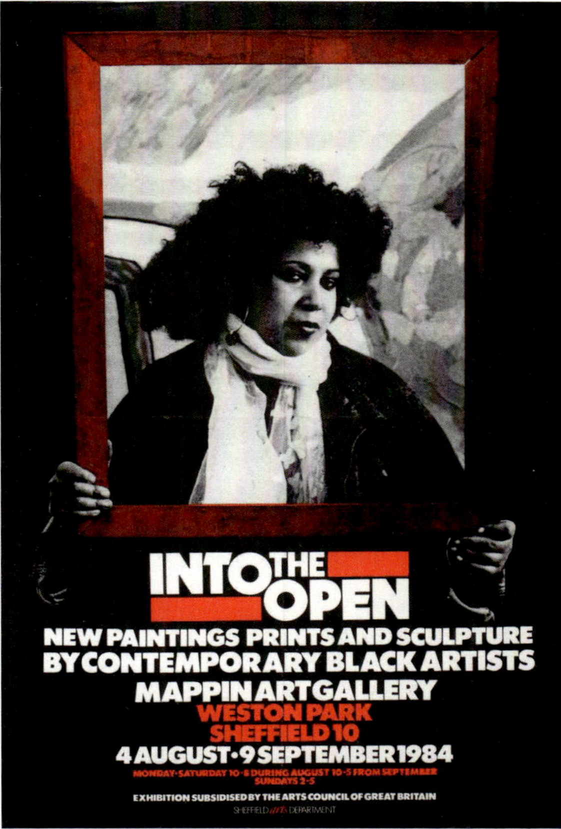

Poster for the exhibition 'Into the Open: New paintings, prints and sculptures by contemporary Black artists', Mappin Art Gallery, Sheffield, 1984, curated by Lubaina Himid and Pogus Caesar. Courtesy Museums Sheffield

Smith and Donald Rodney. Exhibitions such as 'Black Art an' done', held at Wolverhampton Art Gallery in 1981, unequivocally sought to assert the tangible notion of a 'Black art' that existed to respond to the realities of the lives, challenges and struggles of Black people, at home and abroad.[3]

Up until the 1970s, with exceptions limited to occasional contributions from artists such as Bowling or Anish Kapoor, 'British Art' had been, by and large, taken to be the preserve of white, overwhelmingly male artists. But by the mid-1980s, Black artists appeared to have built up a formidable head of steam, moving on from self-initiated exhibitions to celebrated ones at high-profile London galleries, whether the Institute of Contemporary Arts (ICA) or the Whitechapel Gallery. Whilst unprecedented, their emergence into such institutional spaces was not without problems, since they tended to be shown in insistent proximity to *raced* audiences, funding and programming. For instance, 1985 saw 'The Thin Black Line' at the ICA, a group exhibition organised and selected by Lubaina Himid and featuring the work of eleven Black women artists; their work was primarily displayed in the concourse area of the building, hence the 'Thin Black Line' of the title, which, according to Himid, was meant 'to illustrate that there was not enough room for the amount of visual endeavour being produced'.[4] Though it was reviewed in the mainstream media as 'angry', in reality the exhibition attempted to present a multiplicity of experiences through a variety of media, bringing together a survey of Black women's creativity at that time. Sadly, however, 'The Thin Black Line' only came about after the Greater London Council 'had threatened to withdraw its considerable contribution to the ICA if something black did not appear in that financial year'. As Himid makes clear, though, this wasn't an isolated case: in the 1980s and early 90s 'extra money was given to established galleries if they wanted to stage black exhibitions. No questions were asked of them! It was a way of getting money into the coffers.'[5] The following year, the Whitechapel Gallery hosted 'From Two Worlds: Sixteen Artists of Non-European Background', an exhibition initiated by Nicholas Serota and Gavin Jantjes that included practitioners such as Piper, Rasheed Araeen, Zarina Bhimji, the Black Audio Film Collective and Sonia Boyce.[6] 'From Two Worlds' was the most substantial exhibition of Black artists' work to be held at a major London gallery until 'The Other Story: Afro-Asian Artists in Post-War Britain',[7] Araeen's groundbreaking curatorial venture of 1989. At the same time, however, in grouping artists on the sole basis of their being non-white, 'From Two Worlds' and like-minded exhibitions inadvertently contributed to the skewed exposure of Black artists in the 1980s, which in effect meant that, as individual practitioners, these artists were being kept at arm's length by many of London's leading galleries.

Though to a lesser extent other funders played a part, the Arts Council funded much of this bold, brassy and new activity, on something of a piecemeal basis. Though continuing to encounter notable resistance or indifference, Black artists of the 1980s looked to be tearing up the 'British art' script. In this endeavour, artists were aided by their own cogent, insistent voices, as well as those of activists and advocates such as Araeen and Jantjes, who were calling for greater recognition of changes and developments that they felt had long been taking place in British art but were only latterly gaining halting recognition. Jantjes asserted that Black British artists represented a hitherto largely unacknowledged yet compelling fusion of experiences, histories, sensibilities and identities that meant there were many reasons why their work should be taken seriously and institutional support for them provided with more certainty and commitment.[8] Araeen, meanwhile, had, for a number of years, been arguing that Black artists' work needed to be viewed and engaged with through mechanisms radically different to the dominant framings. In his writings and activism, he sought to offer a profoundly different interpretation of Black artists' contributions to art history and the contemporary art scene, whilst simultaneously taking to task what he regarded as the art world's discriminatory pathologies.[9] Further, he contended that culturally ingrained prejudices on the part of the art establishment prevented Black artists from taking up rightful positions within the mainstream of British art, and that the pronounced institutional gravitation towards seeing Black artists' work as 'ethnic arts' did a grave disservice to the most accomplished amongst these practitioners.

Notwithstanding Araeen's continued accusations of cultural obstinacy on the part of the Arts Council, senior figures within the organisation persuaded themselves of the need to formulate some sort of institutional bolstering of this new artistic activity. Thus, in time, the idea emerged of an 'institute' that was to be named, somewhat curiously, 'of new international visual arts'. Perhaps with an organisation such as Artangel as its blueprint, Iniva was, in the first instance, envisaged not as a gallery-centred initiative but as an altogether more curatorially and philosophically agile entity, with a focus on discursive and expansive programming, to be executed in collaboration with a range of partners and supplementary funders.

This conception of Iniva as an institute without its own gallery was fundamental to its early identity, which was formed through a layered series of overlapping phases. The first, undertaken in the early 1990s, comprised research, consultation and development work initiated by Jantjes together with Sarah Wason of the Arts Council's Art Department. The second phase involved activity generated by 'franchises': a publishing one (allocated to Araeen) and two for exhibitions (allocated to Sunil Gupta and myself). Araeen brought several publications into existence through his Kala Press operation, whilst Gupta channelled a range of curatorial activities through his Organisation for the Visual Arts (OVA). For my part, I curated a number of shows for galleries around the country during the mid-1990s. The idea of these franchises was to give Iniva something of a public face whilst the development work of making Iniva an art world reality was undertaken. With the appointment of Gilane Tawadros in 1994 as the project's first director, Iniva entered its third phase of development, during which Tawadros headed a team based in independent offices in central London, very much setting its own programme of activity. Iniva at this time had no explicit relationship with considerations of class and gender, nor with, perhaps most importantly, the notions of 'diversity' that were, within less than a decade, to take on decidedly hegemonic forms. Tawadros, by far Iniva's most accomplished and successful director to date, undertook an adept balancing act between supporting British artists from a plurality of cultural backgrounds and making forays into the international arena.

Had Iniva remained a non-building-based project, articulated as a series of collaborations launched from its modest suite of offices, its history might well have taken a different course. In reality (particularly in the years following Tawadros's departure in 2005), Iniva was unmistakably gravitating towards becoming a bricks-and-mortar entity. This was to have profound consequences. Drawn into the millennial, Blairite wisdom of bringing a plethora of new museums and galleries into existence, and the attendant rhetoric of a more cultured nation at peace with itself in the twenty-first century, Iniva became fixated on becoming a contemporary art gallery modelled upon existing public institutions. In 2007, together with Autograph ABP (the Association of Black Photographers),[10] Iniva finally moved into its current premises at Rivington Place: a new building designed by David Adjaye in East London's booming culture and tech quarter of Shoreditch.

In appraising Iniva's trajectory, it seemed that the Arts Council was now thinking in terms that amounted to separate development for Black artists – something with which seemingly few people had difficulty. Even fewer

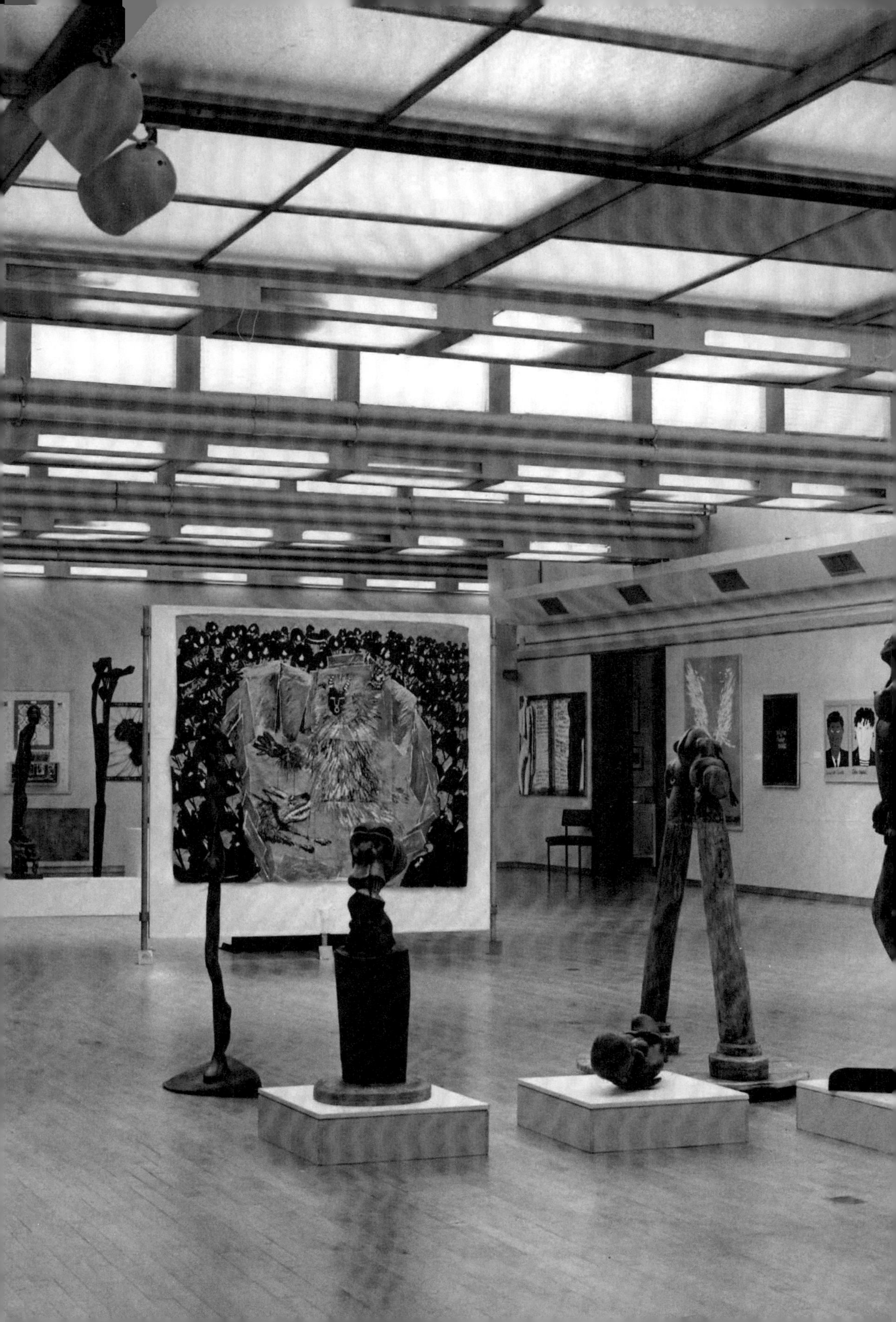

predicted the arguably disastrous consequences and implications of this, though Tawadros recalls that a clear sentiment arising out of Iniva's early consultation meetings was the widely expressed view that 'whatever you do, don't build a Black art gallery'.[11] Despite the not insignificant costs associated with the establishment of Iniva, it was, frankly, infinitely easier for the Arts Council to disregard this plea than it was for it to address ingrained manifestations of cultural or racial intransigence within many of the galleries it funded. Therein lay the seeds of the Arts Council's and, to a far greater extent, Iniva's problems, both then and into the future.

An ominous forecast for Iniva could already be identified in a high-profile feature that appeared in *The Independent* in the summer of 1992. Written by the paper's arts reporter, Dalya Alberge, the article presented Iniva as 'a public gallery that aims to place "artists of colour" in a wider contemporary art context [and] to strengthen London's position as the cultural capital of the world'.[12] The unasked, let alone unanswered question was this: Why should London, the supposed 'cultural capital of the world' need a 'public' gallery to show Black artists' work, when all across the capital (and indeed, the country) were galleries in receipt of substantial amounts of public funding that ought to be showing Black artists' work as part of ongoing, integrated programming? According to Alberge, 'In setting up Iniva, the intention was to move away from the mainstream and take a new look at society and the interplay of different cultures. Artists of all colours, including white, would be shown together.' Why 'artists of all colours, including white', could not be shown together within the existing gallery infrastructure was a question not addressed in the article, nor, it seems, anywhere else. Alberge continued:

> *The Institute of New International Visual Arts (Iniva) – inspired by post-War migration and the breaking-down of cultural boundaries – sets out to place artists from Africa, the Caribbean and Asia alongside their European and American peers. Although the council has, since 1987, supported 'initiatives in cultural diversity', it feels that they have not kept pace with the achievements of black artists in the West.*[13]

Fatally for Iniva, at precisely the same time that the Arts Council was rolling out these plans, the art world was formulating what would, in time, become its own formidable strategy of placing work by 'artists from Africa, the Caribbean and Asia alongside their European and American peers'. Put simply, it did this by unceremoniously bypassing artists of African, Caribbean or Asian origin born, brought up or living in the UK, and went straight to art and artists living in these regions or living elsewhere in the world and taken to be representative of these regions. One of the means by which the art world sought to diversify itself and its programmes was the 'international' exhibition. Much publicised exhibitions such as 'Aratjara: Art of the First Australians: Traditional and Contemporary Works by Aboriginal and Torres Strait Islander Artists', staged at the Hayward Gallery in 1993, and 'Art from South Africa', staged at the Museum of Modern Art, Oxford in 1990, were examples of this new manifestation of internationalism. These were decidedly liberal ventures, in which the curators (and, by extension, exhibition

Installation view, 'Into the Open: New paintings, prints and sculptures by contemporary Black artists', Mappin Art Gallery, Sheffield, 1984. Courtesy the artists

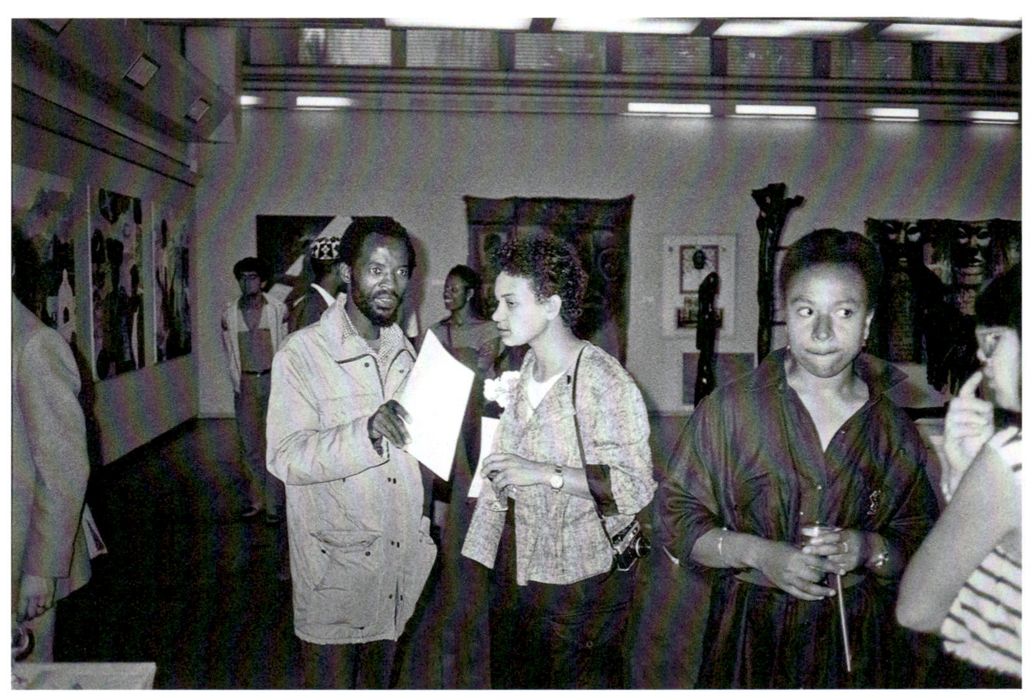

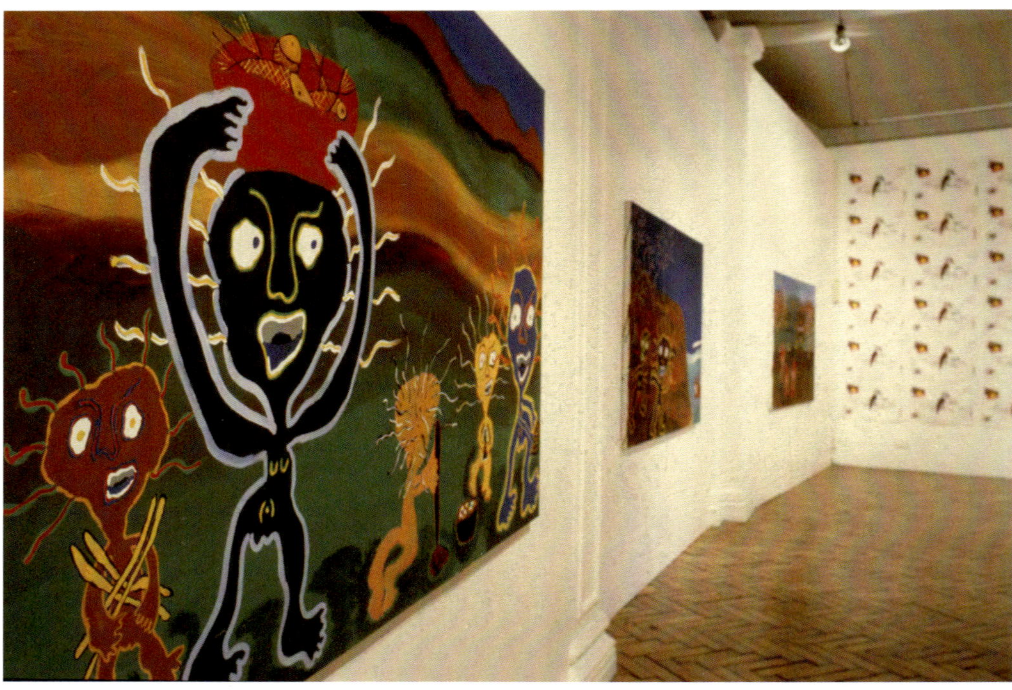

audiences) sought to find common cause with put-upon constituencies in the international arena whilst leaving the dominant society's pathologies untroubled and intact.

Consequently, Iniva became only one manifestation of 'internationalism', as pretty much every gallery with ambitions to maintain or expand its profile turned to the global arena as a means by which it could demonstrate artistic plurality. In this regard, Iniva inadvertently became something of a symbol of the sidelining of Black British artists. Though its development had grown out of the Arts Council's response to Black artists' activity and activism, Iniva only ever declared its embrace of Black artists in the most furtive of ways. A *raced* space that presented itself and sought to function as an *international* space was always likely to be found wanting, particularly when it found itself competing with structurally more secure galleries that were likewise seeking to function as *international* spaces.

'Internationalism' was, in almost every respect, an already ambiguous notion that lent itself to a variety of meanings and interpretations. But as to what exactly 'new internationalism' was or might be, this was anyone's guess. In conversation with Nikos Papastergiadis, Tawadros alluded with candour to Iniva's struggle to articulate its mission: 'I have problems with the term "new internationalism". It is not an appropriate label to define the artistic or intellectual propositions of this organisation. It triggers memories of nationalism and internationalism that presume another sort of utopian structure for wholeness and coherence.'[14] Rather than regarding Iniva as a final destination, Tawadros, with a certain intellectual agility, saw it as a vehicle through which the concerns and questions of artists, curators and thinkers could be channelled, developing an ambitious discursive programme during her tenure.[15] Speaking soon after Iniva's first conference, 'A New Internationalism', held at Tate Gallery, London in April 1994, Tawadros argued that Iniva was 'about posing questions. For instance, the Iniva conference ended with a series of questions, no answers. I think that was right, that's absolutely the tone of the organisation. Artists, to my mind, pose questions, they don't provide answers.'[16] In the autumn of that same year, the 'new' was mercifully dropped, in favour of the altogether more plausible Institute of International Visual Arts – though, by this time, many of London's galleries could in all honesty claim the same sort of identity. By the mid-1990s, not only had the international exhibition become an entrenched feature of the art world, it rapidly came to act as a stand-in for 'diversity', a term which had pretty much always been taken to refer to Black artists' practice and Black culture.

To an extent, one needs to differentiate between the art world's relationship to 'internationalism' and its relationship to 'diversity'. Whilst the former now seems to be pretty much an embedded aspect of the visual arts, the latter is resisted and regarded as a byword for governmentally or state-enforced tinkering – very much to the detriment of society, quality and the settled order of things.[17] In contrast, 'internationalism' exists as a godsend, for its ability to suggest 'diversity' whilst leaving intact pre-existing art world hierarchies of employment and curatorial programming. Artists from beyond the UK, over

Iniva Agenda,
January–April
1999. Cover
image: Cildo
Meireles, *O
Sermão da
Montanha: Fiat
Lux* (*The Sermon
on the Mount:
Let There Be
Light*), 1979,
performance.
Photography:
Luiz Alphonsus
Guimaraes.
Courtesy the
artist and iniva

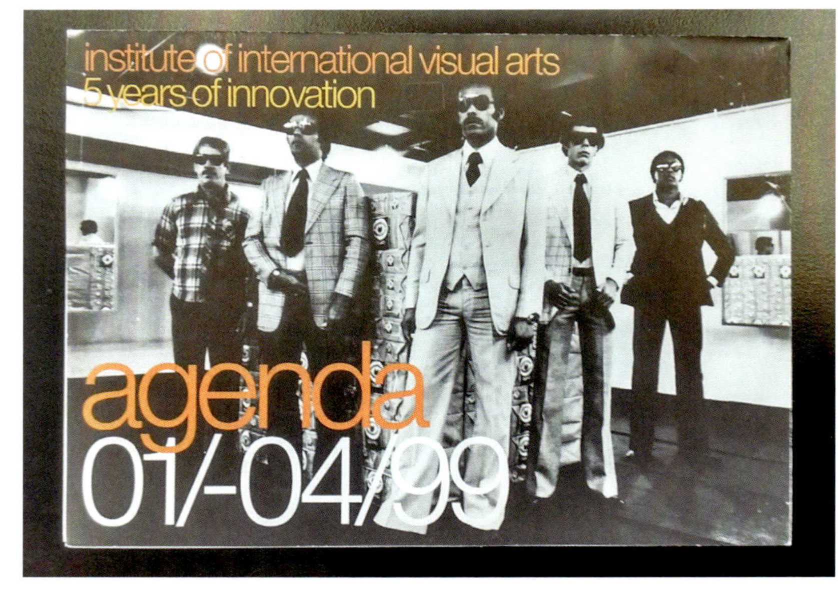

*Global Visions:
Towards a New
Internationalism
in the Visual Arts*,
edited by Jean
Fisher (Kala
Press and Iniva,
1994). Cover
image: Eponce,
Untitled, 1994, oil
on canvas, 112 ×
91.5cm. Courtesy
the artist and
iniva

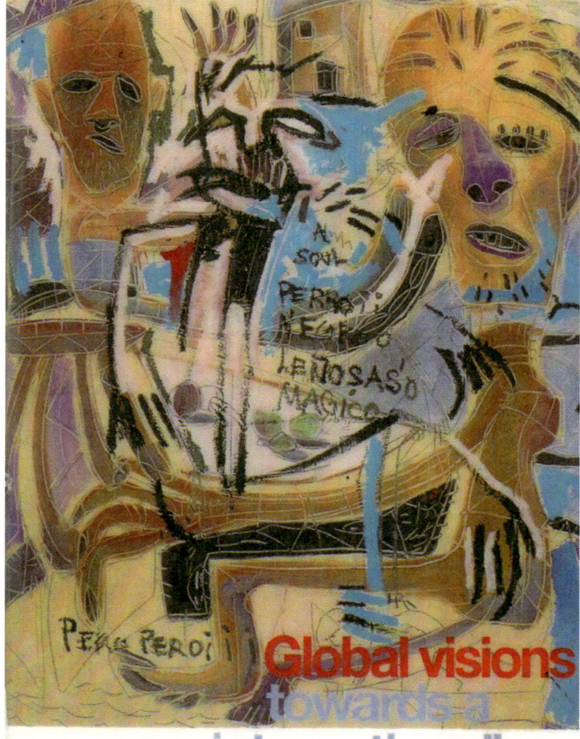

400

the course of the past two decades or more, have grown increasingly attractive to British curators and gallery directors keen to demonstrate 'diversity' within their gallery programmes but not particularly minded to work with Black British artists, who might in earlier times have represented and benefitted from such gestures.

A hegemonic homogeneity has emerged as the dominant characteristic of globalisation, it now being possible to see the same sorts of artists from one city to the next, from one country to another, as long as they are validated by Western European/US art establishment axes of power. For the want of perhaps more global perspectives, insularity and parochialism can take hold. However, the headlong rush to a skewed internationalism has left certain British artists as net losers rather than any sort of beneficiaries. With Iniva having to now chase the same sorts of internationalism as the major players in the London art world, it becomes an easy enough undertaking to appreciate the scale of the organisation's current difficulties. In effect, Iniva has found itself wrong-footed or outflanked by the art world's emphatic embrace of internationalism.

A small number of Black British artists, within a larger pool of British artists, have of course found fabulous success in the international arena, but it is difficult to avoid the somewhat dispiriting conclusion that *internationalism* (or particular manifestations thereof) has failed certain artists, no less than state-sponsored and cack-handed notions of *diversity* have likewise failed certain artists. The defining characteristic of the internationalism of which Iniva is now a part is the hierarchical blueprint of the hegemonic art world. There is within Iniva's programming little or no conceding or transferring of curatorial power, thereby ensuring that hierarchies of power and privilege remain intact. Iniva has moved away from being a dynamic hub from which a variety of exhibitions, publications, residencies and other art projects were initiated, with a range of partners, and become a somewhat lumpen organisation, practising a dull top-down approach to its projects, with little to nothing in the way of lateral working relationships and collaborations. Iniva today is a crash of confusions, contradictions, rigid hierarchy and institutionally mandated cultural difference. It perhaps goes without saying that it has failed those for whom it was, in part at least, established.

Notes

Editors' note: This essay was commissioned in 2015 to explore the political circumstances that led to the establishment of Iniva and offer historical perspective at a time of intense contestation and change for the institution. The 'crisis' described here has now passed: for details of current and future programmes, see http://www.iniva.org.

[1] 'Everything Crash' was a popular Jamaican reggae song by The Ethiopians, from 1968. The song bemoaned the political paralysis and widespread labour unrest occurring in Jamaica at the time. Most significantly, perhaps, it lamented the catastrophic floundering of the hopes and dreams of independence, which had been ushered in just a few years earlier. It reiterated sorrowfully the Jamaican proverb 'What gone bad a mornin' can't come good a evenin'' (in other words, if you start off wrong, you end up wrong). For many Jamaicans, by 1968, it seemed that *everything crash*. Though Iniva's slide into difficulties has taken place over a timescale of several decades, it is now difficult to escape the sense that for Iniva, too, *everything crash*.

[2] The latest and most notorious of these was the announcement, in July 2014, that the Arts Council England had decided to cut Iniva's National Portfolio Organisation grant by 62.3 per cent for the period 2015–18 (following a previous 43 per cent slash in 2012–13). In contrast, the NPO organisation Autograph ABP (the Association of Black Photographers), saw its allocated budget almost doubled so that it could assume management of the building it shares with Iniva. See Morgan Quaintance, 'Iniva: Fit for Purpose?', *Art Monthly*, no.380, October 2014, pp.33–35; and Grant Watson, 'Response to Morgan Quaintance's "Iniva: Fit for Purpose?"', *Art Monthly*, no.382, December 2014–January 2015, pp.14–15. Iniva's director, Tessa Jackson, stepped down in May 2015.

[3] 'Black Art an' done', Wolverhampton Art Gallery, 9–27 June 1981, with works by Dominic Dawes, Andrew Hazell, Ian Palmer, Keith Piper and myself. We organised the exhibition ourselves, as art students and young artists, with guidance from Eric Pemberton, a local schoolteacher who mentored our group.

[4] Lubaina Himid, 'Letters to Susan', *Thin Black Line(s): Tate Britain 2011/2012* (exh. cat.), Newcastle upon Tyne: University of Central Lancashire, 2011, pp.12–13. At the Institute of Contemporary Arts, London, 'The Thin Black Line' (15 November 1985–26 January 1986) included works by Brenda Agard, Sutapa Biswas, Sonia Boyce, Chila Kumari Burman, Jennifer Comrie, Lubaina Himid, Claudette Johnson, Ingrid Pollard, Veronica Ryan, Marlene Smith and Maud Sulter.

[5] L. Himid, 'Mapping: A Decade of Black Women Artists 1980–90', in Maud Sulter (ed.), *Passion: Discourses on Black Women's Creativity*, Hebden Bridge: Urban Fox Press, 1990, p.65.

[6] 'From Two Worlds: Sixteen Artists of Non-European Background', Whitechapel Gallery, London, 30 July–7 September 1986.

[7] 'The Other Story: Afro-Asian Artists in Post-War Britain', Hayward Gallery, London, 29 November 1989–4 February 1990, curated by Rasheed Araeen and featuring works by Araeen, Frank Bowling, Sonia Boyce, Mona Hatoum, Lubaina Himid, Gavin Jantjes, David Medalla and myself, amongst others. The exhibition later travelled to Wolverhampton and Manchester.

[8] See G. Jantjes, 'Black Artists, White Institutions: A Paper', *Artrage*, issue 11, Winter 1985, pp.3–4; and G. Jantjes, 'Art & Cultural Reciprocity', *The Essential Black Art* (exh. cat.), London: Chisenhale Gallery and Kala Press, 1988, pp.42–45.

[9] See Rasheed Araeen, *Making Myself Visible*, London: Kala Press, 1984. The range of practitioners whose contributions and practices urged the Arts Council to action is broad. Alongside the artists mentioned above, in a recent essay Jessica Harrington also includes Pan-Afrikan Connection (later known as the Blk Art Group, which I co-founded in the early 1980s with Keith Piper, Donald Rodney and Marlene Smith), the Sankofa Collective (set up in 1983 by Martina Attille, Maureen Blackwood, Robert Crusz, Isaac Julien and Nadine Marsh-Edwards), the Black Audio Film Collective (founded in 1982 by John Akomfrah, Reece Auguiste, Edward Georg, Lina Gopaul, Avril Johnson, David Lawson and Trevor Mathison) and artists such as Sunil Gupta, Chila Kumari Burman and Ingrid Pollard. See J. Harrington, 'Thinking Through Diversity', *Journal of Museum Education*, vol.34, no.3, September 2009, pp.203–13.

[10] Autograph ABP was established in 1988 as a photographic arts organisation seeking to present a programme of photography-related exhibition, research and publishing activities, with a particular emphasis on addressing issues of cultural identity.

[11] 'Global Proposals: Nikos Papastergiadis talks to Gilane Tawadros', *frieze*, November–December 1994, p.28.

[12] Dalya Alberge, '"Artists of colour" gallery redraws the cultural map', *The Independent*, 25 August 1992, available at http://www.independent.co.uk/news/uk/artists-of-colour-gallery-redraws-the-cultural-map-1542292.html.

[13] *Ibid.*

[14] 'Global Proposals', *op. cit.*, p.29.

[15] For more on the breadth of Gilane Tawadros's programming, see her recent open letter 'The Importance of Iniva', *Art Monthly*, no.385, April 2015, p.11.

[16] 'Global Proposals', *op. cit.* The proceedings of the conference were published in Jean Fisher (ed.), *Global Visions: Towards a New Internationalism in the Visual Arts*, London: Kala Press in association with the Institute of International Visual Arts, 1994.

[17] Though there is no space here to explore this issue in depth, it is worth noting that the diversity policies that were established in the UK at around the same time as Iniva was being set up compounded the marginalisation of Black artists and Black people. For a discussion of Arts Council England's policies regarding cultural diversity, see Richard Hylton, *The Nature of the Beast: Cultural Diversity and the Visual Arts Sector*, Bath: Institute of Contemporary Interdisciplinary Arts, 2007.

My Post-Catastrophic Glossary

Zdenka Badovinac

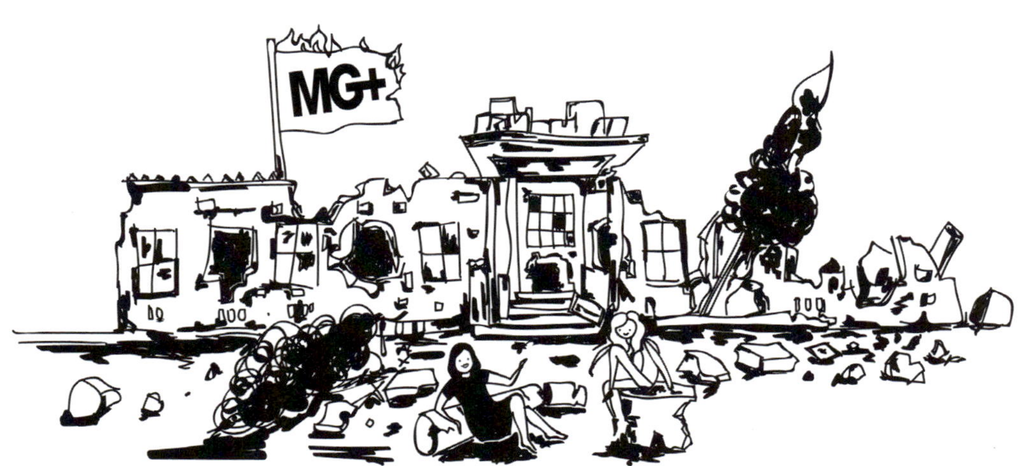

Illustrations by Nika
von Ham, 2018

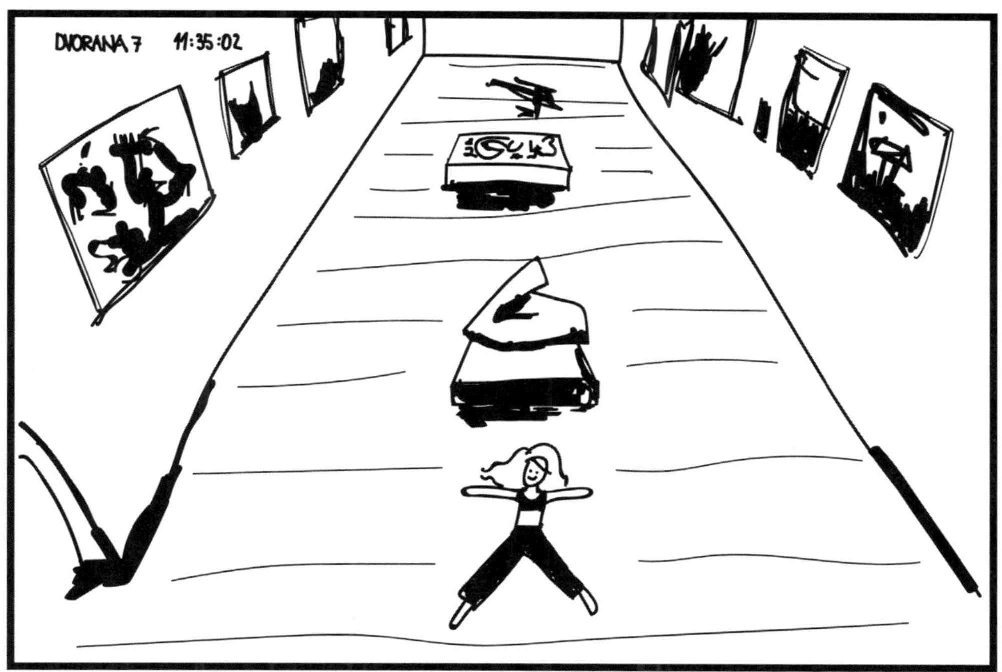

We had nice weather last week in Ljubljana, though I am unsure it still deserves that name. The young artist Nika von Ham and I were hanging out among the ruins of Moderna galerija and stretching our muscles. In the old days, Nika used to guard our collections. I remember she had a strange habit of laying down on the floor and posing for the security cameras. That, she remembers, was her art project. As we chatted, recounting the old days before the catastrophe, she recalled some useful things about the museum. I asked her if she would describe her recollections through drawing. Memories, after all, are the only thing left.

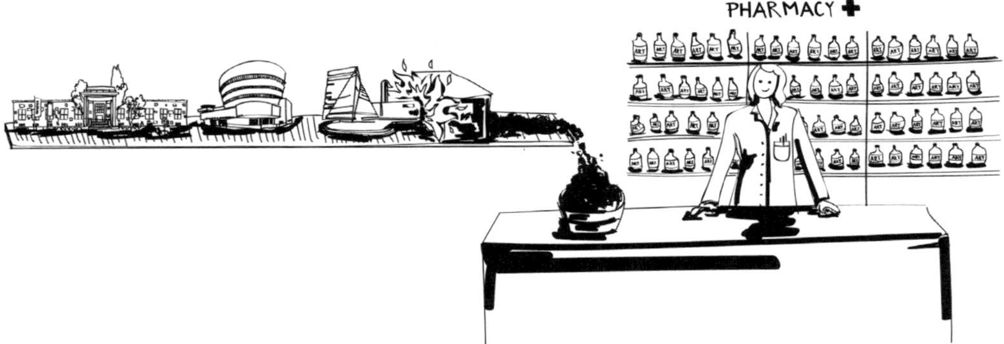

Destruction

These days my thoughts often drift back to Malevich … to his demand that all museums be burned to the ground. The only way the artworks they housed could be made relevant again, he said, was if they were incinerated – reduced to ashes, collected in jars and placed in a pharmacy. Then, he allowed, contemporary artists could use them as a kind of medicine. I also think about Boris Groys, who sometimes reminded me that Malevich's black square touched on the essence of revolution. It was not constructive, it did not imagine a new society, but instead pictured the radical destruction of his society and, indeed, every existing society. As Boris described it, the black square was an image of that destruction; destruction is all that survives permanent change. As such, it countermanded all the imagery of construction that followed the revolution – and, indeed, the project of building an ideal communist society altogether. *Material forces are non-teleological*, Boris said; *they never attain their telos, never reach their end*. Destruction was the only thing Malevich expected from the future. Being a revolutionary artist, on Boris's terms, meant accepting a universal materialistic flow that destroyed all temporary and political orders.

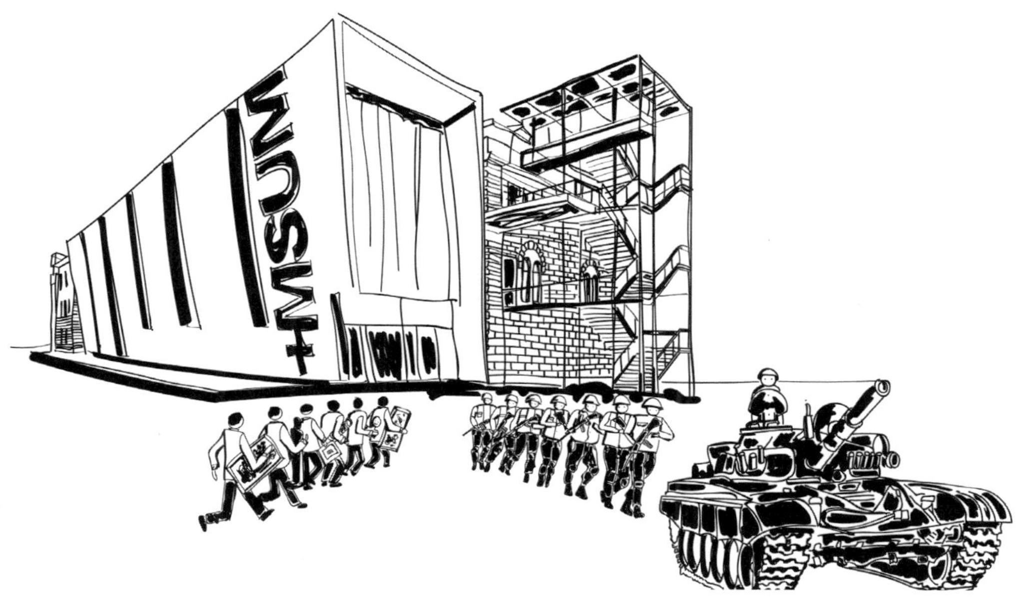

War Time

Today, we can speak only about one time, the time of catastrophe. When our museum still existed, we organised its collections around the idea of eleven times, one of which was the time of war. War time was the time of irruption; it brought contemporaneity. When the barracks of the Yugoslav People's Army were vacated after the army's departure of Slovenia, the building they left behind became a museum of contemporary art. The wars in the Balkans therefore directly inaugurated our contemporaneity. Every second there was a war happening somewhere in the 90s. Contemporary time, as we experienced it, was the time of war. How we should respond to war, and specifically the war in our vicinity, was thus a constant question. We assembled a symposium, called 'Living with Genocide' (1996), dedicated to the war in Bosnia and the genocide enacted against the Muslim population, and we organised an exhibition: artists donated their works to the future Ars Aevi museum in Sarajevo. Later this was called a museum of solidarity.

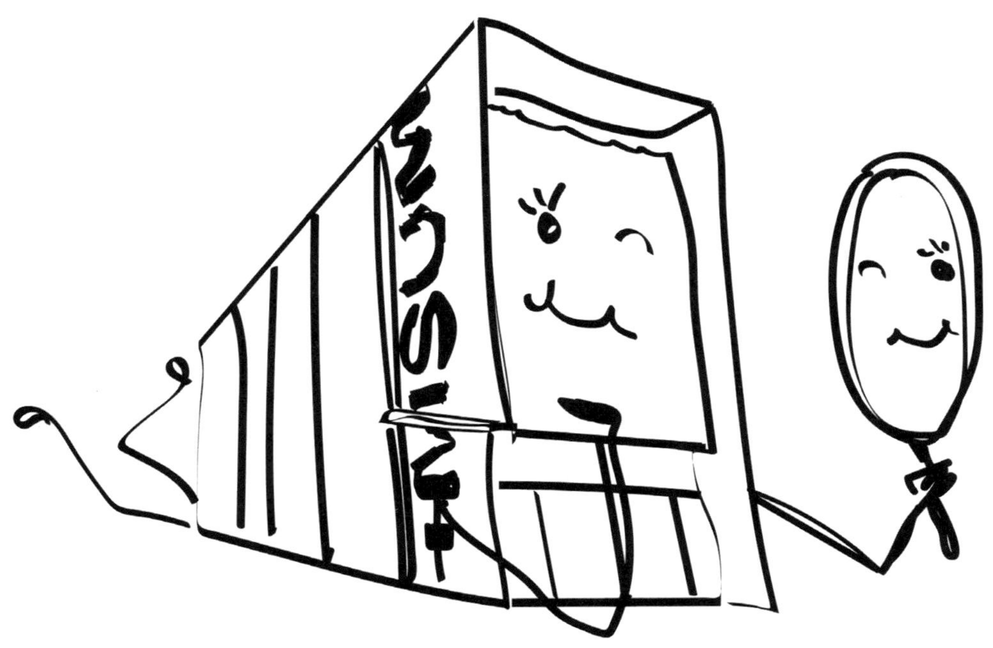

The Self-Reflection of the Museum

Those times, when a museum could be concerned with its own history, seem far away. Before the catastrophe, I believed the museum should be more open, should extend itself outward, into the world. At the same time, I thought it should be more and more concerned with itself, should understand itself as an independent system with its own history. Let me put it another way: a museum was a system that constantly re-established its relationship toward the outside world. It did so by introducing certain strategies of art into the logic of its work. Not only did it represent art but it tried to observe itself from an outside position. By doing so, though, the museum was confronted by its own traumas and complicities: its instrumentalisation by capitalism and ideology, its imbrication in hegemonic systems of knowledge. These pressures had only intensified before the catastrophe, taking forms that were new and hard to recognise.

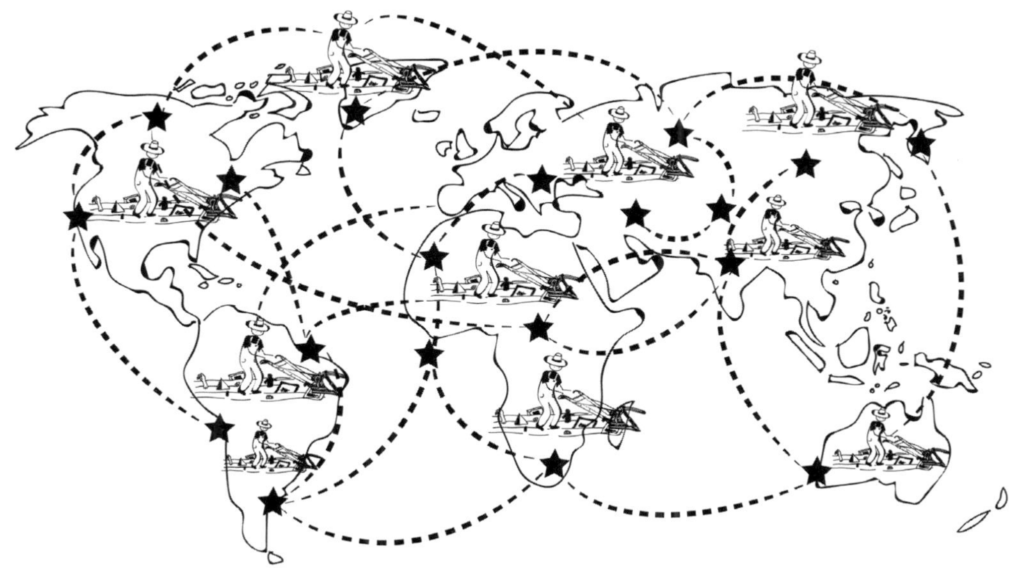

The Authentic Interest of the Museum

Everything is gone now. Yet I remember it so clearly, as if it was right in front of me. Long ago, my work concerned the need to reclaim concepts that had been absorbed by capitalism – ideas like 'authenticity' that had come to seem useless or outdated. Capitalism was of two minds about authenticity. On the one hand, it was seen merely as an illusion. On the other, it was presented, within the world of consumption, however cynically, as a quality that commodities may nevertheless possess. We sought to reclaim the idea from this contradiction. Once the master narrative of the West began to crumble, and with it the universalist models of the museum, it became necessary to define the authentic interests of local institutions: their needs and the methods by which they could join international networks. Making connections was the imperative of the time, and it required adjusting to the circulation systems of global capitalism. Authentic interest meant the opposite: a kind of not-adjusting to global capitalist norms. This had little to do with either the cultivation of traditional identities or with isolationism. Rather, we sought connections of a different kind, with institutions and with people around the world who shared our urgencies.

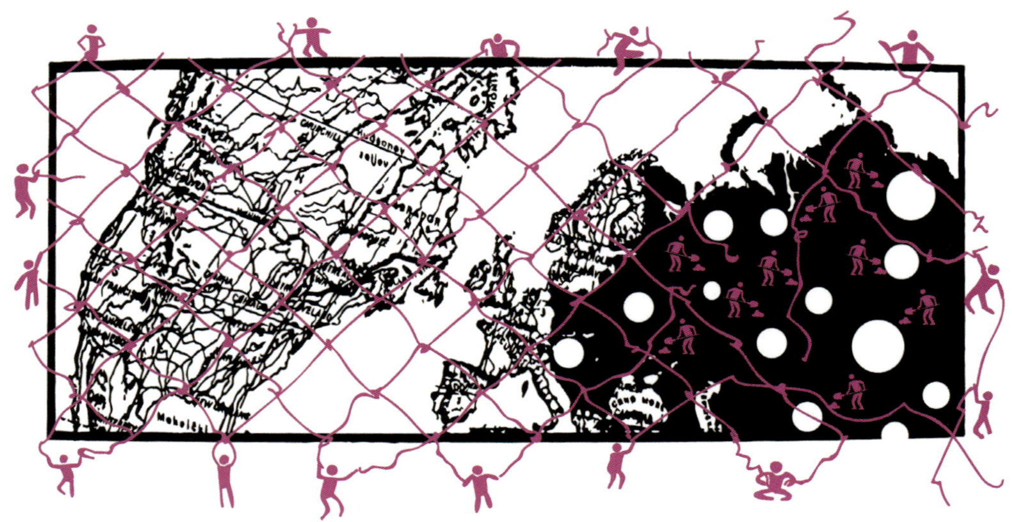

Historicisation

It seemed at the time that capitalism would last forever. Our museum aimed to resist that system, and the cultural hegemonies that had grown from it. I was committed to the historicisation of Eastern European art; that word, *historicisation*, had a specific meaning in my work. It was associated with what was then arriving to history: not only new information into an existing system of knowledge but new ways of thinking that would necessarily transform that system. One of the aims of this kind of historicisation was to oppose the single master narrative of history. I imagined a form of history that was not linear, that did not speak of mastery. Historicisation was history-in-process, constantly supplementing and interrupting itself.

Local Avantgarde

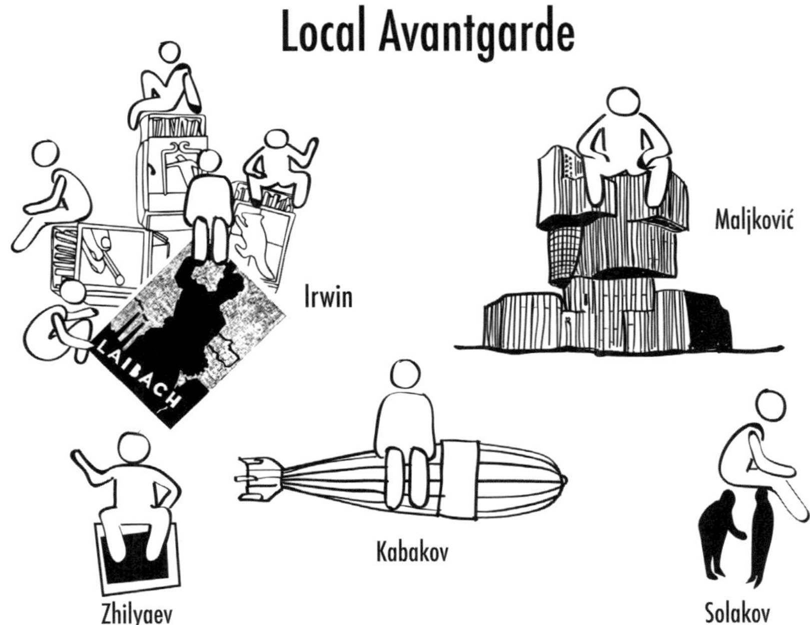

Self-Historicisation

To this idea I added the notion of self-historicisation – an idea that emerged from my encounter with certain features of Eastern European art in the socialist era. The local institutions of the non-Western world, when they existed at all, took a dismissive attitude toward such art. Self-historicisation was an informal system practiced by artists who, in the absence of any suitable collective history, were compelled to search for their own historical and interpretive contexts. Artists archived documents of their own work, of other artists, of broad art movements and their conditions of production. In the post-socialist period, this practice continued, but assumed new forms and took on new subjects. Critical toward new forces in society that aimed to instrumentalise history, their subjects included the cultural legacy of socialism and, among artists living in the territory of the former Yugoslavia, the Yugoslav partisan movement.

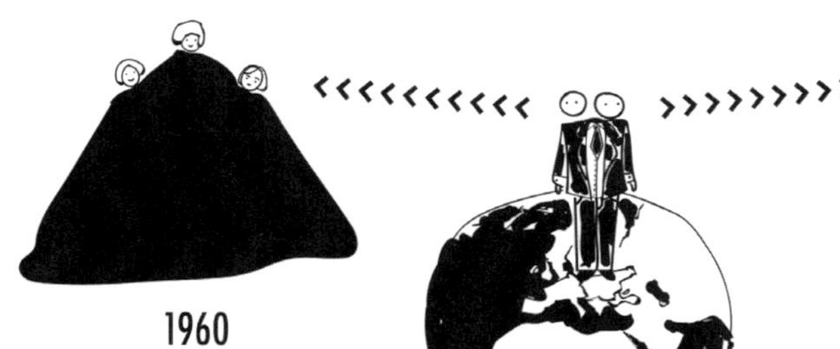
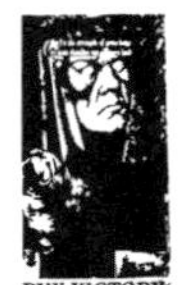
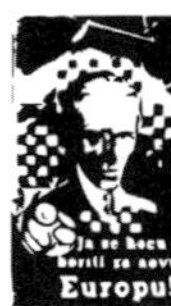
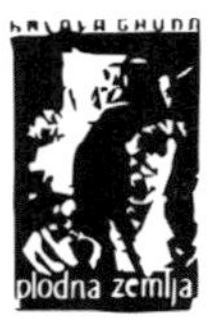

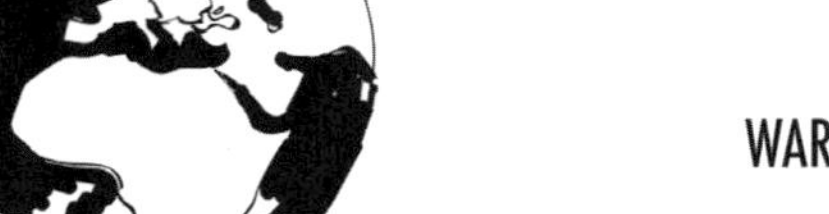

1960
NEW ARTISTIC PRACTICES

1991
WAR IN SLOVENIA

Contemporary Art

I remember it vividly. In 2011, we started operating in two locations – not only in the existing Moderna galerija but now also in the Muzej sodobne umetnosti Metelkova (Museum of Contemporary Art, +MSUM). Working across these two sites made it necessary for us to define the difference between a modern museum and a museum of contemporary art. As I thought about it then, contemporary art had two beginnings. The first came in the 1960s with the introduction of conceptual art, Land art and performance art – or, as we called all of this in Yugoslavia, new art practices. These artists assumed a critical position toward modernism, including its central concepts of the autonomy of art, the originality of the artwork and the neutrality of the white cube. A second beginning then arrived in the early 1990s with the fall of the communist regimes, the acceleration of the processes of globalisation and the expanded use of digital technology. Contemporaneity was therefore not easily demarcated in simple chronological terms. It did not have just one beginning. Contemporary art engaged most deeply with matters associated with its second beginning: the processes of globalisation and their impact on individual local spaces; the instrumentalisation of technology, science, ecology and other forms of knowledge; the colonisation of the private sphere; marginalised art traditions; and searching out the potentials of emancipatory social political traditions.

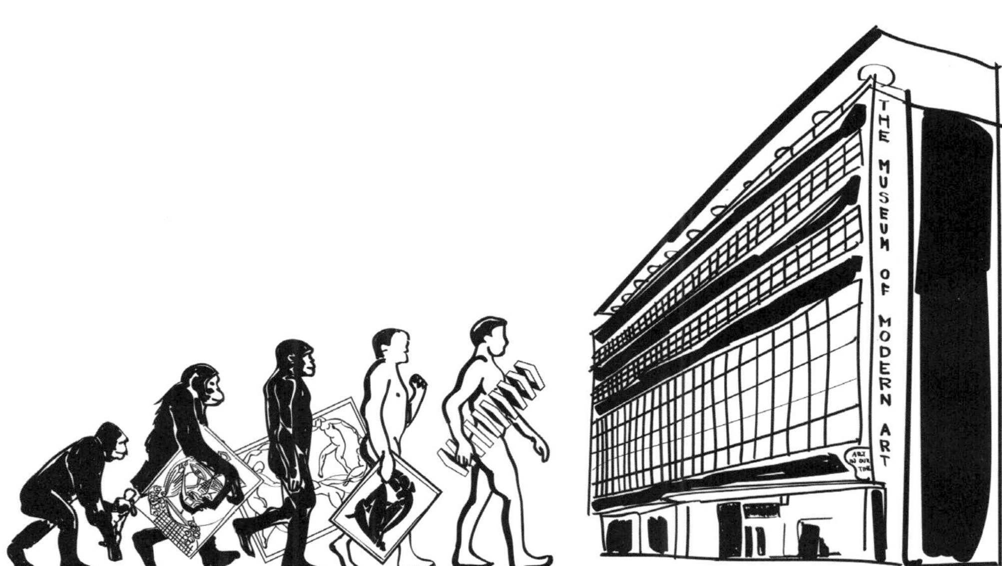

The Museum of Modern Art

Before the founding of the Museum of Modern Art in New York, museums looked primarily to the past and largely organised art into national schools. With the founding of MoMA, the museum's director, Alfred H. Barr, Jr, inaugurated a new understanding of history that differed significantly from that model: a genealogy based on linear time and advancing universal styles (like geometrical abstraction) over national schools. The museums of modernism that have followed have therefore been more interested in time than geography. Time determined quality for museums of modern art. In other words, a work of art of the highest order should, in a sense, be the quintessence of art's development up to that point, while, at the same time, should also represent the transition to the new. Barr had imagined that this commitment to time would require the museum constantly to move forward – to be both contemporary and modern – yet over time it became primarily a museum of the modern past – a past that accumulated as time moved on.

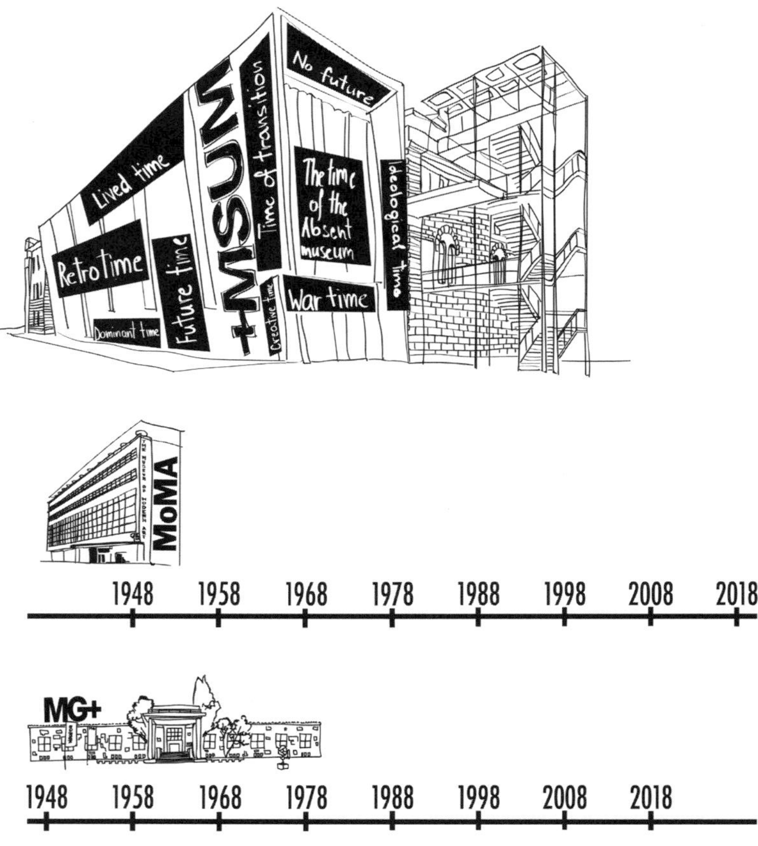

The Museum of Contemporary Art and Its Time

The modern and the contemporary were not discrete periods; indeed, the two categories can be said to overlap. The tradition of modernism remained alive right until the end (rumours suggest it may have contributed to the catastrophe); contemporary art in many ways encompassed the history of the modern. Where the two types of museums differed absolutely was in their respective models of time. The modern museum embraced a teleological and linear view of time. The contemporary art museum was characterised, in contrast, by a critique of that model, as well as of the modernist understanding of quality. Quality was connected to newness. What happened first was venerated, and therefore recorded in history. Anything that followed chronologically was automatically seen to lag behind and was, therefore, both irrelevant to the historical record and of questionable quality. Modern art in the non-Western world was, for a very long time, written of in this way as behind the times, a verdict that can only be handed down if one presumes the universal applicability of an unproblematised single and linear time. Today, such matters of order and priority are less important. With no more museums, nothing is 'behind' anything else.

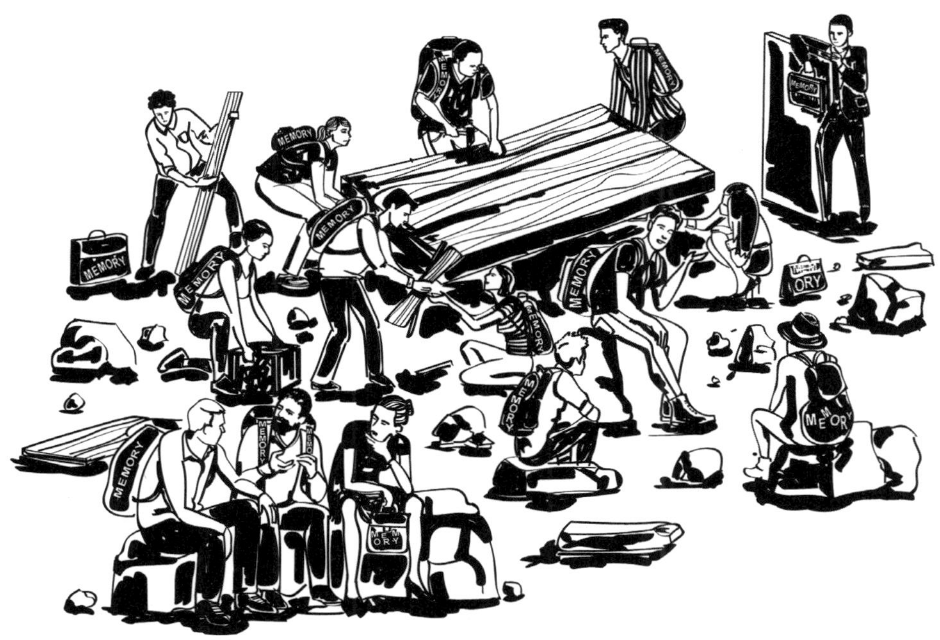

Narrators

Memories are all we have left today. All books, artefacts and archives have been destroyed. Not only museums but schools and libraries have been wiped from the face of the earth. Our future will therefore be built only from our memories and what we tell each other, as it was in pre-modern times. I can still recall whole sentences of Alessandro Portelli's essay on oral histories, though the title escapes me. He wrote that *oral histories were fragmented and tied to the memory and subjective perspective of the individual, group or class concerned.* He wrote that *while orality is saturated by writing, the memory behind it is not a passive depository of facts but an active process of creation of meanings.* In pre-modern times, people remembered by telling stories. Only some of those stories were ever written down – and not even by the people who told them but by learned individuals. After the collapse of the educational system, all memories are now equal, whether the one who recalls them is rich or poor, male or female, black or white. Today we are all narrators, and all narratives count the same. I have to say that I am relieved that I no longer must sit for whole days in front of a computer checking emails. People are listening to each other again! We realise how precious and unique our memories are.

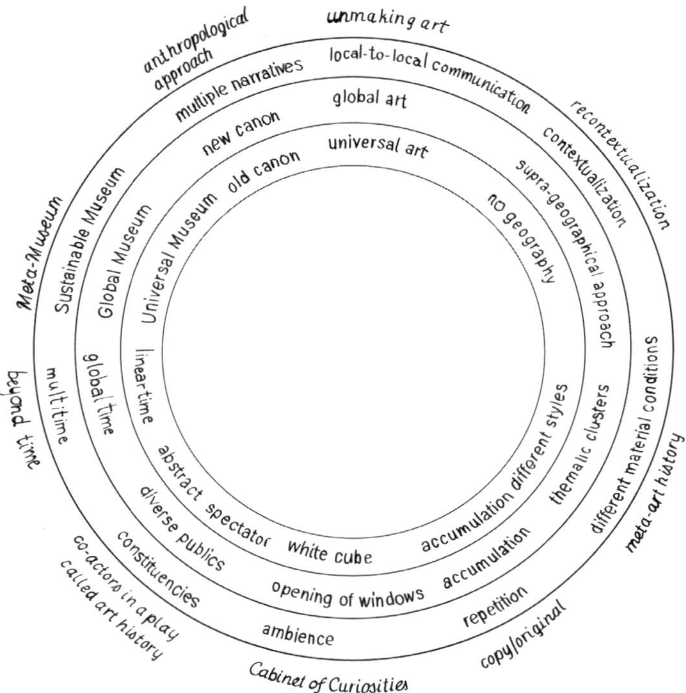

The Sustainable Museum

These days we meet and talk in underground chambers, beneath the ruins of our former institutions; all we have left are our human resources. A diagram from an exhibition close to the end, 'Low-Budget Utopias' (2016), comes to mind, in which I illustrated four models of the museum. The first two, the universal museum and the global museum, were for me associated with MoMA. Such ideas seem absurd today, when there are no more museums. Then there was the sustainable museum. That one didn't have much to do with the eco-friendly, energy-saving 'green' museum people were talking about back then. The sustainable museum operated in a low-budget environment. Though Slovenia was not such a poor country, it afforded little money to culture, so we were always enduring little catastrophes, budget-wise. Such a museum, which rested on human efforts in specific material conditions, could even operate without a building. Finally, there was the meta-museum of Walter Benjamin, which offered an outside perspective on both art and the museum. Comprised of both copies and originals, this museum contained symbols testifying to what we once called the canon. The sustainable and meta-museums did not require constant expansion or the perpetual acquisition of more and more objects. They were designed to survive catastrophes like this one. Such catastrophes do not mean the end of the human needs embodied by museums, even if we do not use that name. What matters is collective memory: not only the memories of experts or museum guards but the public and the fire brigades.

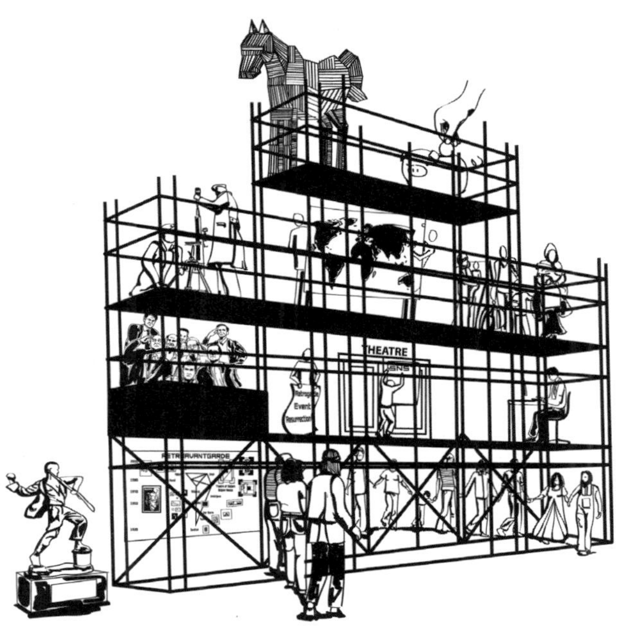

Institutional Building

These days I often think back to the 1980s. As their world was about to collapse into war, Yugoslav artists were already thinking about how to build a new world: one that might resurrect the spirit of the avant-garde, if not the Reformation. On the night of 23 October 1984 – the date is etched into consciousness – the Sisters of Scipio Nasica Theatre staged an event called the *Retrogarde Event Resurrection*. Members of the group went to all the institutional theatres in Ljubljana and, like Martin Luther calling the Catholic church to order, nailed on their doors a call for theatre's renewal. The Sisters had no mercy for anything institutionalised; indeed, on their founding in 1983 they had announced their eventual self-termination, seeking to avoid becoming an institution themselves. True to their word, the group resolved itself in 1987 and was resurrected with a new vision and name. I have often thought that if institutions of art followed the dictates of art, they would be inevitably changed in just this way: transformed from inside by the very art that they housed, or perhaps birthing new and parallel institutions. 'Institutional building' was my term for this. I first used the phrase when assembling a retrospective of the collective project Neue Slowenische Kunst (NSK), which included the Sisters alongside IRWIN, Laibach and five other departments. Unhappy with the institutions of the socialist era, the NSK groups sometimes infiltrated the institution like a Trojan Horse, aiming to transform it from the inside. As often, they accorded to themselves the institutions' duties, building for themselves the history the institutions had ignored. Unwilling to accept the marginalisation or underfunding of Slovene art, they developed their own international networks and sources of funding. NSK could have survived without museums. That is a good lesson for our present situation.

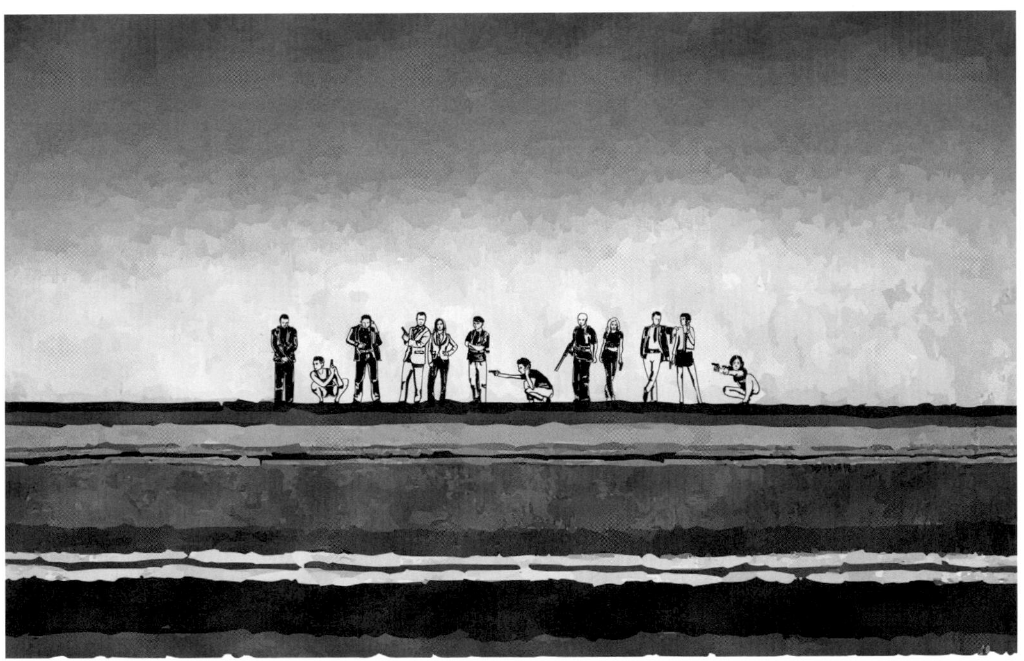

Comradeship

No museums, no careers, no Documenta, no Venice. No competition over prestige, no funding, no government. Just a bloody fight for survival, with no hypocrisy or masquerades. I recognise now that this struggle did not start with the catastrophe. My years at the Moderna galerija were already a battle, one I hardly would have survived without a community held together not just by family ties or personal friendship but by a cause bigger than any of us as individuals. Through war to peace, through socialism to capitalism, from the Yugoslav dinar to the Slovene tolar and finally to the euro. The last moment, remember, when Slovenia joined the European Union, was somehow meant to signal the end of the great social transition! How ironic, then, that this transition was accompanied by the election of a right-wing government in Slovenia and, we feared, a new era of fascism. But that bad future didn't last. The living memory of civil society from the 1980s was too strong. That spirit reawakened and answered the threat. A spirit of collectivism lives on, too, in L'Internationale, the international confederation of institutions launched in the very place where Nika and I sit now. Our museums are gone, and we don't meet as often since we can no longer travel by plane. But our friendship has only grown stronger. Cynical reason having lost its purchase, there is now even greater idealism among us. The senses of solidarity and shared humanity once left in the dustbin of history are in the new light of aftermath being revived and redefined. I think we will survive this disaster. My friends are alive and I can hardly wait to see them roar again like young lions – to sit down with them again in some ruin and start planning a renewed world.

Translated by Rawley Grau.

Postscript, 2021

'My Post-Catastrophic Glossary' owes its origins to a taxi ride in Johannesburg in early 2017, shared by a few participants in the 'Museal Episodes' (2015–17) initiated by the Goethe-Institut São Paulo. The 'Museal Episodes' involved the exchange of ideas between various agents in the field of contemporary art and its institutions from all around the globe. The common thread to all the debates was the South, seen as more than just a geo-political dimension – some participants would even describe it as a state of mind. We might add that the South is the experience of everyone working outside the hyper-regulated and hyper-professionalised art world. I was sharing the backseat of that taxi with Marcelo Rezende, who had recently lost his job as the director of one of the Brazilian museums due to his radical views and innovative approach. We joked a little about ourselves participating in the discussions on collaboration with the South – the other participants were mostly directors of German museums. The city around us further fuelled our banter, and we came up with an idea of a theatrical play that would tell the world that the only possible globally equal collaboration would be after some total global disaster that would bring us all on an equal footing in terms of our conditions of work. Not long after, I wrote 'My Post-Catastrophic Glossary', presenting it at the final 'Museal Episode' event in the context of the Ninth Berlin Biennale (2017); instead of the play imagined in Johannesburg, we presented our fictional stories about museums after some disaster.

Needless to say, none of us had any inkling at the time what a global catastrophe was in store for us so soon. While museum buildings, collections and archives remain intact in this pandemic time, we who work in museums have found ourselves stripped of them, in a way. In a way, I say, because having started to work mostly from home, we feel for the first time what it means to not have physical contact with our co-workers and museum objects. We have all found ourselves in a virtual cloud, in a fog still emanating from the ruins of physical reality. To what extent has this common disaster really united us, to what extent have we become more human? In my glossary, I write about how only we remain after a catastrophe – people with memories that are, as we learned in *Blade Runner* already, not necessarily true. Old and new forces of total surveillance have come together in this fog, new technology and authoritarians from times long ago. The robes of the latter have been donned especially by the leaders of Eastern European countries, who have started their long march through the museums. The new order will show in clear contours only once the fog of the pandemic has lifted. We can only guess at how strong our advocacy of an equal exchange of ideas will be then, and what will bind us. From the perspective of the current state of affairs, only two possibilities seem plausible: new totalitarian horizons, or else numerous new museal episodes giving their different particular explanations of how successfully we have developed the emancipatory potentials arisen in the long-ago year of 2020.

Ground Provisions

Tonika Sealy Thompson

Stefano Harney

Reading Camp

At its source, Ground Provisions is a reading camp. We do many things together. We write, we organise with others, we make movies, work with artists and curate music and film. We travel the Afro-Asian century. We work in the Caribbean and we work in Asia. But if we were to return to the source, this source would be our reading camp. We conceived of the reading camp as a kind of refuge where people can read together. We use the word 'refuge' because the camp involves reading in a quiet place, a place of contemplation and reflection. We read together and to each other and by reading together we make this refuge a place of conversation, discussion and conviviality. It's a retreat, but one we make together. And this is why we call it a refuge. We retreat together. We read together. We read to each other. When we offer a reading residency at our base in Barbados, we offer it to read together.

But why call it a reading camp, and not a school? We have had experiences with autonomous schools, wonderful experiences, from the Decolonial Black Feminism School in Cachoeira, Brazil to ESC in the San Lorenzo neighbourhood of Rome. But the specific idea to create a reading camp came from two sources. First, it came from our experience with the formal, 'official' university. Because we came to see that in the official university *reading is outsourced*. One could even say reading becomes 'piecework' – that system of outsourcing work to individual workers in their homes. We used to think piecework belonged to a certain period in the history of capitalism. Now we know that piecework is a persistent feature of capitalism, a way to avoid the true cost of workers and to keep them separated, as well as to take advantage of gender and racial hierarchies in society. So what do we mean by using this term and saying that reading is outsourced in the university? We think of the classroom as a place of work for the students. It's not the only place of work. Students work all over and around the campus, in the neighbourhood and in the home too. But students also do the bulk of the academic work done inside the university. Yet in their work in the classroom, reading is absent or hidden. It has been outsourced to the privacy of their homes, studies or more typically bus seats and lunch breaks. This hidden production makes it easier to deny the fact that the students do the bulk of the academic work in the university. But it is more than that.

The classroom is a reading-free zone. Indeed anyone caught reading is thought somehow to have not done her or his work! Students are supposed to read at home, alone. Even study groups are supposed to discuss assignments, not spend time in each other's company reading, much less reading to each other. It is almost as if reading is something about which we are embarrassed. We can do yoga together, pray or meditate together, eat together, but somehow we should read in isolation. And this is also true of art schools and art academies, by the way. Reading becomes a profound moment not of togetherness and entangled being, but of individuation. Maybe only the experience of reading with a child escapes this model, but unfortunately such reading is designed precisely to create the individuated child who no longer needs, or wants, to read with the elder.

Meanwhile in the classroom, as they say, everyone is supposed to have 'done the reading'. In this way each person can be measured, in discussion, or on an exam, to see how much she or he absorbed the reading as an individual. To have 'done the reading' is to have completed the work required outside the classroom, the piecemeal work, the outsourced work. The teacher, already the subject supposed to know, is characterised by having done 'all the reading'. But again, by herself, before she came in the room, as a paragon of outsourced work. Another word for outsourced work in our present economy is of course, consultancy. The teacher is at risk of taking on this role of consultant, and the students of becoming apprentice consultants, young entrepreneurs. Hiding reading is the way we hide the work we do outside the workplace, just as the consultant does. The teacher and the student become only as good as the secret work they have done before they arrive, just like consultants. All because the common source of the discussion has been individuated. It is true that the text is now in the classroom, but it is in a sense already finished, already worked upon by each 'individual'. This privatisation of reading compounds a better-known problem in the official university: metrics.

We know as people who have experienced being students and teachers in the university that despite the fact that we have become used to forsaking reading together, discussions in the classroom can generate something special. We can feel each other's energies, lose ourselves in the conversation, feel the presence of something in the room. In these moments, we begin to lose our individual status as producers and feel our common materials and our common and differentiated materiality. And then we have to be graded or to give out grades, and we have to graduate or consider the class completed. The collective product in the room (which is firstly us) gets divided again into marks, rankings, metrics. We get divided away from what we have become together in the room. Even most teachers today get marked and ranked. In other words, our lives together in the classroom get individuated at the end of our experience. But the outsourcing of reading means we are all too ready for this. After all, we came into the class 'by ourselves' through this piecemeal work of reading. And everyone has experienced the collective spell being broken by someone shamed for not reading, whose secret is exposed, or someone who, like a good consultant, disrupts the collectivity but claims to have secretly read more. Thus, Ground Provisions reading camp is conceived in the first instance to allow us to read together, in each other's presence, even if we are in a corner of the yard while someone else is on the porch. Even if reading together is only a feel, an open we dwell in together.

Reading Together as Study
But there is a second immediate source for the reading camp, and that is the (undercommon of the) concept of study itself. Stefano has been speaking of the concept of study with Fred Moten for many years now, and practising it in what might be called 'visitations' with Fred, when they are invited to spend time with students or artists or community workers somewhere. And all of us have been discussing and practising it together. And these visitations have some of the quality of bearing witness and of prophecy. Fred and Stefano do arrive with 'the good word', but only because they know people already have it. And what they already have is study, and study is what they call a base faith, a material practice, mysticism in the flesh. Study is what we do when we come together on our own terms, rather than theirs. It is as Fred and Stefano said in an interview, 'talking and walking around with other people, working, dancing, suffering, some irreducible convergence of all three, held under the name of speculative practice'.[1] And we should add here also: reading together, maybe in silence, or laughter, or occasional comment, or restlessness or stillness, but together. Anyone who has read with a kid knows that authority breaks down. Kids are said not to read as well as adults, but it turns out kids have interpretations and these readings can make the adult readings partial and incomplete. But this is true for all reading together. Reading together makes us incomplete together, and partial towards each other, for each other.

Refuge
So reading, pushed from the university, comes together again in our practice of study. Ground Provisions reading camp and reading residency are a rematerialisation and resocialisation of reading. And therefore Ground Provisions is a refuge, a place to receive visits, wherever Ground Provisions sets up. In an alternation between visitation and refuge, Ground Provisions is the speculative practice of inviting others to be with us, and visiting others to be with them. In other words, it brings speculation down to earth through its invitation, its refuge, its visitation. Or as Walter Rodney would say, Ground Provisions is about groundings, *groundations* with our sisters and brothers. These groundations, this rootedness with others, reflect our grounding in the Caribbean. But in the Caribbean roots do not go just into the earth. They grow out of it, radiating outwards in waves and coming to our shores in waves, in what the Barbadian poet Edward Kamau Brathwaite calls *tidalectics*. Our presence in Asia is therefore not only part of our commitment to the ongoing Afro-Asian century but, for us, it is also a matter of roots, too, roots carried by the tide. We practise *groundations* in Asia too. As Vijay Prashad said, the Third World is a project, and we would add it is also an enmeshment of tides and roots.

Refuge and Reproduction
And there is more to say about refuge and visitation, and about reading, in the practices of Ground Provisions. Because reading can also be thought of as a form of social reproduction, that kind of work necessary for everything

to continue. And if we think of it this way, we may have a way to refuse it as work, and engage it as art. Of course, there are two ways that people use the term 'social reproduction'. There is the question of how we keep 'their thing' going, and the question of how we keep 'our thing' going. Reading on the bus on the way to class is mostly about keeping their thing going. Keeping the university going, and with the university the channelling of our academic labour and ourselves as students and teachers into their machine. This sense of reading as the social reproduction of capital is both accurate and necessary to refuse. But social reproduction also means all that work traditionally done especially by black women, women in general, slaves, the indigenous, queer peoples and peasants to keep that machine profitable by working for free, especially in care, culture and cultivation, the life-giving arts. This sense of social reproduction is the sense we want from reading together, but for ourselves, and not for this machine. This sense is the kind for which we want to provide refuge. To find refuge is to find the arts, be taken into them. To find refuge to read, then, is to find these arts aimed towards the support of reading together. But it is also to return reading from its outsourcing to its home in these arts, which is to say to return study to its home, where it has always been, and always been on the run, fugitive.

A visitation is when we come to others and make our camp. This term echoes we know with a religious reverberation but this is a profane visitation, one where the prophecy is already known, already among us. We announce study that is, we know, already going on, and we propose reading together because reading together belongs with studying together. But visitation is also the practice of acknowledging the refuge that a visit requires and, most importantly, of seeing that refuge as the point of the visit. Another way to say this is that refuge and visitation are practices of grounding 'our thing', of social reproduction for us, not them. Bringing reading into these groundations is just a tactic, but an important one, with a larger practice of honouring the way we make the conditions to continue our thing, and bringing it home into refuge, or taking it with us into visitation. And we do this in different configurations. Ground Provisions is one version of our ensemble, and even it is a version with versions, as we offer refuge and embark on visitations.

Slow Reading

All of our efforts with the reading camp, with visitation and refuge, travelling through the Afro-Asian century offer us the chance to take a different position towards the art we curate, the art we make and the art we organise with others. For us, reading is a condition of making, and reading together is a condition of making together. Like the work and the concepts we produce in the official university, the art we make, curate and organise is vulnerable to breaking loose from its groundings in reading, and therefore its social reproduction, and in particular it is vulnerable to breaking loose from its groundings in study, in reading together, in social reproduction for our thing, not for their machine. We think that making reading visible, making reading together visible, helps to keep the making visible too. It helps us to see what is made through a vision and a feel for where and how it was made together. We can slow down in what we see, hear, feel, touch in this making. We can both recall and foretell the slow reading that makes possible the continuation of this making. We are reminded – during a visitation – by our friend Amaryah Jones-Armstrong, a young scholar of black liberation theology, that one of the roots of 'slow reading' is in Jewish religious reading practices of keeping the text bodily, keeping it among us. This is opposed to a 'close reading' that suggests very careful examination can yield a transcendent meaning from within the text. Our reading is slow because we read together not to master the reading but to unlearn each time what we know. We don't study to graduate, to get credit, to finish. We study to help each other get incompletes. We study to go into debt with each other. We read slow to let things fall apart, to help each other fall apart, to hold each as we fall apart. This means in turn that when we make, curate and organise art we are not culminating our practice, finishing our projects. We are slow reading, we are studying with others by other means. Our art practice is an extension of our reading practice, as coming from and returning to the sources, as a temporary emanation of our groundations, our base arts of being together by reading together. And what we make under these conditions also has to come back to us, come back into study after it is made, or else it will lose its groundations in our social reproduction and join the machine.

Anti-Colonial Correspondences

But of course the social reproduction of 'our thing' in general, the life-giving arts, care, culture and cultivation perpetually risk being called partial, incomplete, in need of the masculine energies of 'proper' politics, 'active' resistance, of policies and strategies. The same is true of reading and studying when they are only understood as the support for something else, rather than the life-giving arts themselves, rather than as a vital part of our thing. Indeed some might say our slow reading is not urgent enough given the state of the 'world'. But travels in the Afro-Asian century teach us otherwise. Amílcar Cabral never minimised these arts, nor Qiu Jin, nor Claudia Jones. Jones did not start Notting Hill's carnival because she gave up on politics. Nor did the Black Panthers think of these life-giving arts as only support systems. Some say the Panthers started as a study group. And this is true, but they did not start as a study group because they wanted to be included in the university. They started as a study group because they saw the impossibility of the university, and the need for something else. Study was at the heart of their revolutionary practice, not a preface to it, as in so much scholarship in the university today. Such was equally the case among the many anti-colonial movements we try to visit in our travels through the Afro-Asian century. The legendary Tan Malaka was said to have gone before the Comintern to try to convince them to take Islam seriously as part of the life-giving arts. They thought he was talking about organising tactics and refused his request. But he was urging them to see the study going on in front of them, in Indonesia and elsewhere, urging them to see that communism and Islam could read slow together, that this could be our thing.

The Futurism of Ground Provisions

Reading together, silently or aloud, belongs with dancing together, cooking together, drinking together, watching movies together, building and cultivating together – and making together. Rather than understanding making as the result of successful social reproduction, we practise it as a temporary emanation, a stepping out without stepping away, where art remains part of the life-giving arts, not a superior comment on them or achievement based on their reproductive support. Support *is* our thing, as Shannon Jackson might say. Support *is* as Fania and Angela Davis say, the process of creating the society we want right now.

A good illustration of our creative practices can be found in Tonika's study of processions and her film practice emerging from this study. When we read together, when we read slowly around her research we see a kind of Afro-Asian futurism sent to us from other centuries before and after ours, a history in procession. By procession Tonika points us towards the fourth coordinate. There is time, space, motion and blackness. Blackness is the process of the procession that entangles time, space and movement. In the procession we feel the non-local in the local, as in the work of Denise Ferreira da Silva on blackness as matter, rather than category. The procession is different from the parade but also different from the carnival. The movement of the procession is not in time like the parade but nor is it the occupation of the parade ground by the carnival, not the turning of time and space upside down in the carnivalesque. The procession instead is the compression and expansion of time and space in a motion that allows us to feel the entanglement, what Ferreira da Silva calls the difference without separability, non-determinate, a being in blackness.[2] In the procession blackness is not just the limit of the world but its enfolding back into earth. The procession is the living archive of the life-giving arts performed together in the ongoing ensemble of blackness. It is no surprise that women, and black women especially, make the procession possible, and no surprise that the procession can show up in any number of ways and places, in the under-common, in the non-local intimate moments of blackness. These moments we find too in Asia in the roots and waves, in the *subnautical* ongoing emergency alternative to the world. We find such moments in the highlands of Thailand, and the struggles of West Papua, under the underpasses in Hong Kong and the nightlife of Taipei. Reading together we feel these roots and waves in the one procession, the procession that is always less and more than one, that is always different, indeterminate and inseparable.

It allows us also to say that in studying, and our reading together, we are returning not so much to a physical activity, but to a spooky state, to a material entanglement and entangled materialism, to a possession without property. This is our black metaphysics, our metaphysics of non-local travel in the Afro-Asian centuries. At Ground Provisions – in every visitation and refuge – when we read slow, when we read to each other, when we read out loud, when we read together, we conjure the life-giving arts. And these are, as they have been, the black arts.

Notes

[1] Stefano Harney and Fred Moten, *The Undercommons: Fugitive Planning and Black Study*, New York and Winvenhoe: Autonomedia/Minor Compositions, 2013, p.110.
[2] Denise Ferreira da Silva, 'On Difference Without Separability', in *Incerteza Viva, 32 Bienal de São Paulo*, São Paulo: Fundacion Bienal de São Paulo, 2016.

Acknowledgements

The editors would like to thank the authors, artists and photographers for their contributions to this book.

For support in the research process that led to this publication we are additionally grateful to: Choi Yan Chi; Garfield Chow; Lauren Cornell; Alice Creischer; Ntone Edjabe; Line Ellegaard; Joseph Grigely; Louis Hartnoll; Sylvia Katende; Lee Weng Choy; Lo Yin Shan; Rolando Vazquez Melken; Adeena Mey; Walter Mignolo; Julian Myers-Szupinska; Lilian Nabulime; Margaret Nagawa; Hans Ulrich Obrist; Colin Perry; Farid Rakun; Grace Samboh; Max Shackleton; Louise Shelley; Andreas Siekmann; Regina Souli; John Tain; Anthony Yung; and Mia Yu.

We would like to thank all the people and organisations that have become fellow travellers over the years of the *Exhibition Histories project*. We are also grateful to current and former students on the Exhibition Studies research masters' programme at Central Saint Martins for continued inspiration.

Afterall journal is also the work of and inspired by many. We would like to acknowledge the editors of journal issues from which texts have been selected, in particular: Ute Meta Bauer, Charles Esche, Candice Hopkins, Anders Kreuger, Wanda Nanibush, Anca Rujoiu and Charles Stankievech, for original editorial input regarding selected texts; former publishing director Caroline Woodley; and Ana Bilbao, Melissa Gronlund, Pablo Lafuente, David Morris and Helena Vilalta, who were responsible for the bulk of the editorial work on the core of essays anthologised here.

The *Exhibition Histories* research and publishing project is made possible through generous support from: Asia Art Archive; Central Saint Martins, University of the Arts London; the Center for Curatorial Studies, Bard College; the Faculty of Fine, Applied and Performing Arts, University of Gothenburg; and public funding through Arts Council England.

Picture and text credits

'Cities on the Move in Public Space: A Journey through the Archive', Bo Choy's 'Womanifesto' and John Tain's 'On the Subject of *Object-act-ivities*: 1989 in Hong Kong' benefitted greatly from the research collections held at Asia Art Archive and the support of the AAA team. AAA's collections on 'Cities on the Move', Womanifesto and *Object-act-ivities* can be accessed online. See *https://aaa.org.hk/en*.

Courtesy Asia Art Archive (p.137 bottom, p.138 top, p.139 bottom, p.140, p.141 top right, middle, bottom, p.142 top, bottom, p.143, p.144 bottom, pp.145–47, pp.234–41)

Courtesy Choi Yan Chi (p.258 bottom)

Courtesy Hayward Gallery, London. Photography: Marcus Leith (p.144 top right)

Courtesy Helsinki: PHOTO Finnish National Gallery / Petri Virtanen (p.138 bottom)

Courtesy Hou Hanru (p.141 top left)

Courtesy Louisiana Museum of Modern Art. Photography: Poul Buchard/Brøndum & Co. (p.142 middle and p.144 top left)

Courtesy Wong Chi Fai and Ellen Pau (pp.254–55)

Photography: Lau Ching-Ping / Kwan Pun Leung / Choi Yan Chi. Courtesy Choi Yan Chi and Yau Ching (p.253 and pp.256–61)

Photography: Margherita Spiluttini © Architekturzentrum Wien, Collection (p.137 top and p.139 top)

***

Articles from *Afterall* journal appear courtesy of the University of Chicago Press, and by kind permission of the authors. Occasional edits have been made to reflect their republication in 2021. Original publication details are as follows:

Adjoa Armah, 'In our language the word for sea means "the spirit that returns"', *Afterall* online, 8 September 2020, https://afterall.org/article/in-our-language-the-word-for-the-sea-means-the-spirit-that-returns

María Berríos, ''Struggle as Culture': The Museum of Solidarity', *Afterall*, issue 44, Autumn/Winter 2017, pp.133–43

Eddie Chambers, 'Iniva: Everything Crash', *Afterall*, issue 39, Summer 2015, pp.51–59

Silvia Rivera Cusicanqui, 'Amo la montaña/I Love the Mountain', *Afterall*, issue 44, Autumn/Winter 2017, pp.145–59

Ekaterina Degot 'The Artist as Director: 'Artist Organisations International' and its Contradictions', *Afterall*, issue 40, Autumn/Winter 2015, pp.21–27

Clémentine Deliss, 'Brothers in Arms: Laboratoire AGIT'art and Tenq in Dakar in the 1990s', *Afterall*, issue 36, Spring/Summer 2014, pp.5–19

Ntone Edjabe, 'How to Eat a Forest', *Afterall*, issue 43, Spring/Summer 2017, pp.74–79

Khwezi Gule, 'Center for Historical Reenactments: Is The Tale Chasing Its Own Tail?', *Afterall*, issue 39, Summer 2015, pp.91–100

Geeta Kapur and Natasha Ginwala, 'On the Curatorial in India (Part 1)' and 'On the Curatorial in India (Part 2)', *Afterall* online, https://www.afterall.org/article/geeta-kapur-part1 and https://www.afterall.org/article/geeta-kapur-on-the-curatorial-in-india-part2, 12 July and 3 October 2011. The conversation was first published by *Art & Deal* magazine, issue 32, 2010, and revised for *Afterall*

Pablo Lafuente, 'Art and the Foreigner's Gaze: A Report on Contemporary Arab Representations', *Afterall*, issue 15, Spring/Summer 2007, pp.13–23

Miguel A. López, 'How Do We Know What Latin American Conceptualism Looks Like?', *Afterall*, issue 23, Spring 2010, pp.5–21

Lee-Ann Martin, 'Anger and Reconciliation: A Very Brief History of Exhibiting Contemporary Indigenous Art in Canada', *Afterall*, issue 43, Spring/Summer 2017, pp.109–15

Serubiri Moses 'Counter-Imaginaries: "Women Artists on the Move", "Second to None" and "Like A Virgin…"', *Afterall*, issue 47, Spring/Summer 2019, pp.115–25

Mujeres Creando, 'La creatividad es un instrumento de lucha y el cambio social un hecho creativo (Creativity Is an Instrument of Struggle, and Social Change a Creative Act)', *Afterall*, issue 46, Autumn/Winter 2018, pp.38–53

Ana Teixeira Pinto 'The Art of Gentrification: The Lisbon Version', *Afterall*, issue 45, Spring/Summer 2018, pp.89–97

Francesca Recchia, 'Aftermaths?: dOCUMENTA (13) in Kabul', *Afterall*, issue 40, Autumn/Winter 2015, pp.67–75

Tonika Sealy Thompson and Stefano Harney 'Ground Provisions', *Afterall*, issue 45, Spring/Summer 2018, pp.121–25

Picture and text credits (continued)

David Teh 'Who Cares a Lot? Ruangrupa as
Curatorship', *Afterall,* issue 30, Summer 2012, p.111–17

Steven ten Thije 'The Joy of Meta: On the Museum
of American Art', *Afterall,* issue 37, Autumn/Winter
2014, pp.75–83

***

The following articles are reproduced by kind
permission of their authors and publishers:

Zdenka Badovinac, 'My Post-Catastrophic Glossary',
in *Comradeship: Curating, Art, and Politics in Post-
Socialist Europe,* New York: Independent Curators
International, 2019, pp.304–33

Elena Filipovic, 'David Hammons, *Untitled
(Knobkerry),* 1994', in *The artist as curator: an
anthology,* London: Koenig Books, 2017, pp.261–81

Yaiza Hernández Velázquez, 'Who Needs "Exhibition
Studies"?', in Ekaterina Álvarez Romero (ed.), *Critical
Museology: Selected Themes,* Ciudad de México: Centro
Cultural Universitario, 2019, pp.286–302

Adeena Mey and David Morris, '*In Real Life* :
réflexions sur "l'exposition virtuelle"' / 'In Real Life
– A Reflection on the "Online Exhibition"', *Critique
d'art,* no.55, Autumn/Winter 2020, pp.189–200

Authors' biographies

Genaro Amaro Altamirano is a founder of the Museo Comunitario del Valle de Xico and a chronicler who has published ethnographic texts on the history of the Xico Valley. He is also an activist who works to protect the rights and heritage of indigenous culture and is involved in founding and supporting community organisations.

Brook Garru Andrew (Wiradjuri/Celtic, Australia) is an artist, curator and scholar. He was Artistic Director of 'NIRIN', the 22nd Biennale of Sydney (2020) and is currently Enterprise Professor in Interdisciplinary Practice at the University of Melbourne and Associate Professor Fine Art at Monash University.

Zdenka Badovinac is a curator and writer. From 1993 to 2020, she has been the Director of the Moderna galerija in Ljubljana (MG+MSUM). Her most recent book is *Comradeship: Curating, Art, and Politics in Post-Socialist Europe* (Independent Curators International (ICI), New York, 2019). Badovinac is a founding member of the museum confederation L'Internationale.

Khairani Barokka is a Minang-Javanese writer and artist, Research Fellow at UAL's Decolonising Arts Institute, and Associate Artist at Delfina Foundation and the National Centre for Writing (UK). Among her honours, she was an *Artforum* Must-See and an NYU Tisch Departmental Fellow. Okka's latest book is *Ultimatum Orangutan* (Nine Arches).

María Berríos is a sociologist, writer and independent curator. Her work explores issues traversing art, culture, and politics, focusing on Latin America, with a special interest in collective experiments of "Third World" alliances and their exhibition formats. She co-curated the 11th Berlin Biennale for Contemporary Art in 2019–20. She has been teaching, as a professor and as a guest tutor, in several universities and art academies in Europe and Latin America.

Ana Bilbao is a Lecturer in Modern and Contemporary Art at the University of York. Her research explores histories of exhibition-making and arts organisations, as well as contemporary art from the Global South. Prior to joining York, she was an editor and research fellow at Afterall Research Centre at Central Saint Martins (UAL), and teaching fellow at the University of Essex. In 2017 she was Visiting Scholar in the Art History Department at KU Leuven, Belgium.

Eddie Chambers gained his PhD from Goldsmiths College, University of London in 1998, for his study of press and other responses to the work of a new generation of Black artists in Britain, active during the 1980s. His latest book is *World is Africa: Writings on Diaspora Art* (Bloomsbury, London and New York, 2021), which brings together a range of texts written over the past two decades.

Bo Choy is an artist and teacher. With an interest in folklore traditions and the mythological, she uses fictioning, costumes and sound as narrative devices to make films and performances. She is Assistant Editor for Afterall Exhibition Histories and Associate Lecturer in BA Fine Art at Chelsea College of Art.

Silvia Rivera Cusicanqui is an Aymara sociologist, activist, oral historian and public intellectual who has worked with indigenous movements in Bolivia over the last four decades. Her book Oppressed but Not Defeated: Peasant Struggles Among the Aymara and Quechua in Bolivia, 1910–1980 (United Nations Research Institute for Social Development, 1982) is considered a classic in Bolivian studies.

Ekaterina Degot is an art historian, art writer and curator. She is a regular contributor to international art journals and magazines such as Artforum, frieze, and e-flux magazine. She is a professor at the Alexander Rodchenko School of Photography and New Media in Moscow. In 2014, she was appointed the Artistic Director at the Academy of Arts of the World, Cologne. Since 2017, she is the Director and Chief Curator of Steirischer Herbst.

Clémentine Deliss is Associate Curator of KW Institute for Contemporary Art. She works across the borders of contemporary art, curatorial practice, and critical anthropology. Her recent book "The Metabolic Museum" is published by Hatje Cantz in co-production with KW. clementinedeliss.academia.edu

Ntone Edjabe is the founder and editor of Chimurenga and its siblings, including the Chronic and Pan African Space Station (PASS).

Charles Esche is director of Van Abbemuseum, Eindhoven (NL) and professor in contemporary art and curating at University of the Arts, London (UK). He is currently researching demodernising art and museums in the context of decoloniality and working on an exhibition on "The Soils" for Melbourne, Yogyakarta and Eindhoven in 2023–24. He works with colleague museums in the L'Internationale confederation of art museums and is an advisor at the Jan van Eyck Academy, Maastricht (NL).

Elena Filipovic is director and curator of Kunsthalle Basel. She previously served as senior curator of WIELS, Brussels and was co-curator, with Adam Szymczyk, of the 5th Berlin Biennale in 2008. Her writings have appeared in numerous artists' catalogues and journals and she has edited several compendiums on exhibition histories, including *The Artist as Curator: An Anthology* (Mousse Publications, 2017). She is author of *David Hammons, Bliz-aard Ball Sale* (Afterall Books, 2017) and *The Apparently Marginal Activities of Marcel Duchamp* (MIT Press, 2016).

Authors' biographies (cont.)

Anthony Gardner (Narrm/Melbourne, Australia) is Professor of Contemporary Art History at the University of Oxford, where he teaches at the Ruskin School of Art and The Queen's College.

Natasha Ginwala is Associate Curator at Gropius Bau, Berlin and Artistic Director of Colomboscope Festival and the 13th Gwangju Biennale with Defne Ayas. Ginwala has curated Contour Biennale 8, Polyphonic Worlds: Justice as Medium and was part of the curatorial team of documenta 14, 2017. Ginwala writes on contemporary art and visual culture in various periodicals and has contributed to numerous publications. She is a recipient of the 2018 visual arts research grant from the Berlin Senate Department for Culture and Europe.

Khwezi Gule is a curator and writer based in Johannesburg. He is currently Chief Curator at the Soweto Museums, which includes, the Hector Pieterson Memorial and Museum and the Kliptown Open Air Museum. Prior to that, Gule held the position of curator of contemporary collections at the Johannesburg Art Gallery.

Ground Provisions is Tonika Sealy Thompson and Stefano Harney. Tonika Sealy Thompson is Barbados's Ambassador to Brazil. Stefano Harney is Honorary Professor in the Institute of Gender, Race, Sexuality, and Social Justice at the University of British Columbia.

Yaiza Hernández Velázquez is a lecturer in the Visual Cultures department at Goldsmiths-UoL. Prior to this, she led the Mres Art: Exhibition Studies programme at Central Saint Martins-UAL. Before returning to academia, she worked for a number of art institutions for over a decade, including as the Head of Public Programmes at MACBA in Barcelona, the director of CENDEAC in Murcia and Curator of Collections and Exhibitions at CAAM in Las Palmas de Gran Canaria.

Geeta Kapur is a Delhi-based critic and curator. Her books include *Contemporary Indian Artists* (1978); *When Was Modernism: Essays on Contemporary Cultural Practice in India* (2000); and *Critic's Compass: Navigating Practice* (forthcoming). She has written widely anthologised essays on such topics as national paradigms, alternative modernisms and critical contemporaneity. Her editorial engagements include Journal of Arts & Ideas, Third Text and Marg. Her curation/co-curation includes: Johannesburg Biennale (1994); 'Century City', Tate Modern (2001); 'subterrain', HKW, Berlin (2003), 'Aesthetic Bind', Chemould, Mumbai (2013–14). She has served as jury member for Venice, Dakar and Sharjah biennials (2005–07).

Pablo Lafuente is a writer, editor and curator who lives in Rio de Janeiro, and whose work is invested in collaborative and educational practices. He was co-curator of the 31st Bienal de São Paulo (2014), the 'Zarigüeya/Alabado Contemporáneo' project (Museo de Arte Precolombino Casa del Alabado, Quito, 2015–ongoing), the exhibitions 'Dja Guata Porã: Rio de Janeiro indígena' (MAR, Rio de Janeiro, 2017–18) and 'Sawé: Liderança indígena e a luta pelo território' (Sesc Ipiranga, São Paulo, scheduled for 2021). Since September 2020, he is the Artistic Director of the Museu de Arte Moderna do Rio de Janeiro, together with Keyna Eleison.

Miguel A. López (Lima, 1983) is a writer and curator. His work investigates collaborative dynamics and feminist rearticulations of art and culture in recent decades. He curated the retrospective exhibition 'Cecilia Vicuña: Seehearing the Enlightened Failure' (2019). Recent books include *Ficciones disidentes en la tierra de la misoginia* (2019) and *Robar la historia* (2017).

Lee-Ann Martin is an independent curator of contemporary Indigenous art. Among Martin's numerous curatorial projects are the national billboard project, 'Resilience', 2018; the international exhibition, 'Close Encounters: The Next 500 Years' (2011); the nationally touring exhibitions, 'Bob Boyer: His Life's Work' (2008); and 'Alex Janvier: His First Thirty Years, 1960–1990' (1993); and the internationally touring exhibition, 'INDIGENA: Perspectives of Indigenous Peoples on 500 Years' (1992).

Naeem Mohaiemen combines films, drawings, sculpture, and essays to research the many forms of utopia-dystopia – beginning from Bangladesh's two postcolonial markers (1947, 1971) and radiating outward to unlikely, and unstable, transnational alliances. He was a 2014 Guggenheim Fellow and finalist for the 2018 Turner Prize.

David Morris lives in London. He is a research fellow and editor at Afterall Research Centre, working particularly on the *Exhibition Histories* series. His work explores different approaches to artistic research, education and exhibition, with a particular focus on experimental and collective practice. He is co-editor, with Sylvère Lotringer, of *Schizo-Culture: The Event, The Book* (Semiotext(e)/The MIT Press, 2014); with David Teh, of *Artist-to-Artist: Independent Art Festivals in Chiang Mai 1992–98* (Afterall Books, 2018) among other publications. With Helena Vilalta he leads a research masters' programme in Exhibition Studies at Central Saint Martins, University of the Arts London.